NEW YORK, MASON BROTHERS

THE

HUMOROUS POETRY

OF THE

ENGLISH LANGUAGE,

FROM CHAUCER TO SAXE.

NARRATIVES,	BURLESQUES,	EPIGRAMS,
SATIRES,	PARODIES,	EPITAPHS,
ENIGMAS,	TRAVESTIES,	TRANSLATIONS.

INCLUDING THE MOST

CELEBRATED COMIC POEMS

OF

THE ANTI-JACOBIN, REJECTED ADDRESSES, THE INGOLDSBY LEGENDS, BLACKWOOD'S MAGAZINE, BENTLEY'S MISCELLANY, AND PUNCH.

WITH MORE THAN

TWO HUNDRED EPIGRAMS,

AND THE CHOICEST HUMOROUS POETRY OF

WOLCOTT,	PRAED,	AYTOUN,	SAXE,	BYRON,
COWPER,	SWIFT,	GAY,	HOOD,	MOORE,
LAMB,	SCOTT,	BURNS,	PRIOR,	LOWELL,
THACKERAY,	HOLMES,	SOUTHEY,	COLERIDGE,	ETC.

WITH NOTES, EXPLANATORY AND BIOGRAPHICAL,

By J PARTON.

SEVENTH EDITION.

NEW YORK:
PUBLISHED BY MASON BROTHERS.
BOSTON: MASON & HAMLIN. PHILADELPHIA: J. B. LIPPINCOTT & CO.
CHICAGO: S. C. GRIGGS & CO.

STEREOTYPED BY
THOMAS B. SMITH,
82 & 84 Beekman Street.

PRINTED BY
C. A. ALVORD,
15 Vandewater St.

PREFACE.

THE design of the projector of this volume was, that it should contain the Best of the shorter humorous poems in the literatures of England and the United States, except:

Poems so local or cotemporary in subject or allusion, as not to be readily understood by the modern American reader;

Poems which, from the freedom of expression allowed in the healthy ages, can not now be read aloud in a company of men and women;

Poems that have become perfectly familiar to every body, from their incessant reproduction in school-books and newspapers; and

Poems by living American authors, who have collected their humorous pieces from the periodicals in which most of them originally appeared, and given them to the world in their own names.

Holmes, Saxe, and Lowell are, therefore, only *represented* in this collection. To have done more than fairly represent them, had been to infringe rights which are doubly sacred, because they are not protected by law. To have done less would have deprived the reader of a most convenient means of observing that, in a kind of composition confessed to be among the most difficult, our native wits are not excelled by foreign.

The editor expected to be embarrassed with a profusion of material for his purpose. But, on a survey of the poetical literature of the two countries, it was discovered that, of really excellent humorous poetry, of the kinds universally interesting, untainted by obscenity, not marred by coarseness of language, nor obscured by remote allusion, the quantity in existence is not great. It is thought that this volume contains a very large proportion of the best pieces that have appeared.

An unexpected feature of the book is, that there is not a line in it by a female hand. The alleged foibles of the Fair have given occasion to libraries of comic verse; yet, with diligent search, no humorous poems by women have been found which are of merit sufficient to give them claim to a place in a collection like this. That lively wit and graceful gayety, that quick perception of the absurd, which ladies are continually displaying in their conversation and correspondence, never, it seems, suggest the successful epigram, or inspire happy satirical verse.

The reader will not be annoyed by an impertinent superfluity of notes. At the end of the volume may be found a list of the sources from which its contents have been taken. For the convenience of those who live remote from biographical dictionaries, a few dates and other particulars have been added to the mention of each name. For valuable contributions to this portion of the volume, and for much well-directed work upon other parts of it, the reader is indebted to Mr. T. BUTLER GUNN, of this city.

There is, certainly, nothing more delightful than the fun of a man of genius. Humor, as Mr. Thackeray observes, is charming, and poetry is charming, but the blending of the two in the same composition is irresistible. There is much nonsense in this book, and some folly, and a little ill-nature; but there is more wisdom than either. They who possess it may congratulate themselves upon having the largest collection ever made of the sportive effusions of genius.

INDEX.

MISCELLANEOUS.

NARRATIVE.

SATIRICAL.

1*

PARODIES AND BURLESQUES.

EPIGRAMMATIC.

ECCENTRIC AND NONDESCRIPT.

ENIGMATIC.

MISCELLANEOUS.

MISCELLANEOUS.

TO MY EMPTY PURSE.

CHAUCER.

To you, my purse, and to none other wight,
Complain I, for ye be my lady dere;
I am sorry now that ye be light,
For, certes, ye now make me heavy chere;
Me were as lefe be laid upon a bere,
For which unto your mercy thus I crie,
Be heavy againe, or els mote I die.

Now vouchsafe this day or it be night,
That I of you the blissful sowne may here,
Or see your color like the sunne bright,
That of yellowness had never pere;
Ye are my life, ye be my hertes stere,
Queen of comfort and of good companie,
Be heavy again, or else mote I die.

Now purse, thou art to me my lives light,
And saviour, as downe in this world here,
Out of this towne helpe me by your might,
Sith that you will not be my treasure,
For I am slave as nere as any frere,
But I pray unto your curtesie,
Be heavy again, or els mote I die.

TO CHLOE.

AN APOLOGY FOR GOING INTO THE COUNTRY.

PETER PINDAR.

Chloe, we must not always be in heaven,
  For ever toying, ogling, kissing, billing;
The joys for which I thousands would have given,
  Will presently be scarcely worth a shilling.

Thy neck is fairer than the Alpine snows,
  And, sweetly swelling, beats the down of doves;
Thy cheek of health, a rival to the rose;
  Thy pouting lips, the throne of all the loves;
Yet, though thus beautiful beyond expression,
That beauty fadeth by too much possession.

Economy in love is peace to nature,
Much like economy in worldly matter;
We should be prudent, never live too fast;
Profusion will not, can not, always last.

Lovers are really spendthrifts—'t is a shame—
Nothing their thoughtless, wild career can tame,
  Till penury stares them in the face;
And when they find an empty purse,
Grown calmer, wiser, how the fault they curse,
  And, limping, look with such a sneaking grace!
Job's war-horse fierce, his neck with thunder hung,
Sunk to an humble hack that carries dung.

Smell to the queen of flowers, the fragrant rose—
Smell twenty times—and then, my dear, thy nose
Will tell thee (not so much for scent athirst)
The twentieth drank less flavor than the *first*.

Love, doubtless, is the sweetest of all fellows;
  Yet often should the little god retire—
Absence, dear Chloe, is a pair of bellows,
  That keeps alive the sacred fire.

TO A FLY,

TAKEN OUT OF A BOWL OF PUNCH.

PETER PINDAR.

Ah! poor intoxicated little knave,
Now senseless, floating on the fragrant wave;
  Why not content the cakes alone to munch?
Dearly thou pay'st for buzzing round the bowl;
Lost to the world, thou busy sweet-lipped soul—
  Thus Death, as well as Pleasure, dwells with Punch.

Now let me take thee out, and moralize—
Thus 't is with mortals, as it is with flies,
  Forever hankering after Pleasure's cup:
Though Fate, with all his legions, be at hand,
The beasts, the draught of Circe can't withstand,
  But in goes every nose—they must, will sup.

Mad are the passions, as a colt untamed!
  When Prudence mounts their backs to ride them mild,
They fling, they snort, they foam, they rise inflamed,
  Insisting on their own sole will so wild.

Gadsbud! my buzzing friend, thou art not dead;
The Fates, so kind, have not yet snapped thy thread;
By heavens, thou mov'st a leg, and now its brother,
And kicking, lo, again, thou mov'st another!

And now thy little drunken eyes unclose,
And now thou feelest for thy little nose,
  And, finding it, thou rubbest thy two hands
Much as to say, "I 'm glad I 'm here again."
And well mayest thou rejoice—'t is very plain,
  That near wert thou to Death's unsocial lands.

And now thou rollest on thy back about,
Happy to find thyself alive, no doubt—
  Now turnest—on the table making rings,
Now crawling, forming a wet track,
Now shaking the rich liquor from thy back,
  Now fluttering nectar from thy silken wings.

Now standing on thy head, thy strength to find,
And poking out thy small, long legs behind;
And now thy pinions dost thou briskly ply;
Preparing now to leave me—farewell, fly!

Go, join thy brothers on yon sunny board,
And rapture to thy family afford—
  There wilt thou meet a mistress, or a wife,
That saw thee drunk, drop senseless in the stream;
Who gave, perhaps, the wide-resounding scream,
  And now sits groaning for thy precious life.

Yes, go and carry comfort to thy friends,
And wisely tell them thy imprudence ends.

Let buns and sugar for the future charm;
These will delight, and feed, and work no harm—
While Punch, the grinning, merry imp of sin,
Invites th' unwary wanderer to a kiss,
Smiles in his face, as though he meant him bliss,
Then, like an alligator, drags him in.

MAN MAY BE HAPPY.

PETER PINDAR.

"Man may be happy, if he will:"
I 've said it often, and I think so still;
Doctrine to make the million stare!
Know then, each mortal is an actual Jove;
Can brew what weather he shall most approve,
Or wind, or calm, or foul, or fair.

But here 's the mischief—man's an ass, I say;
Too fond of thunder, lightning, storm, and rain;
He hides the charming, cheerful ray
That spreads a smile o'er hill and plain!
Dark, he must court the skull, and spade, and shroud—
The mistress of his soul must be a cloud!

Who told him that he must be cursed on earth?
The God of Nature?—No such thing;
Heaven whispered him, the moment of his birth,
"Don't cry, my lad, but dance and sing;
Don't be too wise, and be an ape:—
In colors let thy soul be dressed, not crape.

"Roses shall smooth life's journey, and adorn;
Yet mind me—if, through want of grace,
Thou mean'st to fling the blessing in my face,
Thou hast full leave to tread upon a thorn."

Yet some there are, of men, I think the worst,
Poor imps! unhappy, if they can't be cursed—

Forever brooding over Misery's eggs,
As though life's pleasure were a deadly sin;
Mousing forever for a gin
To catch their happiness by the legs.

Even at a dinner some will be unblessed,
However good the viands, and well dressed:
They always come to table with a scowl,
Squint with a face of verjuice o'er each dish,
Fault the poor flesh, and quarrel with the fish,
Curse cook and wife, and, loathing, eat and growl.

A cart-load, lo, their stomachs steal,
Yet swear they can not make a meal.
I like not the blue-devil-hunting crew!
I hate to drop the discontented jaw!
O let me Nature's simple smile pursue,
And pick even pleasure from a straw.

ADDRESS TO THE TOOTHACHE.

WRITTEN WHEN THE AUTHOR WAS GRIEVOUSLY TORMENTED BY THAT DISORDER.

ROBERT BURNS.

My curse upon thy venom'd stang,
That shoots my tortur'd gums alang;
And thro' my lugs gies mony a twang,
Wi' gnawing vengeance;
Tearing my nerves wi' bitter pang,
Like racking engines!

When fevers burn, or ague freezes,
Rheumatics gnaw, or cholic squeezes;
Our neighbors' sympathy may ease us,
Wi' pitying moan;
But thee—thou hell o' a' diseases,
Aye mocks our groan!

Adown my beard the slavers trickle!
I kick the wee stools o'er the mickle,

As round the fire the giglets keckle,
To see me loup;
While, raving mad, I wish a heckle
Were in their doup.

O' a' the num'rous human dools,
Ill har'sts, daft bargains, cutty-stools,
Or worthy friends rak'd i' the mools,
Sad sight to see!
The tricks o' knaves, or fash o' fools,
Thou bear'st the gree.

Where'er that place be priests ca' hell,
Whence a' the tones o' mis'ry yell,
And ranked plagues their numbers tell,
In dreadfu' raw,
Thou, Toothache, surely bear'st the bell,
Amang them a';

O thou grim mischief-making chiel,
That gars the notes of discord squeel,
'Till daft mankind aft dance a reel
In gore a shoe-thick;—
Gie a' the faes o' Scotland's weal
A towmond's Toothache!

THE PIG.

A COLLOQUIAL POEM.

ROBERT SOUTHEY

Jacob! I do not like to see thy nose
Turn'd up in scornful curve at yonder pig,
It would be well, my friend, if we, like him,
Were perfect in our kind! . . And why despise
The sow-born grunter? . . He is obstinate,
Thou answerest; ugly, and the filthiest beast
That banquets upon offal. . . . Now I pray you
Hear the pig's counsel.
Is he obstinate?
We must not, Jacob, be deceived by words;
We must not take them as unheeding hands

Receive base money at the current worth,
But with a just suspicion try their sound,
And in the even balance weigh them well.
See now to what this obstinacy comes:
A poor, mistreated, democratic beast,
He knows that his unmerciful drivers seek
Their profit, and not his. He hath not learned
That pigs were made for man, . . born to be brawn'd
And baconized: that he must please to give
Just what his gracious masters please to take;
Perhaps his tusks, the weapons Nature gave
For self-defense, the general privilege;
Perhaps, . . hark, Jacob! dost thou hear that horn?
Woe to the young posterity of Pork!
Their enemy is at hand.
Again. Thou say'st
The pig is ugly. Jacob, look at him!
Those eyes have taught the lover flattery.
His face, . . nay, Jacob! Jacob! were it fair
To judge a lady in her dishabille?
Fancy it dressed, and with saltpeter rouged.
Behold his tail, my friend; with curls like that
The wanton hop marries her stately spouse:
So crisp in beauty Amoretta's hair
Rings round her lover's soul the chains of love.
And what is beauty, but the aptitude
Of parts harmonious? Give thy fancy scope,
And thou wilt find that no imagined change
Can beautify this beast. Place at his end
The starry glories of the peacock's pride,
Give him the swan's white breast; for his horn-hoofs
Shape such a foot and ankle as the waves
Crowded in eager rivalry to kiss
When Venus from the enamor'd sea arose; . .
Jacob, thou canst but make a monster of him!
All alteration man could think, would mar
His pig-perfection.
The last charge, . . he lives
A dirty life. Here I could shelter him
With noble and right-reverend precedents,
And show by sanction of authority
That 'tis a very honorable thing

To thrive by dirty ways. But let me rest
On better ground the unanswerable defense.
The pig is a philosopher, who knows
No prejudice. Dirt? .. Jacob, what is dirt?
If matter, .. why the delicate dish that tempts
An o'ergorged epicure to the last morsel
That stuffs him to the throat-gates, is no more.
If matter be not, but as sages say,
Spirit is all, and all things visible
Are one, the infinitely modified,
Think, Jacob, what that pig is, and the mire
Wherein he stands knee-deep!
                                        And there! the breeze
Pleads with me, and has won thee to a smile
That speaks conviction. O'er yon blossom'd field
Of beans it came, and thoughts of bacon rise.

SNUFF.

ROBERT SOUTHEY.

A DELICATE pinch! oh how it tingles up
The titillated nose, and fills the eyes
And breast, till in one comfortable sneeze
The full-collected pleasure bursts at last!
Most rare Columbus! thou shalt be for this
The only Christopher in my calendar.
Why, but for thee the uses of the nose
Were half unknown, and its capacity
Of joy. The summer gale that from the heath,
At midnoon glowing with the golden gorse,
Bears its balsamic odor, but provokes
Not satisfies the sense; and all the flowers,
That with their unsubstantial fragrance tempt
And disappoint, bloom for so short a space,
That half the year the nostrils would keep Lent,
But that the kind tobacconist admits
No winter in his work; when Nature sleeps
His wheels roll on, and still administer
A plenitude of joy, a tangible smell.

What are Peru and those Golcondan mines
To thee, Virginia? miserable realms,

The produce of inhuman toil, they send
Gold for the greedy, jewels for the vain.
But thine are *common* comforts! . . To omit
Pipe-panegyric and tobacco-praise,
Think what a general joy the snuff-box gives,
Europe, and far above Pizarro's name
Write Raleigh in thy records of renown!
Him let the school-boy bless if he behold
His master's box produced, for when he sees
The thumb and finger of authority
Stuffed up the nostrils: when hat, head, and wig
Shake all; when on the waistcoat black, brown dust,
From the oft-reiterated pinch profuse
Profusely scattered, lodges in its folds,
And part on the magistral table lights,
Part on the open book, soon blown away,
Full surely soon shall then the brow severe
Relax; and from vituperative lips
Words that of birch remind not, sounds of praise,
And jokes that *must* be laughed at shall proceed.

A FAREWELL TO TOBACCO.

CHARLES LAMB.

MAY the Babylonish curse
Straight confound my stammering verse,
If I can a passage see
In this word-perplexity,
Or a fit expression find,
Or a language to my mind,
(Still the phrase is wide or scant)
To take leave of thee, GREAT PLANT!
Or in any terms relate
Half my love, or half my hate:
For I hate, yet love thee, so,
That, whichever thing I show,
The plain truth will seem to be
A constrain'd hyperbole,
And the passion to proceed
More from a mistress than a weed.

Sooty retainer to the vine,
Bacchus' black servant, negro fine;
Sorcerer, that mak'st us dote upon
Thy begrimed complexion,
And, for thy pernicious sake,
More and greater oaths to break
Than reclaimèd lovers take
'Gainst women: thou thy siege dost lay
Much too in the female way,
While thou suck'st the lab'ring breath
Faster than kisses or than death,

Thou in such a cloud dost bind us,
That our worst foes can not find us,
And ill fortune, that would thwart us
Shoots at rovers, shooting at us;
While each man, through thy height'ning steam,
Does like a smoking Etna seem,
And all about us does express
(Fancy and wit in richest dress)
A Sicilian fruitfulness.

Thou through such a mist dost show us,
That our best friends do not know us,
And, for those allowèd features,
Due to reasonable creatures,
Liken'st us to fell Chimeras,
Monsters that, who see us, fear us;
Worse than Cerberus or Geryon,
Or, who first loved a cloud, Ixion.

Bacchus we know, and we allow
His tipsy rites. But what art thou,
That but by reflex canst show
What his deity can do,
As the false Egyptian spell
Aped the true Hebrew miracle?
Some few vapors thou may'st raise,
The weak brain may serve to amaze,
But to the reins and nobler heart
Canst nor life nor heat impart.

Brother of Bacchus, later born,
The old world was sure forlorn
Wanting thee, that aidest more
The god's victories than before
All his panthers, and the brawls
Of his piping Bacchanals.
These, as stale, we disallow,
Or judge of *thee* meant: only thou
His true Indian conquest art;
And, for ivy round his dart,
The reformèd god now weaves
A finer thyrsus of thy leaves.

Scent to match thy rich perfume
Chemic art did ne'er presume
Through her quaint alembic strain,
None so sov'reign to the brain;
Nature, that did in thee excel,
Framed again no second smell.
Roses, violets, but toys
For the smaller sort of boys,
Or for greener damsels meant;
Thou art the only manly scent.
Stinking'st of the stinking kind,
Filth of the mouth and fog of the mind,
Africa, that brags her foison,
Breeds no such prodigious poison
Henbane, nightshade, both together,
Hemlock, aconite———

Nay, rather,
Plant divine, of rarest virtue;
Blisters on the tongue would hurt you.
'Twas but in a sort I blamed thee;
None e'er prosper'd who defamed thee;
Irony all, and feign'd abuse,
Such as perplex'd lovers use,
At a need, when, in despair
To paint forth their fairest fair,
Or in part but to express
That exceeding comeliness
Which their fancies doth so strike,
They borrow language of dislike;

And, instead of Dearest Miss,
Jewel, Honey, Sweetheart, Bliss,
And those forms of old admiring,
Call her Cockatrice and Siren,
Basilisk, and all that's evil,
Witch, Hyena, Mermaid, Devil,
Ethiop, Wench, and Blackamoor,
Monkey, Ape, and twenty more;
Friendly Trait'ress, loving Foe—
Not that she is truly so,
But no other way they know
A contentment to express,
Borders so upon excess,
That they do not rightly wot
Whether it be pain or not.

Or, as men, constrain'd to part
With what's nearest to their heart,
While their sorrow 's at the height,
Lose discrimination quite,
And their hasty wrath let fall,
To appease their frantic gall,
On the darling thing whatever,
Whence they feel it death to sever,
Though it be, as they, perforce,
Guiltless of the sad divorce.

For I must (nor let it grieve thee,
Friendliest of plants, that I must) leave thee.
For thy sake, TOBACCO, I
Would do any thing but die,
And but seek to extend my days
Long enough to sing thy praise.
But, as she, who once hath been
A king's consort, is a queen
Ever after, nor will bate
Any title of her state,
Though a widow, or divorced,
So I, from thy converse forced,
The old name and style retain,
A right Katherine of Spain;
And a seat, too, 'mongst the joys
Of the blest Tobacco Boys;

Where, though I, by sour physician,
Am debarr'd the full fruition
Of thy favors, I may catch
Some collateral sweets, and snatch
Sidelong odors, that give life
Like glances from a neighbor's wife;
And still live in the by-places
And the suburbs of thy graces;
And in thy borders take delight,
An unconquer'd Canaanite.

WRITTEN AFTER SWIMMING FROM SESTOS TO ABYDOS.

BYRON.

If, in the month of dark December,
  Leander, who was nightly wont
(What maid will not the tale remember?)
  To cross thy stream broad Hellespont!

If, when the wint'ry tempest roar'd,
  He sped to Hero nothing loth,
And thus of old thy current pour'd,
  Fair Venus! how I pity both!

For *me*, degenerate, modern wretch,
  Though in the genial month of May,
My dripping limbs I faintly stretch,
  And think I 've done a feat to-day.

But since he crossed the rapid tide,
  According to the doubtful story,
To woo—and—Lord knows what beside,
  And swam for Love, as I for Glory;

'T were hard to say who fared the best:
  Sad mortals! thus the gods still plague you!
He lost his labor, I my jest;
  For he was drowned, and I 've the ague

2*

THE LISBON PACKET.

BYRON.

Huzza! Hodgson, we are going,
  Our embargo 's off at last;
Favorable breezes blowing
  Bend the canvas o'er the mast.
From aloft the signal 's streaming,
  Hark! the farewell gun is fired;
Women screeching, tars blaspheming,
  Tell us that our time 's expired.
    Here 's a rascal
    Come to task all,
  Prying from the custom-house;
    Trunks unpacking,
    Cases cracking,
  Not a corner for a mouse
'Scapes unsearched amid the racket,
Ere we sail on board the Packet.

Now our boatmen quit their mooring,
  And all hands must ply the oar;
Baggage from the quay is lowering,
  We 're impatient—push from shore.
"Have a care! that case holds liquor—
  Stop the boat—I 'm sick—O Lord!"
"Sick, ma'am, damme, you 'll be sicker
  Ere you 've been an hour on board."
    Thus are screaming
    Men and women,
Gemmen, ladies, servants, Jacks;
    Here entangling,
    All are wrangling,
  Stuck together close as wax.—
Such the general noise and racket,
Ere we reach the Lisbon Packet.

Now we 've reached her, lo! the captain,
  Gallant Kid, commands the crew;
Passengers their berths are clapped in,
  Some to grumble, some to spew.

"Hey day! call you that a cabin?
Why, 'tis hardly three feet square;
Not enough to stow Queen Mab in—
Who the deuce can harbor there?"
"Who, sir? plenty—
Nobles twenty
Did at once my vessel fill."—
"Did they? Jesus,
How you squeeze us!
Would to God they did so still:
Then I'd 'scape the heat and racket
Of the good ship Lisbon Packet."

Fletcher! Murray! Bob! where are you?
Stretched along the decks like logs—
Bear a hand, you jolly tar, you!
Here's a rope's end for the dogs.
Hobhouse muttering fearful curses,
As the hatchway down he rolls,
Now his breakfast, now his verses,
Vomits forth—and damns our souls.
"Here's a stanza
On Braganza—
Help!"—"A couplet?"—"No, a cup
Of warm water—"
"What's the matter?"
"Zounds! my liver's coming up;
I shall not survive the racket
Of this brutal Lisbon Packet."

Now at length we're off for Turkey,
Lord knows when we shall come back!
Breezes foul and tempests murky
May unship us in a crack.
But, since life at most a jest is,
As philosophers allow,
Still to laugh by far the best is,
Then laugh on—as I do now.
Laugh at all things,
Great and small things.

Sick or well, at sea or shore;
While we 're quaffing,
Let 's have laughing—
Who the devil cares for more?—
Some good wine! and who would lack it,
Even on board the Lisbon Packet?

TO FANNY.

THOMAS MOORE.

NEVER mind how the pedagogue proses,
You want not antiquity's stamp,
The lip that 's so scented by roses,
Oh! never must smell of the lamp.

Old Chloe, whose withering kisses
Have long set the loves at defiance,
Now done with the science of blisses,
May fly to the blisses of science!

Young Sappho, for want of employments,
Alone o'er her Ovid may melt,
Condemned but to read of enjoyments,
Which wiser Corinna had felt.

But for *you* to be buried in books—
Oh, FANNY! they're pitiful sages;
Who could not in *one* of your looks
Read more than in millions of pages!

Astronomy finds in your eye
Better light than she studies above,
And music must borrow your sigh
As the melody dearest to love.

In Ethics—'tis you that can check,
In a minute, their doubts and their quarrels
Oh! show but that mole on your neck,
And 'twill soon put an end to their morals.

Your Arithmetic only can trip
When to kiss and to count you endeavor;
But eloquence glows on your lip
When you swear that you'll love me forever

Thus you see what a brilliant alliance
  Of arts is assembled in you—
A course of more exquisite science
  Man never need wish to go through!

And, oh!—if a fellow like me
  May confer a diploma of hearts,
With my lip thus I seal your degree,
  My divine little Mistress of Arts!

YOUNG JESSICA.

THOMAS MOORE

Young Jessica sat all the day,
  In love-dreams languishingly pining,
Her needle bright neglected lay,
  Like truant genius idly shining.
Jessy, 'tis in idle hearts
  That love and mischief are most nimble;
The safest shield against the darts
  Of Cupid, is Minerva's thimble.

A child who with a magnet play'd,
  And knew its winning ways so wily,
The magnet near the needle laid,
  And laughing, said, "We'll steal it slily."
The needle, having naught to do,
  Was pleased to let the magnet wheedle,
Till closer still the tempter drew,
  And off, at length, eloped the needle.

Now, had this needle turn'd its eye
  To some gay reticule's construction,
It ne'er had stray'd from duty's tie,
  Nor felt a magnet's sly seduction.
Girls would you keep tranquil hearts,
  Your snowy fingers must be nimble;
The safest shield against the darts
  Of Cupid, is Minerva's thimble.

RINGS AND SEALS.

THOMAS MOORE.

"Go!" said the angry weeping maid,
"The charm is broken!—once betray'd,
Oh! never can my heart rely
On word or look, on oath or sigh.
Take back the gifts, so sweetly given,
With promis'd faith and vows to heaven;
That little ring, which, night and morn,
With wedded truth my hand hath worn;
That seal which oft, in moments blest,
Thou hast upon my lip imprest,
And sworn its dewy spring should be
A fountain seal'd for only thee!
Take, take them back, the gift and vow,
All sullied, lost, and hateful, now!"

I took the ring—the seal I took,
While oh! her every tear and look
Were such as angels look and shed,
When man is by the world misled!
Gently I whisper'd, "FANNY, dear!
Not half thy lover's gifts are here:
Say, where are all the seals he gave
To every ringlet's jetty wave,
And where is every one he printed
Upon that lip, so ruby-tinted—
Seals of the purest gem of bliss,
Oh! richer, softer, far than this!

"And then the ring—my love! recall
How many rings, delicious all,
His arms around that neck hath twisted,
Twining warmer far than this did!
Where are they all, so sweet, so many?
Oh! dearest, give back all, if any!"

While thus I murmur'd, trembling too
Lest all the nymph had vow'd was true,
I saw a smile relenting rise
'Mid the moist azure of her eyes,

Like day-light o'er a sea of blue,
While yet the air is dim with dew!
She let her cheek repose on mine,
She let my arms around her twine—
Oh! who can tell the bliss one feels
In thus exchanging rings and seals!

NETS AND CAGES.

THOMAS MOORE.

COME, listen to my story, while
Your needle's task you ply;
At what I sing some maids will smile,
While some, perhaps, may sigh.
Though Love's the theme, and Wisdom blames
Such florid songs as ours,
Yet Truth, sometimes, like eastern dames,
Can speak her thoughts by flowers.
Then listen, maids, come listen, while
Your needle's task you ply;
At what I sing there's some may smile,
While some, perhaps, will sigh.

Young Cloe, bent on catching Loves,
Such nets had learn'd to frame,
That none, in all our vales and groves,
Ere caught so much small game:
While gentle Sue, less given to roam,
When Cloe's nets were taking
These flights of birds, sat still at home,
One small, neat Love-cage making.
Come, listen, maids, etc.

Much Cloe laugh'd at Susan's task;
But mark how things went on:
These light-caught Loves, ere you could ask
Their name and age, were gone!
So weak poor Cloe's nets were wove,
That, though she charm'd into them
New game each hour, the youngest Love
Was able to break through them.
Come, listen, maids, etc.

Meanwhile, young Sue, whose cage was wrought
  Of bars too strong to sever,
One Love with golden pinions caught,
  And caged him there forever;
Instructing thereby, all coquettes,
  Whate'er their looks or ages,
That, though 'tis pleasant weaving Nets,
  'Tis wiser to make Cages.
Thus, maidens, thus do I beguile
  The task your fingers ply—
May all who hear, like Susan smile,
  Ah! not like Cloe sigh!

SALAD.

SYDNEY SMITH.

To make this condiment, your poet begs
The pounded yellow of two hard-boiled eggs;
Two boiled potatoes, passed through kitchen-sieve,
Smoothness and softness to the salad give;
Let onion atoms lurk within the bowl,
And, half-suspected, animate the whole.
Of mordant mustard add a single spoon,
Distrust the condiment that bites so soon;
But deem it not, thou man of herbs, a fault,
To add a double quantity of salt.
And, lastly, o'er the flavored compound toss
A magic soup-spoon of anchovy sauce.
Oh, green and glorious! Oh, herbaceous treat!
'T would tempt the dying anchorite to eat;
Back to the world he 'd turn his fleeting soul,
And plunge his fingers in the salad bowl!
Serenely full, the epicure would say,
Fate can not harm me, I have dined to-day!

MY LETTERS.

R. HARRIS BARHAM.

"Litera scripta manet."—OLD SAW.

ANOTHER mizzling, drizzling day!
Of clearing up there 's no appearance;
So I 'll sit down without delay,
And here, at least, I 'll make a clearance!

Oh ne'er "on such a day as this,"
Would Dido with her woes oppressèd
Have woo'd Æneas back to bliss,
Or Trolius gone to hunt for Cressid!

No, they 'd have stay'd at home, like me,
And popp'd their toes upon the fender,
And drank a quiet cup of tea:
On days like this one can't be tender.

So, Molly, draw that basket nigher,
And put my desk upon the table—
Bring that portfolio—stir the fire—
Now off as fast as you are able!

First here 's a card from Mrs. Grimes,
"A ball!"—she knows that I 'm no dancer—
That woman 's ask'd me fifty times,
And yet I never send an answer.

"DEAR JACK,—
Just lend me twenty pounds,
Till Monday next, when I 'll return it.
Yours truly,
HENRY GIBBS."
Why Z—ds!
I 've seen the man but twice—here, burn it.

One from my cousin Sophy Daw—
Full of Aunt Margery's distresses;
"The cat has kitten'd 'in the *draw*,'
And ruin'd two bran-new silk dresses."

From Sam, "The Chancellor's motto,"—nay
Confound his puns, he knows I hate 'em;
"Pro Rege, Lege, Grege,"—Ay,
"For King read Mob!" Brougham's old *erratum.*

From Seraphina Price—"At two"—
"Till then I can't, my dearest John, stir;"
Two more because I did not go,
Beginning "Wretch" and "Faithless Monster!"

"Dear Sir,—
"This morning Mrs. P——
Who 's doing quite as well as may be,
Presented me at half past three
Precisely, with another baby.

"We 'll name it John, and know with pleasure
You 'll stand"—Five guineas more, confound it!—
I wish they 'd call it Nebuchadnezzar,
Or thrown it in the Thames and drown'd it.

What have we next? A civil dun:
"John Brown would take it as a favor"—
Another, and a surlier one,
"I can't put up with *sich* behavior."

"Bill so long standing,"—"quite tired out,"—
"Must sit down to insist on payment,"
"Called ten times,"—Here 's a fuss about
A few coats, waistcoats, and small raiment!

For once I'll send an answer, and in-
form Mr. Snip he need n't "call" so;
But when his bill 's as "tired of standing"
As he is, beg 't will "sit down also."

This from my rich old Uncle Ned,
Thanking me for my annual present;
And saying he last Tuesday wed
His cook-maid, Molly—vastly pleasant!

An ill-spelt note from Tom at school,
Begging I 'll let him learn the fiddle;
Another from that precious fool,
Miss Pyefinch, with a stupid riddle.

"D' ye give it up?" Indeed I do!
  Confound those antiquated minxes;
I won't play "*Billy Black*" to a "*Blue*,"
  Or Œdipus to such old sphinxes.

A note sent up from Kent to show me,
  Left with my bailiff, Peter King;
"'I 'll burn them precious stacks down, blow me!
  "Yours most sincerely,
    "CAPTAIN SWING."

Four begging letters with petitions,
  One from my sister Jane, to pray
I 'll execute a few commissions"
  In Bond-street, "when I go that way."

"And buy at Pearsall's in the city
  Twelve skeins of silk for netting purses:
Color no matter, so it's pretty;—
  Two hundred pens"—two hundred curses!

From Mistress Jones: "My little Billy
  Goes up his schooling to begin,
Will you just step to Piccadilly,
  And meet him when the coach comes in?

"And then, perhaps, you will as well, see
  The poor dear fellow safe to school
At Dr. Smith's in Little Chelsea!"
  Heaven send he flog the little fool!

From Lady Snooks: "Dear Sir, you know
  You promised me last week a Rebus;
A something smart and *apropos*,
  For my new Album?"—Aid me, Phœbus!

"My first is follow'd by my second;
  Yet should my first my second see,
A dire mishap it would be reckon'd,
  And sadly shock'd my first would be.

"Were I but what my whole implies,
  And pass'd by chance across your portal
You'd cry 'Can I believe my eyes?
  I never saw so queer a mortal!'

"For then my head would not be on,
My arms their shoulders must abandon;
My very body would be gone,
I should not have a leg to stand on."

Come that's dispatch'd—what follows?—Stay
"Reform demanded by the nation;
Vote for Tagrag and Bobtail!" Ay,
By Jove a blessed *Reformation!*

Jack, clap the saddle upon Rose—
Or no!—the filly—she's the fleeter;
The devil take the rain—here goes,
I'm off—a plumper for Sir Peter!

THE POPLAR.

R. HARRIS BARHAM.

Ay, here stands the Poplar, so tall and so stately,
On whose tender rind—'twas a little one then—
We carved *her* initials; though not very lately,
We think in the year eighteen hundred and ten.

Yes, here is the G which proclaimed Georgiana;
Our heart's empress then; see, 'tis grown all askew;
And it's not without grief we perforce entertain a
Conviction, it now looks much more like a Q.

This should be the great D too, that once stood for Dobbin,
Her lov'd patronymic—ah! can it be so?
Its once fair proportions, time, too, has been robbing;
A D?—we'll be *Deed* if it isn't an O!

Alas! how the soul sentimental it vexes,
That thus on our labors stern *Chronos* should frown:
Should change our soft liquids to izzards and Xes,
And turn true-love's alphabet all upside down!

SPRING.

A NEW VERSION.

THOMAS HOOD.

"*Ham.* The air bites shrewdly—it is very cold.
Hor. It is a nipping and eager air."—HAMLET.

COME, *gentle* Spring! ethereal *mildness*, come!"
O! Thomson, void of rhyme as well as reason,
How couldst thou thus poor human nature hum?
There's no such season.

The Spring! I shrink and shudder at her name!
For why, I find her breath a bitter blighter!
And suffer from her *blows* as if they came
From Spring the Fighter.

Her praises, then, let hardy poets sing,
And be her tuneful laureates and upholders,
Who do not feel as if they had a *Spring*
Poured down their shoulders!

Let others eulogize her floral shows;
From me they can not win a single stanza.
I know her blooms are in full blow—and so's
The Influenza.

Her cowslips, stocks, and lilies of the vale,
Her honey-blossoms that you hear the bees at,
Her pansies, daffodils, and primrose pale,
Are things I sneeze at!

Fair is the vernal quarter of the year!
And fair its early buddings and its blowings—
But just suppose Consumption's seeds appear
With other sowings!

For me, I find, when eastern winds are high,
A frigid, not a genial inspiration;
Nor can, like Iron-Chested Chubb, defy
An inflammation.

Smitten by breezes from the land of plague,
  To me all vernal luxuries are fables,
O! where 's the *Spring* in a rheumatic leg,
  Stiff as a table's?

I limp in agony—I wheeze and cough;
  And quake with Ague, that great Agitator;
Nor dream, before July, of leaving off
  My Respirator.

What wonder if in May itself I lack
  A peg for laudatory verse to hang on?—
Spring, mild and gentle!—yes, a Spring-heeled Jack
  To those he sprang on.

In short, whatever panegyrics lie
  In fulsome odes too many to be cited,
The tenderness of Spring is all my eye,
  And that is blighted!

ODE.

ON A DISTANT PROSPECT OF CLAPHAM ACADEMY.

THOMAS HOOD.

Ah me! those old familiar bounds!
That classic house, those classic grounds,
  My pensive thought recalls!
What tender urchins now confine,
What little captives now repine,
  Within yon irksome walls!

Ay, that 's the very house! I know
Its ugly windows, ten a row!
  Its chimneys in the rear!
And there 's the iron rod so high,
That drew the thunder from the sky
  And turned our table-beer!

There I was birched! there I was bred!
There like a little Adam fed
  From Learning's woeful tree!
The weary tasks I used to con!—
The hopeless leaves I wept upon!—
  Most fruitful leaves to me!

The summoned class!—the awful bow!—
I wonder who is master now
  And wholesome anguish sheds!
How many ushers now employs,
How many maids to see the boys
  Have nothing in their heads!

And Mrs. S * * *?—Doth she abet
(Like Pallas in the palor) yet
  Some favored two or three—
The little Crichtons of the hour,
Her muffin-medals that devour,
  And swill her prize—bohea?

Ay, there 's the playground! there 's the lime,
Beneath whose shade in summer's prime
  So wildly I have read!—
Who sits there *now*, and skims the cream
Of young Romance, and weaves a dream
  Of Love and Cottage-bread?

Who struts the Randall of the walk?
Who models tiny heads in chalk?
  Who scoops the light canoe?
What early genius buds apace?
Where 's Poynter? Harris? Bowers? Chase?
  Hal Baylis? blithe Carew?

Alack! they 're gone—a thousand ways!
And some are serving in "the Greys,"
  And some have perished young!—
Jack Harris weds his second wife;
Hal Baylis drives the *wayne* of life;
  And blithe Carew—is hung!

Grave Bowers teaches A B C
To Savages at Owhyee;
   Poor Chase is with the worms!—
All are gone—the olden breed!—
New crops of mushroom boys succeeds,
   "And push us from our *forms!*"

Lo! where they scramble forth, and shout,
And leap, and skip, and mob about,
   At play where we have played!
Some hop, some run (some fall), some twine
Their crony arms; some in the shine,
   And some are in the shade!

Lo there what mixed conditions run!
The orphan lad; the widow's son;
   And Fortune's favored care—
The wealthy born, for whom she hath
Macadamized the future path—
   The nabob's pampered heir!

Some brightly starred—some evil born—
For honor some, and some for scorn—
   For fair or foul renown!
Good, bad, indifferent—none they lack!
Look, here's a white, and there's a black!
   And there's a creole brown!

Some laugh and sing, some mope and weep,
And wish *their* frugal sires would keep
   Their only sons at home;—
Some tease the future tense, and plan
The full-grown doings of the man,
   And pant for years to come!

A foolish wish! There's one at hoop;
And four at *fives!* and five who stoop
   The marble taw to speed!
And one that curvets in and out,
Reining his fellow-cob about,
   Would I were in his *steed!*

Yet he would gladly halt and drop
That boyish harness off, to swop
  With this world's heavy van—
To toil, to tug. O little fool!
While thou can be a horse at school
  To wish to be a man!

Perchance thou deem'st it were a thing
To wear a crown—to be a king!
  And sleep on regal down!
Alas! thou know'st not kingly cares;
Far happier is thy head that wears
  That hat without a crown!

And dost thou think that years acquire
New added joys? Dost think thy sire
  More happy than his son?
That manhood's mirth?—O, go thy ways
To Drury-lane when ——— *plays*,
  And see how *forced* our fun!

Thy taws are brave!—thy tops are rare!—
Our tops are spun with coils of care,
  Our *dumps* are no delight!—
The Elgin marbles are but tame,
And 'tis at best a sorry game
  To fly the Muse's kite!

Our hearts are dough, our heels are lead,
Our topmost joys fall dull and dead,
  Like balls with no rebound!
And often with a faded eye
We look behind, and send a sigh
  Toward that merry ground!

Then be contented. Thou hast got
The most of heaven in thy young lot;
  There's sky-blue in thy cup!
Thou 'lt find thy manhood all too fast—
Soon come, soon gone! and age at last
  A sorry *breaking up!*

SCHOOL AND SCHOOL-FELLOWS.

W. MACKWORTH PRAED.

Twelve years ago I made a mock
 Of filthy trades and traffics:
I wondered what they meant by stock;
 I wrote delightful sapphics:
I knew the streets of Rome and Troy,
 I supped with fates and furies;
Twelve years ago I was a boy,
 A happy boy at Drury's.

Twelve years ago!—how many a thought
 Of faded pains and pleasures,
Those whispered syllables have brought
 From memory's hoarded treasures!
The fields, the forms, the beasts, the books,
 The glories and disgraces,
The voices of dear friends, the looks
 Of old familiar faces.

Where are my friends?—I am alone,
 No playmate shares my beaker—
Some lie beneath the church-yard stone,
 And some before the Speaker;
And some compose a tragedy,
 And some compose a rondo;
And some draw sword for liberty,
 And some draw pleas for John Doe.

Tom Mill was used to blacken eyes,
 Without the fear of sessions;
Charles Medler loathed false quantities,
 As much as false professions;
Now Mill keeps order in the land,
 A magistrate pedantic;
And Medler's feet repose unscanned
 Beneath the wide Atlantic.

Wild Nick, whose oaths made such a din,
 Does Dr. Martext's duty;
And Mullion, with that monstrous chin,
 Is married to a beauty;

And Darrel studies, week by week,
  His Mant and not his Manton;
And Ball, who was but poor at Greek,
  Is very rich at Canton.

And I am eight-and-twenty now—
  The world's cold chain has bound me;
And darker shades are on my brow,
  And sadder scenes around me:
In Parliament I fill my seat,
  With many other noodles;
And lay my head in Germyn-street,
  And sip my hock at Doodle's.

But often when the cares of life,
  Have set my temples aching,
When visions haunt me of a wife,
  When duns await my waking,
When Lady Jane is in a pet,
  Or Hobby in a hurry,
When Captain Hazard wins a bet,
  Or Beaulieu spoils a curry:

For hours and hours, I think and talk
  Of each remembered hobby:
I long to lounge in Poet's Walk—
  Or shiver in the lobby;
I wish that I could run away
  From House, and court, and levee,
Where bearded men appear to-day,
  Just Eton boys, grown heavy;

That I could bask in childhood's sun,
  And dance o'er childhood's roses;
And find huge wealth in one pound one,
  Vast wit and broken noses;
And pray Sir Giles at Datchet Lane,
  And call the milk-maids Houris;
That I could be a boy again—
  A happy boy at Drury's!

THE VICAR.

W. MACKWORTH PRAED.

SOME years ago, ere Time and Taste
  Had turned our parish topsy-turvy,
When Darnel Park was Darnel Waste,
  And roads as little known as scurvy,
The man who lost his way between
  St. Marys' Hill and Sandy Thicket,
Was always shown across the Green,
  And guided to the Parson's Wicket.

Back flew the bolt of lisson lath;
  Fair Margaret in her tidy kirtle,
Led the lorn traveler up the path,
  Through clean-clipped rows of box and myrtle:
And Don and Sancho, Tramp and Tray,
  Upon the parlor steps collected,
Wagged all their tails, and seemed to say,
  "Our master knows you; you 're expected!"

Up rose the Reverend Doctor Brown,
  Up rose the Doctor's "winsome marrow;"
The lady lay her knitting down,
  Her husband clasped his ponderous Barrow;
Whate'er the stranger's caste or creed,
  Pundit or papist, saint or sinner,
He found a stable for his steed,
  And welcome for himself, and dinner.

If, when he reached his journey's end,
  And warmed himself in court or college,
He had not gained an honest friend,
  And twenty curious scraps of knowledge:—
If he departed as he came,
  With no new light on love or liquor,—
Good sooth the traveler was to blame,
  And not the Vicarage, or the Vicar.

His talk was like a stream which runs
  With rapid change from rocks to roses;
It slipped from politics to puns:
  It passed from Mohammed to Moses:

Beginning with the laws which keep
  The planets in their radiant courses,
And ending with some precept deep
  For dressing eels or shoeing horses.

He was a shrewd and sound divine,
  Of loud Dissent the mortal terror;
And when, by dint of page and line,
  He 'stablished Truth, or started Error,
The Baptist found him far too deep;
  The Deist sighed with saving sorrow;
And the lean Levite went to sleep,
  And dreamed of tasting pork to-morrow.

His sermons never said or showed
  That Earth is foul, that Heaven is gracious,
Without refreshment on the road
  From Jerome, or from Athanasius;
And sure a righteous zeal inspired
  The hand and head that penned and planned them,
For all who understood, admired,
  And some who did not understand them.

He wrote, too, in a quiet way,
  Small treatises and smaller verses;
And sage remarks on chalk and clay,
  And hints to noble lords and nurses;
True histories of last year's ghost,
  Lines to a ringlet or a turban;
And trifles for the Morning Post,
  And nothing for Sylvanus Urban.

He did not think all mischief fair,
  Although he had a knack of joking;
He did not make himself a bear,
  Although he had a taste for smoking:
And when religious sects ran mad,
  He held, in spite of all his learning,
That if a man's belief is bad,
  It will not be improved by burning.

And he was kind, and loved to sit
  In the low hut or garnished cottage,

And praise the farmer's homely wit,
  And share the widow's homelier pottage:
At his approach complaint grew mild,
  And when his hand unbarred the shutter,
The clammy lips of Fever smiled
  The welcome which they could not utter.

He always had a tale for me
  Of Julius Cæsar or of Venus:
From him I learned the rule of three,
  Cat's cradle, leap-frog, and Quæ genus;
I used to singe his powdered wig,
  To steal the staff he put such trust in;
And make the puppy dance a jig
  When he began to quote Augustin.

Alack the change! in vain I look
  For haunts in which my boyhood trifled;
The level lawn, the trickling brook,
  The trees I climbed, the beds I rifled:
The church is larger than before:
  You reach it by a carriage entry:
It holds three hundred people more:
  And pews are fitted up for gentry.

Sit in the Vicar's seat: you 'll hear
  The doctrine of a gentle Johnian,
Whose hand is white, whose tone is clear,
  Whose tone is very Ciceronian.
Where is the old man laid?—look down,
  And construe on the slab before you,
HIC JACET GULIELMUS BROWN,
  VIR NULLA NON DONANDUS LAURA.

THE BACHELOR'S CANE-BOTTOMED CHAIR.

W. M. THACKERAY.

IN tattered old slippers that toast at the bars,
And a ragged old jacket perfumed with cigars,
Away from the world and its toils and its cares,
I 've a snug little kingdom up four pair of stairs.

To mount to this realm is a toil, to be sure,
But the fire there is bright and the air rather pure;
And the view I behold on a sunshiny day
Is grand through the chimney-pots over the way.

This snug little chamber is crammed in all nooks,
With worthless old knicknacks and silly old books,
And foolish old odds and foolish old ends,
Cracked bargains from brokers, cheap keepsakes from friends.

Old armor, prints, pictures, pipes, china (all cracked),
Old rickety tables, and chairs broken-backed;
A twopenny treasury, wondrous to see;
What matter? 'tis pleasant to you, friend, and me.

No better divan need the Sultan require,
Than the creaking old sofa that basks by the fire;
And 'tis wonderful, surely, what music you get
From the rickety, ramshackle, wheezy spinet.

That praying-rug came from a Turcoman's camp;
By Tiber once twinkled that brazen old lamp;
A Mameluke fierce yonder dagger has drawn:
'Tis a murderous knife to toast muffins upon.

Long, long through the hours, and the night, and the chimes,
Here we talk of old books, and old friends, and old times;
As we sit in a fog made of rich Latakie
This chamber is pleasant to you, friend, and me.

But of all the cheap treasures that garnish my nest,
There 's one that I love and I cherish the best;
For the finest of couches that 's padded with hair
I never would change thee, my cane-bottomed chair.

'Tis a bandy-legged, high-shouldered, worm-eaten seat,
With a creaking old back, and twisted old feet;
But since the fair morning when Fanny sat there,
I bless thee and love thee, old cane-bottomed chair.

If chairs have but feeling in holding such charms,
A thrill must have passed through your withered old arms!
I looked, and I longed, and I wished in despair;
I wished myself turned to a cane-bottomed chair.

It was but a moment she sat in this place,
She 'd a scarf on her neck, and a smile on her face!
A smile on her face, and a rose in her hair,
And she sat there, and bloomed in my cane-bottomed chair.

And so I have valued my chair ever since,
Like the shrine of a saint, or the throne of a prince;
Saint Fanny, my patroness sweet I declare,
The queen of my heart and my cane-bottomed chair.

When the candles burn low, and the company 's gone,
In the silence of night as I sit here alone—
I sit here alone, but we yet are a pair—
My Fanny I see in my cane-bottomed chair.

She comes from the past and revisits my room;
She looks as she then did, all beauty and bloom;
So smiling and tender, so fresh and so fair,
And yonder she sits in my cane-bottomed chair.

STANZAS TO PALE ALE.

PUNCH.

Oh! I have loved thee fondly, ever
Preferr'd thee to the choicest wine;
From thee my lips they could not sever
By saying thou contain'dst strychnine.
Did I believe the slander? Never!
I held thee still to be divine.

For me thy color hath a charm,
Although 'tis true they call thee Pale;
And be thou cold when I am warm,
As late I 've been—so high the scale
Of Fahrenheit—and febrile harm
Allay, refrigerating Ale!

How sweet thou art!—yet bitter, too
And sparkling, like satiric fun;
But how much better thee to brew,
Than a conundrum or a pun,
It is, in every point of view,
Must be allow'd by every one.

Refresh my heart and cool my throat,
  Light, airy child of malt and hops!
That dost not stuff, engross, and bloat
  The skin, the sides, the chin, the chops,
And burst the buttons off the coat,
  Like stout and porter—fattening slops!

"CHILDREN MUST BE PAID FOR."

PUNCH.

Sweet is the sound of infant voice;
  Young innocence is full of charms:
There 's not a pleasure half so choice,
  As tossing up a child in arms.
Babyhood is a blessed state,
  Felicity expressly made for;
But still, on earth it is our fate,
  That even "Children must be paid for."

If in an omnibus we ride,
  It is a beauteous sight to see,
When full the vehicle inside,
  Age taking childhood on its knee.
But in the dog-days' scorching heat,
  When a slight breath of air is pray'd for,
Half suffocated in our seat,
  We feel that "Children must be paid for."

There is about the sports of youth
  A charm that reaches every heart,
Marbles or tops are games of truth,
  The bat plays no deceiver's part.
But if we hear a sudden crash,
  No explanation need be stay'd for,
We know there 's something gone to smash;
  We feel that "Children must be paid for."

How exquisite the infant's grace,
  When, clambering upon the knee,
The cherub, smiling, takes his place
  Upon his mother's lap at tea;

Perchance the beverage flows o'er,
  And leaves a stain there is no aid for,
On carpet, dress, or chair. Once more
  We feel that "Children must be paid for."

Presiding at the festive board,
  With many faces laughing round,
Dull melancholy is ignored
  While mirth and jollity abound:
We see our table amply spread
  With knives and forks a dozen laid for;
Then pause to think:—"How are they fed?"
  Yes, "Children must indeed be paid for!"

THE MUSQUITO.

WILLIAM CULLEN BRYANT.

Fair insect! that, with thread-like legs spread out,
  And blood-extracting bill, and filmy wing,
Dost murmur, as thou slowly sail'st about,
  In pitiless ears full many a plaintive thing,
And tell how little our large veins should bleed,
Would we but yield them to thy bitter need.

Unwillingly, I own, and, what is worse,
  Full angrily men hearken to thy plaint;
Thou gettest many a brush and many a curse,
  For saying thou art gaunt, and starved, and faint:
Even the old beggar, while he asks for food,
Would kill thee, hapless stranger, if he could.

I call thee stranger, for the town, I ween,
  Has not the honor of so proud a birth—
Thou com'st from Jersey meadows, fresh and green,
  The offspring of the gods, though born on earth;
For Titan was thy sire, and fair was she,
The ocean-nymph that nursed thy infancy.

Beneath the rushes was thy cradle swung,
  And when, at length, thy gauzy wings grew strong,
Abroad to gentle airs their folds were flung,
  Rose in the sky, and bore thee soft along;

The south wind breathed to waft thee on thy way,
And danced and shone beneath the billowy bay.

Calm rose afar the city spires, and thence
  Came the deep murmur of its throng of men,
And as its grateful odors met thy sense,
  They seemed the perfumes of thy native fen.
Fair lay its crowded streets, and at the sight
Thy tiny song grew shriller with delight.

At length thy pinion fluttered in Broadway—
  Ah, there were fairy steps, and white necks kissed
By wanton airs, and eyes whose killing ray
  Shone through the snowy vails like stars through mist;
And fresh as morn, on many a cheek and chin,
Bloomed the bright blood through the transparent skin.

Sure these were sights to tempt an anchorite!
  What! do I hear thy slender voice complain?
Thou wailest when I talk of beauty's light,
  As if it brought the memory of pain:
Thou art a wayward being—well—come near,
And pour thy tale of sorrow in my ear.

What say'st thou, slanderer!—rouge makes thee sick?
  And China Bloom at best is sorry food?
And Rowland's Kalydor, if laid on thick,
  Poisons the thirsty wretch that bores for blood?
Go! 't was a just reward that met thy crime—
But shun the sacrilege another time.

That bloom was made to look at—not to touch;
  To worship—not approach—that radiant white;
And well might sudden vengeance light on such
  As dared, like thee, most impiously to bite.
Thou should'st have gazed at distance, and admired—
Murmured thy admiration, and retired.

Thou 'rt welcome to the town—but why come here
  To bleed a brother poet, gaunt like thee?
Alas! the little blood I have is dear,
  And thin will be the banquet drawn from me.

Look round—the pale-eyed sisters in my cell,
Thy old acquaintance, Song and Famine, dwell.

Try some plump alderman, and suck the blood
  Enriched by generous wine and costly meat;
On well-filled skins, sleek as thy native mud,
  Fix thy light pump, and press thy freckled feet:
Go to the men for whom, in ocean's halls,
The oyster breeds, and the green turtle sprawls.

There corks are drawn, and the red vintage flows,
  To fill the swelling veins for thee, and now
The ruddy cheek, and now the ruddier nose
  Shall tempt thee, as thou flittest round the brow;
And when the hour of sleep its quiet brings,
No angry hand shall rise to brush thy wings.

TO THE LADY IN THE CHEMISETTE WITH BLACK BUTTONS.

N. P. WILLIS.

I KNOW not who thou art, thou lovely one,
Thine eyes were drooped, thy lips half sorrowful,
Yet didst thou eloquently smile on me,
While handing up thy sixpence through the hole
Of that o'er-freighted omnibus!—ah, me!—
The world is full of meetings such as this;
A thrill—a voiceless challenge and reply,
And sudden partings after—we may pass,
And know not of each other's nearness now,
Thou in the Knickerbocker line, and I
Lone in the Waverley! Oh! life of pain;
And even should I pass where thou dost dwell—
Nay, see thee in the basement taking tea—
So cold is this inexorable world,
I must glide on, I dare not feast mine eye,
I dare not make articulate my love,
Nor o'er the iron rails that hem thee in
Venture to throw to thee my innocent card,
Not knowing thy papa.

Hast thou papa?
Is thy progenitor alive, fair girl?
And what doth he for lucre? Lo again!
A shadow o'er the face of this fair dream!
For thou may'st be as beautiful as Love
Can make thee, and the ministering hands
Of milliners, incapable of more,
Be lifted at thy shapeliness and air,
And still 'twixt me and thee, invisibly,
May rise a wall of adamant. My breath
Upon my pale lip freezes as I name
Manhattan's orient verge, and eke the west
In its far down extremity. Thy sire
May be the signer of a temperance pledge,
And clad all decently may walk the earth—
Nay—may be number'd with that blessed few
Who never ask for discount—yet, alas!
If, homeward wending from his daily cares,
He go by Murphy's Line, thence eastward tending—
Or westward from the Line of Kipp & Brown—
My vision is departed! Harshly falls
The doom upon the ear, "She 's not genteel!"
And pitiless is woman who doth keep
Of "good society" the golden key!
And gentlemen are bound, as are the stars,
To stoop not after rising!

But farewell,
And I shall look for thee in streets where dwell
The passengers by Broadway Lines alone!
And if my dreams be true, and thou, indeed,
Art only not more lovely than genteel—
Then, lady of the snow-white chemisette,
The heart which vent'rously cross'd o'er to thee
Upon that bridge of sixpence, may remain—
And, with up-town devotedness and truth,
My love shall hover round thee!

COME OUT, LOVE.

N. P. WILLIS.

Argument.—The poet starts from the Bowling Green to take his sweetheart up to Thompson's for an ice, or (if she is inclined for more) ices. He confines his muse to matters which any every-day man and young woman may see in taking the same promenade for the same innocent refreshment.

COME out, love—the night is enchanting!
  The moon hangs just over Broadway;
The stars are all lighted and panting—
  (Hot weather up there, I dare say!)
'Tis seldom that "coolness" entices,
  And love is no better for chilling—
But come up to Thompson's for ices,
  And cool your warm heart for a shilling!

What perfume comes balmily o'er us?
  Mint juleps from City Hotel!
A loafer is smoking before us—
  (A nasty cigar, by the smell!)
O Woman! thou secret past knowing!
  Like lilacs that grow by the wall,
You breathe every air that is going,
  Yet gather but sweetness from all!

On, on! by St. Paul's, and the Astor!
  Religion seems very ill-plann'd!
For one day we list to the pastor,
  For six days we list to the band!
The sermon may dwell on the future,
  The organ your pulses may calm—
When—pest!—that remember'd cachucha
  Upsets both the sermon and psalm!

Oh, pity the love that must utter
  While goes a swift omnibus by!
(Though sweet is *I scream** when the flutter
  Of fans shows thermometers high)—
But if what I bawl, or I mutter,
  Falls into your ear but to die,
Oh, the dew that falls into the gutter
  Is not more unhappy than I!

* *Query*—Should this be *Ice cream*, or *I scream?*—*Printer's Devil.*

THE WHITE CHIP HAT.

N. P. WILLIS.

I PASS'D her one day in a hurry,
  When late for the Post with a letter—
I think near the corner of Murray—
  And up rose my heart as I met her!
I ne'er saw a parasol handled
  So like to a duchess's doing—
I ne'er saw a slighter foot sandal'd,
  Or so fit to exhale in the shoeing—
          Lovely thing!

Surprising!—one woman can dish us
  So many rare sweets up together!
Tournure absolutely delicious—
  Chip hat without flower or feather—
Well-gloved and enchantingly boddiced,
  Her waist like the cup of a lily—
And an air, that, while daintily modest,
  Repell'd both the saucy and silly—
          Quite the thing!

For such a rare wonder you 'll say, sir,
  There 's reason in tearing one's tether—
And, to see her again in Broadway, sir,
  Who would not be lavish of leather!
I met her again, and as *you* know
  I 'm sage as old Voltaire at Ferney—
But I said a bad word—for my Juno
  Look'd sweet on a sneaking attorney—
          Horrid thing!

Away flies the dream I had nourish'd—
  My castles like mockery fall, sir!
And, now, the fine airs that she flourish'd
  Seem varnish and crockery all, sir!
The bright cup which angels might handle
  Turns earthy when finger'd by asses—
And the star that "swaps" light with a candle,
  Thenceforth for a pennyworth passes!—
          Not the thing!

YOU KNOW IF IT WAS YOU.

N. P. WILLIS.

As the chill'd robin, bound to Florida
Upon a morn of autumn, crosses flying
The air-track of a snipe most passing fair—
Yet colder in her blood than she is fair—
And as that robin lingers on the wing,
And feels the snipe's flight in the eddying air,
And loves her for her coldness not the less—
But fain would win her to that warmer sky
Where love lies waking with the fragrant stars—
Lo I—a languisher for sunnier climes,
Where fruit, leaf, blossom, on the trees forever
Image the tropic deathlessness of love—
Have met, and long'd to win thee, fairest lady,
To a more genial clime than cold Broadway!

Tranquil and effortless thou glidest on,
As doth the swan upon the yielding water,
And with a cheek like alabaster cold!
But as thou didst divide the amorous air
Just opposite the Astor, and didst lift
That vail of languid lashes to look in
At Leary's tempting window—lady! then
My heart sprang in beneath that fringéd vail,
Like an adventurous bird that would escape
To some warm chamber from the outer cold!
And there would I delightedly remain,
And close that fringéd window with a kiss,
And in the warm sweet chamber of thy breast,
Be prisoner forever!

THE DECLARATION.

N. P. WILLIS.

'T WAS late, and the gay company was gone,
And light lay soft on the deserted room
From alabaster vases, and a scent
Of orange-leaves, and sweet verbena came
Through the unshutter'd window on the air,

And the rich pictures with their dark old tints
Hung like a twilight landscape, and all things
Seem'd hush'd into a slumber. Isabel,
The dark-eyed, spiritual Isabel
Was leaning on her harp, and I had stay'd
To whisper what I could not when the crowd
Hung on her look like worshipers. I knelt,
And with the fervor of a lip unused
To the cool breath of reason, told my love.
There was no answer, and I took the hand
That rested on the strings, and press'd a kiss
Upon it unforbidden—and again
Besought her, that this silent evidence
That I was not indifferent to her heart,
Might have the seal of one sweet syllable.
I kiss'd the small white fingers as I spoke,
And she withdrew them gently, and upraised
Her forehead from its resting-place, and look'd
Earnestly on me—*She had been asleep!*

LOVE IN A COTTAGE.

N. P. WILLIS.

They may talk of love in a cottage,
  And bowers of trellised vine—
Of nature bewitchingly simple,
  And milkmaids half divine;
They may talk of the pleasure of sleeping
  In the shade of a spreading tree,
And a walk in the fields at morning,
  By the side of a footstep free!

But give me a sly flirtation
  By the light of a chandelier—
With music to play in the pauses,
  And nobody very near:
Or a seat on a silken sofa,
  With a glass of pure old wine,
And mamma too blind to discover
  The small white hand in mine.

Your love in a cottage is hungry,
  Your vine is a nest for flies—
Your milkmaid shocks the Graces,
  And simplicity talks of pies!
You lie down to your shady slumber
  And wake with a bug in your ear,
And your damsel that walks in the morning
  Is shod like a mountaineer.

True love is at home on a carpet,
  And mightily likes his ease—
And true love has an eye for a dinner,
  And starves beneath shady trees.
His wing is the fan of a lady,
  His foot's an invisible thing,
And his arrow is tipp'd with a jewel,
  And shot from a silver string.

TO HELEN IN A HUFF.

N. P. WILLIS.

Nay, lady, one frown is enough
  In a life as soon over as this—
And though minutes seem long in a huff,
  They 're minutes 'tis pity to miss!
The smiles you imprison so lightly
  Are reckon'd, like days in eclipse;
And though you may smile again brightly,
  You 've lost so much light from your lips!
    Pray, lady, smile!

The cup that is longest untasted
  May be with our bliss running o'er,
And, love when we will, we have wasted
  An age in not loving before!
Perchance Cupid 's forging a fetter
  To tie us together some day,
And, just for the chance, we had better
  Be laying up love, I should say!
    Nay, lady, smile!

THE HEIGHT OF THE RIDICULOUS.

OLIVER WENDELL HOLMES.

I WROTE some lines, once on a time,
In wondrous merry mood,
And thought, as usual, men would say
They were exceeding good.

They were so queer, so very queer,
I laughed as I would die;
Albeit, in the general way,
A sober man am I.

I called my servant, and he came;
How kind it was of him,
To mind a slender man like me,
He of the mighty limb!

"These to the printer," I exclaimed,
And, in my humorous way,
I added (as a trifling jest),
"There 'll be the devil to pay."

He took the paper, and I watched,
And saw him peep within;
At the first lne he read, his face
Was all upon the grin.

He read the next; the grin grew broad,
And shot from ear to ear;
He read the third; a chuckling noise
I now began to hear.

The fourth; he broke into a roar;
The fifth; his waistband split;
The sixth; he burst five buttons off,
And tumbled in a fit.

Ten days and nights, with sleepless eye,
I watched that wretched man,
And since, I never dare to write
As funny as I can.

THE BRIEFLESS BARRISTER.

A BALLAD.

JOHN G. SAXE.

An Attorney was taking a turn,
  In shabby habiliments drest;
His coat it was shockingly worn,
  And the rust had invested his vest.

His breeches had suffered a breach,
  His linen and worsted were worse;
He had scarce a whole crown in his hat,
  And not half-a-crown in his purse.

And thus as he wandered along,
  A cheerless and comfortless elf,
He sought for relief in a song,
  Or complainingly talked to himself:

"Unfortunate man that I am!
  I've never a client but grief;
The case is, I've no case at all,
  And in brief, I've ne'er had a brief!

"I've waited and waited in vain,
  Expecting an 'opening' to find,
Where an honest young lawyer might gain
  Some reward for the toil of his mind.

"'Tis not that I'm wanting in law,
  Or lack an intelligent face,
That others have cases to plead,
  While I have to plead for a case.

"O, how can a modest young man
  E'er hope for the smallest progression—
The profession's already so full
  Of lawyers so full of profession!"

While thus he was strolling around,
  His eye accidentally fell
On a very deep hole in the ground,
  And he sighed to himself, "It is well!"

To curb his emotions, he sat
  On the curb-stone the space of a minute,
Then cried, "Here 's an opening at last!"
  And in less than a jiffy was in it!

Next morning twelve citizens came
  ('Twas the coroner bade them attend),
To the end that it might be determined
  How the man had determined his end!

"The man was a lawyer, I hear,"
  Quoth the foreman who sat on the corse;
"A lawyer? Alas!" said another,
  "Undoubtedly he died of remorse!"

A third said, "He knew the deceased,
  An attorney well versed in the laws,
And as to the cause of his death,
  'Twas no doubt from the want of a cause."

The jury decided at length,
  After solemnly weighing the matter,
"That the lawyer was drownded, because
  He could not keep his head above water!"

SONNET TO A CLAM.

JOHN G. SAXE.

Dum tacent *clam*ant.

INGLORIOUS FRIEND! most confident I am
  Thy life is one of very little ease;
  Albeit men mock thee with their similes
And prate of being "happy as a clam!"
What though thy shell protects thy fragile head
  From the sharp bailiffs of the briny sea?
  Thy valves are, sure, no safety-valves to thee,
While rakes are free to desecrate thy bed,
And bear thee off—as foemen take their spoil—
  Far from thy friends and family to roam;
  Forced, like a Hessian, from thy native home,
To meet destruction in a foreign broil!
  Though thou art tender, yet thy humble bard
  Declares, O clam! thy case is shocking hard!

VENUS OF THE NEEDLE.

WILLIAM ALLINGHAM.

O Maryanne, you pretty girl,
Intent on silky labor,
Of sempstresses the pink and pearl,
Excuse a peeping neighbor!

Those eyes, forever drooping, give
The long brown lashes rarely;
But violets in the shadows live,—
For once unvail them fairly.

Hast thou not lent that flounce enough
Of looks so long and earnest?
Lo, here 's more "penetrable stuff,"
To which thou never turnest.

Ye graceful fingers, deftly sped!
How slender, and how nimble!
O might I wind their skeins of thread,
Or but pick up their thimble!

How blest the youth whom love shall bring,
And happy stars embolden,
To change the dome into a ring,
The silver into golden!

Who 'll steal some morning to her side
To take her finger's measure,
While Maryanne pretends to chide,
And blushes deep with pleasure.

Who 'll watch her sew her wedding-gown,
Well conscious that it *is* hers,
Who 'll glean a tress, without a frown,
With those so ready scissors.

Who 'll taste those ripenings of the south,
The fragrant and delicious—
Don't put the pins into your mouth,
O Maryanne, my precious!

I almost wish it were my trust
  To teach how shocking that is;
I wish I had not, as I must,
  To quit this tempting lattice.

Sure aim takes Cupid, fluttering foe,
  Across a street so narrow;
A thread of silk to string his bow,
  A needle for his arrow!

NARRATIVE.

NARRATIVE.

TAKE THY OLD CLOAK ABOUT THEE.

[OLD BALLAD, QUOTED BY SHAKSPEARE, IN OTHELLO.]

PERCY RELIQUES.

THIS winters weather itt waxeth cold,
  And frost doth freese on every hill,
And Boreas blowes his blasts soe bold,
  That all our cattell are like to spill;
Bell, my wiffe, who loves noe strife,
  Shee sayd unto me quietlye,
Rise up, and save cow Cumbockes liffe,
  Man, put thine old cloake about thee.

HE.

O Bell, why dost thou flyte and scorne?
  Thou kenst my cloak is very thin:
Itt is soe bare and overworne
  A cricke he theron cannot renn:
Then Ile no longer borrowe nor lend,
  For once Ile new appareld bee,
To-morrow Ile to towne and spend,
  For Ile have a new cloake about mee.

SHE.

Cow Crumbocke is a very good cowe,
  Shee ha beene alwayes true to the payle,
She has helpt us to butter and cheese, I trow,
  And other things shee will not fayle;
I wold be loth to see her pine,
  Good husband councell take of mee,
It is not for us to go soe fine,
  Man, take thine old cloake about thee.

He.

My cloake it was a very good cloake
  Itt hath been alwayes true to the weare,
But now it is not worth a groat;
  I have had it four and forty yeere;
Sometime itt was of cloth in graine,
  'Tis now but a sigh clout as you may see,
It will neither hold out winde nor raine;
  And Ile have a new cloake about mee.

She.

It is four and fortye yeeres agoe
  Since the one of us the other did ken,
And we have had betwixt us towe
  Of children either nine or ten;
Wee have brought them up to women and men;
  In the feare of God I trow they bee;
And why wilt thou thyselfe misken?
  Man, take thine old cloake about thee.

He.

O Bell, my wiffe, why dost thou floute!
  Now is nowe, and then was then:
Seeke now all the world throughout,
  Thou kenst not clownes from gentlemen.
They are cladd in blacke, greene, yellowe, or gray,
  Soe far above their owne degree:
Once in my life Ile doe as they,
  For Ile have a new cloake about mee.

She.

King Stephen was a worthy peere,
  His breeches cost him but a crowne,
He held them sixpence all too deere;
  Therefore he calld the taylor Lowne.
He was a wight of high renowne,
  And thouse but of a low degree:
Itt's pride that putts this countrye downe,
  Man, take thine old cloake about thee.

HE.

"Bell, my wife, she loves not strife,
Yet she will lead me if she can;
And oft, to live a quiet life,
I am forced to yield, though Ime good-man;"
Itt 's not for a man with a woman to threape,
Unlesse he first gave oer the plea:
As wee began wee now will leave,
And Ile take mine old cloake about mee.

KING JOHN AND THE ABBOT.

[AN OLD ENGLISH BALLAD—LONG VERY POPULAR.]

PERCY RELIQUES.

An ancient story Ile tell you anon
Of a notable prince, that was called King John;
And he ruled England with maine and with might,
For he did great wrong, and maintein'd little right.

And Ile tell you a story, a story so merrye,
Concerning the Abbot of Canterbùrye;
How for his house-keeping, and high renowne,
They rode poste for him to fair London towne.

An hundred men, the king did heare say,
The abbot kept in his house every day;
And fifty golde chaynes, without any doubt,
In velvet coates waited the abbot about.

How now, father abbot, I heare it of thee,
Thou keepest a farre better house than mee,
And for thy house-keeping and high renowne,
I feare thou work'st treason against my crown.

My liege, quo' the abbot, I would it were knowne
I never spend nothing but what is my owne;
And I trust your grace will doe me no deere
For spending of my owne true-gotten geere.

Yes, yes, father abbot, thy fault it is highe,
And now for the same thou needest must dye;
For except thou canst answer me questions three,
Thy head shall be smitten from thy bodìe.

And first, quo' the king, when I 'm in this stead,
With my crowne of golde so faire on my head,
Among all my liege-men, so noble of birthe,
Thou must tell me to one penny what I am worthe.

Secondlye, tell me, without any doubt,
How soone I may ride the whole world about,
And at the third question thou must not shrink,
But tell me here truly what I do think.

O, these are hard questions for my shallow witt,
Nor I cannot answer your grace as yet;
But if you will give me but three weekes space,
Ile do my endeavour to answer your grace.

Now three weeks space to thee will I give,
And that is the longest time thou hast to live;
For if thou dost not answer my questions three,
Thy lands and thy livings are forfeit to mee.

Away rode the abbot, all sad at that word,
And he rode to Cambridge and Oxenford;
But never a doctor there was so wise,
That could with his learning an answer devise.

Then home rode the abbot, of comfort so cold,
And he mett his shepheard agoing to fold:
How now, my lord abbot, you are welcome home,
What newes do you bring us from good King John?

Sad newes, sad newes, shepheard, I must give:
That I have but three days more to live;
For if I do not answer him questions three,
My head will be smitten from my bodìe.

The first is to tell him there in that stead,
With his crowne of golde so fair on his head,
Among all his liege-men so noble of birth,
To within one penny of what he is worth.

The seconde, to tell him, without any doubt,
How soone he may ride this whole world about:
And at the third question I must not shrinke,
But tell him there truly what he does thinke.

Now cheare up, sire abbot, did you never hear yet,
That a fool he may learne a wise man witt?
Lend me horse, and serving-men, and your apparel,
And I'll ride to London to answere your quarrel.

Nay frowne not, if it hath bin told unto mee,
I am like your lordship, as ever may bee:
And if you will but lend me your gowne,
There is none shall knowe us in fair London towne.

Now horses and serving-men thou shalt have,
With sumptuous array most gallant and brave;
With crozier, and miter, and rochet, and cope,
Fit to appeare 'fore our fader the pope.

Now welcome, sire abbot, the king he did say,
'Tis well thou'rt come back to keepe thy day;
For and if thou canst answer my questions three,
Thy life and thy living both saved shall bee.

And first, when thou seest me here in this stead,
With my crown of golde so fair on my head,
Among all my liege-men so noble of birthe,
Tell me to one penny what I am worth.

For thirty pence our Saivour was sold
Among the false Jewes, as I have bin told:
And twenty-nine is the worth of thee,
For I thinke, thou art one penny worser than hee.

The king he laughed, and swore by St. Bittel,
I did not think I had been worth so littel!
—Now secondly tell me, without any doubt,
How soone I may ride this whole world about.

You must rise with the sun, and ride with the same,
Until the next morning he riseth againe;
And then your grace need not make any doubt
But in twenty-four hours you'll ride it about.

The king he laughed, and swore by St. Jone,
I did not think it could be gone so soone!
—Now from the third question thou must not shrinke,
But tell me here truly what I do thinke.

Yea, that shall I do, and make your grace merry:
You thinke I'm the abbot of Canterbùry;
But I'm his poor shepheard, as plain you may see,
That am come to beg pardon for him and for mee.

The king he laughed, and swore by the masse,
Ile make thee lord abbot this day in his place!
Now naye, my liege, be not in such speede,
For alacke I can neither write, ne reade.

Four nobles a week, then, I will give thee,
For this merry jest thou hast showne unto mee:
And tell the old abbot, when thou comest home,
Thou hast brought him a pardon from good King John.

THE BAFFLED KNIGHT, OR LADY'S POLICY.

[A VERY FAVORITE ANCIENT BALLAD.]

PERCY RELIQUES.

THERE was a knight was drunk with wine,
A riding along the way, sir;
And there he met with a lady fine,
Among the cocks of hay, sir.

Shall you and I, O lady faire,
Among the grass lye down-a:
And I will have a special care,
Of rumpling of your gowne-a.

Upon the grass there is a dewe,
Will spoil my damask gowne, sir:
My gowne and kirtle they are newe,
And cost me many a crowne, sir.

I have a cloak of scarlet red,
  Upon the ground I 'll throwe it;
Then, lady faire, come lay thy head;
  We 'll play, and none shall knowe it.

O yonder stands my steed so free
  Among the cocks of hay, sir,
And if the pinner should chance to see,
  He 'll take my steed away, sir.

Upon my finger I have a ring,
  Its made of finest gold-a,
And, lady, it thy steed shall bring
  Out of the pinner's fold-a.

O go with me to my father's hall;
  Fair chambers there are three, sir:
And you shall have the best of all,
  And I 'll your chamberlaine bee, sir.

He mounted himself on his steed so tall,
  And her on her dapple gray, sir:
And there they rode to her father's hall,
  Fast pricking along the way, sir.

To her father's hall they arrived strait;
  'T was moated round about-a;
She slipped herself within the gate,
  And lockt the knight without-a.

Here is a silver penny to spend,
  And take it for your pain, sir;
And two of my father's men I 'll send
  To wait on you back again, sir.

He from his scabbard drew his brand,
  And wiped it upon his sleeve-a!
And cursed, he said, be every man,
  That will a maid believe-a!

She drew a bodkin from her haire,
  And wip'd it upon her gown-a;
And curs'd be every maiden faire,
  That will with men lye down-a!

A herb there is, that lowly grows,
  And some do call it rue, sir:
The smallest dunghill cock that crows,
  Would make a capon of you, sir.

A flower there is, that shineth bright,
  Some call it mary-gold-a:
He that wold not when he might,
  He shall not when he wold-a.

The knight was riding another day,
  With cloak, and hat, and feather:
He met again with that lady gay,
  Who was angling in the river.

Now, lady faire, I've met with you,
  You shall no more escape me;
Remember, how not long agoe
  You falsely did intrap me.

He from his saddle down did light,
  In all his riche attyer;
And cryed, As I'm a noble knight,
  I do thy charms admyer.

He took the lady by the hand,
  Who seemingly consented;
And would no more disputing stand:
  She had a plot invented.

Looke yonder, good sir knight, I pray,
  Methinks I now discover
A riding upon his dapple gray,
  My former constant lover.

On tip-toe peering stood the knight,
  Fast by the rivers brink-a;
The lady pusht with all her might:
  Sir knight, now swim or sink-a.

O'er head and ears he plunged in,
  The bottom faire he sounded;
Then rising up, he cried amain,
  Help, helpe, or else I'm drownded!

Now, fare-you-well, sir knight, adieu!
  You see what comes of fooling:
That is the fittest place for you;
  Your courage wanted cooling.

Ere many days, in her fathers park,
  Just at the close of eve-a,
Again she met with her angry sparke;
  Which made this lady grieve-a.

False lady, here thou 'rt in my powre,
  And no one now can hear thee:
And thou shalt sorely rue the hour
  That e'er thou dar'dst to jeer me.

I pray, sir knight, be not so warm
  With a young silly maid-a:
I vow and swear I thought no harm,
  'Twas a gentle jest I playd-a.

A gentle jest, in soothe he cry'd,
  To tumble me in and leave me!
What if I had in the river dy'd?——
  That fetch will not deceive me.

Once more I 'll pardon thee this day,
  Tho' injur'd out of measure;
But thou prepare without delay
  To yield thee to my pleasure.

Well then, if I must grant your suit,
  Yet think of your boots and spurs, sir:
Let me pull off both spur and boot,
  Or else you cannot stir, sir.

He set him down upon the grass,
  And begg'd her kind assistance:
Now, smiling, thought this lovely lass,
  I 'll make you keep your distance.

Then pulling off his boots half-way;
  Sir knight, now I 'm your betters:
You shall not make of me your prey;
  Sit there like a knave in fetters.

The knight, when she had served him soe,
He fretted, fum'd, and grumbled:
For he could neither stand nor goe,
But like a cripple tumbled.

Farewell, sir knight, the clock strikes ten,
Yet do not move nor stir, sir:
I 'll send you my father's serving men,
To pull off your boots and spurs, sir.

This merry jest you must excuse,
You are but a stingless nettle:
You 'd never have stood for boots or shoes,
Had you been a man of mettle.

All night in grievous rage he lay,
Rolling upon the plain-a;
Next morning a shepherd past that way,
Who set him right again-a.

Then mounting upon his steed so tall,
By hill and dale he swore-a:
I 'll ride at once to her father's hall;
She shall escape no more-a.

I 'll take her father by the beard,
I 'll challenge all her kindred;
Each dastard soul shall stand affeard;
My wrath shall no more be hindred.

He rode unto her father's house,
Which every side was moated:
The lady heard his furious vows,
And all his vengeance noted.

Thought shee, sir knight, to quench your rage
Once more I will endeavour:
This water shall your fury 'swage,
Or else it shall burn for ever.

Then faining penitence and feare,
She did invite a parley:
Sir knight, if you 'll forgive me heare,
Henceforth I 'll love you dearly.

My father he is now from home,
  And I am all alone, sir:
Therefore across the water come,
  And I am all your own, sir.

False maid, thou canst no more deceive;
  I scorn the treacherous bait-a;
If thou would'st have me thee believe,
  Now open me the gate-a.

The bridge is drawn, the gate is barr'd,
  My father he has the keys, sir;
But I have for my love prepar'd
  A shorter way, and easier.

Over the moate I've laid a plank
  Full seventeen feet in measure,
Then step across to the other bank,
  And there we'll take our pleasure.

These words she had no sooner spoke,
  But straight he came tripping over:
The plank was saw'd, it snapping broke,
  And sous'd the unhappy lover.

TRUTH AND FALSEHOOD.

A TALE.

MATTHEW PRIOR.

Once on a time, in sunshine weather,
Falsehood and Truth walk'd out together,
The neighboring woods and lawns to view,
As opposites will sometimes do.
Through many a blooming mead they passed,
And at a brook arriv'd at last.
The purling stream, the margin green,
With flowers bedeck'd, a vernal scene,
Invited each itinerant maid,
To rest a while beneath the shade.
Under a spreading beach they sat,
And pass'd the time with female chat;

Whilst each her character maintain'd;
One spoke her thoughts, the other feign'd.
At length, quoth Falsehood, sister Truth
(For so she call'd her from her youth),
What if, to shun yon sultry beam,
We bathe in this delightful stream;
The bottom smooth, the water clear,
And there 's no prying shepherd near?–
With all my heart, the nymph replied,
And threw her snowy robes aside,
Stript herself naked to the skin,
And with a spring leapt headlong in.
Falsehood more leisurely undrest,
And, laying by her tawdry vest,
Trick'd herself out in Truth's array,
And 'cross the meadows tript away.
From this curst hour, the fraudful dame
Of sacred Truth usurps the name,
And, with a vile, perfidious mind,
Roams far and near, to cheat mankind;
False sighs suborns, and artful tears,
And starts with vain pretended fears;
In visits, still appears most wise,
And rolls at church her saint-like eyes;
Talks very much, plays idle tricks,
While rising stock* her conscience pricks;
When being, poor thing, extremely gravel'd,
The secrets op'd, and all unravel'd.
But on she will, and secrets tell
Of John and Joan, and Ned and Nell,
Reviling every one she knows,
As fancy leads, beneath the rose.
Her tongue, so voluble and kind,
It always runs before her mind;
As times do serve, she slyly pleads,
And copious tears still show her needs.
With promises as thick as weeds—
Speaks pro and con., is wondrous civil,
To-day a saint, to-morrow devil.
Poor Truth she stript, as has been said,
And naked left the lovely maid,

* South Sea, 1720.

Who, scorning from her cause to wince,
Has gone stark-naked ever since;
And ever naked will appear,
Belov'd by all who Truth revere.

FLATTERY.

A FABLE.

SIR CHARLES HANBURY WILLIAMS.

Fanny, beware of flattery,
Your sex's much-lov'd enemy;
For other foes we are prepar'd,
And Nature puts us on our guard:
In that alone such charms are found,
We court the dart, we nurse the hand;
And this, my child, an Æsop's Fable
Will prove much better than I 'm able.

A young vain female Crow,
Had perch'd upon a pine tree's bough,
  And sitting there at ease,
Was going to indulge her taste,
In a most delicious feast,
  Consisting of a slice of cheese.
A sharp-set Fox (a wily creature)
    Pass'd by that way
    In search of prey;
  When to his nose the smell of cheese,
  Came in a gentle western breeze;
No Welchman knew, or lov'd it better:
  He bless'd th' auspicious wind,
  And strait look'd round to find,
What might his hungry stomach fill,
    And quickly spied the Crow,
    Upon a lofty bough,
Holding the tempting prize within her bill.
    But she was perch'd too high,
    And Reynard could not fly:

She chose the tallest tree in all the wood,
What then could bring her down?
Or make the prize his own?
Nothing but flatt'ry could.
He soon the silence broke,
And thus ingenious hunger spoke:
"Oh, lovely bird,
Whose glossy plumage oft has stirr'd
The envy of the grove;
Thy form was Nature's pleasing care,
So bright a bloom, so soft an air,
All that behold must love.
But, if to suit a form like thine,
Thy voice be as divine;
If both in these together meet,
The feather'd race must own
Of all their tribe there's none,
Of form so fair, of voice so sweet.
Who 'll then regard the linnet's note,
Or heed the lark's melodious throat?
What pensive lovers then shall dwell
With raptures on their Philomel?
The goldfinch shall his plumage hide,
The swan abate her stately pride,
And Juno's bird no more display
His various glories to the sunny day:
Then grant thy Suppliant's prayer,
And bless my longing ear
With notes that I would die to hear!"
Flattery prevail'd, the Crow believ'd
The tale, and was with joy deceiv'd;
In haste to show her want of skill,
She open'd wide her bill:
She scream'd as if the de'el was in her
Her vanity became so strong
That, wrapt in her own frightful song,
She quite forgot, and dropt her dinner:
The morsel fell quick by the place
Where Reynard lay,
Who seized the prey
And eat it without saying grace.

He, sneezing, cried "The day's my own,
My end's obtain'd,
The prize is gain'd,
And now I 'll change my note.
Vain, foolish, cheated Crow,
Lend your attention now,
A truth or two I 'll tell you!
For, since I 've fill'd my belly,
Of course my flatt'ry's done:
Think you I took such pains,
And spoke so well only to hear you croak?
No, 't was the luscious bait,
And a keen appetite to eat,
That first inspir'd, and carried on the cheat.
'T was hunger furnish'd hands and matter,
Flatterers must live by those they flatter;
But weep not, Crow; a tongue like mine
Might turn an abler head than thine;
And though reflection may displease,
If wisely you apply your thought,
To learn the lesson I have taught,
Experience, sure, is cheaply bought,
And richly worth a slice of cheese."

THE PIG AND MAGPIE.

PETER PINDAR.

Cocking his tail, a saucy prig,
A Magpie hopped upon a Pig,
To pull some hair, forsooth, to line his nest;
And with such ease began the hair attack,
As thinking the fee simple of the back
Was by himself, and not the Pig, possessed.

The Boar looked up as thunder black to Mag,
Who, squinting down on him like an arch wag,
Informed Mynheer some bristles must be torn;
Then briskly went to work, not nicely culling:
Got a good handsome beakful by good pulling,
And flew, without a "Thank ye" to his thorn.

The Pig set up a dismal yelling:
Followed the robber to his dwelling,
Who like a fool had built it 'midst a bramble:
In manfully he sallied, full of might,
Determined to obtain his right,
And 'midst the bushes now began to scramble.

He drove the Magpie, tore his nest to rags,
And, happy on the downfall, poured his brags:
But ere he from the brambles came, alack!
His ears and eyes were miserably torn,
His bleeding hide in such a plight forlorn,
He could not count ten hairs upon his back.

ADVICE TO YOUNG WOMEN;

OR, THE ROSE AND STRAWBERRY.

PETER PINDAR.

YOUNG women! don't be fond of killing,
Too well I know your hearts unwilling
To hide beneath the vail a charm—
Too pleased a sparkling eye to roll,
And with a neck to thrill the soul
Of every swain with love's alarm.

Yet, yet, if prudence be not near
Its snow may melt into a tear.

The dimple smile, and pouting lip,
Where little Cupids nectar sip,
Are very pretty lures I own:
But, ah! if prudence be not nigh,
Those lips where all the Cupids lie,
May give a passage to a groan.

A Rose, in all the pride of bloom,
Flinging around her rich perfume
Her form to public notice pushing,
Amid the summer's golden glow
Peeped on a Strawberry below,
Beneath a leaf, in secret blushing.

"Miss Strawberry," exclaimed the Rose,
"What's beauty that no mortal knows?
What is a charm, if never seen?
You really are a pretty creature:
Then wherefore hide each blooming feature?
Come up, and show your modest mien."

"Miss Rose," the Strawberry replied,
"I never did possess a pride
That wished to dash the public eye:
Indeed, I own that I'm afraid—
I think there's safety in the shade,
Ambition causes many a sigh."

"Go, simple child," the Rose rejoined,
"See how I wanton in the wind:
I feel no danger's dread alarms:
And then observe the god of day,
How amorous with his golden ray,
To pay his visits to my charms!"

No sooner said, but with a scream
She started from her favorite theme—
A clown had on her fixed his pat.
In vain she screeched—Hob did but smile;
Rubbed with her leaves his nose awhile,
Then bluntly stuck her in his hat.

ECONOMY.

PETER PINDAR

ECONOMY'S a very useful broom;
Yet should not ceaseless hunt about the room
To catch each straggling pin to make a plumb:
Too oft Economy's an iron vice,
That squeezes even the little guts of mice,
That peep with fearful eyes, and ask a crumb.

Proper Economy's a comely thing—
Good in a subject—better in a king;

Yet pushed too far, it dulls each finer feeling—
Most easily inclined to make folks mean;
Inclines them too, to villainy to lean,
To over-reaching, perjury, and stealing.

Even when the heart should only think of grief,
It creeps into the bosom like a thief,
And swallows up th' affections all so mild—
Witness the Jewess, and her only child:—

THE JEWESS AND HER SON.

Poor Mistress Levi had a luckless son,
Who, rushing to obtain the foremost seat,
In imitation of th' ambitious great,
High from the gallery, ere the play begun,
He fell all plump into the pit,
Dead in a minute as a nit:
In short, he broke his pretty Hebrew neck;
Indeed and very dreadful was the wreck!

The mother was distracted, raving, wild—
Shrieked, tore her hair, embraced and kissed her child—
Afflicted every heart with grief around:
Soon as the shower of tears was somewhat past,
And moderately calm th' hysteric blast,
She cast about her eyes in thought profound·
And being with a saving knowledge blessed,
She thus the playhouse manager addressed:

"Sher, I'm de moder of de poor Chew lad,
Dat meet mishfartin here so bad—
Sher, I muss haf de shilling back, you know,
Ass Moses haf not see de show."

But as for Avarice, 'tis the very devil;
The fount, alas! of every evil:
The cancer of the heart—the worst of ills:
Wherever sown, luxuriantly it thrives;
No flower of virtue near it lives:
Like aconite, where'er it spreads, it kills.

In every soil behold the poison spring!
Can taint the beggar, and infect the king.

The mighty Marlborough pilfered cloth and bread;
So says that gentle satirist Squire Pope;
And Peterborough's Earl upon this head,
Affords us little room to hope,
That what the Twitnam bard avowed,
Might not be readily allowed.

THE COUNTRY LASSES.

PETER PINDAR.

Peter lasheth the Ladies.—He turneth Story-teller.—Peter grieveth.

ALTHOUGH the ladies with such beauty blaze,
They very frequently my passion raise—
Their charms compensate, scarce, their want of *taste.*
Passing amidst the Exhibition crowd,
I heard some damsels *fashionably* loud;
And thus I give the dialogue that pass'd.

"Oh! the dear man!" cried one, "look! here's a bonnet!
He shall paint *me*—I am determin'd on it—
Lord! cousin, see! how beautiful the gown!
What charming colors! here 's fine lace, here 's gauze!
What pretty sprigs the fellow draws!
Lord, cousin! he 's the cleverest man in town!"

"Ay, cousin," cried a second, "very true—
And here, here's charming green, and red, and blue!
There 's a complexion beats the *rouge* of Warren!
See those red lips; oh, la! they seem so nice!
What rosy cheeks then, cousin, to entice!—
Compar'd to this, all other heads are carrion.

Cousin, this limner quickly will be seen,
Painting the Princess Royal, and the Queen:
Pray, don't you think as I do, *Coz?*
But we 'll be painted *first* that's *poz.*"

Such was the very *pretty* conversation
  That pass'd between the *pretty* misses,
While unobserv'd, the glory of our nation,
  Close by them hung Sir Joshua's matchless pieces.
Works! that a Titian's hand could form alone—
Works! that a Reubens had been proud to own.

Permit me, ladies, now to lay before ye
What lately happen'd—therefore a true story:—

A STORY.

Walking one afternoon along the Strand,
My wond'ring eyes did suddenly expand
  Upon a pretty leash of country lasses.

"Heav'ns! my dear beauteous angels, how d'ye do?
  Upon my soul I'm monstrous glad to see ye."
"Swinge! Peter, we are glad to meet with *you;*
  We're just to London come—well, pray how be ye;

"We're just a going, while 'tis light,
  To see St. Paul's before 'tis dark.
Lord! come, for once, be so polite,
  And condescend to be our spark."

"With all my heart, my angels."—On we walk'd,
And much of London—much of Cornwall talk'd.
  Now did I hug myself to think
How much that glorious structure would surprise,
  How from its awful grandeur they would shrink
With open mouths, and marv'ling eyes!

As near to Ludgate-Hill we drew,
St. Paul's just opening on our view;
Behold, my lovely strangers, one and all,
Gave, all at once, a diabolic squawl,
As if they had been tumbled on the stones,
And some confounded cart had crush'd their bones.

After well fright'ning people with their cries,
And sticking to a ribbon-shop their eyes,

They all rush'd in, with sounds enough to stun,
And clattering all together, thus begun:—

"Swinge! here are colors then, to please!
Delightful things, I vow to heav'n!
Why! not to see such things as these,
We never should have been forgiv'n.

"Here, here, are clever things—good Lord!
And, sister, here, upon my word—
Here, here!—look! here are beauties to delight:
Why! how a body's heels might dance
Along from Launceston to Penzance,
Before that one might meet with such a sight!"

"Come, ladies. 't will be dark," cried I—"I fear:
Pray let us view St. Paul's, it is so near"—
"Lord! Peter," cried the girls, "don't mind St. Paul!
Sure! you're a most *incurious* soul—
Why—we can see the church another day;
Don't be afraid—St. Paul's can't *run away.*"

Reader,
If e'er thy bosom felt a thought *sublime*,
Drop tears of pity with the man of rhyme!

THE PILGRIMS AND THE PEAS.

PETER PINDAR.

Peter continueth to give great Advice, and to exhibit deep reflection—He telleth a miraculous Story.

There is a knack in doing many a thing,
Which labor can not to perfection bring:
Therefore, however great in your own eyes,
Pray do not hints from other folks despise:

A fool on something great, at times, may stumble,
And consequently be a good adviser:
On which, forever, your wise men may fumble,
And never be a whit the wiser.

Yes! I advise you, for there 's wisdom in 't,
Never to be superior to a hint—
The genius of each man, with keenness view—
A spark from this, or t'other, caught,
May kindle, quick as thought,
A glorious bonfire up in you.

A question of you let me beg—
Of fam'd Columbus and his egg,
Pray, have you heard? "Yes."—O, then, if you please
I 'll give you the two Pilgrims and the Peas.

THE PILGRIMS AND THE PEAS.

A TRUE STORY.

A brace of sinners, for no good,
Were order'd to the Virgin Mary's shrine,
Who at Loretto dwelt, in wax, stone, wood,
And in a fair white wig look'd wondrous fine.

Fifty long miles had those sad rogues to travel,
With something in their shoes much worse than gravel'
In short, their toes so gentle to amuse,
The priest had order'd peas into their shoes:

A nostrum famous in old Popish times
For purifying souls that stunk of crimes:
A sort of apostolic salt,
Which Popish parsons for its powers exalt,
For keeping souls of sinners sweet,
Just as our kitchen salt keeps meat.

The knaves set off on the same day,
Peas in their shoes, to go and pray:
But very diff'rent was their speed, I wot:
One of the sinners gallop'd on,
Swift as a bullet from a gun;
The other limp'd, as if he had been shot.

One saw the Virgin soon—*peccavi* cried—
Had his soul white-wash'd all so clever;
Then home again he nimbly hied,
Made fit, with saints above, to live forever.

In coming back, however, let me say,
He met his brother rogue about half way—
Hobbling, with out-stretch'd hands and bending knees;
Damning the souls and bodies of the peas:
His eyes in tears, his cheeks and brows in sweat,
Deep sympathizing with his groaning feet.

"How now," the light-toed, white-wash'd pilgrim broke,
"You lazy lubber!"
"Ods curse it," cried the other, "'tis no joke—
My feet, once hard as any rock,
Are now as soft as any blubber.

"Excuse me, Virgin Mary, that I swear—
As for Loretto I shall not get there;
No! to the Dev'l my sinful soul must go,
For damme if I ha'nt lost ev'ry toe.

"But, brother sinner, pray explain
How 'tis that you are not in pain:
What pow'r hath work'd a wonder for *your* toes:
While *I*, just like a snail am crawling,
Now swearing, now on saints devoutly bawling,
While not a rascal comes to ease my woes?

"How is't that *you* can like a greyhound go,
Merry, as if that naught had happen'd, burn ye?"
"Why," cried the other, grinning, "you must know,
That just before I ventur'd on my journey,
To walk a little more at ease,
I took the liberty to boil *my* peas.'"

ON THE DEATH OF A FAVORITE CAT,

DROWNED IN A TUB OF GOLDFISHES.

THOMAS GRAY.

'T WAS on a lofty vase's side,
Where China's gayest art had dyed
The azure flowers that blow,
Demurest of the tabby kind,
The pensive Selimă, reclined,
Gazed on the lake below.

Her conscious tail her joy declared;
The fair round face, the snowy beard,
The velvet of her paws,
Her coat that with the tortoise vies,
Her ears of jet, and emerald eyes,
She saw, and purred applause.

Still had she gaz'd, but, 'midst the tide,
Two angel forms were seen to glide,
The Genii of the stream:
Their scaly armor's Tyrian hue,
Through richest purple, to the view
Betrayed a golden gleam.

The hapless nymph with wonder saw:
A whisker first, and then a claw,
With many an ardent wish,
She stretched in vain to reach the prize:
What female heart can gold despise?
What Cat 's averse to fish?

Presumptuous maid! with looks intent,
Again she stretched, again she bent,
Nor knew the gulf between:
(Malignant Fate sat by and smiled)
The slippery verge her feet beguiled;
She tumbled headlong in.

Eight times emerging from the flood,
She mewed to every watery god
Some speedy aid to send.
No Dolphin came, no Nereid stirred,
Nor cruel Tom or Susan heard:
A fav'rite has no friend!

From hence, ye Beauties! undeceived,
Know one false step is ne'er retrieved,
And be with caution bold:
Not all that tempts your wandering eyes,
And heedless hearts, is lawful prize,
Nor all that glistens gold.

THE RETIRED CAT.

WILLIAM COWPER.

A Poet's Cat, sedate and grave
As poet well could wish to have,
Was much addicted to inquire
For nooks to which she might retire,
And where, secure as mouse in chink,
She might repose, or sit and think.
I know not where she caught the trick;
Nature perhaps herself had cast her
In such a mold PHILOSOPHIQUE,
Or else she learned it of her master.
Sometimes ascending, debonair,
An apple-tree, or lofty pear,
Lodged with convenience in the fork,
She watched the gardener at his work;
Sometimes her ease and solace sought
In an old empty watering-pot,
There wanting nothing, save a fan,
To seem some nymph in her sedan,
Appareled in exactest sort,
And ready to be borne to court.

But love of change it seems has place
Not only in our wiser race;
Cats also feel, as well as we,
That passion's force, and so did she.
Her climbing, she began to find,
Exposed her too much to the wind,
And the old utensil of tin
Was cold and comfortless within:
She therefore wished, instead of those,
Some place of more serene repose,
Where neither cold might come, nor air
Too rudely wanton in her hair,
And sought it in the likeliest mode
Within her master's snug abode.

A drawer, it chanced, at bottom lined
With linen of the softest kind,

With such as merchants introduce
From India, for the ladies' use;
A drawer, impending o'er the rest,
Half open, in the topmost chest,
Of depth enough, and none to spare,
Invited her to slumber there;
Puss with delight beyond expression,
Surveyed the scene and took possession.
Recumbent at her ease, ere long,
And lulled by her own humdrum song,
She left the cares of life behind,
And slept as she would sleep her last,
When in came, housewifely inclined,
The chambermaid, and shut it fast,
By no malignity impelled,
But all unconscious whom it held.

Awakened by the shock (cried puss)
" Was ever cat attended thus!
The open drawer was left, I see,
Merely to prove a nest for me,
For soon as I was well composed,
Then came the maid, and it was closed.
How smooth those 'kerchiefs, and how sweet!
Oh what a delicate retreat!
I will resign myself to rest
Till Sol declining in the west,
Shall call to supper, when, no doubt,
Susan will come, and let me out."

The evening came, the sun descended,
And puss remained still unattended.
The night rolled tardily away
(With her indeed 't was never day),
The sprightly morn her course renewed,
The evening gray again ensued,
And puss came into mind no more
Than if entombed the day before;
With hunger pinched, and pinched for room,
She now presaged approaching doom.
Nor slept a single wink, nor purred,
Conscious of jeopardy incurred.

That night, by chance, the poet, watching,
Heard an inexplicable scratching;
His noble heart went pit-a-pat,
And to himself he said—" What 's that?"
He drew the curtain at his side,
And forth he peeped, but nothing spied.
Yet, by his ear directed, guessed
Something imprisoned in the chest;
And, doubtful what, with prudent care
Resolved it should continue there.
At length a voice which well he knew,
A long and melancholy mew,
Saluting his poetic ears,
Consoled him, and dispelled his fears;
He left his bed, he trod the floor,
He 'gan in haste the drawers explore,
The lowest first, and without stop
The next in order to the top.
For 'tis a truth well know to most,
That whatsoever thing is lost,
We seek it, ere it come to light,
In every cranny but the right.
Forth skipped the cat, not now replete
As erst with airy self-conceit,
Nor in her own fond comprehension,
A theme for all the world's attention,
But modest, sober, cured of all
Her notions hyperbolical,
And wishing for a place of rest,
Any thing rather than a chest.
Then stepped the poet into bed
With this reflection in his head:

MORAL.

Beware of too sublime a sense
Of your own worth and consequence.
The man who dreams himself so great,
And his importance of such weight,
That all around in all that 's done
Must move and act for him alone,
Will learn in school of tribulation
The folly of his expectation.

SAYING NOT MEANING.

WILLIAM BASIL WAKE

Two gentlemen their appetite had fed,
When opening his toothpick-case, one said,
"It was not until lately that I knew
That *anchovies* on *terrâ firmâ* grew.
"Grow!" cried the other, "yes, they *grow*, indeed,
  Like other fish, but not upon the land;
You might as well say grapes grow on a reed,
  Or in the Strand!"

"Why, sir," returned the irritated other,
          "My brother,
    When at Calcutta
Beheld them *bonâ fide* growing;
    He would n't utter
A lie for love or money, sir; so in
  This matter you are thoroughly mistaken."
"Nonsense, sir! nonsense! I can give no credit
To the assertion—none e'er saw or read it;
  Your brother, like his evidence, should be shaken."

"Be shaken, sir! let me observe, you are
    Perverse—in short—"
"Sir," said the other, sucking his cigar,
    And then his port—
"If you will say impossibles are true,
  You may affirm just any thing you please—
That swans are quadrupeds, and lions blue,
  And elephants inhabit Stilton cheese!
Only you must not *force* me to believe
What's propagated merely to deceive."

"Then you force me to say, sir, you're a fool,"
    Return'd the bragger.
Language like this no man can suffer cool:
    It made the listener stagger;
  So, thunder-stricken, he at once replied,
    "The traveler *lied*

Who had the impudence to tell it you ;"
"Zounds! then d'ye mean to swear before my face
That anchovies *don't* grow like cloves and mace ?"
"I *do!*"

Disputants often after hot debates
Leave the contention as they found it—bone,
And take to duelling or thumping *têtes ;*
Thinking by strength of artery to atone
For strength of argument; and he who winces
From force of words, with force of arms convinces!

With pistols, powder, bullets, surgeons, lint,
Seconds, and smelling-bottles, and foreboding,
Our friends advanced; and now portentous loading
(Their hearts already loaded) serv'd to show
It might be better they shook hands—but no;
When each opines himself, though frighten'd, right,
Each is, in courtesy, oblig'd to fight!
And they *did* fight: from six full measured paces
The unbeliever pulled his trigger first;
And fearing, from the braggart's ugly faces,
The whizzing lead had whizz'd its very worst,
Ran up, and with a *duelistic* fear
(His ire evanishing like morning vapors),
Found him possess'd of one remaining ear,
Who in a manner sudden and uncouth,
Had given, not lent, the other ear to truth;
For while the surgeon was applying lint,
He, wriggling, cried—"The deuce is in't—
"Sir! I *meant*—CAPERS!"

JULIA.

SAMUEL TAYLOR COLERIDGE.

—— medio de fonte leporum
Surgit amari aliquid.—*Lucret.*

JULIA was blest with beauty, wit, and grace:
Small poets loved to sing her blooming face.
Before her altars, lo! a numerous train
Preferr'd their vows; yet all preferr'd in vain:
Till charming Florio, born to conquer, came,
And touch'd the fair one with an equal flame.
The flame she felt, and ill could she conceal
What every look and action would reveal.
With boldness then, which seldom fails to move,
He pleads the cause of marriage and of love;
The course of hymeneal joys he rounds,
The fair one's eyes dance pleasure at the sounds.
Naught now remain'd but "Noes"—how little meant—
And the sweet coyness that endears consent.
The youth upon his knees enraptured fell:—
The strange misfortune, oh! what words can tell?
Tell! ye neglected sylphs! who lap-dogs guard,
Why snatch'd ye not away your precious ward?
Why suffer'd ye the lover's weight to fall
On the ill-fated neck of much-loved Ball?
The favorite on his mistress casts his eyes,
Gives a melancholy howl, and—dies!
Sacred his ashes lie, and long his rest!
Anger and grief divide poor Julia's breast.
Her eyes she fix'd on guilty Florio first,
On him the storm of angry grief must burst.
That storm he fled:—he woos a kinder fair,
Whose fond affections no dear puppies share.
'T were vain to tell how Julia pined away;—
Unhappy fair, that in one luckless day
(From future almanacs the day be cross'd!)
At once her lover and her lap-dog lost!

A COCK AND HEN STORY.

ROBERT SOUTHEY.

PART I.

ONCE on a time three Pilgrims true,
Being Father and Mother and Son,
For pure devotion to the Saint,
A pilgrimage begun.

Their names, little friends, I am sorry to say,
In none of my books can I find;
But the son, if you please, we 'll call Pierre,
What the parents were called, never mind.

From France they came, in which fair land
They were people of good renown;
And they took up their lodging one night on the way
In La Calzada town.

Now, if poor Pilgrims they had been,
And had lodged in the Hospice instead of the Inn,
My good little women and men,
Why then you never would have heard,
This tale of the Cock and the Hen.

For the Innkeepers they had a daughter,
Sad to say, who was just such another
As Potiphar's daughter, I think, would have been
If she followed the ways of her mother.

This wicked woman to our Pierre
Behaved like Potiphar's wife;
And because she failed to win his love,
She resolved to take his life.

So she packed up a silver cup
In his wallet privily;
And then, as soon as they were gone,
She raised a hue and cry.

The Pilgrims were overtaken,
The people gathered round,
Their wallets were searched, and in Pierre's
The silver cup was found.

They dragged him before the Alcayde;
A hasty Judge was he,
"The theft," he said, "was plain and proved,
And hang'd the thief must be."
So to the gallows our poor Pierre
Was hurried instantly.

If I should now relate
The piteous lamentation,
Which for their son these parents made,
My little friends, I am afraid
You'd weep at the relation.

But Pierre in Santiago still
His constant faith profess'd;
When to the gallows he was led,
"'T was a short way to Heaven," he said,
"Though not the pleasantest."

And from their pilgrimage he charged
His parents not to cease,
Saying that unless they promised this,
He could not be hanged in peace.

They promised it with heavy hearts;
Pierre then, therewith content,
Was hang'd: and they upon their way
To Compostella went.

PART II.

Four weeks they travel'd painfully,
They paid their vows, and then
To La Calzada's fatal town
Did they come back again.

The Mother would not be withheld,
But go she must to see
Where her poor Pierre was left to hang
Upon the gallows tree.

Oh tale most marvelous to hear,
Most marvelous to tell!
Eight weeks had he been hanging there,
And yet was alive and well!

"Mother," said he, "I am glad you 're return'd,
It is time I should now be released:
Though I can not complain that I 'm tired,
And my neck does not ache in the least.

"The Sun has not scorch'd me by day,
The Moon has not chilled me by night;
And the winds have but helped me to swing,
As if in a dream of delight.

"Go you to the Alcayde,
That hasty Judge unjust,
Tell him Santiago has saved me,
And take me down he must!"

Now, you must know the Alcayde,
Not thinking himself a great sinner,
Just then at table had sate down,
About to begin his dinner.

His knife was raised to carve
The dish before him then;
Two roasted fowls were laid therein,
That very morning they had been
A Cock and his faithful Hen.

In came the Mother, wild with joy:
"A miracle!" she cried;
But that most hasty Judge unjust
Repell'd her in his pride.

"Think not," quoth he, "to tales like this
That I should give belief!
Santiago never would bestow
His miracles, full well I know,
On a Frenchman and a thief."

And pointing to the Fowls, o'er which
He held his ready knife,
"As easily might I believe
These birds should come to life!"

The good Saint would not let him thus
The Mother's true tale withstand;
So up rose the Fowls in the dish,
And down dropt the knife from his hand.

The Cock would have crow'd if he could:
To cackle the Hen had a wish;
And they both slipt about in the gravy
Before they got out of the dish.

And when each would have open'd its eyes,
For the purpose of looking about them,
They saw they had no eyes to open,
And that there was no seeing without them.

All this was to them a great wonder,
They stagger'd and reel'd on the table;
And either to guess where they were,
Or what was their plight, or how they came there
Alas! they were wholly unable:

Because, you must know, that that morning,
A thing which they thought very hard,
The Cook had cut off their heads,
And thrown them away in the yard.

The Hen would have pranked up her feathers,
But plucking had sadly deform'd her;
And for want of them she would have shiver'd with cold.
If the roasting she had had not warm'd her.

And the Cock felt exceedingly queer;
He thought it a very odd thing
That his head and his voice were he did not know where,
And his gizzard tuck'd under his wing.

The gizzard got into its place,
But how Santiago knows best:
And so, by the help of the Saint,
Did the liver and all the rest.

The heads saw their way to the bodies,
In they came from the yard without check,
And each took its own proper station,
To the very great joy of the neck.

And in flew the feathers, like snow in a shower,
For they all became white on the way;
And the Cock and the Hen in a trice were refledged,
And then who so happy as they!

Cluck! cluck! cried the Hen right merrily then,
The Cock his clarion blew,
Full glad was he to hear again
His own cock-a-doo-del-doo!

PART III.

"A MIRACLE! a miracle!"
The people shouted, as they might well,
When the news went through the town,
And every child and woman and man
Took up the cry, and away they ran
To see Pierre taken down.

They made a famous procession·
My good little women and men,
Such a sight was never seen before,
And I think will never again.

Santiago's Image, large as life,
Went first with banners and drum and fife;
And next, as was most meet,
The twice-born Cock and Hen were borne
Along the thronging street.

Perched on a cross-pole hoisted high,
They were raised in sight of the crowd;
And when the people set up a cry,
The Hen she cluck'd in sympathy,
And the Cock he crow'd aloud.

And because they very well knew for why
They were carried in such solemnity,
And saw the Saint and his banners before 'em,
They behaved with the greatest propriety,
And most correct decorum.

The Knife, which had cut off their heads that morn,
Still red with their innocent blood, was borne,
The scullion boy he carried it;
And the Skewers also made part of the show,
With which they were truss'd for the spit.

The Cook in triumph bore that Spit
As high as he was able;
And the Dish was display'd wherein they were laid
When they had been served at table.

With eager faith the crowd prest round;
There was a scramble of women and men
For who should dip a finger-tip
In the blessed Gravy then.

Next went the Alcayde, beating his breast,
Crying aloud like a man distrest,
And amazed at the loss of his dinner,
"Santiago, Santiago!
Have mercy on me a sinner!"

And lifting oftentimes his hands
Toward the Cock and Hen,
"*Orate pro nobis!*" devoutly he cried,
And as devoutly the people replied,
Whenever he said it, "Amen!"

The Father and Mother were last in the train;
Rejoicingly they came,
And extoll'd, with tears of gratitude,
Santiago's glorious name.

So, with all honors that might be,
They gently unhang'd Pierre;
No hurt or harm had he sustain'd,
But, to make the wonder clear,
A deep biack halter-mark remain'd
Just under his left ear.

PART IV.

And now, my little listening dears
With open mouths and open ears,
Like a rhymer whose only art is
That of telling a plain unvarnish'd tale,
To let you know I must not fail,
What became of all the parties.

Pierre went on to Compostella
To finish his pilgrimage,
His parents went back with him joyfully,
After which they returned to their own country,
And there, I believe, that all the three
Lived to a good old age.

For the gallows on which Pierre
So happily had swung,
It was resolved that never more
On it should man be hung.

To the Church it was transplanted,
As ancient books declare:
And the people in commotion,
With an uproar of devotion,
Set it up for a relic there.

What became of the halter I know not,
Because the old books show not;
But we may suppose and hope,
That the city presented Pierre
With that interesting rope.

For in his family, and this
The Corporation knew,
It rightly would be valued more
Than any *cordon bleu.*

The Innkeeper's wicked daughter
Confess'd what she had done,
So they put her in a Convent,
And she was made a Nun.

The Alcayde had been so frighten'd
That he never ate fowls again;
And he always pulled off his hat
When he saw a Cock and Hen.
Wherever he sat at table
Not an egg might there be placed;
And he never even muster'd courage for a custard,
Though garlic tempted him to taste
Of an omelet now and then.

But always after such a transgression
He hastened away to make confession;
And not till he had confess'd,
And the Priest had absolved him, did he feel
His conscience and stomach at rest.

The twice-born Birds to the Pilgrim's Church
As by miracle consecrated,
Were given; and there unto the Saint
They were publicly dedicated.

At their dedication the Corporation
A fund for their keep supplied;
And after following the Saint and his banners,
This Cock and Hen were so changed in their manners,
That the Priests were edified.

Gentle as any turtle-dove,
Saint Cock became all meekness and love;
Most dutiful of wives,
Saint Hen she never peck'd again,
So they led happy lives.

The ways of ordinary fowls
You must know they had clean forsaken;
And if every Cock and Hen in Spain
Had their example taken,
Why then—the Spaniards would have had
No eggs to eat with bacon.

These blessed Fowls, at seven years end,
In the odor of sanctity died:
They were carefully pluck'd and then
They were buried, side by side.

And lest the fact should be forgotten
(Which would have been a pity),
'T was decreed, in honor of their worth,
That a Cock and Hen should be borne thenceforth,
In the arms of that ancient City.

Two eggs Saint Hen had laid—no more—
The chickens were her delight;
A Cock and Hen they proved,
And both, like their parents, were virtuous and white.

The last act of the Holy Hen
Was to rear this precious brood; and when
Saint Cock and she were dead,
This couple, as the lawful heirs,
Succeeded in their stead.

They also lived seven years,
And they laid eggs but two,
From which two milk-white chickens
To Cock and Henhood grew;
And always their posterity
The self-same course pursue.

Not one of these eggs ever addled,
(With wonder be it spoken!)
Not one of them ever was lost,
Not one of them ever was broken.

Sacred they are; neither magpie nor rat,
Snake, weasel, nor marten approaching them:
And woe to the irreverent wretch
Who should even dream of poaching them!

Thus then is this great miracle
Continued to this day;
And to their Church all Pilgrims go,
When they are on the way;
And some of the feathers are given them;
For which they always pay.

No price is set upon them,
And this leaves all persons at ease;
The Poor give as much as they can,
The Rich as much as they please.

But that the more they give the better,
Is very well understood;
Seeing whatever is thus disposed of,
Is for their own souls' good;

For Santiago will always
Befriend his true believers;
And the money is for him, the Priests
Being only his receivers.

To make the miracle the more,
Of these feathers there is always store,

And all are genuine too;
All of the original Cock and Hen,
Which the Priests will swear is true.

Thousands a thousand times told have bought them,
And if myriads and tens of myriads sought them,
They would still find some to buy;
For however great were the demand,
So great would be the supply.

And if any of you, my small friends,
Should visit those parts, I dare say
You will bring away some of the feathers,
And think of old Robin Gray.

THE SEARCH AFTER HAPPINESS;

OR, THE QUEST OF SULTAUN SOLIMAUN.

SIR WALTER SCOTT.

Oh, for a glance of that gay Muse's eye,
That lighten'd on Bandello's laughing tale,
And twinkled with a luster shrewd and sly,
When Giam Batttista bade her vision hail!—
Yet fear not, ladies, the *naïve* detail
Given by the natives of that land canorous;
Italian license loves to leap the pale,
We Britons have the fear of shame before us,
And, if not wise in mirth, at least must be decorous.

In the far eastern clime, no great while since,
Lived Sultaun Solimaun, a mighty prince,
Whose eyes, as oft as they perform'd their round,
Beheld all others fix'd upon the ground;
Whose ears received the same unvaried phrase,
"Sultaun! thy vassal hears, and he obeys!"
All have their tastes—this may the fancy strike
Of such grave folks as pomp and grandeur like;
For me, I love the honest heart and warm
Of monarch who can amble round his farm,
Or when the toil of state no more annoys,
In chimney corner seek domestic joys—

I love a prince will bid the bottle pass,
Exchanging with his subjects glance and glass;
In fitting time, can, gayest of the gay,
Keep up the jest, and mingle in the lay—
Such Monarchs best our free-born humors suit,
But Despots must be stately, stern, and mute.

This Solimaun, Serendib had in sway—
And where's Serendib? may some critic say—
Good lack, mine honest friend, consult the chart,
Scare not my Pegasus before I start!
If Rennell has it not, you'll find, mayhap,
The isle laid down in Captain Sinbad's map—
Famed mariner! whose merciless narrations
Drove every friend and kinsman out of patience,
Till, fain to find a guest who thought them shorter,
He deign'd to tell them over to a porter—
The last edition see, by Long and Co.,
Rees, Hurst, and Orme, our fathers in the Row.

Serendib found, deem not my tale a fiction—
This Sultaun, whether lacking contradiction—
(A sort of stimulant which hath its uses,
To raise the spirits and reform the juices,
—Sovereign specific for all sorts of cures
In my wife's practice, and perhaps in yours),
The Sultaun lacking this same wholesome bitter,
Of cordial smooth for prince's palate fitter—
Or if some Mollah had hag-rid his dreams
With Degial, Ginnistan, and such wild themes
Belonging to the Mollah's subtle craft,
I wot not—but the Sultaun never laugh'd,
Scarce ate or drank, and took a melancholy
That scorn'd all remedy profane or holy;
In his long list of melancholies, mad,
Or mazed, or dumb, hath Burton none so bad.

Physicians soon arrived, sage, ware, and tried,
  As e'er scrawl'd jargon in a darken'd room;
With heedful glance the Sultaun's tongue they eyed,
Peep'd in his bath, and God knows where beside,
  And then in solemn accent spoke their doom,

"His majesty is very far from well."
Then each to work with his specific fell;
The Hakim Ibrahim *instanter* brought
His unguent Mahazzim al Zerdukkaut,
While Roompot, a practitioner more wily,
Relied on his Munaskif all fillfily.
More and yet more in deep array appear,
And some the front assail, and some the rear;
Their remedies to reinforce and vary,
Came surgeon eke, and eke apothecary;
Till the tired Monarch, though of words grown chary,
Yet dropt, to recompense their fruitless labor,
Some hint about a bowstring or a saber.
There lack'd, I promise you, no longer speeches,
To rid the palace of those learned leeches.

Then was the council call'd—by their advice
(They deem'd the matter ticklish all, and nice,
   And sought to shift it off from their own shoulders)
Tartars and couriers in all speed were sent,
To call a sort of Eastern Parliament
   Of feudatory chieftains and freeholders—
Such have the Persians at this very day,
My gallant Malcolm calls them *couroultai*;—
I'm not prepared to show in this slight song
That to Serendib the same forms belong—
E'en let the learn'd go search, and tell me if I'm wrong.

The Omrahs, each with hand on scimitar,
Gave, like Sempronius, still their voice for war—
"The saber of the Sultaun in its sheath
Too long has slept, nor own'd the work of death;
Let the Tambourgi bid his signal rattle,
Bang the loud gong, and raise the shout of battle!
This dreary cloud that dims our sovereign's day,
Shall from his kindled bosom flit away,
When the bold Lootie wheels his courser round,
And the arm'd elephant shall shake the ground.
Each noble pants to own the glorious summons—
And for the charges—Lo! your faithful Commons!"

The Riots who attended in their places
  (Serendib language calls a farmer Riot)
Look'd ruefully in one another's faces,
  From this oration auguring much disquiet,
Double assessment, forage, and free quarters;
And fearing these as China-men the Tartars,
Or as the whisker'd vermin fear the mousers,
Each fumbled in the pockets of his trowsers.

And next came forth the reverend Convocation,
  Bald heads, white beards, and many a turban green,
Imaum and Mollah there of every station,
  Santon, Fakir, and Calendar were seen.
Their votes were various—some advised a Mosque
  With fitting revenues should be erected,
With seemly gardens and with gay Kiosque,
  To create a band of priests selected;
Others opined that through the realms a dole
  Be made to holy men, whose prayers might profit
The Sultaun's weal in body and in soul.
  But their long-headed chief, the Sheik Ul-Sofit,
More closely touch'd the point;—"Thy studious mood,"
Quoth he, "O Prince! hath thicken'd all thy blood,
And dull'd thy brain with labor beyond measure;
Wherefore relax a space and take thy pleasure,
And toy with beauty, or tell o'er thy treasure;
From all the cares of state, my Liege, enlarge thee,
And leave the burden to thy faithful clergy."

These counsels sage availed not a whit,
  And so the patient (as is not uncommon
Where grave physicians lose their time and wit)
  Resolved to take advice of an old woman;
His mother she, a dame who once was beauteous,
And still was called so by each subject duteous.
Now whether Fatima was witch in earnest,
  Or only made believe, I can not say—
But she profess'd to cure disease the sternest,
  By dint of magic amulet or lay;
And, when all other skill in vain was shown,
She deem'd it fitting time to use her own.

"*Sympathia magica* hath wonders done"
(Thus did old Fatima bespeak her son),
"It works upon the fibers and the pores,
And thus, insensibly, our health restores,
And it must help us here.—Thou must endure
The ill, my son, or travel for the cure.
Search land and sea, and get, where'er you can,
The inmost vesture of a happy man:
I mean his SHIRT, my son; which, taken warm
And fresh from off his back, shall chase your harm,
Bid every current of your veins rejoice,
And your dull heart leap light as shepherd-boy's."
Such was the counsel from his mother came;—
I know not if she had some under-game,
As doctors have, who bid their patients roam
And live abroad, when sure to die at home;
Or if she thought, that, somehow or another,
Queen-Regent sounded better than Queen-Mother;
But, says the Chronicle (who will go look it?)
That such was her advice—the Sultaun took it.

All are on board—the Sultaun and his train,
In gilded galley prompt to plow the main.
  The old Rais was the first who question'd, "Whither?"
They paused—"Arabia," thought the pensive Prince,
"Was call'd The Happy many ages since—
  For Mokha, Rais."—And they came safely thither.
But not in Araby, with all her balm,
Not where Judea weeps beneath her palm,
Not in rich Egypt, not in Nubian waste,
Could there the step of Happiness be traced.
One Copt alone profess'd to have seen her smile
When Bruce his goblet fill'd at infant Nile:
She bless'd the dauntless traveler as he quaff'd,
But vanish'd from him with the ended draught.

"Enough of turbans," said the weary King,
"These dolimans of ours are not the thing;
Try we the Giaours, these men of coat and cap, I
Incline to think some of them must be happy;
At least they have as fair a cause as any can,
They drink good wine and keep no Ramazan.

Then northward, ho!"—The vessel cuts the sea,
And fair Italia lies upon her lee.—
But fair Italia, she who once unfurl'd
Her eagle-banners o'er a conquer'd world,
Long from her throne of domination tumbled,
Lay, by her quondam vassals, sorely humbled,
The Pope himself look'd pensive, pale, and lean,
And was not half the man he once had been.
"While these the priest and those the noble fleeces,
Our poor old boot," they said, "is torn to pieces.
Its tops the vengeful claws of Austria feel,
And the Great Devil is rending toe and heel.
If happiness you seek, to tell you truly,
We think she dwells with one Giovanni Bulli;
A tramontane, a heretic—the buck,
Poffaredio! still has all the luck;
By land or ocean never strikes his flag—
And then—a perfect walking money-bag."
Off set our Prince to seek John Bull's abode,
But first took France—it lay upon the road.

Monsieur Baboon, after much late commotion,
Was agitated like a settling ocean,
Quite out of sorts, and could not tell what ail'd him,
Only the glory of his house had fail'd him;
Besides, some tumors on his noddle biding,
Gave indication of a recent hiding.
Our Prince, though Sultauns of such things are heedless,
Thought it a thing indelicate and needless
  To ask, if at that moment he was happy.
And Monsieur, seeing that he was *comme il faut*, a
Loud voice muster'd up, for "*Vive le Roi!*"
  Then whisper'd, "'Ave you any news of Nappy?"
The Sultaun answer'd him with a cross question—
  "Pray, can you tell me aught of one John Bull,
  That dwells somewhere beyond your herring-pool?"
The query seem'd of difficult digestion,
The party shrugg'd, and grinn'd, and took his snuff,
And found his whole good-breeding scarce enough.

Twitching his visage into as many puckers
As damsels wont to put into their tuckers

(Ere liberal Fashion damn'd both lace and lawn,
And bade the vail of modesty be drawn),
Replied the Frenchman, after a brief pause,
"Jean Bool!—I vas not know him—yes, I vas—
I vas remember dat, von year or two,
I saw him at von place call'd Vaterloo—
Ma foi! il s'est tres joliment battu,
Dat is for Englishman—m'entendez-vous?
But den he had wit him one damn son-gun,
Rogue I no like—dey call him Vellington."
Monsieur's politeness could not hide his fret,
So Solimaun took leave, and cross'd the strait.

John Bull was in his very worst of moods,
Raving of sterile farms and unsold goods;
His sugar-loaves and bales about he threw,
And on his counter beat the devil's tattoo.
His wars were ended, and the victory won,
But then, 't was reckoning-day with honest John;
And authors vouch, 'twas still this Worthy's way,
"Never to grumble till he came to pay;
And then he always thinks, his temper's such,
The work too little, and the pay too much."
Yet grumbler as he is, so kind and hearty,
That when his mortal foe was on the floor,
And past the power to harm his quiet more,
Poor John had well-nigh wept for Bonaparte!
Such was the wight whom Solimaun salam'd—
"And who are you," John answer'd, "and be d—d?"

"A stranger come to see the happiest man—
So, signior, all avouch—in Frangistan."—
"Happy? my tenants breaking on my hand;
Unstock'd my pastures, and untill'd my land;
Sugar and rum a drug, and mice and moths
The sole consumers of my good broadcloths—
Happy?—why, cursed war and racking tax
Have left us scarcely raiment to our backs."—
"In that case, signior, I may take my leave;
I came to ask a favor—but I grieve."—
"Favor?" said John, and eyed the Sultaun hard,
"It's my belief you came to break the yard!—

But, stay, you look like some poor foreign sinner—
Take that to buy yourself a shirt and dinner."—
With that he chuck'd a guinea at his head;
But, with due dignity, the Sultaun said,
"Permit me, sir, your bounty to decline;
A *shirt* indeed I seek, but none of thine.
Signior, I kiss your hands, so fare you well,"—
"Kiss and be d—d," quoth John, "and go to hell!"

Next door to John there dwelt his sister Peg,
Once a wild lass as ever shook a leg
When the blithe bagpipe blew—but, soberer now,
She *doucely* span her flax and milk'd her cow.
And whereas erst she was a needy slattern,
Nor now of wealth or cleanliness a pattern,
Yet once a month her house was partly swept,
And once a week a plenteous board she kept.
And, whereas, eke, the vixen used her claws
  And teeth of yore, on slender provocation,
She now was grown amenable to laws,
  A quiet soul as any in the nation;
The sole remembrance of her warlike joys
Was in old songs she sang to please her boys.
John Bull, whom, in their years of early strife,
She wont to lead a cat-and-doggish life,
Now found the woman, as he said, a neighbor,
Who look'd to the main chance, declined no labor,
Loved a long grace, and spoke a northern jargon,
And was d—d close in making of a bargain.

The Sultaun enter'd, and he made his leg,
And with decorum courtesy'd sister Peg;
(She loved a book, and knew a thing or two,
And guess'd at once with whom she had to do).
She bade him "Sit into the fire," and took
Her dram, her cake, her kebbuck from the nook;
Ask'd him "About the news from Eastern parts;
And of her absent bairns, puir Highland hearts!
If peace brought down the price of tea and pepper,
And if the *nitmugs* were grown *ony* cheaper;—
Were there nae *speerings* of our Mungo Park—
Ye'll be the gentleman that wants the sark?

If ye wad buy a web o' auld wife's spinning,
I 'll warrant ye it's a weel-wearing linen."

Then up got Peg, and round the house 'gan scuttle
In search of goods her customer to nail,
Until the Sultaun strain'd his princely throttle
And hallo'd—"Ma'am, that is not what I ail.
Pray, are you happy, ma'am, in this snug glen?"—
"Happy?" said Peg; "What for d'ye want to ken?
Besides, just think upon this by-gane year,
Grain wadna pay the yoking of the pleugh."—
"What say you to the present?"—"Meal's sae dear,
To make their *brose* my bairns have scarce aneugh."—
"The devil take the shirt," said Solimaun,
"I think my quest will end as it began.—
Farewell, ma'am; nay, no ceremony, I beg"—
"Ye 'll no be for the linen then?" said Peg.

Now, for the land of verdant Erin,
The Sultaun's royal bark is steering,
The Emerald Isle, where honest Paddy dwells,
The cousin of John Bull, as story tells.
For a long space had John, with words of thunder
Hard looks, and harder knocks, kept Paddy under,
Till the poor lad, like boy that's flogg'd unduly,
Had gotten somewhat restive and unruly.
Hard was his lot and lodging, you 'll allow,
A wigwam that would hardly serve a sow;
His landlord, and of middle men two brace,
Had screw'd his rent up to the starving-place;
His garment was a top-coat, and an old one,
His meal was a potato, and a cold one;
But still for fun or frolic, and all that,
In the round world was not the match of Pat.
The Sultaun saw him on a holiday,
Which is with Paddy still a jolly day;
When mass is ended, and his load of sins
Confess'd, and Mother Church hath from her binns
Dealt forth a bonus of imputed merit,
Then is Pat's time for fancy, whim, and spirit!
To jest, to sing, to caper fair and free,
And dance as light as leaf upon the tree.

"By Mahomet," said Sultaun Solimaun,
"That ragged fellow is our very man!
Rush in and seize him—do not do him hurt,
But, will he nill he, let me have his *shirt*."

Shilela their plan was well-nigh after baulking
(Much less provocation will set it a-walking),
But the odds that foil'd Hercules foil'd Paddy Whack;
They seized, and they floor'd, and they stripp'd him—Alack!
Up-bubboo! Paddy had not—a shirt to his back!!!
And the King, disappointed, with sorrow and shame,
Went back to Serendib as sad as he came.

THE DONKEY AND HIS PANNIERS.

THOMAS MOORE

A DONKEY whose talent for burden was wondrous,
 So much that you 'd swear he rejoiced in a load,
One day had to jog under panniers so pond'rous,
 That—down the poor donkey fell, smack on the road.

His owners and drivers stood round in amaze—
 What! Neddy, the patient, the prosperous Neddy
So easy to drive through the dirtiest ways,
 For every description of job-work so ready!

One driver (whom Ned might have "hail'd" as a "brother")
 Had just been proclaiming his donkey's renown,
For vigor, for spirit, for one thing or other—
 When, lo! 'mid his praises, the donkey came down.

But, how to upraise him?—one shouts, *t'other* whistles,
 While Jenky, the conjurer, wisest of all,
Declared that an "over-production" of thistles—
 (Here Ned gave a stare)—was the cause of his fall.

Another wise Solomon cries, as he passes—
 "There, let him alone, and the fit will soon cease;
The beast has been fighting with other jack-asses,
 And this is his mode of '*transition to peace.*'"

Some look'd at his hoofs, and, with learned grimaces,
  Pronounced that too long without shoes he had gone—
" Let the blacksmith provide him a *sound metal basis*
  (The wiseacres said), and he 's sure to jog on."

But others who gabbled a jargon half Gaelic,
  Exclaim'd, " Hoot awa, mon, you 're a' gane astray"—
And declared that " whoe'er might prefer the *metallic*,
  They 'd shoe their *own* donkeys with *papier mache*."

Meanwhile the poor Neddy, in torture and fear,
  Lay under his panniers, scarce able to groan,
And, what was still dolefuler—lending an ear
  To advisers whose ears were a match for his own.

At length, a plain rustic, whose wit went so far
  As to see others' folly, roar'd out as he pass'd—
" Quick—off with the panniers, all dolts as ye are,
  Or your prosperous Neddy will soon kick his last."

MISADVENTURES AT MARGATE.

A LEGEND OF JARVIS'S JETTY.

R. HARRIS BARHAM.

MR. SIMPKINSON (*loquitur*).

I WAS in Margate last July, I walk'd upon the pier,
I saw a little vulgar Boy—I said " What make you here ?—
The gloom upon your youthful cheek speaks any thing but joy;"
Again I said, " What make you here, you little vulgar Boy ?"

He frown'd, that little vulgar Boy—he deem'd I meant to scoff—
And when the little heart is big, a little " sets it off ;"
He put his finger in his mouth, his little bosom rose,—
He had no little handkerchief to wipe his little nose !

" Hark ! don't you hear, my little man ?—it 's striking nine," I said,
" An hour when all good little boys and girls should be in bed.
Run home and get your supper, else your Ma' will scold—Oh ! fie !—
It 's very wrong indeed for little boys to stand and cry !"

The tear-drop in his little eye again began to spring,
His bosom throbb'd with agony—he cried like any thing!
I stoop'd, and thus amidst his sobs I heard him murmur—"Ah!
I haven't got no supper! and I haven't got no Ma'! !—

"My father, he is on the seas,—my mother's dead and gone!
And I am here, on this here pier, to roam the world alone;
I have not had, this live-long day, one drop to cheer my heart,
Nor '*brown*' to buy a bit of bread with,—let alone a tart.

"If there's a soul will give me food, or find me in employ,
By day or night, then blow me tight!" (he was a vulgar Boy;)
"And now I'm here, from this here pier it is my fixed intent
To jump, as Mr. Levi did from off the Monu-ment!"

"Cheer up! cheer up! my little man—cheer up!" I kindly said,
You are a naughty boy to take such things into your head:
If you should jump from off the pier, you'd surely break your legs,
Perhaps your neck—then Bogey'd have you, sure as eggs are eggs!

"Come home with me, my little man, come home with me and sup;
My landlady is Mrs. Jones—we must not keep her up—
There's roast potatoes on the fire,—enough for me and you—
Come home,—you little vulgar Boy—I lodge at Number 2."

I took him home to Number 2, the house beside "The Foy,"
I bade him wipe his dirty shoes,—that little vulgar Boy,—
And then I said to Mistress Jones, the kindest of her sex,
"Pray be so good as go and fetch a pint of double X!"

But Mrs. Jones was rather cross, she made a little noise,
She said she "did not like to wait on little vulgar Boys."
She with her apron wiped the plates, and, as she rubb'd the delf,
Said I might "go to Jericho, and fetch my beer myself!"

I did not go to Jericho—I went to Mr. Cobb—
I changed a shilling—(which in town the people call "a Bob")—
It was not so much for myself as for that vulgar child—
And I said, "A pint of double X, and please to draw it mild!"

When I came back I gazed about—I gazed on stool and chair—
I could not see my little friend—because he was not there!
I peep'd beneath the table-cloth—beneath the sofa too—
I said "You little vulgar Boy! why what's become of you?"

I could not see my table-spoons—I look'd, but could not see
The little fiddle-pattern'd ones I use when I'm at tea;
—I could not see my sugar-tongs—my silver watch—oh, dear!
I know 't was on the mantle-piece when I went out for beer.

I could not see my Mackintosh!—it was not to be seen!
Nor yet my best white beaver hat, broad-brimm'd and lined with green;
My carpet-bag—my cruet-stand, that holds my sauce and soy,—
My roast potatoes!—all are gone!—and so's that vulgar Boy!

I rang the bell for Mrs. Jones, for she was down below,
"—Oh, Mrs. Jones! what *do* you think?—ain't this a pretty go?
—That horrid little vulgar Boy whom I brought here to-night,
—He's stolen my things and run away!!"—Says she, "And sarve you right!!"

* * * * * * *

Next morning I was up betimes—I sent the Crier round,
All with his bell and gold-laced hat, to say I'd give a pound
To find that little vulgar Boy, who'd gone and used me so;
But when the Crier cried "O Yes!" the people cried, "O No!"

I went to "Jarvis' Landing-place," the glory of the town,
There was a common sailor-man a-walking up and down;
I told my tale—he seem'd to think I'd not been treated well,
And called me "Poor old Buffer!" what that means I cannot tell.

That sailor-man, he said he'd seen that morning on the shore,
A son of—something—'t was a name I'd never heard before,
A little "gallows-looking chap"—dear me; what could he mean?
With a "carpet-swab" and "muckingtogs," and a hat turned up with green.

He spoke about his "precious eyes," and said he'd seen him "sheer,"
—It's very odd that sailor-men should talk so very queer—
And then he hitch'd his trowsers up, as is, I'm told, their use,
—It's very odd that sailor-men should wear those things so loose.

I did not understand him well, but think he meant to say
He 'd seen that little vulgar Boy, that morning swim away
In Captain Large's Royal George about an hour before,
And they were now, as he supposed, "some*wheres*" about the Nore.

A landsman said, "I *twig* the chap—he 's been upon the Mill—
And 'cause he *gammons* so the *flats*, ve calls him Veeping Bill!"
He said "he 'd done me wery brown," and "nicely *stow'd* the *swag*."
—That 's French, I fancy, for a hat—or else a carpet-bag.

I went and told the constable my property to track;
He asked me if "I did not wish that I might get it back?"
I answered, "To be sure I do!—it 's what I come about."
He smiled and said, "Sir, does your mother know that you are out?"

Not knowing what to do, I thought I 'd hasten back to town,
And beg our own Lord Mayor to catch the Boy who 'd "done me brown."
His Lordship very kindly said he 'd try and find him out,
But he "rather thought that there were several vulgar boys about."

He sent for Mr. Whithair then, and I described "the swag,"
My Mackintosh, my sugar-tongs, my spoons, and carpet-bag;
He promised that the New Police should all their powers employ;
But never to this hour have I beheld that vulgar Boy!

MORAL.

Remember, then, what when a boy I 've heard my Grandma' tell,
"BE WARN'D IN TIME BY OTHERS' HARM, AND YOU SHALL DO FULL WELL!"
Don't link yourself with vulgar folks, who 've got no fix'd abode,
Tell lies, use naughty words, and say they "wish they may be blow'd!"
Don't take too much of double X!—and don't at night go out
To fetch your beer yourself, but make the pot-boy bring your stout!
And when you go to Margate next, just stop and ring the bell,
Give my respects to Mrs. Jones, and say I 'm pretty well!

THE GHOST.

R. HARRIS BARHAM

THERE stands a City,—neither large nor small,
Its air and situation sweet and pretty;
It matters very little—if at all—
Whether its denizens are dull or witty,
Whether the ladies there are short or tall,
Brunettes or blondes, only, there stands a city!—
Perhaps 'tis also requisite to minute
That there's a Castle, and a Cobbler in it.

A fair Cathedral, too, the story goes,
And kings and heroes lie entombed within her;
There pious Saints, in marble pomp repose,
Whose shrines are worn by knees of many a Sinner;
There, too, full many an Aldermanic nose
Roll'd its loud diapason after dinner;
And there stood high the holy sconce of Becket,
—Till four assassins came from France to crack it.

The Castle was a huge and antique mound,
Proof against all th' artillery of the quiver,
Ere those abominable guns were found,
To send cold lead through gallant warrior's liver.
It stands upon a gently rising ground,
Sloping down gradually to the river,
Resembling (to compare great things with smaller)
A well-scooped, moldy Stilton cheese—but taller.

The Keep, I find, 's been sadly alter'd lately,
And 'stead of mail-clad knights, of honor jealous,
In martial panoply so grand and stately,
Its walls are filled with money-making fellows,
And stuff'd, unless I'm misinformed greatly,
With leaden pipes, and coke, and coal, and bellows;
In short, so great a change has come to pass,
'Tis now a manufactory of Gas.

But to my tale.—Before this profanation,
  And ere its ancient glories were cut short all,
A poor hard-working Cobbler took his station
  In a small house, just opposite the portal;
His birth, his parentage, and education,
  I know but little of—a strange, odd mortal;
His aspect, air, and gait, were all ridiculous;
His name was Mason—he 'd been christened Nicholas.

Nick had a wife possessed of many a charm,
  And of the Lady Huntingdon persuasion;
But, spite of all her piety, her arm
  She 'd sometimes exercise when in a passion;
And, being of a temper somewhat warm,
  Would now and then seize, upon small occasion,
A stick, or stool, or any thing that round did lie,
And baste her lord and master most confoundedly.

No matter;—'tis a thing that's not uncommon,
  'Tis what we all have heard, and most have read of,—
I mean, a bruising, pugilistic woman,
  Such as I own I entertain a dread of,
—And so did Nick,—whom sometimes there would come on
  A sort of fear his Spouse might knock his head off,
Demolish half his teeth, or drive a rib in,
She shone so much in "facers" and in "fibbing."

"There 's time and place for all things," said a sage
  (King Solomon, I think), and this I can say,
Within a well-roped ring, or on a stage,
  Boxing may be a very pretty *Fancy*,
When Messrs. Burke or Bendigo engage;
  —'Tis not so well in Susan or in Nancy:—
To get well mill'd by any one's an evil,
But by a lady—'tis the very Devil.

And so thought Nicholas, whose only trouble
  (At least his worst) was this, his rib's propensity;
For sometimes from the ale-house he would hobble,
  His senses lost in a sublime immensity
Of cogitation—then he could n't cobble—
  And then his wife would often try the density
Of his poor skull, and strike with all her might,
As fast as kitchen wenches strike a light.

Mason, meek soul, who ever hated strife,
  Of this same striking had a morbid dread,
He hated it like poison—or his wife—
  A vast antipathy!—but so he said—
And very often, for a quiet life,
  On these occasions he 'd sneak up to bed,
Grope darkling in, and soon as at the door
He heard his lady—he 'd pretend to snore.

One night, then, ever partial to society,
  Nick, with a friend (another jovial fellow),
Went to a Club—I should have said Society—
  At the "City Arms," once call'd the "Porto Bello;"
A Spouting party, which, though some decry it, I
  Consider no bad lounge when one is mellow;
There they discuss the tax on salt, and leather,
And change of ministers and change of weather.

In short, it was a kind of British Forum,
  Like John Gale Jones', erst in Piccadilly,
Only they managed things with more decorum,
  And the Orations were not *quite* so silly;
Far different questions, too, would come before 'em
  Not always politics, which, will ye nill ye,
Their London prototypes were always willing,
To give one *quantum suff.* of—for a shilling.

It more resembled one of later date,
  And tenfold talent, as I 'm told, in Bow-street,
Where kindlier nurtured souls do congregate,
  And, though there are who deem that same a low street,
Yet, I 'm assured, for frolicsome debate
  And genuine humor it 's surpassed by no street,
When the "Chief Baron" enters, and assumes
To "rule" o'er mimic "Thesigers" and "Broughams."

Here they would oft forget their Rulers' faults,
  And waste in ancient lore the midnight taper,
Inquire if Orpheus first produced the Waltz,
  How Gas-lights differ from the Delphic Vapor.
Whether Hippocrates gave Glauber's Salts,
  And what the Romans wrote on ere they'd paper,—
This night the subject of their disquisitions
Was Ghosts, Hobgoblins, Sprites, and Apparitions.

One learned gentleman, "a sage grave man,"
  Talk'd of the Ghost in Hamlet, "sheath'd in steel:"—
His well-read friend, who next to speak began,
  Said, "That was Poetry, and nothing real;"
A third, of more extensive learning, ran
  To Sir George Villiers' Ghost, and Mrs. Veal;
Of sheeted Specters spoke with shorten'd breath,
And thrice he quoted "Drelincourt on Death."

Nick, smoked, and smoked, and trembled as he heard
  The point discuss'd, and all they said upon it,
How frequently some murder'd man appear'd,
  To tell his wife and children who had done it;
Or how a Miser's Ghost, with grisly beard,
  And pale lean visage, in an old Scotch bonnet,
Wander'd about to watch his buried money!
When all at once Nick heard the clock strike One—he

Sprang from his seat, not doubting but a lecture
  Impended from his fond and faithful She;
Nor could he well to pardon him expect her,
  For he had promised to "be home to tea;"
But having luckily the key o' the back door,
  He fondly hoped that, unperceived, he
Might creep up stairs again, pretend to doze,
And hoax his spouse with music from his nose.

Vain fruitless hope!—The wearied sentinel
  At eve may overlook the crouching foe,
Till, ere his hand can sound the alarum-bell,
  He sinks beneath the unexpected blow;
Before the whiskers of Grimalkin fell,
  When slumb'ring on her post, the mouse may go,—
But woman, wakeful woman, 's never weary,
—Above all, when she waits to thump her deary.

Soon Mrs. Mason heard the well-known tread;
  She heard the key slow creaking in the door,
Spied through the gloom obscure, toward the bed
  Nick creeping soft, as oft he had crept before;
When, bang, she threw a something at his head,
  And Nick at once lay prostrate on the floor;
While she exclaim'd with her indignant face on,—
"How dare you use your wife so, Mr. Mason?"

Spare we to tell how fiercely she debated,
  Especially the length of her oration,—
Spare we to tell how Nick expostulated,
  Roused by the bump into a good set passion,
So great, that more than once he execrated,
  Ere he crawl'd into bed in his usual fashion;
—The Muses hate brawls; suffice it then to say,
He duck'd below the clothes—and there he lay:

'Twas now the very witching time of night,
  When church-yards groan, and graves give up their dead,
And many a mischievous, enfranchised Sprite
  Had long since burst his bonds of stone or lead,
And hurried off, with schoolboy-like delight,
  To play his pranks near some poor wretch's bed,
Sleeping, perhaps, serenely as a porpoise,
Nor dreaming of this fiendish Habeas Corpus.

Not so our Nicholas, his meditations
  Still to the same tremendous theme recurred,
The same dread subject of the dark narrations,
  Which, back'd with such authority, he 'd heard;
Lost in his own horrific contemplations,
  He pondered o'er each well-remembered word;
When at the bed's foot, close beside the post,
He verily believed he saw—a Ghost!

Plain and more plain the unsubstantial Sprite
  To his astonish'd gaze each moment grew;
Ghastly and gaunt, it rear'd its shadowy height,
  Of more than mortal seeming to the view,
And round its long, thin, bony fingers drew
  A tatter'd winding-sheet, of course *all white*;—
The moon that moment peeping through a cloud,
Nick very plainly saw it *through the shroud!*

And now those matted locks, which never yet
  Had yielded to the comb's unkind divorce,
Their long-contracted amity forget,
  And spring asunder with elastic force;
Nay, e'en the very cap, of texture coarse,
  Whose ruby cincture crown'd that brow of jet,
Uprose in agony—the Gorgon's head
Was but a type of Nick's up-squatting in the bed.

From every pore distill'd a clammy dew,
  Quaked every limb,—the candle too no doubt,
En règle, *would* have burnt extremely blue,
  But Nick unluckily had put it out;
And he, though naturally bold and stout,
  In short, was in a most tremendous stew;—
The room was fill'd with a sulphureous smell,
But where that came from Mason could not tell.

All motionless the Specter stood,—and now
  Its reverend form more clearly shone confest;
From the pale cheek a beard of purest snow
  Descended o'er its venerable breast;
The thin gray hairs, that crown'd its furrow'd brow,
  Told of years long gone by.—An awful guest
It stood, and with an action of command,
Beckon'd the Cobbler with its wan right hand.

"Whence, and what art thou, Execrable Shape?"
  Nick *might* have cried, could he have found a tongue,
But his distended jaws could only gape,
  And not a sound upon the welkin rung.
His gooseberry orbs seem'd as they would have sprung
  Forth from their sockets,—like a frightened Ape
He sat upon his haunches, bolt upright,
And shook, and grinn'd, and chatter'd with affright.

And still the shadowy finger, long and lean,
  Now beckon'd Nick, now pointed to the door;
And many an ireful glance, and frown, between,
  The angry visage of the Phantom wore,
As if quite vexed that Nick would do no more
  Than stare, without e'en asking, "What d' ye mean?"
Because, as we are told,—a sad old joke too,—
Ghosts, like the ladies, "never speak till spoke to."

Cowards, 'tis said, in certain situations,
  Derive a sort of courage from despair,
And then perform, from downright desperation,
  Much more than many a bolder man would dare.
Nick saw the Ghost was getting in a passion,
  And therefore, groping till he found the chair,
Seized on his awl, crept softly out of bed,
And follow'd quaking where the Specter led.

And down the winding stair, with noiseless tread,
The tenant of the tomb pass'd slowly on,
Each mazy turning of the humble shed
Seem'd to his step at once familiar grown,
So safe and sure the labyrinth did he tread
As though the domicile had been his own,
Though Nick himself, in passing through the shop,
Had almost broke his nose against the mop.

Despite its wooden bolt, with jarring sound,
The door upon its hinges open flew;
And forth the Spirit issued,—yet around
It turn'd as if its follower's fears it knew,
And once more beckoning, pointed to the mound,
The antique Keep, on which the bright moon threw
With such effulgence her mild silvery gleam,
The visionary form seem'd melting in her beam.

Beneath a pond'rous archway's somber shade,
Where once the huge portcullis swung sublime,
'Mid ivied battlements in ruin laid,
Sole, sad memorials of the olden time,
The Phantom held its way,—and though afraid
Even of the owls that sung their vesper chime,
Pale Nicholas pursued, its steps attending,
And wondering what on earth it all would end in.

Within the moldering fabric's deep recess
At length they reach a court obscure and lone;
It seemed a drear and desolate wilderness,
The blackened walls with ivy all o'ergrown;
The night-bird shrieked her note of wild distress,
Disturb'd upon her solitary throne,
As though indignant mortal step should dare,
So led, at such an hour, should venture there!

—The Apparition paused, and would have spoke,
Pointing to what Nick thought an iron ring,
But then a neighboring chanticleer awoke,
And loudly 'gan his early matins sing;
And then "it started like a guilty thing,"
As that shrill clarion the silence broke.
—We know how much dead gentlefolks eschew
The appalling sound of "Cock-a-doodle-do!"

The vision was no more—and Nick alone—
  "His streamer's waving" in the midnight wind,
Which through the ruins ceased not to groan;
  —His garment, too, was somewhat short behind,—
And, worst of all, he knew not where to find
  The ring,—which made him most his fate bemoan—
The iron ring,—no doubt of some trap door,
'Neath which the old dead Miser kept his store.

"What's to be done?" he cried, "'t were vain to stay
  Here in the dark without a single clew—
Oh, for a candle now, or moonlight ray!
  'Fore George, I 'm sadly puzzled what to do."
(Then clapped his hand behind)—"'Tis chilly too—
  I 'll mark the spot, and come again by day.
What can I mark it by?—Oh, here 's the wall—
The mortar's yielding—here I 'll stick my awl!"

Then rose from earth to sky a withering shriek,
  A loud, a long-protracted note of woe,
Such as when tempests roar, and timbers creak,
  And o'er the side the masts in thunder go;
While on the deck resistless billows break,
  And drag their victims to the gulfs below;—
Such was the scream when, for the want of candle,
Nick Mason drove his awl in up to the handle.

Scared by his Lady's heart-appalling cry,
  Vanished at once poor Mason's golden dream—
For dream it was;—and all his visions high,
  Of wealth and grandeur, fled before that scream—
And still he listens, with averted eye,
  When gibing neighbors make "the Ghost" their theme
While ever from that hour they all declare
That Mrs. Mason used a cushion in her chair!

A LAY OF ST. GENGULPHUS.

R. HARRIS BARHAM.

Gengulphus comes from the Holy Land,
  With his scrip, and his bottle, and sandal shoon;
Full many a day hath he been away,
  Yet his lady deems him return'd full soon.

Full many a day hath he been away,
Yet scarce had he crossed ayont the sea,
Ere a spruce young spark of a Learned Clerk
Had called on his Lady, and stopp'd to tea.

This spruce young guest, so trimly drest,
Stay'd with that Lady, her revels to crown;
They laugh'd, and they ate, and they drank of the best,
And they turn'd the old castle quite upside down.

They would walk in the park, that spruce young Clerk,
With that frolicsome Lady so frank and free,
Trying balls and plays, and all manner of ways,
To get rid of what French people call *Ennui.*

* * * * * *

Now the festive board with viands is stored,
Savory dishes be there, I ween,
Rich puddings and big, and a barbacued pig,
And ox-tail soup in a China tureen.

There 's a flagon of ale as large as a pail—
When, cockle on hat, and staff in hand,
While on naught they are thinking save eating and drinking,
Gengulphus walks in from the Holy Land!

"You must be pretty deep to catch weasels asleep,"
Says the proverb: that is "take the Fair unawares:"
A maid o'er the banisters chancing to peep,
Whispers, "Ma'am, here 's Gengulphus a-coming up-stairs.'

Pig, pudding, and soup, the electrified group,
With the flagon pop under the sofa in haste,
And contrive to deposit the Clerk in the closet,
As the dish least of all to Gengulphus's taste.

Then oh! what rapture, what joy was exprest,
When "poor dear Gengulphus" at last appear'd!
She kiss'd and she press'd "the dear man" to her breast,
In spite of his great, long, frizzly beard."

Such hugging and squeezing! 't was almost unpleasing,
A smile on her lip, and a tear in her eye;
She was so very glad, that she seem'd half mad,
And did not know whether to laugh or to cry.

Then she calls up the maid and the table-cloth 's laid,
  And she sends for a pint of the best Brown Stout;
On the fire, too, she pops some nice mutton-chops,
  And she mixes a stiff glass of "Cold Without."

Then again she began at the "poor dear" man;
  She press'd him to drink, and she press'd him to eat,
And she brought a foot-pan, with hot water and bran,
  To comfort his "poor dear" travel-worn feet.

"Nor night nor day since he 'd been away,
  Had she had any rest," she "vow'd and declared."
She "never could eat one morsel of meat,
  For thinking how 'poor dear' Gengulphus fared."

She "really did think she had not slept a wink
  Since he left her, although he 'd been absent so long,"
Here he shook his head,—right little he said,
  But he thought she was "coming it rather too strong."

Now his palate she tickles with the chops and the pickles,
  Till, so great the effect of that stiff gin grog,
His weaken'd body, subdued by the toddy,
  Falls out of the chair, and he lies like a log.

Then out comes the Clerk from his secret lair;
  He lifts up the legs, and she lifts up the head,
And, between them, this most reprehensible pair
  Undress poor Gengulphus and put him to bed.

Then the bolster they place athwart his face,
  And his night-cap into his mouth they cram;
And she pinches his nose underneath the clothes,
  Till the "poor dear soul" goes off like a lamb.

* * * * * * *

And now they tried the deed to hide;
  For a little bird whisper'd "Perchance you may swing;
Here 's a corpse in the case, with a sad swell'd face,
  And a Medical Crowner 's a queer sort of thing!"

So the Clerk and the wife, they each took a knife,
  And the nippers that nipp'd the loaf-sugar for tea;
With the edges and points they sever'd the joints
  At the clavicle, elbow, hip, ankle, and knee.

Thus, limb from limb, they dismember'd him
  So entirely, that e'en when they came to his wrists,
With those great sugar-nippers they nipped off his "flippers,"
  As the Clerk, very flippantly, termed his fists.

When they cut off his head, entertaining a dread
  Lest the folks should remember Gengulphus's face,
They determined to throw it where no one could know it,
  Down the well,—and the limbs in some different place.

But first the long beard from the chin they shear'd,
  And managed to stuff that sanctified hair,
With a good deal of pushing, all into the cushion
  That filled up the seat of a large arm-chair.

They contriv'd to pack up the trunk in a sack,
  Which they hid in an osier-bed outside the town,
The Clerk bearing arms, legs, and all on his back,
  As that vile Mr. Greenacre served Mrs. Brown.

But to see now how strangely things sometimes turn out,
  And that in a manner the least expected!
Who could surmise a man ever could rise
  Who'd been thus carbonado'd, cut up, and dissected?

No doubt 't would surprise the pupils at Guy's;
  I am no unbeliever—no man can say that o' me—
But St. Thomas himself would scarce trust his own eyes
  If he saw such a thing in his School of Anatomy.

You may deal as you please with Hindoos and Chinese,
  Or a Mussulman making his heathen *salaam*, or
A Jew or a Turk, but it's rather guess work
  When a man has to do with a Pilgrim or Palmer.

* * * * * * *

By chance the Prince Bishop, a Royal Divine,
  Sends his cards round the neighborhood next day, and urges his
Wish to receive a snug party to dine,
  Of the resident clergy, the gentry, and burgesses.

At a quarter past five they are all alive,
  At the palace, for coaches are fast rolling in,
And to every guest his card had express'd
  "Half-past" as the hour for "a greasy chin."

Some thirty are seated, and handsomely treated
  With the choicest Rhine wine in his Highness's stock;
When a Count of the Empire, who felt himself heated,
  Requested some water to mix with his Hock.

The Butler, who saw it, sent a maid out to draw it,
  But scarce had she given the windlass a twirl,
Ere Gengulphus's head, from the well's bottom, said
  In mild accents, "Do help us out, that's a good girl!"

Only fancy her dread when she saw a great head
  In her bucket;—with fright she was ready to drop:—
Conceive, if you can, how she roar'd and she ran,
  With the head rolling after her, bawling out "Stop!"

She ran and she roar'd, till she came to the board
  Where the Prince Bishop sat with his party around,
When Gengulphus's poll, which continued to roll
  At her heels, on the table bounced up with a bound.

Never touching the cates, or the dishes or plates,
  The decanters or glasses, the sweetmeats or fruits,
The head smiles, and begs them to bring his legs,
  As a well-spoken gentleman asks for his boots.

Kicking open the casement, to each one's amazement
  Straight a right leg steps in, all impediment scorns,
And near the head stopping, a left follows hopping
  Behind,—for the left leg was troubled with corns.

Next, before the beholders, two great brawny shoulders,
  And arms on their bent elbows dance through the throng,
While two hands assist, though nipped off at the wrist,
  The said shoulders in bearing the body along.

They march up to the head, not one syllable said,
  For the thirty guests all stare in wonder and doubt,
As the limbs in their sight arrange and unite,
  Till Gengulphus, though dead, looks as sound as a trout

I will venture to say, from that hour to this day,
  Ne'er did such an assembly behold such a scene;
Or a table divide fifteen guests of a side
  With a dead body placed in the center between.

Yes, they stared—well they might at so novel a sight:
  No one utter'd a whisper, a sneeze, or a hem,
But sat all bolt upright, and pale with affright;
  And they gazed at the dead man, the dead man at them.

The Prince Bishop's Jester, on punning intent,
  As he view'd the whole thirty, in jocular terms
Said "They put him in mind of a Council of *Trente*
  Engaged in reviewing the Diet of Worms."

But what should they do?—Oh! nobody knew
  What was best to bè done, either stranger or resident;
The Chancellor's self read his Puffendorf through
  In vain, for his book could not furnish a precedent.

The Prince Bishop mutter'd a curse, and a prayer,
  Which his double capacity hit to a nicety;
His Princely, or Lay, half induced him to swear,
  His Episcopal moiety said "*Benedicite!*"

The Coroner sat on the body that night,
  And the jury agreed,—not a doubt could they harbor,—
"That the chin of the corpse—the sole thing brought to light--
  Had been recently shav'd by a very bad barber."

They sent out Van Taünsend, Von Bürnie, Von Roe,
  Von Maine, and Von Rowantz—through châlets and châteaux,
Towns, villages, hamlets, they told them to go,
  And they stuck up placards on the walls of the Stadthaus.

"MURDER!!

"WHEREAS, a dead gentleman, surname unknown,
  Has been recently found at his Highness's banquet,
Rather shabbily dressed in an Amice, or gown
  In appearance resembling a second-hand blanket;

"And WHEREAS, there 's great reason indeed to suspect
  That some ill-disposed person, or persons, with malice
Aforethought, have kill'd, and begun to dissect
  The said Gentleman, not far from this palace·

"This is to give Notice!—Whoever shall seize,
And such person or persons, to justice surrender,
Shall receive—such Reward—as his Highness shall please,
On conviction of him, the aforesaid offender.

"And, in order the matter more clearly to trace
To the bottom, his Highness, the Prince Bishop, further,
Of his clemency, offers free Pardon and Grace
To all such as have *not* been concern'd in the murther.

"Done this day, at our palace,—July twenty-five,—
By command,
(Signed)
Johann Von Rüssell,
N.B.
Deceased rather in years—had a squint when alive;
And smells slightly of gin—linen marked with a G."

The Newspapers, too, made no little ado,
Though a different version each managed to dish up:
Some said "The Prince Bishop had run a man through,"
Others said "an assassin had kill'd the Prince Bishop."

The "Ghent Herald" fell foul of the "Bruxelles Gazette,"
The "Bruxelles Gazette," with much sneering ironical,
Scorn'd to remain in the "Ghent Herald's" debt,
And the "Amsterdam Times" quizz'd the "Nuremberg Chronicle."

In one thing, indeed, all the journals agreed,
Spite of "politics," "bias," or "party collision;"
Viz.: to "give," when they'd "further accounts" of the deed,
"Full particulars" soon, in "a later Edition."

But now, while on all sides they rode and they ran,
Trying all sorts of means to discover the caitiffs,
Losing patience, the holy Gengulphus began
To think it high time to "astonish the natives."

First, a Rittmeister's Frau, who was weak in both eyes,
And supposed the most short-sighted woman in Holland,
Found greater relief, to her joy and surprise,
From one glimpse of his "squint" than from glasses by Dollond.

By the slightest approach to the tip of his Nose,
  Meagrims, headache, and vapors were put to the rout;
And one single touch of his precious Great Toes
  Was a certain specific for chillblains and gout.

Rheumatics,—sciatica,—tic-douloureux!
  Apply to his shin-bones—not one of them lingers;—
All bilious complaints in an instant withdrew,
  If the patient was tickled with one of his fingers.

Much virtue was found to reside in his thumbs:
  When applied to the chest, they cured scantness of breathing,
Sea-sickness, and colic; or, rubb'd on the gums,
  Were "A blessing to Mothers," for infants in teething.

Whoever saluted the nape of his neck,
  Where the mark remain'd visible still of the knife,
Notwithstanding east winds perspiration might check,
  Was safe from sore-throat for the rest of his life.

Thus, while each acute and each chronic complaint
  Giving way, proved an influence clearly Divine,
They perceived the dead Gentleman must be a Saint,
  So they lock'd him up, body and bones, in a shrine.

Through country and town his new Saintship's renown
  As a first-rate physician kept daily increasing,
Till, as Alderman Curtis told Alderman Brown,
  It seem'd as if "Wonders had never *done ceasing*."

The Three Kings of Cologne began, it was known,
  A sad falling off in their offerings to find,
His feats were so many—still the greatest of any,—
  In every sense of the word, was—behind·

For the German Police were beginning to cease
  From exertions which each day more fruitless appear'd,
When Gengulphus himself, his fame still to increase,
  Unravell'd the whole by the help of—his beard!

If you look back you'll see the aforesaid *barbe gris*,
  When divorced from the chin of its murder'd proprietor,
Had been stuffed in the seat of a kind of settee,
  Or double-arm'd chair, to keep the thing quieter.

It may seem rather strange, that it did not arrange
  Itself in its place when the limbs join'd together;
Perhaps it could not get out, for the cushion was stout,
  And constructed of good, strong, maroon-color'd leather

Or what is more likely, Gengulphus might choose,
  For saints, e'en when dead, still retain their volition,
It should rest there, to aid some particular views,
  Produced by his very peculiar position.

Be that as it may, on the very first day
  That the widow Gengulphus sat down on that settee,
What occur'd almost frightened her senses away,
  Beside scaring her hand-maidens, Gertrude and Betty.

They were telling their mistress the wonderful deeds
  Of the new Saint, to whom all the Town said their orisons:
And especially how, as regards invalids,
  His miraculous cures far outrival'd Von Morison's.

"The cripples," said they, "fling their crutches away,
  And people born blind now can easily see us!"
But she (we presume, a disciple of Hume)
  Shook her head, and said angrily, "'*Credat Judæus!*'

"Those rascally liars, the Monks and the Friars,
  To bring grist to their mill, these devices have hit on.
He works miracles!—pooh!—I 'd believe it of you
  Just as soon, you great Geese,—or the Chair that I sit on!"

The Chair—at that word—it seems really absurd,
  But the truth must be told,—what contortions and grins
Distorted her face!—She sprang up from her place
  Just as though she'd been sitting on needles and pins!

For, as if the Saint's beard the rash challenge had heard
  Which she utter'd, of what was beneath her forgetful,
Each particular hair stood on end in the chair,
  Like a porcupine's quills when the animal 's fretful.

That stout maroon leather, they pierced altogether,
  Like tenter-hooks holding when clench'd from within,
And the maids cried—"Good gracious! how very tenacious!"
  —They as well might endeavor to pull off her skin!—

She shriek'd with the pain, but all efforts were vain;
  In vain did they strain every sinew and muscle,—
The cushion stuck fast!—From that hour to her last
  She could never get rid of that comfortless "Bustle"!

And e'en as Macbeth, when devising the death
  Of his King, heard "the very stones prate of his whereabouts;"
So this shocking bad wife heard a voice all her life
  Crying "Murder!" resound from the cushion,—or thereabouts.

With regard to the Clerk, we are left in the dark
  As to what his fate was; but I can not imagine he
Got off scot-free, though unnoticed it be
  Both by Ribadaneira and Jacques de Voragine:

For cut-throats, we 're sure, can be never secure,
  And "History's Muse" still to prove it her pen holds,
As you 'll see, if you 'll look in a rather scarce book,
  "*God's Revenge against Murder*," by one Mr. Reynolds.

MORAL.

Now, you grave married Pilgrims, who wander away,
  Like Ulysses of old (*vide* Homer and Naso),
Don't lengthen your stay to three years and a day,
  And when you *are* coming home, just write and say so!

And you, learned Clerks, who 're *not* given to roam,
  Stick close to your books, nor lose sight of decorum,
Don't visit a house when the master's from home!
  Shun drinking,—and study the "*Vitæ Sanctorum!*"

Above all, you gay ladies, who fancy neglect
  In your spouses, allow not your patience to fail;
But remember Gengulphus's wife!—and reflect
  On the moral enforced by her terrible tale!

SIR RUPERT THE FEARLESS.

A LEGEND OF GERMANY.

R. HARRIS BARHAM.

Sir Rupert the Fearless, a gallant young knight,
Was equally ready to tipple or fight,
Crack a crown, or a bottle,
Cut sirloin, or throttle;
In brief, or as Hume says, "to sum up the tottle,"
Unstain'd by dishonor, unsullied by fear,
All his neighbors pronounced him a *preux chevalier*.

Despite these perfections, corporeal and mental,
He had one slight defect, viz., a rather lean rental;
Besides, 'tis own'd there are spots in the sun,
So it must be confess'd that Sir Rupert had one;
Being rather unthinking,
He'd scarce sleep a wink in
A night, but addict himself sadly to drinking;
And what moralists say,
Is as naughty—to play,
To *Rouge et Noir*, Hazard, Short Whist, *Ecarté;*
Till these, and a few less defensible fancies
Brought the Knight to the end of his slender finances.

When at length through his boozing,
And tenants refusing
Their rents, swearing "times were so bad they were losing,"
His steward said, "O, sir,
It's some time ago, sir,
Since aught through my hands reach'd the baker or grocer,
And the tradesmen in general are grown great complainers."
Sir Rupert the brave thus address'd his retainers:

"My friends, since the stock
Of my father's old hock
Is out, with the Kürchwasser, Barsac, Moselle,
And we 're fairly reduced to the pump and the well,
I presume to suggest,
We shall all find it best
For each to shake hands with his friends ere he goes,
Mount his horse, if he has one, and—follow his nose;

As to me, I opine,
Left *sans* money or wine,
My best way is to throw myself into the Rhine,
Where pitying trav'lers may sigh, as they cross over,
'Though he lived a *roué*, yet he died a philosopher.' "

The Knight, having bow'd out his friends thus politely,
Got into his skiff, the full moon shining brightly,
By the light of whose beam,
He soon spied on the stream
A dame, whose complexion was fair as new cream;
Pretty pink silken hose
Cover'd ankles and toes,
In other respects she was scanty of clothes;
For, so says tradition, both written and oral,
Her *one* garment was loop'd up with bunches of coral.

Full sweetly she sang to a sparkling guitar,
With silver chords stretch'd over Derbyshire spar,
And she smiled on the Knight,
Who, amazed at the sight,
Soon found his astonishment merged in delight;
But the stream by degrees
Now rose up to her knees,
Till at length it invaded her very chemise,
While the heavenly strain, as the wave seem'd to swallow her
And slowly she sank, sounded fainter and hollower;
—Jumping up in his boat
And discarding his coat,
"Here goes," cried Sir Rupert, "by jingo I'll follow her!"
Then into the water he plunged with a souse
That was heard quite distinctly by those in the house.

Down, down, forty fathom and more from the brink,
Sir Rupert the Fearless continues to sink,
And, as downward he goes,
Still the cold water flows
Through his ears, and his eyes, and his mouth, and his nose,
Till the rum and the brandy he'd swallow'd since lunch
Wanted nothing but lemon to fill him with punch;
Some minutes elapsed since he enter'd the flood,
Ere his heels touch'd the bottom, and stuck in the mud.

But oh! what a sight
Met the eyes of the Knight,
When he stood in the depth of the stream bolt upright!—
A grand stalactite hall,
Like the cave of Fingal,
Rose above and about him;—great fishes and small
Came thronging around him, regardless of danger,
And seem'd all agog for a peep at the stranger.
Their figures and forms to describe, language fails—
They 'd such very odd heads, and such very odd tails;
Of their genus or species a sample to gain,
You would ransack all Hungerford market in vain;
E'en the famed Mr. Myers,
Would scarcely find buyers,
Though hundreds of passengers doubtless would stop
To stare, were such monsters exposed in his shop.

But little reck'd Rupert these queer-looking brutes,
Or the efts and the newts
That crawled up his boots,
For a sight, beyond any of which I 've made mention,
In a moment completely absorb'd his attention.
A huge crystal bath, which, with water far clearer
Than George Robins' filters, or Thorpe's (which are dearer),
Have ever distill'd,
To the summit was fill'd,
Lay stretch'd out before him—and every nerve thrill'd
As scores of young women
Were diving and swimming,
Till the vision a perfect quandary put him in;—
All slightly accoutred in gauzes and lawns,
They came floating about him like so many prawns.

Sir Rupert, who (barring the few peccadilloes
Alluded to), ere he lept into the billows
Possess'd irreproachable morals, began
To feel rather queer, as a modest young man;
When forth stepp'd a dame, whom he recognized soon
As the one he had seen by the light of the moon,
And lisp'd, while a soft smile attended each sentence,
"Sir Rupert, I 'm happy to make your acquaintance;

My name is Lurline,
And the ladies you 've seen,
All do me the honor to call me their Queen;
I 'm delighted to see you, sir, down in the Rhine here,
And hope you can make it convenient to dine here."

The Knight blush'd, and bow'd,
As he ogled the crowd
Of subaqueous beauties, then answer'd aloud:
"Ma'am, you do me much honor—I can not express
The delight I shall feel—if you 'll pardon my dress—
May I venture to say, when a gentleman jumps
In the river at midnight for want of the 'dumps,'
He rarely puts on his knee-breeches and pumps;
If I could but have guess'd—what I sensibly feel—
Your politeness—I 'd not have come *en dishabille*,
But have put on my *silk* tights in lieu of my *steel*."
Quoth the lady, "Dear sir, no apologies, pray,
You will take our 'pot-luck' in the family way;
We can give you a dish
Of some decentish fish,
And our water's thought fairish; but here in the Rhine,
I can't say we pique ourselves much on our wine."

The Knight made a bow more profound than before,
When a Dory-faced page oped the dining-room door,
And said, bending his knee,
"*Madame, on a servi!*"
Rupert tender'd his arm, led Lurline to her place,
And a fat little Mer-man stood up and said grace.

What boots it to tell of the viands, or how she
Apologized much for their plain water-souchy,
Want of Harvey's, and Cross's,
And Burgess's sauces?
Or how Rupert, on his side, protested, by Jove, he
Preferr'd his fish plain, without soy or anchovy.
Suffice it the meal
Boasted trout, perch, and eel,
Besides some remarkably fine salmon peel.
The Knight, sooth to say, thought much less of the fishes
Than what they were served on, the massive gold dishes;

While his eye, as it glanced now and then on the girls,
Was caught by thëir persons much less than their pearls,
And a thought came across him and caused him to muse,
If I could but get hold
Of some of that gold,
I might manage to pay off my rascally Jews!"

When dinner was done, at a sign to the lasses,
The table was clear'd, and they put on fresh glasses;
Then the lady addrest
Her redoubtable guest
Much as Dido, of old, did the pious Eneas,
"Dear sir, what induced you to come down and see us?"—
Rupert gave her a glance most bewitchingly tender,
Loll'd back in his chair, put his toes on the fender,
And told her outright
How that he, a young Knight,
Had never been last at a feast or a fight;
But that keeping good cheer
Every day in the year,
And drinking neat wines all the same as small-beer,
Had exhausted his rent,
And, his money all spent,
How he borrow'd large sums at two hundred per cent.;
How they follow'd—and then,
The once civilest of men,
Messrs. Howard and Gibbs, made him bitterly rue it he
'd ever raised money by way of annuity;
And, his mortgages being about to foreclose,
How he jumped into the river to finish his woes!

Lurline was affected, and own'd, with a tear,
That a story so mournful had ne'er met her ear:
Rupert, hearing her sigh,
Look'd uncommonly sly,
And said, with some emphasis, "Ah! miss, had I
A few pounds of those metals
You waste here on kettles,
Then, Lord once again
Of my spacious domain,
A free Count of the Empire once more I might reign

With Lurline at my side,
My adorable bride
(For the parson should come, and the knot should be tied);
No couple so happy on earth should be seen
As Sir Rupert the brave and his charming Lurline;
Not that money's my object—No, hang it! I scorn it—
And as for my rank—but that *you'd* so adorn it—
I'd abandon it all
To remain your true thrall,
And, instead of 'the *Great*,' be call'd 'Rupert the *Small*;'
—To gain but your smiles, were I Sardanapalus,
I'd descend from my throne, and be boots at an alehouse."

Lurline hung her head
Turn'd pale, and then red,
Growing faint at this sudden proposal to wed,
As though his abruptness, in "popping the question"
So soon after dinner, disturb'd her digestion.
Then, averting her eye,
With a lover-like sigh,
"You are welcome," she murmur'd in tones most bewitching,
"To every utensil I have in my kitchen!"
Upstarted the Knight,
Half mad with delight,
Round her finely-form'd waist
He immediately placed
One arm, which the lady most closely embraced,
Of her lily-white fingers the other made capture,
And he press'd his adored to his bosom with rapture.
"And, oh!" he exclaim'd, "let them go catch my skiff, I
'll be home in a twinkling and back in a jiffy,
Nor one moment procrastinate longer my journey
Than to put up the bans and kick out the attorney."

One kiss to her lip, and one squeeze to her hand
And Sir Rupert already was half-way to land,
For a sour-visaged Triton,
With features would frighten
Old Nick, caught him up in one hand, though no light one,
Sprang up through the waves, popp'd him into his funny,
Which some others already had half-fill'd with money;

In fact, 't was so heavily laden with ore
And pearls, 't was a mercy he got it to shore;
    But Sir Rupert was strong,
    And while pulling along,
Still he heard, faintly sounding, the water-nymphs' song.

LAY OF THE NAIADS.

"Away! away! to the mountain's brow,
  Where the castle is darkly frowning;
And the vassals, all in goodly row,
  Weep for their lord a-drowning!
Away! away! to the steward's room,
  Where law with its wig and robe is;
Throw us out John Doe and Richard Roe,
  And sweetly we'll tickle their tobies!"

The unearthly voices scarce had ceased their yelling,
When Rupert reach'd his old baronial dwelling.

    What rejoicing was there!
    How the vassals did stare!
The old housekeeper put a clean shirt down to air,
    For she saw by her lamp
    That her master's was damp,
And she fear'd he 'd catch cold, and lumbago, and cramp;
    But, scorning what she did,
    The Knight never heeded
Wet jacket, or trousers, or thought of repining,
Since their pockets had got such a delicate lining.
    But, oh! what dismay
    Fill'd the tribe of *Ca Sa*,
When they found he 'd the cash, and intended to pay!
Away went "*cognovits*," "bills," "bonds," and "escheats,"
Rupert cleared off old scores, and took proper receipts.

    Now no more he sends out,
    For pots of brown stout,
Or *schnapps*, but resolves to do henceforth without,
Abjure from this hour all excess and ebriety,
Enroll himself one of a Temp'rance Society,

All riot eschew,
Begin life anew,
And new-cushion and hassock the family pew!
Nay, to strengthen him more in this new mode of life
He boldly determined to take him a wife.

Now, many would think that the Knight, from a nice sense
Of honor, should put Lurline's name in the license,
And that, for a man of his breeding and quality,
To break faith and troth,
Confirm'd by an oath,
Is not quite consistent with rigid morality;
But whether the nymph was forgot, or he thought her
From her essence scarce wife, but at best wife-and-water,
And declined as unsuited,
A bride so diluted—
Be this as it may,
He, I'm sorry to say
(For, all things consider'd, I own 't was a rum thing),
Made proposals in form to Miss *Una Von*—something
(Her name has escaped me), sole heiress, and niece
To a highly respectable Justice of Peace.

"Thrice happy 's the wooing
That 's not long a-doing!"
So much time is saved in the billing and cooing—
The ring is now bought, the white favors, and gloves,
And all the *et cetera* which crown people's loves;
A magnificent bride-cake comes home from the baker,
And lastly appears, from the German Long Acre,
That shaft which the sharpest in all Cupid's quiver is,
A plumb-color'd coach, and rich Pompadour liveries.

'T was a comely sight
To behold the Knight,
With his beautiful bride, dress'd all in white,
And the bridemaids fair with their long lace vails,
As they all walk'd up to the altar rails,
While nice little boys, the incense dispensers,
March'd in front with white surplices, bands, and gilt censers.

7*

With a gracious air, and a smiling look,
Mess John had open'd his awful book,
And had read so far as to ask if to wed he meant?
And if "he knew any just cause or impediment?"
When from base to turret the castle shook!!!
Then came a sound of a mighty rain
Dashing against each storied pane,
        The wind blew loud,
        And coal-black cloud
O'ershadow'd the church, and the party, and crowd;
How it could happen they could not divine,
The morning had been so remarkably fine!

Still the darkness increased, till it reach'd such a pass
That the sextoness hasten'd to turn on the gas;
        But harder it pour'd,
        And the thunder roar'd,
As if heaven and earth were coming together;
None ever had witness'd such terrible weather.
        Now louder it crash'd,
        And the lightning flash'd,
        Exciting the fears
        Of the sweet little dears
In the vails, as it danced on the brass chandeliers;
The parson ran off, though a stout-hearted Saxon,
When he found that a flash had set fire to his caxon.

Though all the rest trembled, as might be expected,
Sir Rupert was perfectly cool and collected,
        And endeavor'd to cheer
        His bride, in her ear
Whisp'ring tenderly, "Pray don't be frighten'd, my dear
Should it even set fire to the castle, and burn it, you 're
Amply insured, both for buildings and furniture."
        But now, from without,
        A trustworthy scout
        Rush'd hurriedly in,
        Wet through to the skin,
Informing his master "the river was rising,
And flooding the grounds in a way quite surprising."

He'd no time to say more,
For already the roar
Of the waters was heard as they reach'd the church-door,
While, high on the first wave that roll'd in, was seen,
Riding proudly, the form of the angry Lurline;
And all might observe, by her glance fierce and stormy,
She was stung by the *spretæ injuria formæ.*

What she said to the Knight, what she said to the bride,
What she said to the ladies who stood by her side,
What she said to the nice little boys in white clothes,
Oh, nobody mentions—for nobody knows;
For the roof tumbled in, and the walls tumbled out,
And the folks tumbled down, all confusion and rout,
The rain kept on pouring,
The flood kept on roaring,
The billows and water-nymphs roll'd more and more in;
Ere the close of the day
All was clean wash'd away—
One only survived who could hand down the news,
A little old woman that open'd the pews;
She was borne off, but stuck,
By the greatest good luck,
In an oak-tree, and there she hung, crying and screaming,
And saw all the rest swallow'd up the wild stream in;
In vain, all the week,
Did the fishermen seek
For the bodies, and poke in each cranny and creek;
In vain was their search
After aught in the church,
They caught nothing but weeds, and perhaps a few perch.
The Humane Society
Tried a variety
Of methods, and brought down, to drag for the wreck, tackles,
But they only fished up the clerk's tortoise-shell spectacles.

MORAL.

This tale has a moral. Ye youths, oh, beware
Of liquor, and how you run after the fair!
Shun playing at *shorts*—avoid quarrels and jars—
And don't take to smoking those nasty cigars!

—Let no run of bad-luck, or despair for some Jewess-eyed
Damsel, induce *you to contemplate* suicide!
Don't sit up much later than ten or eleven!—
Be up in the morning by half after seven!
Keep from flirting—nor risk, warn'd by Rupert's miscarriage,
An action for breach of a promise of marriage;—
          Don't fancy odd fishes!
          Don't prig silver dishes!
And to sum up the whole, in the shortest phrase I know,
BEWARE OF THE RHINE, AND TAKE CARE OF THE RHINO!

LOOK AT THE CLOCK.

R. HARRIS BARHAM.

"LOOK at the Clock!" quoth Winifred Pryce,
   As she opened the door to her husband's knock,
Then paused to give him a piece of advice,
   "You nasty Warmint, look at the Clock!
          Is this the way, you
          Wretch, every day you
Treat her who vow'd to love and obey you?—
          Out all night!
          Me in a fright!
Staggering home as it 's just getting light!
You intoxified brute!—you insensible block!—
Look at the Clock!—Do!—Look at the Clock!

Winifred Pryce was tidy and clean,
Her gown was a flower'd one, her petticoat green,
Her buckles were bright as her milking-cans,
Her hat was a beaver, and made like a man's;
Her little red eyes were deep set in their socket-holes,
Her gown-tail was turn'd up, and tuck'd through the pocket-
          holes;
          A face like a ferret
          Betoken'd her spirit:
To conclude, Mrs. Pryce was not over young,
Had very short legs, and a very long tongue.

Now David Pryce
Had one darling vice;
Remarkably partial to any thing nice,
Nought that was good to him came amiss,
Whether to eat, or to drink or to kiss!
Especially ale—
If it was not too stale
I really believe he 'd have emptied a pail;
Not that in Wales
They talk of their Ales:
To pronounce the word they make use of might trouble you,
Being spelt with a C, two R's, and a W.

That particular day,
As I 've heard people say,
Mr. David Pryce had been soaking his clay,
And amusing himself with his pipe and cheroots,
The whole afternoon at the Goat-in-Boots,
With a couple more soakers,
Thoroughbred smokers,
Both, like himself, prime singers and jokers;
And, long after day had drawn to a close,
And the rest of the world was wrapp'd in repose,
They were roaring out "Shenkin!" and "Ar hydd y nos;"
While David himself, to a Sassenach tune,
Sang, "We 've drunk down the Sun, boys! let 's drink down the Moon!
What have we with day to do?
Mrs. Winifred Pryce, 't was made for you!"—
At length, when they could n't well drink any more,
Old "Goat-in-Boots" showed them the door:
And then came that knock,
And the sensible shock
David felt when his wife cried, "Look at the Clock!"
For the hands stood as crooked as crooked might be,
The long at the Twelve, and the short at the Three!

That self-same clock had long been a bone
Of contention between this Darby and Joan;
And often, among their pother and rout,
When this otherwise amiable couple fell out,

Pryce would drop a cool hint,
With an ominous squint
At its case, of an "Uncle" of his, who 'd a "Spout."
That horrid word "Spout"
No sooner came out
Than Winifred Pryce would turn her about,
And with scorn on her lip,
And a hand on each hip,
"Spout" herself till her nose grew red at the tip,
"You thundering Willin,
I know you 'd be killing
Your wife,—ay, a dozen of wives,—for a shilling!
You may do what you please,
You may sell my chemise
(Mrs. P. was too well-bred to mention her stock),
But I never will part with my Grandmother's Clock!'

Mrs. Pryce's tongue ran long and ran fast,
But patience is apt to wear out at last,
And David Pryce in temper was quick,
So he stretch'd out his hand, and caught hold of a stick;
Perhaps in its use he might mean to be lenient,
But walking just then was n't very convenient,
So he threw it, instead,
Direct at her head;
It knock'd off her hat;
Down she fell flat;
Her case, perhaps, was not much mended by that:
But whatever it was,—whether rage and pain
Produced apoplexy, or burst a vein,
Or her tumble induced a concussion of brain,
I can't say for certain,—but *this* I can,
When sober'd by fright, to assist her he ran,
Mrs. Winifred Pryce was dead as Queen Anne!

The fatal catastrophe
Named in my last strophe
As adding to grim Death's exploits such a vast trophy,
Made a great noise; and the shocking fatality,
Ran over, like wild-fire, the whole Principality.
And then came Mr. Ap Thomas, the Coroner,
With his jury to sit, some dozen or more, on her.

Mr. Pryce to commence
His "ingenious defense,"
Made a "powerful appeal" to the jury's "good sense,"
"The world he must defy
Ever to justify
Any presumption of 'Malice Prepense;' "—
The unlucky lick
From the end of his stick
He "deplored"—he was "apt to be rather too quick;"—
But, really, her prating
Was so aggravating:
Some trifling correction was just what he meant;—all
The rest, he assured them, was "quite accidental!"

Then he calls Mr. Jones,
Who depones to her tones,
And her gestures and hints about "breaking his bones."
While Mr. Ap Morgan, and Mr. Ap Rhys
Declared the deceased
Had styled him "a Beast,"
And swear they had witness'd, with grief and surprise,
The allusion she made to his limbs and his eyes.

The jury, in fine, having sat on the body
The whole day, discussing the case, and gin-toddy,
Return'd about half-past eleven at night
The following verdict, "We find, *Sarve her right!*"

Mr. Pryce, Mrs. Winifred Pryce being dead,
Felt lonely, and moped; and one evening he said
He would marry Miss Davis at once in her stead.

Not far from his dwelling,
From the vale proudly swelling,
Rose a mountain; it's name you'll excuse me from telling,
For the vowels made use of in Welsh are so few
That the A and the E, the I, O, and the U,
Have really but little or nothing to do;
And the duty, of course, falls the heavier by far,
On the L, and the H, and the N, and the R,
Its first syllable "Pen,"
Is pronounceable;—then
Come two L L's, and two H H's, two F F's, and an N;

About half a score R's and some W's follow,
Beating all my best efforts at euphony hollow:
But we shan't have to mention it often, so when
We do, with your leave, we 'll curtail it to "PEN."

Well—the moon shone bright
Upon "PEN" that night,
When Pryce, being quit of his fuss and his fright,
Was scaling its side
With that sort of stride
A man puts out when walking in search of a bride·
Mounting higher and higher,
He began to perspire,
Till, finding his legs were beginning to tire,
And feeling opprest
By a pain in his chest,
He paus'd, and turn'd round to take breath, and to rest;
A walk all up hill is apt, we know,
To make one, however robust, puff and blow,
So he stopp'd, and look'd down on the valley below.

O'er fell, and o'er fen,
Over mountain and glen,
All bright in the moonshine, his eye roved, and then
All the Patriot rose in his soul, and he thought
Upon Wales, and her glories, and all he 'd been taught
Of her Heroes of old,
So brave and so bold,—
Of her Bards with long beards, and harps mounted in gold;
Of King Edward the First,
Of memory accurst;
And the scandalous manner in which he behaved,
Killing Poets by dozens,
With their uncles and cousins,
Of whom not one in fifty had ever been shaved—
Of the Court Ball, at which, by a lucky mishap,
Owen Tudor fell into Queen Katherine's lap;
And how Mr. Tudor,
Successfully woo'd her,
Till the Dowager put on a new wedding ring,
And so made him Father-in law to the King.

He thought upon Arthur, and Merlin of yore,
On Gryffith ap Conan, and Owen Glendour;
On Pendragon, and Heaven knows how many more.
He thought of all this, as he gazed, in a trice,
On all things, in short, but the late Mrs. Pryce;
When a lumbering noise from behind made him start,
And sent the blood back in full tide to his heart,
Which went pit-a-pat
As he cried out " What 's that?"—
That very queer sound?—
Does it come from the ground?
Or the air,—from above,—or below,—or around?—
It is not like Talking,
It is not like Walking,
It 's not like the clattering of pot or of pan,
Or the tramp of a horse,—or the tread of a man,—
Or the hum of a crowd,—or the shouting of boys,—
It 's really a deuced odd sort of a noise!
Not unlike a cart's,—but that can't be;—for when
Could " all the King's horses, and all the King's men,"
With Old Nick for a wagoner, drive one up " PEN?"

Pryce, usually brimful of valor when drunk,
Now experienced what school-boys denominate "funk."
In vain he look'd back
On the whole of the track
He had traversed; a thick cloud, uncommonly black,
At this moment obscured the broad disc of the moon,
And did not seem likely to pass away soon;
While clearer and clearer,
'T was plain to the hearer,
Be the noise what it might, it drew nearer and nearer,
And sounded, as Pryce to this moment declares,
Very much " like a coffin a-walking up stairs."

Mr. Pryce had begun
To " make up" for a run,
As in such a companion he saw no great fun,
When a single bright ray
Shone out on the way
He had passed, and he saw, with no little dismay,
Coming after him, bounding o'er crag and o'er rock,
The deceased Mrs. Winifred's " Grandmother's Clock!!"

'T was so !—it had certainly moved from its place,
And come, lumbering on thus, to hold him in chase;
'T was the very same Head, and the very same Case,
And nothing was altered at all—but the Face!
In that he perceived, with no little surprise,
The two little winder-holes turn'd into eyes
Blazing with ire,
Like two coals of fire;
And the "Name of the Maker" was changed to a Lip,
And the Hands to a Nose with a very red tip.
No!—he could not mistake it,—'t was SHE to the life!
The identical face of his poor defunct Wife!

One glance was enough
Completely "*Quant. suff.*"
As the doctors write down when they send you their "stuff,"—
Like a Weather-cock whirled by a vehement puff,
David turned himself round;
Ten feet of ground
He clear'd, in his start, at the very first bound!

I've seen people run at West End Fair for cheeses—
I've seen Ladies run at Bow Fair for chemises—
At Greenwich Fair twenty men run for a hat,
And one from a Bailiff much faster than that—
At foot-ball I've seen lads run after the bladder—
I've seen Irish Bricklayers run up a ladder—
I've seen little boys run away from a cane—
And I've seen (that is, *read of*) good running in Spain;
But I never did read
Of, or witness such speed
As David exerted that evening.—Indeed
All I have ever heard of boys, women, or men,
Falls far short of Pryce, as he ran over "PEN!"

He reaches its brow,—
He has past it,—and now
Having once gained the summit, and managed to cross it, he
Rolls down the side with uncommon velocity;
But, run as he will,
Or roll down the hill,
That bugbear behind him is after him still!

And close at his heels, not at all to his liking,
The terrible clock keeps on ticking and striking,
Till, exhausted and sore,
He can't run any more,
But falls as he reaches Miss Davis's door,
And screams when they rush out, alarm'd at his knock,
" Oh ! Look at the Clock !—Do !—Look at the Clock ! !"

Miss Davis look'd up, Miss Davis look'd down,
She saw nothing there to alarm her ;—a frown
Came o'er her white forehead,
She said, " It was horrid
A man should come knocking at that time of night,
And give her Mamma and herself such a fright ;—
To squall and to bawl
About nothing at all !"
She begg'd " he 'd not think of repeating his call ;
His late wife's disaster
By no means had past her,"
She 'd " have him to know she was meat for his Master !"
Then regardless alike of his love and his woes,
She turn'd on her heel and she turn'd up her nose.

Poor David in vain
Implored to remain,
He " dared not," he said, " cross the mountain again."
Why the fair was obdurate
None knows,—to be sure it
Was said she was setting her cap at the Curate ;—
Be that as it may, it is certain the sole hole
Pryce found to creep into that night was the Coal-hole !
In that shady retreat
With nothing to eat
And with very bruised limbs, and with very sore feet,
All night close he kept ;
I can't say he slept ;
But he sigh'd, and he sobb'd, and he groan'd, and he wept ;
Lamenting his sins,
And his two broken shins,
Bewailing his fate with contortions and grins,
And her he once thought a complete *Rara Avis*,
Consigning to Satan,—viz., cruel Miss Davis !

Mr. David has since had a "serious call,"
He never drinks ale, wine, or spirits, at all,
And they say he is going to Exeter Hall
    To make a grand speech,
    And to preach, and to teach
People that "they can't brew their malt liquor too small!"
That an ancient Welsh Poet, one PYNDAR AP TUDOR,
Was right in proclaiming "ARISTON MEN UDOR!"
    Which means "The pure Element
    Is for Man's belly meant!"
And that *Gin's* but a *Snare* of Old Nick the deluder!

And "still on each evening when pleasure fills up,"
At the old Goat-in-Boots, with Metheglin, each cup,
    Mr. Pryce, if he's there,
    Will get into "The Chair,"
And make all his *quondam* associates stare
By calling aloud to the Landlady's daughter,
"Patty, bring a cigar, and a glass of Spring Water!"
The dial he constantly watches; and when
The long hand's at the "XII.," and the short at the "X.,"
    He gets on his legs,
    Drains his glass to the dregs,
Takes his hat and great-coat off their several pegs,
With his President's hammer bestows his last knock,
And says solemnly—"Gentlemen!
                    LOOK AT THE CLOCK ! ! !"

THE BAGMAN'S DOG.

R. HARRIS BARHAM.

Stant littore Puppies!—VIRGIL.

IT was a litter, a litter of five,
Four are drown'd, and one left alive,
He was thought worthy alone to survive;
And the Bagman resolved upon bringing him up,
To eat of his bread, and to drink of his cup,
He was such a dear little cock-tail'd pup!

The Bagman taught him many a trick;
He would carry, and fetch, and run after a stick,
He could well understand
The word of command,
And appear to doze
With a crust on his nose
Till the Bagman permissively waved his hand:
Then to throw up and catch it he never would fail,
As he sat up on end, on his little cock-tail.
Never was puppy so *bien instruit*,
Or possess'd of such natural talent as he;
And as he grew older,
Every beholder
Agreed he grew handsomer, sleeker, and bolder.

Time, however his wheels we may clog,
Wends steadily still with onward jog,
And the cock-tail'd puppy 's a curly-tail'd dog!
When, just at the time
He was reaching his prime,
And all thought he 'd be turning out something sublime,
One unlucky day,
How no one could say,
Whether soft *liaison* induced him to stray,
Or some kidnapping vagabond coaxed him away,
He was lost to the view,
Like the morning dew;—
He had been, and was not—that 's all that they knew
And the Bagman storm'd, and the Bagman swore
As never a Bagman had sworn before;
But storming or swearing but little avails
To recover lost dogs with great curly tails.

In a large paved court, close by Billiter Square,
Stands a mansion, old, but in thorough repair,
The only thing strange, from the general air
Of its size and appearance, is how it got there;
In front is a short semicircular stair
Of stone steps—some half score—
Then you reach the ground floor,
With a shell-pattern'd architrave over the door.

It is spacious, and seems to be built on the plan
Of a Gentleman's house in the time of Queen Anne;
Which is odd, for, although
As we very well know,
Under Tudors and Stuarts the City could show
Many Noblemen's seats above Bridge and below,
Yet that fashion soon after induced them to go
From St. Michael Cornhill, and St. Mary-le-Bow,
To St. James, and St. George, and St. Anne in Soho.—
Be this as it may—at the date I assign
To my tale—that 's about Seventeen Sixty-Nine—
This mansion, now rather upon the decline,
Had less dignified owners—belonging, in fine,
To Turner, Dry, Weipersyde, Rogers, and Pyne—
A respectable House in the Manchester line.

There were a score
Of Bagmen, and more,
Who had travel'd full oft for the firm before;
But just at this period they wanted to send
Some person on whom they could safely depend—
A trust-worthy body, half agent, half friend—
On some mercantile matter, as far as Ostend;
And the person they pitch'd on was Anthony Blogg
A grave, steady man, not addicted to grog—
The Bagman, in short, who had lost the great dog.

* * * * * *

"The Sea! the Sea! the open Sea!—
That is the place where we all wish to be,
Rolling about on it merrily!"
So all sing and say
By night and by day,
In the *boudoir*, the street, at the concert, and play,
In a sort of coxcombical roundelay;—
You may roam through the City, transversely or straight,
From Whitechapel turnpike to Cumberland gate,
And every young Lady who thrums a guitar,
Ev'ry mustached Shopman who smokes a cigar,
With affected devotion
Promulgates his notion
Of being a "Rover" and "Child of the Ocean"—

Whate'er their age, sex, or condition may be,
They all of them long for the "Wide, Wide Sea!"
But, however they dote,
Only set them afloat
In any craft bigger at all than a boat,
Take them down to the Nore,
And you 'll see that, before
The "Wessel" they "Woyage" in has made half her way
Between Shell-Ness Point and the pier at Herne Bay,
Let the wind meet the tide in the slightest degree,
They 'll be all of them heartily sick of "the Sea!"

* * * * * *

I 've stood in Margate, on a bridge of size
Inferior far to that described by Byron,
Where "palaces and pris'ns on each hand rise—"
—That too 's a stone one, this is made of iron—
And little donkey-boys your steps environ,
Each proffering for your choice his tiny hack,
Vaunting its excellence; and, should you hire one,
For sixpence, will he urge, with frequent thwack,
The much-enduring beast to Buenos Ayres—and back.

And there, on many a raw and gusty day,
I 've stood, and turn'd my gaze upon the pier,
And seen the crews, that did embark so gay
That self-same morn, now disembark so queer;
Then to myself I 've sigh'd and said, "Oh dear!
Who would believe yon sickly-looking man 's a
London Jack Tar—a Cheapside Buccaneer!—"
But hold, my Muse!—for this terrific stanza
Is all too stiffly grand for our Extravaganza.

* * * * *

"So now we 'll go up, up, up,
And now we 'll go down, down, down,
And now we 'll go backward and forward,
And now we 'll go roun', roun', roun'."—
—I hope you 've sufficient discernment to see,
Gentle Reader, that here the discarding the *d*
Is a fault which you must not attribute to me;
Thus my Nurse cut it off when, "with counterfeit glee,"
She sung, as she danced me about on her knee,

In the year of our Lord eighteen hundred and three:
All I mean to say is, that the Muse is now free
From the self-imposed trammels put on by her betters,
And no longer like Filch, midst the felons and debtors,
At Drury Lane, dances her hornpipe in fetters.
    Resuming her track,
    At once she goes back
To our hero, the Bagman—Alas! and Alack!
    Poor Anthony Blogg
    Is as sick as a dog,
Spite of sundry unwonted potations of grog,
By the time the Dutch packet is fairly at sea,
With the sands called the Goodwins a league on her lee.

And now, my good friends, I 've a fine opportunity
To obfuscate you all by sea terms with impunity,
    And talking of "calking,"
    And "quarter-deck walking,"
    "Fore and aft,"
    And "abaft,"
"Hookers," "barkeys," and "craft,"
(At which Mr. Poole has so wickedly laughed),
Of binnacles—bilboes—the boom call'd the spanker,
The best bower-cable—the jib—and sheet-anchor;
Of lower-deck guns—and of broadsides and chases,
Of taffrails and topsails, and splicing main-braces,
And "Shiver my timbers!" and other odd phrases
Employ'd by old pilots with hard-featured faces;—
Of the expletives sea-faring Gentlemen use,
The allusions they make to the eyes of their crews;—
    How the Sailors, too, swear,
    How they cherish their hair,
And what very long pigtails a great many wear.—
But, Reader, I scorn it—the fact is, I fear,
To be candid, I can't make these matters so clear
As Marryat, or Cooper, or Captain Chamier,
Or Sir E. Lytton Bulwer, who brought up the rear
Of the "Nauticals," just at the end of the year
Eighteen thirty-nine—(how Time flies!—Oh, dear!)—
With a well-written preface, to make it appear
That his play, the "Sea-Captain," 's by no means small beer;

There!—"brought up the rear"—you see there's a mistake
Which none of the authors I've mentioned would make,
I ought to have said, that he "sail'd in their wake."—
So I'll merely observe, as the water grew rougher
The more my poor hero continued to suffer,
Till the Sailors themselves cried, in pity, "Poor Buffer!"

Still rougher it grew,
And still harder it blew,
And the thunder kick'd up such a hullibaloo,
That even the Skipper began to look blue;
While the crew, who were few,
Look'd very queer, too,
And seem'd not to know what exactly to do,
And they who'd the charge of them wrote in the logs,
"Wind N. E.—blows a hurricane—rains cats and dogs."
In short it soon grew to a tempest as rude as
That Shakspeare describes near the "still vex'd Bermudas,"
When the winds, in their sport,
Drove aside from its port
The King's ship, with the whole Neapolitan Court,
And swamp'd it to give "the King's Son, Ferdinand," a
Soft moment or two with the Lady Miranda,
While her Pa met the rest, and severely rebuked 'em
For unhandsomely doing him out of his Dukedom.
You don't want me, however, to paint you a Storm,
As so many have done, and in colors so warm;
Lord Byron, for instance, in manner facetious,
Mr. Ainsworth, more gravely,—see also Lucretius,
—A writer who gave me no trifling vexation
When a youngster at school, on Dean Colet's foundation.—
Suffice it to say
That the whole of that day,
And the next, and the next, they were scudding away
Quite out of their course,
Propell'd by the force
Of those flatulent folks known in Classical story as
Aquilo, Libs, Notus, Auster, and Boreas,
Driven quite at their mercy
'Twixt Guernsey and Jersey,
Till at length they came bump on the rocks and the shallows,
In West longitude, One, fifty-seven, near St. Maloes;

There you will not be surprised
That the vessel capsized,
Or that Blogg, who had made, from intestine commotions,
His specific gravity less than the Ocean's,
Should go floating away,
'Mid the surges and spray,
Like a cork in a gutter, which, swoll'n by a shower,
Runs down Holborn-hill about nine knots an hour.

You 've seen, I 've no doubt, at Bartholomew fair,
Gentle Reader,—that is, if you 've ever been there,—
With their hands tied behind them, some two or three pair
Of boys round a bucket set up on a chair,
Skipping, and dipping
Eyes, nose, chin, and lip in,
Their faces and hair with the water all dripping,
In an anxious attempt to catch hold of a pippin,
That bobs up and down in the water whenever
They touch it, as mocking the fruitless endeavor;
Exactly as Poets say,—how, though, they can't tell us,—
Old Nick's Nonpareils play at bob with poor Tantalus.
—Stay!—I 'm nòt clear,
But I 'm rather out here;
'T was the water itself that slipp'd from him, I fear;
Faith, I can't recollect, and I have n't Lempriere.—
No matter,—poor Blogg went on ducking and bobbing,
Sneezing out the salt water, and gulping and sobbing,
Just as Clarence, in Shakspeare, describes all the qualms he
Experienced while dreaming they 'd drown'd him in Malmsey.

"O Lord," he thought, "what pain it was to drown!"
And saw great fishes with great goggling eyes,
Glaring as he was bobbing up and down,
And looking as they thought him quite a prize;
When, as he sank, and all was growing dark,
A something seized him with its jaws!—A shark?—

No such thing, Reader:—most opportunely for Blogg,
'T was a very large, web-footed, curly-tail'd Dog!

* * * * * * *

I 'm nòt much of a trav'ler, and really can't boast
That I knôw a great deal of the Brittany coast,

But I 've often heard say
That e'en to this day,
The people of Granville, St. Maloes, and thereabout,
Are a class that society does n't much care about;
Men who gain their subsistence by contraband dealing,
And a mode of abstraction strict people call "stealing;"
Notwithstanding all which, they are civil of speech,
Above all to a stranger who comes within reach;
And they were so to Blogg,
When the curly-tail'd Dog
At last dragged him out, high and dry on the beach.
But we all have been told,
By the proverb of old,
By no means to think "all that glitters is gold;"
And, in fact, some advance
That most people in France
Join the manners and air of a *Maître de Danse*,
To the morals—(as Johnson of Chesterfield said)—
Of an elderly Lady, in Babylon bred,
Much addicted to flirting, and dressing in red.—
Be this as it might,
It embarrass'd Blogg quite
To find those about him so very polite.

A suspicious observer perhaps might have traced
The *petites soins*, tendered with so much good taste,
To the sight of an old-fashion'd pocket-book, placed
In a black leather belt well secured round his waist,
And a ring set with diamonds, his finger that graced,
So brilliant, no one could have guess'd they were paste.
The group on the shore
Consisted of four;
You will wonder, perhaps, there were not a few more;
But the fact is they 've not, in that part of the nation,
What Malthus would term, a "too dense population,"
Indeed the sole sign of man's habitation
Was merely a single
Rude hut, in a dingle
That led away inland direct from the shingle,
Its sides clothed with underwood, gloomy and dark,
Some two hundred yards above high-water mark;

And thither the party,
So cordial and hearty,
Viz., an old man, his wife, two lads, made a start, he
The Bagman, proceeding,
With equal good breeding,
To express, in indifferent French, all he feels,
The great curly-tail'd Dog keeping close to his heels.—
They soon reach'd the hut, which seem'd partly in ruin,
All the way bowing, chattering, shrugging, *Mon-Dieu*ing,
Grimacing, and what sailors call *parley-vooing.*

* * * * * * *

Is it Paris, or Kitchener, Reader, exhorts
You, whenever your stomach 's at all out of sorts,
To try, if you find richer viands won't stop in it,
A basin of good mutton broth with a chop in it?
(Such a basin and chop as I once heard a witty one
Call, at the Garrick, "a c—d Committee one,"
An expression, I own, I do not think a pretty one.)
However, it 's clear
That with sound table beer,
Such a mess as I speak of is very good cheer;
Especially too
When a person 's wet through,
And is hungry, and tired, and don't know what to do.
Now just such a mess of delicious hot pottage
Was smoking away when they enter'd the cottage,
And casting a truly delicious perfume
Through the whole of an ugly ill-furnish'd room;
"Hot, smoking hot,"
On the fire was a pot
Well replenish'd, but really I can't say with what;
For, famed as the French always are for ragouts,
No creature can tell what they put in their stews,
Whether bull-frogs, old gloves, or old wigs, or old shoes
Notwithstanding, when offer'd I rarely refuse,
Any more than poor Blogg did, when seeing the reeky
Repast placed before him, scarce able to speak, he
In ecstasy mutter'd, "By Jove, Cocky-leeky!"
In an instant, as soon
As they gave him a spoon,

Every feeling and faculty bent on the gruel, he
No more blamed Fortune for treating him cruelly,
But fell tooth and nail on the soup and the *bouilli.*

* * * * * *

Meanwhile that old man standing by,
Subducted his long coat-tails on high,
With his back to the fire, as if to dry
A part of his dress which the watery sky
Had visited rather inclemently.—
Blandly he smil'd, but still he look'd sly,
And something sinister lurk'd in his eye.
Indeed, had you seen him his maritime dress in,
You'd have own'd his appearance was not prepossessing;
He 'd a "dreadnought" coat, and heavy *sabots*,
With thick wooden soles turn'd up at the toes,
His nether man cased in a striped *quelque chose*,
And a hump on his back, and a great hook'd nose,
So that nine out of ten would be led to suppose
That the person before them was Punch in plain clothes.

Yet still, as I told you, he smiled on all present,
And did all that lay in his power to look pleasant.
The old woman, too,
Made a mighty ado,
Helping her guest to a deal of the stew;
She fish'd up the meat, and she help'd him to that,
She help'd him to lean, and she help'd him to fat.
And it look'd like Hare—but it might have been Cat.
The little *garçons* too strove to express
Their sympathy toward the "Child of distress"
With a great deal of juvenile French *politesse;*
But the Bagman bluff
Continued to "stuff"
Of the fat, and the lean, and the tender, and tough,
Till they thought he would never cry "Hold, enough!"
And the old woman's tones became far less agreeable,
Sounding like *peste!* and *sacre!* and *diable!*

I 've seen an old saw, which is well worth repeating,
That says,
"Good Eatynge
Deserveth good Drynkynge."

You 'll find it so printed by Caxton or Wynkyn,
And a very good proverb it is to my thinking.
Blogg thought so too;—
As he finish'd his stew,
His ear caught the sound of the word "*Morbleu!*"
Pronounced by the old woman under her breath.
Now, not knowing what she could mean by "Blue Death!"
He conceiv'd she referr'd to a delicate brewing
Which is almost synonymous,—namely, "Blue Ruin."
So he pursed up his lip to a smile, and with glee,
In his cockneyfy'd accent, responded "Oh, *Vee!*"
Which made her understand he
Was asking for brandy;
So she turn'd to the cupboard, and, having some handy,
Produced, rightly deeming he would not object to it,
An oracular bulb with a very long neck to it;
In fact you perceive her mistake was the same as his,
Each of them "reasoning right from wrong premises;"—
—And here by the way
Allow me to say,
Kind Reader—you sometimes permit me to stray—
'Tis strange the French prove, when they take to aspersing,
So inferior to us in the science of cursing:
Kick a Frenchman down stairs,
How absurdly he swears!
And how odd 'tis to hear him, when beat to a jelly,
Roar out in a passion, "Blue Death!" and "Blue Belly!"

"To return to our sheep" from this little digression:—
Blogg's features assumed a complacent expression
As he emptied his glass, and she gave him a fresh one;
Too little he heeded,
How fast they succeeded.
Perhaps you or I might have done, though, as he did;
For when once Madam Fortune deals out her hard raps,
It 's amazing to think
How one "cottons" to Drink!
At such times, of all things in nature, perhaps,
There 's not one that is half so seducing as *Schnaps.*

Mr. Blogg, beside being uncommonly dry,
Was, like most other Bagmen, remarkably shy,

—" Did not like to deny"—
" Felt obliged to comply"
Every time that she ask'd him to " wet t' other eye;"
For 't was worthy remark that she spared not the stoup,
Though before she had seem'd so to grudge him the soup.
At length the fumes rose
To his brain; and his nose
Gave hints of a strong disposition to doze,
And a yearning to seek " horizontal repose."—
His queer-looking host,
Who, firm at his post,
During all the long meal had continued to toast
That garment 't were rude to
Do more than allude to,
Perceived, from his breathing and nodding, the views
Of his guest were directed to " taking a snooze:"
So he caught up a lamp in his huge dirty paw,
With (as Blogg used to tell it) "*Mounseer, swivvy maw!*"
And " marshal'd" him so
" The way he should go,"
Up stairs to an attic, large, gloomy, and low,
Without table or chair,
Or a movable there,
Save an old-fashion'd bedstead, much out of repair,
That stood at the end most remov'd from the stair.—
With a grin and a shrug
The host points to the rug,
Just as much as to say, " There! — I think you 'll be snug!"
Puts the light on the floor,
Walks to the door,
Makes a formal *Salaam*, and is then seen no more;
When just as the ear lost the sound of his tread,
To the Bagman's surprise, and, at first, to his dread,
The great curly tail'd Dog crept from under the bed!—

—It 's a very nice thing when a man 's in a fright,
And thinks matters all wrong, to find matters all right;
As, for instance, when going home late-ish at night
Through a Church-yard, and seeing a thing all in white,
Which, of course, one is led to consider a Sprite,

To find that the Ghost
Is merely a post,
Or a miller, or chalky-faced donkey at most;
Or, when taking a walk as the evenings begin
To close, or, as some people call it, " draw in,"
And some undefined form, " looming large" through the haze,
Presents itself, right in your path, to your gaze,
Inducing a dread
Of a knock on the head,
Or a sever'd carotid, to find that, instead
Of one of those ruffians who murder and fleece men,
It's your uncle, or one of the " Rural Policemen;"—
Then the blood flows again
Through artery and vein;
You 're delighted with what just before gave you pain;
You laugh at your fears—and your friend in the fog
Meets a welcome as cordial as Anthony Blogg
Now bestow'd on *his* friend—the great curly-tail'd Dog.

For the Dog leap'd up, and his paws found a place
On each side his neck in a canine embrace,
And he lick'd Blogg's hands, and he lick'd his face,
And he waggled his tail as much as to say,
"Mr. Blogg, we 've foregather'd before to-day!"
And the Bagman saw, as he now sprang up,
What, beyond all doubt,
He might have found out
Before, had he not been so eager to sup,
'T was Sancho!—the Dog he had rear'd from a pup!—
The Dog who when sinking had seized his hair—
The Dog who had saved, and conducted him there—
The Dog he had lost out of Billiter Square!!

It 's passing sweet,
An absolute treat,
When friends, long sever'd by distance, meet—
With what warmth and affection each other they greet!
Especially too, as we very well know,
If there seems any chance of a little *cadeau*,
A "Present from Brighton," or "Token" to show,
In the shape of a work-box, ring, bracelet, or so,

That our friends don't forget us, although they may go
To Ramsgate, or Rome, or Fernando Po.
If some little advantage seems likely to start,
From a fifty-pound note to a two-penny tart,
It's surprising to see how it softens the heart,
And you 'll find those whose hopes from the other are strongest,
Use, in common, endearments the thickest and longest.
But, it was not so here;
For although it is clear,
When abroad, and we have not a single friend near,
E'en a cur that will love us becomes very dear,
And the balance of interest 'twixt him and the Dog
Of course was inclining to Anthony Blogg,
Yet he, first of all, ceased
To encourage the beast,
Perhaps thinking "Enough is as good as a feast;"
And besides, as we 've said, being sleepy and mellow,
He grew tired of patting, and crying "Poor fellow!"
So his smile by degrees harden'd into a frown,
And his "That's a good dog!" into "Down, Sancho! down!"

But nothing could stop his mute fav'rite's caressing,
Who, in fact, seem'd resolved to prevent his undressing,
Using paws, tail, and head,
As if he had said,
"Most beloved of masters, pray, don't go to bed;
You had much better sit up, and pat me instead!"
Nay, at last, when determined to take some repose,
Blogg threw himself down on the outside the clothes,
Spite of all he could do,
The Dog jump'd up too,
And kept him awake with his very cold nose;
Scratching and whining,
And moaning and pining,
Till Blogg really believed he must have some design in
Thus breaking his rest; above all, when at length
The Dog scratch'd him off from the bed by sheer strength.

Extremely annoy'd by the "tarnation whop," as it
's call'd in Kentuck, on his head and its opposite,
Blogg show'd fight;
When he saw, by the light

Of the flickering candle, that had not yet quite
Burnt down in the socket, though not over bright,
Certain dark-color'd stains, as of blood newly spilt,
Reveal'd by the dog's having scratch'd off the quilt—
Which hinted a story of horror and guilt!—
'T was "no mistake,"—
He was "wide awake"
In an instant; for, when only decently drunk,
Nothing sobers a man so completely as "funk."

And hark!—what's that?—
They have got into chat
In the kitchen below—what the deuce are they at?—
There's the ugly old Fisherman scolding his wife—
And she!—by the Pope! she's whetting a knife!—
At each twist
Of her wrist,
And her great mutton fist,
The edge of the weapon sounds shriller and louder!—
The fierce kitchen fire
Had not made Blogg perspire
Half so much, or a dose of the best James's powder.—
It ceases—all's silent!—and now, I declare
There's somebody crawls up that rickety stair.

* * * * * *

The horrid old ruffian comes, cat-like, creeping;—
He opens the door just sufficient to peep in,
And sees, as he fancies, the Bagman sleeping!
For Blogg, when he'd once ascertain'd that there was some
"Precious mischief" on foot, had resolv'd to play "'Possum;"—
Down he went, legs and head,
Flat on the bed,
Apparently sleeping as sound as the dead;
While, though none who look'd at him would think such a thing,
Every nerve in his frame was braced up for a spring.
Then, just as the villain
Crept, stealthily still, in,
And you'd not have insur'd his guest's life for a shilling,
As the knife gleam'd on high, bright and sharp as a razor,
Blogg, starting upright, "tipped" the fellow "a facer;"—

—Down went man and weapon.—Of all sorts of blows,
From what Mr. Jackson reports, I suppose
There are few that surpass a flush hit on the nose.

Now, had I the pen of old Ossian or Homer,
(Though each of these names some pronounce a misnomer,
And say the first person
Was call'd James M'Pherson,
While, as to the second, they stoutly declare
He was no one knows who, and born no one knows where)
Or had I the quill of Pierce Egan, a writer
Acknowledged the best theoretical fighter
For the last twenty years,
By the lively young Peers,
Who, doffing their coronets, collars, and ermine, treat
Boxers to "Max," at the One Tun in Jermyn Street;
—I say, could I borrow these Gentlemen's Muses,
More skill'd than my meek one in "fibbings" and bruises,
I 'd describe now to you
As "prime a Set-to,"
And "regular turn-up," as ever you knew;
Not inferior in "bottom" to aught you have read of
Since Cribb, years ago, half knock'd Molyneux's head off.
But my dainty Urania says, "Such things are shocking!"
Lace mittens she loves,
Detesting "The Gloves;"
And turning, with air most disdainfully mocking,
From Melpomene's buskin, adopts the silk stocking.
So, as far as I can see,
I must leave you to "fancy"
The thumps, and the bumps, and the ups and the downs,
And the taps, and the slaps, and the raps on the crowns,
That pass'd 'twixt the Husband, Wife, Bagman, and Dog,
As Blogg roll'd over them, and they roll'd over Blogg;
While what 's called "The Claret"
Flew over the garret:
Merely stating the fact.
As each other they whack'd,
The Dog his old master most gallantly back'd;
Making both the *garçons*, who came running in, sheer off,
With "Hippolyte's" thumb, and "Alphonse's" left ear off;

Next making a stoop on
The buffeting group on
The floor, rent in tatters the old woman's *jupon ;*
Then the old man turn'd up, and a fresh bite of Sancho's
Tore out the whole seat of his striped Calimancoes.—
Really, which way
This desperate fray
Might have ended at last, I 'm not able to say,
The dog keeping thus the assassins at bay:
But a few fresh arrivals decided the day;
For bounce went the door,
In came half a score
Of the passengers, sailors, and one or two more
Who had aided the party in gaining the shore!

It 's a great many years ago—mine then were few—
Since I spent a short time in the old *Courageux ;*
I think that they say
She had been, in her day
A First-rate,—but was then what they term a *Rasée*,—
And they took me on board in the Downs, where she lay
(Captain Wilkinson held the command, by the way.)
In her I pick'd up, on that single occasion,
The little I know that concerns Navigation,
And obtained, *inter alia*, some vague information
Of a practice which often, in cases of robbing,
Is adopted on shipboard—I think it 's call'd "Cobbing."
How it 's managed exactly I really can't say,
But I think that a Boot-jack is brought into play,—
That is, if I 'm right:—it exceeds my ability
To tell how 'tis done;
But the system is one
Of which Sancho's exploit would increase the facility.
And, from all I can learn, I 'd much rather be robb'd
Of the little I have in my purse, than be "cobb'd;"—
That 's mere matter of taste:
But the Frenchman was placed—
I mean the old scoundrel whose actions we've traced—
In such a position, that, on his unmasking,
His consent was the last thing the men thought of asking.

The old woman, too,
Was obliged to go through,
With her boys, the rough discipline used by the crew,
Who, before they let one of the set see the back of them,
"Cobb'd" the whole party,—ay, "every man Jack of them."

MORAL.

And now, Gentle Reader, before that I say
Farewell for the present, and wish you good-day,
Attend to the moral I draw from my lay!—

If ever you travel, like Anthony Blogg,
Be wary of strangers!—don't take too much grog!—
And don't fall asleep, if you should, like a hog!—
Above all—carry with you a curly-tail'd Dog!

Lastly, don't act like Blogg, who, I say it with blushing,
Sold Sancho next month for two guineas at Flushing;
But still on these words of the Bard keep a fix'd eye,
Ingratum si dixeris, omnia dixti! ! !

L'Envoye.

I felt so disgusted with Blogg, from sheer shame of him,
I never once thought to inquire what became of him;
If *you* want to know, Reader, the way, I opine,
To achieve your design,—
—Mind, it's no wish of mine,—
Is,—(a penny will do 't)—by addressing a line
To Turner, Dry, Weipersyde, Rogers, and Pyne.

DAME FREDEGONDE.

WILLIAM AYTOUN.

When folks with headstrong passion blind,
To play the fool make up their mind,
They 're sure to come with phrases nice,
And modest air, for your advice.
But, as a truth unfailing make it,
They ask, but never mean to take it.

'Tis not advice they want, in fact,
But confirmation in their act.
Now mark what did, in such a case,
A worthy priest who knew the race.

A dame more buxom, blithe and free,
Than Fredegonde you scarce would see.
So smart her dress, so trim her shape,
Ne'er hostess offer'd juice of grape,
Could for her trade wish better sign;
Her looks gave flavor to her wine,
And each guest feels it, as he sips,
Smack of the ruby of her lips.
A smile for all, a welcome glad,—
A jovial coaxing way she had;
And,—what was more her fate than blame,—
A nine months' widow was our dame.
But toil was hard, for trade was good,
And gallants sometimes will be rude.
"And what can a lone woman do?
The nights are long and eerie too.
Now, Guillot there 's a likely man.
None better draws or taps a can;
He 's just the man, I think, to suit,
If I could bring my courage to 't."
With thoughts like these her mind is cross'd:
The dame, they say, who doubts, is lost.
"But then the risk? I 'll beg a slice
Of Father Raulin's good advice."

Prankt in her best, with looks demure,
She seeks the priest; and, to be sure,
Asks if he thinks she ought to wed:
"With such a business on my head,
I 'm worried off my legs with care,
And need some help to keep things square.
I 've thought of Guillot, truth to tell!
He 's steady, knows his business well.
What do you think?" When thus he met her:
"Oh, take him, dear, you can't do better!"
"But then the danger, my good pastor,
If of the man I make the master.

There is no trusting to these men."
"Well, well, my dear, don't have him then!"
"But help I must have, there's the curse.
I may go further and fare worse."
"Why, take him then!" "But if he should
Turn out a thankless ne'er-do-good,—
In drink and riot waste my all,
And rout me out of house and hall?"
"Don't have him, then! But I've a plan
To clear your doubts, if any can.
The bells a peal are ringing,—hark!
Go straight, and what they tell you mark.
If they say 'Yes!' wed, and be blest—
If 'No,' why—do as you think best."

The bells rung out a triple bob:
Oh, how our widow's heart did throb,
And thus she heard their burden go,
"Marry, mar-marry, mar-Guillot!"
Bells were not then left to hang idle:
A week,—and they rang for her bridal.
But, woe the while, they might as well
Have rung the poor dame's parting knell.
The rosy dimples left her cheek,
She lost her beauties plump and sleek;
For Guillot oftener kick'd than kiss'd,
And back'd his orders with his fist,
Proving by deeds as well as words,
That servants make the worst of lords.

She seeks the priest, her ire to wreak,
And speaks as angry women speak,
With tiger looks, and bosom swelling,
Cursing the hour she took his telling.
To all, his calm reply was this,—
"I fear you've read the bells amiss.
If they have led you wrong in aught,
Your wish, not they, inspired the thought.
Just go, and mark well what they say."
Off trudged the dame upon her way,
And sure enough the chime went so,—
"Don't have that knave, that knave Guillot!"

"Too true," she cried, "there 's not a doubt:
What could my ears have been about!"
She had forgot, that, as fools think,
The bell is ever sure to clink.

THE KING OF BRENTFORD'S TESTAMENT.

W. MAKEPEACE THACKERAY.

The noble king of Brentford
  Was old and very sick;
He summoned his physicians
  To wait upon him quick;
They stepped into their coaches,
  And brought their best physic.

They crammed their gracious master
  With potion and with pill;
They drenched him and they bled him:
  They could not cure his ill.
"Go fetch," says he, "my lawyer;
  I 'd better make my will."

The monarch's royal mandate
  The lawyer did obey;
The thought of six-and-eightpence
  Did make his heart full gay.
"What is't," says he, "your majesty
  Would wish of me to-day?"

"The doctors have belabored me
  With potion and with pill:
My hours of life are counted
  O man of tape and quill!
Sit down and mend a pen or two,
  I want to make my will.

"O'er all the land of Brentford
  I 'm lord and eke of Kew:
I 've three per cents and five per cents;
  My debts are but a few;
And to inherit after me
  I have but children two.

"Prince Thomas is my eldest son,
  A sober prince is he;
And from the day we breeched him,
  Till now he 's twenty-three,
He never caused disquiet
  To his poor mamma or me.

"At school they never flogged him;
  At college, though not fast,
Yet his little go and great go
  He creditably passed,
And made his year's allowance
  For eighteen months to last.

"He never owed a shilling,
  Went never drunk to bed,
He has not two ideas
  Within his honest head;
In all respects he differs
  From my second son, Prince Ned.

"When Tom has half his income
  Laid by at the year's end,
Poor Ned has ne'er a stiver
  That rightly he may spend,
But sponges on a tradesman,
  Or borrows from a friend.

"While Tom his legal studies
  Most soberly pursues,
Poor Ned must pass his mornings
  A-dawdling with the Muse;
While Tom frequents his banker,
  Young Ned frequents the Jews.

"Ned drives about in buggies,
  Tom sometimes takes a 'bus;
Ah, cruel fate, why made you
  My children differ thus?
Why make of Tom a *dullard*,
  And Ned a *genius?*"

"You 'll cut him with a shilling,"
Exclaimed the man of wits:
"I'll leave my wealth," said Brentford,
"Sir Lawyer, as befits;
And portion both their fortunes
Unto their several wits."

"Your grace knows best," the lawyer said,
"On your commands I wait."
"Be silent, sir," says Brentford,
"A plague upon your prate!
Come, take your pen and paper,
And write as I dictate."

The will, as Brentford spoke it,
Was writ, and signed, and closed;
He bade the lawyer leave him,
And turned him round, and dozed;
And next week in the church-yard
The good old king reposed.

Tom, dressed in crape and hatband,
Of mourners was the chief;
In bitter self-upbraidings
Poor Edward showed his grief;
Tom hid his fat, white countenance
In his pocket handkerchief.

Ned's eyes were full of weeping,
He faltered in his walk;
Tom never shed a tear,
But onward he did stalk,
As pompous, black, and solemn,
As any catafalque.

And when the bones of Brentford—
That gentle king and just—
With bell, and book, and candle,
Were duly laid in dust,
"Now, gentlemen," says Thomas,
"Let business be discussed.

"When late our sire beloved
  Was taken deadly ill,
Sir Lawyer, you attended him,
  (I mean to tax your bill;)
And, as you signed and wrote it,
  I pr'ythee read the will."

The lawyer wiped his spectacles,
  And drew the parchment out;
And all the Brentford family
  Sat eager round about:
Poor Ned was somewhat anxious,
  But Tom had ne'er a doubt.

"My son, as I make ready
  To seek my last long home,
Some cares I had for Neddy,
  But none for thee, my Tom:
Sobriety and order
  You ne'er departed from.

"Ned hath a brilliant genius,
  And thou a plodding brain;
On thee I think with pleasure,
  On him with doubt and pain."
("You see, good Ned," says Thomas,
  "What he thought about us twain.")

"Though small was your allowance,
  You saved a little store;
And those who save a little
  Shall get a plenty more."
As the lawyer read this compliment,
  Tom's eyes were running o'er.

"The tortoise and the hare, Tom,
  Set out, at each his pace;
The hare it was the fleeter,
  The tortoise won the race;
And since the world's beginning,
  This ever was the case.

"Ned's genius, blithe and singing,
  Steps gayly o'er the ground;
As steadily you trudge it,
  He clears it with a bound;
But dullness has stout legs, Tom,
  And wind that's wondrous sound.

"O'er fruits and flowers alike, Tom,
  You pass with plodding feet;
You heed not one nor t'other,
  But onward go your beat,
While genius stops to loiter
  With all that he may meet;

"And ever, as he wanders,
  Will have a pretext fine
For sleeping in the morning,
  Or loitering to dine,
Or dozing in the shade,
  Or basking in the shine.

"Your little steady eyes, Tom,
  Though not so bright as those
That restless round about him
  Your flashing genius throws,
Are excellently suited
  To look before your nose.

"Thank heaven, then, for the blinkers
  It placed before your eyes;
The stupidest are weakest,
  The witty are not wise;
O, bless your good stupidity,
  It is your dearest prize!

"And though my lands are wide,
  And plenty is my gold,
Still better gifts from Nature,
  My Thomas, do you hold—
A brain that's thick and heavy,
  A heart that's dull and cold;

"Too dull to feel depression,
Too hard to heed distress,
Too cool to yield to passion,
Or silly tenderness.
March on—your road is open
To wealth, Tom, and success.

"Ned sinneth in extravagance,
And you in greedy lust."
("I' faith," says Ned, "our father
Is less polite than just.")
"In you, son Tom, I 've confidence,
But Ned I can not trust.

"Wherefore my lease and copyholds,
My lands and tenements,
My parks, my farms, and orchards,
My houses and my rents,
My Dutch stock, and my Spanish stock
My five and three per cents;

"I leave to you, my Thomas—"
("What, all?" poor Edward said;
"Well, well, I should have spent them,
And Tom 's a prudent head.")
"I leave to you, my Thomas,—
To you, IN TRUST for Ned."

The wrath and consternation
What poet e'er could trace
That at this fatal passage
Came o'er Prince Tom his face;
The wonder of the company,
And honest Ned's amaze!

"'Tis surely some mistake,"
Good-naturedly cries Ned;
The lawyer answered gravely,
"'Tis even as I said;
'T was thus his gracious majesty
Ordained on his death-bed.

"See, here the will is witnessed,
And here 's his autograph."
"In truth, our father's writing,"
Said Edward, with a laugh;
"But thou shalt not be loser, Tom,
We 'll share it half and half."

"Alas! my kind young gentleman,
This sharing can not be;
'Tis written in the testament
That Brentford spoke to me,
'I do forbid Prince Ned to give
Prince Tom a half-penny.

"'He hath a store of money,
But ne'er was known to lend it;
He never helped his brother;
The poor he ne'er befriended;
He hath no need of property
He knows not how to spend it.

"'Poor Edward knows but how to spend,
And thrifty Tom to hoard;
Let Thomas be the steward then,
And Edward be the lord;
And as the honest laborer
Is worthy his reward,

"'I pray Prince Ned, my second son,
And my successor dear,
To pay to his intendant
Five hundred pounds a year;
And to think of his old father,
And live and make good cheer.'"

Such was old Brentford's honest testament;
He did devise his moneys for the best,
And lies in Brentford church in peaceful rest.
Prince Edward lived, and money made and spent;
But his good sire was wrong, it is confessed,
To say his young son Thomas, never lent.
He did. Young Thomas lent at interest,
And nobly took his twenty-five per cent.

Long time the famous reign of Ned endured,
  O'er Chiswick, Fulham, Brentford, Putney, Kew;
But of extravagance he ne'er was cured.
  And when both died, as mortal men will do,
'T was commonly reported that the steward
  Was very much the richer of the two.

TITMARSH'S CARMEN LILLIENSE.

W. MAKEPEACE THACKERAY.

LILLE, *Sept.* 2, 1843.

My heart is weary, my peace is gone,
  How shall I e'er my woes reveal?
I have no money, I lie in pawn,
  A stranger in the town of Lille.

I.

WITH twenty pounds but three weeks since
  From Paris forth did Titmarsh wheel,
I thought myself as rich a prince
  As beggar poor I'm now at Lille.

Confiding in my ample means—
  In troth, I was a happy chiel!
I passed the gate of Valenciennes.
  I never thought to come by Lille.

I never thought my twenty pounds
  Some rascal knave would dare to steal;
I gayly passed the Belgic bounds
  At Quiévrain, twenty miles from Lille.

To Antwerp town I hastened post,
  And as I took my evening meal
I felt my pouch,—my purse was lost,
  O Heaven! Why came I not by Lille?

I straightway called for ink and pen,
To grandmamma I made appeal;
Meanwhile a load of guineas ten
I borrowed from a friend so leal.

I got the cash from grandmamma
(Her gentle heart my woes could feel),
But where I went, and what I saw,
What matters? Here I am at Lille.

My heart is weary, my peace is gone,
How shall I e'er my woes reveal?
I have no cash, I lie in pawn,
A stranger in the town of Lille.

II.

To stealing I can never come,
To pawn my watch I 'm too genteel,
Besides, I left my watch at home;
How could I pawn it, then, at Lille?

"*La note*," at times the guests will say,
I turn as white as cold boiled veal;
I turn and look another way,
I dare not ask the bill at Lille.

I dare not to the landlord say,
"Good sir, I can not pay your bill:"
He thinks I am a Lord Anglais,
And is quite proud I stay at Lille.

He thinks I am a Lord Anglais,
Like Rothschild or Sir Robert Peel,
And so he serves me every day
The best of meat and drink in Lille.

Yet when he looks me in the face
I blush as red as cochineal;
And think did he but know my case,
How changed he 'd be, my host of Lille.

My heart is weary, my peace is gone,
  How shall I e'er my woes reveal?
I have no money, I lie in pawn,
  A stranger in the town of Lille.

III.

The sun bursts out in furious blaze,
  I perspirate from head to heel;
I 'd like to hire a one-horse chaise;
  How can I, without cash, at Lille?

I pass in sunshine burning hot
  By cafés where in beer they deal;
I think how pleasant were a pot,
  A frothing pot of beer of Lille!

What is yon house with walls so thick,
  All girt around with guard and grille?
O, gracious gods, it makes me sick,
  It is the *prison-house* of Lille!

O cursèd prison strong and barred,
  It does my very blood congeal!
I tremble as I pass the guard,
  And quit that ugly part of Lille.

The church-door beggar whines and prays,
  I turn away at his appeal:
Ah, church-door beggar! go thy ways!
  You 're not the poorest man in Lille.

My heart is weary, my peace is gone,
  How shall I e'er my woes reveal?
I have no money, I lie in pawn,
  A stranger in the town of Lille.

IV.

Say, shall I to yon Flemish church,
  And at a Popish altar kneel?
O do not leave me in the lurch,—
  I 'll cry ye patron-saints of Lille!

Ye virgins dressed in satin hoops,
  Ye martyrs slain for mortal weal,
Look kindly down! before you stoops
  The miserablest man in Lille.

And lo! as I beheld with awe
  A pictured saint (I swear 'tis real)
It smiled, and turned to grandmamma!—
  It did! and I had hope in Lille!

'T was five o'clock, and I could eat,
  Although I could not pay, my meal;
I hasten back into the street
  Where lies my inn, the best in Lille.

What see I on my table stand,—
  A letter with a well-known seal?
'Tis grandmamma's! I know her hand,—
  To Mr. M. A. Titmarsh, Lille."

I feel a choking in my throat,
  I pant and stagger, faint and reel!
It is—it is—a ten pound note,
  And I'm no more in pawn at Lille!

[He goes off by the diligence that evening, and is restored to the bosom of his happy family.]

SHADOWS

LANTERN.

Deep! I own I start at shadows,
  Listen, I will tell you why;
(Life itself is but a taper,
  Casting shadows till we die.)

Once, in Italy, at Florence,
  I a radiant girl adored:
When she came, she saw, she conquered,
  And by Cupid I was floored.

Round my heart her glossy ringlets
 Were mysteriously entwined--
And her soft voluptuous glances
 All my inmost thoughts divined.

"Mia cara Mandolina!
 Are we not, indeed," I cried,
"All the world to one another?"
 Mandolina smiled and sighed.

Earth was Eden, she an angel,
 I a Jupiter enshrined—
Till one night I saw a damning
 Double shadow on her blind!

"Fire and fury! double shadows
 On their bed-room windows ne'er,
To my knowledge, have been cast by
 Ladies virtuous and fair.

"False, abandoned, Mandolina!
 Fare thee well, for evermore!
Vengeance!" shrieked I, "vengeance! vengeance!"
 And I thundered through the door.

This event occurred next morning;
 Mandolina staring sat,
Stark amaz'd, as out I tumbled,
 Raving mad, without a hat!

Six weeks after I 'd a letter,
 On its road six weeks delayed—
With a dozen re-directions
 From the lost one, and it said:

"Foolish, wicked, cruel Albert!
 Base suspicion's doubts resign;
Double lights throw double shadows!
 Mandolina—ever thine."

"Heavens, what an ass!" I muttered,
"Not before to think of that!"—
And again I rushed excited
To the rail, without a hat.

"Mandolina! Mandolina!"
When her house I reached, I cried:
"Pardon, dearest love!" she answered—
"I'm the Russian Consul's bride!"

Thus, by Muscovite barbarian,
And by Fate, my life was crossed;
Wonder ye I start at shadows?
Types of Mandolina lost.

THE RETORT.

GEORGE P. MORRIS.

Old Nick, who taught the village school,
Wedded a maid of homespun habit;
He was stubborn as a mule,
She was playful as a rabbit.

Poor Jane had scarce become a wife,
Before her husband sought to make her
The pink of country-polished life,
And prim and formal as a Quaker.

One day the tutor went abroad,
And simple Jenny sadly missed him;
When he returned, behind her lord
She slyly stole, and fondly kissed him!

The husband's anger rose!—and red
And white his face alternate grew!
"Less freedom, ma'am!"—Jane sighed and said,
"*Oh, dear! I did n't know 't was you!*"

SATIRICAL.

SATIRICAL.

THE RABBLE: OR, WHO PAYS?

SAMUEL BUTLER.

How various and innumerable
Are those who live upon the rabble!
'Tis they maintain the Church and State,
Employ the priest and magistrate;
Bear all the charge of government,
And pay the public fines and rent;
Defray all taxes and excises,
And impositions of all prices;
Bear all th' expense of peace and war,
And pay the pulpit and the bar;
Maintain all churches and religions,
And give their pastors exhibitions;
And those who have the greatest flocks
Are primitive and orthodox;
Support all schismatics and sects,
And pay them for tormenting texts;
Take all their doctrines off their hands,
And pay 'em in good rents and lands;
Discharge all costly offices,
The doctor's and the lawyer's fees,
The hangman's wages, and the scores
Of caterpillar bawds and whores;
Discharge all damages and costs
Of Knights and Squires of the Post;
All statesmen, cut-purses, and padders,
And pay for all their ropes and ladders;
All pettifoggers, and all sorts
Of markets, churches, and of courts;

All sums of money paid or spent,
With all the charges incident,
Laid out, or thrown away, or given
To purchase this world, Hell or Heaven.

THE CHAMELEON.

MATTHEW PRIOR.

As the Chameleon who is known
To have no colors of its own:
But borrows from his neighbor's hue
His white or black, his green or blue;
And struts as much in ready light,
Which credit gives him upon sight:
As if the rainbow were in tail
Settled on him, and his heirs male;
So the young squire, when first he comes
From country school to Will or Tom's:
And equally, in truth is fit
To be a statesman or a wit;
Without one notion of his own,
He saunters wildly up and down;
Till some acquaintance, good or bad,
Takes notice of a staring lad;
Admits him in among the gang:
They jest, reply, dispute, harangue;
He acts and talks, as they befriend him,
Smear'd with the colors which they lend him.
  Thus merely, as his fortune chances,
His merit or his vice advances.
  If haply he the sect pursues,
That read and comment upon news;
He takes up their mysterious face:
He drinks his coffee without lace.
This week his mimic tongue runs o'er
What they have said the week before;
His wisdom sets all Europe right,
And teaches Marlborough when to fight.
  Or if it be his fate to meet
With folks who have more wealth than wit:

He loves cheap port, and double bub;
And settles in the hum-drum club:
He learns how stocks will fall or rise;
Holds poverty the greatest vice;
Thinks wit the bane of conversation;
And says that learning spoils a nation.
But if, at first, he minds his hits,
And drinks champagne among the wits!
Five deep he toasts the towering lasses;
Repeats you verses wrote on glasses;
Is in the chair; prescribes the law;
And lies with those he never saw.

MERRY ANDREW.

MATTHEW PRIOR.

Sly Merry Andrew, the last Southwark fair
(At Barthol'mew he did not much appear:
So peevish was the edict of the Mayor)
At Southwark, therefore, as his tricks he show'd,
To please our masters, and his friends the crowd;
A huge neat's tongue he in his right hand held:
His left was with a huge black pudding fill'd.
With a grave look in this odd equipage,
The clownish mimic traverses the stage:
Why, how now, Andrew! cries his brother droll,
To-day's conceit, methinks, is something dull:
Come on, sir, to our worthy friends explain,
What does your emblematic worship mean?
Quoth Andrew; Honest English let us speak:
Your emble—(what d' ye call 't) is heathen Greek.
To tongue or pudding thou hast no pretense;
Learning thy talent is, but mine is sense.
That busy fool I was, which thou art now;
Desirous to correct, not knowing how:
With very good design, but little wit,
Blaming or praising things, as I thought fit.
I for this conduct had what I deserv'd;
And dealing honestly, was almost starv'd.

But, thanks to my indulgent stars, I eat;
Since I have found the secret to be great.
O, dearest Andrew, says the humble droll,
Henceforth may I obey, and thou control;
Provided thou impart thy useful skill.—
Bow then, says Andrew; and, for once, I will.—
Be of your patron's mind, whate'er he says;
Sleep very much: think little; and talk less;
Mind neither good nor bad, nor right nor wrong,
But eat your pudding, slave; and hold your tongue.
A reverend prelate stopp'd his coach and six,
To laugh a little at our Andrew's tricks;
But when he heard him give this golden rule,
Drive on (he cried); this fellow is no fool.

JACK AND JOAN.

MATTHEW PRIOR.

Stet quicunque volet potens
Aulæ culmine lubrico, &c. SENECA.

INTERR'D beneath this marble stone
Lie sauntering Jack and idle Joan.
While rolling threescore years and one
Did round this globe their courses run;
If human things went ill or well;
If changing empires rose or fell;
The morning past, the evening came,
And found this couple still the same.
They walk'd and eat, good folks: what then?
Why then they walk'd and eat again:
They soundly slept the night away;
They just did nothing all the day;
And having buried children four,
Would not take pains to try for more;
Nor sister either had, nor brother;
They seem'd just tallied for each other.
Their moral and economy
Most perfectly they made agree:
Each virtue kept its proper bound,
Nor trespass'd on the other's ground.

Nor fame, nor censure they regarded;
They neither punish'd nor rewarded.
He cared not what the footman did;
Her maids she neither prais'd nor chid;
So every servant took his course;
And bad at first, they all grew worse.
Slothful disorder filled his stable;
And sluttish plenty deck'd her table.
Their beer was strong; their wine was port;
Their meal was large; their grace was short.
They gave the poor the remnant meat,
Just when it grew not fit to eat.
They paid the church and parish rate;
And took, but read not the receipt:
For which they claim their Sunday's due,
Of slumbering in an upper pew.
No man's defects sought they to know;
So never made themselves a foe,
No man's good deeds did they commend;
So never rais'd themselves a friend.
Nor cherish'd they relations poor;
That might decrease their present store:
Nor barn nor house did they repair;
That might oblige their future heir.
They neither added nor confounded;
They neither wanted nor abounded.
Each Christmas they accompts did clear,
And wound their bottom round the year.
Nor tear or smile did they employ
At news of public grief or joy.
When bells were rung, and bonfires made,
If ask'd they ne'er denied their aid;
Their jug was to the ringers carried,
Whoever either died, or married.
Their billet at the fire was found,
Whoever was depos'd, or crown'd.
Nor good, nor bad, nor fools, nor wise;
They would not learn, nor could advise:
Without love, hatred, joy, or fear,
They led—a kind of—as it were:
Nor wish'd, nor car'd, nor laugh'd, nor cried:
And so they liv'd, and so they died.

THE PROGRESS OF POETRY.

DEAN SWIFT.

THE farmer's goose, who in the stubble
Has fed without restraint or trouble,
Grown fat with corn and sitting still,
Can scarce get o'er the barn-door sill;
And hardly waddles forth to cool
Her belly in the neighboring pool!
Nor loudly cackles at the door;
For cackling shows the goose is poor.
But, when she must be turn'd to graze,
And round the barren common strays,
Hard exercise, and harder fare,
Soon make my dame grow lank and spare;
Her body light, she tries her wings,
And scorns the ground, and upward springs,
While all the parish, as she flies,
Hear sounds harmonious from the skies.
Such is the poet fresh in pay,
The third night's profits of his play;
His morning draughts till noon can swill,
Among his brethren of the quill:
With good roast beef his belly full,
Grown lazy, foggy, fat, and dull,
Deep sunk in plenty and delight,
What poet e'er could take his flight?
Or, stuff'd with phlegm up to the throat,
What poet e'er could sing a note?
Nor Pegasus could bear the load
Along the high celestial road;
The steed, oppress'd, would break his girth,
To raise the lumber from the earth.
But view him in another scene,
When all his drink is Hippocrene,
His money spent, his patrons fail,
His credit out for cheese and ale;
His two-years' coat so smooth and bare,
Through every thread it lets in air;
With hungry meals his body pined,
His guts and belly full of wind;

And like a jockey for a race,
His flesh brought down to flying case:
Now his exalted spirit loathes
Encumbrances of food and clothes;
And up he rises like a vapor,
Supported high on wings of paper.
He singing flies, and flying sings,
While from below all Grub street rings.

TWELVE ARTICLES.

DEAN SWIFT.

I.

Lest it may more quarrels breed,
I will never hear you read.

II.

By disputing, I will never,
To convince you once endeavor.

III.

When a paradox you stick to,
I will never contradict you.

IV.

When I talk and you are heedless,
I will show no anger needless.

V.

When your speeches are absurd,
I will ne'er object a word.

VI.

When you furious argue wrong,
I will grieve and hold my tongue.

VII.

Not a jest or humorous story
Will I ever tell before ye:
To be chidden for explaining,
When you quite mistake the meaning.

VIII.

Never more will I suppose,
You can taste my verse or prose.

IX.

You no more at me shall fret,
While I teach and you forget.

X.

You shall never hear me thunder,
When you blunder on, and blunder.

XI.

Show your poverty of spirit,
And in dress place all your merit;
Give yourself ten thousand airs:
That with me shall break no squares.

XII.

Never will I give advice,
Till you please to ask me thrice:
Which if you in scorn reject,
'T will be just as I expect.

Thus we both shall have our ends,
And continue special friends.

THE BEASTS' CONFESSION.

DEAN SWIFT.

When beasts could speak (the learned say
They still can do so every day),
It seems, they had religion then,
As much as now we find in men.
It happen'd, when a plague broke out
(Which therefore made them more devout),
The king of brutes (to make it plain,
Of quadrupeds I only mean)
By proclamation gave command,
That every subject in the land

Should to the priest confess their sins;
And thus the pious Wolf begins:
Good father, I must own with shame,
That often I have been to blame:
I must confess, on Friday last,
Wretch that I was! I broke my fast:
But I defy the basest tongue
To prove I did my neighbor wrong;
Or ever went to seek my food,
By rapine, theft, or thirst of blood.
The Ass approaching next, confess'd,
That in his heart he loved a jest:
A wag he was, he needs must own,
And could not let a dunce alone:
Sometimes his friend he would not spare,
And might perhaps be too severe:
But yet the worst that could be said,
He was a wit both born and bred;
And, if it be a sin and shame,
Nature alone must bear the blame:
One fault he has, is sorry for 't,
His ears are half a foot too short;
Which could he to the standard bring,
He 'd show his face before the king:
Then for his voice, there 's none disputes
That he 's the nightingale of brutes.
The Swine with contrite heart allow'd,
His shape and beauty made him proud:
In diet was perhaps too nice,
But gluttony was ne'er his vice:
In every turn of life content,
And meekly took what fortune sent:
Inquire through all the parish round,
A better neighbor ne'er was found;
His vigilance might some displease;
'Tis true, he hated sloth like pease.
The mimic Ape began his chatter,
How evil tongues his life bespatter;
Much of the censuring world complain'd,
Who said, his gravity was feign'd:
Indeed, the strictness of his morals
Engaged him in a hundred quarrels:

He saw, and he was grieved to see 't,
His zeal was sometimes indiscreet;
He found his virtues too severe
For our corrupted times to bear;
Yet such a lewd licentious age
Might well excuse a stoic's rage.
The Goat advanced with decent pace,
And first excused his youthful face;
Forgiveness begg'd that he appear'd
('T was Nature's fault) without a beard.
'Tis true, he was not much inclined
To fondness for the female kind:
Not, as his enemies object,
From chance, or natural defect;
Not by his frigid constitution;
But through a pious resolution:
For he had made a holy vow
Of Chastity, as monks do now:
Which he resolved to keep forever hence,
And strictly too, as doth his reverence.
Apply the tale, and you shall find,
How just it suits with human kind.
Some faults we own; but can you guess?
—Why, virtue 's carried to excess,
Wherewith our vanity endows us,
Though neither foe nor friend allows us.
The Lawyer swears (you may rely on 't)
He never squeezed a needy client;
And this he makes his constant rule,
For which his brethren call him fool;
His conscience always was so nice,
He freely gave the poor advice;
By which he lost, he may affirm,
A hundred fees last Easter term;
While others of the learned robe,
Would break the patience of a Job.
No pleader at the bar could match
His diligence and quick dispatch;
Ne'er kept a cause, he well may boast,
Above a term or two at most.
The cringing Knave, who seeks a place
Without success, thus tells his case:

Why should he longer mince the matter?
He fail'd, because he could not flatter:
He had not learn'd to turn his coat,
Nor for a party give his vote:
His crime he quickly understood;
Too zealous for the nation's good:
He found the ministers resent it,
Yet could not for his heart repent it.
  The Chaplain vows, he can not fawn,
Though it would raise him to the lawn
He pass'd his hours among his books;
You find it in his meager looks:
He might, if he were worldly wise,
Preferment get, and spare his eyes;
But owns he had a stubborn spirit,
That made him trust alone to merit;
Would rise by merit to promotion;
Alas! a mere chimeric notion.
  The Doctor, if you will believe him,
Confess'd a sin; (and God forgive him!)
Call'd up at midnight, ran to save
A blind old beggar from the grave:
But see how Satan spreads his snares;
He quite forgot to say his prayers.
He can not help it, for his heart,
Sometimes to act the parson's part:
Quotes from the Bible many a sentence,
That moves his patients to repentance;
And, when his medicines do no good,
Supports their minds with heavenly food:
At which, however well intended,
He hears the clergy are offended;
And grown so bold behind his back,
To call him hypocrite and quack.
In his own church he keeps a seat;
Says grace before and after meat;
And calls, without affecting airs,
His household twice a-day to prayers.
He shuns apothecaries' shops,
And hates to cram the sick with slops:
He scorns to make his art a trade;
Nor bribes my lady's favorite maid.

Old nurse-keepers would never hire,
To recommend him to the squire;
Which others, whom he will not name,
Have often practiced to their shame.
The Statesman tells you, with a sneer,
His fault is to be too sincere;
And having no sinister ends,
Is apt to disoblige his friends.
The nation's good, his master's glory,
Without regard to Whig or Tory,
Were all the schemes he had in view,
Yet he was seconded by few:
Though some had spread a thousand lies,
'T was he defeated the excise.
'T was known, though he had borne aspersion,
That standing troops were his aversion:
His practice was, in every station,
To serve the king, and please the nation.
Though hard to find in every case
The fittest man to fill a place:
His promises he ne'er forgot,
But took memorials on the spot;
His enemies, for want of charity,
Said he affected popularity;
'Tis true, the people understood,
That all he did was for their good;
Their kind affections he has tried;
No love is lost on either side.
He came to court with fortune clear,
Which now he runs out every year;
Must at the rate that he goes on,
Inevitably be undone:
O! if his majesty would please
To give him but a writ of ease,
Would grant him license to retire,
As it has long been his desire,
By fair accounts it would be found,
He 's poorer by ten thousand pound.
He owns, and hopes it is no sin,
He ne'er was partial to his kin;
He thought it base for men in stations,
To crowd the court with their relations:

His country was his dearest mother,
And every virtuous man his brother;
Through modesty or awkward shame
(For which he owns himself to blame),
He found the wisest man he could,
Without respect to friends or blood;
Nor ever acts on private views,
When he has liberty to choose.
The Sharper swore he hated play,
Except to pass an hour away:
And well he might; for, to his cost,
By want of skill he always lost;
He heard there was a club of cheats,
Who had contrived a thousand feats;
Could change the stock, or cog a die,
And thus deceive the sharpest eye:
Nor wonder how his fortune sunk,
His brothers fleece him when he 's drunk.
I own the moral not exact,
Besides, the tale is false, in fact;
And so absurd, that could I raise up,
From fields Elysian, fabling Æsop,
I would accuse him to his face,
For libeling the four-foot race.
Creatures of every kind but ours
Well comprehend their natural powers,
While we, whom reason ought to sway,
Mistake our talents every day.
The Ass was never known so stupid,
To act the part of Tray or Cupid;
Nor leaps upon his master's lap,
There to be stroked, and fed with pap,
As Æsop would the world persuade;
He better understands his trade:
Nor comes whene'er his lady whistles,
But carries loads, and feeds on thistles.
Our author's meaning, I presume, is
A creature *bipes et implumis;*
Wherein the moralist design'd
A compliment on human kind;
For here he owns, that now and then
Beasts may degenerate into men.

A NEW SIMILE FOR THE LADIES.

WITH USEFUL ANNOTATIONS,

DR. THOMAS SHERIDAN.*

To make a writer miss his end,
You've nothing else to do but mend.

I OFTEN tried in vain to find
A simile† for womankind,
A simile, I mean, to fit 'em,
In every circumstance to hit 'em.‡
Through every beast and bird I went,
I ransack'd every element;
And, after peeping through all nature,
To find so whimsical a creature,
A cloud§ presented to my view,
And straight this parallel I drew:
Clouds turn with every wind about,
They keep us in suspense and doubt,
Yet, oft perverse, like womankind,
Are seen to scud against the wind:
And are not women just the same?
For who can tell at what they aim?‖
Clouds keep the stoutest mortals under,
When, bellowing,¶ they discharge their thnnder:
So, when the alarum-bell is rung,
Of Xanti's** everlasting tongue,

* The following foot-notes, which appear to be Dr. Sheridan's, are replaced from the Irish edition. They hit the ignorance of the ladies in that age.

† Most ladies, in reading, call this word a *smile*; but they are to note, it consists of three syllables, sim-i-le. In English, a likeness.

‡ Not to hurt them.

§ Not like a gun or pistol.

‖ This is not meant as to shooting, but resolving.

¶ This word is not here to be understood of a bull, but a cloud, which makes a noise like a bull, when it thunders.

** Xanti, a nick-name of Xantippe, that scold of glorious memory, who never let poor Socrates have one moment's peace of mind; yet with unexampled patience he bore her pestilential tongue. I shall beg the ladies' pardon if I insert a few passages concerning her: and at the same time I assure them it is not to lesson those of the present age, who are possessed of the like laudable talents; for I will confess, that I know three in the city of Dublin, no way inferior to Xantippe, but that they have not as great men to work upon.

When a friend asked Socrates how he could bear the scolding of his wife Xantippe, he retorted, and asked him how he could bear the gaggling of his geese.

The husband dreads its loudness more
Than lightning's flash, or thunder's roar.
  Clouds weep, as they do, without pain·
And what are tears but women's rain?
  The clouds about the welkin roam:*
And ladies never stay at home.
  The clouds build castles in the air,
A thing peculiar to the fair:
For all the schemes of their forecasting,†
Are not more solid nor more lasting.
  A cloud is light by turns, and dark,
Such is a lady with her spark;
Now with a sudden pouting‡ gloom
She seems to darken all the room;
Again she's pleased, his fear's beguiled,§
And all is clear when she has smiled.
In this they're wondrously alike,
(I hope this simile will strike)‖
Though in the darkest dumps¶ you view them,
Stay but a moment, you'll see through them.
  The clouds are apt to make reflection,**
And frequently produce infection:

Ay, but my geese lay eggs for me, replies his friend; So does my wife bear children, said Socrates.—*Diog. Laert.*

Being asked at another time, by a friend, how he could bear her tongue, he said, she was of this use to him, that she taught him to bear the impertinences of others with more ease when he went abroad.—*Plat. de Capiend. ex. host. utilit.*

Socrates invited his friend Euthymedus to supper. Xantippe, in great rage, went into them, and overset the table. Euthymedus, rising in a passion to go off, My dear friend, stay, said Socrates, did not a hen do the same thing at your house the other day, and did I show any resentment?—*Plat. de ira cohibenda.*

I could give many more instances of her termagancy and his philosophy, if such a proceeding might not look as if I were glad of an opportunity to expose the fair sex; but, to show that I have no such design, I declare solemnly, that I had much worse stories to tell of her behavior to her husband, which I rather passed over, on account of the great esteem which I bear the ladies, especially those in the honorable station of matrimony.

* Ramble.

† Not vomiting.

‡ Thrusting out the lip.

§ This is to be understood not in the sense of wort, when brewers put yeast or barm in it; but its true meaning is, deceived or cheated.

‖ Hit your fancy.

¶ Sullen fits. We have a merry jig called Dumpty-Deary, invented to rouse ladies from the dumps.

** Reflection of the sun.

So Celia, with small provocation,
Blasts every neighbor's reputation.
  The clouds delight in gaudy show,
(For they, like ladies, have their bow;)
The gravest matron* will confess,
That she herself is fond of dress.
  Observe the clouds in pomp array'd,
What various colors are display'd;
The pink, the rose, the violet's dye,
In that great drawing-room the sky;
How do these differ from our Graces,†
In garden-silks, brocades, and laces?
Are they not such another sight,
When met upon a birth-day night?
  The clouds delight to change their fashion:
(Dear ladies be not in a passion!)
Nor let this whim to you seem strange,
Who every hour delight in change.
  In them and you alike are seen
The sullen symptoms of the spleen;
The moment that your vapors rise,
We see them dropping from your eyes.
  In evening fair you may behold
The clouds are fring'd with borrow'd gold;
And this is many a lady's case,
Who flaunts about in borrow'd lace.‡
Grave matrons are like clouds of snow,
Where words fall thick, and soft, and slow;
While brisk coquettes,§ like rattling hail,
Our ears on every side assail.
  Clouds when they intercept our sight,
Deprive us of celestial light:
So when my Chloe I pursue,
No heaven besides I have in view.

* Motherly woman.

† Not grace before and after meat, nor their graces the duchesses, but the Graces which attended on Venus.

‡ Not Flanders-lace, but gold and silver lace. By borrowed, I mean such as run into honest tradesmen's debts, for which they were not able to pay, as many of them did for French silver lace, against the last birth-day. *Vide* the shop-keepers' books.

§ Girls who love to hear themselves prate, and put on a number of monkey-airs to catch men.

Thus, on comparison,* you see,
In every instance they agree;
So like, so very much the same,
That one may go by t' other's name.
Let me proclaim† it then aloud,
That every woman is a cloud.

ON A LAPDOG.

JOHN GAY.

Shock's fate I mourn; poor Shock is now no more:
Ye Muses! mourn: ye Chambermaids! deplore.
Unhappy Shock! yet more unhappy fair,
Doom'd to survive thy joy and only care.
Thy wretched fingers now no more shall deck,
And tie the favorite ribbon round his neck;
No more thy hand shall smooth his glossy hair,
And comb the wavings of his pendent ear.
Yet cease thy flowing grief, forsaken maid!
All mortal pleasures in a moment fade:
Our surest hope is in an hour destroy'd,
And love, best gift of Heaven, not long enjoy'd.
Methinks I see her frantic with despair,
Her streaming eyes, wrung hands, and flowing hair·
Her Mechlin pinners, rent, the floor bestrow,
And her torn fan gives real signs of woe.
Hence, Superstition! that tormenting guest,
That haunts with fancied fears the coward breast;
No dread events upon this fate attend,
Stream eyes no more, no more thy tresses rend.
Though certain omens oft forewarn a state,
And dying lions show the monarch's fate,
Why should such fears bid Celia's sorrow rise?
For when a lapdog falls, no lover dies.
Cease, Celia, cease; restrain thy flowing tears,
Some warmer passion will dispel thy cares.
In man you'll find a more substantial bliss,
More grateful toying, and a sweeter kiss.

* I hope none will be so uncomplaisant to the ladies as to think these comparisons are odious.

† Tell the whole world; not to proclaim them as robbers and rapparees.

He 's dead. Oh! lay him gently in the ground!
And may his tomb be by this verse renown'd:
"Here Shock, the pride of all his kind, is laid,
Who fawn'd like man, but ne'er like man betray'd."

THE RAZOR SELLER.

PETER PINDAR.

A FELLOW in a market town,
Most musical, cried razors up and down,
And offered twelve for eighteen-pence;
Which certainly seemed wondrous cheap,
And for the money quite a heap,
As every man would buy, with cash and sense.

A country bumpkin the great offer heard:
Poor Hodge, who suffered by a broad black beard,
That seemed a shoe-brush stuck beneath his nose·
With cheerfulness the eighteen-pence he paid,
And proudly to himself, in whispers, said,
"This rascal stole the razors, I suppose.

"No matter if the fellow *be* a knave,
Provided that the razors *shave;*
It certainly will be a monstrous prize."
So home the clown, with his good fortune, went,
Smiling in heart and soul, content,
And quickly soaped himself to ears and eyes.

Being well lathered from a dish or tub,
Hodge now began with grinning pain to grub,
Just like a hedger cutting furze:
'T was a vile razor!—then the rest he tried—
All were imposters—"Ah," Hodge sighed!
"I wish my eighteen-pence within my purse."

In vain to chase his beard, and bring the graces,
He cut, and dug, and winced, and stamped, and swore,
Brought blood, and danced, blasphemed, and made wry faces,
And cursed each razor's body o'er and o'er:

His muzzle, formed of *opposition* stuff,
Firm as a Foxite, would not lose its ruff:
So kept it—laughing at the steel and suds:
Hodge, in a passion, stretched his angry jaws,
Vowing the direst vengeance, with clenched claws,
On the vile cheat that sold the goods.
"Razors! a damned, confounded dog,
Not fit to scrape a hog!"

Hodge sought the fellow—found him—and begun:
"P'rhaps, Master Razor rogue, to you 'tis fun,
That people flay themselves out of their lives:
You rascal! for an hour have I been grubbing,
Giving my crying whiskers here a scrubbing,
With razors just like oyster knives.
Sirrah! I tell you, you 're a knave,
To cry up razors that can't *shave*."

"Friend," quoth the razor-man, "I 'm not a knave:
As for the razors you have bought,
Upon my soul I never thought
That they would *shave*."
"Not think they'd *shave!*" quoth Hodge, with wond'ring eyes,
And voice not much unlike an Indian yell;
"What were they made for then, you dog?" he cries:
"Made!" quoth the fellow, with a smile—"to *sell*."

THE SAILOR BOY AT PRAYERS.

PETER PINDAR.

A great law Chief, whom God nor demon scares,
Compelled to kneel and pray, who swore his prayers,
The devil behind him pleased and grinning,
Patting the angry lawyer on the shoulder,
Declaring naught was ever bolder,
Admiring such a novel mode of sinning:

Like this, a subject would be reckoned rare,
Which proves what blood game infidels can dare;
Which to my memory brings a fact,
Which nothing but an English tar would act.

In ships of war, on Sunday's, prayers are given;
For though so wicked, sailors think of heaven,
Particularly in a storm;
Where, if they find no brandy to get drunk,
Their souls are in a miserable funk,
Then vow they to th' Almighty to reform,
If in His goodness only once, once more,
He 'll suffer them to clap a foot on shore.

In calms, indeed, or gentle airs,
They ne'er on weekdays pester heaven with prayers;
For 'tis among the Jacks a common saying,
"Where there 's no danger, there 's no need of praying."

One Sunday morning all were met
To hear the parson preach and pray,
All but a boy, who, willing to forget
That prayers were handing out, had stolen away,
And, thinking praying but a useless task,
Had crawled to take a nap, into a cask.

The boy was soon found missing, and full soon
The boatswain's cat, sagacious smelt him out;
Gave him a clawing to some tune—
This cat's a cousin Germain to the Knout.

"Come out, you skulking dog," the boatswain cried,
"And save your d——d young sinful soul."
He then the moral-mending cat applied,
And turned him like a badger from his hole.

Sulky the boy marched on, and did not mind him,
Altho' the boatswain flogging kept behind him:
"Flog," cried the boy, "flog—curse me, flog away—
I 'll go—but mind—G–d d—n me if I 'll *pray*."

BIENSEANCE.

PETER PINDAR.

There is a little moral thing in France,
Called by the natives *bienseance;*
Much are the English mob inclined to scout it,
But rarely is *Monsieur Canaille* without it.

To *bienseance* 'tis tedious to incline,
In many cases;
To flatter, *par example*, keep smooth faces
When kicked, or suffering grievous want of coin.

To vulgars, *bienseance* may seem an oddity—
I deem it a most portable commodity;
A sort of magic wand;
Which, if 'tis used with ingenuity,
Although a utensil of much tenuity,
In place of something solid, it will stand.

For verily I 've marveled times enow
To see an Englishman, the ninny,
Give people for their services a guinea,
Which Frenchmen have rewarded with a bow.

Bows are a bit of *bienseance*
Much practiced too in that same France:
Yet called by Quakers, children of inanity;
But as they pay their court to people's vanity,
Like rolling-pins they smooth where'er they go
The souls and faces of mankind like dough!
With some, indeed, may *bienseance* prevail
To folly—see the under-written tale.

THE PETIT MAITRE, AND THE MAN ON THE WHEEL.

At Paris some time since, a murdering man,
A German, and a most unlucky chap,
Sad, stumbling at the threshold of his plan,
Fell into Justice's strong trap.

The bungler was condemned to grace the wheel,
On which the dullest fibers learn to feel;
His limbs *secundum artem* to be broke
Amid ten thousand people, perhaps, or more;
Whenever Monsieur Ketch applied a stroke,
The culprit, like a bullock, made a roar.

A flippant *petit maître* skipping by,
Stepped up to him, and checked him for his cry—

"Boh!" quoth the German, "an't I 'pon de wheel?
D'ye tink my nerfs and bons can't feel?"

"Sir," quoth the beau, "don't, don't be in a passion;
I've naught to say about your situation;
But making such a hideous noise in France,
Fellow, is contrary to *bienseance*."

KINGS AND COURTIERS.

PETER PINDAR.

How pleasant 'tis the courtier clan to see!
So prompt to drop to majesty the knee;
To start, to run, to leap, to fly,
And gambol in the royal eye;
And, if expectant of some high employ,
How kicks the heart against the ribs, for joy!

How rich the incense to the royal nose!
How liquidly the oil of flattery flows!
But should the monarch turn from sweet to sour,
Which cometh oft to pass in half an hour,
How altered instantly the courtier clan!
How faint! how pale! how woe-begone, and wan!

Thus Corydon, betrothed to Delia's charms,
In fancy holds her ever in his arms:
  In maddening fancy, cheeks, eyes, lips devours;
Plays with the ringlets that all flaxen flow
In rich luxuriance o'er a breast of snow,
  And on that breast the soul of rapture pours.

Night, too, entrances—slumber brings the dream—
  Gives to his lips his idol's sweetest kiss;
Bids the wild heart, high panting, swell its stream,
  And deluge every nerve with bliss:
But if his nymph unfortunately frowns,
Sad, chapfallen, lo! he hangs himself or drowns!

Oh, try with bliss his moments to beguile:
Strive not to make your sovereign frown—but smile:

Sublime are royal nods—most precious things!—
Then, to be whistled to by kings!

To have him lean familiar on one's shoulder,
Becoming thus the royal arm upholder,
  A heart of very stone must grow quite glad.
Oh! would some king so far himself demean,
As on my shoulder but for once to lean,
  The excess of joy would nearly make me mad!
How on the honored garment I should dote,
And think a glory blazed around the coat!

Blessed, I should make this coat my coat of arms,
In fancy glittering with a thousand charms;
  And show my children's children o'er and o'er;
"Here, babies," I should say, "with awe behold
This coat—worth fifty times its weight in gold:
  This very, very coat your grandsire wore!

"Here"—pointing to the shoulder—I should say,
"Here majesty's own hand so sacred lay"—
  Then p'rhaps repeat some speech the king might utter;
As—"Peter, how go sheep a score? what? what?
What's cheapest meat to make a bullock fat?
  Hæ? hæ? what, what's the price of country butter?"

Then should I, strutting, give myself an air,
  And deem myself adorned with immortality:
Then should I make the children, calf-like stare,
  And fancy grandfather a man of quality:
And yet, not stopping here, with cheerful note,
The muse should sing an ode upon the coat.

Poor lost America, high honors missing,
Knows naught of smile, and nod, and sweet hand-kissing;
Knows naught of golden promises of kings;
Knows naught of coronets, and stars, and strings;
  In solitude the lovely rebel sighs!
But vainly drops the penitential tear—
  Deaf as the adder to the woman's cries,
We suffer not her wail to wound our ear:
For food we bid her hopeless children prowl,
And with the savage of the desert howl.

PRAYING FOR RAIN.

PETER PINDAR

How difficult, alas! to please mankind!
One or the other every moment *mutters:*
This wants an eastern, that a western wind:
A third, petition for a southern, utters.
Some pray for rain, and some for frost and snow:
How can Heaven suit *all* palates?—I don't know.

Good Lamb, the curate, much approved,
Indeed by all his flock *beloved*,
Was one dry summer begged to pray for rain:
The parson most devoutly prayed—
The powers of prayer were soon displayed;
Immediately a *torrent* drenched the plain.

It chanced that the church warden, Robin Jay,
Had of his meadow not yet *saved* the hay:
Thus was his hay to *health* quite past restoring.
It happened too that Robin was from home;
But when he heard the story, in a foam
He sought the parson, like a lion roaring.

"Zounds! Parson Lamb, why, what have you been doing?
A pretty storm, indeed, ye have been brewing!
What! pray for *rain* before I *saved* my hay!
Oh! you're a cruel and ungrateful man!
I that forever help you all I can;
Ask you to dine with me and Mistress Jay,
Whenever we have something on the spit,
Or in the pot a nice and dainty bit;

"Send you a goose, a pair of chicken,
Whose bones you are so fond of picking;
And often too a cag of brandy!
You that were welcome to a treat,
To smoke and chat, and drink and eat;
Making my house so very handy!

"*You*, parson, serve one such a scurvy trick!
Zounds! you must have the bowels of Old Nick.

What! bring the flood of Noah from the skies,
With *my* fine field of hay before your eyes!
A numskull, that I wer'n't of this aware.—
Curse me but I had stopped your pretty prayer!"
"Dear Mister Jay?" quoth Lamb, "alas! alas!
I never thought upon your field of grass."

"Lord! parson, you 're a fool, one might suppose—
Was not the field just underneath your *nose?*
This is a very pretty losing job!"—
"Sir," quoth the curate, "know that Harry Cobb
Your brother warden joined, to have the prayer."—
"Cobb! Cobb! why this for Cobb was only *sport:*
What doth Cobb own that any rain can *hurt?*"
Roared furious Jay as broad as he could stare.

"The fellow owns, as far as I can *larn,*
A few old houses only, and a barn;
As that 's the case, zounds! what are showers to *him?*
Not Noah's flood could make *his* trumpery *swim.*

"Besides—why could you not for *drizzle* pray?
Why force it down in *buckets* on the hay?
Would *I* have played with *your* hay such a freak?
No! I'd have stopped the weather for a week."

"Dear Mister Jay, I do protest,
I acted solely for the best;
I do affirm it, Mister Jay, indeed.
Your anger for this *once* restrain,
I 'll never bring a drop again
Till you and all the parish are *agreed.*"

APOLOGY FOR KINGS.

PETER PINDAR.

As want of candor really is not right,
I own my satire too inclined to bite:
On kings behold it breakfast, dine, and sup—
Now shall she praise, and try to make it up.

Why will the simple world expect wise things,
From lofty folk, particularly kings?
  Look on their poverty of education!
Adored and flattered, taught that they are gods,
And by their awful frowns and nods,
  Jove-like, to shake the pillars of creation!

They scorn that little useful imp called mind,
Who fits them for the circle of mankind!
Pride their companion, and the world their hate;
Immured, they doze in ignorance and state.

Sometimes, indeed, great kings will condescend
A little with their subjects to unbend!
  An instance take:—A king of this great land,
  In days of yore, we understand,
Did visit Salisbury's old church so fair:
  An Earl of Pembroke was the Monarch's guide;
  Incog. they traveled, shuffling side by side;
And into the cathedral stole the pair.

  The verger met them in his blue silk gown,
  And humbly bowed his neck with reverence down,
Low as an ass to lick a lock of hay:
  Looking the frightened verger through and through,
  And with his eye-glass—"Well, sir, who are you?
What, what, sir?—hey, sir?" deigned the king to say.

  "I am the verger here, most mighty king:
  In this cathedral I do every thing;
Sweep it, an't please ye, sir, and keep it clean."
  "Hey? verger! verger!—you the verger?—hey?
  "Yes, please your glorious majesty, I *be*,"
The verger answered, with the mildest mien.

Then turned the king about toward the peer,
And winked, and laughed, then whispered in his ear,
"Hey, hey—what, what—fine fellow, 'pon my word:
I'll knight him, knight him, knight him—hey, my lord?"

[It is a satire-royal: and if any thing were yet wanting to convince us that Master Pindar is no turncoat, here is proof sufficient.]

Then with his glass, as hard as eye could strain,
He kenned the trembling verger o'er again.

"He 's a poor verger, sire," his lordship cried:
  "Sixpence would handsomely requite him."
"Poor verger, verger, hey?" the king replied:
  "No, no, then, we won't knight him—no, won't knight him."

Now to the lofty roof the king did raise
His glass, and skipped it o'er with sounds of praise!
  For thus his marveling majesty did speak:
"Fine roof this, Master Verger, quite complete;
High—high and lofty too, and clean, and neat:
  What, verger, what? *mop, mop* it once a week?"

"An't please your majesty," with marveling chops,
The verger answered, "we have got no mops
  In Salisbury that will reach so high."
"Not mop, no, no, not mop it," quoth the king—
"No, sir, our Salisbury mops do no such thing;
  They might as well pretend to scrub the sky."

Moral.

This little anecdote doth plainly show
  That ignorance, a king too often lurches;
For, hid from art, Lord! how should monarchs know
  The natural history of mops and churches?

STORY THE SECOND.

From Salisbury church to Wilton House, so grand,
Returned the mighty ruler of the land—
  "My lord, you 've got fine statues," said the king.
"A few! beneath your royal notice, sir,"
Replied Lord Pembroke—"Sir, my lord, stir, stir;
  Let's see them all, all, all, all, every thing.

"Who 's this? who 's this?—who 's this fine fellow here?"
"Sesostris," bowing low, replied the peer.
"Sir Sostris, hey?—Sir Sostris?—'pon my word!
Knight or a baronet, my lord?

One of my making?—what, my lord, my making?"
This, with a vengeance, was mistaking?

"*Se*-sostris, sire," so soft, the peer replied—
"A famous king of Egypt, sir, of old."
"Oh, poh!" th' instructed monarch snappish cried,
"I need not that—I need not that be told."

"Pray, pray, my lord, who 's that big fellow there?"
"'Tis Hercules," replies the shrinking peer;
"Strong fellow, hey, my lord? strong fellow, hey?
Cleaned stables!—cracked a lion like a flea;
Killed snakes, great snakes, that in a cradle found him—
The queen, queen's coming! wrap an apron around him."

Our moral is not merely water-gruel—
It shows that curiosity's a jewel!
It shows with kings that ignorance may dwell:
It shows that subjects must not give opinions
To people reigning over wide dominions,
As information to great folk is hell:

It shows that decency may live with kings,
On whom the bold *virtu*-men turn their backs;
And shows (for numerous are the naked things)
That saucy statues should be lodged in sacks.

ODE TO THE DEVIL.

PETER PINDAR.

The devil is not so black as he is painted.

Ingratum Odi.

Prince of the dark abodes! I ween
Your highness ne'er till now hath seen
Yourself in meter shine;
Ne'er heard a song with praise sincere,
Sweet warbled on your smutty ear,
Before this Ode of mine.

Perhaps the reason is too plain,
Thou triest to starve the tuneful train,
Of potent verse afraid!
And yet I vow, in all my time,
I 've not beheld a single rhyme
That ever spoiled thy trade.

I 've often read those pious whims—
John Wesley's sweet damnation hymns,
That chant of heavenly riches.
What have they done?—those heavenly strains,
Devoutly squeezed from canting brains,
But filled John's earthly breeches?

There 's not a shoe-black in the land,
So humbly at the world's command,
As thy old cloven foot;
Like lightning dost thou fly, when called,
And yet no pickpocket 's so mauled
As thou, O Prince of Soot!

What thousands, hourly bent on sin,
With supplication call thee in,
To aid them to pursue it;
Yet, when detected, with a lie
Ripe at their fingers' ends, they cry,
"The Devil made me do it."

Behold the fortunes that are made,
By men through rouguish tricks in trade,
Yet all to thee are owing—
And though we meet it every day,
The sneaking rascals dare not say,
This is the Devil's doing.

As to thy company, I 'm sure,
No man can shun thee on that score;
The very best is thine:
With kings, queens, ministers of state,
Lords, ladies, I have seen thee great,
And many a grave divine.

I 'm sorely grieved at times to find,
The very instant thou art kind,
Some people so uncivil,
When aught offends, with face awry,
With base ingratitude to cry,
"I wish it to the Devil."

Hath some poor blockhead got a wife,
To be the torment of his life,
By one eternal yell—
The fellow cries out coarsely, "Zounds,
I 'd give this moment twenty pounds
To see the jade in hell."

Should Heaven their prayers so ardent grant,
Thou never company wouldst want
To make thee downright mad;
For, mind me, in their wishing mood,
They never offer thee what 's good,
But every thing that 's bad.

My honest anger boils to view
A sniffling, long-faced, canting crew,
So much thy humble debtors,
Rushing, on Sundays, one and all,
With desperate prayers thy head to maul,
And thus abuse their betters.

To seize one day in every week,
On thee their black abuse to wreak,
By whom their souls are fed
Each minute of the other six,
With every joy that heart can fix,
Is impudence indeed!

Blushing I own thy pleasing art
Hath oft seduced my vagrant heart,
And led my steps to joy—
The charms of beauty have been mine
And let me call the merit thine,
Who broughtst the lovely toy.

No, Satan—if I ask thy aid,
To give my arms the blooming maid.
  I will not, though the nation all,
Proclaim thee (like a gracless imp)
A vile old good-for-nothing pimp,
  But say, "'Tis thy vocation, Hal."

Since truth must out—I seldom knew
What 't was high pleasure to pursue,
  Till thou hadst won my heart—
So social were we both together,
And beat the hoof in every weather,
  I never wished to part.

Yet when a child—good Lord! I thought
That thou a pair of horns hadst got,
  With eyes like saucers staring!
And then a pair of ears so stout,
A monstrous tail and hairy snout,
  With claws beyond comparing.

Taught to avoid the paths of evil,
By day I used to dread the devil,
  And trembling when 't was night,
Methought I saw thy horns and ears,
They sung or whistled to my fears,
  And ran to chase my fright.

And every night I went to bed,
I sweated with a constant dread,
  And crept beneath the rug;
There panting, thought that in my sleep
Thou slyly in the dark wouldst creep,
  And eat me, though so snug.

A haberdasher's shop is thine,
With sins of all sorts, coarse and fine,
  To suit both man and maid:
Thy wares they buy, with open eyes;
How cruel then, with constant cries,
  To vilify thy trade!

To speak the *truth*, *indeed*, I 'm loath—
Life 's deemed a mawkish dish of broth,
   Without thy aid, old sweeper;
So mawkish, few will put it down,
Even from the cottage to the crown,
   Without thy salt and pepper.

O Satan, whatsoever geer,
Thy Proteus form shall choose to wear,
   Black, red, or blue, or yellow;
Whatever hypocrites may say,
They think thee (trust my honest lay)
   A most bewitching fellow.

'Tis ordered (to deaf ears, alas!)
To praise the bridge o'er which we pass
   Yet often I discover
A numerous band who daily make
An easy bridge of thy poor back,
   And damn it when they 're over.

Why art thou, then, with cup in hand,
Obsequious to a graceless band,
   Whose souls are scarce worth taking;
O prince, pursue but my advice,
I 'll teach your highness in a trice
   To set them all a quaking.

Plays, operas, masquerades, destroy:
Lock up each charming *fille de joie;*
   Give race-horses the glander—
The dice-box break, and burn each card—
Let virtue be its own reward,
   And gag the mouth of slander;

In one week's time, I 'll lay my life,
There 's not a man, nor maid, nor wife,
   That will not glad agree,
If thou will charm 'em as before,
To show their nose at church no more,
   But quit their God for thee.

'Tis now full time my ode should end:
And now I tell thee like a friend,
  Howe'er the world may scout thee;
Thy ways are all so wond'rous winning,
And folks so very fond of sinning,
  They can not do without thee.

THE KING OF SPAIN AND THE HORSE.

PETER PINDAR.

In seventeen hundred seventy-eight,
  The rich, the proud, the potent King of Spain,
Whose ancestors sent forth their troops to smite
  The peaceful natives of the western main,
With faggots and the blood-delighting sword,
To play the devil, to oblige the Lord!

For hunting, roasting heretics, and boiling,
Baking and barbecuing, frying, broiling,
  Was thought Heaven's cause amazingly to further;
For which most pious reason, hard to work,
They went, with gun and dagger, knife and fork,
  To charm the God of mercy with their murther!

I say, this King, in seventy-eight surveyed,
In tapestry so rich, portrayed,
  A horse with stirrups, crupper, bridle, saddle:
Within the stirrup, lo, the monarch tried
To fix his foot the palfry to bestride;
  In vain!—he could not o'er the palfry straddle!

Stiff as a Turk, the beast of yarn remained,
And every effort of the King disdained,
Who, 'midst his labors, to the ground was tumbled,
And greatly mortified, as well as humbled.

Prodigious was the struggle of the day,
The horse attempted not to run away;
  At which the poor-chafed monarch now 'gan grin,
And swore by every saint and holy martyr,
He would not yield the traitor quarter,
  Until he got possession of his skin.

Not fiercer famed La Mancha's knight,
  Hight Quixote, at a puppet-show,
Did with more valor stoutly fight,
  And terrify each little squeaking foe;
When bold he pierced the lines, immortal fray!
And broke their pasteboard bones, and stabbed their hearts
    of hay.

Not with more energy and fury
The beauteous street-walker of Drury
  Attacks a sister of the smuggling trade,
Whose winks, and nods, and sweet resistless smile,
Ah, me! her paramour beguile,
  And to her bed of healthy straw persuade;
Where mice with music charm, and vermin crawl,
And snails with silver traces deck the wall.

And now a cane, and now a whip he used,
And now he kicked, and sore the palfry bruised;
Yet, lo, the horse seemed patient at each kick,
And bore with Christian spirit whip and stick;
And what excessively provoked this prince,
The horse so stubborn scorned even once to wince.

Now rushed the monarch for a bow and arrow
To shoot the rebel like a sparrow;
And, lo, with shafts well steeled, with all his force,
Just like a pincushion, he stuck the horse!

Now with the fury of the chafed wild boar,
With nails and teeth the wounded horse he tore,
  Now to the floor he brought the stubborn beast;
Now o'er the vanquish'd horse that dared rebel,
Most Indian-like the monarch gave a yell,
  Pleased on the quadruped his eyes to feast;
Blessed as Achilles when with fatal wound
He brought the mighty Hector to the ground.

Yet more to gratify his godlike ire,
He vengeful flung the palfry in the fire!
Showing his pages round, poor trembling things,
How dangerous to resist the will of kings.

THE TENDER HUSBAND.

PETER PINDAR.

Lo, to the cruel hand of fate,
My poor dear Grizzle, meek-souled mate,
Resigns her tuneful breath—
Though dropped her jaw, her lip though pale,
And blue each harmless finger-nail,
She 's beautiful in death.

As o'er her lovely limbs I weep,
I scarce can think her but asleep—
How wonderfully tame!
And yet her voice is really gone,
And dim those eyes that lately shone
With all the lightning's flame.

Death was, indeed, a daring wight,
To take it in his head to smite—
To lift his dart to hit her;
For as she was so great a woman,
And cared a single fig for no man,
I thought he feared to meet her.

Still is that voice of late so strong,
That many a sweet capriccio sung,
And beat in sounds the spheres;
No longer must those fingers play
"Britons strike home," that many a day
Hath soothed my ravished ears.

Ah me! indeed I'm much inclined
To think how I may speak my mind,
Nor hurt her dear repose;
Nor think I now with rage she 'd roar,
Were I to put my fingers o'er,
And touch her precious nose.

Here let me philosophic pause—
How wonderful are nature's laws,

When ladies' breath retires,
Its fate the flaming passions share,
Supported by a little air,
Like culinary fires.

Whene'er I hear the bagpipe's note,
Shall fancy fix on Grizzle's throat,
And loud instructive lungs;
O Death, in her, though only one,
Are lost a thousand charms unknown,
At least a thousand tongues.

Soon as I heard her last sweet sigh,
And saw her gently-closing eye,
How great was my surprise!
Yet have I not, with impious breath,
Accused the hard decrees of death,
Nor blamed the righteous skies.

Why do I groan in deep despair,
Since she 'll be soon an angel fair?
Ah! why my bosom smite?
Could grief my Grizzle's life restore!—
But let me give such ravings o'er—
Whatever is, is right.

O doctor! you are come too late;
No more of physic's virtues prate,
That could not save my lamb:
Not one more bolus shall be given—
You shall not ope her mouth by heaven,
And Grizzle's gullet cram.

Enough of boluses, poor heart,
And pills, she took, to load a cart,
Before she closed her eyes:
But now my word is here a law,
Zounds! with a bolus in her jaw,
She shall not seek the skies.

Good sir, good doctor, go away;
To hear my sighs you must not stay,

For this my poor lost treasure:
I thank you for your pains and skill;
When next you come, pray bring your bill;
I'll pay it, sir, with pleasure.

Ye friends who come to mourn her doom,
For God's sake gently tread the room,
Nor call her from the blessed—
In softest silence drop the tear,
In whispers breathe the fervent prayer,
To bid her spirit rest.

Repress the sad, the wounding scream;
I can not bear a grief extreme—
Enough one little sigh—
Besides, the loud alarm of grief,
In many a mind may start belief,
Our noise is all a lie.

Good nurses, shroud my lamb with care;
Her limbs, with gentlest fingers, spare,
Her mouth, ah! slowly close;
Her mouth a magic tongue that held—
Whose softest tone, at times, compelled
To peace my loudest woes.

And, carpenter, for my sad sake,
Of stoutest oak her coffin make—
I'd not be stingy, sure—
Procure of steel the strongest screws;
For who could paltry pence refuse
To lodge his wife secure?

Ye people who the corpse convey,
With caution tread the doleful way,
Nor shake her precious head;
Since Fame reports a coffin tossed,
With careless swing against a post,
Did once disturb the dead.

Farewell, my love, forever lost!
Ne'er troubled be thy gentle ghost,

That I *again will woo*—
By all our past delights, my dear,
No more the marriage chain I 'll wear,
Deil take me if I do!

THE SOLDIER AND THE VIRGIN MARY.

PETER PINDAR.

A Soldier at Loretto's wondrous chapel,
To parry from his soul the wrath Divine,
That followed mother Eve's unlucky apple,
Did visit oft the Virgin Mary's shrine;
Who every day is gorgeously decked out,
In silks or velvets, jewels, great and small.
Just like a fine young lady for a rout,
A concert, opera, wedding, or a ball.

At first the Soldier at a distance kept,
Begging her vote and interest in heaven—
With seeming bitterness the sinner wept,
Wrung his two hands, and hoped to be forgiven:
Dinned her two ears with Ave-Mary flummery!
Declared what miracles the dame could do,
Even with her garter, stocking, or her shoe,
And such like wonder-working mummery.

What answer Mary gave the wheedling sinner,
Who nearly and more nearly moved to win her,
The mouth of history doth not mention,
And therefore I can't tell but by invention.

One day, as he was making love and praying,
And pious Aves, thick as herring, saying,
And sins so manifold confessing;
He drew, as if to whisper, very near,
And twitched a pretty diamond from her ear,
Instead of taking the good lady's blessing.

Then off he set, with nimble shanks,
Nor once turned back to give her thanks:
A hue and cry the thief pursued,
Who, to his cost, soon understood
That he was not beyond the claw
Of that same long-armed giant, christened Law.

With horror did his judges quake—
  As for the tender-conscienced jury,
They doomed him quickly to the stake,
  Such was their devilish pious fury.

However, after calling him hard names,
  They asked if aught he had in vindication,
To save his wretched body from the flames,
  And sinful soul from terrible damnation.

The Soldier answered them with much *sany froid*,
Which showed, of sin, a conscience void,
  That if they meant to kill him they might kill:
As for the diamond which they found about him,
He hoped they would by no means doubt him,
  That madam gave it him from pure good-will.

The answer turned both judge and jury pale:
  The punishment was for a time deferred,
Until his Holiness should hear the tale,
  And his infallibility be heard.

The Pope, to all his counselors, made known
  This strange affair—to cardinals and friars,
Good pious gentlemen, who ne'er were known
  To act like hypocrites, and thieves, and liars.
The question now was banded to and fro,
  If Mary had the power to *give*, or *no*.

That Mary *could not* give it, was to say
  The wonder-working lady wanted power—
This was the stumbling-block that stopped the way—
  This made Pope, cardinals, and friars lower.

To save the Virgin's credit, lo!
  And keep secure the diamonds that were left:
They said, she *might*, indeed, the gem bestow,
  And consequently it might be no theft:
But then they passed immediately an act,
That every one discovered in the fact
Of taking presents from the Virgin's hand,
Or from the saints of any land,
Should know no mercy, but be led to slaughter,
Flayed here, and fried eternally hereafter.

Ladies, I deem the moral much too clear
  To need poetical assistance;
Which bids you not let men approach too near,
  But keep the saucy fellows at a distance;
Since men you find, so bold, are apt to seize
Jewels from ladies, even upon their knees!

A KING OF FRANCE AND THE FAIR LADY

PETER PINDAR.

A King of France upon a day,
  With a fair lady of his court,
Was pleased at battledore to play—
  A very fashionable sport.

Into the bosom of this fair court dame,
Whose whiteness did the snow's pure whiteness shame.
King Louis by odd mischance did knock
    The shuttlecock,
Thrice happy rogue, upon the town of doves,
To nestle with the pretty little loves!

"Now, sire, pray take it out"—quoth she,
With an arch smile.—But what did he?
  What? what to charming modesty belongs!
Obedient to her soft command,
He raised it—but not with his hand!
  No, marveling reader, but the chimney tongs.

What a chaste thought in this good king!
How clever!
When shall we hear agen of such a thing?
Lord! never.
Now were our princes to be prayed
To such an act by some fair maid,
I'll bet my life not one would mind it:
But handy, without more ado,
The youths would search the bosom through,
Although it took a day to find it!

THE EGGS.

FROM THE SPANISH OF YRIARTE.

G. H. DEVEREUX.

Beyond the sunny Philippines
An island lies, whose name I do not know;
But that's of little consequence, if so
You understand that there they had no hens;
Till, by a happy chance, a traveler,
After a while, carried some poultry there.
Fast they increased as any one could wish;
Until fresh eggs became the common dish.
But all the natives ate them boiled—they say—
Because the stranger taught no other way.
At last the experiment by one was tried—
Sagacious man!—of having his eggs fried.
And, O! what boundless honors, for his pains,
His fruitful and inventive fancy gains!
Another, now, to have them baked devised—
Most happy thought!—and still another, spiced.
Who ever thought eggs were so delicate!
Next, some one gave his friends an omelette:
"Ah!" all exclaimed, "what an ingenious feat!"
But scarce a year went by, an artiste shouts,
"I have it now—ye're all a pack of louts!—
With nice tomatoes all my eggs are stewed."
And the whole island thought the mode so good,
That they would so have cooked them to this day,
But that a stranger, wandering out that way,

Another dish the gaping natives taught,
And showed them eggs cooked *à la Huguenot.*

Successive cooks thus proved their skill diverse;
But how shall I be able to rehearse
All of the new, delicious condiments
That luxury, from time to time, invents?
Soft, hard, and dropped; and now with sugar sweet,
And now boiled up with milk, the eggs they eat;
In sherbet, in preserves; at last they tickle
Their palates fanciful with eggs in pickle.
All had their day—the last was still the best.
But a grave senior thus, one day, addressed
The epicures: "Boast, ninnies, if you will,
These countless prodigies of gastric skill—
But blessings on the man *who brought the hens!*"

Beyond the sunny Philippines
Our crowd of modern authors need not go
New-fangled modes of cooking eggs to show.

THE ASS AND HIS MASTER.

FROM THE SPANISH OF YRIARTE.

G. H. DEVEREUX.

"On good and bad an equal value sets
The stupid mob. From me the worst it gets,
  And never fails to praise." With vile pretense,
The scurrilous author thus his trash excused.
  A poet shrewd, hearing the lame defense,
Indignant, thus exposed the argument abused.

A Donkey's master said unto his beast,
  While doling out to him his lock of straw,
"Here, take it—since such diet suits your taste,
  And much good may it do your vulgar maw!"
Often the slighting speech the man repeated.
The Ass—his quiet mood by insult heated—

Replies: "Just what you choose to give, I take,
  Master unjust! but not because I choose it.
Think you I nothing like but straw? Then make
  The experiment. Bring corn, and see if I refuse it."
Ye caterers for the public, hence take heed
  How your defaults by false excuse you cover!
Fed upon straw—straw it may eat, indeed:
  Try it with generous fare—'t will scorn the other.

THE LOVE OF THE WORLD REPROVED; OR, HYPOCRISY DETECTED.

WILLIAM COWPER.

Thus says the prophet of the Turk,
Good Mussulman, abstain from pork;
There is a part in every swine
No friend or follower of mine
May taste, whate'er his inclination,
On pain of excommunication.
Such Mohammed's mysterious charge,
And thus he left the point at large.
Had he the sinful part expressed,
They might with safety eat the rest;
But for one piece they thought it hard
From the whole hog to be debarred;
And set their wit at work to find
What joint the prophet had in mind.
Much controversy straight arose,
These chose the back, the belly those;
By some 'tis confidently said
He meant not to forbid the head;
While others at that doctrine rail,
And piously prefer the tail.
Thus, conscience freed from every clog,
Mohammedans eat up the hog.
  You laugh—'tis well.—The tale applied
May make you laugh on t' other side.
Renounce the world—the preacher cries.
We do—a multitude replies.

While one as innocent regards
A snug and friendly game at cards;
And one, whatever you may say,
Can see no evil in a play;
Some love a concert, or a race;
And others shooting, and the chase.
Reviled and loved, renounced and followed,
Thus, bit by bit, the world is swallowed;
Each thinks his neighbor makes too free,
Yet likes a slice as well as he;
With sophistry their sauce they sweeten,
Till quite from tail to snout 'tis eaten.

REPORT OF AN ADJUDGED CASE,

NOT TO BE FOUND IN ANY OF THE BOOKS.

WILLIAM COWPER

BETWEEN Nose and Eyes a strange contest arose,
  The spectacles set them unhappily wrong;
The point in dispute was, as all the world knows,
  To which the said spectacles ought to belong.

So Tongue was the lawyer, and argued the cause
  With a great deal of skill, and a wig full of learning;
While chief baron Ear sat to balance the laws,
  So famed for his talent in nicely discerning.

In behalf of the Nose it will quickly appear,
  And your lordship, he said, will undoubtedly find,
That the Nose has had spectacles always to wear,
  Which amounts to possession time out of mind.

Then holding the spectacles up to the court—
  Your lordship observes they are made with a straddle
As wide as the ridge of the Nose is; in short,
  Designed to sit close to it, just like a saddle.

Again, would your lordship a moment suppose
  ('Tis a case that has happened, and may be again)
That the visage or countenance had not a nose,
  Pray who would, or who could, wear spectacles then?

On the whole it appears, and my argument shows,
With a reasoning the court will never condemn,
That the spectacles plainly were made for the Nose,
And the Nose was as plainly intended for them.

Then shifting his side (as a lawyer knows how),
He pleaded again in behalf of the Eyes;
But what were his arguments few people know,
For the court did not think they were equally wise.

So his lordship decreed with a grave solemn tone,
Decisive and clear, without one *if* or *but*—
That, whenever the Nose put his spectacles on,
By daylight or candlelight—Eyes should be shut!

HOLY WILLIE'S PRAYER.*

ROBERT BURNS.

O Thou, wha in the heavens dost dwell,
Wha, as it pleases best thysel',
Sends ane to heaven, and ten to hell,
A' for thy glory,
And no for ony guid or ill
They've done afore thee!

I bless and praise thy matchless might,
When thousands thou hast left in night,
That I am here, afore thy sight,
For gifts an' grace,
A burnin' an' a shinin' light
To a' this place.

* Kennedy gives the following account of the origin of "Holy Willie's Prayer:"—Gavin Hamilton, Esq., Clerk of Ayr, the Poet's friend and benefactor, was accosted one Sunday morning by a mendicant, who begged alms of him. Not recollecting that it was the Sabbath, Hamilton set the man to work in his garden, which lay on the public road, and the poor fellow was discovered by the people on their way to the kirk, and they immediately stoned him from the ground. For this offense, Mr. Hamilton was not permitted to have a child christened, which his wife bore him soon afterward, until he applied to the synod. His most officious opponent was William Fisher, one of the elders of the church: and to revenge the insult to his friend, Burns made him the subject of this humorous ballad.

What was I, or my generation,
That I should get sic exaltation!
I, wha deserve sic just damnation,
For broken laws,
Five thousand years 'fore my creation,
Thro' Adam's cause.

When frae my mither's womb I fell,
Thou might hae plung'd me into hell,
To gnash my gums, to weep and wail,
In burnin' lake,
Whare damned devils roar and yell,
Chain'd to a stake.

Yet I am here a chosen sample;
To show thy grace is great and ample;
I 'm here a pillar in thy temple,
Strong as a rock,
A guide, a buckler, an example
To a' thy flock.

[O L—d, thou kens what zeal I bear,
When drinkers drink, and swearers swear,
And singing there, and dancing here,
Wi' great and sma';
For I am keepit by thy fear,
Free frae them a'.]

But yet, O L—d! confess I must,
At times I 'm fash'd wi' fleshly lust;
And sometimes, too, wi' warldly trust,
Vile self gets in;
But thou remembers we are dust,
Defil'd in sin.

* * * * *

* * * * *

* * * * *

* * * * *

* * * * *

* * * * *

May be thou lets this fleshly thorn
Beset thy servant e'en and morn,
Lest he owre high and proud should turn,
'Cause he 's sae gifted;
If sae, thy han' maun e'en be borne,
Until thou lift it.

L—d, bless thy chosen in this place,
For here thou hast a chosen race:
But G—d confound their stubborn face,
And blast their name,
Wha bring thy elders to disgrace
And public shame.

L—d, mind Gawn Hamilton's deserts,
He drinks, and swears, and plays at cartes,
Yet has sae mony takin' arts,
Wi' great and sma',
Frae G—d's ain priests the people's hearts
He steals awa'.

An' whan we chasten'd him therefore,
Thou kens how he bred sic a splore,
As set the warld in a roar
O' laughin' at us;—
Curse thou his basket and his store,
Kail and potatoes.

L—d, hear my earnest cry and pray'r,
Against the presbyt'ry of Ayr;
Thy strong right hand, L—d, mak' it bare
Upo' their heads,
L—d, weigh it down, and dinna spare,
For their misdeeds.

O L—d my G—d, that glib-tongu'd Aiken,
My very heart and saul are quakin',
To think how we stood groanin', shakin',
And swat wi' dread,
While Auld wi' hinging lip gaed snakin',
And hid his head.

L—d, in the day of vengeance try him,
L—d, visit them wha did employ him,
And pass not in thy mercy by 'em,
Nor hear their pray'r;
But for thy people's sake destroy 'em,
And dinna spare.

But, L—d, remember me and mine,
Wi' mercies temp'ral and divine,
That I for gear and grace may shine,
Excell'd by nane,
An' a' the glory shall be thine,
Amen, Amen!

EPITAPH ON HOLY WILLIE.

Here Holy Willie's sair worn clay
Taks up its last abode;
His saul has ta'en some other way,
I fear, the left-hand road.

Stop! there he is, as sure 's a gun,
Poor, silly body, see him;
Nae wonder he 's as black 's the grun—
Observe wha's standing wi' him!

Your brunstane devilship, I see,
Has got him there before ye;
But haud your nine-tail cat a wee,
Till ance ye've heard my story.

Your pity I will not implore,
For pity ye hae nane!
Justice, alas! has gi'en him o'er,
And mercy's day is gane.

But hear me, sir, deil as ye are,
Look something to your credit;
A coof like him wad stain your name,
If it were kent ye did it.

ADDRESS TO THE DEIL.

ROBERT BURNS.

"O Prince! O Chief of many throned Pow'rs,
That led th' embattled Seraphim to war!"---
MILTON.

O THOU! whatever title suit thee,
Auld Hornie, Satan, Nick, or Clootie,
Wha in yon cavern grim and sootie,
Closed under hatches,
Spairges about the brunstane cootie,
To scaud poor wretches!

Hear me, auld Hangie, for a wee,
An' let poor damned bodies be;
I 'm sure sma' pleasure it can gie,
E'en to a deil,
To skelp an' scaud poor dogs like me,
An' hear us squeel!

Great is thy power, an' great thy fame;
Far kenn'd and noted is thy name:
An' tho' yon lowin heugh's thy hame,
Thou travels far:
An,' faith! thou's neither lag nor lame,
Nor blate nor scaur.

Whyles, ranging like a roaring lion,
For prey, a' holes an' corners tryin';
Whyles on the strong-wing'd tempest flyin'
Tirlin the kirks;
Whyles, in the human bosom pryin',
Unseen thou lurks.

I 've heard my reverend Grannie say,
In lanely glens ye like to stray;

Or where auld ruin'd castles, gray,
Nod to the moon,
Ye fright the nightly wand'rer's way
Wi' eldritch croon.

When twilight did my Grannie summon
To say her prayers, douce, honest woman!
Aft yont the dyke she 's heard you bummin',
Wi' eerie drone;
Or, rustlin, thro' the boortries comin',
Wi' heavy groan.

Ae dreary, windy, winter night,
The stars shot down wi' sklentin' light,
Wi' you, mysel, I gat a fright
Ayont the lough;
Ye, like a rash-bush, stood in sight,
Wi' waving sough.

The cudgel in my nieve did shake,
Each bristl'd hair stood like a stake,
When wi' an eldritch, stoor quaick—quaick—
Amang the springs,
Awa ye squatter'd, like a drake,
On whistling wings.

Let warlocks grim, an' wither'd hags,
Tell how wi' you, on ragweed nags,
They skim the muirs an' dizzy crags,
Wi' wicked speed;
And in kirk-yards renew their leagues
Owre howkit dead.

Thence countra wives, wi' toil an' pain,
May plunge an' plunge the kirn in vain:
For, oh! the yellow treasure 's taen
By witching skill;
An' dawtit, twal-pint hawkie's gaen
As yell's the bill.

Thence mystic knots mak great abuse
On young guidmen, fond, keen, an' crouse;

When the best wark-lume i' the house,
By cantrip wit,
Is instant made no worth a louse,
Just at the bit.

When thowes dissolve the snawy hoord,
An' float the jinglin icy-boord,
Then water-kelpies haunt the foord,
By your direction;
An' nighted trav'lers are allur'd
To their destruction.

An' aft your moss-traversing spunkies
Decoy the wight that late an' drunk is:
The bleezin, curst, mischievous monkeys
Delude his eyes,
Till in some miry slough he sunk is,
Ne'er mair to rise.

When masons' mystic word an' grip
In storms an' tempests raise you up,
Some cock or cat your rage maun stop,
Or, strange to tell!
The youngest brother ye wad whip
Aff straught to hell!

Lang syne, in Eden's bonnie yard,
When youthfu' lovers first were pair'd,
An' all the soul of love they shar'd,
The raptur'd hour,
Sweet on the fragrant, flow'ry sward,
In shady bow'r:

Then you, ye auld, snec-drawing dog!
Ye came to Paradise incog.,
An' play'd on man a cursed brogue,
(Black be your fa'!)
An' gied the infant warld a shog,
Maist ruin'd a'.

D'ye mind that day, when in a bizz,
Wi' reekit duds, an' reestit gizz,

Ye did present your smoutie phiz
'Mang better folk,
An' sklented on the man of Uz
Your spitefu' joke?

An' how ye gat him i' your thrall,
An' brak him out o' house an' hall,
While scabs an' botches did him gall,
Wi' bitter claw,
And lows'd his ill-tongu'd, wicked scawl,
Was warst ava?

But a' your doings to rehearse,
Your wily snares an' fechtin' fierce,
Sin' that day Michael did you pierce,
Down to this time,
Wad ding a Lallan tongue, or Erse,
In prose or rhyme.

An' now, auld Cloots, I ken ye're thinkin
A certain Bardie's rantin', drinkin',
Some luckless hour will send him linkin'
To your black pit;
But, faith! he 'll turn a corner jinkin',
An' cheat you yet.

But, fare you weel, auld Nickie-ben!
O wad ye tak a thought an' men'!
Ye aiblins might—I dinna ken—
Still hae a stake—
I 'm wae to think upo' yon den,
Ev'n for your sake!!

THE DEVIL'S WALK ON EARTH.

ROBERT SOUTHEY

From his brimstone bed at break of day
A walking the Devil is gone,
To look at his snug little farm of the World,
And see how his stock went on.

Over the hill and over the dale,
  And he went over the plain;
And backward and forward he swish'd his tail,
  As a gentleman swishes a cane.

  How then was the Devil drest?
  Oh, he was in his Sunday's best
His coat was red and his breeches were blue,
And there was a hole where his tail came through.

A lady drove by in her pride,
In whose face an expression he spied
  For which he could have kiss'd her;
Such a flourishing, fine, clever woman was she,
With an eye as wicked as wicked can be,
I should take her for my Aunt, thought he,
  If my dam had had a sister.

    He met a lord of high degree,
    No matter what was his name;
Whose face with his own when he came to compare
    The expression, the look, and the air,
  And the character, too, as it seem'd to a hair—
  Such a twin-likeness there was in the pair
  That it made the Devil start and stare,
For he thought there was surely a looking-glass there,
    But he could not see the frame.

He saw a Lawyer killing a viper,
  On a dung-hill beside his stable;
Ha! quoth he, thou put'st me in mind
  Of the story of Cain and Abel.

An Apothecary on a white horse
  Rode by on his vocation;
And the Devil thought of his old friend
  Death in the Revelation.

He pass'd a cottage with a double coach-house,
  A cottage of gentility,
And he own'd with a grin
That his favorite sin,
  Is pride that apes humility.

He saw a pig rapidly
  Down a river float;
The pig swam well, but every stroke
  Was cutting his own throat;

And Satan gave thereat his tail
  A twirl of admiration;
For he thought of his daughter War,
  And her suckling babe Taxation.

Well enough, in sooth, he liked that truth
  And nothing the worse for the jest;
But this was only a first thought
  And in this he did not rest:
Another came presently into his head,
And here it proved, as has often been said
  That second thoughts are best.

For as Piggy plied with wind and tide,
  His way with such celerity,
And at every stroke the water dyed
With his own red blood, the Devil cried,
Behold a swinish nation's pride
  In cotton-spun prosperity.

He walk'd into London leisurely,
  The streets were dirty and dim:
But there he saw Brothers the Prophet,
  And Brothers the Prophet saw him.

He entered a thriving bookseller's shop;
  Quoth he, we are both of one college,
For I myself sate like a Cormorant once
  Upon the Tree of Knowledge.

As he passed through Cold-Bath Fields he look'd
  At a solitary cell;
And he was well-pleased, for it gave him a hint
  For improving the prisons of Hell.

He saw a turnkey tie a thief's hands
  With a cordial tug and jerk;
Nimbly, quoth he, a man's fingers move
  When his heart is in his work.

He saw the same turnkey unfettering a man
With little expedition;
And he chuckled to think of his dear slave-trade,
And the long debates and delays that were made,
Concerning its abolition.

He met one of his favorite daughters
By an Evangelical Meeting:
And forgetting himself for joy at her sight,
He would have accosted her outright,
And given her a fatherly greeting.

But she tipt him the wink, drew back, and cried,
Avaunt! my name 's Religion!
And then she turn'd to the preacher
And leer'd like a love-sick pigeon.

A fine man and a famous Professor was he,
As the great Alexander now may be,
Whose fame not yet o'erpast is:
Or that new Scotch performer
Who is fiercer and warmer,
The great Sir Arch-Bombastes.

With throbs and throes, and ah's and oh's.
Far famed his flock for frightning;
And thundering with his voice, the while
His eyes zigzag like lightning.

This Scotch phenomenon, I trow,
Beats Alexander hollow;
Even when most tame
He breathes more flame
Then ten Fire-Kings could swallow

Another daughter he presently met;
With music of fife and drum,
And a consecrated flag,
And shout of tag and rag,
And march of rank and file,
Which had fill'd the crowded aisle
Of the venerable pile,
From church he saw her come.

He call'd her aside, and began to chide,
For what dost thou here? said he;
My city of Rome is thy proper home,
And there's work enough there for thee.

Thou hast confessions to listen,
And bells to christen,
And altars and dolls to dress;
And fools to coax,
And sinners to hoax,
And beads and bones to bless;
And great pardons to sell
For those who pay well,
And small ones for those who pay less.

Nay, Father, I boast, that this is my post,
She answered; and thou wilt allow,
That the great Harlot,
Who is clothed in scarlet,
Can very well spare me now.

Upon her business I am come here,
That we may extend our powers:
Whatever lets down this church that we hate,
Is something in favor of ours.

You will not think, great Cosmocrat!
That I spend my time in fooling;
Many irons, my sire, have we in the fire,
And I must leave none of them cooling;
For you must know state-councils here,
Are held which I bear rule in.
When my liberal notions,
Produce mischievous motions,
There's many a man of good intent,
In either house of Parliament,
Whom I shall find a tool in;
And I have hopeful pupils too
Who all this while are schooling.

Fine progress they make in our liberal opinions,
My Utilitarians,

My all sorts of—inians
And all sorts of—arians;
My all sorts of—ists,
And my Prigs and my Whigs
Who have all sorts of twists
Train'd in the very way, I know,
Father, you would have them go;
High and low,
Wise and foolish, great and small,
March-of-Intellect-Boys all.

Well pleased wilt thou be at no very far day
When the caldron of mischief boils,
And I bring them forth in battle array
And bid them suspend their broils,
That they may unite and fall on the prey,
For which we are spreading our toils.
How the nice boys all will give mouth at the call,
Hark away! hark away to the spoils!
My Macs and my Quacks and my lawless-Jacks,
My Shiels and O'Connells, my pious Mac-Donnells,
My joke-smith Sydney, and all of his kidney,
My Humes and my Broughams,
My merry old Jerry,
My Lord Kings, and my Doctor Doyles!

At this good news, so great
The Devil's pleasure grew,
That with a joyful swish he rent
The hole where his tail came through.

His countenance fell for a moment
When he felt the stitches go;
Ah! thought he, there 's a job now
That I 've made for my tailor below.

Great news! bloody news! cried a newsman;
The Devil said, Stop, let me see!
Great news? bloody news? thought the Devil,
The bloodier the better for me.

So he bought the newspaper, and no news
  At all for his money he had.
Lying varlet, thought he, thus to take in old Nick!
  But it 's some satisfaction, my lad,
To know thou art paid beforehand for the trick,
  For the sixpence I gave thee is bad.

And then it came into his head
  By oracular inspiration,
That what he had seen and what he had said
  In the course of this visitation,
Would be published in the Morning Post
  For all this reading nation.

Therewith in second sight he saw
  The place and the manner and time,
In which this mortal story
  Would be put in immortal rhyme.

That it would happen when two poets
  Should on a time be met,
In the town of Nether Stowey,
  In the shire of Somerset.

  There while the one was shaving
    Would he the song begin;
And the other when he heard it at breakfast,
    In ready accord join in.

  So each would help the other,
  Two heads being better than one;
    And the phrase and conceit
    Would in unison meet,
And so with glee the verse flow free,
  In ding-dong chime of sing-song rhyme,
    Till the whole were merrily done.

  And because it was set to the razor,
    Not to the lute or harp,
  Therefore it was that the fancy
Should be bright, and the wit be sharp.

But, then, said Satan to himself,
As for that said beginner,
Against my infernal Majesty,
There is no greater sinner.

He hath put me in ugly ballads
With libelous pictures for sale;
He hath scoff'd at my hoofs and my horns,
And has made very free with my tail.

But this Mister Poet shall find
I am not a safe subject for whim;
For I 'll set up a School of my own,
And my Poets shall set upon him.

He went to a coffee-house to dine,
And there he had soy in his dish;
Having ordered some soles for his dinner,
Because he was fond of flat fish.

They are much to my palate, thought he,
And now guess the reason who can,
Why no bait should be better than place,
When I fish for a Parliament-man.

But the soles in the bill were ten shillings;
Tell your master, quoth he, what I say;
If he charges at this rate for all things,
He must be in a pretty good way.

But mark ye, said he to the waiter,
I 'm a dealer myself in this line,
And his business, between you and me,
Nothing like so extensive as mine.

Now soles are exceedingly cheap,
Which he will not attempt to deny,
When I see him at my fish-market,
I warrant him, by-and-by.

As he went along the Strand
Between three in the morning and four
He observed a queer-looking person
Who staggered from Perry's door.

And he thought that all the world over
  In vain for a man you might seek,
Who could drink more like a Trojan
  Or talk more like a Greek.

  The Devil then he prophesied
  It would one day be matter of talk,
    That with wine when smitten,
And with wit moreover being happily bitten,
The erudite bibber was he who had written
    The story of this walk.

  A pretty mistake, quoth the Devil;
    A pretty mistake I opine!
I have put many ill thoughts in his mouth,
  He will never put good ones in mine.

And whoever shall say that to Porson
  These best of all verses belong,
He is an untruth-telling whore-son,
  And so shall be call'd in the song.

And if seeking an illicit connection with fame,
  Any one else should put in a claim,
    In this comical competition;
  That excellent poem will prove
    A man-trap for such foolish ambition,
Where the silly rogue shall be caught by the leg,
    And exposed in a second edition.

Now the morning air was cold for him
  Who was used to a warm abode;
And yet he did not immediately wish,
  To set out on his homeward road.

For he had some morning calls to make
  Before he went back to Hell;
So thought he I'll step into a gaming-house,
  And that will do as well;
But just before he could get to the door
  A wonderful chance befell.

For all on a sudden, in a dark place,
He came upon General ———'s burning face;
And it struck him with such consternation,
That home in a hurry his way did he take,
Because he thought, by a slight mistake
'T was the general conflagration.

CHURCH AND STATE.

THOMAS MOORE.

When Royalty was young and bold,
Ere, touch'd by Time, he had become—
If 't is not civil to say *old*—
At least, a *ci-devant jeune homme*.

One evening, on some wild pursuit,
Driving along, he chanced to see
Religion, passing by on foot,
And took him in his *vis-à-vis*.

This said Religion was a friar,
The humblest and the best of men,
Who ne'er had notion or desire
Of riding in a coach till then.

"I say"—quoth Royalty, who rather
Enjoy'd a masquerading joke—
"I say, suppose, my good old father,
You lend me, for a while, your cloak."

The friar consented—little knew
What tricks the youth had in his head;
Besides, was rather tempted, too,
By a laced coat he got in stead.

Away ran Royalty, slap-dash,
Scampering like mad about the town;
Broke windows—shiver'd lamps to smash,
And knock'd whole scores of watchmen down.

While naught could they whose heads were broke,
  Learn of the "why" or the "wherefore,"
Except that 't was Religion's cloak
  The gentleman, who crack'd them, wore.

Meanwhile, the Friar, whose head was turn'd
  By the laced coat, grew frisky too—
Look'd big—his former habits spurn'd—
  And storm'd about as great men do—

Dealt much in pompous oaths and curses—
  Said "Damn you," often, or as bad—
Laid claim to other people's purses—
  In short, grew either knave or mad.

As work like this was unbefitting,
  And flesh and blood no longer bore it,
The Court of Common Sense then sitting,
  Summon'd the culprits both before it;

Where, after hours in wrangling spent
  (As courts must wrangle to decide well),
Religion to St. Luke's was sent,
  And Royalty pack'd off to Bridewell:

With this proviso—Should they be
  Restored in due time to their senses,
They both must give security
  In future, against such offenses—

Religion ne'er to *lend his cloak*,
  Seeing what dreadful work it leads to;
And Royalty to crack his joke—
  But *not* to crack poor people's heads, too.

LYING.

THOMAS MOORE.

I do confess, in many a sigh,
My lips have breath'd you many a lie,
And who, with such delights in view,
Would lose them for a lie or two?

Nay—look not thus, with brow reproving:
Lies are, my dear, the soul of loving!
If half we tell the girls were true,
If half we swear to think and do,
Were aught but lying's bright illusion,
The world would be in strange confusion!
If ladies' eyes were, every one,
As lovers swear, a radiant sun,
Astronomy should leave the skies,
To learn her lore in ladies' eyes!
Oh no!—believe me, lovely girl,
When nature turns your teeth to pearl,
Your neck to snow, your eyes to fire,
Your yellow locks to golden wire,
Then, only then, can heaven decree,
That you should live for only me,
Or I for you, as night and morn,
We 've swearing kiss'd, and kissing sworn.

And now, my gentle hints to clear,
For once, I 'll tell you truth, my dear!
Whenever you may chance to meet
A loving youth, whose love is sweet,
Long as you 're false and he believes you,
Long as you trust and he deceives you,
So long the blissful bond endures;
And while he lies, his heart is yours:
But, oh! you 've wholly lost the youth
The instant that he tells you truth!

THE MILLENNIUM.

SUGGESTED BY THE LATE WORK OF THE REVEREND MR. IRV-NG "ON PROPHECY."

THOMAS MOORE.

MILLENNIUM at hand!—I 'm delighted to hear it—
  As matters both public and private now go,
With multitudes round us, all starving or near it,
  A good rich millennium will come *à propos*.

Only think, Master Fred, what delight to behold,
  Instead of thy bankrupt old City of Rags,
A bran-new Jerusalem, built all of gold,
  Sound bullion throughout, from the roof to the flags—

A city where wine and cheap corn shall abound—
  A celestial *Cocaigne*, on whose butterfly shelves
We may swear the best things of this world will be found,
  As your saints seldom fail to take care of themselves!

Thanks, reverend expounder of raptures elysian,
  Divine Squintifobus, who, placed within reach
Of two opposite worlds by a twist of your vision
  Can cast, at the same time, a sly look at each;—

Thanks, thanks for the hopes thou hast given us, that we
  May, even in our times a jubilee share,
Which so long has been promised by prophets like thee,
  And so often has fail'd, we began to despair.

There was Whiston, who learnedly took Prince Eugene
  For the man who must bring the Millennium about;
There 's Faber, whose pious predictions have been
  All belied, ere his book's first edition was out;—

There was Counsellor Dobbs, too, an Irish M.P.,
  Who discoursed on the subject with signal *eclat*,
And, each day of his life, sat expecting to see
  A Millennium break out in the town of Armagh!

There was also—but why should I burden my lay
  With your Brotherses, Southcotes, and names less deserving,
When all past Millenniums henceforth must give way
  To the last new Millennium of Orator Irv-ng.

Go on, mighty man—doom them all to the shelf—
  And, when next thou with prophecy troublest thy sconce,
Oh, forget not, I pray thee, to prove that thyself
  Art the Beast (chapter 4) that sees nine ways at once!

THE LITTLE GRAND LAMA.

A FABLE FOR PRINCES ROYAL.

THOMAS MOORE.

In Thibet once there reign'd, we 're told,
A little Lama, one year old— .
Raised to the throne, that realm to bless,
Just when his little Holiness
Had cut—as near as can be reckoned—
Some say his *first* tooth, some his *second.*
Chronologers and verses vary,
Which proves historians should be wary.
We only know the important truth—
His Majesty *had* cut a tooth.

And much his subjects were enchanted,
As well all Lamas' subjects may be,
And would have given their heads, if wanted.
To make tee-totums for the baby
As he was there by Right Divine
(What lawyers call *Jure Divino*
Meaning a right to yours and mine,
And every body's goods and rhino)—
Of course his faithful subjects' purses
Were ready with their aids and succors—
Nothing was seen but pension'd nurses,
And the land groan'd with bibs and tuckers.

Oh! had there been a Hume or Bennet
Then sitting in the Thibet Senate,
Ye gods, what room for long debates
Upon the Nursery Estimates!
What cutting down of swaddling-clothes
And pin-a-fores, in nightly battles!
What calls for papers to expose
The waste of sugar-plums and rattles!
But no—if Thibet *had* M.P.s,
They were far better bred than these;
Nor gave the slightest opposition,
During the Monarch's whole dentition.

But short this calm; for, just when he
Had reach'd the alarming age of three,
When royal natures—and, no doubt
Those of *all* noble beasts—break out,
The Lama, who till then was quiet,
Show'd symptoms of a taste for riot;
And, ripe for mischief, early, late,
Without regard for Church or State,
Made free with whosoe'er came nigh—
Tweak'd the Lord Chancellor by the nose,
Turn'd all the Judges' wigs awry,
And trod on the old General's toes—
Pelted the Bishops with hot buns,
Rode cock-horse on the city maces,
And shot, from little devilish guns,
Hard peas into his subjects' faces.
In short, such wicked pranks he play'd,
And grew so mischievous (God bless him!)
That his chief Nurse—though with the aid
Of an Archbishop—was afraid,
When in these moods, to comb or dress him;
And even the persons most inclined
For Kings, through thick and thin, to stickle,
Thought him (if they 'd but speak their mind
Which they did *not*) an odious pickle.

At length, some patriot lords—a breed
Of animals they have in Thibet,
Extremely rare, and fit, indeed,
For folks like Pidcock to exhibit—
Some patriot lords, seeing the length
To which things went, combined their strength,
And penn'd a manly, plain and free
Remonstrance to the Nursery;
In which, protesting that they yielded,
To none, that ever went before 'em—
In loyalty to him who wielded
The hereditary pap-spoon o'er 'em—
That, as for treason, 't was a thing
That made them almost sick to think of—
That they and theirs stood by the King,
Throughout his measles and his chin-cough,

When others, thinking him consumptive,
Had ratted to the heir Presumptive!—
But still—though much admiring kings
(And chiefly those in leading-strings)—
They saw, with shame and grief of soul,
  There was no longer now the wise
And constitutional control
  Of *birch* before their ruler's eyes;
But that, of late, such pranks and tricks,
  And freaks occurr'd the whole day long,
As all, but men with bishoprics,
  Allow'd, even in a King, were wrong—
Wherefore it was they humbly pray'd
  That Honorable Nursery,
That such reforms be henceforth made,
  As all good men desired to see;—
In other words (lest they might seem
Too tedious) as the gentlest scheme
For putting all such pranks to rest,
  And in its bud the mischief nipping—
They ventured humbly to suggest
  His Majesty should have a whipping!

When this was read—no Congreve rocket
  Discharged into the Gallic trenches,
E'er equall'd the tremendous shock it
  Pròduc'd upon the Nursery Benches.
The Bishops, who, of course had votes,
  By right of age and petticoats,
Were first and foremost in the fuss—
  "What, whip a Lama!—suffer birch
To touch his sacred —— infamous!
Deistical!—assailing thus
  The fundamentals of the Church!
No—no—such patriot plans as these
(So help them Heaven—and their sees!)
They held to be rank blasphemies."

The alarm thus given, by these and other
  Grave ladies of the Nursery side,
Spread through the land, till, such a pother
  Such party squabbles, far and wide,

Never in history's page had been
Recorded, as were then between
The Whippers and Non-whippers seen.
Till, things arriving at a state
  Which gave some fears of revolution,
The patriot lords' advice, though late,
  Was put at last in execution.
The Parliament of Thibet met—
  The little Lama call'd before it,
Did, then and there, his whipping get,
And (as the Nursery Gazette
Assures us) like a hero bore it.

And though 'mong Thibet Tories, some
Lament that Royal Martyr*d*om
(Please to observe, the letter D
In this last word 's pronounced like B),
Yet to the example of that Prince
  So much is Thibet's land a debtor,
'Tis said her little Lamas since
  Have all behaved themselves *much* better.

ETERNAL LONDON.

THOMAS MOORE.

And is there then no earthly place
  Where we can rest, in dream Elysian,
Without some cursed, round English face,
  Popping up near, to break the vision!

'Mid northern lakes, 'mid southern vines,
  Unholy cits we 're doom'd to meet;
Nor highest Alps nor Appenines
  Are sacred from Threadneedle-street.

If up the Simplon's path we wind,
Fancying we leave this world behind,
Such pleasant sounds salute one's ear
As—" Baddish news from 'Change, my dear--

"The Funds—(phew, curse this ugly hill!)
Are lowering fast—(what! higher still?)—
And—(zooks, we're mounting up to Heaven!)—
Will soon be down to sixty-seven."

Go where we may—rest where we will,
Eternal London haunts us still.
The trash of Almack's or Fleet-Ditch—
And scarce a pin's head difference *which*—
Mixes, though even to Greece we run,
With every rill from Helicon!
And if this rage for traveling lasts,
If Cockneys of all sets and castes,
Old maidens, aldermen, and squires,
Will leave their puddings and coal fires,
To gape at things in foreign lands
No soul among them understands—
If Blues desert their coteries,
To show off 'mong the Wahabees—
If neither sex nor age controls,
  Nor fear of Mamelukes forbids
Young ladies, with pink parasols,
  To glide among the Pyramids—
Why, then, farewell all hope to find
A spot that's free from London-kind!
Who knows, if to the West we roam,
But we may find some *Blue* "at home"
  Among the *Blacks* of Carolina—
Or, flying to the eastward, see
Some Mrs. Hopkins, taking tea
  And toast upon the Wall of China.

ON FACTOTUM NED.

THOMAS MOORE.

Here lies Factotum Ned at last:
  Long as he breath'd the vital air,
Nothing throughout all Europe pass'd
  In which he had n't some small share.

Whoe'er was *in*, whoe'er was *out*—
  Whatever statesmen did or said—
If not exactly brought about,
  Was all, at least, contrived by Ned.

With NAP if Russia went to war,
  'T was owing, under Providence,
To certain hints Ned gave the Czar—
  (*Vide* his pamphlet—price six pence).

If France was beat at Waterloo—
  As all, but Frenchmen, think she was—
To Ned, as Wellington well knew,
  Was owing half that day's applause.

Then for his news—no envoy's bag
  E'er pass'd so many secrets through it—
Scarcely a telegraph could wag
  Its wooden finger, but Ned knew it.

Such tales he had of foreign plots,
  With foreign names one's ear to buzz in—
From Russia *chefs* and *ofs* in lots,
  From Poland *owskis* by the dozen.

When GEORGE, alarm'd for England's creed,
  Turn'd out the last Whig ministry,
And men ask'd—who advised the deed?
  Ned modestly confess'd 't was he.

For though, by some unlucky miss,
  He had not downright *seen* the King,
He sent such hints through Viscount *This*,
  To Marquis *That*, as clench'd the thing.

The same it was in science, arts,
  The drama, books, MS. and printed—
Kean learn'd from Ned his cleverest parts,
  And Scott's last work by him was hinted.

Childe Harold in the proofs he read,
  And, here and there, infused some soul in 't—
Nay, Davy's lamp, till seen by Ned,
  Had—odd enough—a dangerous hole in 't.

'T was thus, all doing and all knowing,
  Wit, statesman, boxer, chemist, singer,
Whatever was the best pie going,
  In *that* Ned—trust him—had his finger.
  *   *   *   *   *

LETTERS

FROM MISS BIDDY FUDGE AT PARIS TO MISS DOROTHY —— IN IRELAND.

THOMAS MOORE.

WHAT a time since I wrote!—I 'm a sad naughty girl—
Though, like a tee-totum, I 'm all in a twirl,
Yet even (as you wittily say) a tee-totum
Between all its twirls gives a *letter* to note 'em.
But, Lord, such a place! and then, Dolly, my dresses,
My gowns, so divine!—there 's no language expresses,
Except just the *two* words "superbe," "magnifique,"
The trimmings of that which I had home last week!
It is call'd—I forget—*à la*—something which sounded
Like *alicampane*—but, in truth, I 'm confounded
And bother'd, my dear, 'twixt that troublesome boy's
(Bob's) cookery language, and Madame Le Roi's:
What with fillets of roses, and fillets of veal,
Things *garni* with lace, and things *garni* with eel,
One's hair, and one's cutlets both *en papillote*,
And a thousand more things I shall ne'er have by rote,
I can scarce tell the difference, at least as to phrase,
Between beef *à la Psyché* and curls *à la braise.*—
But, in short, dear, I 'm trick'd out quite *à la Française*,
With my bonnet—so beautiful!—high up and poking,
Like things that are put to keep chimneys from smoking.

Where *shall* I begin with the endless delights
Of this Eden of milliners, monkeys, and sights—
This dear busy place, where there 's nothing transacting,
But dressing and dinnering, dancing and acting?

Imprimis, the Opera—mercy, my ears!
  Brother Bobby's remark t' other night was a true one;
"This *must* be the music," said he, "of the *spears*,
  For I 'm curst if each note of it does n't run through one!"

Pa says (and you know, love, his book 's to make out),
'T was the Jacobins brought every mischief about;
That this passion for roaring has come in of late,
Since the rabble all tried for a *voice* in the State.
What a frightful idea, one's mind to o'erwhelm!
  What a chorus, dear Dolly, would soon be let loose of it!
If, when of age, every man in the realm
  Had a voice like old Laïs, and chose to make use of it!
No—never was known in this riotous sphere
Such a breach of the peace as their singing, my dear;
So bad, too, you 'd swear that the god of both arts,
  Of Music and Physic, had taken a frolic
For setting a loud fit of asthma in parts,
  And composing a fine rumbling base to a cholic!

But, the dancing—*ah parlez moi*, Dolly, *de ça*—
There, indeed, is a treat that charms all but Papa.
Such beauty—such grace—oh ye sylphs of romance!
  Fly, fly to Titania, and ask her if *she* has
One light-footed nymph in her train, that can dance
  Like divine Bigottini and sweet Fanny Bias!
Fanny Bias in Flora—dear creature!—you 'd swear,
When her delicate feet in the dance twinkle round,
That her steps are of light, that her home is the air,
  And she only *par complaisance* touches the ground.
And when Bigottini in Psyche dishevels
  Her black flowing hair, and by demons is driven,
Oh! who does not envy those rude little devils,
  That hold her, and hug her, and keep her from heaven?
Then, the music—so softly its cadences die,
So divinely—oh, Dolly! between you and I,
It 's as well for my peace that there 's nobody nigh
To make love to me then—*you've* a soul, and can judge
What a crisis 't would be for your friend Biddy Fudge!

The next place (which Bobby has near lost his heart in),
They call it the Play-house—I think—of Saint Martin:
Quite charming—and *very* religious—what folly
To say that the French are not pious, dear Dolly,
When here one beholds, so correctly and rightly,
The Testament turn'd into melo-drames nightly:

And, doubtless, so fond they 're of scriptural facts,
They will soon get the Pentateuch up in five acts.
Here Daniel, in pantomime, bids bold defiance
To Nebuchadnezzar and all his stuff'd lions,
While pretty young Israelites dance round the Prophet,
In very thin clothing, and *but* little of it;—
Here Bégrand, who shines in this scriptural path,
 As the lovely Susanna, without even a relic
Of drapery round her, comes out of the Bath
 In a manner, that, Bob says, is quite *Eve-angelic!*

But, in short, dear, 't would take me a month to recite
All the exquisite places we 're at, day and night;
And, besides, ere I finish, I think you 'll be glad
Just to hear one delightful adventure I 've had.

Last night, at the Beaujon, a place where—I doubt
If I well can describe—there are cars that set out
From a lighted pavilion, high up in the air,
And rattle you down, Doll—you hardly know where.
These vehicles, mind me, in which you go through
This delightfully dangerous journey, hold *two*.
Some cavalier asks, with humility, whether
 You 'll venture down with him—you smile—'tis a match;
In an instant you 're seated, and down both together
 Go thundering, as if you went post to old Scratch;
Well, it was but last night, as I stood and remark'd
On the looks and odd ways of the girls who embark'd,
The impatience of some for the perilous flight,
The forc'd giggle of others, 'twixt pleasure and fright,
That there came up—imagine, dear Doll, if you can—
A fine sallow, sublime, sort of Werter-fac'd man,
With mustaches that gave (what we read of so oft),
The dear Corsair expression, half savage, half soft,
As Hyænas in love may be fancied to look, or
A something between Abelard and old Blucher!
Up he came, Doll, to me, and uncovering his head
(Rather bald, but so warlike!) in bad English said,
"Ah! my dear—if Ma'mselle vil be so very good—
Just for von little course"—though I scarce understood
What he wish'd me to do, I said, thank him, I would.

Off we set—and, though 'faith, dear, I hardly knew whether
  My head or my heels were the uppermost then,
For 't was like heaven and earth, Dolly, coming together—
  Yet, spite of the danger, we dared it again.
And oh! as I gazed on the features and air
  Of the man, who for me all this peril defied,
I could fancy almost he and I were a pair
  Of unhappy young lovers, who thus, side by side,
Were taking, instead of rope, pistol, or dagger, a
Desperate dash down the falls of Niagara!

This achiev'd, through the gardens we saunter'd about,
  Saw the fire-works, exclaim'd "magnifique!" at each cracker,
And, when 't was all o'er, the dear man saw us out
  With the air, I *will* say, of a prince, to our *fiacre.*
Now, hear me—this stranger—it may be mere folly—
But *who* do you think we all think it is, Dolly?
Why, bless you, no less than the great King of Prussia,
Who 's here now incog.—he, who made such a fuss, you
Remember, in London, with Blucher and Platoff,
When Sal was near kissing old Blucher's cravat off!
Pa says he 's come here to look after his money
(Not taking things now as he used under Boney),
Which suits with our friend, for Bob saw him, he swore,
Looking sharp to the silver received at the door.
Besides, too, they say that his grief for his Queen
(Which was plain in this sweet fellow's face to be seen)
Requires such a stimulant dose as this car is,
Used three times a day with young ladies in Paris.
Some Doctor, indeed, has declared that such grief
  Should—unless 't would to utter despairing its folly push—
Fly to the Beaujon, and there seek relief
  By rattling, as Bob says, "like shot through a holly-bush."

I must now bid adieu—only think, Dolly, think
If this *should* be the King—I have scarce slept a wink
With imagining how it will sound in the papers,
  And how all the Misses my good luck will grudge,
When they read that Count Buppin, to drive away vapors,
  Has gone down the Beaujon with Miss Biddy Fudge.

Nota Bene.—Papa's almost certain 'tis he—
For he knows the L*git**ate cut, and could see,
In the way he went poising, and managed to tower
So erect in the car, the true *Balance of Power.*

SECOND LETTER.

Well, it *is n't* the King, after all, my dear creature!
  But *don't* you go laugh, now—there 's nothing to quiz in 't—
For grandeur of air and for grimness of feature,
  He *might* be a King, Doll, though, hang him, he is n't.
At first I felt hurt, for I wish'd it, I own,
If for no other cause than to vex Miss MALONE—
(The great heiress, you know, of Shandangan, who 's here,
Showing off with *such* airs and a real Cashmere,
While mine's but a paltry old rabbit-skin, dear!)
But says Pa, after deeply considering the thing,
"I am just as well pleased it should *not* be the King;
As I think for my BIDDY, so *gentilie jolie*,
  Whose charms may their price in an *honest* way fetch,
That a Brandenburg—(what *is* a Brandenburg, DOLLY?)—
  Would be, after all, no such very great catch.
If the R—G—T, indeed—" added he, looking sly—
(You remember that comical squint of his eye)
But I stopp'd him—"La, Pa, how *can* you say so,
When the R—G—T loves none but old women, you know!"
Which is fact, my dear Dolly—we, girls of eighteen,
And so slim—Lord, he 'd think us not fit to be seen;
And would like us much better as old—ay, as old
As that Countess of Desmond, of whom I 've been told
That she lived to much more than a hundred and ten,
And was kill'd by a fall from a cherry-tree then!
What a frisky old girl! but—to come to my lover,
  Who, though not a king, is a *hero* I 'll swear—
You shall hear all that 's happen'd just briefly run over,
  Since that happy night, when we whisk'd through the air!

Let me see—'t was on Saturday—yes, Dolly, yes—
From that evening I date the first dawn of my bliss;
When we both rattled off in that dear little carriage,
Whose journey, Bob says, is so like love and marriage,

"Beginning gay, desperate, dashing down-hilly;
And ending as dull as a six-inside Dilly!"
Well, scarcely a wink did I sleep the night through,
And, next day, having scribbled my letter to you,
With a heart full of hope this sweet fellow to meet,
Set out with Papa, to see Louis Dix-huit
Make his bow to some half-dozen women and boys,
Who get up a small concert of shrill *Vive le Rois*—
And how vastly genteeler, my dear, even this is,
Than vulgar Pall-Mall's oratorio of hisses!
The gardens seem'd full—so, of course, we walk'd o'er 'em,
'Mong orange-trees, clipp'd into town-bred decorum,
And Daphnes, and vases, and many a statue
There staring, with not even a stitch on them, at you!
The ponds, too, we view'd—stood awhile on the brink
  To contemplate the play of those pretty gold fishes—
"*Live Bullion*," says merciless Bob, "which I think,
  Would, if *coin'd*, with a little *mint* sauce, be delicious!"

But *what*, Dolly, what is the gay orange-grove,
Or gold fishes, to her that's in search of her love?
In vain did I wildly explore every chair
Where a thing *like* a man was—no lover sat there!
In vain my fond eyes did I eagerly cast
At the whiskers, mustaches, and wigs that went past,
To obtain, if I could, but a glance at that curl,
But a glimpse of those whiskers, as sacred, my girl,
As the lock that, Pa says, is to Mussulmen given,
For the angel to hold by that "lugs them to heaven!"
Alas, there went by me full many a quiz,
And mustaches in plenty, but nothing like his!
Disappointed, I found myself sighing out "well-a-day,"
Thought of the words of T—M M—RE's Irish melody,
Something about the "green spot of delight,"
  (Which you know, Captain Macintosh sung to us one day:)
Ah, Dolly! *my* "spot" was that Saturday night,
  And its verdure, how fleeting, had wither'd by Sunday!

We dined at a tavern—La, what do I say?
  If Bob was to know!—a *Restaurateur's*, dear;
Where your *properest* ladies go dine every day,
  And drink Burgundy out of large tumblers, like beer.

Fine Bob (for he 's really grown *super*-fine)
  Condescended, for once, to make one of the party;
Of course, though but three, we had dinner for nine,
  And, in spite of my grief, love, I own I ate hearty;
Indeed, Doll, I know not how 'tis, but in grief,
I have always found eating a wondrous relief;
And Bob, who 's in love, said he felt the same *quite*—
  "My sighs," said he "ceased with the first glass I drank you;
The *lamb* made me tranquil, the *puffs* made me light,
  And now that 's all o'er—why, I 'm—pretty well, thank you!"

To *my* great annoyance, we sat rather late;
For Bobby and Pa had a furious debate
About singing and cookery—Bobby, of course,
Standing up for the latter Fine Art in full force;
And Pa saying, "God only knows which is worst,
  The French singers or cooks, but I wish us well over it—
What with old Laïs and Véry, I 'm curst
  If *my* head or my stomach will ever recover it!"
'T was dark when we got to the Boulevards to stroll,
  And in vain did I look 'mong the street Macaronis,
When sudden it struck me—last hope of my soul—
  That some angel might take the dear man to Tortoni's!
We enter'd—and scarcely had Bob, with an air,
  For a *grappe a la jardiniere* call'd to the waiters,
When, oh! Doll, I saw him—my hero was there
  (For I knew his white small-clothes and brown leather
      gaiters),
A group of fair statues from Greece smiling o'er him,
And lots of red currant-juice sparkling before him!
Oh Dolly, these heroes—what creatures they are!
  In the *boudoir* the same as in fields full of slaughter;
As cool in the Beaujon's precipitous car
  As when safe at Tortoni's, o'er iced currant-water!
He joined us—imagine, dear creature my ecstacy—
Join'd by the man I'd have broken ten necks to see!
Bob wish'd to treat him with punch *à la glace*,
But the sweet fellow swore that my *beauté*, my *grace*,
And my *je-ne-sais-quoi* (then his whiskers he twirl'd)
Were, to *him*, "on de top of all ponch in de vorld."—
How pretty!—though oft (as, of course, it must be)
Both his French and his English are Greek, Doll, to me.

But, in short, I felt happy as ever fond heart did:
And, happier still, when 't was fix'd, ere we parted,
That, if the next day should be *pastoral* weather,
We all would set off in French buggies, together,
To see *Montmorency*—that place which, you know,
Is so famous for cherries and Jean Jacques Rousseau.
His card then he gave us—the *name*, rather creased—
But 't was Calicot—something—a colonel, at least!
After which—sure there never was hero so civil—he
Saw us safe home to our door in *Rue Rivoli*,
Where his *last* words, as at parting, he threw
A soft look o'er his shoulders, were—"how do you do?"

But, Lord—there 's Papa for the post—I 'm so vex'd—
Montmorency must now, love, be kept for my next.
That dear Sunday night!—I was charmingly dress'd,
And—*so* providential—was looking my best;
Such a sweet muslin gown, with a flounce—and my frills,
You 've no notion how rich—(though Pa has by the bills)—
And you 'd smile had you seen, when we sat rather near,
Colonel Calicot eyeing the cambric, my dear.
Then the flowers in my bonnet—but, la, it's in vain—
So, good by, my sweet Doll—I shall soon write again.

B. F.

Nota bena—our love to all neighbors about—
Your papa in particular—how is his gout?

P. S.—I 've just open'd my letter to say,
In your next you must tell me (now *do*, Dolly, pray
For I hate to ask Bob, he 's so ready to quiz)
What sort of a thing, dear, a *Brandenburg* is.

THIRD LETTER.

At last, Dolly—thanks to a potent emetic
Which Bobby and Pa, with grimace sympathetic,
Have swallowed this morning to balance the bliss
Of an eel *matelote*, and a *bisque d'ecrevisses*—
I 've a morning at home to myself, and sit down
To describe you our heavenly trip out of town.

How agog you must be for this letter, my dear!
Lady JANE in the novel less languish'd to hear
If that elegant cornet she met at Lord NEVILLE'S
Was actually dying with love or—blue devils.
But love, DOLLY, love is the theme *I* pursue;
With, blue devils, thank heaven, I 've nothing to do—
Except, indeed, dear Colonel CALICOT spies
Any imps of that color in *certain* blue eyes,
Which he stares at till *I*, DOLL, at *his* do the same;
Then he simpers—I blush—and would often exclaim,
If I knew but the French for it, "Lord, sir, for shame!"

Well, the morning was lovely—the trees in full dress
For the happy occasion—the sunshine *express*—
Had we order'd it dear, of the best poet going,
It scarce could be furnish'd more golden and glowing.
Though late when we started, the scent of the air
Was like GATTIE'S rose-water, and bright here and there
On the grass an odd dew-drop was glittering yet,
Like my aunt's diamond pin on her green tabinet!
And the birds seemed to warble, as blest on the boughs,
As if *each* a plumed CALICOT had for her spouse,
And the grapes were all blushing and kissing in rows,
And—in short, need I tell you, wherever one goes
With the creature one loves, 'tis all *couleur de rose;*
And ah, I shall ne'er, lived I ever so long, see
A day such as that at divine Montmorency!

There was but *one* drawback—at first when we started,
The Colonel and I were inhumanly parted;
How cruel—young hearts of such moments to rob!
He went in Pa's buggy, and I went with BOB:
And, I own, I felt spitefully happy to know
That Papa and his comrade agreed but *so-so.*
For the Colonel, it seems, is a stickler of BONEY'S—
Served with him, of course—nay, I 'm sure they were cronies;
So martial his features, dear DOLL, you can trace
Ulm, Austerlitz, Lodi, as plain in his face
As you do on that pillar of glory and brass
Which the poor Duc de B**RI must hate so to pass.
It appears, too, he made—as most foreigners do—
About English affairs an odd blunder or two.

For example—misled by the names, I dare say—
He confounded JACK CASTLES with Lord CASTLEREAGH;
And—such a mistake as no mortal hit ever on—
Fancied the *present* Lord CAMDEN the *clever* one!

But politics ne'er were the sweet fellow's trade;
'T was for war and the ladies my Colonel was made.
And, oh, had you heard, as together we walk'd
Through that beautiful forest, how sweetly he talk'd;
And how perfectly well he appear'd, DOLL, to know
All the life and adventures of JEAN JACQUES ROUSSEAU!—
"'T was there," said he—not that his *words* I can state—
'T was a gibberish that Cupid alone could translate;—
But "there," said he (pointing where, small and remote,
The dear Hermitage rose), "there his JULIE he wrote,
Upon paper gilt-edged, without blot or erasure,
Then sanded it over with silver and azure,
And—oh, what will genius and fancy not do?—
Tied the leaves up together with *nompareille* blue!"
What a trait of Rousseau! what a crowd of emotions
From sand and blue ribbons are conjured up here!
Alas! that a man of such exquisite notions,
Should send his poor brats to the Foundling, my dear!

"'T was here, too, perhaps," Colonel CALICOT said—
As down the small garden he pensively led—
(Though once I could see his sublime forehead wrinkle
With rage not to find there the loved periwinkle)—
"'T was here he received from the fair D'EPINAY,
(Who call'd him so sweetly *her Bear*, every day),
That dear flannel petticoat, pull'd off to form
A waistcoat to keep the enthusiast warm!"

Such, DOLL, were the sweet recollections we ponder'd,
As, full of romance, through that valley we wander'd,
The flannel (one's train of ideas, how odd it is!)
Led us to talk about other commodities,
Cambric, and silk, and I ne'er shall forget,
For the sun was then hastening in pomp to its set,
And full on the Colonel's dark whiskers shone down,
When he ask'd me, with eagerness—who made my gown?

The question confused me—for, Doll, you must know,
And I *ought* to have told my best friend long ago,
That, by Pa's strict command, I no longer employ
That enchanting *couturiere*, Madame Le Roi,
But am forc'd, dear, to have Victorine, who—deuce take her—
It seems is, at present, the king's mantua-maker—
I mean *of his party*—and, though much the smartest,
Le Roi is condemned as a rank B*n*pa*t*st.

Think, Doll, how confounded I look'd—so well knowing
The Colonel's opinions—my cheeks were quite glowing;
I stammer'd out something—nay, even half named
The *legitimate* semptress, when, loud, he exclaimed,
"Yes, yes, by the stiching 'tis plain to be seen
It was made by that B**rb*n**t b——h, Victorine!"
What a word for a hero, but heroes *will* err,
And I thought, dear, I'd tell you things *just* as they were.
Besides, though the word on good manners intrench,
I assure you, 'tis not *half* so shocking in French.

But this cloud, though embarrassing, soon pass'd away,
And the bliss altogether, the dreams of that day,
The thoughts that arise when such dear fellows woo us—
The *nothings* that then, love, are *every thing* to us—
That quick correspondence of glances and sighs,
And what Bob calls the "Twopenny-Post of the Eyes"—
Ah Doll, though I *know* you've a heart, 'tis in vain
To a heart so unpracticed these things to explain.
They can only be felt in their fullness divine
By her who has wander'd, at evening's decline,
Through a valley like that, with a Colonel like mine!

But here I must finish—for Bob, my dear Dolly,
Whom physic, I find, always makes melancholy,
Is seized with a fancy for church-yard reflections;
And full of all yesterday's rich recollections,
Is just setting off for Montmartre—"for *there* is,"
Said he, looking solemn, "the tomb of the Verys!
Long, long have I wish'd, as a votary true,
  O'er the grave of such talents to utter my moans;
And to-day, as my stomach is not in good cue
  For the *flesh* of the Verys—I'll visit their *bones*!"

He insists upon *my* going with him—how teasing!
This letter, however, dear DOLLY, shall lie
Unseal'd in my drawer, that if any thing pleasing
Occurs while I 'm out, I may tell you—Good-by.

B. F.

Four o'clock.

Oh, DOLLY, dear DOLLY, I 'm ruin'd forever—
I ne'er shall be happy again, DOLLY, never;
To think of the wretch!—what a victim was I!
'Tis too much to endure—I shall die, I shall die!
My brain 's in a fever—my pulses beat quick—
I shall die, or, at least, be exceedingly sick!
Oh what do you think? after all my romancing,
My visions of glory, my sighing, my glancing,
This Colonel—I scarce can commit it to paper—
This Colonel 's no more than a vile linen-draper!!
'Tis true as I live—I had coax'd brother BOB so
(You 'll hardly make out what I 'm writing, I sob so),
For some little gift on my birth-day—September
The thirtieth, dear, I 'm eighteen, you remember—
That BOB to a shop kindly order'd the coach
(Ah, little thought I who the shopman would prove),
To bespeak me a few of those *mouchoirs de poche*,
Which, in happier hours, I have sighed for, my love—
(The most beautiful things—two Napoleons the price—
And one 's name in the corner embroidered so nice!)
Well, with heart full of pleasure, I enter'd the shop,
But—ye gods, what a phantom!—I thought I should drop—
There he stood, my dear DOLLY—no room for a doubt—
There, behind the vile counter, these eyes saw him stand,
With a piece of French cambric before him roll'd out,
And that horrid yard-measure upraised in his hand!
Oh—Papa all along knew the secret, 'tis clear—
'T was a *a shopman* he meant by a "Brandenburg," dear!
The man, whom I fondly had fancied a King,
And when *that* too delightful illusion was past,
As a hero had worship'd—vile treacherous thing—
To turn out but a low linen-draper at last!
My head swam round—the wretch smil'd, I believe,
But his smiling, alas! could no longer deceive—
I fell back on BOB—my whole heart seem'd to wither,
And, pale as a ghost, I was carried back hither!

I only remember that Bob, as I caught him,
  With cruel facetiousness said—"Curse the Kiddy,
A staunch Revolutionist always I've thought him,
  But now I find out he's a *Counter* one, Biddy!"

Only think, my dear creature, if this should be known
To that saucy satirical thing, Miss Malone!
What a story 't will be at Shandangen forever!
  What laughs and what quizzing she 'll have with the men!
It will spread through the country—and never, oh never
  Can Biddy be seen at Kilrandy again!

Farewell—I shall do something desperate, I fear—
And ah! if my fate ever reaches your ear,
One tear of compassion my Doll will not grudge
To her poor—broken-hearted—young friend,
Biddy Fudge.

Nota Bene.—I 'm sure you will hear with delight,
That we 're going, all three, to see Brunet to-night.
A laugh will revive me—and kind Mr. Cox
(Do you know him?) has got us the Governor's box.

THE LITERARY LADY.

RICHARD BRINSLEY SHERIDAN.

What motley cares Corilla's mind perplex,
Whom maids and metaphors conspire to vex!
In studious dishabille behold her sit,
A lettered gossip and a household wit;
At once invoking, though for different views,
Her gods, her cook, her milliner and muse.
Round her strewed room a frippery chaos lies,
A checkered wreck of notable and wise,
Bills, books, caps, couplets, combs, a varied mass,
Oppress the toilet and obscure the glass;
Unfinished here an epigram is laid,
And there a mantua-maker's bill unpaid.
There new-born plays foretaste the town's applause,
There dormant patterns pine for future gauze.

A moral essay now is all her care,
A satire next, and then a bill of fare.
A scene she now projects, and now a dish;
Here Act the First, and here, Remove with Fish.
Now, while this eye in a fine frenzy rolls,
That soberly casts up a bill for coals;
Black pins and daggers in one leaf she sticks,
And tears, and threads, and bowls, and thimbles mix.

NETLEY ABBEY.*

R. HARRIS BARHAM

I SAW thee, Netley, as the sun
Across the western wave
Was sinking slow,
And a golden glow
To thy roofless towers he gave;
And the ivy sheen
With its mantle of green
That wrapt thy walls around,
Shone lovelily bright
In that glorious light,
And I felt 't was holy ground.

Then I thought of the ancient time—
The days of thy monks of old,—
When to matin, and vesper, and compline chime,
The loud Hosanna roll'd,
And, thy courts and "long-drawn aisles" among,
Swell'd the full tide of sacred song.

And then a vision pass'd
Across my mental eye;
And silver shrines, and shaven crowns,
And delicate ladies, in bombazeen gowns,
And long white vails, went by;
Stiff, and staid, and solemn, and sad,—
—But one, methought, wink'd at the Gardener-lad!

* A noted ruin, much frequented by pleasure-parties.

Then came tne Abbot, with miter and ring,
And pastoral staff, and all that sort of thing,
And a monk with a book, and a monk with a bell,
And "dear linen souls,"
In clean linen stoles,
Swinging their censers, and making a smell.—
And see where the Choir-master walks in the rear
With front severe
And brow austere,
Now and then pinching a little boy's ear
When he chants the responses too late or too soon,
Or his *Do*, *Re*, *Mi*, *Fa*, *Sol*, *La 's* not quite in tune.
(Then you know
They 'd a "movable *Do*,"
Not a fix'd one as now—and of course never knew
How to set up a musical Hullah-baloo.)
It was, in sooth, a comely sight,
And I welcom'd the vision with pure delight.

But then "a change came o'er"
My spirit—a change of fear—
That gorgeous scene I beheld no more,
But deep beneath the basement floor
A dungeon dark and drear!
And there was an ugly hole in the wall—
For an oven too big,—for a cellar too small!
And mortar and bricks
All ready to fix,
And I said, "Here 's a Nun has been playing some tricks!—
That horrible hole!—it seems to say,
'I 'm a grave that gapes for a living prey!' "
And my heart grew sick, and my brow grew sad—
And I thought of that wink at the Gardener-lad.
Ah me! ah me!—'tis sad to think
That maiden's eye, which was made to wink,
Should here be compelled to grow blear and blink,
Or be closed for aye
In this kind of way,
Shut out forever from wholesome day,
Wall'd up in a hole with never a chink,
No light,—no air,—no victuals,—no drink!—

And that maiden's lip,
Which was made to sip,
Should here grow wither'd and dry as a chip!
—That wandering glance and furtive kiss,
Exceedingly naughty, and wrong, I wis,
Should yet be considered so much amiss
As to call for a sentence severe as this!—
And I said to myself, as I heard with a sigh
The poor lone victim's stifled cry,
"Well, I can't understand
How any man's hand
Could wall up that hole in a Christian land!
Why, a Mussulman Turk
Would recoil from the work,
And though, when his ladies run after the fellows, he
Stands not on trifles, if madden'd by jealousy,
Its objects, I'm sure, would declare, could they speak,
In their Georgian, Circassian, or Turkish, or Greek,
'When all's said and done, far better it was for us,
Tied back to back
And sewn up in a sack,
To be pitch'd neck-and-heels from a boat in the Bosphorus!'
—Oh! a saint 't would vex
To think that the sex
Should be no better treated than Combe's double X!
Sure some one might run to the Abbess, and tell her
A much better method of stocking her cellar."

If ever on polluted walls
Heaven's right arm in vengeance falls,—
If e'er its justice wraps in flame
The black abodes of sin and shame,
That justice, in its own good time,
Shall visit, for so foul a crime,
Ope desolation's floodgate wide,
And blast thee, Netley, in thy pride!

Lo where it comes!—the tempest lowers,—
It bursts on thy devoted towers;
Ruthless Tudor's bloated form
Rides on the blast, and guides the storm;

I hear the sacrilegious cry,
"Down with the nests, and the rooks will fly!"

Down! down they come—a fearful fall—
Arch, and pillar, and roof-tree, and all,
Stained pane, and sculptured stone,
There they lie on the greensward strown—
Moldering walls remain alone!
Shaven crown
Bombazeen gown,
Miter, and crozier, and all are flown!

And yet, fair Netley, as I gaze
Upon that gray and moldering wall,
The glories of thy palmy days
Its very stones recall!—
They "come like shadows, so depart"—
I see thee as thou wert—and art—

Sublime in ruin!—grand in woe!
Lone refuge of the owl and bat;
No voice awakes thine echoes now!
No sound—good gracious!—what was that?
Was it the moan,
The parting groan
Of her who died forlorn and alone,
Embedded in mortar, and bricks, and stone?—
Full and clear
On my listening ear
It comes—again—near and more near—
Why zooks! it's the popping of Ginger Beer
—I rush to the door—
I tread the floor,
By abbots and abbesses trodden before,
In the good old chivalric days of yore,
And what see I there?—
In a rush-bottom'd chair
A hag surrounded by crockery-ware,
Vending, in cups, to the credulous throng
A nasty decoction miscall'd Souchong,—
And a squeaking fiddle and "wry-necked fife"
Are screeching away, for the life!—for the life!
Danced to by "All the World and his Wife."

Tag, Rag, and Bobtail, are capering there,
Worse scene, I ween, than Bartlemy Fair!—
Two or three chimney-sweeps, two or three clowns,
Playing at "pitch and toss," sport their "Browns,"
Two or three damsels, frank and free,
Are ogling, and smiling, and sipping Bohea.
Parties below, and parties above,
Some making tea, and some making love.
Then the "toot—toot—toot"
Of that vile demi-flute,—
The detestable din
Of that cracked violin,
And the odors of "Stout," and tobacco, and gin!
"—Dear me!" I exclaim'd, "what a place to be in!"
And I said to the person who drove my "shay"
(A very intelligent man, by the way),
"This, all things considered, is rather too gay!
It don't suit my humor,—so take me away!
Dancing! and drinking!—cigar and song!
If not profanation, it's 'coming it strong,'
And I really consider it all very wrong.—
—Pray, to whom does this property now belong?"—
He paus'd, and said,
Scratching his head,
"Why I really *do* think he's a little to blame,
But I can't say I knows the gentleman's name!"

"Well—well!" quoth I,
As I heaved a sigh,
And a tear-drop fell from my twinkling eye,
"My vastly good man, as I scarcely doubt
That some day or other you'll find it out,
Should he come in your way,
Or ride in your 'shay'
(As perhaps he may),
Be so good as to say
That a Visitor whom you drove over one day,
Was exceedingly angry, and very much scandalized,
Finding these beautiful ruins so Vandalized,
And thus of their owner to speak began,
As he ordered you home in haste,
NO DOUBT HE'S A VERY RESPECTABLE MAN,
But—'*I can't say much for his taste!*'"

FAMILY POETRY.

R. HARRIS BARHAM

Zooks! I must woo the Muse to-day,
  Though line before I never wrote!
"On what occasion?" do you say?
  Our Dick has got a long-tail'd coat!!

Not a coatee, which soldiers wear
  Button'd up high about the throat,
But easy, flowing, debonair,
  In short a *civil* long-tail'd coat.

A smarter you'll not find in town,
  Cut by Nugee, that snip of note;
A very quiet olive brown
  's the color of Dick's long-tail'd coat.

Gay jackets clothe the stately Pole,
  The proud Hungarian, and the Croat,
Yet Esterhazy, on the whole
  Looks best when in a long-tail'd coat

Lord Byron most admired, we know,
  The Albanian dress, or Suliote,
But then he died some years ago,
  And never saw Dick's long-tail'd coat;

Or past all doubt the poet's theme
  Had never been the "White Capote,"
Had he once view'd in Fancy's dream,
  The glories of Dick's long-tail'd coat!

We also know on Highland kilt
  Poor dear Glengarry used to dote,
And had esteem'd it actual guilt
  I' "the Gael" to wear a long-tail'd coat!

No wonder 't would his eyes annoy,
  Monkbarns himself would never quote
"Sir Robert Sibbald," "Gordon," "Ray,"
  Or "Stukely" for a long-tail'd coat.

Jackets may do to ride or race,
  Or row in, when one 's in a boat,
But in the boudoir, sure, for grace
  There 's nothing like Dick's long-tail'd coat.

Of course in climbing up a tree,
  On terra-firma, or afloat,
To mount the giddy topmast, he
  Would doff awhile his long-tail'd coat.

What makes you simper, then, and sneer?
  From out your own eye pull the mote!
A *pretty* thing for you to jeer—
  Have n't *you*, too, got a long-tail'd coat?

Oh! "Dick 's scarce old enough," you mean
  Why, though too young to give a note,
Or make a will, yet, sure Fifteen
  's a ripe age for a long-tail'd coat.

What! would you have him sport a chin
  Like Colonel Stanhope, or that goat
O' Gorman Mahon, ere begin
  To figure in a long-tail'd coat?

Suppose he goes to France—can he
  Sit down at any *table d' hôte*,
With any sort of decency,
  Unless he 's got a long-tail'd coat?

Why Louis Philippe, Royal Cit,
  There soon may be a *sans culotte*,
And Nugent's self may then admit
  The advantage of a long-tail'd coat.

Things are not now as when, of yore,
  In tower encircled by a moat,
The lion-hearted chieftain wore
  A corselet for a long-tail'd coat;

Then ample mail his form embraced,
  Not like a weasel or a stoat,
"Cribb'd and confined" about the waist,
  And pinch'd in like Dick's long-tail'd coat.

With beamy spear or biting ax,
To right and left he thrust and smote—
Ah! what a change! no sinewy thwacks
Fall from a modern long-tail'd coat!

More changes still! now, well-a-day!
A few cant phrases learned by rote,
Each beardless booby spouts away,
A Solon, in a long-tail'd coat!

Prates of the "March of Intellect"—
"The Schoolmaster." A *Patriote*
So noble, who could e'er suspect
Had just put on a long-tail'd coat?

Alack! alack! that every thick-
Skull'd lad must find an antidote
For England's woes, because, like Dick,
He has put on a long-tail'd coat!

But lo! my rhyme 's begun to fail,
Nor can I longer time devote;
Thus rhyme and time cut short the *tale*,
The *long tale* of Dick's long-tail'd coat.

THE SUNDAY QUESTION.

THOMAS HOOD.

"It is the king's highway that we are in, and in this way it is that thou hast placed the lions."—BUNYAN.

WHAT! shut the Gardens! lock the latticed gate!
Refuse the shilling and the fellow's ticket!
And hang a wooden notice up to state,
On Sundays no admittance at this wicket!
The Birds, the Beasts, and all the Reptile race,
Denied to friends and visitors till Monday!
Now, really, this appears the common case
Of putting too much Sabbath into Sunday—
But what is your opinion, Mrs. Grundy?

The Gardens—so unlike the ones we dub
  Of Tea, wherein the artisan carouses—
Mere shrubberies without one drop of shrub—
  Wherefore should they be closed like public-houses?
No ale is vended at the wild Deer's Head—
  No rum—nor gin—not even of a Monday—
The Lion is not carved—or gilt—or red,
  And does not send out porter of a Sunday—
  But what is your opinion, Mrs. Grundy?

The Bear denied! the Leopard under locks!
  As if his spots would give contagious fevers!
The Beaver close as hat within its box;
  So different from other Sunday beavers!
The Birds invisible—the Gnaw-way Rats—
  The Seal hermetically sealed till Monday—
The Monkey tribe—the Family of Cats—
  We visit other families on Sunday—
  But what is your opinion, Mrs. Grundy

What is the brute profanity that shocks
  The super-sensitively serious feeling?
The Kangaroo—is he not orthodox
  To bend his legs, the way he does, in kneeling?
Was strict Sir Andrew, in his Sabbath coat,
  Struck all a-heap to see a *Coati mundi?*
Or did the Kentish Plumtree faint to note
  The Pelicans presenting bills on Sunday?—
  But what is your opinion, Mrs. Grundy?

What feature has repulsed the serious set?
  What error in the bestial birth or breeding,
To put their tender fancies on the fret?
  One thing is plain—it is not in the feeding!
Some stiffish people think that smoking joints
  Are carnal sins 'twixt Saturday and Monday—
But then the beasts are pious on these points,
  For they all eat cold dinners on a Sunday—
  But what is your opinion, Mrs. Grundy?

What change comes o'er the spirit of the place,
  As if transmuted by some spell organic?

Turns fell Hyena of the Ghoulish race?
  The Snake, *pro tempore*, the true Satanic?
Do Irish minds—(whose theory allows
  That now and then Good Friday falls on Monday)—
Do Irish minds suppose that Indian Cows
  Are wicked Bulls of Bashan on a Sunday?—
  But what is your opinion, Mrs. Grundy?

There are some moody Fellows, not a few,
  Who, turned by nature with a gloomy bias,
Renounce black devils to adopt the blue,
  And think when they are dismal they are pious:
Is 't possible that Pug's untimely fun
  Has sent the brutes to Coventry till Monday?—
Or perhaps some animal, no serious one,
  Was overheard in laughter on a Sunday—
  But what is your opinion, Mrs. Grundy?

What dire offense have serious Fellows found
  To raise their spleen against the Regent's spinney?
Were charitable boxes handed round,
  And would not Guinea Pigs subscribe their guinea?
Perchance, the Demoiselle refused to molt
  The feathers in her head—at least till Monday;
Or did the Elephant, unseemly, bolt
  A tract presented to be read on Sunday?—
  But what is your opinion, Mrs. Grundy?

At whom did Leo struggle to get loose?
  Who mourns through Monkey-tricks his damaged clothing?
Who has been hissed by the Canadian Goose?
  On whom did Llama spit in utter loathing?
Some Smithfield Saint did jealous feelings tell
  To keep the Puma out of sight till Monday,
Because he preyed extempore as well
  As certain wild Itinerants on Sunday—
  But what is your opinion, Mrs. Grundy?

To me it seems that in the oddest way
  (Begging the pardon of each rigid Socius)

Our would-be Keepers of the Sabbath-day
  Are like the Keepers of the brutes ferocious—
As soon the Tiger might expect to stalk
  About the grounds from Saturday till Monday,
As any harmless man to take a walk,
  If Saints could clap him in a cage on Sunday—
  But what is your opinion, Mrs. Grundy?

In spite of all hypocrisy can spin,
  As surely as I am a Christian scion,
I cannot think it is a mortal sin—
  (Unless he 's loose)—to look upon a lion.
I really think that one may go, perchance,
  To see a bear, as guiltless as on Monday—
(That is, provided that he did not dance)—
  Bruin 's no worse than bakin' on a Sunday—
  But what is your opinion, Mrs. Grundy?

In spite of all the fanatic compiles,
  I can not think the day a bit diviner,
Because no children, with forestalling smiles,
  Throng, happy, to the gates of Eden Minor—
It is not plain, to my poor faith at least,
  That what we christen "Natural" on Monday,
The wondrous history of Bird and Beast,
  Can be unnatural because it's Sunday—
  But what is your opinion, Mrs. Grundy?

Whereon is sinful fantasy to work?
  The Dove, the winged Columbus of man's haven?
The tender Love-Bird—or the filial Stork?
  The punctual Crane—the providential Raven?
The Pelican whose bosom feeds her young?
  Nay, must we cut from Saturday till Monday
That feathered marvel with a human tongue,
  Because she does not preach upon a Sunday—
  But what is your opinion, Mrs. Grundy?

The busy Beaver—that sagacious beast!
  The Sheep that owned an Oriental Shepherd—
That Desert-ship, the Camel of the East,
  The horned Rhinoceros—the spotted Leopard—

The Creatures of the Great Creator's hand
  Are surely sights for better days than Monday—
The Elephant, although he wears no band,
  Has he no sermon in his trunk for Sunday?—
  But what is your opinion, Mrs. Grundy?

What harm if men who burn the midnight-oil,
  Weary of frame, and worn and wan of feature,
Seek once a week their spirits to assoil,
  And snatch a glimpse of "Animated Nature?"
Better it were if, in his best of suits,
  The artisan, who goes to work on Monday,
Should spend a leisure-hour among the brutes,
  Than make a beast of his own self on Sunday—
  But what is your opinion, Mrs. Grundy?

Why, zounds! what raised so Protestant a fuss
  (Omit the zounds! for which I make apology)
But that the Papists, like some Fellows, thus
  Had somehow mixed up *Dens* with their Theology?
Is Brahma's Bull—a Hindoo god at home—
  A Papal Bull to be tied up till Monday?—
Or Leo, like his namesake, Pope of Rome,
  That there is such a dread of them on Sunday—
  But what is your opinion, Mrs. Grundy?

Spirit of Kant! have we not had enough
  To make Religion sad, and sour, and snubbish,
But Saints Zoological must cant their stuff,
  As vessels cant their ballast—rattling rubbish!
Once let the sect, triumphant to their text,
  Shut Nero up from Saturday till Monday,
And sure as fate they will deny us next
  To see the Dandelions on a Sunday—
  But what is your opinion, Mrs. Grundy?

ODE TO RAE WILSON, ESQUIRE.*

THOMAS HOOD.

"Close, close your eyes with holy dread,
And weave a circle round him thrice;
For he on honey-dew hath fed,
And drunk the milk of Paradise!"—COLERIDGE.

"It's very hard them kind of men
Won't let a body be."—OLD BALLAD.

A WANDERER, Wilson, from my native land,
Remote, O Rae, from godliness and thee,
Where rolls between us the eternal sea,
Besides some furlongs of a foreign sand—
Beyond the broadest Scotch of London Wall;
Beyond the loudest Saint that has a call;
Across the wavy waste between us stretched,
A friendly missive warns me of a stricture,
Wherein my likeness you have darkly etched,
And though I have not seen the shadow sketched,
Thus I remark prophetic on the picture.

I guess the features:—in a line to paint
Their moral ugliness, I'm not a saint.
Not one of those self-constituted saints,
Quacks—not physicians—in the cure of souls,
Censors who sniff out moral taints,
And call the devil over his own coals—
Those pseudo Privy Councillors of God,
Who write down judgments with a pen hard-nibbed:
Ushers of Beelzebub's Black Rod,
Commending sinners not to ice thick-ribbed,
But endless flames, to scorch them like flax—
Yet sure of heaven themselves, as if they'd cribbed
The impression of St. Peter's keys in wax!

Of such a character no single trace
Exists, I know, in my fictitious face;
There wants a certain cast about the eye;

* Who had, in one of his books, characterized some of Hood's verses as "profaneness and ribaldry."

A certain lifting of the nose's tip;
A certain curling of the nether lip,
In scorn of all that is, beneath the sky;
In brief, it is an aspect deleterious,
A face decidedly not serious,
A face profane, that would not do at all
To make a face at Exeter Hall—
That Hall where bigots rant, and cant, and pray,
And laud each other face to face,
Till every farthing-candle *ray*
Conceives itself a great gas-light of grace!

Well!—be the graceless lineaments confest!
I do enjoy this bounteous beauteous earth;
    And dote upon a jest
"Within the limits of becoming mirth;"—
No solemn sanctimonious face I pull,
Nor think I 'm pious when I 'm only bilious—
Nor study in my sanctum supercilious
To frame a Sabbath Bill or forge a Bull.
I pray for grace—repent each sinful act—
Peruse, but underneath the rose, my Bible;
And love my neighbor, far too well, in fact,
To call and twit him with a godly tract
That 's turned by application to a libel.
My heart ferments not with the bigot's leaven,
All creeds I view with toleration thorough,
And have a horror of regarding heaven
    As any body's rotten borough.

What else? No part I take in party fray,
With tropes from Billingsgate's slang-whanging Tartars,
I fear no Pope—and let great Ernest play
At Fox and Goose with Fox's Martyrs!
I own I laugh at over-righteous men,
I own I shake my sides at ranters,
And treat sham Abr'am saints with wicked banters,
I even own, that there are times—but then
It 's when I 've got my wine—I say d—— canters!

I 've no ambition to enact the spy
On fellow-souls, a spiritual Pry—

'Tis said that people ought to guard their noses
Who thrust them into matters none of theirs:
And, though no delicacy discomposes
Your saint, yet I consider faith and prayers
Among the privatest of men's affairs.

I do not hash the Gospel in my books,
And thus upon the public mind intrude it,
As if I thought, like Otaheitan cooks,
No food was fit to eat till I had chewed it.

On Bible stilts I don't affect to stalk;
Nor lard with Scripture my familiar talk—
For man may pious texts repeat,
And yet religion have no inward seat;
'Tis not so plain as the old Hill of Howth,
A man has got his belly full of meat
Because he talks with victuals in his mouth!

Mere verbiage—it is not worth a carrot!
Why, Socrates or Plato—where 's the odds?—
Once taught a Jay to supplicate the gods,
And made a Polly-theist of a Parrot!

A mere professor, spite of all his cant, is
Not a whit better than a Mantis—
An insect, of what clime I can't determine,
That lifts its paws most parson-like, and thence,
By simple savages—through sheer pretense—
Is reckoned quite a saint among the vermin.
But where 's the reverence, or where the *nous*,
To ride on one's religion through the lobby,
Whether as stalking-horse or hobby,
To show its pious paces to "the house."

I honestly confess that I would hinder
The Scottish member's legislative rigs,
That spiritual Pindar,
Who looks on erring souls as straying pigs,
That must be lashed by law, wherever found,
And driven to church as to the parish pound.

I do confess, without reserve or wheedle,
I view that groveling idea as one
Worthy some parish clerk's ambitious son,
A charity-boy who longs to be a beadle.
On such a vital topic sure 'tis odd
How much a man can differ from his neighbor;
One wishes worship freely given to God,
Another wants to make it statute-labor—
The broad distinction in a line to draw,
As means to lead us to the skies above,
You say—Sir Andrew and his love of law,
And I—the Saviour with his law of love.

Spontaneously to God should tend the soul,
Like the magnetic needle to the Pole;
But what were that intrinsic virtue worth,
Suppose some fellow with more zeal than knowledge,
Fresh from St. Andrew's college,
Should nail the conscious needle to the north?
I do confess that I abhor and shrink
From schemes, with a religious willy-nilly,
That frown upon St. Giles' sins, but blink
The peccadilloes of all Piccadilly—
My soul revolts at such bare hypocrisy,
And will not, dare not, fancy in accord
The Lord of hosts with an exclusive lord
Of this world's aristocracy.
It will not own a nation so unholy,
As thinking that the rich by easy trips
May go to heaven, whereas the poor and lowly
Must work their passage as they do in ships.

One place there is—beneath the burial-sod,
Where all mankind are equalized by death;
Another place there is—the Fane of God,
Where all are equal who draw living breath;—
Juggle who will *elsewhere* with his own soul,
Playing the Judas with a temporal dole—
He who can come beneath that awful cope,
In the dread presence of a Maker just,
Who metes to every pinch of human dust
One even measure of immortal hope—

He who can stand within that holy door,
With soul unbowed by that pure spirit-level,
And frame unequal laws for rich and poor,—
Might sit for Hell, and represent the Devil!

Such are the solemn sentiments, O Rae,
In your last journey-work, perchance, you ravage,
Seeming, but in more courtly terms, to say
I 'm but a heedless, creedless, godless, savage;
A very Guy, deserving fire and faggots,—
    A scoffer, always on the grin,
And sadly given to the mortal sin
Of liking Mawworms less than merry maggots!

The humble records of my life to search,
I have not herded with mere pagan beasts:
But sometimes I have "sat at good men's feasts,"
And I have been "where bells have knolled to church."
Dear bells! how sweet the sound of village bells
When on the undulating air they swim!
Now loud as welcomes! faint, now, as farewells!
And trembling all about the breezy dells,
As fluttered by the wings of Cherubim.
Meanwhile the bees are chanting a low hymn;
And lost to sight the ecstatic lark above
Sings, like a soul beatified, of love,
With, now and then, the coo of the wild pigeon:—
O pagans, heathens, infidels, and doubters!
If such sweet sounds can't woo you to religion,
Will the harsh voices of church cads and touters?

A man may cry Church! Church! at every word,
With no more piety than other people—
A daw's not reckoned a religious bird
Because it keeps a-cawing from a steeple;
The Temple is a good, a holy place,
But quacking only gives it an ill savor;
While saintly mountebanks the porch disgrace,
And bring religion's self into disfavor!

Behold yon servitor of God and Mammon,
Who, binding up his Bible with his ledger,

Blends Gospel texts with trading gammon,
A black-leg saint, a spiritual hedger,
Who backs his rigid Sabbath, so to speak,
Against the wicked remnant of the week,
A saving bet against his sinful bias—
"Rogue that I am," he whispers to himself,
"I lie—I cheat—do any thing for pelf,
But who on earth can say I am not pious!"

In proof how over-righteousness re-acts,
Accept an anecdote well based on facts;
On Sunday morning—(at the day don't fret)—
In riding with a friend to Ponder's End
Outside the stage, we happened to commend
A certain mansion that we saw To Let.
"Ay," cried our coachman, with our talk to grapple,
"You 're right! no house along the road comes nigh it!
'T was built by the same man as built yon chapel,
And master wanted once to buy it,—
But t' other driv' the bargain much too hard,—
He axed sure-*ly* a sum prodigious!
But being so particular religious,
Why, *that* you see, put master on his guard!"
Church is "a little heaven below,
I have been there and still would go,"
Yet I am none of those who think it odd
A man can pray unbidden from the cassock,
And, passing by the customary hassock
Kneel down remote upon the simple sod,
And sue in *formâ pauperis* to God.

As for the rest,—intolerant to none,
Whatever shape the pious rite may bear,
Even the poor Pagan's homage to the sun
I would not harshly scorn, lest even there
I spurned some elements of Christian prayer—
An aim, though erring, at a "world ayont"—
Acknowledgment of good—of man's futility,
A sense of need, and weakness, and indeed
That very thing so many Christians want—
Humility.

Such, unto Papists, Jews or Turbaned Turks,
Such is my spirit—(I don't mean my wraith!)
Such, may it please you, is my humble faith;
I know, full well, you do not like my *works!*

I have not sought, 'tis true, the Holy Land,
As full of texts as Cuddie Headrigg's mother,
The Bible in one hand,
And my own common-place-book in the other—
But you have been to Palestine—alas!
Some minds improve by travel—others, rather,
Resemble copper wire or brass,
Which gets the narrower by going further!

Worthless are all such pilgrimages—very!
If Palmers at the Holy Tomb contrive
The humans heats and rancor to revive
That at the Sepulcher they ought to bury.
A sorry sight it is to rest the eye on,
To see a Christian creature graze at Sion,
Then homeward, of the saintly pasture full,
Rush bellowing, and breathing fire and smoke,
At crippled Papistry to butt and poke,
Exactly as a skittish Scottish bull
Haunts an old woman in a scarlet cloak.

Why leave a serious, moral, pious home,
Scotland, renowned for sanctity of old,
Far distant Catholics to rate and scold
For—doing as the Romans do at Rome?
With such a bristling spirit wherefore quit
The Land of Cakes for any land of wafers,
About the graceless images to flit,
And buzz and chafe importunate as chafers,
Longing to carve the carvers to Scotch collops?—
People who hold such absolute opinions
Should stay at home in Protestant dominions,
Not travel like male Mrs. Trollopes.

Gifted with noble tendency to climb,
Yet weak at the same time,

Faith is a kind of parasitic plant,
That grasps the nearest stem with tendril rings;
And as the climate and the soil may grant,
So is the sort of tree to which it clings.
Consider, then, before, like Hurlothrumbo,
You aim your club at any creed on earth,
That, by the simple accident of birth,
You might have been High Priest to Mungo Jumbo.

For me—through heathen ignorance perchance,
Not having knelt in Palestine,—I feel
None of that griffinish excess of zeal,
Some travelers would blaze with here in France.
Dolls I can see in Virgin-like array,
Nor for a scuffle with the idols hanker
Like crazy Quixotte at the puppet's play,
If their "offense be rank," should mine be *rancor?*

Mild light, and by degrees, should be the plan
To cure the dark and erring mind;
But who would rush at a benighted man,
And give him two black eyes for being blind?

Suppose the tender but luxuriant hop
Around a cankered stem should twine,
What Kentish boor would tear away the prop
So roughly as to wound, nay, kill the bine?

The images, 'tis true, are strangely dressed,
With gauds and toys extremely out of season;
The carving nothing of the very best,
The whole repugnant to the eye of Reason,
Shocking to Taste, and to Fine Arts a treason—
Yet ne'er o'erlook in bigotry of sect
One truly *Catholic*, one common form,
At which unchecked
All Christian hearts may kindle or keep warm.

Say, was it to my spirit's gain or loss
One bright and balmy morning, as I went
From Liege's lovely environs to Ghent,
If hard by the wayside I found a cross,

That made me breathe a prayer upon the spot—
While Nature of herself, as if to trace
The emblem's use, had trailed around its base
The blue significant Forget-Me-Not?
Methought, the claims of Charity to urge
More forcibly along with Faith and Hope,
The pious choice had pitched upon the verge
    Of a delicious slope,
Giving the eye much variegated scope!—
"Look round," it whispered, "on that prospect rare,
Those vales so verdant, and those hills so blue;
Enjoy the sunny world, so fresh, and fair,
But"—(how the simple legend pierced me through!)
    "Priez pour les Malheureux."

With sweet kind natures, as in honeyed cells,
Religion lives and feels herself at home;
But only on a formal visit dwells
Where wasps instead of bees have formed the comb

Shun pride, O Rae!—whatever sort beside
You take in lieu, shun spiritual pride!
A pride there is of rank—a pride of birth,
A pride of learning, and a pride of purse,
A London pride—in short, there be on earth
A host of prides, some better and some worse;
But of all prides, since Lucifer's attaint,
The proudest swells a self-elected Saint.

To picture that cold pride so harsh and hard,
Fancy a peacock in a poultry-yard.
Behold him in conceited circles sail,
Strutting and dancing, and now planted stiff,
In all his pomp of pageantry, as if
He felt "the eyes of Europe" on his tail!
As for the humble breed retained by man,
  He scorns the whole domestic clan—
    He bows, he bridles,
    He wheels, he sidles,
As last, with stately dodgings in a corner,
He pens a simple russet hen, to scorn her
Full in the blaze of his resplendent fan!

"Look here," he cries (to give him words),
"Thou feathered clay—thou scum of birds!"
Flirting the rustling plumage in her eyes—
"Look here, thou vile predestined sinner,
Doomed to be roasted for a dinner,
Behold these lovely variegated dyes!
These are the rainbow colors of the skies,
That heaven has shed upon me *con amore*—
A Bird of Paradise?—a pretty story!
I am that Saintly Fowl, thou paltry chick!
Look at my crown of glory!
Thou dingy, dirty, dabbled, draggled jill!"
And off goes Partlett, wriggling from a kick,
With bleeding scalp laid open by his bill!

That little simile exactly paints
How sinners are despised by saints.
By saints!—the Hypocrites that ope heaven's door
Obsequious to the sinful man of riches—
But put the wicked, naked, bare-legged poor,
In parish stocks, instead of breeches.

The Saints?—the Bigots that in public spout,
Spread phosphorus of zeal on scraps of fustian,
And go like walking "Lucifers" about—
Mere living bundles of combustion.

The Saints!—the aping Fanatics that talk
All cant and rant and rhapsodies high flown—
That bid you balk
A Sunday walk,
And shun God's work as you should shun your own.

The Saints!—the Formalists, the extra pious,
Who think the mortal husk can save the soul,
By trundling, with a mere mechanic bias,
To church, just like a lignum-vitæ bowl!

The Saints!—the Pharisees, whose beadle stands
Beside a stern coercive kirk,
A piece of human mason-work,
Calling all sermons contrabands,
In that great Temple that 's not made with hands!

Thrice blessed, rather, is the man with whom
The gracious prodigality of nature,
The balm, the bliss, the beauty, and the bloom,
The bounteous providence in every feature,
Recall the good Creator to his creature,
Making all earth a fane, all heaven its dome!
To *his* tuned spirit the wild heather-bells
 Ring Sabbath knells;
The jubilate of the soaring lark
 Is chant of clerk;
For Choir, the thrush and the gregarious linnet;
The sod 's a cushion for his pious want;
And, consecrated by the heaven within it,
The sky-blue pool, a font.
Each cloud-capped mountain is a holy altar;
 An organ breathes in every grove;
 And the full heart 's a Psalter,
Rich in deep hymns of gratitude and love!

Sufficiently by stern necessitarians
Poor Nature, with her face begrimmed by dust,
Is stoked, coked, smoked, and almost choked: but must
Religion have its own Utilitarians,
Labeled with evangelical phylacteries,
To make the road to heaven a railway trust,
And churches—that 's the naked fact—mere factories?

O! simply open wide the temple door,
And let the solemn, swelling organ greet,
 With *Voluntaries* meet,
The *willing* advent of the rich and poor!
And while to God the loud Hosannas soar,
With rich vibrations from the vocal throng—
From quiet shades that to the woods belong,
 And brooks with music of their own,
Voices may come to swell the choral song
With notes of praise they learned in musings lone.

How strange it is, while on all vital questions,
That occupy the House and public mind,
We always meet with some humane suggestions
Of gentle measures of a healing kind,

Instead of harsh severity and vigor,
The saint alone his preference retains
For bills of penalties and pains,
And marks his narrow code with legal rigor!
Why shun, as worthless of affiliation,
What men of all political persuasion
Extol—and even use upon occasion—
That Christian principle, conciliation?
But possibly the men who make such fuss
With Sunday pippins and old Trots infirm,
Attach some other meaning to the term,
As thus:

One market morning, in my usual rambles,
Passing along Whitechapel's ancient shambles,
Where meat was hung in many a joint and quarter,
I had to halt a while, like other folks,
To let a killing butcher coax
A score of lambs and fatted sheep to slaughter.
A sturdy man he looked to fell an ox,
Bull-fronted, ruddy, with a formal streak
Of well-greased hair down either cheek,
As if he dee-dashed-dee'd some other flocks
Besides those woolly-headed stubborn blocks
That stood before him, in vexatious huddle—
Poor little lambs, with bleating wethers grouped,
While, now and then, a thirsty creature stooped
And meekly snuffed, but did not taste the puddle.

Fierce barked the dog, and many a blow was dealt,
That loin, and chump, and scrag and saddle felt,
Yet still, that fatal step they all declined it—
And shunned the tainted door as if they smelt
Onions, mint-sauce, and lemon-juice behind it.
At last there came a pause of brutal force;
The cur was silent, for his jaws were full
Of tangled locks of tarry wool;
The man had whooped and bellowed till dead hoarse,
The time was ripe for mild expostulation,
And thus it stammered from a stander-by—
"Zounds!—my good fellow—it quite makes me—why
It really—my dear fellow—do just try
Conciliation!"

Stringing his nerves like flint,
The sturdy butcher seized upon the hint—
At least he seized upon the foremost wether—
And hugged and lugged and tugged him neck and crop
Just *nolens volens* through the open shop—
If tails come off he did n't care a feather—
Then walking to the door, and smiling grim,
He rubbed his forehead and his sleeve together—
"There!—I 've *con*ciliated him!"

Again—good-humoredly to end our quarrel—
(Good humor should prevail!)
I 'll fit you with a tale
Whereto is tied a moral.
Once on a time a certain English lass
Was seized with symptoms of such deep decline,
Cough, hectic flushes, every evil sign,
That, as their wont is at such desperate pass,
The doctors gave her over—to an ass.

Accordingly, the grisly Shade to bilk,
Each morn the patient quaffed a frothy bowl
Of assinine new milk,
Robbing a shaggy suckling of a foal
Which got proportionably spare and skinny—
Meanwhile the neighbors cried "Poor Mary Ann!
She can't get over it! she never can!"
When lo! to prove each prophet was a ninny,
The one that died was the poor wet-nurse Jenny.

To aggravate the case,
There were but two grown donkeys in the place;
And, most unluckily for Eve's sick daughter,
The other long-eared creature was a male,
Who never in his life had given a pail
Of milk, or even chalk and water.
No matter: at the usual hour of eight
Down trots a donkey to the wicket-gate,
With Mister Simon Gubbins on his back—
"Your sarvant, Miss—a werry spring-like day—
Bad time for hasses, though! good lack! good lack!
Jenny be dead, Miss—but I 'ze brought ye Jack—
He doesn 't give no milk—but he can bray."

So runs the story,
And, in vain self-glory,
Some Saints would sneer at Gubbins for his blindness;
But what the better are their pious saws
To ailing souls, than dry hee-haws,
Without the milk of human kindness?

DEATH'S RAMBLE.

THOMAS HOOD.

One day the dreary old King of Death
Inclined for some sport with the carnal,
So he tied a pack of darts on his back,
And quietly stole from his charnel.

His head was bald of flesh and of hair,
His body was lean and lank;
His joints at each stir made a crack, and the cur
Took a gnaw, by the way, at his shank.

And what did he do with his deadly darts,
This goblin of grisly bone?
He dabbled and spilled man's blood, and he killed
Like a butcher that kills his own.

The first he slaughtered it made him laugh
(For the man was a coffin-maker),
To think how the mutes, and men in black suits,
Would mourn for an undertaker.

Death saw two Quakers sitting at church;
Quoth he, "We shall not differ."
And he let them alone, like figures of stone,
For he could not make them stiffer.

He saw two duellists going to fight,
In fear they could not smother;
And he shot one through at once—for he knew
They never would shoot each other.

He saw a watchman fast in his box,
  And he gave a snore infernal;
Said Death, "He may keep his breath, for his sleep
  Can never be more eternal."

He met a coachman driving a coach
  So slow that his fare grew sick;
But he let him stray on his tedious way,
  For Death only wars on the *quick*.

Death saw a tollman taking a toll,
  In the spirit of his fraternity;
But he knew that sort of man would extort,
  Though summoned to all eternity.

He found an author writing his life,
  But he let him write no further;
For Death, who strikes whenever he likes,
  Is jealous of all self-murther!

Death saw a patient that pulled out his purse,
  And a doctor that took the sum;
But he let them be—for he knew that the "fee"
  Was a prelude to "faw" and "fum."

He met a dustman ringing a bell,
  And he gave him a mortal thrust;
For himself, by law, since Adam's flaw,
  Is contractor for all our dust.

He saw a sailor mixing his grog,
  And he marked him out for slaughter;
For on water he scarcely had cared for death,
  And never on rum-and-water.

Death saw two players playing at cards,
  But the game was n't worth a dump,
For he quickly laid them flat with a spade,
  To wait for the final trump!

THE BACHELOR'S DREAM.

THOMAS HOOD.

My pipe is lit, my grog is mixed,
My curtains drawn and all is snug;
Old Puss is in her elbow chair,
And Tray is sitting on the rug.
Last night I had a curious dream,
Miss Susan Bates was Mistress Mogg—
What d' ye think of that, my cat?
What d' ye think of that, my dog?

She look'd so fair, she sang so well,
I could but woo and she was won;
Myself in blue, the bride in white,
The ring was placed, the deed was done!
Away we went in chaise-and-four,
As fast as grinning boys could flog—
What d' ye think of that my cat?
What d' ye think of that my dog?

What loving *tête-à-têtes* to come!
What *tête-à-têtes* must still defer!
When Susan came to live with me,
Her mother came to live with her!
With sister Belle she could n't part,
But all *my* ties had leave to jog—
What d' ye think of that, my cat?
What d' ye think of that, my dog?

The mother brought a pretty Poll—
A monkey, too, what work he made!
The sister introduced a beau—
My Susan brought a favorite maid.
She had a tabby of her own,—
A snappish mongrel christened Gog,—
What d' ye think of that, my cat?
What d' ye think of that, my dog?

The monkey bit—the parrot screamed,
All day the sister strummed and sung;

The petted maid was such a scold!
My Susan learned to use her tongue;
Her mother had such wretched health,
She sat and croaked like any frog—
What d' ye think of that, my cat?
What d' ye think of that, my dog?

No longer Deary, Duck, and Love,
I soon came down to simple "M!"
The very servants crossed my wish,
My Susan let me down to them.
The poker hardly seemed my own,
I might as well have been a log—
What d' ye think of that, my cat?
What d' ye think of that, my dog?

My clothes they were the queerest shape!
Such coats and hats she never met!
My ways they were the oddest ways!
My friends were such a vulgar set!
Poor Tompkinson was snubbed and huffed,
She could not bear that Mister Blogg—
What d' ye think of that, my cat?
What d' ye think of that, my dog?

At times we had a spar, and then
Mamma must mingle in the song—
The sister took a sister's part—
The maid declared her master wrong—
The parrot learned to call me "Fool!"
My life was like a London fog—
What d' ye think of that, my cat?
What d' ye think of that, my dog?

My Susan's taste was superfine,
As proved by bills that had no end;
I never had a decent coat—
I never had a coin to spend!
She forced me to resign my club,
Lay down my pipe, retrench my grog—
What d' ye think of that, my cat?
What d' ye think of that, my dog?

Each Sunday night we gave a rout
To fops and flirts, a pretty list;
And when I tried to steal away
I found my study full of whist!
Then, first to come, and last to go,
There always was a Captain Hogg—
What d' ye think of that, my cat?
What d' ye think of that, my dog?

Now was not that an awful dream
For one who single is and snug—
With Pussy in the elbow-chair,
And Tray reposing on the rug?—
If I must totter down the hill
'Tis safest done without a clog—
What d' ye think of that, my cat?
What d' ye think of that, my dog?

ON SAMUEL ROGERS.

LORD BYRON.

Question.

Nose and chin would shame a knocker,
Wrinkles that would puzzle Cocker:
Mouth which marks the envious scorner,
With a scorpion in each corner,
Turning its quick tail to sting you
In the place that most may wring you:
Eyes of lead-like hue, and gummy;
Carcass picked out from some mummy;
Bowels (but they were forgotten,
Save the liver, and that's rotten);
Skin all sallow, flesh all sodden—
Form the Devil would frighten God in.
Is't a corpse stuck up for show,
Galvanized at times to go
With the Scripture in connection,
New proof of the resurrection?
Vampyre, ghost, or ghoul, what is it?
I would walk ten miles to miss it.

Answer.

Many passengers arrest one,
To demand the same free question.
Shorter 's my reply, and franker—
That 's the Bard, the Beau, the Banker.
Yet if you could bring about,
Just to turn him inside out,
Satan's self would seem less sooty,
And his present aspect—Beauty.
Mark that (as he masks the bilious
Air, so softly supercilious)
Chastened bow, and mock humility,
Almost sickened to servility;
Hear his tone, (which is to talking
That which creeping is to walking --
Now on all-fours, now on tiptoe),
Hear the tales he lends his lip to;
Little hints of heavy scandals,
Every friend in turn he handles;
All which women or which men do,
Glides forth in an innuendo,
Clothed in odds and ends of humor—
Herald of each paltry rumor.
From divorces down to dresses,
Women's frailties, men's excesses,
All which life presents of evil
Make for him a constant revel.
You 're his foe—for that he fears you,
And in absence blasts and sears you:
You 're his friend—for that he hates you,
First caresses, and then baits you,
Darting on the opportunity
When to do it with impunity:
You are neither—then he 'll flatter
Till he finds some trait for satire;
Hunts your weak point out, then shows it
Where it injures to disclose it,
In the mode that 's most invidious,
Adding every trait that 's hideous,
From the bile, whose blackening river
Rushes through his Stygian liver.

Then he thinks himself a lover:
Why I really can't discover
In his mind, age, face, or figure:
Viper-broth might give him vigor:
Let him keep the caldron steady,
He the venom has already.
For his faults, he has but *one*—
'Tis but envy, when all 's done.
He but pays the pain he suffers;
Clipping, like a pair of snuffers,
Lights which ought to burn the brighter
For this temporary blighter.
He 's the cancer of his species,
And will eat himself to pieces;
Plague personified, and famine;
Devil, whose sole delight is damning!

For his merits, would you know 'em?
Once he wrote a pretty Poem.

MY PARTNER.

W. MACKWORTH PRAED.

At Cheltenham, where one drinks one's fill
  Of folly and cold water,
I danced, last year, my first quadrille
  With old Sir Geoffrey's daughter.
Her cheek with summer's rose might vie,
  When summer's rose is newest;
Her eyes were blue as autumn's sky,
  When autumn's sky is bluest;
And well my heart might deem her one
  Of life's most precious flowers,
For half her thoughts were of its sun,
  And half were of its showers.

I spoke of novels:—"Vivian Gray"
  Was positively charming,
And "Almack's" infinitely gay,
  And "Frankenstein" alarming;

I said "De Vere" was chastely told,
  Thought well of "Herbert Lacy,"
Called Mr. Banim's sketches "bold,"
  And Lady Morgan's "racy;"
I vowed the last new thing of Hook's
  Was vastly entertaining;
And Laura said—"I dote on books,
  Because it's always raining!"

I talked of music's gorgeous fane,
  I raved about Rossini,
Hoped Ronzo would come back again,
  And criticized Paccini;
I wished the chorus singers dumb
  The trumpets more pacific,
And eulogized Brocard's *aplomb*
  And voted Paul "terrific."
What cared she for Medea's pride
  Or Desdemona's sorrow?
"Alas!" my beauteous listener sighed,
  "We *must* have storms to-morrow!"

I told her tales of other lands;
  Of ever-boiling fountains,
Of poisonous lakes, and barren sands,
  Vast forests, trackless mountains;
I painted bright Italian skies,
  I lauded Persian roses,
Coined similes for Spanish eyes,
  And jests for Indian noses;
I laughed at Lisbon's love of mass,
  And Vienna's dread of treason;
And Laura asked me where the glass
  Stood at Madrid last season.

I broached whate'er had gone its rounds,
  The week before, of scandal;
What made Sir Luke lay down his hounds,
  And Jane take up her Handel;
Why Julia walked upon the heath,
  With the pale moon above her;
Where Flora lost her false front teeth,
  And Anne her false lover;

How Lord de B. and Mrs. L.
  Had crossed the sea together;
My shuddering partner cried—"Oh, Ciel!
  How *could* they in such weather?"

Was she a blue?—I put my trust
  In strata, petals, gases;
A boudoir pedant?—I discussed
  The toga and the fasces;
A cockney-muse?—I mouthed a deal
  Of folly from Endymion:
A saint?—I praised the pious zeal
  Of Messrs. Way and Simeon;
A politician?—It was vain
  To quote the morning paper;
The horrid phantoms come again,
  Rain, hail, and snow, and vapor.

Flat flattery was my only chance,
  I acted deep devotion,
Found magic in her every glance,
  Grace in her every motion;
I wasted all a stripling's lore,
  Prayer, passion, folly, feeling;
And wildly looked upon the floor,
  And wildly on the ceiling;
I envied gloves upon her arm,
  And shawls upon her shoulder;
And when my worship was most warm,
  She "never found it colder."

I don't object to wealth or land·
  And she will have the giving
Of an extremely pretty hand,
  Some thousands, and a living.
She makes silk purses, broiders stools,
  Sings sweetly, dances finely,
Paints screens, subscribes to Sunday-schools,
  And sits a horse divinely.
But to be linked for life to her!—
  The desperate man who tried it,
Might marry a barometer,
  And hang himself beside it!

THE BELLE OF THE BALL.

W. MACKWORTH PRAED.

YEARS—years ago—ere yet my dreams
  Had been of being wise and witty;
Ere I had done with writing themes,
  Or yawn'd o'er this infernal Chitty;
Years, years ago, while all my joys
  Were in my fowling-piece and filly:
In short, while I was yet a boy,
  I fell in love with Laura Lilly.

I saw her at a country ball;
  There when the sound of flute and fiddle
Gave signal sweet in that old hall,
  Of hands across and down the middle,
Hers was the subtlest spell by far
  Of all that sets young hearts romancing:
She was our queen, our rose, our star;
  And when she danced—oh, heaven, her dancing!

Dark was her hair, her hand was white;
  Her voice was exquisitely tender,
Her eyes were full of liquid light;
  I never saw a waist so slender;
Her every look, her every smile,
  Shot right and left a score of arrows;
I thought 't was Venus from her isle,
  I wondered where she 'd left her sparrows.

She talk'd of politics or prayers;
  Of Southey's prose, or Wordsworth's sonnets;
Of daggers or of dancing bears,
  Of battles, or the last new bonnets;
By candle-light, at twelve o'clock,
  To me it matter'd not a tittle,
If those bright lips had quoted Locke,
  I might have thought they murmured Little.

Through sunny May, through sultry June,
  I loved her with a love eternal;
I spoke her praises to the moon,
  I wrote them for the Sunday Journal.

My mother laughed; I soon found out
  That ancient ladies have no feeling;
My father frown'd; but how should gout
  Find any happiness in kneeling?

She was the daughter of a dean,
  Rich, fat, and rather apoplectic;
She had one brother just thirteen,
  Whose color was extremely hectic;
Her grandmother, for many a year,
  Had fed the parish with her bounty;
Her second cousin was a peer,
  And lord-lieutenant of the county.

But titles and the three per cents,
  And mortgages, and great relations,
And India bonds, and tithes and rents,
  Oh! what are they to love's sensations?
Black eyes, fair forehead, clustering locks,
  Such wealth, such honors, Cupid chooses;
He cares as little for the stocks,
  As Baron Rothschild for the muses.

She sketch'd; the vale, the wood, the beach,
  Grew lovelier from her pencil's shading;
She botanized; I envied each
  Young blossom in her boudoir fading;
She warbled Handel; it was grand—
  She made the Catalina jealous;
She touch'd the organ; I could stand
  For hours and hours and blow the bellows.

She kept an album, too, at home,
  Well fill'd with all an album's glories;
Paintings of butterflies and Rome,
  Patterns for trimming, Persian stories;
Soft songs to Julia's cockatoo,
  Fierce odes to famine and to slaughter;
And autographs of Prince Laboo,
  And recipes of elder water.

And she was flatter'd, worship'd, bored,
  Her steps were watch'd, her dress was noted,

Her poodle dog was quite adored,
  Her sayings were extremely quoted.
She laugh'd, and every heart was glad,
  As if the taxes were abolish'd;
She frown'd, and every look was sad,
  As if the opera were demolishd.

She smil'd on many just for fun—
  I knew that there was nothing in it;
I was the first the only one
  Her heart thought of for a minute;
I knew it, for she told me so,
  In phrase which was divinely molded;
She wrote a charming hand, and oh!
  How sweetly all her notes were folded!

Our love was like most other loves—
  A little glow, a little shiver;
A rosebud and a pair of gloves,
  And "Fly Not Yet," upon the river;
Some jealousy of some one's heir,
  Some hopes of dying broken-hearted,
A miniature, a lock of hair,
  The usual vows—and then we parted.

We parted—months and years roll'd by;
  We met again for summers after;
Our parting was all sob and sigh—
  Our meeting was all mirth and laughter;
For in my heart's most secret cell,
  There had been many other lodgers;
And she was not the ball-room belle,
  But only Mrs.—Something—Rogers.

SORROWS OF WERTHER.

W. MAKEPEACE THACKERAY.

Werther had a love for Charlotte
  Such as words could never utter;
Would you know how first he met her?
  She was cutting bread and butter.

Charlotte was a married lady,
And a moral man was Werther,
And for all the wealth of Indies,
Would do nothing for to hurt her.

So he sighed and pined and ogled,
And his passion boiled and bubbled,
Till he blew his silly brains out,
And no more was by it troubled.

Charlotte, having seen his body
Borne before her on a shutter,
Like a well-conducted person,
Went on cutting bread and butter.

THE YANKEE VOLUNTEERS.

W. MAKEPEACE THACKERAY.

["A surgeon of the United States army says, that on inquiring of the Captain of his company, he found *that nine tenths* of the men had enlisted on account of some female difficulty."]—*Morning Paper.*

YE Yankee volunteers!
It makes my bosom bleed
When I your story read,
Though oft 'tis told one.
So—in both hemispheres
The woman are untrue,
And cruel in the New,
As in the Old one!

What—in this company
Of sixty sons of Mars,
Who march 'neath Stripes and Stars,
With fife and horn,
Nine tenths of all we see
Along the warlike line
Had but one cause to join
This Hope Folorn?

Deserters from the realm
Where tyrant Venus reigns,
You slipped her wicked chains,
Fled and out-ran her.
And now, with sword and helm,
Together banded are
Beneath the Stripe and Star-
embroidered banner!

And so it is with all
The warriors ranged in line,
With lace bedizened fine
And swords gold-hilted—
Yon lusty corporal,
Yon color-man who gripes
The flag of Stars and Stripes—
Has each been jilted?

Come, each man of this line,
The privates strong and tall,
"The pioneers and all,"
The fifer nimble—
Lieutenant and Ensign,
Captain with epaulets,
And Blacky there, who beats
The clanging cymbal—

O cymbal-beating black,
Tell us, as thou canst feel,
Was it some Lucy Neal
Who caused thy ruin?
O nimble fifing Jack,
And drummer making din
So deftly on the skin,
With thy rat-tattooing.

Confess, ye volunteers,
Lieutenant and Ensign,
And Captain of the line,
As bold as Roman—

Confess, ye grenadiers,
However strong and tall,
The Conqueror of you all
Is Woman, Woman!

No corselet is so proof,
But through it from her bow,
The shafts that she can throw
Will pierce and rankle.
No champion e'er so tough,
But 's in the struggle thrown,
And tripped and trodden down
By her slim ankle.

Thus, always it has ruled,
And when a woman smiled,
The strong man was a child,
The sage a noodle.
Alcides was befooled,
And silly Samson shorn,
Long, long ere you were born,
Poor Yankee Doodle!

COURTSHIP AND MATRIMONY.

A POEM, IN TWO CANTOS.

PUNCH.

CANTO THE FIRST.

COURTSHIP.

Fairest of earth! if thou wilt hear my vow,
Lo! at thy feet I swear to love thee ever;
And by this kiss upon thy radiant brow,
Promise affection which no time shall sever;
And love which e'er shall burn as bright as now,
To be extinguished—never, dearest, never!
Wilt thou that naughty, fluttering heart resign?
Catherine! my own sweet Kate! wilt thou be mine?

Thou shalt have pearls to deck thy raven hair—
  Thou shalt have all this world of ours can bring;
And we will live in solitude, nor care
  For aught save for each other. We will fling
Away all sorrow—Eden shall be there!
  And thou shalt be my queen, and I thy king!
Still coy, and still reluctant? Sweetheart say,
When shall we monarchs be? and which the day?

CANTO THE SECOND.

MATRIMONY.

Now Mrs. Pringle, once for all, I say
  I will not such extravagance allow!
Bills upon bills, and larger every day,
  Enough to drive a man to drink, I vow!
Bonnets, gloves, frippery and trash—nay, nay,
  Tears, Mrs. Pringle, will not gull me now—
I say I won't allow ten pounds a week;
I can't afford it; madam, do not speak!

In wedding you I thought I had a treasure;
  I find myself most miserably mistaken!
You rise at ten, then spend the day in pleasure;—
  In fact, my confidence is slightly shaken.
Ha! what's that uproar? This, ma'am, is my leisure;
  Sufficient noise the slumbering dead to waken!
I seek retirement, and I find—a riot;
Confound those children, but I'll make them quiet!

CONCERNING SISTERS-IN-LAW.

PUNCH.

I.

They looked so alike as they sat at their work,
(What a pity it is that one isn't a Turk!)
The same glances and smiles, the same habits and arts,
The same tastes, the same frocks, and (no doubt) the same hearts.

The same irresistible cut in their jibs,
The same little jokes, and the same little fibs—
That I thought the best way to get out of my pain
Was by—*heads* for Maria, and *woman* for Jane;
For hang *me* if it seemed it could matter a straw,
Which dear became wife, and which sister-in-law.

II.

But now, I will own, I feel rather inclined
To suspect I 've some reason to alter my mind;
And the doubt in my breast daily grows a more strong one,
That they 're not *quite* alike, and I 've taken the wrong one.
Jane is always so gentle, obliging, and cool;
Never calls me a monster—not even a fool;
All our little contentions, 'tis she makes them up,
And she knows how much sugar to put in my cup:—
Yes, I sometimes *have* wished—Heav'n forgive me the flaw!—
That my very dear wife was my sister-in-law.

III.

Oh, your sister-in-law, is a dangerous thing!
The daily comparisons, too, she will bring!
Wife—curl-papered, slip-shod, unwashed and undressed;
She—ringleted, booted, and "fixed in her best;"
Wife—sulky, or storming, or preaching, or prating;
She—merrily singing, or laughing, or chatting:
Then the innocent freedom her friendship allows
To the happy half-way between mother and spouse.
In short, if the Devil e'er needs a cat's-paw,
He can't find one more sure than a sister-in-law.

IV.

That no good upon earth can be had undiluted
Is a maxim experience has seldom refuted;
And preachers and poets have proved it is so
With abundance of tropes, more or less *apropos*.
Every light has its shade, every rose has its thorn,
The cup has its head-ache, its poppy the corn;
There 's a fly in the ointment, a spot on the sun—
In short, they 've used all illustrations—but one;
And have left it to me the most striking to draw—
Viz.: that none, without *wives*, can have *sisters-in-law*.

THE LOBSTERS.*

PUNCH.

As a young Lobster roamed about,
Itself and mother being out,
Their eyes at the same moment fell
On a boiled lobster's scarlet shell.
"Look," said the younger; "is it true
That we might wear so bright a hue?
No coral, if I trust mine eye,
Can with its startling brilliance vie;
While you and I must be content
A dingy aspect to present."
"Proud heedless fool," the parent cried;
"Know'st thou the penalty of pride?
The tawdry finery you wish,
Has ruined this unhappy fish.
The hue so much by you desired
By his destruction was acquired—
So be contented with your lot,
Nor seek to change by going to pot."

TO SONG-BIRDS ON A SUNDAY.

PUNCH.

Silence, all! ye winged choir;
Let not yon right reverend sire
Hear your happy symphony:
'Tis too good for such as he.

On the day of rest divine,
He poor townsfolk would confine
In their crowded streets and lanes,
Where they can not hear your strains.

All the week they drudge away,
Having but one holiday;
No more time for you, than that—
Unlike bishops, rich and fat.

* Appeared at the time of the Anti-popery excitement, produced by the titles of Cardinal Wiseman, etc.

Utter not your cheerful sounds,
Therefore, in the bishop's grounds;
Make him melody no more,
Who denies you to the poor.

Linnet, hist! and blackbird, hush!
Throstle, be a songless thrush;
Nightingale and lark, be mute;
Never sing to such a brute.

Robin, at the twilight dim,
Never let thine evening hymn,
Bird of red and ruthful breast,
Lend the bishop's Port a zest.

Soothe not, birds, his lonesome hours,
Keeping us from fields and flowers,
Who to pen us tries, instead,
'Mong the intramural dead.

Only let the raven croak
At him from the rotten oak;
Let the magpie and the jay
Chatter at him on his way.

And when he to rest has laid him,
  Let his ears the screech-owl harry;
And the night-jar serenade him
  With a proper charivari.

THE FIRST SENSIBLE VALENTINE.

(ONE OF THE MOST ASTONISHING FRUITS OF THE EMIGRATION MANIA.)

PUNCH.

LET other swains, upon the best cream-laid
  Or wire-wove note, their amorous strains indite;
Or, in despair, invoke the limner's aid
  To paint the sufferings they can not write:

Upon their page, transfixed with numerous darts,
  Let slender youths in agony expire;
Or, on one spit, let two pale pink calves' hearts
  Roast at some fierce imaginary fire.

Let Angelina there, as in a bower
  Of shrubs, unknown to Lindley, she reposes,
See her own Alfred to the old church tower
  Led on by Cupid, in a chain of roses;
Or let the wreath, when raised, a cage reveal,
  Wherein two doves their little bills entwine;
(A vile device, which always makes me feel
  Marriage would only add your bills to mine.)

For arts like these I've neither skill nor time;
  But if you'll seek the Diggings, dearest maid,
And share my fortune in that happier clime,
  Your berth is taken, and your passage paid.
For reading, lately, in my list of things,
  "Twelve dozen shirts! twelve dozen collars," too!
The horrid host of buttons and of strings
  Flashed on my spirit, and I thought—of you.

"Surely," I said, as in my chest I dived—
  That vast receptacle of all things known—
"To teach this truth my outfit was contrived,
  It is not good for man to be alone!"
Then fly with me! My bark is on the shore
  (Her mark A 1, her size eight hundred tons),
And though she's nearly full, can take some more
  Dry goods, by measurement—say Green and Sons.

Yes, fly with me! Had all our friends been blind,
  We might have married, and been happy *here;*
But since young married folks the means must find
  The eyes of stern society to cheer,
And satisfy its numerous demands,
  I think 'twill save us many a vain expense,
If on our wedding cards this Notice stands,
  "At Home, at Ballarat, just three months hence!"

A SCENE ON THE AUSTRIAN FRONTIER.

PUNCH.

"DEY must not pass!" was the warning cry of the Austrian sentinel
To one whose little knapsack bore the books he loved so well.
"They must not pass? Now, wherefore not?" the wond'ring tourist cried;
"No English book can pass mit me;" the sentinel replied.
The tourist laughed a scornful laugh; quoth he, "Indeed, I hope
There are few English books would please a Kaiser or a Pope;
But these are books in common use: plain truths and facts they tell—"
"Der Teufel! Den dey *most not* pass!" said the startled sentinel.

"This Handbook to North Germany, by worthy Mr. MURRAY,
Need scarcely put your government in such a mighty flurry;
If tourists' handbooks be proscribed, pray have you ever tried
To find a treasonable page in *Bradshaw's Railway Guide?*
This map, again, of Switzerland—nay, man, you need n't start or
Look black at such a little map, as if 't were Magna Charta;
I know it is the land of TELL, but, curb your idle fury—
We 've not the slightest hope, to-day, to find a TELL in your eye (Uri)."

"Sturmwetter!" said the sentinel, "Come! cease dis idle babbles!
Was ist dis oder book I see? Das Haus mit sieben Gabbles?
I nevvare heard of him bifor, ver mosh I wish I had,
For now Ich kann nicht let him pass, for fear he should be bad.
Das Haus of Commons it must be; Ja wohl! 'tis so, and den
Die Sieben Gabbles are de talk of your chief public men;
Potzmiekchen! it is dreadful books. Ja! Ja! I know him well;
Hoch Himmel! here he most not pass:" said the learned sentinel.

"Dis PLATO, too, I ver mosh fear, he will corrupt the land,
He has soch many long big words, Ich kann nicht onderstand."
"My friend," the tourist said, "I fear you 're really in the way to
Quite change the proverb, and be friends with neither Truth nor PLATO.

My books, 'tis true, are little worth, but they have served me long,
And I regard the greatness less than the nature of the wrong;
So, if the books must stay behind, I stay behind as well."
"Es ist mir nichts, mein lieber Freund," said the courteous sentinel.

ODE TO THE GREAT SEA-SERPENT ON HIS WONDERFUL REAPPEARANCE.

PUNCH.

FROM what abysses of the unfathom'd sea
  Turnest thou up, Great Serpent, now and then,
If we may venture to believe in thee,
  And affidavits of sea-faring men?

What whirlpool gulf to thee affords a home!
  Amid the unknown depths where dost thou dwell?
If—like the mermaid, with her glass and comb—
  Thou art not what the vulgar call a Sell.

Art thou, indeed, a serpent and no sham?
  Or, if no serpent, a prodigious eel,
An entity, though modified by flam,
  A basking shark, or monstrous kind of seal?

I'll think that thou a true Ophidian art;
  I can not say a reptile of the deep,
Because thou dost not play a reptile's part;
  Thou swimmest, it appears, and dost not creep.

The Captain was not WALKER but M'QUHÆ,
  I'll trust, by whom thou some time since wast seen;
And him who says he saw thee t'other day,
  I will not bid address the corps marine.

Sea-Serpent, art thou venomous or not?
  What sort of snake may be thy class and style?
That of Mud-Python, by APOLLO shot,
  And mentioned—rather often—by CARLYLE?

Or, art thou but a serpent of the mind?
  Doubts, though subdued, will oft recur again—
A serpent of the visionary kind,
  Proceeding from the grog-oppressed brain?

Art thou a giant adder, or huge asp,
  And hast thou got a rattle at thy tail?
If of the Boa species, couldst thou clasp
  Within thy fold, and suffocate, a whale?

How long art thou?—Some sixty feet, they say,
  And more—but how much more they do not know:
I fancy thou couldst reach across a bay
  From head to head, a dozen miles or so.

Scales hast thou got, of course—but what's thy weight?
  On either side 'tis said thou hast a fin,
A crest, too, on thy neck, deponents state,
  A saw-shaped ridge of flabby, dabby skin.

If I could clutch thee—in a giant's grip—
  Could I retain thee in that grasp sublime?
Wouldst thou not quickly through my fingers slip,
  Being all over glazed with fishy slime?

Hast thou a forked tongue—and dost thou hiss
  If ever thou art bored with Ocean's play?
And is it the correct hypothesis
  That thou of gills or lungs dost breathe by way?

What spines, or spikes, or claws, or nails, or fin,
  Or paddle, Ocean-Serpent, dost thou bear?
What kind of teeth show'st thou when thou dost grin?—
  A set that probably would make one stare.

What is thy diet? Canst thou gulp a shoal
  Of herrings? Or hast thou the gorge and room
To bolt fat porpoises and dolphins, whole,
  By dozens, e'en as oysters we consume?

Art thou alone, thou serpent, on the brine,
  The sole surviving member of thy race?
Is there no brother, sister, wife, of thine,
  But thou alone, afloat on Ocean's face?

If such a calculation may be made,
  Thine age at what a figure may we take?
When first the granite mountain-stones were laid,
  Wast thou not present there and then, old Snake?

What fossil Saurians in thy time have been?
  How many Mammoths crumbled into mold?
What geologic periods hast thou seen,
  Long as the tail thou doubtless canst unfold?

As a dead whale, but as a whale, though dead,
  Thy floating bulk a British crew did strike;
And, so far, none will question what they said,
  That thou unto a whale wast very like.

A flock of birds a record, rather loose,
  Describes as hovering o'er thy lengthy hull;
Among them, doubtless, there was many a Goose,
  And also several of the genus Gull.

THE FEAST OF VEGETABLES, AND THE FLOW OF WATER.

PUNCH.

New Year comes,—so let's be jolly;
  On the board the Turnip smokes,
While we sit beneath the holly,
  Eating Greens and passing jokes

How the Cauliflower is steaming,
  Sweetest flower that ever blows!
See, good old Sir Kidney, beaming,
  Shows his jovial famed red nose.

Here behold the reign of Plenty,—
  Help the Carrots, hand the Kail;
Roots how nice, and herbs how dainty,
  Well washed down with Adam's Ale!

Feed your fill,—untasted only
  Let the fragrant onion go;
Or, amid the revels lonely,
  Go not nigh the mistletoe!"

KINDRED QUACKS.

PUNCH.

I OVERHEARD two matrons grave, allied by close affinity
(The name of one was PHYSIC, and the other's was DIVINITY),
As they put their groans together, both so doleful and lugubrious:

Says PHYSIC, "To unload the heart of grief, ma'am, is salubrious:
Here am I, at my time of life, in this year of our deliverance;
My age gives me a right to look for some esteem and reverence.
But, ma'am, I feel it is too true what every body says to me,—
Too many of my children are a shame and a disgrace to me."

"Ah!" says DIVINITY, "my heart can suffer with another, ma'am;
I'm sure I can well understand your feelings as a mother, ma'am.
I've some, as well,—no doubt but what you're perfectly aware on't, ma'am,
Whose doings bring derision and discredit on their parent, ma'am."

"There are boys of mine," says PHYSIC, "ma'am, such silly fancies nourishing,
As curing gout and stomach-ache by pawing and by flourishing."

"Well," says DIVINITY, "I've those that teach that Heaven's beatitudes
Are to be earned by postures, genuflexions, bows, and attitudes."

"My good-for-nothing sons," says PHYSIC, "some have turned hydropathists,
Some taken up with mesmerism, or joined the homœopathists."

"Mine," says DIVINITY, "pursue a system of gimcrackery,
Called Puseyism, a pack of stuff, and quite as arrant quackery."

Says PHYSIC, "Mine have sleep-walkers, pretending through the hide of you,
To look, although their eyes are shut, and tell you what's inside of you."

"Ah!" says DIVINITY, "so mine, with quibbling and with caviling,
Would have you, ma'am, to blind yourself, to see the road to travel in."

"Mine," PHYSIC says, "have quite renounced their good old pills and potions, ma'am,
For doses of a billionth of a grain, and such wild notions, ma'am."

"So," says DIVINITY, "have mine left wholesome exhortation, ma'am,
For credence-tables, reredoses, rood-lofts, and maceration, ma'am."

"But hospitals," says PHYSIC, "my misguided boys are founding, ma'am."

"Well," says DIVINITY, "of mine, the chapels are abounding, ma'am."
"Mine are trifling with diseases, ma'am," says PHYSIC, "not attacking them."

"Mine," says DIVINITY, "instead of curing souls, are quacking them."

"Ah, ma'am," says PHYSIC, "I'm to blame, I fear, for these absurdities."

"That's my fear too," DIVINITY says; "ma'am, upon my word it is."

Says PHYSIC, "Fees, not science, have been far too much my wishes, ma'am."

"Truth," says DIVINITY, "I've loved much less than loaves and fishes, ma'am."

Says each to each, "We 're simpletons, or sad deceivers, some of
us;
And I am sure, ma'am, I don't know whatever will become of
us."

THE RAILWAY TRAVELER'S FAREWELL TO HIS FAMILY.

PUNCH.

'T WAS business call'd a Father to travel by the Rail;
His eye was calm, his hand was firm, although his cheek was pale.
He took his little boy and girl, and set them on his knee;
And their mother hung about his neck, and her tears flowed fast
and free.

I 'm going by the Rail, my dears—ELIZA, love, don't cry—
Now, kiss me both before I leave, and wish Papa good-by.
I hope I shall be back again, this afternoon, to tea,
And then, I hope, alive and well, that your Papa you 'll see.

I 'm going by the Rail, my dears, where the engines puff and hiss;
And ten to one the chances are that something goes amiss;
And in an instant, quick as thought—before you could cry "Ah!"
An accident occurs, and—say good-by to poor Papa!

Sometimes from scandalous neglect, my dears, the sleepers sink,
And then you have the carriages upset, as you may think.
The progress of the train, sometimes, a truck or coal-box checks,
And there 's a risk for poor Papa's, and every body's necks.

Or there may be a screw loose, a hook, or bolt, or pin—
Or else an ill-made tunnel may give way, and tumble in;
And in the wreck the passengers and poor Papa remain
Confined, till down upon them comes the next Excursion-train.

If a policeman 's careless, dears, or if not over-bright,
When he should show a red flag, it may be he shows a white;
Between two trains, in consequence, there 's presently a clash,
If poor Papa is only bruised, he 's lucky in the smash.

Points may be badly managed, as they were the other day,
Because a stingy Company for hands enough won't pay;
Over and over goes the train—the engine off the rail,
And poor Papa 's unable, when he 's found, to tell the tale.

And should your poor Papa escape, my darlings, with his life,
May he return on two legs, to his children and his wife—
With both his arms, my little dears, return your fond embrace,
And present to you, unalter'd, every feature of his face.

I hope I shall come back, my dears—but, mind, I am insured—
So, in case the worst may happen, you are so far all secured.
An action then will also lie for you and your Mamma—
And don't forget to bring it—on account of poor Papa.

A LETTER AND AN ANSWER.

PUNCH.

THE PRESBYTERS TO PALMERSTON.

The Plague has come among us,
Miserable sinners!
Fear and remorse have stung us,
Miserable sinners!
We ask the State to fix a day,
Whereon all men may fast and pray,
That Heaven will please to turn away
The Plague that works us sore dismay,
Miserable sinners!

PALMERSTON TO THE PRESBYTERS.

The Plague that comes among you,
Miserable sinners!
To effort hath it strung you?
Miserable sinners!
You ask that all should fast and pray;
Better all wake and work, I say;
Sloth and supineness put away,
That so the Plague may cease to slay;
Miserable sinners!

For Plagues, like other evils,
Miserable sinners!
Are God's and not the Devil's,
Miserable sinners!
Scourges they are, but in a hand
Which love and pity do command;
And when the heaviest stripes do fall,
'Tis where they're wanted most of all,
Miserable sinners!

Look round about your city,
Miserable sinners!
Arouse to shame and pity,
Miserable sinners!
Pray: but use brush and limewash pail;
Fast: but feed those for want who fail;
Bow down, gude town, to ask for grace,
But bow with cleaner hands and face,
Miserable sinners!

All Time God's Law hath spoken,
Miserable sinners!
That Law may not be broken,
Miserable sinners!
But he that breaks it must endure
The penalty which works the cure.
To us, for God's great laws transgressed,
Is doomsman Pestilence addressed,
Miserable sinners!

We can not juggle Heaven,
Miserable sinners!
With one day out of seven,
Miserable sinners!
Shall any force of fasts atone
For years of duty left undone?
How expiate with prayer or psalm,
Deaf ear, blind eye, and folded palm?
Miserable sinners!

Let us be up and stirring,
Miserable sinners!

'Mong ignorant and erring,
Miserable sinners!
Sloth and self-seeking from us cast,
Believing this the fittest fast,
For of all prayers prayed 'neath the sun
There is no prayer like work well done,
Miserable sinners!

PAPA TO HIS HEIR,

A FAST MINOR.

PUNCH.

My son, a father's warning heed;
I think my end is nigh:
And then, you dog, you will succeed
Unto my property.

But, seeing you are not, just yet,
Arrived at man's estate,
Before you full possession get,
You'll have a while to wait.

A large allowance I allot
You during that delay;
And I don't recommend you not
To throw it all away.

To such advice you'd ne'er attend;
You won't let prudence rule
Your courses; but, I know, will spend
Your money like a fool.

I do not ask you to eschew
The paths of vice and sin;
You'll do as all young boobies, who
Are left, as you say, tin.

You 'll sot, you 'll bet; and, being green.
At all that 's right you 'll joke;
Your life will be a constant scene
Of billiards and of smoke.

With bad companions you 'll consort,
With creatures vile and base,
Who 'll rob you; yours will be, in short.
The puppy's common case.

But oh, my son! although you must
Through this ordeal pass,
You will not be, I hope—I trust—
A wholly senseless ass.

Of course at prudence you will sneer,
On that theme I won't harp;
Be good, I won't say—that 's severe;
But be a little sharp.

All rascally associates shun
To bid you were too much,
But, oh! beware, my spooney son,
Beware one kind of such.

It asks no penetrative mind
To know these fellows: when
You meet them, you, unless you 're blind,
At once discern the men.

The turgid lip, the piggish eye,
The nose in form of hook,
The rings, the pins, you tell them by,
The vulgar flashy look.

Spend every sixpence, if you please,
But do not, I implore,
Oh! do not go, my son, to these
Vultures to borrow more.

Live at a foolish wicked rate,
  My hopeful, if you choose,
But don't your means anticipate
  Through bill-discounting Jews.

SELLING OFF AT THE OPERA HOUSE

A POETICAL CATALOGUE.

PUNCH.

Lot One, The well-known village, with bridge, and church, and green,
Of half a score *divertissements* the well-remembered scene,
Including six substantial planks, forming the eight-inch ridge
On which the happy peasantry came dancing down the bridge.
Lot Two, A Sheet of Thunder. Lot Three, A Box of Peas
Employed in sending storms of hail to rattle through the trees.
Lot Four, A Canvas Mossy Bank for Cupids to repose.
Lot Five, The old Stage Watering-pot, complete—except the nose.
Lot Six, The favorite Water-mill, used for *Amina's* dream,
Complete, with practicable wheel, and painted canvas stream.
Lots Seven to Twelve, Some sundries—A Pair of Sylphide's Wings;
Three dozen Druid's Dresses (one of them wanting strings).
Lots Thirteen, Fourteen, Fifteen—Three Services of Plate
In real *papier mâché*—all in a decent state;
One of these services includes—its value to increase—
A full dessert, each plate of fruit forming a single piece.
Lot Seventeen, The Gilded Cup, from which *Genarro* quaffed,
'Mid loud applause, night after night, *Lucrezia's* poisoned draught.
Lots Eighteen, Nineteen, Twenty, Three rich White Satin Skirts.
Lot Twenty-one, A set of six Swiss Peasants' Cotton Shirts.
Lot Twenty-two, The sheet that backed *Masaniello's* tent.
Lot Twenty-three, The Long White Wig—in wool—of *Bide-the-Bent.*
Lots Twenty-three to Forty, The Fish—Soles, Cod, and Dace—
For pelting the Vice-regal Guard in Naples' Market-place.
Lot Forty-one, Vesuvius, rather the worse for wear.
Lots Forty-two to Fifty, Priests' Leggings—at per pair.
Lot Fifty-one, The well-known Throne, with canopy and seat,
And plank in front, for courtiers to kneel at Sovereigns' feet.

Lot Fifty-two, A Royal Robe of Flannel, nearly white,
Warranted equal to Cashmere—upon the stage at night—
With handsome ermine collar thrown elegantly back;
The tails of twisted worsted—pale yellow, tipped with black.
Lots Fifty-three to Sixty, Some Jewellery rare—
The Crown of *Semiramide*—complete, with false back hair;
The Order worn by *Ferdinand*, when he proceeds to fling
His sword and medals at the feet of the astonished king.
Lot Sixty-one, The Bellows used in *Cinderella's* song.
Lot Sixty-two, A Document. Lot Sixty-three, A Gong.
Lots Sixty-four to Eighty, Of Wigs a large array,
Beginning at the Druids down to the present day.
Lot Eighty-one, The Bedstead on which *Amina* falls.
Lots Eighty-two to Ninety, Some sets of Outer Walls.
Lot Ninety-one, The Furniture of a Grand Ducal Room,
Including Chair and Table. Lot Ninety-two, A Tomb.
Lot Ninety-three, A set of Kilts. Lot Ninety-four, A Rill.
Lot Ninety-five, A Scroll, To form death-warrant, deed, or will.
Lot Ninety-six, An ample fall of best White Paper Snow.
Lot Ninety-seven, A Drinking-cup, brimmed with stout extra tow.
Lot Ninety-eight, A Set of Clouds, a Moon, to work on flat;
Water with practicable boat. Lot Ninety-nine, A Hat.
Lot Hundred, Massive Chandelier. Hundred and one, A Bower.
Hundred and two, A Canvas Grove. Hundred and three, A Tower.
Hundred and four, A Fountain. Hundred and five, Some Rocks.
Hundred and six, The Hood that hides the Prompter in his box.

WONDERS OF THE VICTORIAN AGE.

PUNCH.

Our gracious Queen—long may she fill her throne—
Has been to see Louis Napoleon.
The Majesty of England—bless her heart!—
Has cut her mutton with a Bonaparte;
And Cousin Germans have survived the view
Of Albert taking luncheon at St. Cloud.

In our young days we little thought to see
Such legs stretched under such mahogany;

That British Royalty would ever share
At a French Palace, French Imperial fare:
Nor eat—as we should have believed at school—
The croaking tenant of the marshy pool.
At the *Trois Frères* we had not feasted then,
As we have since, and hope to do again.

This great event of course could not take place
Without fit prodigies for such a case;
The brazen pig-tail of King George the Third
Thrice with a horizontal motion stirr'd,
Then rose on end, and stood so all day long,
Amid the cheers of an admiring throng.
In every lawyer's office Eldon shed
From plaster nose three heavy drops of red.
Each Statue, too, of Pitt turn'd up the point
Of its proboscis—was that out of joint?
While Charles James Fox's grinn'd from ear to ear,
And Peel's emitted frequent cries of "Hear!"

TO THE PORTRAIT OF "A GENTLEMAN,"

IN THE ATHENÆUM GALLERY.

OLIVER WENDELL HOLMES.

It may be so—perhaps thou hast
A warm and loving heart;
I will not blame thee for thy face,
Poor devil as thou art.

That thing, thou fondly deem'st a nose,
Unsightly though it be,—
In spite of all the cold world's scorn,
It may be much to thee.

Those eyes,—among thine elder friends
Perhaps they pass for blue;—
No matter,—if a man can see,
What more have eyes to do?

Thy mouth—that fissure in thy face
By something like a chin,—
May be a very useful place
To put thy victual in.

I know thou hast a wife at home,
I know thou hast a child,
By that subdued, domestic smile
Upon thy features mild.

That wife sits fearless by thy side,
That cherub on thy knee;
They do not shudder at thy looks,
They do not shrink from thee.

Above thy mantel is a hook,—
A portrait once was there;
It was thine only ornament,—
Alas! that hook is bare.

She begged thee not to let it go,
She begged thee all in vain:
She wept,—and breathed a trembling prayer
To meet it safe again.

It was a bitter sight to see
That picture torn away;
It was a solemn thought to think
What all her friends would say!

And often in her calmer hours,
And in her happy dreams,
Upon its long-deserted hook
The absent portrait seems.

Thy wretched infant turns his head
In melancholy wise,
And looks to meet the placid stare
Of those unbending eyes.

I never saw thee, lovely one,—
Perchance I never may;
It is not often that we cross
Such people in our way;

But if we meet in distant years,
Or on some foreign shore,
Sure I can take my Bible oath
I 've seen that face before.

MY AUNT.

OLIVER WENDELL HOLMES.

My aunt! my dear unmarried aunt!
Long years have o'er her flown;
Yet still she strains the aching clasp
That binds her virgin zone;
I know it hurts her—though she looks
As cheerful as she can;
Her waist is ampler than her life,
For life is but a span.

My aunt! my poor deluded aunt!
Her hair is almost gray;
Why will she train that winter curl
In such a spring-like way?
How can she lay her glasses down,
And say she reads as well,
When, through a double convex lens,
She just makes out to spell?

Her father—grandpapa! forgive
This erring lip its smiles—
Vowed she should make the finest girl
Within a hundred miles;
He sent her to a stylish school;
'T was in her thirteenth June;
And with her, as the rules required,
"Two towels and a spoon."

They braced my aunt against a board,
To make her straight and tall;
They laced her up, they starved her down,
To make her light and small.
They pinched her feet, they singed her hair,
They screwed it up with pins;—
O never mortal suffered more
In penance for her sins.

So, when my precious aunt was done,
My grandsire brought her back;
(By daylight, lest some rabid youth
Might follow on the track;)
"Ah!" said my grandsire, as he shook
Some powder in his pan,
"What could this lovely creature do
Against a desperate man!"

Alas! nor chariot, nor barouche,
Nor bandit cavalcade,
Tore from the trembling father's arms
His all-accomplished maid.
For her how happy had it been!
And heaven had spared to me
To see one sad, ungathered rose
On my ancestral tree.

COMIC MISERIES.

JOHN G. SAXE.

My dear young friend, whose shining wit
Sets all the room a-blaze,
Don't think yourself a "happy dog,"
For all your merry ways;
But learn to wear a sober phiz,
Be stupid, if you can,
It's such a very serious thing
To be a funny man!

You 're at an evening party, with
  A group of pleasant folks,—
You venture quietly to crack
  The least of little jokes,—
A lady does n't catch the point,
  And begs you to explain—
Alas for one that drops a jest
  And takes it up again!

You 're talking deep philosophy
  With very special force,
To edify a clergyman
  With suitable discourse,—
You think you 've got him—when he calls
  A friend across the way,
And begs you 'll say that funny thing
  You said the other day!

You drop a pretty *jeu-de-mot*
  Into a neighbor's ears,
Who likes to give you credit for
  The clever thing he hears,
And so he hawks your jest about,
  The old authentic one,
Just breaking off the point of it,
  And leaving out the pun!

By sudden change in politics,
  Or sadder change in Polly,
You, lose your love, or loaves, and fall
  A prey to melancholy,
While every body marvels why
  Your mirth is under ban,—
They think your very grief "a joke,"
  You 're such a funny man!

You follow up a stylish card
  That bids you come and dine,
And bring along your freshest wit
  (To pay for musty wine),

You 're looking very dismal, when
  My lady bounces in,
And wonders what you 're thinking of,
  And why you don't begin!

You 're telling to a knot of friends
  A fancy-tale of woes
That cloud your matrimonial sky,
  And banish all repose—
A solemn lady overhears
  The story of your strife,
And tells the town the pleasant news:
  You quarrel with your wife!

My dear young friend, whose shining wit
  Sets all the room a-blaze,
Don't think yourself "a happy dog,"
  For all your merry ways;
But learn to wear a sober phiz,
  Be stupid, if you can,
It 's such a very serious thing
  To be a funny man!

IDÉES NAPOLÉONIENNES.

WILLIAM AYTOUN.

The impossibility of translating this now well-known expression (imperfectly rendered in a companion-work, "Ideas of Napoleonism"), will excuse the title and burden of the present ballad being left in the original French.—TRANSLATOR.

Come, listen all who wish to learn
  How nations should be ruled,
From one who from his youth has been
  In such-like matters school'd;
From one who knows the art to please,
  Improve and govern men—
Eh bien! Ecoutez, aux Idées,
  Napoléoniennes!

To keep the mind intently fixed
  On number One alone—

To look to no one's interest,
  But push along your own,
Without the slightest reference
  To how, or what, or when—
*Eh bien! c'est la première Idée
  Napoléonienne.*

To make a friend, and use him well,
  By which, of course, I mean
To use him up—until he 's drain'd
  Completely dry and clean
Of all that makes him useful, and
  To kick him over then
Without remorse—*c'est une Idée
  Napoléonienne.*

To sneak into a good man's house
  With sham credentials penn'd—
To sneak into his heart and trust,
  And seem his children's friend—
To learn his secrets, find out where
  He keeps his keys—and then
To bone his spoons—*c'est une Idée
  Napoléonienne.*

To gain your point in view—to wade
  Through dirt, and slime, and blood—
To stoop to pick up what you want
  Through any depth of mud.
But always in the fire to thrust
  Some helpless cat's-paw, when
Your chestnuts burn—*c'est une Idée
  Napoléonienne.*

To clutch and keep the lion's share—
  To kill or drive away
The wolves, that you upon the lambs
  May, unmolested, prey—
To keep a gang of jackals fierce
  To guard and stock your den,
While you lie down—*c'est une Idée
  Napoléonienne.*

To bribe the base, to crush the good,
  And bring them to their knees—
To stick at nothing, or to stick
  At what or whom you please—
To stoop, to lie, to brag, to swear,
  Forswear, and swear again—
To rise—*Ah! voià des Idées*
  Napoléoniennes.

THE LAY OF THE LOVER'S FRIEND.

WILLIAM AYTOUN.

AIR—"The days we went a-gipsying."

I WOULD all womankind were dead,
  Or banished o'er the sea;
For they have been a bitter plague
  These last six weeks to me:
It is not that I'm touched myself,
  For that I do not fear;
No female face hath shown me grace
  For many a bygone year.
    But 'tis the most infernal bore,
      Of all the bores I know,
    To have a friend who's lost his heart
      A short time ago.

Whene'er we steam it to Blackwall,
  Or down to Greenwich run,
To quaff the pleasant cider cup,
  And feed on fish and fun;
Or climb the slopes of Richmond Hill,
  To catch a breath of air:
Then, for my sins, he straight begins
  To rave about his fair.
    Oh, 'tis the most tremendous bore,
  Of all the bores I know,
    To have a friend who's lost his heart
  A short time ago

In vain you pour into his ear
  Your own confiding grief;
In vain you claim his sympathy,
  In vain you ask relief;
In vain you try to rouse him by
  Joke, repartee, or quiz;
His sole reply 's a burning sigh,
  And "What a mind it is!"
    O Lord! it is the greatest bore,
      Of all the bores I know,
    To have a friend who 's lost his heart
      A short time ago.

I 've heard her thoroughly described
  A hundred times, I 'm sure;
And all the while I 've tried to smile,
  And patiently endure;
He waxes strong upon his pangs,
  And potters o'er his grog;
And still I say, in a playful way—
  "Why you 're a lucky dog!"
    But oh! it is the heaviest bore,
      Of all the bores I know,
    To have a friend who 's lost his heart
      A short time ago.

I really wish he 'd do like me
  When I was young and strong;
I formed a passion every week,
  But never kept it long.
But he has not the sportive mood
  That always rescued me,
And so I would all women could
  Be banished o'er the sea.
    For 'tis the most egregious bore,
      Of all the bores I know,
    To have a friend who 's lost his heart
      A short time ago.

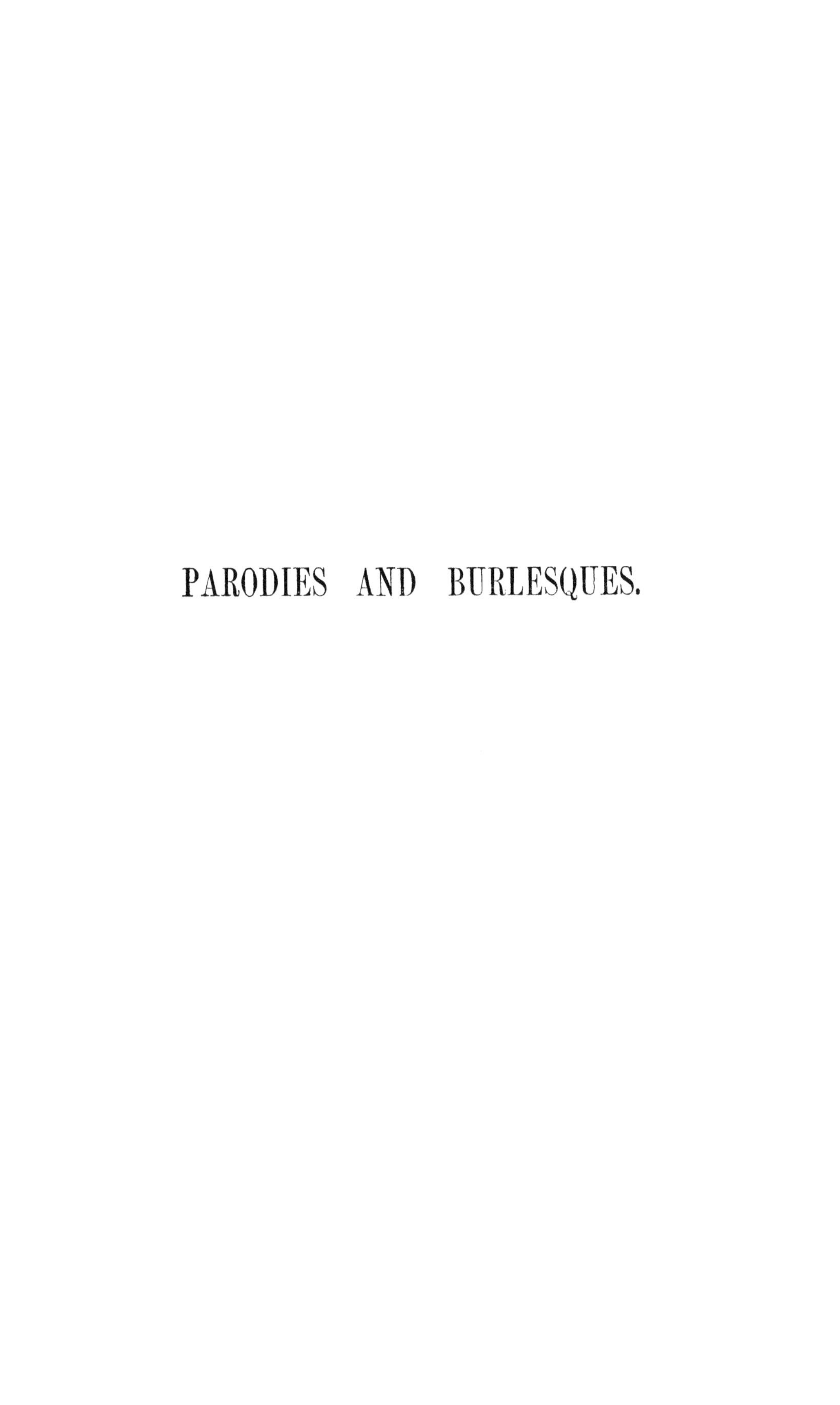

PARODIES AND BURLESQUES.

PARODIES AND BURLESQUES.

WINE.

JOHN GAY.

Nulla placere diu, nec vivere carmina possunt,
Quæ scribuntur aquæ potoribus. Hor.

Of happiness terrestrial, and the source
Whence human pleasures flow, sing, heavenly Muse!
Of sparkling juices, of the enlivening grape,
Whose quickening taste adds vigor to the soul,
Whose sovereign power revives decaying nature,
And thaws the frozen blood of hoary Age,
A kindly warmth diffusing;—youthful fires
Gild his dim eyes, and paint with ruddy hue
His wrinkled visage, ghastly wan before:
Cordial restorative to mortal man,
With copious hand by bounteous gods bestow'd!
Bacchus divine! aid my adventurous song,
"That with no middle flight intends to soar:"
Inspir'd sublime, on Pegasean wing,
By thee upborne, I draw Miltonic air.
When fumy vapors clog our loaded brows
With furrow'd frowns, when stupid downcast eyes,
The external symptoms of remorse within,
Express our grief, or when in sullen dumps,
With head incumbent on expanded palm,
Moping we sit, in silent sorrow drown'd;
Whether inveigling Hymen has trepann'd
The unwary youth, and tied the gordian knot
Of jangling wedlock not to be dissolv'd;
Worried all day by loud Xantippe's din,
Who fails not to exalt him to the stars,
And fix him there among the branched crew

(Taurus, and Aries, and Capricorn,
The greatest monsters of the Zodiac),
Or for the loss of anxious worldly pelf,
Or Celia's scornful slights, and cold disdain,
Which check'd his amorous flame with coy repulse,
The worst events that mortals can befall;
By cares depress'd, in pensive hippish mood,
With slowest pace the tedious minutes roll,
Thy charming sight, but much more charming gust,
New life incites, and warms our chilly blood.
Straight with pert looks we raise our drooping fronts,
And pour in crystal pure thy purer juice;—
With cheerful countenance and steady hand
Raise it lip-high, then fix the spacious rim
To the expecting mouth:—with grateful taste
The ebbing wine glides swiftly o'er the tongue;
The circling blood with quicker motion flies:
Such is thy powerful influence, thou straight
Dispell'st those clouds that, lowering dark, eclips'd
The whilom glories of the gladsome face;—
While dimpled cheeks, and sparkling rolling eyes,
Thy cheering virtues, and thy worth proclaim.
So mists and exhalations that arise
From "hills or steamy lake, dusky or gray,"
Prevail, till Phœbus sheds Titanian rays,
And paints their fleecy skirts with shining gold;
Unable to resist, the foggy damps,
That vail'd the surface of the verdant fields,
At the god's penetrating beams disperse!
The earth again in former beauty smiles,
In gaudiest livery drest, all gay and clear.
When disappointed Strephon meets repulse,
Scoff'd at, despis'd, in melancholic mood
Joyless he wastes in sighs the lazy hours,
Till reinforc'd by thy most potent aid
He storms the breach, and wins the beauteous fort.
To pay thee homage, and receive thy blessing,
The British seaman quits his native shore,
And ventures through the trackless, deep abyss,
Plowing the ocean, while the upheav'd oak,
"With beaked prow, rides tilting o'er the waves;"
Shock'd by tempestuous jarring winds, she rolls

In dangers imminent, till she arrives
At those blest climes thou favor'st with thy presence.
Whether at Lusitania's sultry coast,
Or lofty Teneriffe, Palma, Ferro,
Provence, or at the Celtiberian shores,
With gazing pleasure and astonishment,
At Paradise (seat of our ancient sire)
He thinks himself arrived: the purple grapes,
In largest clusters pendent, grace the vines
Innumerous: in fields grotesque and wild,
They with implicit curls the oak entwine,
And load with fruit divine his spreading boughs:
Sight most delicious! not an irksome thought,
Or of left native isle, or absent friends,
Or dearest wife, or tender sucking babe,
His kindly treacherous memory now presents;
The jovial god has left no room for cares.
Celestial Liquor! thou that didst inspire
Maro and Flaccus, and the Grecian bard,
With lofty numbers, and heroic strains
Unparallel'd, with eloquence profound,
And arguments convictive, didst enforce
Fam'd Tully, and Demosthenes renown'd;
Ennius, first fam'd in Latin song, in vain
Drew Heliconian streams, ungrateful whet
To jaded Muse, and oft with vain attempt,
Heroic acts, in flagging numbers dull,
With pains essay'd; but, abject still and low,
His unrecruited Muse could never reach
The mighty theme, till, from the purple fount
Of bright Lenæan sire, her barren drought
He quench'd, and with inspiring nectarous juice
Her drooping spirits cheer'd:—aloft she towers,
Borne on stiff pennons, and of war's alarms,
And trophies won, in loftiest numbers sings.
'Tis thou the hero's breast to martial acts,
And resolution bold, and ardor brave,
Excit'st: thou check'st inglorious lolling ease,
And sluggish minds with generous fires inflam'st.
O thou! that first my quickened soul didst warm,
Still with thy aid assist me, that thy praise,
Thy universal sway o'er all the world,

In everlasting numbers, like the theme,
I may record, and sing thy matchless worth.
Had the Oxonian bard thy praise rehears'd,
His Muse had yet retain'd her wonted height;
Such as of late o'er Blenheim's field she soar'd
Aerial; now in Ariconian bogs
She lies inglorious, floundering, like her theme,
Languid and faint, and on damp wing, immerg'd
In acid juice, in vain attempts to rise.
With what sublimest joy from noisy town,
At rural seat, Lucretius retir'd:
Flaccus, untainted by perplexing cares,
Where the white poplar and the lofty pine
Join neighboring boughs, sweet hospitable shade,
Creating, from Phœbean rays secure,
A cool retreat, with few well-chosen friends,
On flowery mead recumbent, spent the hours
In mirth innocuous, and alternate verse!
With roses interwoven, poplar wreaths,
Their temples bind, dress of sylvestrian gods!
Choicest nectarean juice crown'd largest bowls,
And overlook'd the brim, alluring sight,
Of fragrant scent, attractive, taste divine!
Whether from Formian grape depressed, Falern,
Or Setin, Massic, Gauran, or Sabine,
Lesbian, or Cœcuban, the cheering bowl
Mov'd briskly round, and spurr'd their heighten'd wit
To sing Mecæna's praise, their patrôn kind.
But we not as our pristine sires repair
To umbrageous grot or vale; but when the sun
Faintly from western skies his rays oblique
Darts sloping, and to Thetis' wat'ry lap
Hastens in prone career, with friends select
Swiftly we hie to Devil,* young or old,
Jocund and boon; where at the entrance stands
A stripling, who with scrapes and humil cringe
Greets us in winning speech, and accent bland:
With lightest bound, and safe unerring step,
He skips before, and nimbly climbs the stairs.
Melampus thus, panting with lolling tongue,
And wagging tail, gambols and frisks before

* The Devil Tavern, Temple Bar.

His sequent lord, from pensive walk return'd,
Whether in shady wood or pasture green,
And waits his coming at the well-known gate.
Nigh to the stairs' ascent, in regal port,
Sits a majestic dame, whose looks denounce
Command and sovereignty: with haughty air,
And studied mien, in semicircular throne
Enclos'd, she deals around her dread commands;
Behind her (dazzling sight!) in order rang'd,
Pile above pile, crystalline vessels shine:
Attendant slaves with eager strides advance,
And, after homage paid, bawl out aloud
Words unintelligible, noise confus'd:
She knows the jargon sounds, and straight describes,
In characters mysterious, words obscure:
More legible are algebraic signs,
Or mystic figures by magicians drawn,
When they invoke the infernal spirit's aid.
  Drive hence the rude and barbarous dissonance
Of savage Thracians and Croatian boors;
The loud Centaurian broils with Lapithæ
Sound harsh, and grating to Lenæan god;
Chase brutal feuds of Belgian skippers hence
(Amid their cups whose innate temper 's shown),
In clumsy fist wielding scymetrian knife,
Who slash each other's eyes, and blubber'd face,
Profaning Bacchanalian solemn rites:
Music's harmonious numbers better suit
His festivals, from instruments or voice,
Or Gasperani's hand the trembling string
Should touch; or from the dulcet Tuscan dames,
Or warbling Toft's far more melodious tongue,
Sweet symphonies should flow: the Delian god
For airy Bacchus is associate meet.
  The stair's ascent now gain'd, our guide unbars
The door of spacious room, and creaking chairs
(To ear offensive) round the table sets.
We sit; when thus his florid speech begins:
"Name, sirs! the wine that most invites your taste;
Champaign, or Burgundy, or Florence pure,
Or Hock antique, or Lisbon new or old,
Bourdeaux, or neat French white, or Alicant."

For Bourdeaux we with voice unanimous
Declare, (such sympathy's in boon compeers).
He quits the room alert, but soon returns;
One hand capacious glistering vessels bears
Resplendent, the other, with a grasp secure,
A bottle (mighty charge!) upstaid, full fraught
With goodly wine. He, with extended hand
Rais'd high, pours forth the sanguine frothy juice,
O'erspread with bubbles, dissipated soon:
We straight to arms repair, experienc'd chiefs:
Now glasses clash with glasses (charming sound!)
And glorious Anna's health, the first, the best,
Crowns the full glass; at her inspiring name
The sprightly wine results, and seems to smile:
With hearty zeal and wish unanimous,
Her health we drink, and in her health our own.
  A pause ensues: and now with grateful chat
We improve the interval, and joyous mirth
Engages our rais'd souls; pat repartee,
Or witty joke, our airy senses moves
To pleasant laughter; straight the echoing room
With universal peals and shouts resounds.
  The royal Dane, blest consort of the Queen,
Next crowns the ruby'd nectar, all whose bliss
In Anna's plac'd: with sympathetic flame,
And mutual endearments, all her joys,
Like to the kind turtle's pure untainted love,
Center in him, who shares the grateful hearts
Of loyal subjects, with his sovereign queen;
For by his prudent care united shores
Were sav'd from hostile fleets' invasion dire.
  The hero Marlborough next, whose vast exploits
Fame's clarion sounds; fresh laurels, triumphs new
We wish, like those he won at Hockstet's field.
  Next Devonshire illustrious, who from race
Of noblest patriots sprang, whose worthy soul
Is with each fair and virtuous gift adorn'd,
That shone in his most worthy ancestors;
For then distinct in separate breasts were seen
Virtues distinct, but all in him unite.
  Prudent Godolphin, of the nation's weal
Frugal, but free and generous of his own,

Next crowns the bowl; with faithful Sunderland,
And Halifax, the Muses' darling son,
In whom conspicuous, with full luster, shine
The surest judgment and the brightest wit,
Himself Mecænas and a Flaccus too;
And all the worthies of the British realm,
In order rang'd succeed; such healths as tinge
The dulcet wine with a more charming gust.
Now each his mistress toasts, by whose bright eye
He 's fired; Cosmelia fair, or Dulcibell',
Or Sylvia, comely black, with jetty eyes
Piercing, or airy Celia, sprightly maid!—
Insensibly thus flow unnumber'd hours;
Glass succeeds glass, till the Dircean god
Shines in our eyes, and with his fulgent rays
Enlightens our glad looks with lovely dye;
All blithe and jolly, that like Arthur's knights
Of Rotund Table, fam'd in old records,
Now most we seem'd—such is the power of Wine!
Thus we the winged hours in harmless mirth
And joys unsullied pass, till humid Night
Has half her race perform'd; now all abroad
Is hush'd and silent, nor the rumbling noise
Of coach, or cart, or smoky link-boy's call,
Is heard—but universal silence reigns;
When we in merry plight, airy and gay,
Surpris'd to find the hours so swiftly fly,
With hasty knock, or twang of pendant cord,
Alarm the drowsy youth from slumbering nod:
Startled he flies, and stumbles o'er the stairs
Erroneous, and with busy knuckles plies
His yet clung eyelids, and with staggering reel
Enters confus'd, and muttering asks our wills;
When we with liberal hand the score discharge,
And homeward each his course with steady step
Unerring steers, of cares and coin bereft.

ODE ON SCIENCE.

DEAN SWIFT.

O, HEAVENLY born! in deepest dells
If fairer science ever dwells
   Beneath the mossy cave;
Indulge the verdure of the woods,
With azure beauty gild the floods,
   And flowery carpets lave.

For, Melancholy ever reigns
Delighted in the sylvan scenes
   With scientific light
While Dian, huntress of the vales,
Seeks lulling sounds and fanning gales,
   Though wrapt from mortal sight.

Yet, goddess, yet the way explore
With magic rites and heathen lore
   Obstructed and depress'd;
Till Wisdom give the sacred Nine,
Untaught, not uninspired, to shine,
   By Reason's power redress'd.

When Solon and Lycurgus taught
To moralize the human thought
   Of mad opinion's maze,
To erring zeal they gave new laws,
Thy charms, O Liberty, the cause,
   That blends congenial rays.

Bid bright Astræa gild the morn,
Or bid a hundred suns be born,
   To hecatomb the year;
Without thy aid, in vain the poles,
In vain the zodiac system rolls,
   In vain the lunar sphere.

Come, fairest princess of the throng,
Bring sweet philosophy along,
   In metaphysic dreams:

While raptured bards no more behold
A vernal age of purer gold,
  In Heliconian streams.

Drive thraldom with malignant hand,
To curse some other destined land,
  By Folly led astray:
Ierne bear on azure wing;
Energic let her soar, and sing
  Thy universal sway.

So when Amphion bade the lyre
To more majestic sound aspire,
  Behold the mad'ning throng,
In wonder and oblivion drowned,
To sculpture turned by magic sound,
  And petrifying song.

A LOVE SONG,

IN THE MODERN TASTE.

DEAN SWIFT.

Fluttering spread thy purple pinions
  Gentle Cupid, o'er my heart:
I a slave in thy dominions;
  Nature must give way to art.

Mild Arcadians, ever blooming,
  Nightly nodding o'er your flocks,
See my weary days consuming
  All beneath yon flowery rocks.

Thus the Cyprian goddess weeping
  Mourned Adonis, darling youth;
Him the boar, in silence creeping,
  Gored with unrelenting tooth.

Cynthia, tune harmonious numbers;
  Fair Discretion, string the lyre:
Soothe my ever-waking slumbers:
  Bright Apollo, lend thy choir.

Gloomy Pluto, king of terrors,
  Arm'd in adamantine chains,
Lead me to the crystal mirrors,
  Watering soft Elysian plains.

Mournful cypress, verdant willow,
  Gilding my Aurelia's brows,
Morpheus, hovering o'er my pillow,
  Hear me pay my dying vows.

Melancholy smooth Meander,
  Swiftly purling in a round,
On thy margin lovers wander,
  With thy flowery chaplets crown'd.

Thus when Philomela drooping,
  Softly seeks her silent mate,
See the bird of Juno stooping;
  Melody resigns to fate.

BAUCIS AND PHILEMON.

ON THE EVER-LAMENTED LOSS OF THE TWO YEW-TREES IN THE PARISH OF CHILTHORNE, SOMERSET. IMITATED FROM THE EIGHTH BOOK OF OVID.

DEAN SWIFT.

In ancient time, as story tells,
The saints would often leave their cells,
And stroll about, but hide their quality,
To try good people's hospitality.
  It happen'd on a winter night,
As authors of the legend write,
Two brother hermits, saints by trade,
Taking their tour in masquerade,
Disguised in tatter'd habits, went
To a small village down in Kent;
Where, in the strollers' canting strain,
They begg'd from door to door in vain,
Tried every tone might pity win;
But not a soul would let them in.

Our wandering saints, in woeful state,
Treated at this ungodly rate,
Having through all the village past,
To a small cottage came at last
Where dwelt a good old honest ye'man,
Call'd in the neighborhood Philemon;
Who kindly did these saints invite
In his poor hut to pass the night;
And then the hospitable sire
Bid Goody Baucis mend the fire;
While he from out the chimney took
A flitch of bacon off the hook,
And freely from the fattest side
Cut out large slices to be fried;
Then stepp'd aside to fetch them drink,
Fill'd a large jug up to the brink,
And saw it fairly twice go round;
Yet (what was wonderful) they found
'T was still replenish'd to the top,
As if they ne'er had touch'd a drop.
The good old couple were amazed,
And often on each other gazed;
For both were frighten'd to the heart,
And just began to cry, "What ar't!"
Then softly turn'd aside, to view
Whether the lights were burning blue.
The gentle pilgrims, soon aware on't,
Told them their calling and their errand:
"Good folks, you need not be afraid,
We are but saints," the hermits said;
"No hurt shall come to you or yours:
But for that pack of churlish boors,
Not fit to live on Christian ground,
They and their houses shall be drown'd;
While you shall see your cottage rise,
And grow a church before your eyes."
They scarce had spoke, when fair and soft,
The roof began to mount aloft;
Aloft rose every beam and rafter;
The heavy wall climb'd slowly after.
The chimney widen'd, and grew higher,
Became a steeple with a spire.

The kettle to the top was hoist,
And there stood fasten'd to a joist,
But with the upside down, to show
Its inclination for below:
In vain; for a superior force
Applied at bottom stops its course:
Doom'd ever in suspense to dwell,
'Tis now no kettle, but a bell.
A wooden jack, which had almost
Lost by disuse the art to roast,
A sudden alteration feels,
Increased by new intestine wheels;
And, what exalts the wonder more,
The number made the motion slower.
The flier, though it had leaden feet,
Turn'd round so quick you scarce could see't;
But, slacken'd by some secret power,
Now hardly moves an inch an hour.
The jack and chimney, near allied,
Had never left each other's side;
The chimney to a steeple grown,
The jack would not be left alone;
But, up against the steeple rear'd,
Became a clock, and still adhered;
And still its love to household cares,
By a shrill voice at noon, declares,
Warning the cook-maid not to burn
That roast meat, which it can not turn.
The groaning-chair began to crawl,
Like a huge snail, along the wall;
There stuck aloft in public view,
And with small change, a pulpit grew.
The porringers, that in a row
Hung high, and made a glittering show,
To a less noble substance changed,
Were now but leathern buckets ranged.
The ballads, pasted on the wall,
Of Joan of France, and English Moll,
Fair Rosamond, and Robin Hood,
The little Children in the Wood,
Now seem'd to look abundance better,
Improved in picture, size, and letter:

And, high in order placed, describe
The heraldry of every tribe.
A bedstead of the antique mode,
Compact of timber many a load,
Such as our ancestors did use,
Was metamorphosed into pews;
Which still their ancient nature keep
By lodging folks disposed to sleep.
The cottage, by such feats as these,
Grown to a church by just degrees,
The hermits then desired their host
To ask for what he fancied most.
Philemon, having paused a while,
Return'd them thanks in homely style;
Then said, "My house is grown so fine,
Methinks, I still would call it mine.
I 'm old, and fain would live at ease;
Make me the parson if you please."
He spoke, and presently he feels
His grazier's coat fall down his heels:
He sees, yet hardly can believe,
About each arm a pudding sleeve;
His waistcoat to a cassock grew,
And both assumed a sable hue;
But, being old, continued just
As threadbare, and as full of dust.
His talk was now of tithes and dues:
He smoked his pipe, and read the news;
Knew how to preach old sermons next,
Vamp'd in the preface and the text;
At christenings well could act his part,
And had the service all by heart;
Wish'd women might have children fast,
And thought whose sow had farrow'd last;
Against dissenters would repine,
And stood up firm for "right divine;"
Found his head fill'd with many a system;
But classic authors—he ne'er miss'd 'em.
Thus having furbish'd up a parson,
Dame Baucis next they play'd their farce on.
Instead of homespun coifs, were seen
Good pinners edged with colberteen;

Her petticoat transform'd apace,
Became black satin, flounced with lace.
"Plain Goody" would no longer down,
'T was "Madam," in her grogram gown.
Philemon was in great surprise,
And hardly could believe his eyes.
Amazed to see her look so prim,
And she admired as much at him.
Thus happy in their change of life,
Were several years this man and wife:
When on a day, which proved their last,
Discoursing o'er old stories past,
They went by chance, amid their talk,
To the church-yard to take a walk;
When Baucis hastily cried out,
"My dear, I see your forehead sprout!"—
"Sprout," quoth the man; "what's this you tell us?
I hope you don't believe me jealous!
But yet, methinks I feel it true,
And really yours is budding too—
Nay—now I can not stir my foot;
It feels as if 't were taking root."
Description would but tire my Muse,
In short, they both were turn'd to yews.
Old Goodman Dobson of the green
Remembers he the trees has seen;
He 'll talk of them from noon till night,
And goes with folks to show the sight;
On Sundays, after evening prayer,
He gathers all the parish there;
Points out the place of either yew,
Here Baucis, there Philemon, grew:
Till once a parson of our town,
To mend his barn, cut Baucis down;
At which, 'tis hard to be believed
How much the other tree was grieved,
Grew scrubbed, died a-top, was stunted,
So the next parson stubb'd and burnt it.

A DESCRIPTION OF A CITY SHOWER.

IN IMITATION OF VIRGIL'S GEORGICS.

DEAN SWIFT.

Careful observers may foretell the hour,
(By sure prognostics), when to dread a shower.
While rain depends, the pensive cat gives o'er
Her frolics, and pursues her tail no more.
Returning home at night, you'll find the sink
Strike your offended sense with double stink.
If you be wise, then, go not far to dine:
You'll spend in coach-hire more than save in wine.
A coming shower your shooting corns presage,
Old aches will throb, your hollow tooth will rage;
Sauntering in coffee-house is Dulman seen;
He damns the climate, and complains of spleen.
Meanwhile the South, rising with dabbled wings,
A sable cloud athwart the welkin flings,
That swill'd more liquor than it could contain,
And, like a drunkard, gives it up again.
Brisk Susan whips her linen from the rope,
While the first drizzling shower is borne aslope;
Such is that sprinkling which some careless quean
Flirts on you from her mop, but not so clean:
You fly, invoke the gods; then, turning, stop
To rail; she singing, still whirls on her mop.
Not yet the dust had shunn'd the unequal strife,
But, aided by the wind, fought still for life,
And wafted with its foe by violent gust,
'T was doubtful which was rain, and which was dust.
Ah! where must needy poet seek for aid,
When dust and rain at once his coat invade?
Sole coat! where dust, cemented by the rain,
Erects the nap, and leaves a cloudy stain!
Now in contiguous drops the flood comes down,
Threatening with deluge this *devoted* town.
To shops in crowds the daggled females fly,
Pretend to cheapen goods, but nothing buy.
The Templar spruce, while every spout's abroach,
Stays till 'tis fair, yet seems to call a coach.

The tuck'd up sempstress walks with hasty strides,
While streams run down her oil'd umbrella's sides.
Here various kinds, by various fortunes led,
Commence acquaintance underneath a shed.
Triumphant Tories, and desponding Whigs,
Forget their feuds, and join to save their wigs.
Box'd in a chair the beau impatient sits,
While spouts run clattering o'er the roof by fits,
And ever and anon with frightful din
The leather sounds; he trembles from within.
So when Troy chairmen bore the wooden steed,
Pregnant with Greeks impatient to be freed,
(Those bully Greeks, who, as the moderns do,
Instead of paying chairmen, ran them through),
Laocoon struck the outside with his spear,
And each imprison'd hero quaked for fear.
  Now from all parts the swelling kennels flow,
And bear their trophies with them as they go:
Filth of all hues and odor, seem to tell
What street they sail'd from by their sight and smell.
They, as each torrent drives with rapid force,
From Smithfield to St. Pulchre's shape their course,
And in huge confluence join'd at Snowhill ridge,
Fall from the conduit prone to Holborne bridge.
Sweeping from butchers' stalls, dung, guts, and blood;
Drown'd puppies, stinking sprats, all drench'd in mud,
Dead cats, and turnip-tops, come tumbling down the flood.

THE PROGRESS OF CURIOSITY;

OR A ROYAL VISIT TO WHITBREAD'S BREWERY.

PETER PINDAR.

Sic transit gloria mundi!—Old Sun Dials.

From House of Buckingham, in grand parade,
To Whitbread's *Brewhouse*, moved the cavalcade.

THE ARGUMENT.—Peter's loyalty.—He suspecteth Mr. Warton* of joking.—Complimenteth the poet Laureate.—Peter differeth in opinion from Mr. Warton.—Taketh up the cudgels for King Edward, King Harry V., and Queen Bess.—Feats on Blackheath and Wimbledon performed by our most gracious sovereign.—King Charles the Second half damned by Peter, yet praised for keeping company with gentlemen.—Peter praiseth himself.—Peter reproved by Mr. Warton.—Desireth Mr. Warton's prayers.—A fine simile.—Peter still suspecteth the Laureate of ironical dealings—Peter expostulateth with Mr. Warton.—Mr. Warton replieth.—Peter administereth bold advice.—Wittily calleth death and physicians poachers.—Praiseth the king for parental tenderness.—Peter maketh a natural simile.—Peter furthermore telleth Thomas Warton what to say.—Peter giveth a beautiful example of ode-writing.

THE CONTENTS OF THE ODE.—His Majesty's† love for the arts and sciences, even in quadrupeds.—His resolution to know the history of brewing beer.—Billy Ramus sent ambassador to Chiswell street.—Interview between Messrs. Ramus and Whitbread.—Mr. Whitbread's bow, and compliments to Majesty.—Mr. Ramus's return from his embassy.—Mr. Whitbread's terrors described to Majesty by Mr. Ramus.—The King's pleasure thereat.—Description of people of worship. —Account of the Whitbread preparation.—The royal cavalcade to Chiswell-street. —The arrival at the brewhouse.—Great joy of Mr. Whitbread.—His Majesty's nod, the Queen's dip, and a number of questions.—A West India simile.—The marvelings of the draymen described.—His Majesty peepeth into a pump.—Beautifully compared to a magpie peeping into a marrow-bone.—The *minute* curiosity of the King.—Mr. Whitbread endeavoreth to surprise Majesty.—His Majesty puzzleth Mr. Whitbread.—Mr. Whitbread's horse expresseth wonder.—Also Mr. Whitbread's dog.—His Majesty maketh laudable inquiry about Porter.—Again puzzleth Mr. Whitbread.—King noteth *notable* things.—Profound questions proposed by Majesty.—As profoundly answered by Mr. Whitbread.—Majesty in a mistake.—Corrected by the brewer.—A nose simile.—Majesty's admiration of the bell.—Good manners of the bell.—Fine appearance of Mr. Whitbread's pigs.—Majesty proposeth questions, but benevolently waiteth not for answers.—Peter telleth the duty of Kings.—Discovereth one of his shrewd maxims.—Sublime sympathy of a water-spout and a king.—The great use of asking questions.—The habitation of truth.—The collation.—The wonders performed by the Royal Visitors.—Majesty proposeth to take leave.—Offereth knighthood to Whitbread.—Mr. Whitbread's objections.—The king runneth a rig on his host.—Mr. Whitbread thanketh Majesty.—Miss Whitbread curtsieth.—The queen dippeth.—The Cavalcade departeth.

Peter triumpheth.—Admonisheth the Laureate.—Peter croweth over the Laureate.—Discovereth deep knowledge of kings, and surgeons, and men who have lost their legs.—Peter reasoneth.—Vaunteth.—Even insulteth the Laureate.—Pe-

* The Poet Laureate.

† George III.

ter proclaimeth his peaceable disposition.—Praiseth Majesty, and concludeth with a prayer for curious kings.

Tom, soon as e'er thou strik'st thy golden lyre,
Thy brother Peter's muse is all on fire,
  To sing of kings and queens, and such rare folk:
Yet, 'midst thy heap of compliments so fine,
Say, may we venture to believe a line?
  You Oxford wits most dearly love a joke.

Son of the Nine, thou writest well on naught;
Thy thundering stanza, and its pompous thought,
  I think, must put a dog into a laugh:
Edward and Harry were much braver men
Than this new-christened hero of thy pen.
  Yes, laurelled Odeman, braver far by half;

Though on Blackheath and Wimbledon's wide plain,
George keeps his hat off in a shower of rain;
Sees swords and bayonets without a dread,
Nor at a volley winks, nor ducks his head:

  Although at grand reviews he seems so blest,
  And leaves at six o'clock his downy nest,
Dead to the charms of blanket, wife, and bolster;
  Unlike his officers, who, fond of cramming,
  And at reviews afraid of thirst and famine,
With bread and cheese and brandy fill their holsters.

  Sure, Tom, we should do justice to Queen Bess:
  His present majesty, whom Heaven long bless
With wisdom, wit, and art of choicest quality,
  Will never get, I fear, so fine a niche
  As that old queen, though often called old b—ch,
In fame's colossal house of immortality.

  As for John Dryden's Charles—that king
  Indeed was never any mighty thing;
He merited few honors from the pen:
  And yet he was a devilish hearty fellow,
  Enjoyed his beef, and bottle, and got mellow,
And mind—kept company with *gentlemen:*

For, like some kings, in hobby grooms,
Knights of the manger, curry-combs, and brooms,
Lost to all glory, Charles did not delight—
Nor joked by day with pages, servant-maids,
Large, red-polled, blowzy, hard two-handed jades:
Indeed I know not what Charles did by night.

Thomas, I am of candor a great lover;
In short, I 'm candor's self all over;
Sweet as a candied cake from top to toe;
Make it a rule that Virtue shall be praised,
And humble Merit from the ground be raised:
What thinkest thoŭ of Peter now?

Thou cryest "Oh! how false! behold thy king,
Of whom thou scarcely say'st a handsome thing;
That king has virtues that should make thee stare."
Is it so?—Then the sin 's in me—
'Tis my vile optics that can't see;
Then pray for them when next thou sayest a prayer.

But, p'rhaps aloft on his imperial throne,
So distant, O ye gods! from every one,
The royal virtues are like many a star,
From this our pigmy system rather far:
Whose light, though flying ever since creation,
Has not yet pitched upon our nation.*

Then may the royal ray be soon explored—
And Thomas, if thou 'lt swear thou art not humming,
I 'll take my spying-glass and bring thee word
The instant I behold it coming.
But, Thomas Warton, without joking,
Art thou, or art thou not, thy sovereign smoking?

How canst thou seriously declare,
That George the Third
With Cressy's Edward can compare,
Or Harry?—'Tis too bad, upon my word:
George is a clever king, I needs must own,
And cuts a jolly figure on the throne.

* Such was the sublime opinion of the Dutch astronomer, Huygens.

Now thou exclaim'st, "God rot it! Peter, pray
What to the devil shall I sing or say?"

I'll tell thee what to say, O tuneful Tom:
  Sing how a monarch, when his son was dying,
  His gracious eyes and ears was edifying,
By abbey company and kettle drum:
Leaving that son to death and the physician,
Between two fires—a forlorn-hope condition;
Two poachers, who make man their game,
And, special marksmen! seldom miss their aim.

Say, though the monarch did not see his son,
  He kept aloof through fatherly affection;
Determined nothing should be done,
  To bring on useless tears, and dismal recollection.
For what can tears avail, and piteous sighs?
Death heeds not howls nor dripping eyes;
And what are sighs and tears but wind and water,
That show the leakiness of feeble nature?

Tom, with my simile thou wilt not quarrel;
  Like air and any sort of drink,
  Whizzing and oozing through each chink,
That proves the weakness of the barrel.

Say—for the prince, when wet was every eye,
And thousands poured to heaven the pitying sigh
    Devout;
Say how a King, unable to dissemble,
Ordered Dame Siddons to his house, and Kemble,
    To spout:

Gave them ice creams and wines, so dear!
Denied till then a thimble full of beer;
For which they've thanked the author of this meter,
Videlicet, the moral mender, Peter
Who, in his Ode on Ode, did dare exclaim,
And call such royal avarice, a shame.

Say—but I'll teach thee how to make an ode;
Thus shall thy labors visit fame's abode,

In company with my immortal lay;
And look, Tom—thus I fire away—

BIRTH-DAY ODE.

This day, this very day, gave birth,
Not to the brightest monarch upon earth,
Because there are some brighter and as big;
  Who love the arts that man exalt to heaven,
  George loves them also, when they 're given
To four-legged Gentry, christened dog and pig.*
Whose deeds in this our wonder-hunting nation
Prove what a charming thing is education.

Full of the art of brewing beer,
  The monarch heard of Mr. Whitbread's fame:
Quoth he unto the queen "My dear, my dear,
  Whitbread hath got a marvelous great name;
Charly, we must, must, must see Whitbread brew—
Rich as us, Charly, richer than a Jew:
Shame, shame, we have not yet his brewhouse seen!"
Thus sweetly said the king unto the queen!

Red-hot with novelty's delightful rage,
To Mr. Whitbread forth he sent a page,
  To say that majesty proposed to view,
With thirst of wondrous knowledge deep inflamed,
His vats, and tubs, and hops, and hogsheads famed,
  And learn the noble secret how to brew.

Of such undreamt-of honor proud,
Most reverently the brewer bowed;
So humbly (so the humble story goes,)
He touched even *terra firma* with his nose;

Then said unto the page, *hight* Billy Ramus,
"Happy are we that our great king should name us,
As worthy unto majesty to show,
How we poor Chiswell people brew."

* The dancing dogs and wise pig have formed a considerable part of the royal amusement.

Away sprung Billy Ramus quick as thought,
To majesty the welcome tidings brought,
  How Whitbread, staring, stood like any stake,
And trembled—then the civil things he said—
On which the king did smile and nod his head:
  For monarchs like to see their subjects quake:

Such horrors unto kings most pleasant are,
  Proclaiming reverence and humility:
High thoughts, too, all those shaking fits declare
  Of kingly grandeur and great capability!

People of worship, wealth, and birth,
Look on the humbler sons of earth,
  Indeed in a most humble light, God knows!
High stations are like Dover's towering cliffs,
Where ships below appear like little skiffs,
  While people walking on the strand like crows.

Muse, sing the stir that Mr. Whitbread made;
Poor gentleman! most terribly afraid
  He should not charm enough his guests divine:
He gave his maids new aprons, gowns and smocks;
And lo! two hundred pounds were spent in frocks,
  To make the apprentices and draymen fine:

Busy as horses in a field of clover,
Dogs, cats, and chairs, and stools, were tumbled over,
Amid the Whitbread rout of preparation,
To treat the lofty ruler of the nation.

Now moved king, queen, and princesses so grand,
To visit the first brewer in the land;
Who sometimes swills his beer and grinds his meat
In a snug corner christened Chiswell-street;
But oftener charmed with fashionable air,
Amid the gaudy great of Portman-square.

Lord Aylesbury, and Denbigh's Lord *also*,
  His grace the Duke of Montague *likewise*,
With Lady Harcourt joined the raree-show,
  And fixed all Smithfield's marveling eyes:

For lo! a greater show ne'er graced those quarters,
Since Mary roasted, just like crabs, the martyrs.

Arrived, the king broad grinned, and gave a nod
To smiling Whitbread, who, had God
   Come with his angels to behold his beer,
With more respect he never could have met--
Indeed the man was in a sweat,
   So much the brewer did the king revere.

Her majesty contrived to make a dip:
Light as a feather then the king did skip,
And asked a thousand questions, with a laugh,
Before poor Whitbread comprehended half.

Reader, my Ode should have a simile—
Well, in Jamaica, on a tamarind tree,
   Five hundred parrots, gabbling just like Jews,
I 've seen—such noise the feathered imps did make,
As made my very *pericranium* ache—
   Asking and telling parrot news:

Thus was the brewhouse filled with gabbling noise,
Whilst draymen and the brewer's boys,
   Devoured the questions that the king did ask:
In different parties were they staring seen,
Wondering to think they saw a king and queen!
   Behind a tub were some, and some behind a cask.

Some draymen forced themselves (a pretty luncheon)
Into the mouth of many a gaping puncheon;
And through the bung-hole winked with curious eye,
   To view, and be assured what sort of things
   Were princesses, and queens, and kings,
For whose most lofty station thousands sigh!
And lo! of all the gaping puncheon clan,
Few were the mouths that had not got a man!

Now majesty into a pump so deep
Did with an opera-glass so curious peep:
Examining with care each wondrous matter
            That brought up water!

Thus have I seen a magpie in the street,
A chattering bird we often meet,
A bird for curiosity well known;
With head awry,
And cunning eye,
Peep knowingly into a marrow-bone.

And now his curious majesty did stoop
To count the nails on every hoop;
And, lo! no single thing came in his way,
That, full of deep research, he did not say,
"What's this! hæ, hæ? what's that? what's this? what's that?"
So quick the words, too, when he deigned to speak,
As if each syllable would break his neck.

Thus, to the world of *great* whilst others crawl,
Our sovereign peeps into the world of *small;*
Thus microscopic genuises explore
Things that too oft provoke the public scorn,
Yet swell of useful knowledges the store,
By finding systems in a pepper-corn.

Now boasting Whitbread serious did declare,
To make the majesty of England stare,
That he had butts enough, he knew,
Placed side by side, to reach along to Kew:
On which the king with wonder swiftly cried,
"What, if they reach to Kew then, side by side,
What would they do, what, what, placed end to end?"
To whom with knitted, calculating brow,
The man of beer most solemnly did vow,
Almost to Windsor that they would extend;
On which the king, with wondering mien,
Repeated it unto the wondering queen:
On which, quick turning round his haltered head,
The brewer's horse, with face astonished neighed;
The brewer's dog too poured a note of thunder,
Rattled his chain, and wagged his tail for wonder.

Now did the king for other beers inquire,
For Calvert's, Jordan's, Thrale's entire·

And, after talking of these different beers,
Asked Whitbread if his porter equalled theirs?

This was a puzzling, diagreeing question;
Grating like arsenic on his host's digestion :
A kind of question to the man of cask,
That not even Solomon himself would ask.

Now majesty, alive to knowledge, took
A very pretty memorandum-book,
With gilded leaves of asses' skin so white,
And in it legibly began to write—

Memorandum.

A charming place beneath the grates
For roasting chestnuts or potates.

Mem.

'Tis hops that give a bitterness to beer—
Hops grow in Kent, says Whitbread, and elsewhere.

Quœre.

Is there no cheaper stuff? where doth it dwell?
Would not horse-aloes bitter it as well?

Mem.

To try it soon on our small beer—
'T will save us several pound a year.

Mem.

To remember to forget to ask
  Old Whitbread to my house one day.

Mem.

Not to forget to take of beer the cask,
  The brewer offered me, away.

Now having penciled his remarks so shrewd,
  Sharp as the point indeed of a new pin,
His majesty his watch most sagely viewed,
  And then put up his asses' skin.

To Whitbread now deigned majesty to say,
"Whitbread, are all your horses fond of hay!"
"Yes, please your majesty," in humble notes,
The brewer answered—"also, sir, of oats:
Another thing my horses too maintains,
And that, an't please your majesty, are grains."

"Grains, grains," said majesty, "to fill their crops?
Grains, grains?—that comes from hops—yes, hops, hops?
hops?"

Here was the king, like hounds sometimes, at fault—
"Sire," cried the humble brewer, "give me leave
Your sacred majesty to undeceive;
Grains, sire, are never made from hops, but malt."

"True," said the cautious monarch, with a smile:
"From malt, malt, malt—I meant malt all the while."
"Yes," with the sweetest bow, rejoined the brewer,
"An't please your majesty, you did, I'm sure."
"Yes," answered majesty, with quick reply,
"I did, I did, I did I, I, I, I."

Now this was wise in Whitbread—here we find
A very pretty knowledge of mankind;
As monarchs never must be in the wrong,
'T was really a bright thought in Whitbread's tongue,
To tell a little fib, or some such thing,
To save the sinking credit of a king.

Some brewers, in a rage of information,
Proud to instruct the ruler of a nation,
Had on the folly dwelt, to seem damned clever!
Now, what had been the consequence? Too plain!
The man had cut his consequence in twain;
The king had hated the *wise* fool forever!

Reader, whene'er thou dost espy a nose
That bright with many a ruby glows,
That nose thou mayest pronounce, nay safely swear,
Is nursed on something better than small-beer.

Thus when thou findest kings in brewing wise,
  Or natural history holding lofty station,
Thou mayest conclude, with marveling eyes,
  Such kings have had a goodly education.

Now did the king admire the bell so fine,
That daily asks the draymen all to dine:
On which the bell rung out (how very proper!)
To show it was a bell, and had a clapper.

And now before their sovereign's curious eye,
  Parents and children, fine, fat, hopeful sprigs,
All snuffling, squinting, grunting in their style,
  Appeared the brewer's tribe of handsome pigs:
On which the observant man, who fills a throne,
Declared the pigs were vastly like his own:

On which the brewer, swallowed up in joys,
Tears and astonishment in both his eyes,
His soul brim full of sentiments so loyal,
  Exclaimed, "O heavens! and can my swine
  Be deemed by majesty so fine!
Heavens! can my pigs compare, sire, with pigs royal!
To which the king assented with a nod;
On which the brewer bowed, and said, "Good God!"
Then winked significant on Miss;
Significant of wonder and of bliss;
  Who, bridling in her chin divine,
Crossed her fair hands, a dear old maid,
And then her lowest courtesy made
  For such high honor done her father's swine.

Now did his majesty so gracious say
To Mr. Whitbread, in his flying way,
  "Whitbread, d'ye nick the excisemen now and then?
Hæ, Whitbread, when d'ye think to leave off trade?
Hæ? what? Miss Whitbread's still a maid, a maid?
  What, what's the matter with the men?

"D'ye hunt!—hæ, hunt? No, no, you are too old—
  You'll be lord mayor—lord mayor one day—
Yes, yes, I've heard so—yes, yes, so I'm told:
  Don't, don't the fine for sheriff pay?

I 'll prick you every year, man, I declare:
Yes, Whitbread—yes, yes—you shall be lord mayor.

"Whitbread, d'ye keep a coach, or job one, pray?
  Job, job, that's cheapest; yes, that's best, that's best.
You put your liveries on the draymen—hæ?
Hæ, Whitbread? you have feather'd well your nest.
What, what's the price now, hæ, of all your stock?
But, Whitbread, what's o'clock, pray, what's o'clock?"

Now Whitbread inward said, "May I be cursed
If I know what to answer first;"
  Then searched his brains with ruminating eye:
But e'er the man of malt an answer found,
Quick on his heel, lo, majesty turned round,
  Skipped off, and baulked the pleasure of reply.

Kings in inquisitiveness should be strong—
  From curiosity doth wisdom flow:
For 'tis a maxim I 've adopted long,
  The more a man inquires, the more he 'll know.

Reader, didst ever see a water-spout?
  'Tis possible that thou wilt answer, "No."
Well then! he makes a most infernal rout;
  Sucks, like an elephant, the waves below,
With huge proboscis reaching from the sky,
As if he meant to drink the ocean dry:
At length so full he can't hold one drop more—
He bursts—down rush the waters with a roar
On some poor boat, or sloop, or brig, or ship,
And almost sinks the wand'rer of the deep:
Thus have I seen a monarch at reviews,
Suck from the tribe of officers the news,
Then bear in triumph off each *wondrous* matter,
And souse it on the queen with such a clatter!

I always would advise folks to ask questions;
  For, truly, questions are the keys of knowledge:
Soldiers, who forage for the mind's digestions,
  Cut figures at the Old Bailey, and at college;
Make chancellors, chief justices, and judges,
Even of the lowest green-bag drudges.

The sages say, Dame Truth delights to dwell,
Strange mansion! in the bottom of a well,
Questions are then the windlass and the rope
That pull the grave old gentlewoman up:
Damn jokes then, and unmannerly suggestions,
Reflecting upon kings for asking questions.

Now having well employed his royal lungs
On nails, hoops, staves, pumps, barrels, and their bungs,
The king and Co. sat down to a collation
Of flesh and fish, and fowl of every nation.
Dire was the clang of plates, of knife and fork,
That merciless fell like tomahawks to work,
And fearless scalped the fowl, the fish, and cattle,
While Whitbread, in the rear, beheld the battle.

The conquering monarch, stopping to take breath
Amidst the regiments of death,
Now turned to Whitbread with complacence round,
And, merry, thus addressed the man of beer
"Whitbread, is't true? I hear, I hear,
You're of an ancient family—renowned—
What? what? I'm told that you're a limb
Of Pym, the famous fellow Pym:
What Whitbread, is it true what people say?
Son of a round-head are you? hæ? hæ? hæ?
I'm told that you send Bibles to your votes—
A snuffling round-headed society—
Prayer-books instead of cash to buy them coats—
Bunyans, and Practices of Piety:
Your Bedford votes would wish to change their fare—
Rather see cash—yes, yes—than books of prayer.
Thirtieth of January don't you *feed?*
Yes, yes, you eat calf's head, you eat calf's head."

Now having wonders done on flesh, fowl, fish,
Whole hosts o'erturned—and seized on all supplies;
The royal visitors expressed a wish
To turn to House of Buckingham their eyes.

But first the monarch, so polite,
Asked Mr. Whitbread if he'd be a *knight.*

Unwilling in the list to be enrolled,
Whitbread contemplated the knights of Peg,
Then to his generous sovereign made a leg,
And said, "He was afraid he was too old.
He thanked however his most gracious king,
For offering to make him *such a thing.*"

But, ah! a different reason 't was I fear!
It was not age that bade the man of beer
The proffered honor of the monarch shun:
The tale of Margaret's knife, and royal fright,
Had almost made him damn the *name* of knight,
A tale that farrowed such a world of fun.

He mocked the prayer too by the king appointed,
Even by himself the Lord's Anointed :—
A foe to *fast* too, is he, let me tell ye;
And though a Presbyterian, can not think
Heaven (quarrelling with meat and drink)
Joys in the grumble of a hungry belly!

Now from the table with Cæsarean air
Up rose the monarch with his laureled brow,
When Mr. Whitbread, waiting on his chair,
Expressed much thanks, much joy, and made a bow.
Miss Whitbread now so quick her curtsies drops,
Thick as her honored father's Kentish hops;
Which hop-like curtsies were returned by dips
That never hurt the royal knees and hips;
For hips and knees of queens are sacred things,
That only bend on gala days
Before the best of kings,
When odes of triumph sound his praise.—

Now through a thundering peal of kind huzzas,
Proceeding some from hired* and unhired jaws,

* When his majesty goes to a play-house, or brew-house, or parliament, the Lord Chamberlain provides some pounds' worth of mob to huzza their beloved monarch. At the play-house about forty wide-mouthed fellows are hired on the night of their majesties' appearance, at two shillings and sixpence per head, with the liberty of seeing the play *gratis*. These *Stentors* are placed in different parts of the theater, who, immediately on the royal entry into the stage-box, set up their howl of loyalty; to whom their majesties, with sweetest smiles, acknowledge

The raree-show thought proper to retire;
Whilst Whitbread and his daughter fair
Surveyed all Chiswell-street with lofty air;
For, lo! they felt themselves some six feet higher

Such, Thomas, is the way to write!
Thus shouldst thou birth-day songs indite;
Then stick to earth, and leave the lofty sky:
No more of ti tum tum, and ti tum ti.

Thus should an honest laureate write of kings—
Not praise them for *imaginary things;*
I own I can not make my stubborn rhyme
Call every king a character sublime;
For conscience will not suffer me to wander
So very widely from the paths of candor.
I know full well *some* kings are to be seen,
To whom my verse so bold would give the spleen,
Should that bold verse declare they wanted *brains.*
I won't say that they *never* brains possessed—
They *may* have been with such a present blessed,
And therefore fancy that some *still* remains;

For every well-experienced surgeon knows,
That men who with their legs have parted,
Swear that they 've felt a pain in all their *toes,*
And often at the twinges started;
They stared upon their oaken stumps in vain!
Fancying the toes were all come back again.

If men, then, who their absent toes have mourned,
Can fancy those same toes at times returned;
So kings, in matters of intelligences,
May fancy they have stumbled on their senses.

Yes, Tom—mine is the way of writing ode—
Why liftest thou thy pious eyes to God!

the obligation by a genteel bow, and an elegant curtesy. This congratulatory noise of the *Stentors* is looked on by many, particularly country ladies and gentlemen, as an infallible thermometer, that ascertains the warmth of the national regard.—*P. P.*

Strange disappointment in thy looks I read;
  And now I hear thee in proud triumph cry,
"Is this an action, Peter, this a deed
  To raise a monarch to the sky?
Tubs, porter, pumps, vats, all the Whitbread throng,
Rare things to figure in the Muse's song!"

Thomas, I here protest, I want no quarrels
On kings and brewers, porter, pumps, and barrels—
  Far from the dove-like Peter be such strife,
But this I tell thee, Thomas, for a fact—
        Thy Cæsar never did an act
  More wise, more glorious in his life.

Now God preserve all wonder-hunting kings,
  Whether at Windsor, Buckingham, or Kew-house:
And may they never do more foolish things
  Than visiting Sam Whitbread and his brewhouse.

THE AUTHOR AND THE STATESMAN

[ADDRESSED BY FIELDING TO SIR ROBERT WALPOLE.]

While at the helm of state you ride,
Our nation's envy, and its pride;
While foreign courts with wonder gaze,
And curse those councils which they praise;
Would you not wonder, sir, to view
Your bard a greater man than you?
Which that he is you can not doubt,
When you have read the sequel out.

You know, great sir, that ancient fellows,
Philosophers, and such folks, tell us,
No great analogy between
Greatness and happiness is seen.
If then, as it might follow straight,
Wretched to be, is to be *great;*
Forbid it, gods, that you should try
What 'tis to be so great as I!

The family that dines the latest,
Is in our street esteem'd the greatest;
But latest hours must surely fall
'Fore him who never dines at all.

Your taste in architect, you know,
Hath been admired by friend and foe:
But can your earthly domes compare
With all my castles—in the air?

We 're often taught it doth behoove us
To think those greater who 're above us:
Another instance of my glory,
Who live above you, twice two story;
And from my garret can look down
On the whole street of *Arlington.*

Greatness by poets still is painted
With many followers acquainted:
This too doth in my favor speak;
Your levee is but twice a week;
From mine I can exclude but one day,
My door is quiet on a Sunday.

Nor in the manner of attendance,
Doth your great bard claim less ascendance.
Familiar you to admiration
May be approached by all the nation;
While I, like the Mogul in *Indo*,
Am never seen but at my window.
If with my greatness you 're offended,
The fault is easily amended;
For I 'll come down, with wondrous ease,
Into whatever *place* you please.
I 'm not ambitious; little matters
Will serve us great, but humble creatures.

Suppose a secretary o' this isle,
Just to be doing with a while;
Admiral, gen'ral, judge, or bishop:
Or I can foreign treaties dish up.
If the good genius of the nation
Should call me to negotiation,

Tuscan and French are in my head,
Latin I write, and *Greek*—I read.

If you should ask, what pleases best?
To get the most, and do the least.
What fittest for?—You know, I' m sure;
I 'm fittest for—a *sine-cure.*

THE FRIEND OF HUMANITY AND THE KNIFE-GRINDER.*

ANTI-JACOBIN.

FRIEND OF HUMANITY.†

"NEEDY Knife-grinder! whither are you going?
Rough is the road, your wheel is out of order—
Bleak blows the blast; your hat has got a hole in 't,
So have your breeches!

Some stanzas of the original poem, by Southey, are here subjoined:

THE WIDOW.

SAPPHICS.

Cold was the night wind; drifting fast the snows fell;
Wide were the downs, and shelterless and naked;
When a poor wand'rer struggled on her journey,
Weary and way-sore.

Drear were the downs, more dreary her reflections;
Cold was the night wind, colder was her bosom:
She had no home, the world was all before her,
She had no shelter.

Fast o'er the heath a chariot rattled by her:
"Pity me!" feebly cried the poor night wanderer,
"Pity me, strangers! lest with cold and hunger
Here I should perish."

† The "Friend of Humanity" was intended for MR. TIERNEY, M. P. for Southwark, who in early times was among the more forward of the Reformers. "He was," says Lord Brougham, "an assiduous member of the *Society of Friends of the People*, and drew up the much and justly celebrated Petition in which that useful body laid before the House of Commons all the more striking particulars of its defective title to the office of representing the people, which that House then, as now, but with far less reason, assumed.

"Weary Knife-grinder! little think the proud ones,
Who in their coaches roll along the turnpike-
road, what hard work 'tis crying all day 'Knives and
"'Scissors to grind O!'

Tell me, Knife-grinder, how came you to grind knives?
Did some rich man tyrannically use you?
Was it the squire? or parson of the parish?
Or the attorney?

"Was it the squire, for killing of his game? or
Covetous parson, for his tithes distraining?
Or roguish lawyer, made you lose your little
All in a lawsuit?

"(Have you not read the Rights of Man, by Tom Paine?)
Drops of compassion tremble on my eyelids,
Ready to fall, as soon as you have told your
Pitiful story."

KNIFE-GRINDER.

"Story! God bless you! I have none to tell, sir,
Only last night a-drinking at the Chequers,
This poor old hat and breeches, as you see, were
Torn in a scuffle.

"Constables came up, for to take me into
Custody; they took me before the justice;
Justice Oldmixon put me in the parish-
Stocks for a vagrant.

"I should be glad to drink your Honor's health in
A pot of beer, if you will give me sixpence;
But for my part, I never love to meddle
With politics, sir."

FRIEND OF HUMANITY.

"*I* give thee sixpence! I will see thee damned first—
Wretch! whom no sense of wrongs can rouse to vengeance—
Sordid, unfeeling, reprobate, degraded,
Spiritless outcast!"

[Kicks the Knife-grinder, overturns his wheel, and exit in a transport of Republican enthusiasm and universal philanthropy.]

INSCRIPTION

FOR THE DOOR OF THE CELL IN NEWGATE, WHERE MRS. BROWNRIGG, THE 'PRENTICE-CIDE WAS CONFINED PREVIOUS TO HER EXECUTION.*

FROM THE ANTI-JACOBIN. 1797.

For one long term, or e'er her trial came,
Here Brownrigg linger'd. Often have these cells
Echoed her blasphemies, as with shrill voice
She screamed for fresh Geneva. Not to her
Did the blithe fields of Tothill, or thy street,
St. Giles, its fair varieties expand;
Till at the last, in slow-drawn cart she went
To execution. Dost thou ask her crime?
SHE WHIPP'D TWO FEMALE 'PRENTICES TO DEATH,
AND HID THEM IN THE COAL-HOLE. For her mind
Shaped strictest plans of discipline. Sage schemes!
Such as Lycurgus taught, when at the shrine
Of the Orthyan goddess he bade flog
The little Spartans; such as erst chastised
Our Milton, when at college. For this act
Did Brownrigg swing. Harsh laws! But time shall come
When France shall reign, and laws be all repeal'd!

* INSCRIPTION BY SOUTHEY

FOR THE APARTMENT IN CHEPSTOW CASTLE, WHERE HENRY MARTEN, THE REGICIDE, WAS IMPRISONED THIRTY YEARS.

For thirty years, secluded from mankind,
Here Marten lingered. Often have these walls
Echoed his footsteps, as with even tread
He paced around his prison: not to him
Did Nature's fair varieties exist;
He never saw the sun's delightful beams,
Save when through yon high bars he pour'd a sad
And broken splendor. Dost thou ask his crime?
He had REBELL'D AGAINST THE KING, AND SAT
IN JUDGMENT ON HIM; for his ardent mind
Shaped goodliest plans of happiness on earth,
And peace and liberty. Wild dreams! but such
As Plato loved; such as with holy zeal
Our Milton worship'd. Bless'd hopes! awhile
From man withheld, even to the latter days
When Christ shall come, and all things be fulfill'd!

SONG.*

SUNG BY ROGERO IN THE BURLESQUE PLAY OF "THE ROVER."
FROM THE ANTI-JACOBIN, 1798.

CANNING.

I.

WHENE'ER with haggard eyes I view
This dungeon that I'm rotting in,
I think of those companions true
Who studied with me at the U
—niversity of Gottingen—
—niversity of Gottingen.

[Weeps, and pulls out a blue kerchief, with which he wipes his eyes; gazing tenderly at it, he proceeds—

II.

Sweet kerchief, check'd with heavenly blue,
Which once my love sat knotting in!—
Alas! Matilda *then* was true!
At least I thought so at the U—
—niversity of Gottingen—
—niversity of Gottingen.

[At the repetition of this line *Rogero* clanks his chains in cadence.

III.

Barbs! Barbs! alas! how swift you flew
Her neat post-wagon trotting in!
Ye bore Matilda from my view;
Forlorn I languish'd at the U—
—niversity of Gottingen—
—niversity of Gottingen.

IV.

This faded form! this pallid hue!
This blood my veins is clotting in,

* There is a curious circumstance connected with the composition of this song, the first five stanzas of which were written by Mr. Canning. Having been accidentally seen, previous to its publication, by Mr. Pitt, who was cognizant of the proceedings of the "Anti-Jacobin" writers, he was so amused with it, that he took up a pen and composed the last stanza on the spot.

My years are many—they were few
When first I entered at the U—
—niversity of Gottingen—
—niversity of Gottingen.

V.

There first for thee my passion grew,
Sweet! sweet Matilda Pottingen!
Thou wast the daughter of my tu—
—tor, law professor at the U—
—niversity at Gottingen—
—niversity of Gottingen.

VI.

Sun, moon and thou, vain world, adieu,
That kings and priests are plotting in;
Here doom'd to starve on water gru—
—el, never shall I see the U—
—niversity of Gottingen—
—niversity of Gottingen.

[During the last stanza *Rogero* dashes his head repeatedly against the walls of his prison; and, finally, so hard as to produce a visible contusion; he then throws himself on the floor in an agony. The curtain drops; the music still continuing to play till it is wholly fallen.

THE AMATORY SONNETS OF ABEL SHUFFLE-BOTTOM.

ROBERT SOUTHEY.

I.

DELIA AT PLAY.

SHE held a *Cup and Ball* of ivory white,
Less white the ivory than her *snowy* hand!
Enrapt, I watched her from my secret stand,
As now, intent, in *innocent* delight,
Her *taper* fingers twirled the giddy ball,
Now tost it, following still with EAGLE *sight*,
Now on the pointed end *infixed* its fall.
Marking her sport I mused, and musing sighed.

Methought the BALL she played with was my HEART;
(Alas! that sport like *that* should be her pride!)
And the *keen point* which steadfast still she eyed
Wherewith to pierce it, that was Cupid's *dart;*
Shall I not then the cruel Fair condemn
Who *on that dart* IMPALES my BOSOM'S GEM?

II.

THE POET PROVES THE EXISTENCE OF A SOUL FROM HIS LOVE FOR DELIA.

Some have denied a soul! THEY NEVER LOVED.
Far from my Delia now by fate removed,
At home, abroad, I view her everywhere:
Her ONLY in the FLOOD OF NOON I see,
My *Goddess-Maid*, my OMNIPRESENT FAIR.
For LOVE *annihilates the world to me!*
And when the weary SOL *around his bed*
Closes the SABLE CURTAINS *of the night*,
SUN OF MY SLUMBERS, on my dazzled sight
She shines confest. When *every sound is dead*,
The SPIRIT OF HER VOICE comes then to *roll*
The surge of music o'er my wavy brain.
Far, far from her my *Body* drags its chain,
But sure with Delia *I exist* A SOUL!

III.

THE POET EXPRESSES HIS FEELINGS RESPECTING A PORTRAIT IN DELIA'S PARLOR.

I would I were that portly gentleman
With gold-laced hat and golden-headed cane,
Who hangs in Delia's parlor! For whene'er
From book or needlework her looks arise,
On him *converge the* SUN-BEAMS *of her eyes*,
And he *unblamed* may gaze upon MY FAIR,
And oft MY FAIR his *favored* form surveys.
O HAPPY PICTURE! still on HER to gaze;
I envy him! and jealous fear alarms,
Lest the STRONG *glance* of those *divinest* charms
WARM HIM TO LIFE, as in the ancient days,
When MARBLE MELTED in Pygmalion's arms.
I would I were that portly gentleman,
With gold-laced hat and golden-headed cane!

THE LOVE ELEGIES OF ABEL SHUFFLEBOTTOM.

ROBERT SOUTHEY.

I.

THE POET RELATES HOW HE OBTAINED DELIA'S POCKET-HANDKERCHIEF.

'Tis mine! what accents can my joy declare?
  Blest be the pressure of the thronging rout!
Blest be the hand so hasty of my fair,
  That left the *tempting corner* hanging out!

I envy not the joy the pilgrim feels,
  After long travel to some distant shrine,
When at the relic of his saint he kneels,
  For Delia's POCKET-HANDKERCHIEF IS MINE.

When first with *filching fingers* I drew near,
  Keen hopes shot tremulous through every vein;
And when the *finished deed* removed my fear,
  Scarce could my bounding heart its joy contain.

What though the EIGHTH COMMANDMENT rose to mind,
  It only served a moment's qualm to move;
For thefts like this it could not be designed—
  THE *eighth commandment* WAS NOT MADE FOR LOVE!

Here, when she took the maccaroons from me,
  She wiped her mouth to clear the crumbs so sweet!
Dear napkin! yes, she wiped her lips on thee!
  Lips *sweeter* than the *maccaroons* she eat.

And when she took that pinch of Moccabaw,
  That made my love so *delicately* sneeze,
Thee to her Roman nose applied I saw,
  And thou art doubly dear for things like these.

No washerwoman's filthy hand shall e'er,
  SWEET POCKET-HANDKERCHIEF! thy worth profane;
For thou hast touched the *rubies* of my fair,
  And I will kiss thee o'er and o'er again.

II.

THE POET EXPATIATES ON THE BEAUTY OF DELIA'S HAIR.

The comb between whose ivory teeth she strains
The straightning curls of gold so *beamy bright*,
Not spotless merely from the touch remains,
But issues forth *more pure*, more *milky white*.

The rose pomatum that the FRISEUR spreads
Sometimes with honored fingers for my fair,
No added perfume on her tresses sheds,
But borrows sweetness from her sweeter hair.

Happy the FRISEUR who in Delia's hair
With licensed fingers uncontrolled may rove!
And happy in his death the DANCING BEAR,
Who died to make pomatum for my love.

Oh could I hope that e'er my favored lays
Might *curl those lovely locks* with conscious pride,
Nor Hammond, nor the Mantuan shepherd's praise,
I 'd envy them, nor wish reward beside.

Cupid has strung from you, O tresses fine,
The bow that in my breast impell'd his dart;
From you, sweet locks! he wove the subtile line
Wherewith the urchin *angled* for MY HEART.

Fine are my Delia's tresses as the threads
That from the silk-worm, *self-interr'd*, proceed;
Fine as the GLEAMY GOSSAMER that spreads
His filmy net-work o'er the tangled mead.

Yet with these tresses Cupid's power, elate,
My captive *heart* has *handcuff'd* in a chain,
Strong as the cables of some huge first-rate,
THAT BEARS BRITANNIA'S THUNDERS O'ER THE MAIN.

The SYLPHS that round her radiant locks repair,
In *flowing luster* bathe their bright'ning wings;
And ELFIN MINSTRELS with assiduous care,
The ringlets rob for FAIRY FIDDLESTRINGS.

III.

THE POET RELATES HOW HE STOLE A LOCK OF DELIA'S HAIR, AND HER ANGER.

Oh! be the day accurst that gave me birth!
 Ye Seas! to swallow me, in kindness rise!
Fall on me, mountains! and thou merciful earth,
 Open, and hide me from my Delia's eyes.

Let universal Chaos now return,
 Now let the central fires their prison burst,
And EARTH, and HEAVEN, and AIR, and OCEAN burn,
 For Delia *frowns.* SHE FROWNS, and I am curst.

Oh! I could dare the fury of the fight,
 Where hostile MILLIONS sought my single life;
Would storm VOLCANOES, BATTERIES, with delight,
 And grapple with GRIM DEATH in glorious strife.

Oh! I could brave the bolts of angry JOVE,
 When ceaseless lightnings fire the midnight skies;
What is *his wrath* to that of HER I love?
 What is his LIGHTNING to my Delia's eyes?

Go, fatal lock! I cast thee to the wind;
 Ye *serpent* CURLS, ye *poison tendrils*, go!
Would I could tear thy memory from my mind,
 ACCURSED LOCK; thou cause of all my woe!

Seize the CURST CURLS, ye Furies, as they fly!
 Demons of darkness, guard the infernal roll,
That thence your cruel vengeance, when I die,
 May *knit the* KNOTS OF TORTURE *for my* SOUL.

Last night—Oh hear me, heaven, and grant my prayer!
 The BOOK OF FATE before thy suppliant lay,
And let me from its ample records tear
 Only the single PAGE OF YESTERDAY!

Or let me meet OLD TIME upon his flight,
 And I will STOP HIM on his restless way;
Omnipotent in love's resistless might,
 I'll force him back the ROAD OF YESTERDAY.

Last night, as o'er the page of love's despair,
My Delia bent *deliciously* to grieve,
I stood a *treacherous loiterer* by her chair,
And drew the FATAL SCISSORS from my sleeve:

And would at that instant o'er my thread
The SHEARS OF ATROPOS had opened then;
And when I reft the lock from Delia's head,
Had cut me sudden from the sons of men!

She heard the scissors that fair lock divide,
And while my heart with transport parted big,
She cast a FURY frown on me, and cried,
"You stupid puppy—you have spoiled my wig!"

THE BABY'S DEBUT.*

[A BURLESQUE IMITATION OF WORDSWORTH.—REJECTED ADDRESSES.]

JAMES SMITH.

[Spoken in the character of Nancy Lake, a girl eight years of age, who is drawn upon the stage in a child's chaise by Samuel Hughes, her uncle's porter.]

My brother Jack was nine in May,
And I was eight on New-year's-day;
So in Kate Wilson's shop
Papa (he 's my papa and Jack's)
Bought me, last week, a doll of wax,
And brother Jack a top.
Jack 's in the pouts, and this it is—
He thinks mine came to more than his;
So to my drawer he goes,
Takes out the doll, and, O, my stars!
He pokes her head between the bars,
And melts off half her nose!

* "The author does not, in this instance, attempt to copy any of the higher attributes of Mr. Wordsworth's poetry; but has succeeded perfectly in the imitation of his mawkish affectations of childish simplicity and nursery stammering. We hope it will make him ashamed of his *Alice Fell*, and the greater part of his last volumes—of which it is by no means a parody, but a very fair, and indeed we think a flattering, imitation."—*Edinburg Review.*

Quite cross, a bit of string I beg,
And tie it to his peg-top's peg,
And bang, with might and main,
Its head against the parlor-door:
Off flies the head, and hits the floor,
And breaks a window-pane.

This made him cry with rage and spite:
Well, let him cry, it serves him right.
A pretty thing, forsooth!
If he's to melt, all scalding hot,
Half my doll's nose, and I am not
To draw his peg-top's tooth!

Aunt Hannah heard the window break,
And cried, "O naughty Nancy Lake,
Thus to distress your aunt:
No Drury Lane for you to-day!"
And while papa said, "Pooh, she may!"
Mamma said, "No, she sha'n't!"

Well, after many a sad reproach,
They got into a hackney-coach,
And trotted down the street.
I saw them go: one horse was blind,
The tails of both hung down behind,
Their shoes were on their feet.

The chaise in which poor brother Bill
Used to be drawn to Pentonville,
Stood in the lumber-room:
I wiped the dust from off the top,
While Molly mopped it with a mop,
And brushed it with a broom.

My uncle's porter, Samuel Hughes,
Came in at six to black the shoes,
(I always talk to Sam:)
So what does he, but takes, and drags
Me in the chaise along the flags,
And leaves me where I am.

My father's walls are made of brick,
But not so tall and not so thick
As these; and, goodness me!
My father's beams are made of wood,
But never, never half so good
As those that now I see.

What a large floor! 'tis like a town!
The carpet, when they lay it down,
Won't hide it, I'll be bound;
And there's a row of lamps!—my eye!
How they do blaze! I wonder why
They keep them on the ground.

At first I caught hold of the wing,
And kept away; but Mr. Thing-
umbob, the prompter man,
Gave with his hand my chaise a shove,
And said, "Go on, my pretty love;
Speak to 'em little Nan.

"You've only got to curtsy, whisp-
er, hold your chin up, laugh and lisp,
And then you're sure to take:
I've known the day when brats, not quite
Thirteen, got fifty pounds a night;
Then why not Nancy Lake?"

But while I'm speaking, where's papa?
And where's my aunt? and where's mamma?
Where's Jack? O there they sit!
They smile, they nod; I'll go my ways,
And order round poor Billy's chaise,
To join them in the pit.

And now, good gentlefolks, I go
To join mamma, and see the show;
So, bidding you adieu,
I curtsy like a pretty miss,
And if you'll blow to me a kiss,
I'll blow a kiss to you.

[Blows a kiss, and exit.]

PLAY-HOUSE MUSINGS.

[A BURLESQUE IMITATION OF COLERIDGE.—REJECTED ADDRESSES.]

JAMES SMITH

My pensive Public, wherefore look you sad?
I had a grandmother, she kept a donkey
To carry to the mart her crockery-ware,
And when that donkey looked me in the face,
His face was sad! and you are sad, my Public.

Joy should be yours: this tenth day of October
Again assembles us in Drury Lane.
Long wept my eye to see the timber planks
That hid our ruins; many a day I cried,
Ah me! I fear they never will rebuild it!
Till on one eve, one joyful Monday eve,
As along Charles-street I prepared to walk,
Just at the corner, by the pastrycook's,
I heard a trowel tick against a brick.
I looked me up, and straight a parapet
Uprose at least seven inches o'er the planks.
Joy to thee, Drury! to myself I said:
He of the Blackfriars' Road, who hymned thy downfall
In loud Hosannahs, and who prophesied
That flames, like those from prostrate Solyma,
Would scorch the hand that ventured to rebuild thee,
Has proved a lying prophet. From that hour,
As leisure offered, close to Mr. Spring's
Box-office door, I 've stood and eyed the builders.
They had a plan to render less their labors;
Workmen in olden times would mount a ladder
With hodded heads, but these stretched forth a pole
From the wall's pinnacle, they placed a pulley
Athwart the pole, a rope athwart the pulley;
To this a basket dangled; mortar and bricks
Thus freighted, swung securely to the top,
And in the empty basket workmen twain
Precipitate, unhurt, accosted earth.

Oh! 't was a goodly sound, to hear the people
Who watched the work, express their various thoughts!

While some believed it never would be finished,
Some, on the contrary, believed it would.

I've heard our front that faces Drury Lane
Much criticised; they say 'tis vulgar brick-work,
A mimic manufactory of floor-cloth.
One of the morning papers wished that front
Cemented like the front in Brydges-street;
As now it looks, they call it Wyatt's Mermaid,
A handsome woman with a fish's tail.

White is the steeple of St. Bride's in Fleet-street,
The Albion (as its name denotes) is white;
Morgan and Saunders' shop for chairs and tables
Gleams like a snow-ball in the setting sun;
White is Whitehall. But not St. Bride's in Fleet-street,
The spotless Albion, Morgan, no, nor Saunders,
Nor white Whitehall, is white as Drury's face.

Oh, Mr. Whitbread! fie upon you, sir!
I think you should have built a colonnade;
When tender Beauty, looking for her coach,
Protrudes her gloveless hand, perceives the shower,
And draws the tippet closer round her throat,
Perchance her coach stands half a dozen off,
And, ere she mounts the step, the oozing mud
Soaks through her pale kid slipper. On the morrow,
She coughs at breakfast, and her gruff papa
Cries, "There you go! this comes of playhouses!"
To build no portico is penny wise:
Heaven grant it prove not in the end pound foolish!

Hail to thee, Drury! Queen of Theaters!
What is the Regency in Tottenham-street,
The Royal Amphitheater of Arts,
Astley's, Olympic, or the Sans Pareil,
Compared with thee? Yet when I view thee pushed
Back from the narrow street that christened thee,
I know not why they call thee Drury Lane.
Amid the freaks that modern fashion sanctions,
It grieves me much to see live animals
Brought on the stage. Grimaldi has his rabbit,
Laurent his cat, and Bradbury his pig;

Fie on such tricks! Johnson, the machinist
Of former Drury, imitated life
Quite to the life. The elephant in Blue Beard,
Stuffed by his hand, wound round his lithe proboscis
As spruce as he who roared in Padmanaba.*

Naught born on earth should die. On hackney stands
I reverence the coachman who cries "Gee,"
And spares the lash. When I behold a spider
Prey on a fly, a magpie on a worm,
Or view a butcher with horn-handled knife
Slaughter a tender lamb as dead as mutton,
Indeed, indeed, I'm very, very sick!

[*Exit hastily.*

THE THEATER.†

[A BURLESQUE IMITATION OF CRABBE.—REJECTED ADDRESSES.]

JAMES SMITH.

Interior of a Theater described.—Pit gradually fills.—The Check-taker.—Pit full.—The Orchestra tuned.—One Fiddle rather dilatory.—Is reproved—and repents.—Evolutions of a Play-bill.—Its final Settlement on the Spikes.—The Gods taken to task—and why.—Motley Group of Play-goers.—Holywell-street, St. Pancras.—Emanuel Jennings binds his Son apprentice—not in London—and why.—Episode of the Hat.

'Tis sweet to view, from half-past five to six,
Our long wax-candles, with short cotton wicks,
Touched by the lamplighter's Promethean art,
Start into light, and make the lighter start;

* "Padmanaba," viz., in a pantomime called *Harlequin in Padmanaba.* This elephant, some years afterward, was exhibited over Exeter 'Change, where it was found necessary to destroy the poor animal by discharges of musketry. When he made his entrance in the pantomime above-mentioned, Johnson, the machinist of the rival house, exclaimed, "I should be very sorry if I could not make a better elephant than that!"

† "'The Theater,' by the Rev. G. Crabbe, we rather think, is the best piece in the collection. It is an exquisite and most masterly imitation, not only of the peculiar style, but of the taste, temper, and manner of description of that most original author. * * * It does not aim, of course, at any shadow of his pathos or moral sublimity, but seems to us to be a singularly faithful copy of his pas sages of mere description."—*Edinburg Review.*

To see red Phœbus through the gallery-pane
Tinge with his beams the beams of Drury Lane;
While gradual parties fill our widened pit,
And gape, and gaze, and wonder, ere they sit.

At first, while vacant seats give choice and ease,
Distant or near, they settle where they please;
But when the multitude contracts the span,
And seats are rare, they settle where they can.

Now the full benches to late comers doom
No room for standing, miscalled *standing-room.*

Hark! the check-taker moody silence breaks,
And bawling "Pit full!" gives the checks he takes;
Yet onward still the gathering numbers cram,
Contending crowders shout the frequent damn,
And all is bustle, squeeze, row, jabbering, and jam.

See to their desks Apollo's sons repair—
Swift rides the rosin o'er the horse's hair!
In unison their various tones to tune,
Murmurs the hautboy, growls the coarse bassoon;
In soft vibration sighs the whispering lute,
Tang goes the harpsichord, too-too the flute,
Brays the loud trumpet, squeaks the fiddle sharp,
Winds the French horn, and twangs the tingling harp
Till, like great Jove, the leader, fingering in,
Attunes to order the chaotic din.
Now all seems hushed—but, no, one fiddle will
Give half-ashamed, a tiny flourish still.
Foiled in his clash, the leader of the clan
Reproves with frowns the dilatory man:
Then on his candlestick thrice taps his bow,
Nods a new signal, and away they go.

Perchance, while pit and gallery cry "Hats off!"
And awed Consumption checks his chided cough,
Some giggling daughter of the Queen of Love
Drops, 'reft of pin, her play-bill from above:

Like Icarus, while laughing galleries clap,
Soars, ducks, and dives in air the printed scrap;
But, wiser far than he, combustion fears,
And, as it flies, eludes the chandeliers;
Till, sinking gradual, with repeated twirl,
It settles, curling, on a fiddler's curl;
Who from his powdered pate the intruder strikes,
And, for mere malice, sticks it on the spikes.

Say, why these Babel strains from Babel tongues?
Who 's that calls "Silence!" with such leathern lungs?
He who, in quest of quiet, "Silence!" hoots,
Is apt to make the hubbub he imputes.

What various swains our motley walls contain!
Fashion from Moorfields, honor from Chick Lane;
Bankers from Paper Buildings here resort,
Bankrupts from Golden Square and Riches Court;
From the Haymarket canting rogues in grain,
Gulls from the Poultry, sots from Water Lane;
The lottery cormorant, the auction shark,
The full-price master, and the half-price clerk;
Boys who long linger at the gallery-door,
With pence twice five—they want but twopence more;
Till some Samaritan the two-pence spares,
And sends them jumping up the gallery-stairs.

Critics we boast who ne'er their malice balk,
But talk their minds—we wish they 'd mind their talk:
Big-worded bullies, who by quarrels live—
Who give the lie, and tell the lie they give;
Jews from St. Mary's Ax, for jobs so wary,
That for old clothes they 'd even ax St. Mary;
And bucks with pockets empty as their pate,
Lax in their gaiters, laxer in their gait;
Who oft, when we our house lock up, carouse
With tippling tipstaves in a lock-up house.

Yet here, as elsewhere, Chance can joy bestow,
Where scowling fortune seemed to threaten woe.

John Richard William Alexander Dwyer
Was footman to Justinian Stubbs, Esquire;
But when John Dwyer listed in the Blues,
Emanuel Jennings polished Stubb's shoes.
Emanuel Jennings brought his youngest boy
Up as a corn-cutter—a safe employ;
In Holywell Street, St. Pancras, he was bred
(At number twenty-seven, it is said),
Facing the pump, and near the Granby's Head:
He would have bound him to some shop in town,
But with a premium he could not come down.
Pat was the urchin's name—a red haired youth,
Fonder of purl and skittle-grounds than truth.

Silence, ye gods! to keep your tongue in awe,
The Muse shall tell an accident she saw.

Pat Jennings in the upper gallery sat,
But, leaning forward, Jennings lost his hat:
Down from the gallery the beaver flew,
And spurned the one to settle in the two.
How shall he act? Pay at the gallery-door
Two shillings for what cost, when new, but four?
Or till half-price, to save his shilling, wait,
And gain his hat again at half-past eight?
Now, while his fears anticipate a thief,
John Mullins whispers, "Take my handkerchief."
"Thank you," cries Pat; "but one won't make a line."
"Take mine," cries Wilson; and cries Stokes, "Take mine."
A motley cable soon Pat Jennings ties,
Where Spitalfields with real India vies.
Like Iris' bow, down darts the painted clew,
Starred, striped, and spotted, yellow, red, and blue,
Old calico, torn silk, and muslin new.
George Green below, with palpitating hand
Loops the last 'kerchief to the beaver's band—
Up soars the prize! The youth, with joy unfeigned,
Regained the felt, and felt the prize regained;
While to the applauding galleries grateful Pat
Made a low bow, and touched the ransomed hat.

A TALE OF DRURY LANE.*

[A BURLESQUE OF SIR WALTER SCOTT'S METRICAL ROMANCES. REJECTED ADDRESSES.]

HORACE SMITH.

[To be spoken by Mr. Kemble, in a suit of the Black Prince's Armor, borrowed from the Tower.]

SURVEY this shield, all bossy bright—
These cuisses twin behold!
Look on my form in armor dight
Of steel inlaid with gold;
My knees are stiff in iron buckles,
Stiff spikes of steel protect my knuckles.
These once belonged to sable prince,
Who never did in battle wince;
With valor tart as pungent quince,
He slew the vaunting Gaul.
Rest there awhile, my bearded lance,
While from green curtain I advance
To yon foot-lights, no trivial dance,
And tell the town what sad mischance
Did Drury Lane befall.

THE NIGHT.

On fair Augusta's towers and trees
Flittered the silent midnight breeze,
Curling the foliage as it past,
Which from the moon-tipped plumage cast
A spangled light, like dancing spray,
Then reassumed its still array;
When, as night's lamp unclouded hung,
And down its full effulgence flung,

* "From the parody of Sir Walter Scott we know not what to select—it is all good. The effect of the fire on the town, and the description of a fireman in his official apparel, may be quoted as amusing specimens of the *misapplication* of the style and meter of Mr. Scott's admirable romances."—*Quarterly Review.*

"'A Tale of Drury,' by Walter Scott, is, upon the whole, admirably executed; though the introduction is rather tame. The burning is described with the mighty minstrel's characteristic love of localities. The catastrophe is described with a spirit not unworthy of the name so venturously assumed by the describer."—*Edinburg Review.*

It shed such soft and balmy power
That cot and castle, hall and bower,
And spire and dome, and turret height,
Appear'd to slumber in the light.
From Henry's chapel, Rufus' Hall,
To Savoy, Temple, and St. Paul,
From Knightsbridge, Pancras, Camden Town,
To Redriff Shadwell, Horsleydown,
No voice was heard, no eye unclosed,
But all in deepest sleep reposed.
They might have thought, who gazed around
Amid a silence so profound,
It made the senses thrill,
That 't was no place inhabited,
But some vast city of the dead—
All was so hushed and still.

THE BURNING.

As chaos, which, by heavenly doom,
Had slept in everlasting gloom,
Started with terror and surprise
When light first flashed upon her eyes—
So London's sons in night-cap woke,
In bed-gown woke her dames;
For shouts were heard 'mid fire and smoke,
And twice ten hundred voices spoke—
"The playhouse is in flames!"
And, lo! where Catharine street extends,
A fiery tail its luster lends
To every window-pane;
Blushes each spout in Martlet Court,
And Barbican, moth-eaten fort,
And Covent Garden kennels sport,
A bright ensanguined drain;
Meux's new brewhouse shows the light,
Rowland Hill's chapel, and the height
Where patent shot they sell;
The Tennis-Court, so fair and tall,
Partakes the ray, with Surgeons' Hall,
The ticket-porters' house of call,

Old Bedlam, close by London Wall,
Wright's shrimp and oyster shop withal,
 And Richardson's Hotel.
Nor these alone, but far and wide,
Across red Thames's gleaming tide,
To distant fields the blaze was borne,
And daisy white and hoary thorn
In borrowed luster seemed to sham
The rose of red sweet Wil-li-am.
To those who on the hills around
Beheld the flames from Drury's mound,
 As from a lofty altar rise,
It seemed that nations did conspire
To offer to the god of fire
 Some vast stupendous sacrifice!
The summoned firemen woke at call,
And hied them to their stations all:
Starting from short and broken snooze,
Each sought his pond'rous hobnailed shoes,
But first his worsted hosen plied,
Plush breeches next, in crimson dyed,
 His nether bulk embraced;
Then jacket thick, of red or blue,
Whose massy shoulder gave to view
The badge of each respective crew,
 In tin or copper traced.
The engines thundered through the street,
Fire-hook, pipe, bucket, all complete,
And torches glared, and clattering feet
 Along the pavement paced.
And one, the leader of the band,
From Charing Cross along the Strand,
Like stag by beagles hunted hard,
Ran till he stopped at Vin'gar Yard.
The burning badge his shoulder bore,
The belt and oil-skin hat he wore,
The cane he had, his men to bang,
Showed foreman of the British gang—
His name was Higginbottom. Now
'Tis meet that I should tell you how
 The others came in view:
The Hand-in-Hand the race begun,

Then came the Phœnix and the Sun,
Th' Exchange, where old insurers run,
    The Eagle, where the new;
With these came Rumford, Bumford, Cole,
Robins from Hockley in the Hole,
Lawson and Dawson, cheek by jowl,
    Crump from St. Giles's Pound:
Whitford and Mitford joined the train,
Huggins and Muggins from Chick Lane,
And Clutterbuck, who got a sprain
    Before the plug was found.
Hobson and Jobson did not sleep,
But ah! no trophy could they reap
For both were in the Donjon Keep
    Of Bridewell's gloomy mound!
E'en Higginbottom now was posed,
For sadder scene was ne'er disclosed,
Without, within, in hideous show,
Devouring flames resistless glow,
And blazing rafters downward go,
And never halloo "Heads below!"
    Nor notice give at all.
The firemen terrified are slow
To bid the pumping torrent flow,
    For fear the roof would fall.
Back, Robins, back; Crump, stand aloof!
Whitford, keep near the walls!
Huggins, regard your own behoof,
For lo! the blazing rocking roof
Down, down, in thunder falls!
An awful pause succeeds the stroke,
And o'er the ruins volumed smoke,
Rolling around its pitchy shroud,
Concealed them from th' astonished crowd.
At length the mist awhile was cleared,
When, lo! amid the wreck upreared,
Gradually a moving head appeared,
    And Eagle firemen knew
'T was Joseph Muggins, name revered,
    The foreman of their crew.
Loud shouted all in signs of woe,
"A Muggins! to the rescue, ho!"

And poured the hissing tide:
Meanwhile the Muggins fought amain,
And strove and struggled all in vain,
For, rallying but to fall again,
He tottered, sunk, and died!

Did none attempt, before he fell,
To succor one they loved so well?
Yes, Higginbottom did aspire
(His fireman's soul was all on fire),
His brother chief to save;
But ah! his reckless generous ire
Served but to share his grave!
'Mid blazing beams and scalding streams,
Through fire and smoke he dauntless broke,
Where Muggins broke before.
But sulphury stench and boiling drench
Destroying sight o'erwhelmed him quite,
He sunk to rise no more.
Still o'er his head, while Fate he braved,
His whizzing water-pipe he waved;
"Whitford and Mitford, ply your pumps,
You, Clutterbuck, come, stir your stumps,
Why are you in such doleful dumps?
A fireman, and afraid of bumps!—
What are they fear'd on? fools: 'od rot 'em!"
Were the last words of Higginbottom.

THE REVIVAL.

Peace to his soul! new prospects bloom,
And toil rebuilds what fires consume!
Eat we and drink we, be our ditty,
"Joy to the managing committee!"
Eat we and drink we, join to rum
Roast beef and pudding of the plum;
Forth from thy nook, John Horner, come,
With bread of ginger brown thy thumb,
For this is Drury's gay day:
Roll, roll thy hoop, and twirl thy tops,
And buy, to glad thy smiling chops,

Crisp parliament with lollypops,
  And fingers of the Lady.
Didst mark, how toiled the busy train,
From morn to eve, till Drury Lane
Leaped like a roebuck from the plain?
Ropes rose and sunk, and rose again,
  And nimble workmen trod;
To realize bold Wyatt's plan
Rushed may a howling Irishman;
Loud clattered many a porter-can,
And many a ragamuffin clan,
  With trowel and with hod.
Drury revives! her rounded pate
Is blue, is heavenly blue with slate;
She "wings the midway air," elate,
  As magpie, crow, or chough;
White paint her modish visage smears,
Yellow and pointed are her ears.
No pendant portico appears
Dangling beneath, for Whitbread's shears
  Have cut the bauble off.
Yes, she exalts her stately head;
And, but that solid bulk outspread,
Opposed you on your onward tread,
And posts and pillars warranted
That all was true that Wyatt said,
You might have deemed her walls so thick,
Were not composed of stone or brick,
But all a phantom, all a trick,
Of brain disturbed and fancy-sick,
So high she soars, so vast, so quick!

DRURY'S DIRGE.

[BY LAURA MATILDA.—REJECTED ADDRESSES.]

HORACE SMITH.

"You praise our sires: but though they wrote with force,
Their rhymes were vicious, and their diction coarse:
We want their *strength*, agreed; but we atone
For that and more, by *sweetness* all our own."—GIFFORD.

BALMY zephyrs, lightly flitting,
Shade me with your azure wing;
On Parnassus' summit sitting,
Aid me, Clio, while I sing.

Softly slept the dome of Drury
O'er the empyreal crest,
When Alecto's sister-fury
Softly slumbering sunk to rest.

Lo! from Lemnos, limping lamely,
Lags the lowly Lord of Fire,
Cytherea yielding tamely
To the Cyclops dark and dire.

Clouds of amber, dreams of gladness,
Dulcet joys and sports of youth,
Soon must yield to haughty sadness,
Mercy holds the vail to Truth.

See Erostratus the second
Fires again Diana's fane;
By the Fates from Orcus beckoned,
Clouds envelop Drury Lane.

Lurid smoke and frank suspicion
Hand in hand reluctant dance:
While the god fulfills his mission,
Chivarly, resign thy lance.

Hark! the engines blandly thunder,
Fleecy clouds disheveled lie,
And the firemen, mute with wonder,
On the son of Saturn cry.

See the bird of Ammon sailing,
Perches on the engine's peak,
And, the Eagle firemen hailing,
Soothes them with its bickering beak.

Juno saw, and mad with malice,
Lost the prize that Paris gave;
Jealousy's ensanguined chalice,
Mantling pours the orient wave.

Pan beheld Patrocles dying,
Nox to Niobe was turned;
From Busiris Bacchus flying,
Saw his Semele inurned.

Thus fell Drury's lofty glory,
Leveled with the shuddering stones;
Mars, with tresses black and gory,
Drinks the dew of pearly groans.

Hark! what soft Æolian numbers
Gem the blushes of the morn!
Break, Amphion, break your slumbers,
Nature's ringlets deck the thorn.

Ha! I hear the strain erratic
Dimly glance from pole to pole;
Raptures sweet, and dreams ecstatic
Fire my everlasting soul.

Where is Cupid's crimson motion?
Billowy ecstasy of woe,
Bear me straight, meandering ocean,
Where the stagnant torrents flow.

Blood in every vein is gushing,
Vixen vengeance lulls my heart;
See, the Gorgon gang is rushing!
Never, never, let us part!

WHAT IS LIFE?

BY "ONE OF THE FANCY."

BLACKWOOD'S MAGAZINE.

AND do you ask me, "What is LIFE?"
And do you ask me, "What is pleasure?"
My muse and I are not at strife,
So listen, lady, to my measure:—
Listen amid thy graceful leisure,
To what is LIFE, and what *is* pleasure.
'Tis LIFE to see the first dawn stain
With sallow light the window-pane:
To dress—to wear a rough drab coat,
With large pearl buttons all afloat
Upon the waves of plush: to tie
A kerchief of the King-cup dye
(White spotted with a small bird's-eye)
Around the neck, and from the nape
Let fall an easy fan-like cape:
To quit the house at morning's prime,
At six or so—about the time
When watchmen, conscious of the day
Puff out their lantern's rush-light ray;
Just when the silent streets are strewn
With level shadows, and the moon
Takes the day's wink and walks aside
To nurse a nap till eventide.
'Tis LIFE to reach the livery stable,
Secure the *ribbons* and the *day-bill*,
And mount a gig that had a spring
Some summer's back: and then take wing
Behind (in Mr. Hamlet's tongue)
A jade whose "withers are unwrung;
Who stands erect, and yet forlorn,
And from a *half-pay* life of corn,
Showing as many *points* each way
As Martial's Epigrammata,
Yet who, when set a-going, goes
Like one undestined to repose.
'Tis LIFE to revel down the road,
And *queer* each o'erfraught chaise's load,

To rave and rattle at the *gate*,
And shower upon the gatherer's pate
Damns by the dozens, and such speeches
As well betokens one 's *slang* riches:
To take of Deady's bright *stark naked*
A glass or so—'tis LIFE to take it!
To see the *Hurst* with tents encampt on;
Lurk around Lawrence's at Hampton;
Join the *flash* crowd (the horse being led
Into the yard, and clean'd and fed);
Talk to Dav' Hudson, and Cy' Davis
(The last a fighting *rara avis*),
And, half in secret, scheme a plan
For trying the hardy *Gas-light-Man.*
'Tis LIFE to cross the laden ferry,
With boon companions, wild and merry,
And see the ring upon the *Hurst*
With carts encircled—hear the burst
At distance of the eager crowd.
Oh, it *is* LIFE! to see a proud
And dauntless man step, full of hopes,
Up to the P. C. stakes and ropes,
Throw in his hat, and with a spring,
Get gallantly within the ring;
Eye the wide crowd, and walk awhile,
Taking all cheerings with a smile:
To see him skip—his well-trained form,
White, glowing, muscular, and warm,
All beautiful in conscious power,
Relaxed and quiet, till the hour;
His glossy and transparent frame,
In radiant plight to strive for fame!
To look upon the clean shap'd limb
In silk and flannel clothed trim;
While round the waist the 'kerchief tied,
Makes the flesh glow in richer pride.
'Tis more than LIFE, to watch him hold
His hand forth, tremulous yet bold,
Over his second's, and to clasp
His rival's in a quiet grasp;
To watch the noble attitude
He takes—the crowd in breathless mood:

And then to see, with adamant start,
The muscles set, and the great heart
Hurl a courageous splendid light
Into the eye—and then—the FIGHT!

FRAGMENTS.

[BY A FREE-LOVER.]

BLACKWOOD'S MAGAZINE, 1823.

THEY were not married by a muttering priest,
With superstitious rites, and senseless words,
Out-snuffled from an old worm-eaten book,
In a dark corner (railed off like a sheep-pen)
Of an old house, that fools do call a *Church!*
Their altar was the flowery lap of earth—
The starry empyrean their vast temple—
Their book each other's eyes—and Love himself,
Parson, and Clerk, and Father to the bride!—
Holy espousals! whereat wept with joy
The spirit of the universe.—In sooth
There was a sort of drizzling rain that day,
For I remember (having left at home
My parapluie, a name than *umbrella*
Far more expressive) that I stood for shelter
Under an entry not twelve paces off
(It might be ten) from Sheriff Waithman's shop,
For half an hour or more, and there I mused
(Mine eyes upon the running kennel fixed,
That hurried as a het'rogenous mass
To the common sewer, it 's dark reservoir),
I mused upon the running stream of *life!*

But that 's not much to the purpose—I was telling
Of these most pure espousals.—Innocent pair!
Ye were not shackled by the vulgar chains
About the yielding mind of credulous youth,
Wound by the nurse and priest—*your* energies,
Your unsophisticated impulses,
Taught ye to soar above their "settled rules
Of Vice and Virtue." Fairest creature! He

Whom the world called thy husband, was in truth
Unworthy of thee.—A dull plodding wretch!
With whose ignoble nature *thy free spirit*
Held no communion.—'T was well done, fair creature!
T' assert the independence of a mind
Created—generated I would say—
Free as "that chartered libertine, the air."
Joy to thy chosen partner! blest exchange!
Work of mysterious sympathy! that drew
Your kindred souls by * * *
* * * * * *

There fled the noblest spirit!—The most pure,
Most sublimated essence that ere dwelt
In earthly tabernacle. Gone thou art,
Exhaled, dissolved, diffused, commingled now
Into and *with* the all-absorbing frame
Of Nature, the great mother. Ev'n in life,
While still, pent-up in flesh, and skin, and bones,
My thoughts and feelings like electric flame
Shot through the solid mass, toward the source,
And blended with the general elements,
When thy young star o'er life's horizon hung
Far from it's zenith yet low lagging clouds
(Vapors of earth) obscured its heaven-born rays—
Dull joys of prejudice and superstition
And vulgar decencies begirt thee round;
And thou didst wear awhile th' unholy bonds
Of "holy matrimony!" and didst vail
Awhile thy lofty spirit to the cheat.—
But reason came—and firm philosophy,
And mild philanthropy, and pointed out
The shame it was—the crying, crushing shame,
To curb within a little paltry pale
The love that over *all* created things
Should be diffusive as the atmosphere.
Then did thy boundless tenderness expand
Over all space—all animated things
And things inanimate. Thou hadst a heart,
A ready tear for *all*.—The dying whale,
Stranded and gasping—ripped up for his blubber
By Man the Tyrant.—The small sucking pig

Slain for his riot.—The down-trampled flower
Crushed by his cruel foot.—*All*, *each*, and *all*
Shared in thy boundless sympathies, and then—
(*Sublime* perfection of perfected *love*)
Then didst thou spurn the whimp'ring wailing thing
That dared to call *thee* "husband," and to claim,
As her just right, support and love from *thee*—
Then didst thou * * * *
* * * * * * *

THE CONFESSION.

BLACKWOOD'S MAGAZINE.

There 's somewhat on my breast father,
There 's somewhat on my breast!
The live-long day I sigh, father,
At night I can not rest;
I can not take my rest, father,
Though I would fain do so,
A weary weight oppresseth me—
The weary weight of woe!

'Tis not the lack of gold, father
Nor lack of worldly gear;
My lands are broad and fair to see,
My friends are kind and dear;
My kin are leal and true, father,
They mourn to see my grief,
But oh! 'tis not a kinsman's hand
Can give my heart relief!

'Tis not that Janet's false, father,
'Tis not that she's unkind;
Though busy flatterers swarm around,
I know her constant mind.
'Tis not her coldness, father,
That chills my laboring breast—
Its that confounded cucumber
I 've ate, and can't digest.

THE MILLING-MATCH BETWEEN ENTELLUS AND DARES.

TRANSLATED FROM THE FIFTH BOOK OF THE ÆNEID, BY ONE OF THE FANCY.

THOMAS MOORE.

WITH *daddles** high upraised, and *nob* held back,
In awful prescience of the impending *thwack*,
Both *Kiddies*† stood—and with prelusive *spar*,
And light manœuv'ring, kindled up the war!
The One, in bloom of youth—a *light-weight blade*—
The Other, vast, gigantic, as if made,
Express, by Nature for the *hammering* trade;
But aged, slow, with stiff limbs, tottering much,
And lungs, that lack'd the *bellows-mender's* touch.

Yet, sprightly *to the Scratch* both *Buffers* came,
While *ribbers* rung from each resounding frame,
And divers *digs*, and many a ponderous *pelt*,
Were on their broad *bread-baskets* heard and felt.
With roving aim, but aim that rarely miss'd,
Round *lugs* and *ogles* ‡ flew the frequent fist;
While showers of *facers* told so deadly well,
That the crush'd jaw-bones crackled as they fell!
But firmly stood ENTELLUS—and still bright,
Though bent by age, with all THE FANCY'S light,
Stopp'd with a skill, and *rallied* with a fire
The Immortal FANCY could alone inspire!
While DARES, *shifting* round, with looks of thought,
An opening to the *Cove's* huge carcase sought
(Like General PRESTON, in that awful hour,
When on *one* leg he hopp'd to—take the Tower!)
And here, and there, explored with active *fin* §
And skillful *feint*, some guardless pass to win,
And prove a *boring* guest when once *let in.*
And now ENTELLUS, with an eye that plann'd
Punishing deeds, high raised his heavy hand,
But, ere the *sledge* came down, young DARES spied
His shadow o'er his brow, and slipp'd aside—

* Hands. † Fellows, usually *young* fellows.
‡ Ears and Eyes. § Arm.

So nimbly slipp'd, that the vain *nobber* pass'd
Through empty air; and He, so high, so vast,
Who dealt the stroke, came thundering to the ground!
Not B—CK—GH—M himself, with bulkier sound,
Uprooted from the field of Whiggish glories,
Fell *souse*, of late, among the astonish'd Tories!
Instant the *Ring* was broke, and shouts and yells
From Trojan *Flashmen* and Sicilian *Swells*
Fill'd the wide heaven—while, touch'd with grief to see
His *pal*,* well-known through many a *lark* and *spree*,†
Thus *rumly floor'd*, the kind ACESTES ran,
And pitying raised from earth the *game* old man,
Uncow'd, undamaged to the *sport* he came,
His limbs all muscle, and his soul all flame.
The memory of his *milling* glories past,
The shame that aught but death should see him *grass'd*,
All fired the veteran's *pluck*—with fury flush'd,
Full on his light-limb'd *customer* he rush'd—
And *hammering* right and left, with ponderous swing,
Ruffian'd the reeling youngster round the *Ring*—
Nor rest, nor pause, nor breathing-time was given,
But, rapid as the rattling hail from heaven
Beats on the house-top, showers of RANDALL'S *shot* ‡
Around the Trojan's *lugs* flew peppering hot!
Till now ÆNEAS, fill'd with anxious dread,
Rush'd in between them, and, with words well-bred
Preserved alike the peace and DARES' head,
Both which the veteran much inclined to *break*—
Then kindly thus the *punish'd* youth bespake:
   Poor *Johnny Raw!* what madness could impel
So *rum* a *Flat* to face so *prime* a *Swell?*
Sees't thou not, boy, THE FANCY, heavenly Maid,
Herself descends to this great *Hammerer's* aid,
And, singling *him* from all her *flash* adorers,
Shines in his *hits*, and thunders in his *floorers?*
Then, yield thee, youth—nor such a *spooncy* be,
To think mere man can *mill* a Deity!"

Thus spoke the Chief—and now, the *scrimage* o'er,
His faithful *pals* the *done-up* DARES bore

* Friend. † Party of pleasure and frolic.
‡ A favorite blow of THE NONPARIEL'S, so called.

Back to his home, with tottering *gams*, sunk heart,
And *muns* and *noddle pink'd* in every part.
While from his *gob* the guggling *claret* gush'd,
And lots of *grinders*, from their sockets crush'd,
Forth with the crimson tide in rattling fragments rush'd!

NOT A SOUS HAD HE GOT.

[PARODY ON WOLFE'S "BURIAL OF SIR JOHN MOORE."]

R. HARRIS BARHAM.

Not a *sous* had he got—not a guinea or note,
And he looked confoundedly flurried,
As he bolted away without paying his shot,
And the Landlady after him hurried.

We saw him again at dead of night,
When home from the Club returning;
We twigg'd the Doctor beneath the light
Of the gas-lamp brilliantly burning.

All bare, and exposed to the midnight dews,
Reclined in the gutter we found him;
And he look'd like a gentleman taking a snooze,
With his *Marshall* cloak around him.

"The Doctor's as drunk as the d——," we said,
And we managed a shutter to borrow;
We raised him, and sigh'd at the thought that his head
Whould "consumedly ache" on the morrow.

We bore him home, and we put him to bed,
And we told his wife and his daughter
To give him, next morning, a couple of red
Herrings, with soda-water.—

Loudly they talk'd of his money that 's gone,
And his Lady began to upbraid him;
But little he reck'd, so they let him snore on
'Neath the counterpane just as we laid him.

We tuck'd him in, and had hardly done
When, beneath the window calling,
We heard the rough voice of a son of a gun
Of a watchman "One o'clock!" bawling.

Slowly and sadly we all walk'd down
From his room in the uppermost story;
A rushlight was placed on the cold hearth-stone,
And we left him alone in his glory!!

RAISING THE DEVIL.

A LEGEND OF CORNELIUS AGRIPPA.

R. HARRIS BARHAM.

"And hast thou nerve enough?" he said,
That gray Old Man, above whose head
Unnumbered years have roll'd—
"And hast thou nerve to view," he cried,
"The incarnate Fiend that Heaven defied!—
—Art thou indeed so bold?

"Say, canst Thou, with unshrinking gaze,
Sustain, rash youth, the withering blaze
Of that unearthly eye,
That blasts where'er it lights—the breath
That, like the Simoom, scatters death
On all that yet *can* die!

—"Darest thou confront that fearful form,
That rides the whirlwind, and the storm,
In wild unholy revel!—
The terrors of that blasted brow,
Archangel's once—though ruin'd now—
—Ay—dar'st thou face The Devil?"—

"I dare!" the desperate Youth replied,
And placed him by that Old Man's side,
In fierce and frantic glee,

Unblenched his cheek, and firm his limb
—"No paltry juggling Fiend, but HIM!
—THE DEVIL!—I fain would see!—

"In all his Gorgon terrors clad,
His worst, his fellest shape!" the Lad
Rejoined in reckless tone.—
—"Have then thy wish!" Agrippa said,
And sigh'd and shook his hoary head,
With many a bitter groan.

He drew the mystic circle's bound,
With skull and cross-bones fenc'd around;
He traced full many a sigil there;
He mutter'd many a backward pray'r,
That sounded like a curse—
"He comes!"—he cried with wild grimace,
"The fellest of Apollyon's race!"
—Then in his startled pupil's face
He dash'd—an EMPTY PURSE!!

THE LONDON UNIVERSITY;*

OR, STINKOMALEE TRIUMPHANS.

AN ODE TO BE PERFORMED ON THE OPENING OF THE NEW COLLEGE.

R. HARRIS BARHAM.

WHENE'ER with pitying eye I view
Each operative sot in town,
I smile to think how wondrous few
Get drunk who study at the U-
niversity we 've Got in town—
niversity we 've Got in town.

What precious fools "The People" grew,
Their *alma mater* not in town;
The "useful classes" hardly knew

* See page 387.

Four was composed of two and two,
Until they learned it at the U-
niversity we 've Got in town—
niversity we 've Got in town.

But now they 're taught by JOSEPH HU-
ME, by far the cleverest Scot in town,
Their *items* and their *tottles* too ;
Each may dissect his sister Sue,
From his instructions at the U-
niversity we 've Got in town—
niversity we 've Got in town.

Then L———E comes, like him how few
Can caper and can trot in town,
In *pirouette* or *pas de deux*—
He beats the famed *Monsieur Giroux*,
And teaches dancing at the U-
niversity we 've Got in town—
niversity we 've Got in town.

And GILCHRIST, see, that great Geentoo-
Professor, has a lot in town
Of Cockney boys who fag Hindoo,
And *larn Jem-nastics* at the U-
niversity we 've Got in town—
niversity we 've Got in town.

SAM R—— corpse of vampire hue,
Comes from its grave to rot in town ;
For Bays the dead bard 's crowned with Yew,
And chants, the Pleasures of the U-
niversity we 've Got in town—
niversity we 've Got in town.

FRANK JEFFREY, of the Scotch Review,—
Whom MOORE had nearly shot in town,—
Now, with his pamphlet stitched in blue
And yellow, d—ns the other two,
But lauds the ever-glorious U-
niversity we 've Got in town—
niversity we 've Got in town.

Great BIRBECK, king of chips and glue,
   Who paper oft does blot in town,
From the Mechanics' Institu-
tion, comes to prate of wedge and screw,
Lever and axle at the U-
               niversity we 've Got in town—
               niversity we 've Got in town.

LORD WAITHAM, who long since withdrew
   From Mansion House to cot in town;
Adorn'd with chair of ormolu,
All darkly grand, like Prince Lee Boo,
Lectures on *Free Trade* at the U-
               niversity we 've Got in town—
               niversity we 've Got in town.

Fat F——, with his coat of blue,
   Who speeches makes so hot in town,
In rhetoric, spells his lectures through,
And sounds the V for W,
The *vay they speaks* it at the U-
               niversity we 've Got in town—
               niversity we 've Got in town.

Then H——E comes, who late at New-
   gate Market, sweetest spot in town!
Instead of one clerk popp'd in two,
To make a place for his ne-phew,
Seeking another at the U-
               niversity we 've Got in town—
               niversity we 've Got in town.

There 's Captain Ross, a traveler true,
   Has just presented, what in town-
's an article of great *virtu*
(The telescope he once peep'd through,
And 'spied an Esquimaux canoe
On Croker Mountains), to the U-
               niversity we 've Got in town—
               niversity we 've Got in town.

Since MICHAEL gives no roast nor stew,
   Where Whigs might eat and plot in town,
And swill his port, and mischief brew—

Poor CREEVY sips his water gru-
el as the beadle of the U-
niversity we 've Got in town—
niversity we 've Got in town.

There 's JERRY BENTHAM and his crew,
Names ne'er to be forgot in town,
In swarms like Banquo's long is-sue—
Turk, Papist, Infidel and Jew,
Come trooping on to join the U-
niversity we 've Got in town—
niversity we 've Got in town.

To crown the whole with triple queue—
Another such there 's not in town,
Twitching his restless nose askew,
Behold tremendous HARRY BROUGH-
AM! Law Professor at the U-
niversity we 've Got in town—
niversity we 've Got in town.

Grand chorus:

Huzza! huzza! for HARRY BROUGH-
AM! Law Professor at the U-
niversity we 've Got in town—
niversity we 've Got in town.

DOMESTIC POEMS.

THOMAS HOOD.

I.

GOOD-NIGHT.

THE sun was slumbering in the west, my daily labors past;
On Anna's soft and gentle breast my head reclined at last;
The darkness closed around, so dear to fond congenial souls;
And thus she murmured in my ear, "My love, we 're out of coals!

"That Mister Bond has called again, insisting on his rent;
And all the Todds are coming up to see us, out of Kent;

I quite forgot to tell you John has had a tipsy fall ;—
I'm sure there's something going on with that vile Mary Hall!

"Miss Bell has bought the sweetest silk, and I have bought the rest—
Of course, if we go out of town, Southend will be the best.
I really think the Jones's house would be the thing for us ;
I think I told you Mrs. Pope had parted with her *nus*—

"Cook, by the way, came up to-day, to bid me suit myself—
And, what'd ye think? the rats have gnawed the victuals on the shelf.
And, Lord! there's such a letter come, inviting you to fight!
Of course you don't intend to go—God bless you, dear, good-night!"

II.

A PARENTAL ODE TO MY SON, AGED THREE YEARS AND FIVE MONTHS.

Thou happy, happy elf!
(But stop—first let me kiss away that tear)—
Thou tiny image of myself!
(My love, he's poking peas into his ear!)
Thou merry, laughing sprite!
With spirits feather-light,
Untouched by sorrow, and unsoiled by sin—
(Good heavens! the child is swallowing a pin!)
Thou little tricksy Puck!
With antic toys so funnily bestuck,
Light as the singing bird that wings the air—
(The door! the door! he'll tumble down the stair!)
Thou darling of thy sire!
(Why, Jane, he'll set his pinafore afire!)
Thou imp of mirth and joy!
In Love's dear chain so strong and bright a link,
Thou idol of thy parents—(Drat the boy!
There goes my ink!)

Thou cherub—but of earth ;
Fit playfellow for Fays, by moonlight pale,

In harmless sport and mirth,
(That dog will bite him if he pulls its tail!)
Thou human humming-bee, extracting honey
From every blossom in the world that blows,
Singing in youth's elysium ever sunny,
(Another tumble!—that's his precious nose!)

Thy father's pride and hope!
(He 'll break the mirror with that skipping-rope!)
With pure heart newly stamped from Nature's mint—
(Where did he learn that squint?)
Thou young domestic dove!
(He 'll have that jug off, with another shove!)
Dear nursling of the Hymeneal nest!
(Are those torn clothes his best?)
Little epitome of man!
(He 'll climb upon the table, that 's his plan!)
Touched with the beauteous tints of dawning life—
(He 's got a knife!)

Thou enviable being!
No storms, no clouds, in thy blue sky foreseeing,
Play on, play on,
My elfin John!
Toss the light ball—bestride the stick—
(I knew so many cakes would make him sick!)
With fancies, buoyant as the thistle-down,
Prompting the face grotesque, and antic brisk,
With many a lamb-like frisk,
(He 's got the scissors, snipping at your gown!)

Thou pretty opening rose!
(Go to your mother, child, and wipe your nose!)
Balmy and breathing music like the South,
(He really brings my heart into my mouth!)
Fresh as the morn, and brilliant as its star—
(I wish that window had an iron bar!)
Bold as the hawk, yet gentle as the dove—
(I 'll tell you what, my love,
I can not write, unless he 's sent above!)

III.

A SERENADE.

"LULLABY, O, lullaby!"
Thus I heard a father cry,
"Lullaby, O, lullaby!
The brat will never shut an eye;
Hither come, some power divine!
Close his lids, or open mine!"

"Lullaby, O, lullaby!
What the devil makes him cry?
Lullaby, O, lullaby!
Still he stares—I wonder why,
Why are not the sons of earth
Blind, like puppies, from their birth?"

"Lullaby, O, lullaby!"
Thus I heard the father cry;
"Lullaby, O, lullaby!
Mary, you must come and try!—
Hush, O, hush, for mercy's sake—
The more I sing, the more you wake!"

"Lullaby, O, lullaby!
Fie, you little creature, fie!
Lullaby, O, lullaby!
Is no poppy-syrup nigh?
Give him some, or give him all,
I am nodding to his fall!"

"Lullaby, O, lullaby!
Two such nights and I shall die!
Lullaby, O, lullaby!
He 'll be bruised, and so shall I—
How can I from bed-posts keep,
When I 'm walking in my sleep!"

"Lullaby, O, lullaby!
Sleep his very looks deny—
Lullaby, O lullaby!
Nature soon will stupefy—

My nerves relax—my eyes grow dim—
Who 's that fallen—me or him?"

ODE TO PERRY,

THE INVENTOR OF THE STEEL PEN.

THOMAS HOOD.

"In this good work, Penn appears the greatest, usefullest of God's instruments. Firm and unbending when the exigency requires it—soft and yielding when rigid inflexibility is not a desideratum—fluent and flowing, at need, for eloquent rapidity—slow and retentive in cases of deliberation—never spluttering or by amplification going wide of the mark—never splitting, if it can be helped, with any one, but ready to wear itself out rather in their service—all things as it were with all men—ready to embrace the hand of Jew, Christian, or Mohammedan—heavy with the German, light with the Italian, oblique with the English, upright with the Roman, backward in coming forward with the Hebrew—in short, for flexibility, amiability, constitutional durability, general ability, and universal utility, it would be hard to find a parallel to the great Penn."—PERRY'S CHARACTERISTICS OF A SETTLER.

O! PATENT Pen-inventing Perrian Perry!
Friend of the goose and gander,
That now unplucked of their quill-feathers wander,
Cackling, and gabbling, dabbling, making merry,
About the happy fen,
Untroubled for one penny-worth of pen,
For which they chant thy praise all Britain through,
From Goose-Green unto Gander-Cleugh!—

Friend to all Author-kind—
Whether of Poet or of Proser—
Thou art composer unto the composer
Of pens—yea, patent vehicles for Mind
To carry it on jaunts, or more extensive
*Perry*grinations through the realms of thought;
Each plying from the Comic to the Pensive,
An Omnibus of intellectual sort;

Modern improvements in their course we feel,
And while to iron railroads heavy wares,
Dry goods and human bodies, pay their fares,
Mind flies on steel.

To Penrith, Penrhyn, even to Penzance;
Nay, penetrates, perchance,
To Pennsylvania, or, without rash vaunts,
To where the Penguin haunts!

In times bygone, when each man cut his quill,
With little Perryan skill,
What horrid, awkward, bungling tools of trade
Appeared the writing implements home-made!
What Pens were sliced, hewed, hacked, and haggled out,
Slit or unslit, with many a various snout,
Aquiline, Roman, crooked, square, and snubby,
Stumpy and stubby;
Some capable of ladye-billets neat,
Some only fit for ledger-keeping clerk,
And some to grub down Peter Stubbs his mark,
Or smudge through some illegible receipt;
Others in florid caligraphic plans,
Equal to ships, and wiggy heads, and swans!

To try in any common inkstands, then,
With all their miscellaneous stocks,
To find a decent pen,
Was like a dip into a lucky box:
You drew—and got one very curly,
And split like endive in some hurly-burly;
The next unslit, and square at end, a spade;
The third, incipient pop-gun, not yet made;
The fourth a broom; the fifth of no avail,
Turned upward, like a rabbit's tail;
And last, not least, by way of a relief,
A stump that Master Richard, James or John,
Had tried his candle-cookery upon,
Making "roast-beef!"

Not so thy Perryan Pens!
True to their M's and N's,
They do not with a whizzing zig-zag split,
Straddle, turn up their noses, sulk, and spit,
Or drop large dots,
Hugh full-stop blots,
Where even semicolons were unfit.

They will not frizzle up, or, broom-like, drudge
In sable sludge—
Nay, bought at proper "Patent Perryan" shops,
They write good grammar, sense, and mind their stops
Compose both prose and verse, the sad and merry—
For when the editor, whose pains compile
The grown-up Annual, or the Juvenile,
Vaunteth his articles, not women's, men's,
But lays "by the most celebrated Pens,"
What means he but thy Patent Pens, my Perry?

Pleasant they are to feel!
So firm! so flexible! composed of steel
So finely tempered—fit for tenderest Miss
To give her passion breath,
Or kings to sign the warrant stern of death—
But their supremest merit still is this,
Write with them all your days,
Tragedy, Comedy, all kinds of plays—
(No dramatist should ever be without 'em)—
And, just conceive the bliss—
There is so little of the goose about 'em,
One 's safe from any hiss!
Ah! who can paint that first great awful night,
Big with a blessing or a blight,
When the poor dramatist, all fume and fret,
Fuss, fidget, fancy, fever, funking, fright,
Ferment, fault-fearing, faintness—more f's yet:
Flushed, frigid, flurried, flinching, fitful, flat,
Add famished, fuddled, and fatigued, to that;
Funeral, fate-foreboding—sits in doubt,
Or rather doubt with hope, a wretched marriage,
To see his play upon the stage come out;
No stage to him! it is Thalia's carriage,
And he is sitting on the spikes behind it,
Striving to look as if he did n't mind it!

Witness how Beazley vents upon his hat
His nervousness, meanwhile his fate is dealt:
He kneads, molds, pummels it, and sits it flat,
Squeezes and twists it up, until the felt,
That went a beaver in, comes out a rat!

Miss Mitford had mis-givings, and in fright,
    Upon Rienzi's night,
Gnawed up one long kid glove, and all her bag,
    Quite to a rag.
Knowles has confessed he trembled as for life,
    Afraid of his own "Wife;"
Poole told me that he felt a monstrous pail
Of water backing him, all down his spine—
"The ice-brook's temper"—pleasant to the chine!
For fear that Simpson and his Co. should fail.
Did Lord Glengall not frame a mental prayer,
Wishing devoutly he was Lord knows where?
Nay, did not Jerrold, in enormous drouth,
While doubtful of Nell Gwynne's eventful luck,
    Squeeze out and suck
More oranges with his one fevered mouth
Than Nelly had to hawk from north to south?
Yea, Buckstone, changing color like a mullet,
Refused, on an occasion, once, twice, thrice,
From his best friend, an ice,
Lest it should hiss in his own red-hot gullet.

Doth punning Peake not sit upon the points
Of his own jokes, and shake in all his joints,
        During their trial?
        'Tis past denial.
And does not Pocock, feeling, like a peacock,
All eyes upon him, turn to very meacock?
And does not Planché, tremulous and blank,
Meanwhile his personages tread the boards,
        Seem goaded by sharp swords,
And called upon himself to "walk the plank?"
As for the Dances, Charles and George to boot,
        What have they more
Of ease and rest, for sole of either foot,
Than bear that capers on a hotted floor!

Thus pending—does not Matthews, at sad shift
For voice, croak like a frog in waters fenny?—
Serle seem upon the surly seas adrift?—
And Kenny think he 's going to Kilkenny?—

Haynes Bayly feel Old ditto, with the note
Of Cotton in his ear, a mortal grapple
About his arms, and Adam's apple
Big as a fine Dutch codling in his throat?
Did Rodwell, on his chimney-piece, desire
Or not to take a jump into the fire?
Did Wade feel as composed as music can?
And was not Bernard his own Nervous Man?
Lastly, don't Farley, a bewildered elf,
Quake at the Pantomime he loves to cater,
And ere its changes ring transform himself?
A frightful mug of human delf?
A spirit-bottle—empty of "the cratur?"
A leaden-platter ready for the shelf?
A thunderstruck dumb-waiter?

To clench the fact,
Myself, once guilty of one small rash act,
Committed at the Surrey,
Quite in a hurry,
Felt all this flurry,
Corporal worry,
And spiritual scurry,
Dram-devil—attic curry!
All going well,
From prompter's bell,
Until befell
A hissing at some dull imperfect dunce—
There 's no denying
I felt in all four elements at once!
My head was swimming, while my arms were flying!
My legs for running—all the rest was frying!

Thrice welcome, then, for this peculiar use,
Thy pens so innocent of goose!
For this shall dramatists, when they make merry,
Discarding port and sherry,
Drink—"Perry!"
Perry, whose fame, pennated, is let loose
To distant lands,
Perry, admitted on all hands,

Text, running, German, Roman,
For Patent Perryans approached by no man!
And when, ah me! far distant be the hour!
Pluto shall call thee to his gloomy bower,
Many shall be thy pensive mourners, many!
And Penury itself shall club its penny
To raise thy monument in lofty place,
Higher than York's or any son of War;
While time all meaner effigies shall bury,
On due pentagonal base
Shall stand the Parian, Perryan, periwigged Perry,
Perched on the proudest peak of Penman Mawr!

A THEATRICAL CURIOSITY.

CRUIKSHANK'S OMNIBUS.

Once in a barn theatric, deep in Kent,
A famed tragedian—one of tuneful tongue—
Appeared for that night only—'t was Charles Young.
As Rolla he. And as that Innocent,
The Child of hapless Cora, on there went
A smiling, fair-hair'd girl. She scarcely flung
A shadow, as she walk'd the lamps among—
So light she seem'd, and so intelligent!
That child would Rolla bear to Cora's lap:
Snatching the creature by her tiny gown,
He plants her on his shoulder,—All, all clap!
While all with praise the Infant Wonder crown,
She lisps in Rolla's ear,—"*Look out, old chap,*
Or else I'm blow'd if you don't have me down!"

SIDDONS AND HER MAID

W. S. LANDOR.

Siddons. I leave, and unreluctant, the repast;
The herb of China is its crown at last.
Maiden! hast thou a thimble in thy gear?
Maid. Yes, missus, yes.

Siddons. Then, maiden, place it here,
With penetrated, penetrating eyes.
Maid. Mine? missus! are they?
Siddons. Child! thou art unwise,
Of needles', not of woman's eyes, I spake.
Maid. O dear me! missus, what a sad mistake!
Siddons. Now canst thou tell me what was that which led
Athenian Theseus into labyrinth dread?
Maid. He never told me: I can't say, not I,
Unless, mayhap, 't was curiosity.
Siddons. Fond maiden!
Maid. No, upon my conscience, madam!
If I was fond of 'em I might have had 'em.
Siddons. Avoid! avaunt! beshrew me! 't is in vain
That Shakspeare's language germinates again.

THE SECRET SORROW.

PUNCH.

Oh! let me from the festive board
To thee, my mother, flee;
And be my secret sorrow shared
By thee—by only thee!

In vain they spread the glitt'ring store,
The rich repast, in vain;
Let others seek enjoyment there,
To me 'tis only pain.

There *was* a word of kind advice—
A whisper soft and low,
But oh! that *one* resistless smile!
Alas! why was it so?

No blame, no blame, my mother dear,
Do I impute to *you*,
But since I ate that currant tart
I don't know what to do!

SONG FOR PUNCH DRINKERS.

AFTER SCHILLER.

PUNCH.

Four be the elements,
  Here we assemble 'em,
Each of man's world
  And existence an emblem.

Press from the lemon
  The slow flowing juices—
Bitter is life
  In its lessons and uses.

Bruise the fair sugar lumps—
  Nature intended
Her sweet and severe
  To be everywhere blended.

Pour the still water—
  Unwarning by sound,
Eternity's ocean
  Is hemming us round.

Mingle the spirit,
  The life of the bowl—
Man is an earth-clod
  Unwarmed by a soul!

Drink of the stream
  Ere its potency goes!—
No bath is refreshing
  Except while it glows!

THE SONG OF THE HUMBUGGED HUSBAND.

PUNCH.

She 's not what fancy painted her—
  I'm sadly taken in:
If some one else had won her, I
  Should not have cared a pin.

I thought that she was mild and good
  As maiden e'er could be;
I wonder how she ever could
  Have so much humbugg'd me.

They cluster round and shake my hand—
  They tell me I am blest:
My case they do not understand—
  I think that I know best.

They say she 's fairest of the fair—
  They drive me mad and madder.
What do they mean by it? I swear,
  I only wish they had her.

'Tis true that she has lovely locks,
  That on her shoulders fall;
What would they say to see the box
  In which she keeps them all?

Her taper fingers, it is true,
  'Twere difficult to match:
What would they say if they but knew
  How terribly they scratch?

TEMPERANCE SONG.

PUNCH.

Air—*Friend of my soul.*

Friend of my soul, this water sip,
  Its strength you need not fear;
'Tis not so luscious as egg-flip,
  Nor half so strong as beer.
Like Jenkins when he writes,
  It can not touch the mind;
Unlike what he indites,
  No nausea leaves behind.

LINES

ADDRESSED TO ** **** ***** ON THE 29TH OF SEPTEMBER, WHEN WE PARTED FOR THE LAST TIME.

PUNCH.

I HAVE watch'd thee with rapture, and dwelt on thy charms,
As link'd in Love's fetters we wander'd each day;
And each night I have sought a new life in thy arms,
And sigh'd that our union could last not for aye.

But thy life now depends on a frail silken thread,
Which I even by kindness may cruelly sever,
And I look to the moment of parting with dread,
For I feel that in parting I lose thee forever.

Sole being that cherish'd my poor troubled heart!
Thou know'st all its secrets—each joy and each grief;
And in sharing them all thou did'st ever impart
To its sorrows a gentle and soothing relief.

The last of a long and affectionate race,
As thy days are declining I love thee the more,
For I feel that thy loss I can never replace—
That thy death will but leave me to weep and deplore.

Unchanged, thou shalt live in the mem'ry of years,
I can not—I will not—forget what thou wert!
While the thoughts of thy love as they call forth my tears,
In fancy will wash thee once more—MY LAST SHIRT.

Grub-street.

MADNESS.

PUNCH.

THERE is a madness of the heart, not head—
That in some bosoms wages endless war;
There is a throe when other pangs are dead,
That shakes the system to its utmost core.

There is a tear more scalding than the brine
  That streams from out the fountain of the eye,
And like the lava leaves a scorched line,
  As in its fiery course it rusheth by.

What is that madness? Is it envy, hate,
  Or jealousy more cruel than the grave,
With all the attendants that upon it wait
  And make the victim now despair, now rave?

It is when hunger, clam'ring for relief,
  Hears a shrill voice exclaim, "That graceless sinner,
The cook, has been, and gone, and burnt the beef,
  And spilt the tart—in short, she 's dish 'd the dinner!"

THE BANDIT'S FATE.

PUNCH.

He wore a brace of pistols the night when first we met,
His deep-lined brow was frowning beneath his wig of jet,
His footsteps had the moodiness, his voice the hollow tone,
Of a bandit-chief, who feels remorse, and tears his hair alone—
  I saw him but at half-price, yet methinks I see him now,
  In the tableau of the last act, with the blood upon his brow.

A private bandit's belt and boots, when next we met, he wore;
His salary, he told me, was lower than before;
And standing at the O. P. wing he strove, and not in vain,
To borrow half a sovereign, which he never paid again.
  I saw it but a moment—and I wish I saw it now—
  As he buttoned up his pocket with a condescending bow.

And once again we met; but no bandit chief was there;
His rouge was off, and gone that head of once luxuriant hair:
He lodges in a two-pair back, and at the public near,
He can not liquidate his "chalk," or wipe away his beer.
  I saw him sad and seedy, yet methinks I see him now,
  In the tableau of the last act, with the blood upon his brow.

LINES WRITTEN AFTER A BATTLE.

BY AN ASSISTANT SURGEON OF THE NINETEENTH NANKEENS.

PUNCH.

Stiff are the warrior's muscles,
  Congeal'd, alas! his chyle;
No more in hostile tussles
  Will he excite his bile.
Dry is the epidermis,
  A vein no longer bleeds—
And the communis vermis
  Upon the warrior feeds.

Compress'd, alas! the thorax,
  That throbbed with joy or pain;
Not e'en a dose of borax
  Could make it throb again.
Dried up the warrior's throat is,
  All shatter'd too, his head:
Still is the epiglottis—
  The warrior is dead.

THE PHRENOLOGIST TO HIS MISTRESS.

PUNCH.

Though largely developed's my organ of order,
  And though I possess my destructiveness small,
On suicide, dearest, you 'll force me to border,
  If thus you are deaf to my vehement call.

For thee veneration is daily extending,
  On a head that for want of it once was quite flat;
If thus with my passion I find you contending,
  My organs will swell till they 've knocked off my hat.

I know, of perceptions, I 've none of the clearest;
  For while I believe that by thee I 'm beloved,
I 'm told at my passion thou secretly sneerest;
  But oh! may the truth unto me never be proved!

I 'll fly to Deville, and a cast of my forehead
I 'll send unto thee;—then upon thee I 'll call.
Rejection—alas! to the lover how horrid—
When 'tis passion that *spurs-him*, 'tis bitter as *gall*.

THE CHEMIST TO HIS LOVE.

PUNCH.

I LOVE thee, Mary, and thou lovest me—
Our mutual flame is like th' affinity
That doth exist between two simple bodies:
I am Potassium to thine Oxygen.
'Tis little that the holy marriage vow
Shall shortly make us one. That unity
Is, after all, but metaphysical.
O, would that I, my Mary, were an acid,
A living acid; thou an alkali
Endow'd with human sense, that, brought together,
We both might coalesce into one salt,
One homogeneous crystal. Oh! that thou
Wert Carbon, and myself were Hydrogen;
We would unite to form olefiant gas,
Or common coal, or naphtha—would to heaven
That I were Phosphorus, and thou wert Lime!
And we of Lime composed a Phosphuret.
I 'd be content to be Sulphuric Acid,
So that thou might be Soda. In that case
We should be Glauber's Salt. Wert thou Magnesia
Instead we 'd form that's named from Epsom.
Couldst thou Potassa be, I Aqua-fortis,
Our happy union should that compound form,
Nitrate of Potash—otherwise Saltpeter.
And thus our several natures sweetly blent,
We'd live and love together, until death
Should decompose the fleshly *tertium quid*,
Leaving our souls to all eternity
Amalgamated. Sweet, thy name is Briggs
And mine is Johnson. Wherefore should not we
Agree to form a Johnsonate of Briggs?
We will. The day, the happy day, is nigh,
When Johnson shall with beauteous Briggs combine.

A BALLAD OF BEDLAM.

PUNCH.

O, Lady wake!—the azure moon
Is rippling in the verdant skies,
The owl is warbling his soft tune,
Awaiting but thy snowy eyes.
The joys of future years are past,
To-morrow's hopes have fled away;
Still let us love, and e'en at last,
We shall be happy yesterday.

The early beam of rosy night
Drives off the ebon morn afar,
While through the murmur of the light
The huntsman winds his mad guitar.
Then, lady, wake! my brigantine
Pants, neighs, and prances to be free;
Till the creation I am thine,
To some rich desert fly with me.

STANZAS TO AN EGG.

[BY A SPOON.]

PUNCH.

Pledge of a feather'd pair's affection,
Kidnapped in thy downy nest,
Soon for my breakfast—sad reflection!—
Must thou in yon pot be drest.

What are the feelings of thy mother?
Poor bereaved, unhappy hen!
Though she may lay, perchance, another,
Thee she ne'er will see again.

Yet do not mourn. Although above thee
Never more shall parent brood,
Know, dainty darling! that I love thee
Dearly as thy mother could.

A FRAGMENT.

PUNCH.

His eye was stern and wild,—his cheek was pale and cold as clay;
Upon his tightened lip a smile of fearful meaning lay;
He mused awhile—but not in doubt—no trace of doubt was there;
It was the steady solemn pause of resolute despair.
Once more he look'd upon the scroll—once more its words he read—
Then calmly, with unflinching hand, its folds before him spread.
I saw him bare his throat, and seize the blue cold-gleaming steel,
And grimly try the tempered edge he was so soon to feel!
A sickness crept upon my heart, and dizzy swam my head,—
I could not stir—I could not cry—I felt benumb'd and dead;
Black icy horrors struck me dumb, and froze my senses o'er;
I closed my eyes in utter fear, and strove to think no more.

* * * * * * *

Again I looked,—a fearful change across his face had pass'd—
He seem'd to rave,—on cheek and lip a flaky foam was cast;
He raised on high the glitteirng blade—then first I found a tongue—
"Hold, madman! stay thy frantic deed!" I cried, and forth I sprung;
He heard me, but he heeded not; one glance around he gave;
And ere I could arrest his hand, he had begun to *shave!*

EATING SONG.

PUNCH.

Oh! carve me yet another slice,
O help me to more gravy still,
There 's naught so sure as something nice
To conquer care, or grief to kill.

I always loved a bit of beef,
When Youth and Bliss and Hope were mine;
And now it gives my heart relief
In sorrow's darksome hour—to dine!

THE SICK CHILD.

[BY THE HONORABLE WILHELMINA SKEGGS.]

PUNCH.

A WEAKNESS seizes on my mind—I would more pudding take;
But all in vain—I feel—I feel—my little head will ache.
Oh! that I might alone be left, to rest where now I am,
And finish with a piece of bread that pot of currant jam.

I gaze upon the cake with tears, and wildly I deplore
That I must take a powder if I touch a morsel more,
Or oil of castor, smoothly bland, will offer'd be to me,
In wave pellucid, floating on a cup of milkless tea.

It may be so—I can not tell—I yet may do without;
They need not know, when left alone, what I have been about.
I long to eat that potted beef—to taste that apple-pie;
I long—I long to eat some more, but have not strength to try.

I gasp for breath, and now I know I 've eaten far too much;
Not one more crumb of all the feast before me can I touch.
Susan, oh! Susan, ring the bell, and call for mother, dear,
My brain swims round—I feel it all—mother, your child is queer!

THE IMAGINATIVE CRISIS.

PUNCH.

OH, solitude! thou wonder-working fay,
Come nurse my feeble fancy in your arms,
Though I, and thee, and fancy town-pent lay,
Come, call around, a world of country charms.
Let all this room, these walls dissolve away,
And bring me Surrey's fields to take their place:
This floor be grass, and draughts as breezes play;
Yon curtains trees, to wave in summer's face;
My ceiling, sky; my water-jug a stream;
My bed, a bank, on which to muse and dream.

The spell is wrought: imagination swells
My sleeping-room to hills, and woods, and dells!
I walk abroad, for naught my footsteps hinder,
And fling my arms. Oh! mi! I've broke the *winder!*

LINES TO BESSY.

[BY A STUDENT AT LAW.]

PUNCH.

My head is like a title-deed,
Or abstract of the same:
Wherein, my Bessy, thou may'st read
Thine own long-cherish'd name.

Against thee I my suit have brought,
I am thy plaintiff lover,
And for the heart that thou hast caught,
An action lies—of trover.

Alas, upon me every day
The heaviest costs you levy:
Oh, give me back my heart—but nay!
I feel I can't replevy.

I 'll love thee with my latest breath,
Alas, I can not *you* shun,
Till the hard hand of *sheriff* death
Takes me in execution.

Say, Bessy dearest, if you will
Accept me as a lover?
Must true affection file a bill
The secret to discover?

Is it my income's small amount
That leads to hesitation?
Refer the question of account
To Cupid's arbitration.

MONODY ON THE DEATH OF AN ONLY CLIENT.

PUNCH.

Oh! take away my wig and gown,
  Their sight is mockery now to me:
I pace my chambers up and down,
  Reiterating "Where is *he?*"

Alas! wild echo, with a moan,
  Murmurs above my feeble head:
In the wide world I am alone;
  Ha! ha! my only client's—dead!

In vain the robing-room I seek;
  The very waiters scarcely bow;
Their looks contemptuously speak,
  "He 's lost his only client now."

E'en the mild usher, who, of yore,
  Would hasten when his name I said,
To hand in motions, comes no more,
  He knows my only client's dead.

Ne'er shall I, rising up in court,
  Open the pleadings of a suit:
Ne'er shall the judges cut me short
  While moving them for a compute.

No more with a consenting brief
  Shall I politely bow my head;
Where shall I run to hide my grief?
  Alas! my only client 's dead.

Imagination's magic power
  Brings back, as clear, as clear as can be,
The spot, the day, the very hour,
  When first I sign'd my maiden plea.

In the Exchequer's hindmost row
  I sat, and some one touched my head,
He tendered ten-and-six, but oh!
  That only client now is dead.

In vain I try to sing—I 'm hoarse:
  In vain I try to play the flute,
A phantom seems to flit across—
  It is the ghost of a compute.

I try to read,—but all in vain;
  My chamber listlessly I tread;
Be still, my heart; throb less, my brain;
  Ho! ho! my only client's dead.

I think I hear a double knock:
  I did—alas! it is a dun.
Tailor—avaunt! my sense you shock;
  He 's dead! you know I had but one.

What 's this they thrust into my hand?
  A bill returned!—ten pounds for bread!
My butcher's got a large demand;
  I 'm mad! my only client's dead.

LOVE ON THE OCEAN.

PUNCH.

They met, 't was in a storm
  On the deck of a steamer;
She spoke in language warm,
  Like a sentimental dreamer.
He spoke—at least he tried;
  His position he altered;
Then turned his face aside,
  And his deep-ton'd voice falter'd.

She gazed upon the wave,
  Sublime she declared it;
But no reply he gave—
  He could not have dared it.
A breeze came from the south,
  Across the billows sweeping;
His heart was in his mouth,
  And out he thought 't was leaping.

"O, then, Steward!" he cried,
  With the deepest emotion;
Then totter'd to the side,
  And leant o'er the ocean.
The world may think him cold,
  But they 'll pardon him with quickness,
When the fact they shall be told,
  That he suffer'd from sea-sickness.

"OH! WILT THOU SEW MY BUTTONS ON?"*

AND

"YES, I WILL SEW THY BUTTONS ON!"

PUNCH.

[Just at present no lyrics have so *éclatant* a *succès de société* as the charming companion ballads which, under the above pathetic titles, have made a *fureur* in the fashionable circles, to which the fair composer, to whom they are attributed in the *causeries* of May Fair and Belgravia (The HON. MRS. N—T—N), belongs. The touching event to which they refer, is the romantic union of the HON. MISS BL—CHE DE F—TZ—FL—M to C—PT—N DE B—TS, of the C—DS—M G—DS, which took the *beau monde* by surprise last season. Previous to the *éclaircissement*, the gifted and lovely composer, at a ball given by the distinguished D—CH—SS of S—TH—D, accidentally overheard the searching question of the gallant but penniless Captain, and the passionate and self-devoted answer of his lovely and universally admired *fiancée*. She instantly rushed home and produced these pathetic and powerful ballads.]

"OH! wilt thou sew my buttons on,
  When gayer scenes recall
That fairy face, that stately grace,
  To reign amid the ball?
When Fulham's bowers their sweetest flowers
  For fête-champêtres shall don,
Oh! say, wilt thou, of queenly brow,
  Still sew my buttons on?

"The noble, sweet, are at thy feet,
  To meet a freezing eye;
The gay, the great, in camp and state,
  In vain around thee sigh.

* "Wilt thou love me then as now?" and "I will love thee then as now," were two popular songs in 1849.

Thou turn'st away, in scorn of sway,
   To bless a younger son—
But when we live in lodgings, say,
   Wilt sew his buttons on?"

"Yes, I will sew thy buttons on,
   Though all look dark and drear;
And scant, they say, lieutenant's pay,
   Two hundred pounds a year.
Let How'll and James tempt wealthier dames,
   Of gauds and gems I 'll none;
Nor ask to roam, but sit at home,
   And sew thy buttons on!

"When ladies blush 'neath lusters' flush,
   And fast the waltzers fly,
Though tame at tea I bide with thee,
   No tear shall dim my eye.
When summer's close brings Chiswick shows—
   When all from town have gone,
I 'll sit me down, nor pout nor frown,
   But sew thy buttons on!"

THE PAID BILL.

A BALLAD OF DOMESTIC ECONOMY.

PUNCH.

O fling not this receipt away,
   Given by one who trusted thee;
Mistakes will happen every day
   However honest folks may be.
And sad it is, love, twice to pay;
So cast not that receipt away!

Ah, yes; if e'er, in future hours,
   When we this bill have all forgot,
They send it in again—ye powers!—
   And swear that we have paid it not—
How sweet to know, on such a day
We 've never cast receipts away!

PARODY FOR A REFORMED PARLIAMENT.

PUNCH.

The quality of bribery is deep stained;
It droppeth from a hand behind the door
Into the voter's palm. It is twice dirty:
It dirts both him that gives, and him that takes.
'Tis basest in the basest, and becomes
Low blacklegs more than servants of the Crown.
Those swindlers show the force of venal power,
The attribute to trick and roguery,
Whereby 'tis managed that a bad horse wins:
But bribery is below their knavish "lay."
It is the vilest of dishonest things;
It was the attribute to Gatton's self;
And other boroughs most like Gatton show
When bribery smothers conscience. Therefore, you,
Whose conscience takes the fee, consider this—
That in the cause of just reform, you all
Should lose your franchise: we do dislike bribery;
And that dislike doth cause us to object to
The deeds of W. B.

THE WAITER.

PUNCH.

I met the waiter in his prime
  At a magnificent hotel;
His hair, untinged by care or time,
  Was oiled and brushed exceeding well.
When "waiter," was the impatient cry,
  In accents growing stronger,
He seem'd to murmur "By and by,
  Wait a little longer."

Within a year we met once more,
  'T was in another part of town—
An humbler air the waiter wore,
  I fancied he was going down.

Still, when I shouted "Waiter, bread!"
  He came out rather stronger,
As if he 'd say with toss of head,
  "Wait a little longer."

Time takes us on through many a grade;
  Of "ups and downs" I 've had my run,
Passing full often through the shade
  And sometimes loitering in the sun.
I and the waiter met again
  At a small inn at Ongar;
Still, when I call'd, 't was almost vain—
  He bade me wait the longer.

Another time—years since the last—
  At eating-house I sought relief
From present care and troubles past,
  In a small plate of round of beef.
"One beef, and taturs," was the cry,
  In tones than mine much stronger;
'T was the old waiter standing by,
  "Waiting a little longer."

I 've marked him now for many a year;
  I 've seen his coat more rusty grow;
His linen is less bright and clear,
  His polished pumps are on the go.
Torn are, alas! his Berlin gloves—
  They used to be much stronger;
The waiter's whole appearance proves
  He can not wait much longer.

I sometimes see the waiter still;
  'Gainst want he wages feeble strife;
He 's at the bottom of the hill,
  Downward has been his path through life
Of "waiter, waiter," there are cries,
  Which louder grow and stronger;
'Tis to old Time he now replies,
  "Wait a little longer."

THE LAST APPENDIX TO "YANKEE DOODLE."

PUNCH, 1851.

YANKEE DOODLE sent to Town
His goods for exhibition;
Every body ran him down,
And laugh'd at his position.
They thought him all the world behind;
A goney, muff, or noodle;
Laugh on, good people—never mind—
Says quiet YANKEE DOODLE.

Chorus.—YANKEE DOODLE, etc.

YANKEE DOODLE had a craft,
A rather tidy clipper,
And he challenged, while they laughed,
The Britishers to whip her.
Their whole yacht-squadron she outsped,
And that on their own water;
Of all the lot she went a-head,
And they came nowhere arter.

Chorus.—YANKEE DOODLE, etc.

O'er Panamà there was a scheme
Long talk'd of, to pursue a
Short route—which many thought a dream—
By Lake Nicaragua.
JOHN BULL discussed the plan on foot,
With slow irresolution,
While YANKEE DOODLE went and put
It into execution.

Chorus.—YANKEE DOODLE, etc.

A steamer of the COLLINS line,
A YANKEE DOODLE'S notion,
Has also quickest cut the brine
Across the Atlantic Ocean.
And British agents, no ways slow
Her merits to discover,

Have been and bought her—just to tow
  The CUNARD packets over.

Chorus.—YANKEE DOODLE, etc.

Your gunsmiths of their skill may crack,
  But that again don't mention:
I guess that COLTS' revolvers whack
  Their very first invention.
By YANKEE DOODLE, too, you 're beat
  Downright in Agriculture,
With his machine for reaping wheat,
  Chaw'd up as by a vulture.

Chorus.—YANKEE DOODLE, etc.

You also fancied, in your pride,
  Which truly is tarnation,
Them British locks of yourn defied
  The rogues of all creation;
But CHUBBS' and BRAMAH'S HOBBS has pick'd,
  And you must now be view'd all
As having been completely licked
  By glorious YANKEE DOODLE.

Chorus.—YANKEE DOODLE, etc.

LINES FOR MUSIC.

PUNCH.

COME strike me the harp with its soul-stirring twang,
The drum shall reply with its hollowest bang;
Up, up in the air with the light tamborine,
And let the dull ophecleide's groan intervene;
For such is our life, lads, a chaos of sounds,
Through which the gay traveler actively bounds.
With the voice of the public the statesman must chime,
And change the key-note, boys, exactly in time;
The lawyer will coolly his client survey,
As an instrument merely whereon he can play.
Then harp, drum, and cymbals together shall clang,
With a loud-tooral lira, right tooral, bang, bang!

DRAMA FOR EVERY-DAY LIFE.

LUDGATE HILL.—A MYSTERY.

PUNCH.

DRAMATIS PERSONÆ.

MR. MEADOWS	*A Country Gentleman.*
PRIGWELL	*With a heavy heart and light fingers.*
BROWN . . . . . . JONES	*Friends of each other.*
BLIND VOCALIST	*Who will attempt the song of "Hey the Bonny Breast Knot."*

The Scene represents Ludgate Hill in the middle of the day; Passengers, Omnibuses, etc., etc., passing to and fro.

MEADOWS *enters, musing.*

Meadows. I stand at last on Ludgate's famous hill;
I've traversed Farringdon's frequented vale,
I've quitted Holborn's heights—the slopes of Snow,
Where Skinner's sinuous street, with tortuous track,
Trepans the traveler toward the field of Smith;
That field, whose scents burst on the offended nose
With foulest flavor, while the thrice shocked ear,
Thrice shocked with bellowing blasphemy and blows,
Making one compound of Satanic sound,
Is stunned, in physical and moral sense.
But this is Ludgate Hill—here commerce thrives;
Here, merchants carry trade to such a height
That competition, bursting builders' bonds,
Starts from the shop, and rushing through the roof,
Unites the basement with the floors above;
Till, like a giant, that outgrows his strength,
The whole concern, struck with abrupt collapse,
In one "tremendous failure" totters down!—
'Tis food on which philosophy may fatten.

[Turns round, musing, and looks into a shop window.

Enter PRIGWELL, *talking to himself.*

Prigwell. I've made a sorry day of it thus far;
I've fathomed fifty pockets, all in vain;
I've spent in omnibuses half-a-crown;
I've ransacked forty female reticules—
And nothing found—some business must be done.

By Jove—I 'd rather turn Lascar at once:
Allow the walnut's devastating juice
To track its inky course along my cheek,
And stain my British brow with Indian brown.
Or, failing that, I 'd rather drape myself
In cheap white cotton, or gay colored chintz—
Hang roung my ear the massive curtain-ring—
With strings of bold, effective glassy beads
Circle my neck—and play the Brahmin Priest,
To win the sympathy of passing crowds,
And melt the silver in the stranger's purse.
But ah! (*seeing* MEADOWS) the land of promise looms before me:
The bulging skirts of that provincial coat
Tell tales of well-filled pocket-books within.

[Goes behind Meadows and empties his pockets.

This is indeed a prize!

[Meadows turns suddenly round.

Your pardon, sir;
Is this the way to Newgate?

Meadows. Why, indeed
I scarce can say; I 'm but a stranger here,
I should not like to misdirect you.

Prigwell. Thank you,
I 'll find the way to Newgate by myself.

[Exit.

Meadows (still musing). This is indeed a great Metropolis.

Enter BLIND VOCALIST.

Blind Vocalist (singing). Hey, the bonny! (*Knocks up against* MEADOWS, *who exit*). Ho! the bonny—(*A passenger knocks up against the* BLIND VOCALIST *on the other side*). Hey, the bonny—(*A butcher's tray strikes the* BLIND VOCALIST *in the chest*)—breast knot. *As he continues singing "Hey, the bonny! ho, the bonny," the* BLIND VOCALIST *encounters various collisions, and his breath being taken away by a poke or a push between each bar, he is carried away by the stream of passengers.*

Enter BROWN *and* JONES. *Meeting, they stop and shake hands most cordially for several minutes.*

Brown. How are you, JONES?

Jones. Why, BROWN, I do declare
'Tis quite an age since you and I have met.

Brown. I 'm quite delighted.

Jones. I 'm extremely glad.

[An awkward pause.

Brown. Well! and how are you?

Jones. Thank you, very well;
And you, I hope are well?
Brown. Quite well, I thank you.
[Another awkward pause.

Jones. Oh!—by the way—have you seen THOMSON lately?
Brown. Not very lately. (*After a pause, and as if struck with a happy idea*). But I met with SMITH—
A week ago.
Jones. Oh! did you though, indeed?
And how was SMITH?
Brown. Why, he seemed pretty well.
[Another long pause; at the end of which both appear as if they were going to speak to each other.

Jones. I beg your pardon.
Smith. You were going to speak?
Jones. Oh! nothing. I was only going to say—
Good morning.
Smith. Oh! and so was I. Good-day.
[Both shake hands, and are going off in opposite directions, when Smith turns round. Jones turning round at the same time they both return and look at each other.

Jones. I thought you wished to speak, by looking back.
Brown. Oh no. I thought the same.
Both together. Good-by! Good-by!
[Exeunt finally; and the conversation and the curtain drop together.

PROCLIVIOR.

(*A slight Variation on* LONGFELLOW'S "EXCELSIOR.")

PUNCH.

THE shades of night were falling fast,
As tow'rd the Haymarket there pass'd
A youth, whose look told in a trice
That his taste chose the queer device—
PROCLIVIOR!

His hat, a wide-awake; beneath
He tapp'd a cane against his teeth;
His eye was bloodshot, and there rung,
Midst scraps of slang, in unknown tongue,
PROCLIVIOR!

In calm first-floors he saw the light
Of circles cosy for the night;
But far ahead the gas-lamps glow;
He turn'd his head, and murmur'd "Slow,"
PROCLIVIOR!

"Come early home," his Uncle said,
"We all are early off to bed;
The family blame you far and wide;"
But loud that noisy youth replied—
PROCLIVIOR!

"Stay," said his Aunt, "come home to sup,
Early retire—get early up."
A wink half quivered in his eye;
He answered to the old dame's sigh—
PROCLIVIOR!

"Mind how you meddle with that lamp!
And mind the pavement, for it's damp!"
Such was the Peeler's last good-night.
A faint voice stutter'd out "All right."
PROCLIVIOR!

At break of day, as far West-ward
A cab roll'd o'er the highways hard,
The early mover stopp'd to stare
At the wild shouting of the fare—
PROCLIVIOR!

And by the bailiff's faithful hound,
At breakfast-time, a youth was found,
Upon three chairs, with aspect nice,
True to his young life's queer device,
PROCLIVIOR!

Thence, on a dull and muggy day,
They bore him to the Bench away,
And there for several months he lay,
While friends speak gravely as they say—
PROCLIVIOR!

JONES AT THE BARBER'S SHOP.

PUNCH.

SCENE.—*A Barber's Shop. Barber's men engaged in cutting hair, making wigs, and other barberesque operations.*

Enter JONES, *meeting* OILY *the barber.*

Jones. I wish my hair cut.

Oily. Pray, sir, take a seat.

[OILY puts a chair for JONES, who sits. During the following dialogue OILY continues cutting JONES's hair.

Oily. We 've had much wet, sir.

Jones. Very much, indeed.

Oily. And yet November's early days were fine.

Jones. They were.

Oily. I hoped fair weather might have lasted us
Until the end.

Jones. At one time—so did I.

Oily. But we have had it very wet.

Jones. We have.

[A pause of some minutes.

Oily. I know not, sir, who cut your hair last time;
But this I say, sir, it was badly cut:
No doubt 't was in the country.

Jones. No! in town!

Oily. Indeed! I should have fancied otherwise.

Jones. 'T was cut in town—and in this very room.

Oily. Amazement!—but I now remember well.
We had an awkward, new provincial hand,
A fellow from the country. Sir, he did
More damage to my business in a week
Than all my skill can in a year repair.
He must have cut your hair.

Jones (*looking at him*). No—'t was yourself.

Oily. Myself! Impossible! You must mistake.

Jones. I don't mistake—'t was you that cut my hair.

[A long pause, interrupted only by the clipping of the scissors.

Oily. Your hair is very dry, sir.

Jones. Oh! indeed.

Oily. Our Vegetable Extract moistens it.

Jones. I like it dry.

Oily. But, sir, the hair when dry
Turns quickly gray.
Jones. That color I prefer.
Oily. But hair, when gray, will rapidly fall off,
And baldness will ensue.
Jones. I would be bald.
Oily. Perhaps you mean to say you 'd like a wig.—
We 've wigs so natural they can't be told
From real hair.
Jones. Deception I detest.

[Another pause ensues, during which OILY blows down JONES'S neck, and relieves him from the linen wrapper in which he has been enveloped during the process of hair-cutting.

Oily. We 've brushes, soaps, and scent, of every kind.
Jones. I see you have. (*Pays* 6*d.*) I think you 'll find that right.
Oily. If there is nothing I can show you, sir.
Jones. No: nothing. Yet—there may be something, too,
That you may show me.
Oily. Name it, sir.
Jones. The door.

[*Exit* JONES.

Oily (*to his man*). That 's a rum customer at any rate.
Had I cut him as short as he cut me,
How little hair upon his head would be!
But if kind friends will all our pains requite,
We 'll hope for better luck another night.

[Shop-bell rings and curtain falls.

THE SATED ONE.

[IMPROMPTU AFTER CHRISTMAS DINNER.]

PUNCH.

IT may not be—go maidens, go,
Nor tempt me to the mistletoe;
I once could dance beneath its bough,
But must not, will not, can not, now!

A weight—a load within I bear;
It is not madness nor despair;
But I require to be at rest,
So that my burden may—digest!

SAPPHICS OF THE CABSTAND.*

PUNCH.

Friend of Self-Government.

SEEDY Cab-driver, whither art thou going?
Sad is thy fate—reduced to law and order,
Local self-government yielding to the gripe of
Centralization.

Victim of FITZROY! little think the M.P.s,
Lording it o'er cab, 'bus, lodging-house, and grave-yard,
Of the good times when every Anglo Saxon's
House was his castle.

Say, hapless sufferer, was it Mr. CHADWICK—
Underground foe to the British Constitution—
Or my LORD SHAFTESBURY, put up MR. FITZROY
Thus to assail you?

Was it the growth of Continental notions,
Or was it the Metropolitan police-force
Prompted this blow at *Laissez-faire*, that free and
Easiest of doctrines?

Have you not read Mr. TOULMIN SMITH'S great work on
Centralization? If you have n't, buy it;
Meanwhile I should be glad at once to hear your
View on the subject.

Cab-driver.

View on the subjeck? jiggered if I 've got one;
Only I wants no centrylisin', I don't—
Which I suppose it's a crusher standin' sentry
Hover a cabstand.

Whereby if we gives e'er a word o' cheek to
Parties as rides, they pulls us up like winkin'—
And them there blessed beaks is down upon us
Dead as an 'ammer!

* See page 384.

As for Mr. TOULMIN SMITH, can't say I knows him—
But as you talks so werry like a gem'man,
Perhaps you're goin in 'ansome style to stand a
Shillin' a mile, sir?

Friend of Self-Government.

I give a shilling? I will see thee hanged first—
Sixpence a mile—or drive me straight to Bow-street—
Idle, ill-mannered, dissipated, dirty,
Insolent rascal!

JUSTICE TO SCOTLAND.*

[AN UNPUBLISHED POEM BY BURNS.]

COMMUNICATED BY THE EDINBURG SOCIETY FOR PROMOTING CIVILIZATION IN ENGLAND.

PUNCH.

O MICKLE yeuks the keckle doup,
An' a' unsicker girns the graith,
For wae and wae! the crowdies loup
O'er jouk an' hallan, braw an' baith.
Where ance the coggie hirpled fair,
And blithesome poortith toomed the loof,
There 's nae a burnie giglet rare
But blaws in ilka jinking coof.

The routhie bield that gars the gear
Is gone where glint the pawky een,
And aye the stound is birkin lear
Where sconnered yowies wheeped yestreen,
The creeshie rax wi' skelpin' kaes
Nae mair the howdie bicker whangs,
Nor weanies in their wee bit claes
Glour light as lammies wi' their sangs.

Yet leeze me on my bonnie byke!
My drappie aiblins blinks the noo,

* In this poem the Scottish words and phrases are all ludicrously misapplied.

An' leesome luve has lapt the dyke
  Forgatherin' just a wee bit fou.
And SCOTIA! while thy rantin' lunt
  Is mirk and moop with gowans fine,
I'll stowlins pit my unco brunt,
  An' cleek my duds for auld lang syne.

THE POETICAL COOKERY-BOOK.

PUNCH.

THE STEAK.

AIR.—"*The Sea.*"

OF Steak—of Steak—of prime Rump Steak—
A slice of half-inch thickness take,
Without a blemish, soft and sound;
In weight a little more than a pound.
Who'd cook a Stake—who'd cook a Steak—
Must a fire clear proceed to make:
With the red above and the red below,
In one delicious genial glow.
If a coal should come, a blaze to make,
Have patience! You must n't put on your Steak.

First rub—yes, rub—with suet fat,
The gridiron's bars, then on it flat
Impose the meat; and the fire soon
Will make it sing a delicious tune.
And when 'tis brown'd by the genial glow,
Just turn the upper side below.
Both sides with brown being cover'd o'er,
For a moment you broil your Steak no more,
But on a hot dish let it rest,
And add of butter a slice of the best;
In a minute or two the pepper-box take,
And with it gently dredge your Steak.

When seasoned quite, upon the fire
Some further time it will require;
And over and over be sure to turn
Your Steak till done—nor let it burn;

For nothing drives me half so wild
As a nice Rump Steak in the cooking *spiled.*
I 've lived in pleasure mixed with grief,
On fish and fowl, and mutton and beef;
With plenty of cash, and power to range,
But my Steak I never wished to change:
For a Steak was always a treat to me,
At breakfast, luncheon, dinner, or tea.

ROASTED SUCKING-PIG.

AIR—"*Scots wha hae.*"

COOKS who 'd roast a Sucking-pig,
Purchase one not over big;
Coarse ones are not worth a fig;
So a young one buy.
See that he is scalded well
(That is done by those who sell),
Therefore on that point to dwell,
Were absurdity.

Sage and bread, mix just enough,
Salt and pepper *quantum suff.*,
And the Pig's interior stuff,
With the whole combined.
To a fire that 's rather high,
Lay it till completely dry;
Then to every part apply
Cloth, with butter lined.

Dredge with flour o'er and o'er,
Till the Pig will hold no more;
Then do nothing else before
'Tis for serving fit.
Then scrape off the flour with care;
Then a butter'd cloth prepare;
Rub it well; then cut—not tear—
Off the head of it.

Then take out and mix the brains
With the gravy it contains;
While it on the spit remains,
        Cut the Pig in two.
Chop the sage, and chop the bread
Fine as very finest shred;
O'er it melted butter spread—
        Stinginess won't do.

When it in the dish appears,
Garnish with the jaws and ears;
And when dinner-hour nears,
        Ready let it be.
Who can offer such a dish
May dispense with fowl and fish;
And if he a guest should wish,
        Let him send for me!

BEIGNET DE POMME.

AIR—"*Home, Sweet Home.*"

'MID fritters and lollipops though we may roam,
On the whole, there is nothing like Beignet de Pomme.
Of flour a pound, with a glass of milk share,
And a half pound of butter the mixture will bear.
    Pomme! Pomme! Beignet de Pomme!
    Of Beignets there 's none like the Beignet de Pomme!

A Beignet de Pomme, you will work at in vain,
If you stir not the mixture again and again;
Some beer, just to thin it, may into it fall;
Stir up that, with three whites of eggs, added to all.
    Pomme! Pomme! Beignet de Pomme!
    Of Beignets there 's none like the Beignet de Pomme!

Six apples, when peeled, you must carefully slice,
And cut out the cores—if you 'll take my advice;
Then dip them in batter, and fry till they foam,
And you 'll have in six minutes your Beignet de Pomme.
    Pomme! Pomme! Beignet de Pomme!
    Of Beignets there 's none like the Beignet de Pomme!

CHERRY PIE.

AIR—"*Cherry Ripe.*"

CHERRY PIE! Cherry Pie! Pie! I cry,
Kentish cherries you may buy.
If so be you ask me where
To put the fruit, I 'll answer "There!"
In the dish your fruit must lie,
When you make your Cherry Pie.
Cherry Pie! Cherry Pie! etc.

Cherry Pie! Cherry Pie! Pie! I cry;
Full and fair ones mind you buy
Whereabouts the crust should go,
Any fool, of course will know;
In the midst a cup may lie,
When you make your Cherry Pie.
Cherry Pie! Cherry Pie! etc.

DEVILED BISCUIT.

AIR—"*A Temple of Friendship.*"

"A NICE Devil'd Biscuit," said JENKINS enchanted,
"I 'll have after dinner—the thought is divine!"
The biscuit was bought, and he now only wanted—
To fully enjoy it—a glass of good wine.
He flew to the pepper, and sat down before it,
And at peppering the well-butter'd biscuit he went;
Then, some cheese in a paste mix'd with mustard spread o'er it,
And down to be grill'd to the kitchen 't was sent.

"Oh! how," said the Cook, "can I this think of grilling,
When common the pepper? the whole will be flat.
But here 's the Cayenne; if my master is willing,
I 'll make, if he pleases, a devil with that."
So the Footman ran up with the Cook's observation
To JENKINS, who gave him a terrible look:
"Oh, go to the devil!" forgetting his station,
Was the answer that JENKINS sent down to the Cook

RED HERRINGS.

AIR—"*Meet me by Moonlight.*"

MEET me at breakfast alone,
And then I will give you a dish
Which really deserves to be known,
Though it 's not the genteelest of fish.
You must promise to come, for I said
A splendid Red Herring I 'd buy—
Nay, turn not away your proud head;
You 'll like it, I know, when you try.

If moisture the Herring betray,
Drain, till from moisture 'tis free;
Warm it through in the usual way,
Then serve it for you and for me.
A piece of cold butter prepare,
To rub it when ready it lies;
Egg-sauce and potatoes don't spare,
And the flavor will cause you surprise.

IRISH STEW.

AIR—"*Happy Land.*"

IRISH stew, Irish stew!
Whatever else my dinner be,
Once again, once again,
I 'd have a dish of thee.

Mutton chops, and onion slice,
Let the water cover,
With potatoes, fresh and nice;
Boil, but not quite over,
Irish stew, Irish stew!
Ne'er from thee, my taste will stray.
I could eat
Such a treat
Nearly every day.
La, la, la, la!

BARLEY BROTH.

AIR—"*The King, God bless him!*"

A BASIN of Barley Broth make, make for me;
Give those who prefer it, the plain:
No matter the broth, so of barley it be,
If we ne'er taste a basin again.
For, oh! when three pounds of good mutton you buy,
And of most of its fat dispossess it,
In a stewpan uncover'd, at first, let it lie;
Then in water proceed to dress it.
Hurrah! hurrah! hurrah!
In a stewpan uncover'd, at first, let it lie;
Then in water proceed to dress it.

What a teacup will hold—you should first have been told—
Of barley you gently should boil;
The pearl-barley choose—'tis the nicest that 's sold—
All others the mixture might spoil.
Of carrots and turnips, small onions, green peas
(If the price of the last don't distress one),
Mix plenty; and boil altogether with these
Your basin of Broth when you dress one.
Hurrah! hurrah! hurrah!
Two hours together the articles boil;
There 's your basin of Broth, if you 'd dress one.

CALF'S HEART.

AIR—"*Maid of Athens, ere we part.*"

MAID of all work, as a part
Of my dinner, cook a heart;
Or, since such a dish is best,
Give me that, and leave the rest.
Take my orders, ere I go;
Heart of calf we 'll cook thee so.

Buy—to price you 're not confined—
Such a heart as suits your mind:
Buy some suet—and enough
Of the herbs required to stuff;

Buy some lemon-peel—and, oh!
Heart of calf, we 'll fill thee so.

Buy some onions—just a taste—
Buy enough, but not to waste;
Buy two eggs of slender shell,
Mix, and stir the mixture well;
Crumbs of bread among it throw;
Heart of calf we 'll roast thee so.

Maid of all work, when 'tis done,
Serve it up to me alone:
Rich brown gravy round it roll,
Marred by no intruding coal;
Currant jelly add—and lo!
Heart of calf, I 'll eat thee so.

THE CHRISTMAS PUDDING.

AIR—"*Jeannette and Jeannot.*"

If you wish to make a pudding in which every one delights,
Of a dozen new-laid eggs you must take the yolks and whites;
Beat them well up in a basin till they thoroughly combine,
And shred and chop some suet particularly fine;

Take a pound of well-stoned raisins, and a pound of currants dried,
A pound of pounded sugar, and a pound of peel beside;
Stir them all well up together with a pound of wheaten flour,
And let them stand and settle for a quarter of an hour;

Then tie the pudding in a cloth, and put it in the pot,—
Some people like the water cold, and some prefer it hot;
But though I don't know which of these two methods I should praise,
I know it ought to boil an hour for every pound it weighs.

Oh! if I were Queen of France, or, still better, Pope of Rome,
I'd have a Christmas pudding every day I dined at home;
And as for other puddings whatever they might be,
Why those who like the nasty things should eat them all for me.

APPLE PIE.

AIR—"*All that's bright must fade.*"

ALL new dishes fade—
  The newest oft the fleetest;
Of all the pies now made,
  The Apple's still the sweetest;
Cut and come again,
  The syrup upward springing!
While my life and taste remain,
  To thee my heart is clinging.
Other dainties fade—
  The newest oft the fleetest;
But of all the pies now made,
  The Apple's still the sweetest.

Who absurdly buys
  Fruit not worth the baking?
Who wastes crust on pies
  That do not pay for making?
Better far to be
  An Apple Tartlet buying,
Than to make one at home, and see
  On it there 's no relying:
That all must be weigh'd,
  When thyself thou treatest—
Still a pie home-made
  Is, after all, the sweetest.

Who a pie would make,
  First his apple slices;
Then he ought to take
  Some cloves—the best of spices:
Grate some lemon rind,
  Butter add discreetly;
Then some sugar mix—but mind
  The pie 's not made too sweetly.
Every pie that 's made
  With sugar, is completest;
But moderation should pervade—
  Too sweet is not the sweetest.

Who would tone impart,
  Must—if my word is trusted—
Add to his pie or tart
  A glass of port—old crusted
If a man of taste,
  He, complete to make it,
In the very finest paste
  Will inclose and bake it.
Pies have each their grade;
  But, when this thou eatest,
Of all that e'er were made,
  You 'll say 'tis best and sweetest.

LOBSTER SALAD.

AIR.—"*Blue Bonnets over the Border.*"

TAKE, take, lobsters and lettuces;
  Mind that they send you the fish that you order:
Take, take, a decent-sized salad bowl,
  One that 's sufficiently deep in the border.
      Cut into many a slice
      All of the fish that 's nice,
  Place in the bowl with due neatness and order:
      Then hard-boil'd eggs you may
      Add in a neat array
  All round the bowl, just by way of a border.

Take from the cellar of salt a proportion:
  Take from the castors both pepper and oil,
With vinegar, too—but a moderate portion—
  Too much of acid your salad will spoil.
      Mix them together,
      You need not mind whether
  You blend them exactly in apple-pie order;
      But when you 've stirr'd away,
      Mix up the whole you may—
  All but the eggs, which are used as a border.

Take, take, plenty of seasoning;
  A teaspoon of parsley that 's chopp'd in small pieces:
Though, though, the point will bear reasoning,
  A small taste of onion the flavor increases.

As the sauce curdle may,
Should it: the process stay,
Patiently do it again in due order;
For, if you chance to spoil
Vinegar, eggs, and oil,
Still to proceed would on lunacy border.

STEWED STEAK

AIR.—"*Had I a Heart for Falsehood Framed.*"

HAD I pound of tender Steak,
I'd use it for a stew;
And if the dish you would partake,
I'll tell you what to do.
Into a stew-pan, clean and neat,
Some butter should be flung:
And with it stew your pound of meat,
A tender piece—but young.

And when you find the juice express'd
By culinary art,
To draw the gravy off, were best,
And let it stand apart.
Then, lady, if you'd have a treat,
Be sure you can't be wrong
To put more butter to your meat,
Nor let it stew too long.

And when the steak is nicely done,
To take it off were best;
And gently let it fry alone,
Without the sauce or zest;
Then add the gravy—with of wine
A spoonful in it flung;
And a shalot cut very fine—
Let the shalot be young.

And when the whole has been combined,
More stewing 't will require;
Ten minutes will suffice—but mind,
Don't have too quick a fire.

Then serve it up—'t will form a treat!
  Nor fear you 've cook'd it wrong;
Gourmets in all the old 't will meet,
  And *gourmands* in the young.

GREEN PEA SOUP.

AIR—"*The Ivy Green.*"

OH! a splendid Soup is the true Pea Green·
  I for it often call;
And up it comes in a smart tureen,
  When I dine in my banquet hall.
When a leg of mutton at home is boil'd,
  The liquor I always keep,
And in that liquor (before 'tis spoil'd)
  A peck of peas I steep.
When boil'd till tender they have been,
I rub through a sieve the peas so green.

Though the trouble the indolent may shock,
  I rub with all my power;
And having return'd them to the stock,
  I stew them for more than an hour:
Then of younger peas I take some more,
  The mixture to improve,
Thrown in a little time before
  The soup from the fire I move.
Then seldom a better soup is seen,
Than the old familiar soup Pea Green.

Since first I began my household career,
  How many my dishes have been!
But the one that digestion never need fear,
  Is the simple old soup Pea Green.
The giblet may tire, the gravy pall,
  And the turtle lose its charm;
But the Green Pea triumphs over them all,
  And does not the slightest harm.
Smoking hot in a smart tureen,
A rare soup is the true Pea Green!

TRIFLE.

AIR—"*The Meeting of the Waters.*"

THERE'S not in the wide world so tempting a sweet
As that Trifle where custard and macaroons meet;
Oh! the latest sweet tooth from my head must depart
Ere the taste of that Trifle shall not win my heart.

Yet it is not the sugar that's thrown in between,
Nor the peel of the lemon so candied and green;
'Tis not the rich cream that's whipp'd up by a mill:
Oh, no! it is something more exquisite still.

'Tis that nice macaroons in the dish I have laid,
Of which a delicious foundation is made;
And you'll find how the last will in flavor improve,
When soak'd with the wine that you pour in above.

Sweet *plateau* of Trifle! how great is my zest
For thee, when spread o'er with the jam I love best,
When the cream white of eggs—to be over thee thrown,
With a whisk kept on purpose—is mingled in one!

MUTTON CHOPS.

AIR—"*Come dwell with me.*"

COME dine with me, come dine with me,
And our dish shall be, our dish shall be,
A Mutton Chop from the butcher's shop—
And how I cook it you shall see.
The Chop I choose is not too lean;
For to cut off the fat I mean.
Then to the fire I put it down,
And let it fry until 'tis brown.
Come dine with me; yes, dine with me, etc.

I'll fry some bread cut rather fine,
To place betwixt each chop of mine;
Some spinach, or some cauliflowers,
May ornament this dish of ours.

I will not let thee once repine
At having come with me to dine:
'T will be my pride to hear thee say,
"I have enjoy'd my Chop, to-day."
  Come, dine with me; yes, dine with me;
  Dine, dine, dine, with me, etc.

BARLEY WATER.

AIR—"*On the Banks of Allan Water.*"

FOR a jug of Barley Water
  Take a saucepan not too small;
Give it to your wife or daughter,
  If within your call.
If her duty you have taught her,
  Very willing each will be
To prepare some Barley Water
  Cheerfully for thee.

For a jug of Barley Water,
  Half a gallon, less or more,
From the filter that you bought her,
  Ask your wife to pour.
When a saucepan you have brought her
  Polish'd bright as bright can be,
In it empty all the water,
  Either you or she.

For your jug of Barley Water
  ('Tis a drink by no means bad),
Some two ounces and a quarter
  Of pearl barley add.
When 'tis boiling, let your daughter
  Skim from blacks to keep it free;
Added to your Barley Water
  Lemon rind should be.

For your jug of Barley Water
  (I have made it very oft),
It must boil, so tell your daughter,
  Till the barley's soft.

Juice of a small lemon's quarter
  Add; then sweeten all like tea;
Strain through sieve your Barley Water—
  'T will delicious be.

BOILED CHICKEN.

AIR—"*Norah Creina.*"

LESBIA hath a fowl to cook;
  But, being anxious not to spoil it,
Searches anxiously our book,
  For how to roast, and how to boil it.
Sweet it is to dine upon—
  Quite alone, when small its size is;—
And, when cleverly 'tis done,
  Its delicacy quite surprises.
    Oh! my tender pullet dear!
  My boiled—not roasted—tender Chicken
      I can wish
      No other dish,
With thee supplied, my tender Chicken!

Lesbia, take some water cold,
  And having on the fire placed it,
And some butter, and be bold—
  When 'tis hot enough—taste it.
Oh! the Chicken meant for me
  Boil before the fire grows dimmer,
Twenty minutes let it be
  In the saucepan left to simmer.
    Oh, my tender Chicken dear!
  My boil'd, delicious, tender Chicken!
      Rub the breast
      (To give a zest)
With lemon-juice, my tender Chicken.

Lesbia hath with sauce combined
  Broccoli white, without a tarnish;
'Tis hard to tell if 'tis design'd
  For vegetable or for garnish.

Pillow'd on a butter'd dish,
  My Chicken temptingly reposes,
Making gourmands for it wish,
  Should the savor reach their noses.
    Oh, my tender pullet dear!
  My boiled—not roasted—tender Chicken!
      Day or night,
      Thy meal is light,
  For supper, e'en, my tender Chicken.

STEWED DUCK AND PEAS.

AIR—"*My Heart and Lute.*"

I GIVE thee all, I can no more,
  Though poor the dinner be;
Stew'd Duck and Peas are all the store
  That I can offer thee.
A Duck, whose tender breast reveals
  Its early youth full well;
And better still, a Pea that peels
  From fresh transparent shell.

Though Duck and Peas may fail, alas!
  One's hunger to allay;
At least for luncheon they may pass,
  The appetite to stay.
If seasoned Duck an odor bring
  From which one would abstain,
The Peas, like fragrant breath of Spring,
  Set all to rights again.

I give thee all my kitchen lore,
  Though poor the offering be;
I'll tell thee how 'tis cook'd, before
  You come to dine with me:
The Duck is truss'd from head to heels,
  Then stew'd with butter well;
And streaky bacon, which reveals
  A most delicious smell.

When Duck and Bacon in a mass
  You in the stew-pan lay,
A spoon around the vessel pass,
  And gently stir away:
A table-spoon of flour bring,
  A quart of water bring,
Then in it twenty onions fling,
  And gently stir again.

A bunch of parsley, and a leaf
  Of ever-verdant bay,
Two cloves—I make my language brief—
  Then add your Peas you may!
And let it simmer till it sings
  In a delicious strain,
Then take your Duck, nor let the strings
  For trussing it remain.

The parsley fail not to remove,
  Also the leaf of bay;
Dish up your Duck—the sauce improve
  In the accustom'd way,
With pepper, salt, and other things,
  I need not here explain:
And, if the dish contentment brings,
  You 'll dine with me again.

CURRY.

THREE pounds of veal my darling girl prepares,
And chops it nicely into little squares;
Five onions next prepares the little minx
(The biggest are the best her Samiwel thinks).
And Epping butter, nearly half a pound,
And stews them in a pan until they 're brown'd.

What 's next my dexterous little girl will do?
She pops the meat into the savory stew,
With curry powder, table-spoonfulls three,
And milk a pint (the richest that may be);

And, when the dish has stewed for half-an-hour,
A lemon's ready juice she 'll o'er it pour:
Then, bless her! then she gives the luscious pot
A very gentle boil—and serves quite hot.

P. S. Beef, mutton, rabbit, if you wish;
Lobsters, or prawns, or any kind of fish
Are fit to make A CURRY. 'Tis, when done,
A dish for emperors to feed upon.

THE RAILWAY GILPIN.

PUNCH.

JOHN GILPIN is a citizen;
  For lineage of renown,
The famed JOHN GILPIN'S grandson, he
  Abides in London town.

To our JOHN GILPIN said his dear,
  " Stewed up here as we 've been
Since Whitsuntide, 'tis time that we
  Should have a change of scene.

" To-morrew is a leisure day,
  And we 'll by rail repair
Unto the Nell at Dedmanton,
  And take a breath of air.

" My sister takes our eldest child;
  The youngest of our three
Will go in arms, and so the ride
  Won't so expensive be."

JOHN soon replied, " I don't admire
  That railway, I, for one;
But you know best, my dearest dear,
  And so it must be done.

" I, as a linen-draper bold,
  Will bear myself, and though
'Tis Friday by the calendar,
  Will risk my limbs, and go."

Quoth Mistress Gilpin, "Nicely said:
  And then, besides, look here,
We 'll go by the Excursion Train,
  Which makes it still less dear."

John Gilpin poked his clever wife,
  And slightly smiled to find
That though on peril she was bent,
  She had a careful mind.

The morning came; a cab was sought:
  The proper time allow'd
To reach the station door; but lo!
  Before it stood a crowd.

For half an hour they there were stay'd,
  And when they did get in—
"No train! a hoax!" cried clerks, agog
  To swear through thick and thin.

"Yaa!" went the throats; stamp went the heels:
  Were never folks so mad,
The disappointment dire beneath;
  All cried "it was too bad!"

John Gilpin home would fain have hied,
  But he must needs remain,
Commanded by his willful bride,
  And take the usual train.

'T was long before our passengers
  Another train could find,
When—stop! one ticket for the fares
  Was lost or left behind!

"Good lack!" quoth John, "yet try it on."
  "'T won't do," the Guard replies;
And bearing wife and babes on board,
  The train without him flies.

Now see him in a second train,
  Behind the iron steed,
Borne on, slap dash—for life or bones
  With small concern or heed.

Away went GILPIN, neck or naught,
  Exclaiming, "Dash my wig!
Oh, here's a game! oh, here's a go!
  A running such a rig!"

A signal, hark!—the whistle screamed—
  Smash! went the windows all:
"An accident!" cried out each one,
  As loud as he could bawl.

Away went GILPIN, never mind—
  His brain seemed spinning round;
Thought he, "This speed a killing pace
  Will prove, I'll bet a pound!"

And still, as stations they drew near,
  The whistle shrilly blew,
And in a trice, past signal-men,
  The train like lightning flew.

Thus, all through merry Killbury,
  Without a stop shot they;
But paused, to 'scape a second smash,
  At Dedmanton so gay.

At Dedmanton his loving wife,
  On platform waiting, spied
Her tender husband, striving much
  To let himself outside.

"Hallo! JOHN GILPIN, here we are—
  Come out!" they all did cry;
"To death with waiting we are tired!"
  "Guard!" shouted GILPIN, "Hi!"

But no—the train was not a bit
  Arranged to tarry there,
For why?—because 't was an Express,
  And did dispatches bear.

So, in a second, off it flew
  Again, and dashed along,
As if the deuce 't were going to,
  With motive impulse strong.

Away went GILPIN, on the breath
  Of puffing steam, until
They came unto their journey's end,
  Where they at last stood still.

And then—best thing that he could do—
  He book'd himself for Town;
They stopped at every station up,
  Till he again got down.

Says GILPIN, "Sing, Long live the QUEEN,
  And eke long life to me;
And ere I 'll trust that Line again,
  Myself I blest will see!"

ELEGY,

WRITTEN IN A RAILWAY STATION.

PUNCH.

THE Station clock proclaims the close of day;
  The hard-worked clerks drop gladly off to tea;
The last train starts upon its dangerous way,
  And leaves the place to darkness and to me.

Now fades the panting engine's red tail-light,
  And all the platform solemn stillness holds,
Save where the watchmen, pacing for the night,
  By smothered coughs announce their several colds.

Behind that door of three-inch planking made,
  Those frosted panes placed too high up to peep,
All in their iron safes securely laid,
  The cooked account-books of the Railway sleep.

The Debts to credit side so neatly borne,
  What should be losses, profits proved instead;
The Dividends those pages that adorn
  No more shall turn the fond Shareholder's head.

Oft did the doubtful to their balance yield,
  Their evidence arithmetic could choke:
How jocund were they that to them appealed!
  How many votes of thanks did they provoke!

Let not Derision mock KING HUDSON'S toil,
  Who made things pleasant greenhorns to allure;
Nor prudery give hard names unto the spoil
  'T was glad to share—while it could share secure.

All know the way that he his fortune made,
  How he bought votes and consciences did hire;
How hands that Gold and Silver-sticks have swayed
  To grasp his dirty palm would oft aspire,

Till these accounts at last their doctored page,
  Thanks to mischance and panic, did unroll,
When virtue suddenly became the rage,
  And wiped George Hudson out of fashion's scroll.

Full many a noble Lord who once serene
  The feasts at Albert Gate was glad to share,
For tricks he blushed not at, or blushed unseen,
  Now cuts the Iron King with vacant stare.

For those who, mindful of their money fled,
  Rejoice in retribution, sure though late—
Should they, by ruin to reflection led,
  Ask *Punch* to point the moral of his fate,

Haply that wooden-headed sage may say,
  "Oft have I seen him, in his fortune's dawn,
When at his levees elbowing their way,
  Peer's ermine might be seen and Bishop's lawn.

"There the great man vouchsafed in turn to each
  Advice, what scrip or shares 't was best to buy,
There his own arts his favorites he would teach,
  And put them up to good things on the sly.

"Till to the House by his admirers borne,
  Warmed with Champagne in flustered speech he strove,
And on through commerce, colonies, and corn,
  Like engine, without break or driver, drove.

"Till when he ceased to dip in fortune's till,
  Out came one cooked account—of our M. P.;
Another came—yet men scarce ventured, still,
  To think their idol such a rogue could be.

"Until those figures set in sad array
Proved how his victims he had fleeced and shorn—
Approach and read (if thou canst read) my lay,
Writ on him more in sadness than in scorn."

THE EPITAPH.

Here lies, the gilt rubbed off his sordid earth,
A man whom Fortune made to Fashion known;
Though void alike of breeding, parts, or birth,
God Mammon early marked him for his own.

Large was his fortune, but he bought it dear;
When he won foully he did freely spend.
He plundered no one knows how much a-year,
But Chancery o'ertook him in the end.

No further seek his frailties to disclose:
For many of his sins should share the load:
While he kept rising, who asked how he rose?
While we could reap, what cared we how he sowed?

THE BOA AND THE BLANKET.*

AN APOLOGUE OF THE ZOOLOGICAL GARDENS.—[AFTER WARREN.]

PUNCH.

It is talked of Now! Was talked of Yesterday!
May be muttered to-morrow! What?—
The Boa that Bolted the Blanket,
Speckled Enthusiast!

It was full moon's full moonlight! The Shilling
I had paid down at the Gate
Seem'd hung in Heaven. To Newton's Eye
(As Master of the Mint).
A Splendid, yea, Celestial Shilling!
I was alone, with Nothing to Speak of
But Creation!

* A few days before this burlesque of Warren appeared, a boa-constrictor in the London Zoological Gardens swallowed the blanket that had served as its bed.

Yes! Gigantic NOAH's Ark of twenty times her tonnage,
Lay crouch'd, and purring, and velvety, and fanged
About me!
Cane-colored tigers—rug-spotted Leopards—
Snakes (ah, CUPID!) knit and interknit—to true love knots
Semblable!
Striped Zebra—Onager Calcitrant—Common Ass,
And I—and all were there!
The bushy Squirrel with his half-cracked Nut,
Slept. The Boar of Allemagne snored.
The Lion's Cage was hot with heat of blood:
And Peace in Curtain Ring linked two Ring Doves!

In Gardens Zoological and Regent,
I, meditating, stood!
And still the moon looked wondrous like a Shilling,
Impartial Moon, that showed me all.

My heart fluttered as tho' winged from Mercury!
I moved—approached the Snake-House!
Oh, the balm of Paradise that came and went!
The silver gleams of Eden shooting down the trembling strings
Of my melodious heart!
Down—down to its coral roots!
I dashed aside the human tear; and—yes—prepared myself
With will, drunk from the eyes of Hope, to gaze upon the Snake!
The Boa!!
The Python!!!
The Anaconda!!!!

A Boa was there! A Boa, 'neath Crystal Roof!
And rabbits, taking the very moonlight in their paws,
Washed their meek faces. Washed, then hopped!
"And so (I could n't help it) so," I groaned—"the ancient
Snake—
That milk-white thing—and innocent—trustful!
And then, Death—Death—
And lo! there, typical, it is—it is—
THE BLANKET!!
Death shred of living thing that cropped the flower;
And, thoughtless, bleated forth its little baa-a!"

Away! I will not tarry! Let the Boa sleep,
And Rabbits, that have given bills to destiny,
Meet his demand at three and six months' date!
(We know such Boas and rabbits,
Know we not?)
Let me pass on!
And here 'tis cool; nay, even cold
Without the Snake-House!

The Moon still glistens, and again I think
Of Multitudes who 've paid and stared, and yawned and wandered here!
The city muckworm, who
From peacock orient, scarce could tell a cock
Of hay!
Though be ye sure, a guinea from a guinea-pig
He knows, and (as for money)
Ever has his squeak for 't!
Here, too, paused the wise, sagacious man,
Master of probabilities!
He sees the tusk of elephant—the two tusks—
And, with a thought, cuts 'em into cubes—
And with another thought—another—and another—
Tells (to himself) how oft, in twenty years
Those spotted squares shall come up sixes!
And this in living elephant!

And HER MAJESTY has trod these Walks,
Accompanied
By
PRINCE ALBERT,
THE PRINCE OF WALES,
THE PRINCESS ROYAL,
And
The Rest of the Royal Children!—

She saw the Tiger!
Did she think of TIPPOO SAIB'S Tiger's Head?
She saw the Lion!
Thought she of one of her own Arms?
She did *not* see the Unicorn; but

(With her gracious habits of condescension)
Did she think of him a bit the less?
  Thoughts crowd upon me—cry move on!

And now I am here; and whether I will or no,
I feel I 'm jolly!
The Chameleons are asleep, and, like the Cabinet
(Of course I mean the Whigs),
Know not, when they rise to-morrow,
What color they will wake!—
The baby elephant seems prematurely old:
Its infant hide all corrugate with thoughts
Of cakes and oranges given it by boys;
Alas! in Chancery now, and paralytic!
This is very sad. No more of it!

Ha! ha! here sits the Ape—the many-colored wight!
Thou hast marked him, with nose of scarlet sealing-wax,
And so be-colored with prismatic hues,
As though he had come from sky to earth—
Sliding and wiping a fresh-painted rainbow!

Hush! I have made a perfect circle!
And at the Snake-House once again I stand!
Such is life!
Eh! Oh! Help! Murder! Dreadful Accident!
To be conceived—Oh, perhaps!
Described—Oh, never!
Keepers are up, and crowd about the box—
The Boa's box—with unconcernéd rabbits!
Not so the Boa! Look! Behold!
And where 's the Blanket?
In the Boa's inside place! The Monster mark!
How he writhes and wrestles with the wool, as though
He had within him rolls and rolls
Of choking, suffocating influenza,
That lift his eyes from out their sockets!—Of fleecy phlegm
That will neither in or out, but mid-way
Seem to strangle!
Silence and wonder settle on the crowd;
From whom instinctively and breathlessly,

Ascend two pregnant questions!
"Will the Boa bolt the blanket?
Will the blanket choke the Boa?"
Such the problem!

And then men mark and deduce
Differently.

"The Blanket is England: the Boa the Pope,
Will the Pope disgorge his Bull?"

"The Blanket's Free Trade: the Corn-Gorged Folk
Is the Boa with plenty stifled!"

"The Blanket's Reform to gag the mob,
And naught to satisfy!"

But I, a lofty and an abstract man,
A creature of a higher element
Than ever nourished the wood
Ordained for ballot-boxes—I
Say nothing; until a Keeper comes to me, and,
Hooking his fore-finger in his forehead's lock,
Says—"What 's your opinion, Sir?
If Boas will bolt Blankets, Boas must:
If Snakes will rush upon their end, why not?"
"My friend," said I, "The Blanket and the Boa—
You will conceive me—are a type, yes, just a type,
Of this our day.
The dumb and monstrous, tasteless appetite
Of stupid Boa, to gobble up for food
What needs must scour or suffocate,
Not nourish!
My friend; let the wool of that one blanket
Warm but the back of one live sheep,
And the Boa would bolt the animal entire,
And flourish on his meal, transmuting flesh and bones,
And turning them to healthful nutriment!
Believe this vital truth;
The stomach may take down and digest
And sweetly, too, a leg of mutton;
That would turn at and reject
One little ball of worsted!"

On saying this I turned away,
Feeling adown the small-o'-the back
That gentle warmth that waits upon us, when WE KNOW
We have said a good thing;
Knowing it better than the vain world
Ever can or ever will.
Reader, I have sung my song!
The *Boa and the B——*, like new-found star,
Is mine no longer; but the world's!—
Tell me, how have I sung it? With what note?
With note akin to that immortal bard
The snow-white Swan of Avon?
Or haply, to that
—*Rara avis*,
—That has
—"Tried WARREN'S?"

THE DILLY AND THE D'S,*

[AN APOLOGUE OF THE OXFORD INSTALLATION.]

BY S—L W—RR—N, Q.S., LL.D., F.R.S.

PUNCH.

PART FIRST.

Oh, Spirit! Spirit of Literature,
Alien to Law!
Oh, Muse! ungracious to thy sterner sister, THEMIS,
Whither away?—Away!
Far from my brief—
Brief with a fee upon it,
Tremendous!
And probably—before my business is concluded—
A REFRESHER—nay, several! !
Whither whirlest thou thy thrall?
Thy willing thrall?
"*Now and Then*;"
But not just at this moment,
If you please, Spirit!

* Burlesque of Warren's Poem of "The Lily and the Bee," published at the time of the great Exhibition of 1851.

No, let me read and ponder on
THE PLEADINGS.
Declaration!
  Plea!!
    Replication!!!
      Rejoinder!!!!
        Surrejoinder!!!!!
          Rebutter!!!!!!
            Surrebutter!!!!!!!
ETC! ETC!! ETC!!!
It may not be. The Muse—
As ladies often are—
Though lovely, is obstinate,
And will have her own way!

* * * *

And am I not
As well as a Q.S.,
An F.R.S.
And LL.D.?
Ask BLACKWOOD
The reason why, and he will tell you;
So will the Mayor—
The MAYOR OF HULL!
I obey, Spirit.
Hang my brief—'tis gone!—
To-morrow let my junior cram me in Court.
Whither away? Where am I?
What is it I behold?
In space, or out of space? I know not.
In fact
I've not the least idea if I'm crazy.
Or sprung—sprung?
I've only had a pint of Port at dinner
And can't be sprung—
Oh, no!—Shame on the thought!
I see a coach!—
Is it a coach?
Not exactly.
Yet it has wheels—
Wheels within wheels—and on the box
A driver, and a cad behind,
And Horses—Horses?—

Bethink thee—Worm!—
Are they Horses? or that race
Lower than Horses, but with longer ears
And less intelligence—
In fact—"*equi asini*,"
Or in vernacular
JACKASSES?
'Tis not a coach exactly—
Now I see on the panels—
Pricked out and flourished—
A word! A magic word—
"THE DILLY!"—"THE DERBY DILLY!"
Oh Dilly! Dilly!—all thy passengers
Are outsiders—
The road is rough and rutty—
And thy driver, like NIMSHI'S son—
Driveth
Furiously!
And the cad upon the monkey-board
The monkey-board behind,
Scorneth the drag—but goes
Downhill like mad.
He hath a Caucasian brow!
A son of SHEM, is he,
Not of HAM—
Nor JAPHETH—
In fact a Jew—
But see, the pace
Grows faster—and more fast—in fact—
I may say
A case of Furious driving!
Take care, you'll be upset—
Look out!
Holloa!

* * * *

Horrible! Horrible!! Horrible!!!
The Dilly—
With all its precious freight
Of men and Manners—
Is gone!
Gone to immortal
SMASH!

Pick up the pieces! Let me wipe my eyes!
Oh Muse—lend me my scroll
To do it with, for I have lost
My wipe!

PART SECOND.

* * * Again upon the road
The road to where?
To nowhere in particular!
Ah, no—I thank thee, Muse—
That hint—'tis a finger-post,
And "he that runs may read"—
He that runs?
But I am not running—
I am riding—
How came I here?—what am I riding on?
Who are my fellow-passengers?
Ah, ha!
I recognize them now!
The Coach—
The Box—
The Driver—
And the Cad—
I'm on the Dilly, and the Dilly
Is on the road again
And now I see
That finger-post!
It saith
"To Oxford
Fifty-two miles."
And, hark! a chorus!
From all the joyous load,
Driver and cad, and all!
"We go," they sing—
To Oxford to be doctored."
To be Doctored?
Then, wherefore
Are ye so cheerful?
I was not cheerful in my early days—
Days of my buoyant boyhood—

When, after inglutition
Of too much
Christmas pudding,
Or Twelfth cake saccharine,
I went, as we go now,
To be Doctored!
Salts!
Senna and Rhubarb! !
Jalap and Ipecacuanha! ! !
And Antimonial Wine! ! ! !
"*Worm!*
IDIOT! !
DONKEY! ! !"
Said the free-spoken Muse
"With them thou goest to be doctored, too,
Not in medicine—but in Law—
All these—and thou—
Are going to be made
HONORARY
LL.D.s!
Behold!
And know thy company
Be thou familiar with them,
But by no means vulgar—
For familiarity breeds contempt;
And no man is a hero
To his *valét-de-chambre!*
So ponder and perpend."
DERBY!
The wise, the meek, the chivalrous—
Mirror of knightly graces
And daily dodges;
Who always says the right things
At the right time,
And never forgets himself as others—
Nor changes his side
Nor his opinion—
A STANLEY to the core, as ready
To fight
As erst on FLODDEN FIELD
His mail-clad ancestor.—
See the poem

Of *Marmion*,
By SIR WALTER SCOTT!
DIZZY!
Dark—supple—subtle—
With mind lithe as the limbs
Of ISHMAEL'S sons, his swart progenitors—
With tongue sharp as the spear
That o'er Sahara
Flings the blue shadow
Of the crown of ostrich feathers—
As described so graphically
By LAYARD, in his recent book
On Nineveh!
With tongue as sharp
As aspic's tooth of NILUS,
Or sugary
Upon the occasion
As is the date
Of TAFILAT.
DIZZY, the bounding Arab
Of the political arena—
As swift to whirl
Right about face—
As strong to leap
From premise to conclusion—
As great in balancing
A budget—
Or flinging headlong
His somersets
Over sharp swords of adverse facts,
As were his brethren of *El-Arish*,
Who
Some years ago exhibited—
With rapturous applause—
At Astley's Amphitheater—
And subsequently
At Vauxhall Gardens!

* * * * *

Clustering, front and back
On box and knife-board,
See, petty man;
Behold! and thank thy stars

That led thee—Worm—
Thee, that art merely a writer
And a barrister,
Although a man of elegant acquirements,
A gentleman and a scholar—
Nay, F.R.S. to boot—
Into such high society,
Among such SWELLS,
And REAL NOBS!
Behold! ten live LORDS! and lo! no end
Of Ex-Cabinet Ministers!
Oh! happy, happy, happy,
Oh, happy SAM!
Say, is n't this worth, at the least
"*Ten Thousand a Year!*"

*　　*　　*　　*　　*

And these are all, to day at least—
Thy fellows!
Going to be made
LL.D.s, even as thyself—
And thou shalt walk in silk attire,
And hob and nob with all the mighty of the earth,
And lunch in Hall—
In Hall!
Where lunched before thee,
But on inferior grub,
That first great SAM—
SAM JOHNSON!
And LAUD, and ROGER BACON,
And CRANMER, LATIMER,
And RIDLEY,
And CYRIL JACKSON—and a host besides,
Whom at my leisure
I will look up
In WOOD'S
"*Athenæ Oxonienses!*"
Only to think!
How BLACKWOOD
Is honored!
ALISON! AYTOUN!!
BULWER!!!
And last, not least

The great SAM GANDERAM ! ! ! !
Oh EBONY !
Oh MAGA !
And oh
Our noble selves !

* * * *

"A BOOK IN A BUSTLE."

A TRUE TALE OF THE WARWICK ASSIZES. BY THE GHOST OF CRABBE.

PUNCH.

THE partial power that to the female race
Is charged to apportion gifts of form and grace,
With liberal hand molds beauty's curves in one,
And to another gives as good as none:
But woman still for nature proves a match,
And grace by her denied, from art will snatch.
Hence, great ELIZA, grew thy farthingales ;
Hence, later ANNA, swelled thy hoops' wide pales ;
To this we must refer the use of stays ;
Nor less the bustle of more modern days.

Artful device ! whose imitative pad
Into good figures roundeth off the bad—
Whether of simple sawdust thou art seen,
Or tak'st the guise of costlier crinoline—
How oft to thee the female form doth owe
A grace rotund, a line of ampler flow,
Than flesh and blood thought fit to clothe it with below !

There dwelt in Liverpool a worthy dame,
Who had a friend—JAMES TAYLOR was his name.
He dealt in glass, and drove a thriving trade
And still saved up the profits that he made,
Till when a daughter blessed his marriage bed,
The father in the savings-bank was led
In his child's name a small sum to invest,
From which he drew the legal interest.

Years went and came; JAMES TAYLOR came and went;
Paid in, and drew, his modest three per cent.,
Till, by the time his child reach'd girlhood's bounds,
The sum had ris'n to two-and-twenty pounds.

Our cautious legislature—well 'tis known—
Round savings-banks a guardian fence has thrown:
'Tis easy to pay into them, no doubt,
Though any thing but easy to draw out.
And so JAMES TAYLOR found; for on a day
He wanted twenty pounds a bill to pay,
And, short of cash, unto the bank applied;
Failing some form of law, he was denied!

JAMES TAYLOR humm'd and haw'd—look'd blank and blue;—
In short, JAMES TAYLOR knew not what to do:
His creditor was stern—the bill was over due.

As to a friend he did his plight deplore—
The worthy dame of whom I spoke before—
(It might cause pain to give the name she owns,
So let me use the pseudonym of JONES);
"TAYLOR," said MRS. JONES, "as I'm a friend,
I do not care if I the money lend.
But even friends security should hold:
Give me security—I 'll lend the gold."
"This savings-bank deposit-book!" he cries.
"See—in my daughter's name the sum that lies!"
She saw—and, satisfied, the money lent;
Wherewith JAMES TAYLOR went away content.

But now what cares seize MRS. JONES's breast!
What terrors throng her once unbroken rest!
Cash she could keep, in many a secret nook—
But where to stow away JAMES TAYLOR's book?
Money is heavy: where 'tis put 't will stay;
Paper—as WILLIAM COBBETT used to say—
Will make wings to itself, and fly away!

Long she devised: new plans the old ones chase,
Until at last she hit upon a place.
Was 't VENUS that the strange concealment planned,
Or rather PLUTUS's irreverent hand?

Good Mrs. Jones was of a scraggy make;
But when did woman vanity forsake?
What nature sternly to her form denied,
A Bustle's ample aid had well supplied,
Within whose vasty depths the book might safely hide!

'T was thought—'t was done! by help of ready pin,
The sawdust was let out, the book put in.
Henceforth—at home—abroad—where'er she moved,
Behind her lurk'd the volume that she loved.
She laughed to scorn the cut-purse and his sleight:
No fear of burglars scared her through the night;

But ah, what shrine is safe from greed of gold,
What fort against cupidity can hold?
Can stoutest buckram's triple fold keep in,
The *odor lucri*—the strong scent of *tin*?
For which Chubb's locks are weak, and Milner's safes are thin.

Some time elapsed—the time required by law,
Which past, James Taylor might the money draw,
His kind but cautious creditor to pay,
So to the savings-bank they took their way.
There Mrs. Jones with modesty withdrew—
To do what no rude eye might see her do—
And soon returning—with a blushing look,
Unmarked by Taylor, she produced the book.
Which he, presenting, did the sum demand
Of Mr. Tomkins, the cashier so bland.

What can there be upon the red-lined page
That Tomkins's quick eye should so engage?
What means his invitation to J. T.,
To "Walk in for a moment"—"he would see"—
"Only a moment"—"'t was all right, no-doubt,"
"It could not be"—"and yet"—here he slipped out,
Leaving James Taylor grievously perplexed,
And Mrs. Jones by his behavior vexed.
"What means the man by treating people so?"
Said Taylor, "I am a loss to know."

Too soon, alas, the secret cause they knew!
Tomkins return'd, and, with him, one in blue—

POLICEMAN X, a stern man and a strong,
Who told JAMES TAYLOR he must "come along"—
And TOMKINS, seeing MRS. JONES aghast,
Revealed the book was forged—from first to last!

Who can describe the wrath of MRS. JONES?
The chill of fear that crept through TAYLOR's bones?
The van—the hand-cuffs—and the prison cell
Where pined JAMES TAYLOR—wherefore pause to tell?
Soon came the Assizes—and the legal train;
In form the clerk JAMES TAYLOR did arraign;
And though his council mustered tears at will,
And made black white with true Old Bailey skill,
TAYLOR, though MRS. JONES for mercy sued,
Was doomed to five years' penal servitude;
And in a yellow suit turned up with gray,
To Portland prison was conveyed away!

Time passed: forgot JAMES TAYLOR and his shame—
When lo—one day unto the bank there came
A new JAMES TAYLOR—a new MRS. JONES—
And a new book, which TOMKINS genuine owns!
"Two TAYLORS and two JONESES and two books"—
Thought wary TOMKINS, "this suspicious looks—
"The former TAYLOR, former JONES I knew—
These are imposters—yet the book is true!"
When like a flash upon his mind it burst—
Who brought the second book had forged the first!

Again was summon'd X, the stern, the strong—
Again that pair were bid to "Come along!"
The truth before the justices appear'd,
And wrong'd JAMES TAYLOR's character was clear'd.

In evil hour—by what chance ne'er was known,
Whether the bustle's seam had come unsewn,
Or MRS. JONES by chance had laid aside.
The artificial charms that decked her side—
But so it was, how or whene'er assailed—
The treacherous hiding-place was tried—and failed!

The book was ta'en—a forged one fill'd its place;—
And MRS. JONES was robb'd—not to her face—
And poor JAMES TAYLOR doom'd to trial and disgrace!

Who shall describe her anguish—her remorse?
James Taylor was at once released, of course;
And Mrs. Jones, repentant, inly swore
Henceforth to carry, what she'd keep, before.

My tale is told—and, what is more, 'tis true:
I read it in the papers—so may you.
And this its moral: Mrs. Joneses all—
Though reticules may drop, and purses fall,
Though thieves may unprotected females hustle,
Never invest your money in a bustle.

STANZAS FOR THE SENTIMENTAL.

PUNCH.

I.

ON A TEAR WHICH ANGELINA OBSERVED TRICKLING DOWN MY NOSE AT DINNER TIME.

Nay, fond one! I will ne'er reveal
Whence flowed that sudden tear:
The truth 't were kindness to conceal
From thy too anxious ear.

How often when some hidden spring
Of recollected grief
Is rudely touched, a tear will bring
The bursting breast relief!

Yet 't was no anguish of the soul,
No memory of woes,
Bade that one lonely tearlet roll
Adown my chiseled nose:

But, ah! interrogation's note
Still twinkles in thine eye;
Know then that I have burnt my throat
With this confounded pie!

II.

ON MY REFUSING ANGELINA A KISS UNDER THE MISLETOE

Nay, fond one, shun that misletoe,
  Nor lure me 'neath its fatal bough:
Some other night 't were joy to go,
  But ah! I must not, dare not now!
'Tis sad, I own, to see thy face
  Thus tempt me with its giggling glee,
And feel I can not now embrace
  The opportunity—and thee.

'Tis sad to think that jealousy's
  Sharp scissors may our true love sever;
And that my coldness now may freeze
  Thy warm affection, love, forever.
But ah! to disappoint our bliss,
  A fatal hind'rance now is stuck:
'Tis not that I am loath to kiss,
  But, dearest, list—*I dined off duck!*

III.

ON MY FINDING ANGELINA STOP SUDDENLY IN A RAPID AFTER-SUPPER POLKA AT MRS. TOMPKINS'S BALL.

Edwin. "Maiden, why that look of sadness?
  Whence that dark o'erclouded brow?
What hath stilled thy bounding gladness,
  Changed thy pace from fast to slow?
Is it that by impulse sudden
  Childhood's hours thou paus'st to mourn?
Or hath thy cruel EDWIN trodden
  Right upon thy favorite corn?

"Is it that for evenings wasted
  Some remorse thou 'gin'st to feel?
Or hath that sham champagne we tasted
  Turned thy polka to a reel?
Still that gloom upon each feature?
  Still that sad reproachful frown?"
Angelina. "Can't you see, you clumsy creature,
  All my back hair 's coming down!"

COLLOQUY ON A CAB-STAND.

ADAPTED FOR THE BOUDOIR.

PUNCH.

"Oh! William," James was heard to say—
James drove a hackney cabriolet:
William, the horses of his friend,
With hay and water used to tend.

"Now, tell me, William, can it be,
That Mayne has issued a decree,
Severe and stern, against us, planned
Of comfort to deprive our Stand?"

"I fear the tale is all too true,"
Said William, "on my word I do."
"Are we restricted to the Row
And from the footpath?" "Even so."

"Must our companions be resigned,
We to the Rank alone confined?"
"Yes; or they apprehend the lads
Denominated Bucks and Cads."

"Dear me!" cried James, "how very hard!
And are we, too, from beer debarred?"
Said William, "While remaining here
We also are forbidden beer."

"Nor may we breathe the fragrant weed?"
"That 's interdicted too." "Indeed!"
"Nor in the purifying wave
Must we our steeds or chariots lave."

"For private drivers, at request,
It is Sir Richard Mayne's behest
That we shall move, I understand?"
"Such, I believe, *is* the command"

"Of all remains of food and drink
Left by our animals, I think,

We are required to clear the ground?"
"Yes: to remove them we are bound."

"These mandates should we disobey—"
"They take our licenses away."
"That were unkind. How harsh our lot!"
"It is indeed." "Now is it not?"

"Thus strictly why are we pursued?"
"It is alleged that we are rude;
The people opposite complain,
Our lips that coarse expressions stain."

"Law, how absurd!" "And then, they say
We smoke and tipple all the day,
Are oft in an excited state,
Disturbance, noise, and dirt create."

"What shocking stories people tell!
I never! Did you ever?—Well—
Bless them!" the Cabman mildly sighed.
"May they be blest!" his Friend replied.

THE SONG OF HIAWATHA.

AN ENGLISH CRITICISM.

PUNCH.

You, who hold in grace and honor,
Hold, as one who did you kindness
When he publish'd former poems,
Sang Evangeline the noble,
Sang the golden Golden Legend,
Sang the songs the Voices utter
Crying in the night and darkness,
Sang how unto the Red Planet
Mars he gave the Night's First Watches,
Henry Wadsworth, whose *adnomen*
(Coming awkward, for the accents,

Into this his latest rhythm)
Write we as Protracted Fellow,
Or in Latin, *Longus Comes*—
Buy the Song of Hiawatha.

Should you ask me, Is the poem
Worthy of its predecessors,
Worthy of the sweet conception,
Of the manly nervous diction,
Of the phrase, concise or pliant,
Of the songs that sped the pulses,
Of the songs that gemm'd the eyelash,
Of the other works of Henry?
I should answer, I should tell you,
You may wish that you may get it—
Don't you wish that you may get it?

Should you ask me, Is it worthless,
Is it bosh and is it bunkum,
Merely facile flowing nonsense,
Easy to a practiced rhythmist,
Fit to charm a private circle,
But not worth the print and paper
David Bogue hath here expended?
I should answer, I should tell you,
You 're a fool and most presumptuous.
Hath not Henry Wadsworth writ it?
Hath not *Punch* commanded "Buy it?"

Should you ask me, What 's its nature?
Ask me, What 's the kind of poem?
Ask me in respectful language,
Touching your respectful beaver,
Kicking back your manly hind-leg,
Like to one who sees his betters;
I should answer, I should tell you,
'Tis a poem in this meter,
And embalming the traditions,
Fables, rites, and superstitions,
Legends, charms, and ceremonials
Of the various tribes of Indians,

From the land of the Ojibways,
From the land of the Dacotahs,
From the mountains, moors, and fenlands,
Where the heron, the Shuh-shuh-gah,
Finds its sugar in the rushes:
From the fast-decaying nations,
Which our gentle Uncle Samuel
Is improving, very smartly,
From the face of all creation,
Off the face of all creation.

Should you ask me, By what story,
By what action, plot, or fiction,
All these matters are connected ?
I should answer, I should tell you,
Go to Bogue and buy the poem,
Publish'd neatly, at one shilling,
Publish'd sweetly, at five shillings.
Should you ask me, Is there music
In the structure of the verses,
In the names and in the phrases?
Pleading that, like weaver Bottom,
You prefer your ears well tickled;
I should answer, I should tell you,
Henry's verse is very charming;
And for names—there 's Hiawatha,
Who 's the hero of the poem;
Mudjeekeewis, that 's the West Wind,
Hiawatha's graceless father;
There 's Nokomis, there 's Wenonah—
Ladies both, of various merit;
Puggawangum, that 's a war-club;
Pau-puk-keewis, he 's a dandy,
"Barr'd with streaks of red and yellow;
And the women and the maidens
Love the handsome Pau-puk-keewis,"
Tracing in him *Punch's* likeness.
Then there 's lovely Minnehaha—
Pretty name with pretty meaning—
It implies the Laughing-water;
And the darling Minnehaha
Married noble Hiawatha;

And her story 's far too touching
To be sport for you, you donkey,
With your ears like weaver Bottom's,
Ears like booby Bully Bottom.

Once upon a time in London,
In the days of the Lyceum,
Ages ere keen Arnold let it
To the dreadful Northern Wizard,
Ages ere the buoyant Mathews
Tripp'd upon its boards in briskness—
I remember, I remember
How a scribe, with pen chivalrous,
Tried to save these Indian stories
From the fate of chill oblivion.
Out came sundry comic Indians
Of the tribe of Kut-an-hack-um.
With their Chief, the clean Efmatthews,
With the growling Downy Beaver,
With the valiant Monkey's Uncle,
Came the gracious Mari-Kee-lee,
Firing off a pocket-pistol,
Singing, too, that Mudjee-keewis
(Shorten'd in the song to "Wild Wind,")
Was a spirit very kindly.
Came her Sire, the joyous Kee-lee,
By the waning tribe adopted,
Named the Buffalo, and wedded
To the fairest of the maidens,
But repented of his bargain,
And his brother Kut-an-hack-ums
Very nearly chopp'd his toes off—
Serve him right, the fickle Kee-lee.
If you ask me, What this memory
Hath to do with Hiawatha,
And the poem which I speak of?
I should answer, I should tell you,
You 're a fool, and most presumptuous;
'Tis not for such humble cattle
To inquire what links and unions
Join the thoughts, and mystic meanings,
Of their betters, mighty poets,

Mighty writers—*Punch* the mightiest;
I should answer, I should tell you,
Shut your mouth, and go to David,
David, *Mr. Punch's* neighbor,
Buy the Song of Hiawatha,
Read, and learn, and then be thankful
Unto *Punch* and Henry Wadsworth,
Punch and noble Henry Wadsworth,
Truer poet, better fellow,
Than to be annoyed at jesting,
From his friend, great *Punch*, who loves him.

COMFORT IN AFFLICTION.

WILLIAM AYTOUN.

"Wherefore starts my bosom's lord ?
Why this anguish in thine eye ?
Oh, it seems as thy heart's chord
Had broken with that sigh !

"Rest thee, my dear lord, I pray,
Rest thee on my bosom now !
And let me wipe the dews away,
Are gathering on thy brow.

"There, again ! that fevered start!
What, love! husband! is thy pain ?
There is a sorrow in thy heart,
A weight upon thy brain !

"Nay, nay, that sickly smile can ne'er
Deceive affection's searching eye ;
'Tis a wife's duty, love, to share
Her husband's agony.

"Since the dawn began to peep,
Have I lain with stifled breath ;
Heard thee moaning in thy sleep,
As thou wert at grips with death.

"Oh, what joy it was to see
  My gentle lord once more awake!
Tell me, what is amiss with thee?
  Speak, or my heart will break!"

"Mary, thou angel of my life,
  Thou ever good and kind;
'Tis not, believe me, my dear wife,
  The anguish of the mind!

"It is not in my bosom, dear,
  No, nor my brain, in sooth;
But Mary, oh, I feel it here,
  Here in my wisdom tooth!

"Then give,—oh, first, best antidote,—
  Sweet partner of my bed!
Give me thy flannel petticoat
  To wrap around my head!"

THE HUSBAND'S PETITION.

WILLIAM AYTOUN.

Come hither, my heart's darling,
  Come, sit upon my knee,
And listen, while I whisper,
  A boon I ask of thee.
You need not pull my whiskers
  So amorously, my dove;
'Tis something quite apart from
  The gentle cares of love.

I feel a bitter craving—
  A dark and deep desire,
That glows beneath my bosom
  Like coals of kindled fire.
The passion of the nightingale,
  When singing to the rose,
Is feebler than the agony
  That murders my repose!

Nay, dearest! do not doubt me,
  Though madly thus I speak—
I feel thy arms about me,
  Thy tresses on my cheek:
I know the sweet devotion
  That links thy heart with mine—
I know my soul's emotion
  Is doubly felt by thine:

And deem not that a shadow
  Hath fallen across my love:
No, sweet, my love is shadowless,
  As yonder heaven above.
These little taper fingers—
  Ah! Jane, how white they be!—
Can well supply the cruel want
  That almost maddens me.

Thou wilt not sure deny me
  My first and fond request;
I pray thee, by the memory
  Of all we cherish best—
By all the dear remembrance
  Of those delicicious days,
When, hand in hand, we wandered
  Along the summer braes:

By all we felt, unspoken,
  When 'neath the early moon,
We sat beside the rivulet,
  In the leafy month of June;
And by the broken whisper,
  That fell upon my ear,
More sweet than angel-music,
  When first I woo'd thee, dear!

By that great vow which bound thee
  Forever to my side,
And by the ring that made thee
  My darling and my bride!

Thou wilt not fail nor falter,
  But bend thee to the task—
A BOILED SHEEP'S HEAD ON SUNDAY
  Is all the boon I ask.

THE BITER BIT.

WILLIAM AYTOUN.

THE sun is in the sky, mother, the flowers are springing fair,
And the melody of woodland birds is stirring in the air;
The river, smiling to the sky, glides onward to the sea,
And happiness is everywhere, oh, mother, but with me!

They are going to the church, mother—I hear the marriage bell;
It booms along the upland—oh! it haunts me like a knell;
He leads her on his arm, mother, he cheers her faltering step,
And closely to his side she clings—she does, the demirep!

They are crossing by the stile, mother, where we so oft have stood,
The stile beside the shady thorn, at the corner of the wood;
And the boughs, that wont to murmur back the words that won
  my ear,
Wave their silver branches o'er him, as he leads his bridal fere.

He will pass beside the stream, mother, where first my hand he
  pressed,
By the meadow where, with quivering lip, his passion he
  confessed;
And down the hedgerows where we 've strayed again and yet
  again;
But he will not think of me, mother, his broken-hearted Jane!

He said that I was proud, mother, that I looked for rank and gold,
He said I did not love him—he said my words were cold;
He said I kept him off and on, in hopes of higher game—
And it may be that I did, mother; but who has n't done the same?

I did not know my heart, mother—I know it now too late;
I thought that I without a pang could wed some nobler mate;
But no nobler suitor sought me—and he has taken wing,
And my heart is gone, and I am left a lone and blighted thing.

You may lay me in my bed, mother—my head is throbbing sore;
And, mother, prithee, let the sheets be duly aired before;
And, if you 'd please, my mother dear, your poor desponding child,
Draw me a pot of beer, mother, and, mother, draw it mild!

A MIDNIGHT MEDITATION.

BY SIR E—— B—— L——.

WILLIAM AYTOUN.

Fill me once more the foaming pewter up!
Another board of oysters, ladye mine!
To-night Lucullus with himself shall sup.
These mute inglorious Miltons are divine;
And as I here in slippered ease recline,
Quaffing of Perkins' Entire my fill,
I sigh not for the lymph of Aganippe's rill.

A nobler inspiration fires my brain,
Caught from Old England's fine time-hallowed drink,
I snatch the pot again and yet again,
And as the foaming fluids shrink and shrink,
Fill me once more, I say, up to the brink!
This makes strong hearts—strong heads attest its charm—
This nerves the might that sleeps in Britain's brawny arm!

But these remarks are neither here nor there.
Where was I? Oh, I see—old Southey 's dead!
They 'll want some bard to fill the vacant chair,
And drain the annual butt—and oh, what head
More fit with laurel to be garlanded
Than this, which, curled in many a fragrant coil,
Breathes of Castalia's streams, and best Macassar oil?

I know a grace is seated on my brow,
Like young Apollo's with his golden beams;
There should Apollo's bays be budding now:
And in my flashing eyes the radiance beams
That marks the poet in his waking dreams,

When as his fancies cluster thick and thicker,
He feels the trance divine of poesy and liquor.

They throng around me now, those things of air,
That from my fancy took their being's stamp:
There Pelham sits and twirls his glossy hair,
There Clifford leads his pals upon the tramp;
Their pale Zanoni, bending o'er his lamp,
Roams through the starry wilderness of thought,
Where all is every thing, and every thing is naught.

Yes, I am he, who sung how Aram won
The gentle ear of pensive Madeline!
How love and murder hand in hand may run,
Cemented by philosophy serene,
And kisses bless the spot where gore has been!
Who breathed the melting sentiment of crime,
And for the assassin waked a sympathy sublime!

Yes, I am he, who on the novel shed
Obscure philosophy's enchanting light!
Until the public, wildered as they read,
Believed they saw that which was not in sight—
Of course 't was not for me to set them right;
For in my nether heart convinced I am,
Philosophy 's as good as any other bam.

Novels three-volumed I shall write no more—
Somehow or other now they will not sell;
And to invent new passions is a bore—
I find the Magazines pay quite as well.
Translating 's simple, too, as I can tell,
Who 've hawked at Schiller on his lyric throne,
And given the astonished bard a meaning all my own.

Moore, Campbell, Wordsworth, their best days are grassed;
Battered and broken are their early lyres.
Rogers, a pleasant memory of the past,
Warmed his young hands at Smithfield's martyr fires,
And, worth a plum, nor bays, nor butt desires.
But these are things would suit me to the letter,
For though this Stout is good, old Sherry's greatly better.

A fico for your small poetic ravers,
Your Hunts, your Tennysons, your Milnes, and these!
Shall they compete with him who wrote "Maltravers,"
Prologue to "Alice or the Mysteries?"
No! Even now, my glance prophetic sees
My own high brow girt with the bays about.
What ho, within there, ho! another pint of Stout!

THE DIRGE OF THE DRINKER.

BY W—— E—— A——, ESQ.

WILLIAM AYTOUN.

Brothers, spare awhile your liquor, lay your final tumbler down;
He has dropp'd—that star of honor—on the field of his renown!
Raise the wail, but raise it softly, lowly bending on your knees,
If you find it more convenient, you may hiccup if you please.
Sons of Pantagruel, gently let your hip-hurraing sink,
Be your manly accents clouded, half with sorrow, half with drink!
Lightly to the sofa pillow lift his head from off the floor;
See, how calm he sleeps, unconscious as the deadest nail in door!
Widely o'er the earth I've wander'd; where the drink most freely flow'd,
I have ever reel'd the foremost, foremost to the beaker strode.
Deep in shady Cider Cellars I have dream'd o'er heavy wet,
By the fountains of Damascus I have quaff'd the rich Sherbet,
Regal Montepulciano drained beneath its native rock,
On Johannis' sunny mountain frequent hiccup'd o'er my hock;
I have bathed in butts of Xeres deeper than did e'er Monsoon,
Sangaree'd with bearded Tartars in the Mountains of the Moon;
In beer-swilling Copenhagen I have drunk your Danesman blind,
I have kept my feet in Jena, when each bursch to earth declined;
Glass for glass, in fierce Jamaica, I have shared the planter's rum,
Drank with Highland dhuinie-wassels, till each gibbering Gael grew dumb;
But a stouter, bolder drinker—one that loved his liquor more—
Never yet did I encounter than our friend upon the floor!

Yet the best of us are mortal, we to weakness all are heir,
He has fallen, who rarely stagger'd—let the rest of us beware!
We shall leave him, as we found him—lying where his manhood fell,
'Mong the trophies of the revel, for he took his tipple well.
Better 't were we loosed his neckcloth, laid his throat and bosom bare,
Pulled his Hobies off, and turn'd his toes to taste the breezy air.
Throw the sofa cover o'er him, dim the flaring of the gas,
Calmly, calmly let him slumber, and, as by the bar we pass,
We shall bid that thoughtful waiter place beside him, near and handy,
Large supplies of soda water, tumblers bottomed well with brandy,
So when waking, he shall drain them, with that deathless thirst of his,
Clinging to the hand that smote him, like a good 'un as he is!

FRANCESCA DA RIMINI.

TO BON GAULTIER.

WILLIAM AYTOUN.

ARGUMENT.—An impassioned pupil of Leigh Hunt, having met Bon Gaultier at a Fancy Ball, declares the destructive consequences thus:

Didst thou not praise me, Gaultier, at the ball,
Ripe lips, trim boddice, and a waist so small,
With clipsome lightness, dwindling ever less,
Beneath the robe of pea-y greeniness!
Dost thou remember, when with stately prance,
Our heads went crosswise in the country dance;
How soft, warm fingers, tipp'd like buds of balm,
Trembled within the squeezing of thy palm;
And how a cheek grew flush'd and peachy-wise
At the frank lifting of thy cordial eyes?
Ah, me! that night there was one gentle thing,
Who like a dove, with its scarce-feather'd wing,
Flutter'd at the approach of thy quaint swaggering!
There's wont to be, at conscious times like these,
An affectation of a bright-eyed ease—

A crispy-cheekiness, if so I dare
Describe the swaling of a jaunty air;
And thus, when swirling from the waltz's wheel,
You craved my hand to grace the next quadrille,
That smiling voice, although it made me start,
Boil'd in the meek o'erlifting of my heart;
And, picking at my flowers, I said with free
And usual tone, "Oh yes, sir, certainly!"

Like one that swoons, 'twixt sweet amaze and fear,
I heard the music burning in my ear,
And felt I cared not, so thou wert with me,
If Gurth or Wamba were our vis-à-vis.
So, when a tall Knight Templar ringing came,
And took his place against us with his dame,
I neither turned away, nor bashful shrunk
From the stern survey of the soldier-monk,
Though rather more than full three-quarters drunk;
But threading through the figure, first in rule,
I paused to see thee plunge into La Poule.

Ah, what a sight was that? Not prurient Mars,
Pointing his toe through ten celestial bars—
Not young Apollo, beamily array'd
In tripsome guise for Juno's masquerade—
Not smartest Hermes, with his pinion girth,
Jerking with freaks and snatches down to earth,
Look'd half so bold, so beautiful and strong,
As thou when pranking thro' the glittering throng!
How the calm'd ladies looked with eyes of love
On thy trim velvet doublet laced above;
The hem of gold, that, like a wavy river,
Flowed down into thy back with glancing shiver!
So bare was thy fine throat, and curls of black
So lightsomely dropp'd on thy lordly back,
So crisply swaled the feather in thy bonnet,
So glanced thy thigh, and spanning palm upon it,
That my weak soul took instant flight to thee,
Lost in the fondest gush of that sweet witchery!

But when the dance was o'er, and arm in arm
(The full heart beating 'gainst the elbow warm),

We pass'd to the great refreshment hall,
Where the heap'd cheese-cakes and the comfits small
Lay, like a hive of sunbeams, to burn
Around the margin of the negus urn;
When my poor quivering hand you finger'd twice,
And, with inquiring accents, whisper'd "Ice,
Water, or cream?" I could no more dissemble,
But dropp'd upon the couch all in a tremble.
A swimming faintness misted o'er my brain,
The corks seem'd starting from the brisk champagne,
The custards fell untouch'd upon the floor,
Thine eyes met mine. That night we danced no more!

LOUIS NAPOLEON'S ADDRESS TO HIS ARMY.

WILLIAM AYTOUN.

Guards! who at Smolensko fled—
No—I beg your pardon—bled!
For my Uncle blood you 've shed,
Do the same for me.

Now 's the day and now 's the hour,
Heads to split and streets to scour;
Strike for rank, promotion, power,
Sawg, and *eau de vie.*

Who 's afraid a child to kill?
Who respects a shopman's till?
Who would pay a tailor's bill?
Let him turn and flee.

Who would burst a goldsmith's door,
Shoot a dun, or sack a store?
Let him arm, and go before—
That is, follow me!

See the mob, to madness riled,
Up the barricades have piled;
In among them, man and child,
Unrelentingly!

Shoot the men! there 's scarcely one
In a dozen 's got a gun:
Stop them, if they try to run,
With artillery!

Shoot the boys! each one may grow
Into—of the state—a foe
(Meaning by the state, you know,
My supremacy!)

Shoot the girls and women old!
Those may bear us traitors bold—
These may be inclined to scold
Our severity.

Sweep the streets of all who may
Rashly venture in the way,
Warning for a future day
Satisfactory.

Then, when still'd is ev'ry voice,
We, the nation's darling choice,
Calling on them to rejoice,
Tell them, FRANCE IS FREE.

THE BATTLE OF THE BOULEVARD.

WILLIAM AYTOUN.

ON Paris, when the sun was low,
The gay "Comique" made goodly show,
Habitués crowding every row
To hear Limnandier's opera.

But Paris showed another sight,
When, mustering in the dead of night,
Her masters stood, at morning light,
The crack *chasseurs* of Africa.

By servants in my pay betrayed,
Cavaignac, then, my prisoner made,
Wrote that a circumstance delayed
His marriage rite and revelry.

Then shook small Thiers, with terror riven;
Then stormed Bedeau, while gaol-ward driven;
And, swearing (not alone by Heaven),
Was seized bold Lamoricière.

But louder rose the voice of woe
When soldiers sacked each cit's dépôt,
And tearing down a helpless foe,
Flashed Magnan's red artillery.

More, more arrests! Changarnier brave
Is dragged to prison like a knave:
No time allowed the swell to shave,
Or use the least perfumery.

'Tis morn, and now Hortense's son
(Perchance her spouse's too) has won
The imperial crown. The French are done,
Chawed up most incontestably.

Few, few shall write, and none shall meet;
Suppressed shall be each journal-sheet;
And every serf beneath my feet
Shall hail the soldier's Emperor.

PUFFS POETICAL.

WILLIAM AYTOUN.

I.

PARIS AND HELEN.

As the youthful Paris presses
Helen to his ivory breast,
Sporting with her golden tresses,
Close and ever closer pressed.

He said: "So let me quaff the nectar,
Which thy lips of ruby yield;
Glory I can leave to Hector,
Gathered in the tented field.

"Let me ever gaze upon thee,
 Look into thine eyes so deep;
With a daring hand I won thee,
 With a faithful heart I 'll keep.

"Oh, my Helen, thou bright wonder,
 Who was ever like to thee?
Jove would lay aside his thunder,
 So he might be blest like me.

"How mine eyes so fondly linger
 On thy soft and pearly skin;
Scan each round and rosy finger,
 Drinking draughts of beauty in!

"Tell me, whence thy beauty, fairest!
 Whence thy cheek's enchanting bloom?
Whence the rosy hue thou wearest,
 Breathing round thee rich perfume?"

Thus he spoke, with heart that panted,
 Clasped her fondly to his side,
Gazed on her with look enchanted,
 While his Helen thus replied:

"Be no discord, love, between us,
 If I not the secret tell!
'Twas a gift I had of Venus,—
 Venus who hath loved me well.

"And she told me as she gave it,
 'Let not e'er the charm be known,
O'er thy person freely lave it,
 Only when thou art alone.'

"'Tis inclosed in yonder casket—
 Here behold its golden key;
But its name—love, do not ask it,
 Tell 't I may not, e'en to thee!"

Long with vow and kiss he plied her,
 Still the secret did she keep,
Till at length he sank beside her,
 Seemed as he had dropped to sleep.

Soon was Helen laid in slumber,
When her Paris, rising slow,
Did his fair neck disencumber
From her rounded arms of snow;

Then her heedless fingers oping,
Takes the key and steals away,
To the ebon table groping,
Where the wondrous casket lay;

Eagerly the lid uncloses,
Sees within it, laid aslope,
PEAR'S LIQUID BLOOM OF ROSES,
Cakes of his TRANSPARENT SOAP!

II.

TARQUIN AND THE AUGUR.

GINGERLY is good King Tarquin shaving,
Gently glides the razor o'er his chin,
Near him stands a grim Haruspex raving,
And with nasal whine he pitches in,
Church Extension hints,
Till the monarch squints,
Snicks his chin, and swears—a deadly sin!

"Jove confound thee, thou bare-legged impostor!
From my dressing table get thee gone!
Dost thou think my flesh is double Glo'ster?
There again! That cut was to the bone!
Get ye from my sight;
I'll believe you're right
When my razor cuts the sharping hone!"

Thus spoke Tarquin with a deal of dryness;
But the Augur, eager for his fees,
Answered—"Try it, your Imperial Highness,
Press a little harder, if you please.
There! the deed is done!"
Through the solid stone
Went the steel as glibly as through cheese.

So the Augur touched the tin of Tarquin,
  Who suspected some celestial aid:
But he wronged the blameless Gods; for hearken!
  Ere the monarch's bet was rashly laid,
    With his searching eye
    Did the priest espy
RODGER'S name engraved upon the blade.

REFLECTIONS OF A PROUD PEDESTRIAN.

OLIVER WENDELL HOLMES.

I SAW the curl of his waving lash,
    And the glance of his knowing eye,
And I knew that he thought he was cutting a dash,
    As his steed went thundering by.

And he may ride in the rattling gig,
    Or flourish the Stanhope gay,
And dream that he looks exceeding big
    To the people that walk in the way;

But he shall think, when the night is still,
    On the stable-boy's gathering numbers,
And the ghost of many a veteran bill
    Shall hover around his slumbers;

The ghastly dun shall worry his sleep,
    And constables cluster around him,
And he shall creep from the wood-hole deep
    Where their specter eyes have found him!

Ay! gather your reins, and crack your thong,
    And bid your steed go faster;
He does not know as he scrambles along,
    That he has a fool for his master;

And hurry away on your lonely ride,
    Nor deign from the mire to save me;
I will paddle it stoutly at your side
    With the tandem that nature gave me!

EVENING.

BY A TAILOR.

OLIVER WENDELL HOLMES.

Day hath put on his jacket, and around
His burning bosom buttoned it with stars.
Here will I lay me on the velvet grass,
That is like padding to earth's meager ribs,
And hold communion with the things about me.
Ah me! how lovely is the golden braid,
That binds the skirt of night's descending robe!
The thin leaves, quivering on their silken threads,
Do make a music like to rustling satin,
As the light breezes smooth their downy nap.

Ha! what is this that rises to my touch,
So like a cushion? Can it be a cabbage?
It is, it is that deeply injured flower,
Which boys do flout us with;—but yet I love thee,
Thou giant rose, wrapped in a green surtout.
Doubtless in Eden thou didst blush as bright
As these, thy puny brethren; and thy breath
Sweetened the fragrance of her spicy air;
But now thou seemest like a bankrupt beau,
Stripped of his gaudy hues and essences,
And growing portly in his sober garments.

Is that a swan that rides upon the water?
O no, it is that other gentle bird,
Which is the patron of our noble calling.
I well remember, in my early years,
When these young hands first closed upon a goose;
I have a scar upon my thimble finger,
Which chronicles the hour of young ambition.
My father was a tailor, and his father,
And my sire's grandsire, all of them were tailors;
They had an ancient goose,—it was an heir-loom
From some remoter tailor of our race.
It happened I did see it on a time
When none was near, and I did deal with it,
And it did burn me,—oh, most fearfully!

It is a joy to straighten out one's limbs,
And leap elastic from the level counter,
Leaving the petty grievances of earth,
The breaking thread, the din of clashing shears,
And all the needles that do wound the spirit,
For such a pensive hour of soothing silence.
Kind Nature, shuffling in her loose undress,
Lays bare her shady bosom; I can feel
With all around me;—I can hail the flowers
That sprig earth's mantle,—and yon quiet bird,
That rides the stream, is to me as a brother.
The vulgar know not all the hidden pockets,
Where Nature stows away her loveliness.
But this unnatural posture of my legs
Cramps my extended calves, and I must go
Where I can coil them in their wonted fashion.

PHAETHON;

OR, THE AMATEUR COACHMAN.

JOHN G. SAXE.

DAN PHAETHON—so the histories run—
Was a jolly young chap, and a son of the SUN;
Or rather of PHŒBUS—but as to his mother,
Genealogists make a deuce of a pother,
Some going for one, and some for another!
For myself, I must say, as a careful explorer,
This roaring young blade was the son of AURORA!

Now old Father PHŒBUS, ere railways begun
To elevate funds and depreciate fun,
Drove a very fast coach by the name of "THE SUN;"
    Running, they say,
    Trips every day
(On Sundays and all, in a heathenish way).
And lighted up with a famous array
Of lanterns that shone with a brilliant display,
And dashing along like a gentleman's "shay."
With never a fare, and nothing to pay!

Now PHAETHON begged of his doting old father,
To grant him a favor, and this the rather,
Since some one had hinted, the youth to annoy,
That he was n't by any means PHŒBUS's boy!
Intending, the rascally son of a gun,
To darken the brow of the son of the SUN!
"By the terrible Styx!" said the angry sire,
While his eyes flashed volumes of fury and fire,
"To prove your reviler an infamous liar,
I swear I will grant you whate'er you desire!"
"Then by my head,"
The youngster said,
"I'll mount the coach when the horses are fed!—
For there's nothing I'd choose, as I'm alive,
Like a seat on the box, and a dashing drive!"
"Nay, PHAETHON, don't—
I beg you won't—
Just stop a moment and think upon 't!
You're quite too young," continued the sage,
"To tend a coach at your tender age!
Besides, you see,
'T will really be
Your first appearance on any stage!
Desist, my child,
The cattle are wild,
And when their mettle is thoroughly 'riled,'
Depend upon 't, the coach 'll be 'spiled'—
They 're not the fellows to draw it mild!
Desist, I say,
You'll rue the day—
So mind, and don't be foolish, PHA!"
But the youth was proud,
And swore aloud,
'T was just the thing to astonish the crowd—
He 'd have the horses and would n't be cowed!
In vain the boy was cautioned at large,
He called for the chargers, unheeding the charge,
And vowed that any young fellow of force,
Could manage a dozen coursers, of course!
Now PHŒBUS felt exceedingly sorry
He had given his word in such a hurry,
But having sworn by the Styx, no doubt
He was in for it now, and could n't back out.

So calling PHAETHON up in a trice,
He gave the youth a bit of advice:—
" '*Parce stimulis, utere loris!*'
(A "stage direction," of which the core is,
Don't use the whip—they're ticklish things—
But, whatever you do, hold on to the strings!)
Remember the rule of the Jehu-tribe is,
'*Medio tutissimus ibis*'
(As the Judge remarked to a rowdy Scotchman,
Who was going to quod between two watchmen!)
So mind your eye, and spare your goad,
Be shy of the stones, and keep in the road!"

Now PHAETHON, perched in the coachman's place,
Drove off the steeds at a furious pace,
Fast as coursers running a race,
Or bounding along in a steeple-chase!
Of whip and shout there was no lack,
"Crack—whack—
Whack—crack"
Resounded along the horses' back!—
Frightened beneath the stinging lash,
Cutting their flanks in many a gash,
On—on they sped as swift as a flash,
Through thick and thin away they dash,
(Such rapid driving is always rash!)
When all at once, with a dreadful crash,
The whole "establishment" went to smash!
And PHAETHON, he,
As all agree,
Off the coach was suddenly hurled,
Into a puddle, and out of the world!

MORAL.

Don't rashly take to dangerous courses—
Nor set it down in your table of forces,
That any one man equals any four horses!
Don't swear by the Styx!—
It's one of OLD NICK's
Diabolical tricks
To get people into a regular "fix,"
And hold 'em there as fast as bricks!

THE SCHOOL-HOUSE.

[AFTER GOLDSMITH.]

JAMES RUSSELL LOWELL.

Propt on the marsh, a dwelling now, I see
The humble school-house of my A, B, C,
Where well-drilled urchins, each behind his tire,
Waited in ranks the wished command to fire,
Then all together, when the signal came,
Discharged their *a-b abs* against the dame,
Who, 'mid the volleyed learning, firm and calm,
Patted the furloughed ferule on her palm,
And, to our wonder, could detect at once
Who flashed the pan, and who was downright dunce

There young Devotion learned to climb with ease
The gnarly limbs of Scripture family-trees,
And he was most commended and admired
Who soonest to the topmost twig perspired;
Each name was called as many various ways
As pleased the reader's ear on different days,
So that the weather, or the ferule's stings,
Colds in the head, or fifty other things,
Transformed the helpless Hebrew thrice a week
To guttural Pequot or resounding Greek,
The vibrant accent skipping here and there
Just as it pleased invention or despair;
No controversial Hebraist was the Dame;
With or without the points pleased her the same;
If any tyro found a name too tough,
And looked at her, pride furnished skill enough;
She nerved her larynx for the desperate thing,
And cleared the five-barred syllables at a spring.

Ah, dear old times! there once it was my hap,
Perched on a stool, to wear the long-eared cap;
From books degraded, there I sat at ease,
A drone, the envy of compulsory bees.

EPIGRAMMATIC.

EPIGRAMMATIC

EPIGRAMS OF BEN JONSON.

TO FINE GRAND.

What is 't Fine Grand, makes thee my friendship fly,
Or take an Epigram so fearfully,
As 't were a challenge, or a borrower's letter?
The world must know your greatness is my debtor.
Imprimis, Grand, you owe me for a jest
I lent you, on mere acquaintance, at a feast.
Item, a tale or two some fortnight after,
That yet maintains you, and your house in laughter.
Item, the Babylonian song you sing;
Item, a fair Greek poesy for a ring,
With which a learned madam you bely.
Item, a charm surrounding fearfully
Your *partie-per-pale* picture, one half drawn
In solemn cyprus, th' other cobweb lawn.
Item, a gulling impress for you, at tilt.
Item, your mistress' anagram, in your hilt.
Item, your own, sew'd in your mistress' smock.
Item, an epitaph on my lord's cock,
In most vile verses, and cost me more pain,
Than had I made 'em good, to fit your vein.
Forty things more, dear Grand, which you know true,
For which, or pay me quickly, or I'll pay you.

TO BRAINHARDY.

Hardy, thy brain is valiant, 'tis confest,
Thou more; that with it every day dar'st jest

Thyself into fresh brawls; when call'd upon,
Scarce thy week's swearing brings thee off of one;
So in short time, thou art in arrearage grown
Some hundred quarrels, yet dost thou fight none;
Nor need'st thou; for those few, by oath released,
Make good what thou dar'st in all the rest.
Keep thyself there, and think thy valor right;
He that dares damn himself, dares more than fight.

TO DOCTOR EMPIRIC.

When men a dangerous disease did 'scape,
Of old, they gave a cock to Æsculape;
Let me give two, that doubly am got free;
From my disease's danger, and from thee.

TO SIR ANNUAL FILTER.

Filter, the most may admire thee, though not I;
And thou, right guiltless, may'st plead to it, why?
For thy late sharp device. I say 'tis fit
All brains, at times of triumph, should run wit;
For then our water-conduits do run wine;
But that 's put in, thou 'lt say. Why, so is thine.

ON BANKS THE USURER.

Banks feels no lameness of his knotty gout,
His moneys travel for him in and out,
And though the soundest legs go every day,
He toils to be at hell, as soon as they.

ON CHEVRIL THE LAWYER.

No cause, nor client fat, will Cheveril leese,
But as they come, on both sides he takes fees,
And pleaseth both; for while he melts his grease
For this; that wins, for whom he holds his peace.

EPIGRAMATIC VERSES BY SAMUEL BUTLER.

OPINION.

Opinion governs all mankind,
Like the blind's leading of the blind;
For he that has no eyes in 's head,
Must be by a dog glad to be led;
And no beasts have so little in 'em
As that inhuman brute, Opinion.
'Tis an infectious pestilence,
The tokens upon wit and sense,
That with a venomous contagion
Invades the sick imagination:
And, when it seizes any part,
It strikes the poison to the heart.
This men of one another catch,
By contact, as the humors match;
And nothing 's so perverse in nature
As a profound opiniator.

CRITICS.

Critics are like a kind of flies, that breed
In wild fig-trees, and when they 're grown up, feed
Upon the raw fruit of the nobler kind,
And, by their nibbling on the outward rind,
Open the pores, and make way for the sun
To ripen it sooner than he would have done.

HYPOCRISY.

Hypocrisy will serve as well
To propagate a church, as zeal;
As persecution and promotion
Do equally advance devotion:
So round white stones will serve, they say,
As well as eggs to make hens lay.

POLISH.

All wit and fancy, like a diamond,
The more exact and curious 'tis ground,
Is forced for every carat to abate,
As much in value as it wants in weight.

THE GODLY.

A godly man, that has served out his time
In holiness, may set up any crime;
As scholars, when they 've taken their degrees,
May set up any faculty they please.

PIETY.

Why should not piety be made,
As well as equity, a trade,
And men get money by devotion,
As well as making of a motion?
B' allow'd to pray upon conditions,
As well as suitors in petitions?
And in a congregation pray,
No less than Chancery, for pay?

MARRIAGE.

All sorts of vot'ries, that profess
To bind themselves apprentices
To Heaven, abjure, with solemn vows,
Not Cut and Long-tail, but a Spouse
As the worst of all impediments
To hinder their devout intents.

POETS.

It is not poetry that makes men poor;
For few do write that were not so before;
And those that have writ best, had they been rich,
Had ne'er been clapp'd with a poetic itch;

Had loved their ease too well to take the pains
To undergo that drudgery of brains;
But, being for all other trades unfit,
Only t' avoid being idle, set up wit.

PUFFING.

They that do write in authors' praises,
And freely give their friends their voices,
Are not confined to what is true;
That's not to give, but pay a due:
For praise, that's due, does give no more
To worth, than what it had before;
But to commend without desert,
Requires a mastery of art,
That sets a gloss on what's amiss,
And writes what should be, not what is.

POLITICIANS.

All the politics of the great
Are like the cunning of a cheat,
That lets his false dice freely run,
And trusts them to themselves alone,
But never lets a true one stir,
Without some fingering trick or slur;
And, when the gamester doubts his play,
Conveys his false dice safe away,
And leaves the true ones in the lurch
T' endure the torture of the search.

FEAR.

There needs no other charm, nor conjurer
To raise infernal spirits up, but fear;
That makes men pull their horns in, like a snail
That's both a pris'ner to itself, and jail;
Draws more fantastic shapes, than in the grains
Of knotted wood, in some men's crazy brains;
When all the cocks they think they see, and bulls,
Are only in the insides of their skulls.

THE LAW.

The law can take a purse in open court
While it condemns a less delinquent for 't.

THE SAME.

Who can deserve, for breaking of the laws,
A greater penance than an honest cause.

THE SAME.

All those that do but rob and steal enough,
Are punishment and court-of-justice proof,
And need not fear, nor be concerned a straw
In all the idle bugbears of the law;
But confidently rob the gallows too,
As well as other sufferers, of their due.

CONFESSION.

In the Church of Rome to go to shrift
Is but to put the soul on a clean shift.

SMATTERERS

All smatterers are more brisk and pert
Than those that understand an art;
As little sparkles shine more bright
Than glowing coals, that give them light.

BAD WRITERS.

As he that makes his mark is understood
To write his name, and 'tis in law as good,
So he, that can not write one word of sense
Believes he has as legal a pretense
To scribble what he does not understand,
As idiots have a title to their land

THE OPINIONATIVE.

Opinionators naturally differ
From other men; as wooden legs are stiffer
Than those of pliant joints, to yield and bow,
Which way soever they 're design'd to go.

LANGUAGE OF THE LEARNED.

Were Tully now alive, he 'd be to seek
In all our Latin terms of art and Greek;
Would never understand one word of sense
The most irrefragable schoolman means:
As if the Schools design'd their terms of art,
Not to advance a science, but to divert;
As *Hocus Pocus* conjures to amuse
The rabble from observing what he does.

GOOD WRITING.

As 'tis a greater mystery in the art
Of painting, to foreshorten any part,
Than draw it out; so 'tis in books the chief
Of all perfections to be plain and brief.

COURTIERS.

As in all great and crowded fairs
Monsters and puppet-play are wares,
Which in the less will not go off,
Because they have not money enough;
So men in princes' courts will pass
That will not in another place.

INVENTIONS.

All the inventions that the world contains,
Were not by reason first found out, nor brains;
But pass for theirs who had the luck to light
Upon them by mistake or oversight.

LOGICIANS.

Logicians used to clap a proposition,
As justices do criminals, in prison,
And, in as learn'd authentic nonsense, writ
The names of all their moods and figures fit;
For a logician's one that has been broke
To ride and pace his reason by the book;
And by their rules, and precepts, and examples,
To put his wits into a kind of trammels.

LABORIOUS WRITERS.

Those get the least that take the greatest pains,
But most of all i' th' drudgery of the brains,
A natural sign of weakness, as an ant
Is more laborious than an elephant;
And children are more busy at their play,
Than those that wiseliest pass their time away.

ON A CLUB OF SOTS.

The jolly members of a toping club,
Like pipestaves, are but hoop'd into a tub;
And in a close confederacy link,
For nothing else but only to hold drink.

HOLLAND.

A country that draws fifty feet of water,
In which men live as in the hold of Nature;
And when the sea does in upon them break,
And drown a province, does but spring a leak;
That always ply the pump, and never think
They can be safe, but at the rate they stink;
That live as if they had been run a-ground,
And, when they die, are cast away and drown'd;
That dwell in ships, like swarms of rats, and prey
Upon the goods all nations' fleets convey;
And, when their merchants are blown up and cracked,
Whole towns are cast away and wrecked;

That feed, like cannibals, on other fishes,
And serve their cousin-germans up in dishes:
A land that rides at anchor, and is moor'd,
In which they do not live, but go a-board.

WOMEN.

The souls of women are so small,
That some believe they 've none at all;
Or if they have, like cripples, still
They 've but one faculty, the will;
The other two are quite laid by
To make up one great tyranny;
And though their passions have most pow'r,
They are, like Turks, but slaves the more
To th' abs'lute will, that with a breath
Has sovereign pow'r of life and death,
And, as its little int'rests move,
Can turn 'em all to hate or love;
For nothing, in a moment, turn
To frantic love, disdain, and scorn;
And make that love degenerate
T' as great extremity of hate;
And hate again, and scorn, and piques,
To flames, and raptures, and love-tricks.

EPIGRAMS OF EDMUND WALLER.

ON A PAINTED LADY WITH ILL TEETH.

WERE men so dull they could not see
That LYCE painted; should they flee,
Like simple birds, into a net,
So grossly woven, and ill set,
Her own teeth would undo the knot,
And let all go that she had got.
Those teeth fair LYCE must not show,
If she would bite: her lovers, though

Like birds they stoop at seeming grapes,
Are dis-abus'd, when first she gapes:
The rotten bones discover'd there,
Show 'tis a painted sepulcher.

OF THE MARRIAGE OF THE DWARFS.

Design, or chance, makes others wive;
But nature did this match contrive:
EVE might as well have ADAM fled,
As she denied her little bed
To him, for whom heav'n seem'd to frame,
And measure out, this only dame.
  Thrice happy is that humble pair,
Beneath the level of all care!
Over whose heads those arrows fly
Of sad distrust, and jealousy:
Secured in as high extreme,
As if the world held none but them.
  To him the fairest nymphs do show
Like moving mountains, topp'd with snow:
And ev'ry man a POLYPHEME
Does to his GALATEA seem;
None may presume her faith to prove;
He proffers death that proffers love.
  Ah CHLORIS! that kind nature thus
From all the world had sever'd us:
Creating for ourselves us two,
As love has me for only you!

EPIGRAMS OF MATTHEW PRIOR.

A SIMILE.

DEAR Thomas, didst thou never pop
Thy head into a tin-man's shop?
There, Thomas, didst thou never see
('Tis but by way of simile)

A squirrel spend his little rage,
In jumping round a rolling cage?
The cage, as either side turn'd up,
Striking a ring of bells a-top?—
Mov'd in the orb, pleas'd with the chimes,
The foolish creature thinks he climbs:
But here or there, turn wood or wire,
He never gets two inches higher.
So fares it with those merry blades,
That frisk it under Pindus' shades.
In noble songs, and lofty odes,
They tread on stars, and talk with gods;
Still dancing in an airy round,
Still pleased with their own verses' sound;
Brought back, how fast soe'er they go,
Always aspiring, always low.

THE FLIES.

Say, sire of insects, mighty Sol,
(A Fly upon the chariot pole
Cries out), what Blue-bottle alive
Did ever with such fury drive?
Tell Belzebub, great father, tell
(Says t' other, perch'd upon the wheel),
Did ever any mortal Fly
Raise such a cloud of dust as I?
My judgment turn'd the whole debate:
My valor sav'd the sinking state.
So talk two idle buzzing things;
Toss up their heads, and stretch their wings.
But let the truth to light be brought;
This neither spoke, nor t' other fought:
No merit in their own behavior:
Both rais'd, but by their party's favor.

PHILLIS'S AGE.

How old may Phillis be, you ask,
Whose beauty thus all hearts engages?
To answer is no easy task:
For she has really two ages.

Stiff in brocade, and pinch'd in stays,
Her patches, paint, and jewels on;
All day let envy view her face,
And Phillis is but twenty-one.

Paint, patches, jewels laid aside,
At night astronomers agree,
The evening has the day belied;
And Phillis is some forty-three.

TO THE DUKE DE NOALLES.

Vain the concern which you express,
That uncall'd Alard will possess
Your house and coach, both day and night,
And that Macbeth was haunted less
By Banquo's restless sprite.

With fifteen thousand pounds a-year,
Do you complain, you can not bear
An ill, you may so soon retrieve?
Good Alard, faith, is modester
By much, than you believe.

Lend him but fifty louis-d'or;
And you shall never see him more:
Take the advice; probatum est.
Why do the gods indulge our store,
But to secure our rest?

ON BISHOP ATTERBURY.

Meek Francis lies here, friend: without stop or stay,
As you value your peace, make the best of your way.
Though at present arrested by death's caitiff paw,
If he stirs, he may still have recourse to the law.
And in the King's Bench should a verdict be found,
That by livery and seisin his grave is his ground,

He will claim to himself what is strictly his due,
And an action of trespass will straightway ensue,
That you without right on his premises tread,
On a simple surmise that the owner is dead.

FORMA BONUM FRAGILE.

What a frail thing is beauty! says baron Le Cras,
Perceiving his mistress had one eye of glass:
  And scarcely had he spoke it,
When she more confus'd as more angry she grew,
By a negligent rage prov'd the maxim too true:
  She dropt the eye, and broke it.

EARNING A DINNER.

Full oft doth Mat. with Topaz dine,
Eateth baked meats, drinketh Greek wine;
But Topaz his own werke rehearseth;
And Mat. mote praise what Topaz verseth.
Now sure as priest did e'er shrive sinner,
Full hardly earneth Mat. his dinner.

BIBO AND CHARON.

When Bibo thought fit from the world to retreat,
And full of champagne as an egg's full of meat,
He waked in the boat; and to Charon he said,
He would be row'd back, for he was not yet dead.
Trim the boat, and sit quiet, stern Charon replied:
You may have forgot, you were drunk when you died

THE PEDANT.

Lysander talks extremely well;
On any subject let him dwell,
  His tropes and figures will content ye
He should possess to all degrees
The art of talk; he practices
  Full fourteen hours in four-and-twenty.

EPIGRAMS OF JOSEPH ADDISON.

THE COUNTESS OF MANCHESTER.

Written on his admission to the Kit-Cat Club, in compliance with the rule that every new member should name his toast, and write a verse in her praise.

While haughty Gallia's dames, that spread
O'er their pale cheeks an artful red,
Beheld this beauteous stranger there,
In nature's charms divinely fair;
Confusion in their looks they showed,
And with unborrowed blushes glowed.

TO AN ILL-FAVORED LADY.

[IMITATED FROM MARTIAL.]

While in the dark on thy soft hand I hung,
And heard the tempting syren in thy tongue,
What flames, what darts, what anguish I endured!
But when the candle entered I was cured.

TO A CAPRICIOUS FRIEND.

[IMITATED FROM MARTIAL.]

In all thy humors, whether grave or mellow,
Thou 'rt such a touchy, testy, pleasant fellow;
Hast so much wit, and mirth, and spleen about thee,
There is no living with thee, nor without thee.

TO A ROGUE.

[IMITATED FROM MARTIAL.]

Thy beard and head are of a different dye:
Short of one foot, distorted in an eye:
With all these tokens of a knave complete,
Should'st thou be honest, thou 'rt a dev'lish cheat.

EPIGRAMS OF ALEXANDER POPE.

ON MRS. TOFTS.

(A CELEBRATED OPERA SINGER.)

So bright is thy beauty, so charming thy song,
As had drawn both the beasts and their Orpheus along;
But such is thy avarice, and such is thy pride.
That the beasts must have starved, and the poet have died.

TO A BLOCKHEAD.

You beat your pate, and fancy wit will come:
Knock as you please, there 's nobody at home.

THE FOOL AND THE POET.

Sir, I admit your general rule,
That every poet is a fool,
But you yourself may serve to show it,
That every fool is not a poet.

EPIGRAMS OF DEAN SWIFT.

ON BURNING A DULL POEM.

An ass's hoof alone can hold
That poisonous juice, which kills by cold.
Methought when I this poem read,
No vessel but an ass's head
Such frigid fustian could contain;
I mean the head without the brain.
The cold conceits, the chilling thoughts,
Went down like stupefying draughts;
I found my head begin to swim,
A numbness crept through every limb.

In haste, with imprecations dire,
I threw the volume in the fire;
When (who could think?) though cold as ice,
It burnt to ashes in a trice.
 How could I more enhance its fame?
Though born in snow, it died in flame.

TO A LADY,

On hearing her praise her husband.

You always are making a god of your spouse;
But this neither Reason nor Conscience allows;
Perhaps you will say, 'tis in gratitude due,
And you adore him because he adores you.
Your argument's weak, and so you will find,
For you, by this rule, must adore all mankind.

THE CUDGELED HUSBAND.

As Thomas was cudgel'd one day by his wife,
He took to his heels and fled for his life:
Tom's three dearest friends came by in the squabble,
And saved him at once from the shrew and the rabble;
Then ventured to give him some sober advice—
But Tom is a person of honor so nice,
Too wise to take counsel, too proud to take warning,
That he sent to all three a challenge next morning.
Three duels he fought, thrice ventured his life;
Went home, and was cudgeled again by his wife.

ON SEEING VERSES WRITTEN UPON WINDOWS AT INNS.

The sage, who said he should be proud
 Of windows in his breast,
Because he ne'er a thought allow'd
 That might not be confest;
His window scrawled by every rake,
 His breast again would cover,
And fairly bid the devil take
 The diamond and the lover.

ON SEEING THE BUSTS OF NEWTON, LOCKE, AND OTHERS,

Placed by Queen Caroline in Richmond Hermitage.

Louis the living learned fed,
And raised the scientific head;
Our frugal queen, to save her meat,
Exalts the heads that cannot eat.

ON THE CHURCH'S DANGER.

Good Halifax and pious Wharton cry,
The Church has vapors; there 's no danger nigh.
In those we love not, we no danger see,
And were they hang'd, there would no danger be.
But we must silent be, amid our fears,
And not believe our senses, but the Peers.
So ravishers. that know no sense of shame,
First stop her mouth, and then debauch the dame.

ON ONE DELACOURT'S COMPLIMENTING CARTHY ON HIS POETRY.

Carthy, you say, writes well—his genius true,
You pawn your word for him—he 'll vouch for you.
So two poor knaves, who find their credit fail,
To cheat the world, become each other's bail.

ON A USURER.

Beneath this verdant hillock lies,
Demar, the wealthy and the wise.
His heirs, that he might safely rest,
Have put his carcass in a chest,
The very chest in which, they say,
His other self, his money lay.
And, if his heirs continue kind
To that dear self he left behind,
I dare believe, that four in five
Will think his better half alive.

TO MRS. BIDDY FLOYD;

OR, THE RECEIPT TO FORM A BEAUTY.

When Cupid did his grandsire Jove entreat
To form some Beauty by a new receipt,
Jove sent, and found, far in a country scene,
Truth, innocence, good nature, look serene:
From which ingredients first the dext'rous boy
Pick'd the demure, the awkward, and the coy.
The Graces from the court did next provide
Breeding, and wit, and air, and decent pride:
These Venus cleans from every spurious grain
Of nice coquet, affected, pert, and vain.
Jove mix'd up all, and the best clay employ'd;
Then call'd the happy composition FLOYD.

THE REVERSE;

OR, MRS. CLUDD.

Venus one day, as story goes,
But for what reason no man knows,
In sullen mood and grave deport,
Trudged it away to Jove's high court;
And there his Godship did entreat,
To look out for his best receipt:
And make a monster strange and odd,
Abhorr'd by man and every god.
Jove, ever kind to all the fair,
Nor e'er refused a lady's prayer,
Straight oped 'scrutoire, and forth he took
A neatly bound and well-gilt book;
Sure sign that nothing enter'd there,
But what was very choice and rare.
Scarce had he turn'd a page or two—
It might be more, for aught I know;
But, be the matter more or less,
'Mong friends 't will break no squares, I guess.
Then, smiling, to the dame quoth he,
Here 's one will fit you to a T.

But, as the writing doth prescribe,
'Tis fit the ingredients we provide.
Away he went, and search'd the stews,
And every street about the Mews;
Diseases, impudence, and lies,
Are found and brought him in a trice
From Hackney then he did provide,
A clumsy air and awkward pride;
From lady's toilet next he brought
Noise, scandal, and malicious thought.
These Jove put in an old close-stool,
And with them mix'd the vain, the fool,
But now came on his greatest care,
Of what he should his paste prepare;
For common clay or finer mold
Was much too good, such stuff to hold
At last he wisely thought on mud;
So raised it up, and call'd it—*Cludd.*
With this, the lady well content,
Low curtsey'd, and away she went.

THE PLACE OF THE DAMNED.

All folks who pretend to religion and grace,
Allow there 's a Hell, but dispute of the place:
But, if Hell may by logical rules be defined
The place of the damn'd—I 'll tell you my mind.
Wherever the damn'd do chiefly abound,
Most certainly there is Hell to be found:
Damn'd poets, damn'd critics, damn'd blockheads, damn'd knaves.
Damn'd senators bribed, damn'd prostitute slaves;
Damn'd lawyers and judges, damn'd lords and damn'd squires;
Damn'd spies and informers, damn'd friends and damn'd liars;
Damn'd villains, corrupted in every station;
Damn'd time-serving priests all over the nation;
And into the bargain I 'll readily give you
Damn'd ignorant prelates, and councillors privy.
Then let us no longer by parsons be flamm'd,
For we know by these marks the place of the damn'd:
And Hell to be sure is at Paris or Rome.
How happy for us that it is not at home!

THE DAY OF JUDGMENT.

With a world of thought oppress'd,
I sunk from reverie to rest.
A horrid vision seized my head,
I saw the graves give up their dead!
Jove, arm'd with terrors, bursts the skies,
And thunder roars and lightning flies;
Amazed, confused, its fate unknown,
The world stands trembling at his throne!
While each pale sinner hung his head,
Jove, nodding, shook the heavens, and said:
"Offending race of human kind,
By nature, reason, learning, blind;
You who, through frailty, stepp'd aside;
And you, who never fell from pride:
You who in different sects were shamm'd,
And come to see each other damn'd;
(So some folk told you, but they knew
No more of Jove's designs than you);
—The world's mad business now is o'er,
And I resent these pranks no more.
—I to such blockheads set my wit!
I damn such fools!—Go, go, you 're bit."

PAULUS THE LAWYER.

LINDSAY.

"A slave to crowds, scorch'd with the summer's heats,
In courts the wretched lawyer toils and sweats;
While smiling Nature, in her best attire,
Regales each sense, and vernal joys inspire.
Can he, who knows that real good should please,
Barter for gold his liberty and ease?"
This Paulus preach'd:—When, entering at the door,
Upon his board the client pours the ore:
He grasps the shining gifts, pores o'er the cause,
Forgets the sun, and dozes o'er the laws.

EPIGRAMS BY THOMAS SHERIDAN.

ON A CARICATURE.

IF you say this was made for friend Dan, you belie it,
I 'll swear he 's so like it that he was made by it.

ON DEAN SWIFT'S PROPOSED HOSPITAL FOR LUNATICS.

Great wits to madness nearly are allied,
This makes the Dean for kindred *thus* provide.

TO A DUBLIN PUBLISHER.

Who displayed a bust of Dean Swift in his window, while publishing Lord Orrery's offensive remarks upon the Dean.

Faulkner! for once thou hast some judgment shown,
By representing Swift transformed to stone;
For could he thy ingratitude have known,
Astonishment itself the work had done!

WHICH IS WHICH.

BYROM.

"GOD bless the King! God bless the faith's defender!
God bless—no harm in blessing—the Pretender.
But who that pretender is, and who that king,
God bless us all, is quite another thing."

ON SOME LINES OF LOPEZ DE VEGA.

DR. JOHNSON.

IF the man who turnips cries,
Cry not when his father dies,
'Tis a proof that he had rather
Have a turnip than his father.

ON A FULL-LENGTH PORTRAIT OF BEAU MARSH.

Placed between the busts of Newton and Pope.

LORD CHESTERFIELD.

"Immortal Newton never spoke
More truth than here you 'll find;
Nor Pope himself e'er penn'd a joke
More cruel on mankind.

"The picture placed the busts between,
Gives satire all its strength;
Wisdom and Wit are little seen—
But Folly at full length."

ON SCOTLAND.

CLEVELAND.

"Had Cain been Scot, God would have changed his doom;
Nor forced him wander, but confined him home."

EPIGRAMS OF PETER PINDAR.

EDMUND BURKE'S ATTACK ON WARREN HASTINGS.

Poor Edmund sees poor Britain's setting sun:
Poor Edmund *groans*—and Britain is *undone!*

Reader! thou hast, I do presume
(God knows though) been in a snug room,
By coals or wood made comfortably warm,
And often fancied that a storm *without*,
Hath made a diabolic rout—
Sunk ships, tore trees up—done a world of harm.

Yes, thou hast lifted up thy tearful eyes,
Fancying thou heardst of mariners the cries;
And sigh'd, "How wretched now must thousands be!
Oh! how I pity the poor souls at sea!"

When, lo! this dreadful tempest, and his roar,
A *zephyr*—in the key-hole of the door!

Now may not Edmund's howlings be a sigh
  Pressing through Edmund's lungs for loaves and fishes,
On which he long hath looked with *longing* eye
  To fill poor Edmund's not o'erburden'd dishes?

Give Mun a sup—forgot will be complaint;
Britain be safe, and Hastings prove a *saint.*

ON AN ARTIST

Who boasted that his pictures had hung near those of Sir Joshua Reynolds in the Exhibition.

A shabby fellow chanc'd one day to meet
The British Roscius in the street,
  Garrick, on whom our nation justly brags—
The fellow hugg'd him with a kind embrace—
"Good sir, I do not recollect your face,"
  Quoth Garrick—"No!" replied the man of rags:

"The boards of Drury you and I have trod
  Full many a time together, I am sure—"
"When?" with an oath, cried Garrick—"for by G—
  I never saw that face of yours before!—
        What characters, I pray,
        Did you and I together play?"

"Lord!" quoth the fellow, "think not that I mock—
When you play'd Hamlet, sir—I play'd the cock."

ON THE CONCLUSION OF HIS ODES.

"*Finish'd!*" a disappointed artist cries,
  With open mouth, and straining eyes;
Gaping for praise like a young crow for meat—
  "Lord! why have you not mentioned *me!*"
      Mention *thee!*
Thy *impudence* hath put me in a *sweat*—
What rage for fame attends both great and small:
Better be *d—n'd*, than mention'd *not at all!*

THE LEX TALIONIS UPON BENJAMIN WEST

West tells the world that Peter can not rhyme—
Peter declares, point blank, that West can't paint:
West swears I've not an atom of sublime—
I swear he hath no notion of a saint:

And that his cross-wing'd cherubim are fowls,
Baptized by naturalists, owls:
Half of the meek apostles, gangs of robbers;
His angels, sets of brazen-headed lubbers.

The Holy Scripture says, "All flesh is grass;"
With Mr. West, all flesh is brick and brass;
Except his horse-flesh, that I fairly own
Is often of the choicest Portland stone.
I've said it too, that this artist's faces
Ne'er paid a visit to the graces:

That on expression he can never brag:
Yet for this article hath he been studying,
But in it never could surpass a pudding—
No, gentle reader, nor a pudding-bag.

I dare not say, that Mr. West
Can not sound criticism impart:
I'm told the man with technicals is blest,
That he can talk a deal upon the art;
Yes, he can talk, I do not doubt it—
"About it, goddess, and about it."

Thus, then, is Mr. West deserving praise—
And let my justice the fair laud afford;
For, lo! this far-fam'd artist cuts both ways,
Exactly like the angel Gabriel's sword;
The beauties of the art his *converse* shows,
His *canvas* almost ev'ry thing that's bad!
Thus at th' Academy, we must suppose,
A man more useful never could be had:
Who in himself, a host, so much can do;
Who is both precept and example too!

BARRY'S ATTACK UPON SIR JOSHUA REYNOLDS.

When Barry dares the President to fly on,
'Tis like a mouse, that, work'd into a rage,
Daring some dreadful war to wage,
Nibbles the tail of the Nemæan lion.

Or like a louse, of mettle full,
Nurs'd in some giant's skull—
Because Goliath scratch'd him as he fed,
Employs with vehemence his angry claws,
And gaping, grinning, formidable jaws,
To *carry off* the *giant's head!*

ON THE DEATH OF MR. HONE, R.A.

There 's one R.A. more dead! stiff is poor Hone—
His works be with him under the same stone:
I think the sacred art will not bemoan 'em;
But, Muse!—*De mortuis nil nisi bonum*—
As to his host, a *trav'ler*, with a sneer,
Said of his *dead Small-beer*.
Go, then, poor Hone! and join a numerous train
Sunk in *Oblivion's* wide pacific ocean;
And may its *whale-like* stomach feel no motion
To cast thee, like a Jonah, up again.

ON GEORGE THE THIRD'S PATRONAGE OF BENJAMIN WEST.

Thus have I seen a child, with smiling face,
A little daisy in the garden place,
And strut in triumph round its fav'rite flow'r;
Gaze on the leaves with infant admiration,
Thinking the flow'r the finest in the nation,
Then pay a visit to it ev'ry hour:
Lugging the wat'ring-pot about,
Which John the gard'ner was oblig'd to fill;
The child, so pleas'd, would pour the water out,
To show its marvelous gard'ning skill;

Then staring round, all wild for praises panting,
Tell all the world it was its own sweet planting;
And boast away, too happy elf,
How that it found the daisy all itself!

ANOTHER ON THE SAME.

In *simile* if I may shine agen—
Thus have I seen a fond old hen
With one poor miserable chick,
Bustling about a farmer's yard;
Now on the dunghill laboring hard,
Scraping away through thin and thick,
Flutt'ring her feathers—making such a noise!
Cackling aloud such quantities of joys,
As if this chick, to which her egg gave birth,
Was born to deal prodigious knocks,
To shine the Broughton of game cocks,
And kill the fowls of all the earth!

EPITAPH ON PETER STAGGS.

Poor Peter Staggs, now rests beneath this rail,
Who loved his joke, his pipe, and mug of ale;
For twenty years he did the duties well,
Of ostler, boots, and waiter at the "Bell."
But Death stepp'd in, and order'd Peter Staggs
To feed his worms, and leave the farmers' nags.
The church clock struck one—alas! 't was Peter's knel.,
Who sigh'd, "I 'm coming—that 's the ostler's bell!"

TRAY'S EPITAPH.

Here rest the relics of a friend below,
Blest with more sense than half the folks I know:
Fond of his ease, and to no parties prone,
He damn'd no sect, but calmly gnaw'd his bone;
Perform'd his functions well in ev'ry way—
Blush, *Christians*, if you can, and copy *Tray*.

ON A STONE THROWN AT A VERY GREAT MAN, BUT WHICH MISSED HIM.

Talk no more of the lucky escape of the head
  From a flint so unluckily thrown—
I think very different, with thousands indeed,
  'T was a lucky escape for the stone.

[The following stanza, on the death of Lady Mount E——'s favorite pig Cupid, is verily exceeded by nothing in the annals of impertinence.—P. P.]

A CONSOLATORY STANZA

TO LADY MOUNT E——, ON THE DEATH OF HER PIG CUPID.

O dry that tear, so round and big,
  Nor waste in sighs your precious wind!
Death only takes a single pig—
  Your lord and son are still behind.

EPIGRAMS BY ROBERT BURNS.

THE POET'S CHOICE.

I MURDER hate, by field or flood,
  Though glory's name may screen us;
In wars at hame I'll spend my blood,
  Life-giving wars of Venus.

The deities that I adore,
  Are social peace and plenty;
I'm better pleased to make one more,
  Than be the death of twenty.

ON A CELEBRATED RULING ELDER.

Here souter Hood in death does sleep;—
  To h—ll, if he's gane thither,
Satan, gie him thy gear to keep,
  He'll haud it weel thegither.

ON JOHN DOVE

INNKEEPER OF MAUCHLINE.

Here lies Johnny Pidgeon;
What was his religion?
Wha e'er desires to ken,
To some other warl'
Maun follow the carl,
  For here Johnny Pidgeon had nane!

Strong ale was ablution—
Small beer, persecution,
  A dram was *memento mori:*
But a full flowing bowl
Was the saving his soul,
  And port was celestial glory.

ON ANDREW TURNER.

In se'enteen hunder an' forty-nine,
Satan took stuff to mak' a swine,
  And cuist it in a corner;
But wilily he chang'd his plan,
And shaped it something like a man,
  And ca'd it Andrew Turner.

ON A SCOTCH COXCOMB.

Light lay the earth on Billy's breast,
  His chicken heart so tender;
But build a castle on his head,
  His skull will prop it under.

ON GRIZZEL GRIM.

Here lies with death auld Grizzel Grim,
  Lincluden's ugly witch;
O death, how horrid is thy taste,
  To lie with such a b——!

ON A WAG IN MAUCHLINE.

Lament him, Mauchline husbands a',
  He aften did assist ye;
For had ye stayed whole years awa,
  Your wives they ne'er had missed ye.
Ye Mauchline bairns, as on ye pass
  To school in bands thegither,
O tread ye lightly on his grass—
  Perhaps he was your father.

EPITAPH ON W——.

Stop, thief! dame Nature cried to Death,
As Willie drew his latest breath;
You have my choicest model ta'en;
How shall I make a fool again?

ON A SUICIDE.

Earth'd up here lies an imp o' hell,
  Planted by Satan's dibble—
Poor silly wretch, he 's damn'd himsel'
  To save the Lord the trouble.

EPIGRAMS FROM THE GERMAN OF LESSING.

NIGER.

"He 's gone at last—old Niger's dead!"
  Last night 't was said throughout the city;
Each quidnunc gravely shook his head,
  And *half* the town cried, "What a pity!"

The news proved false—'t was all a cheat—
  The morning came the fact denying;
And *all* the town to-day repeat
  What *half* the town last night was crying.

A NICE POINT.

Say which enjoys the greater blisses,
John, who Dorinda's picture kisses,
Or Tom, his friend, the favor'd elf,
Who kisses fair Dorinda's self?
Faith, 'tis not easy to divine,
While both are thus with raptures fainting,
To which the balance should incline,
Since Tom and John both kiss a painting.

THE POINT DECIDED.

Nay, surely John's the happier of the twain,
Because—the picture can not kiss again!

TRUE NOBILITY.

Young Stirps as any lord is proud,
Vain, haughty, insolent, and loud,
Games, drinks, and in the full career
Of vice, may vie with any peer;
Seduces daughters, wives, and mothers,
Spends his own cash, and that of others,
Pays like a lord—that is to say,
He never condescends to pay,
But bangs his creditor in requital—
And yet this blockhead wants a title!

TO A LIAR.

Lie as long as you will, my fine fellow, believe me,
Your rhodomontading will never deceive me;
Though you took me in *then*, I confess, my good youth,
When moved by caprice you once told me the truth.

MENDAX.

See yonder goes old Mendax, telling lies
To that good easy man with whom he 's walking;
How know I that? you ask, with some surprise;
Why, don't you see, my friend, the fellow's talking.

THE BAD WIFE.

Savans have decided, that search the globe round,
One only bad wife in the world can be found;
The worst of it is, as her name is not known,
Not a husband but swears that bad wife is his own.

THE DEAD MISER.

From the grave where dead Gripeall, the miser, reposes,
What a villainous odor invades all our noses!
It can't be his *body* alone—in the hole
They have certainly buried the usurer's *soul.*

ON FELL.

While Fell was reposing himself on the hay,
A reptile conceal'd bit his leg as he lay;
But all venom himself, of the wound he made light,
And got well, while the scorpion died of the bite.

THE BAD ORATOR.

So vile your grimace, and so croaking your speech,
One scarcely can tell if you 're laughing or crying;
Were you fix'd on one's funeral sermon to preach,
The bare apprehension would keep one from dying.

THE WISE CHILD.

How plain your little darling says "Mamma,"
But still she calls you "Doctor," not "Papa."
One thing is clear: your conscientious rib
Has not yet taught the pretty dear to fib.

SPECIMEN OF THE LACONIC.

"Be less prolix," says Grill. I like advice—
"Grill, you 're an ass!" Now surely that's concise

CUPID AND MERCURY, OR THE BARGAIN.

Sly Cupid late with Maia's son
  Agreed to live as friend and brother;
In proof, his bow and shafts the one
  Chang'd for the well-fill'd purse of t' other.

And now, the transfer duly made,
  Together through the world they rove;
The thieving god in arms array'd,
  And gold the panoply of love!

FRITZ.

Quoth gallant Fritz, "I ran away
To fight again another day."
The meaning of his speech is plain,
He only fled to fly again.

ON DORILIS.

That Dorilis thus, on her lap as he lies,
Should kiss little Pompey, excites no surprise;
But the lapdog whom thus she keeps fondling and praising,
Licks her face in return—that I own is amazing!

TO A SLOW WALKER AND QUICK EATER.

So slowly you walk, and so quickly you eat,
You should march with your mouth, and devour with your feet.

ON TWO BEAUTIFUL ONE-EYED SISTERS.

Give up one eye, and make your sister's two,
Venus she then would be, and Cupid you.

THE PER-CONTRA, OR MATRIMONIAL BALANCE.

How strange, a deaf wife to prefer!
True, but she 's also dumb, good sir.

EPIGRAMS S. T. COLERIDGE.

AN EXPECTORATION,

Or Splenetic Extempore, on my joyful departure from the city of Cologne.

As I am rhymer,
And now, at least, a merry one,
Mr. Mum's Rudesheimer,
And the church of St. Geryon,
Are the two things alone,
That deserve to be known,
In the body-and-soul-stinking town of Cologne.

EXPECTORATION THE SECOND.

In Clon, the town of monks and bones,
And pavements fanged with murderous stones,
And rags, and hags, and hideous wenches,
I counted two-and-seventy stenches,
All well defined and separate stinks!
Ye nymphs that reign o'er sewers and sinks,
The river Rhine, it is well known,
Doth wash your city of Cologne.
But tell me, nymphs, what power divine
Shall henceforth wash the river Rhine?

TO A LADY,

Offended by a sportive observation that women have no souls.

Nay, dearest Anna, why so grave?
I said you had no soul, 'tis true,
For what you *are* you can not *have*;
'Tis *I* that have one since I first had you.

AVARO.

[STOLEN FROM LESSING.]

There comes from old Avaro's grave
A deadly stench– why sure they have
Immured his *soul* within his grave.

BEELZEBUB AND JOB.

Sly Beelzebub took all occasions
To try Job's constancy and patience.
He took his honor, took his health,
He took his children, took his wealth,
His servants, oxen, horses, cows—
But cunning Satan did *not* take his spouse.

But Heaven, that brings out good from evil,
And loves to disappoint the devil,
Had predetermined to restore
Twofold all he had before;
His servants, horses, oxen, cows—
Short-sighted devil, *not* to take his spouse!

SENTIMENTAL.

The rose that blushes like the morn,
  Bedecks the valleys low:
And so dost thou, sweet infant corn,
  My Angelina's toe.

But on the rose there grows a thorn,
  That breeds disastrous woe:
And so dost thou, remorseless corn,
  On Angelina's toe.

AN ETERNAL POEM.

Your poem must *eternal* be,
Dear sir, it can not fail,
For 'tis incomprehensible,
And wants both *head* and *tail.*

BAD POETS.

Swans sing before they die—'t were no bad thing,
Did certain persons die before they sing.

TO MR. ALEXANDRE, THE VENTRILOQUIST.

SIR WALTER SCOTT.

Of yore, in Old England, it was not thought good,
To carry two visages under one hood:
What should folks say to *you?* who have faces so plenty,
That from under one hood you last night showed us twenty!
Stand forth, arch deceiver, and tell us in truth,
Are you handsome or ugly, in age or in youth?
Man, woman or child—a dog or a mouse?
Or are you, at once, each live thing in the house?
Each live thing did I ask?—each dead implement too,
A workshop in your person—saw, chisel, and screw!
Above all, are you one individual?—I know
You must be, at least, Alexandre and Co.
But I think you 're a troop, an assemblage, a mob,
And that I, as the sheriff, should take up the job:
And, instead of rehearsing your wonders in verse,
Must read you the riot-act, and bid you disperse!

THE SWALLOWS.

R. BRINSLEY SHERIDAN.

The Prince of Wales came into Brooke's one day, and complained of cold, but after drinking three glasses of brandy and water, said he felt comfortable.

The prince came in and said 't was cold,
 Then put to his head the rummer,
Till *swallow* after *swallow* came,
 When he pronounced it summer.

FRENCH AND ENGLISH.

ERSKINE.

The French have taste in all they do,
 Which we are quite without;
For Nature, that to them gave *goût*,
 To us gave only gout.

EPIGRAMS BY THOMAS MOORE.

TO SIR HUDSON LOWE.

SIR Hudson Lowe, Sir Hudson *Low*
(By name, and ah! by nature so),
As thou art fond of persecutions,
Perhaps thou 'st read, or heard repeated,
How Captain Gulliver was treated,
When thrown among the Lilliputians.

They tied him down—these little men did—
And having valiantly ascended
Upon the Mighty Man's protuberance,
They did so strut!—upon my soul,
It must have been extremely droll
To see their pigmy pride's exuberance!

And how the doughty mannikins
Amused themselves with sticking pins
And needles in the great man's breeches;
And how some *very* little things,
That pass'd for Lords, on scaffoldings
Got up and worried him with speeches.

Alas! alas! that it should happen
To mighty men to be caught napping!—
Though different, too, these persecutions;
For Gulliver, *there*, took the nap,
While, *here*, the *Nap*, oh sad mishap,
Is taken by the Lilliputians!

DIALOGUE

BETWEEN A CATHOLIC DELEGATE AND HIS ROYAL HIGHNESS THE DUKE OF CUMBERLAND.

Said his Highness to NED, with that grim face of his,
"Why refúse us the *Veto*, dear Catholic NEDDY?"—
"Because, sir," said NED, looking full in his phiz,
"You 're *forbidding* enough, in all conscience, already!"

TO MISS ——.

With woman's form and woman's tricks
So much of man you seem to mix,
One knows not where to take you;
I pray you, if 'tis not too far,
Go, ask of Nature *which* you are,
Or what she meant to make you.

Yet stay—you need not take the pains—
With neither beauty, youth, nor brains,
For man or maid's desiring:
Pert as female, fool as male,
As boy too green, as girl too stale—
The thing 's not worth inquiring!

TO ——.

Die when you will, you need not wear
At heaven's court a form more fair
Than Beauty here on earth has given;
Keep but the lovely looks we see—
The voice we hear and you will be
An angel *ready-made* for heaven!

UPON BEING OBLIGED TO LEAVE A PLEASANT PARTY,

FROM THE WANT OF A PAIR OF BREECHES TO DRESS FOR DINNER IN.

Between Adam and me the great difference is,
Though a paradise each has been forced to resign,
That he never wore breeches till turn'd out of his,
While, for want of my breeches, I 'm banish'd from mine.

WHAT'S MY THOUGHT LIKE?

Quest.—Why is a Pump like Viscount CASTLEREAGH?
Answ.—Because it is a slender thing of wood,
That up and down its awkward arm doth sway,
And coolly spout, and spout, and spout away,
In one weak, washy, everlasting flood!

FROM THE FRENCH.

Of all the men one meets about,
  There 's none like Jack—he 's everywhere:
At church—park—auction—dinner—rout—
  Go when and where you will, he 's there.
Try the West End, he 's at your back—
  Meets you, like Eurus, in the East—
You 're call'd upon for "How do, Jack?"
  One hundred times a-day, at least.
A friend of his one evening said,
  As home he took his pensive way,
"Upon my soul, I fear Jack's dead—
  I 've seen him but three times to-day!"

A JOKE VERSIFIED.

"Come, come," said Tom's father, "at your time of life,
  There 's no longer excuse for thus playing the rake—
It is time you should think, boy, of taking a wife."—
  "Why, so it is, father—whose wife shall I take?"

THE SURPRISE.

Chloris, I swear, by all I ever swore,
  That from this hour I shall not love thee more.—
"What! love no more? Oh! why this alter'd vow?"
Because I *can not* love thee *more*—than *now!*

ON ———.

Like a snuffers, this loving old dame,
  By a destiny grievous enough,
Though so oft she has snapp'd at the flame,
  Hath never more than the snuff.

ON A SQUINTING POETESS.

To no *one* Muse does she her glance confine,
But has an eye, at once, to *all the nine!*

ON A TUFT-HUNTER.

Lament, lament, Sir Isaac Heard,
  Put mourning round thy page, Debrett,
For here lies one, who ne'er preferr'd
  A Viscount to a Marquis yet.

Beside his place the God of Wit,
  Before him Beauty's rosiest girls,
Apollo for a *star* he 'd quit,
  And Love's own sister for an Earl's.

Did niggard fate no peers afford,
  He took, of course, to peers' relations;
And, rather than not sport a lord,
  Put up with even the last creations.

Even Irish names, could he but tag 'em
  With "Lord" and "Duke," were sweet to call,
And, at a pinch, Lord Ballyraggum
  Was better than no Lord at all.

Heaven grant him now some noble nook,
  For, rest his soul, he 'd rather be
Genteelly damn'd beside a Duke,
  Than saved in vulgar company.

THE KISS.

Give me, my love, that billing kiss
  I taught you one delicious night,
When, turning epicures in bliss,
  We tried inventions of delight.

Come, gently steal my lips along,
  And let your lips in murmurs move—
Ah, no!—again—that kiss was wrong—
  How can you be so dull, my love?

"Cease, cease!" the blushing girl replied—
  And in her milky arms she caught me—
"How can you thus your pupil chide;
  You know '*t was in the dark* you taught me!"

EPITAPH ON A WELL-KNOWN POET—(ROBERT SOUTHEY.)

Beneath these poppies buried deep,
The bones of Bob the bard lie hid;
Peace to his manes; and may he sleep
As soundly as his readers did!

Through every sort of verse meandering,
Bob went without a hitch or fall,
Through Epic, Sapphic, Alexandrine,
To verse that was no verse at all;

Till fiction having done enough,
To make a bard at least absurd,
And give his readers *quantum suff.*,
He took to praising George the Third:

And now, in virtue of his crown,
Dooms us, poor whigs, at once to slaughter;
Like Donellan of bad renown,
Poisoning us all with laurel-water.

And yet at times some awkward qualms he
Felt about leaving honor's track;
And though he 's got a butt of Malmsey,
It may not save him from a sack.

Death, weary of so dull a writer,
Put to his works a *finis* thus.
Oh! may the earth on him lie lighter
Than did his quartos upon us!

WRITTEN IN A YOUNG LADY'S COMMON-PLACE BOOK,

Called the "Book of Follies."

This journal of folly 's an emblem of me;
But what book shall we find emblematic of thee?
Oh! shall we not say thou art *Love's Duodecimo?*
None can be prettier, few can be less, you know.
Such a volume in *sheets* were a volume of charms;
Or if *bound*, it should only be *bound in our arms!*

THE RABBINICAL ORIGIN OF WOMEN.

They tell us that Woman was made of a rib
  Just pick'd from a corner so snug in the side;
But the Rabbins swear to you that this is a fib,
  And 't was not so at all that the sex was supplied.

For old Adam was fashion'd, the first of his kind,
  With a tail like a monkey, full a yard and a span;
And when Nature cut off this appendage behind,
  Why—then woman was made of the tail of the man.

If such is the tie between women and men,
  The ninny who weds is a pitiful elf;
For he takes to his tail, like an idiot, again,
  And makes a most damnable ape of himself!

Yet, if we may judge as the fashions prevail,
  Every husband remembers the original plan,
And, knowing his wife is no more than his tail,
  Why—he leaves her behind him as much as he can.

ANACREONTIQUE.

Press the grape, and let it pour
Around the board its purple shower;
And while the drops my goblet steep,
I 'll think—in *woe* the clusters weep.

Weep on, weep on, my pouting vine!
Heaven grant no tears but tears of wine.
Weep on; and, as thy sorrows flow,
I 'll taste the *luxury of woe!*

SPECULATION.

Of all speculations the market holds forth,
  The best that I know for a lover of pelf,
Is to buy —— up at the price he is worth,
  And then sell him at that which he sets on himself.

ON BUTLER'S MONUMENT.

REV. SAMUEL WESLEY.

While Butler, needy wretch, was yet alive,
No generous patron would a dinner give.
See him, when starved to death and turn'd to dust,
Presented with a monumental bust.
The poet's fate is here in emblem shown—
He ask'd for *bread*, and he received a *stone*.

ON THE DISAPPOINTMENT OF THE WHIG ASSOCIATES OF THE PRINCE REGENT, AT NOT OBTAINING OFFICE.

CHARLES LAMB.

Ye politicians, tell me, pray,
Why thus with woe and care rent?
This is the worst that you can say,
Some wind has blown the wig away,
And left the *Hair Apparent*.

TO PROFESSOR AIREY,

On his marrying a beautiful woman.

SIDNEY SMITH

Airey alone has gained that double prize,
Which forced musicians to divide the crown;
His works have raised a mortal to the skies,
His marriage-vows have drawn a mortal down.

ON LORD DUDLEY AND WARD.

SAMUEL ROGERS

"They say Ward has no heart, but I deny it;
He has a heart—and gets his speeches by it."

EPIGRAMS OF LORD BYRON.

TO THE AUTHOR OF A SONNET BEGINNING

"'SAD IS MY VERSE,' YOU SAY, 'AND YET NO TEAR.'"

Thy verse is "sad" enough, no doubt,
A devilish deal more sad than witty!
Why should we weep, I can't find out,
Unless for *thee* we weep in pity.

Yet there is one I pity more,
And much, alas! I think he needs it—
For he, I'm sure, will suffer sore,
Who, to his own misfortune, reads it.

The rhymes, without the aid of magic,
May *once* be read—but never after;
Yet their effect's by no means tragic,
Although by far too dull for laughter.

But would you make our bosoms bleed,
And of no common pang complain?
If you would make us weep indeed,
Tell us you'll read them o'er again.

WINDSOR POETICS.

On the Prince Regent being seen standing between the coffins of Henry VIII. and Charles I., in the royal vault at Windsor.

Famed for contemptuous breach of sacred ties,
By headless Charles see heartless Henry lies;
Between them stands another sceptered thing—
It moves, it reigns—in all but name, a king;
Charles to his people, Henry to his wife,
—In him the double tyrant starts to life;
Justice and death have mixed their dust in vain,
Each royal vampyre wakes to life again.
Ah! what can tombs avail, since these disgorge
The blood and dust of both to mold a George?

ON A CARRIER WHO DIED OF DRUNKENNESS.

John Adams lies here, of the parish of Southwell,
A carrier who carried his can to his mouth well;
He carried so much, and he carried so fast,
He could carry no more—so was carried at last;
For the liquor he drank, being too much for one,
He could not carry off—so he 's now carri*on*.

EPIGRAMS OF BARHAM.

ON THE WINDOWS OF KING'S COLLEGE REMAINING BOARDED.

Loquitur Discipulus Esuriens.

Professors, in your plan there seems
  A something not quite right:
'Tis queer to cherish learning's beams
  By shutting out the light.

While thus we see your windows block'd,
  If nobody complains;
Yet everybody must be shock'd,
  To see you don't take pains.

And tell me why should bodily
  Succumb to mental meat?
Or why should *ητα*, *βητα*, *πι*,
  Be all the pie we eat?

No *helluo librorum* I,
  No literary glutton,
Would veal with Virgil like to try,
  With metaphysics, mutton.

Leave us no longer in the lurch,
  With Romans, Greeks, and Hindoos:
But give us beef instead of birch,
  And *board us*—not your windows.

NEW-MADE HONOR.

[IMITATED FROM MARTIAL.]

A friend I met, some half hour since—
  "*Good-morrow Jack!*" quoth I;
The new-made Knight, like any Prince,
  Frown'd, nodded, and pass'd by;
When up came Jem—"*Sir John, your slave!*"
  "Ah, James; we dine at eight—
Fail not—(low bows the supple knave)
  Don't make my lady wait."
The king can do no wrong? As I'm a sinner,
He's spoilt an honest tradesman and my dinner.

EHEU FUGACES.

What Horace says is,
Eheu fugaces
Anni labunter, Postume, Postume!
Years glide away, and are lost to me, lost to me!
Now, when the folks in the dance sport their merry toes,
Taglionis, and Ellslers, Duvernays and Ceritos,
Sighing, I murmur, "*O mihi præteritos!*"

ANONYMOUS EPIGRAMS.

ON A PALE LADY WITH A RED-NOSED HUSBAND.

Whence comes it that, in Clara's face,
The lily only has its place?
Is it because the absent rose
Has gone to paint her husband's nose?

UPON POPE'S TRANSLATION OF HOMER

So much, dear Pope, thy English Homer charms,
As pity melts us, or as passion warms,
That after ages will with wonder seek
Who 't was translated Homer into Greek.

RECIPE FOR A MODERN BONNET.

Two scraps of foundation, some fragments of lace,
A shower of French rose-buds to droop o'er the face;
Fine ribbons and feathers, with crage and illusions,
Then mix and *de*range them in graceful confusion;
Inveigle some fairy, out roaming for pleasure,
And beg the slight favor of taking her measure,
The length and the breadth of her dear little pate,
And hasten a miniature frame to create;
Then pour, as above, the bright mixture upon it,
And lo! you possess "such a love of a bonnet!"

MY WIFE AND I

As my wife and I, at the window one day,
Stood watching a man with a monkey,
A cart came by, with a "broth of a boy,"
Who was driving a stout little donkey.
To my wife I then spoke, by way of a joke,
"There 's a relation of yours in that carriage."
To which she replied, as the donkey she spied,
"Ah, yes, a relation—*by marriage!*"

ON TWO GENTLEMEN,

One of whom, O'Connell, delayed a duel on the plea of his wife's illness; the other declined on account of the illness of his daughter.

Some men, with a horror of slaughter,
Improve on the Scripture command,
And honor their wife and their daughter,
That their days may be long in the land.

WELLINGTON'S NOSE.

"Pray, why does the great Captain's nose
Resemble Venice?" Duncomb cries.
"Why," quoth Sam Rogers, "I suppose
Because it has a bridge of size (sighs)."

THE SMOKER.

All dainty meats I do defy
  Which feed men fat as swine,
He is a frugal man indeed
  That on a leaf can dine!
He needs no napkin for his hands,
  His finger's ends to wipe,
That keeps his kitchen in a box,
  And roast meat in his pipe!

AN ESSAY ON THE UNDERSTANDING.

"Harry, I can not think," says Dick,
"What makes my *ankles* grow so thick:"
"You do not recollect," says Harry,
"How great a *calf* they have to carry."

TO A LIVING AUTHOR.

Your comedy I 've read, my friend,
  And like the half you pilfer'd best;
But sure the piece you yet may mend:
  Take courage, man! and steal the rest.

EPIGRAMS BY THOMAS HOOD.

ON THE ART-UNIONS.

THAT picture-raffles will conduce to nourish
Design, or cause good coloring to flourish,
Admits of logic-chopping and wise sawing,
But surely lotteries encourage drawing.

THE SUPERIORITY OF MACHINERY.

A mechanic his labor will often discard
  If the rate of his pay he dislikes:
But a clock—and its *case* is uncommonly hard—
  Will continue to work though it *strikes*.

EPIGRAMS BY W. SAVAGE LANDOR.

ON OBSERVING A VULGAR NAME ON THE PLINTH OF AN ANCIENT STATUE.

BARBARIANS must we always be?
Wild hunters in pursuit of fame?
Must there be nowhere stone or tree
Ungashed with some ignoble name.
O Venus! in thy Tuscan dome
May every god watch over thee!
Apollo! bend thy bow o'er Rome,
And guard thy sister's chastity.
Let Britons paint their bodies blue
As formerly, but touch not you.

LYING IN STATE.

Now from the chamber all are gone
Who gazed and wept o'er Wellington;
Derby and Dis do all they can
To emulate so great a man:
If neither can be quite so great,
Resolved is each to LIE *in state.*

EPIGRAMS FROM PUNCH.

THE CAUSE.

LISETTE has lost her wanton wiles—
What secret care consumes her youth,
And circumscribes her smiles?—
A speck on a front tooth?

IRISH PARTICULAR.

Shiel's oratory 's like bottled Dublin stout—
For, draw the cork, and only froth comes out.

ONE GOOD TURN DESERVES ANOTHER.

A poor man went to hang himself,
  But treasure chanced to find:
He pocketed the miser's pelf
  And left the rope behind.

His money gone, the miser hung
  Himself in sheer despair:
Thus each the other's wants supplied,
  And that was surely fair.

STICKY.

I 'm going to seal a letter, Dick,
  Some *wax* pray give to me.
I have not got a *single stick*,
  Or *whacks* I 'd give to thee.

THE POET FOILED.

To win the maid the poet tries,
And sometimes writes to Julia's eyes;—
She likes a *verse*—but, cruel whim,
She still appears *a-verse* to him.

BLACK AND WHITE.

The Tories vow the Whigs are black as night,
And boast that they are only blessed with light.
Peel's politics to both sides so incline,
His may be called the *equinoctial line*.

INQUEST—NOT EXTRAORDINARY.

Great Bulwer's works fell on Miss Basbleu's head,
And, in a moment, lo! the maid was dead!
A jury sat, and found the verdict plain—
She died of *milk* and *water on the brain*.

DOMESTIC ECONOMY.

Said Stiggins to his wife, one day,
 "We 've nothing left to eat;
If things go on in this queer way,
 We shan't make *both ends meet.*"

The dame replied, in words discreet,
 "We 're not so badly fed,
If we can make but *one* end *meat,*
 And make the other *bread.*"

ON SEEING AN EXECUTION.

One morn, two friends before the Newgate drop,
To see a culprit throttled, chanced to stop:
"Alas!" cried one, as round in air he spun,
"That miserable wretch's *race is run.*"
"True," said the other, drily, "to his cost,
The race is run—but, by a *neck* 'tis lost."

A VOICE, AND NOTHING ELSE.

"I wonder if Brougham thinks as much as he talks,"
 Said a punster, perusing a trial:
"I vow, since his lordship was made Baron Vaux,
 He 's been *Vaux et prœterea nihil!*"

THE AMENDE HONORABLE.

Quoth Will, "On that young servant-maid
 My heart its life-string stakes."
"Quite safe!" cries Dick, "don't be afraid—
 She pays for all she breaks."

THE CZAR.

Czar NICHOLAS is so devout, they say,
His majesty does nothing else than prey.

BAS BLEU.

Ma'amselle Bas Bleu, erudite virgin,
With learned zeal is ever urging
The love and reverence due
From modern men to things antique,
Egyptian, British, Roman, Greek,
Relic of Gaul or Jew.

No wonder that, Ma'amselle, the love
Due to antiquity to prove
And urge is ever prone;
She knows where'er there cease to be
Admirers of Antiquity,
She needs must lose her own!

TO A RICH YOUNG WIDOW.

I will not ask if thou canst touch
The tuneful ivory key?
Those silent notes of thine are such
As quite suffice for me.

I'll make no question if thy skill
The pencil comprehends,
Enough for me, love, if thou still
Canst draw thy dividends!

THE RAILWAY OF LIFE.

Short was the passage through this earthly vale,
By turnpike roads when mortals used to wend,
But now we travel by the way of rail,
As soon again we reach the journey's end.

A CONJUGAL CONUNDRUM.

Which is of greater value, prythee, say,
The Bride or Bridegroom?—must the truth be told?
Alas, it must! The Bride is given away—
The Bridegroom's often regularly sold.

NUMBERS ALTERED.

The lounger must oft, as he walks through the streets,
Be struck with the grace of some girl that he meets;
So graceful behind in dress—ringlets—all that—
But one gaze at the front—what a horrid old cat!
You then think of the notice you 've seen on a door,
Which informs you, of "70 late 24."

GRAMMAR FOR THE COURT OF BERLIN

His majesty you should not say of *Fritz*,
That king is neuter; so for *His*, use *Its*.

THE EMPTY BOTTLE.

WILLIAM AYTOUN

Ah, liberty! how like thou art
To this large bottle lying here,
Which yesterday from foreign mart,
Came filled with potent English beer!

A touch of steel—a hand—a gush—
A pop that sounded far and near—
A wild emotion—liquid rush—
And I had drunk that English beer!

And what remains?—An empty shell!
A lifeless form both sad and queer,
A temple where no god doth dwell—
The simple memory of beer!

THE DEATH OF DOCTOR MORRISON.

BENTLEY'S MISCELLANY.

What 's the news?—Why, they say Death has killed Dr. Morrison.
The Pill-maker? Yes. Then Death will be sorry soon.

EPIGRAMS BY JOHN G. SAXE.

ON A RECENT CLASSIC CONTROVERSY.

Nay, marvel not to see these scholars fight,
  In brave disdain of certain scath and scar;
'Tis but the genuine, old, Hellenic spite,—
  "When Greek meets Greek, then comes the tug of war!"

ANOTHER.

Quoth David to Daniel—"Why is it these scholars
  Abuse one another whenever they speak?"
Quoth Daniel to David—it nat'rally follers
  Folks come to hard words if they meddle with Greek!"

ON AN ILL-READ LAWYER.

An idle attorney besought a brother
For "something to read—some novel or other,
    That was really fresh and new."
"Take Chitty!" replied his legal friend,
"There is n't a book that I could lend
    Would prove more 'novel' to you!"

ON AN UGLY PERSON SITTING FOR A DAGUERREOTYPE.

Here Nature in her glass—the wanton elf—
Sits gravely making faces at herself;
And while she scans each clumsy feature o'er,
Repeats the blunders that she made before!

WOMAN'S WILL.

Men dying make their wills—but wives
    Escape a work so sad;
Why should they make what all their lives
    The gentle dames have had?

FAMILY QUARRELS.

"A fool," said Jeanette, "is a creature I hate!"
"But hating," quoth John, "is immoral;
Besides, my dear girl, it's a terrible fate
To be found in a family quarrel!"

A REVOLUTIONARY HERO.

JAMES RUSSELL LOWELL.

OLD JOE is gone, who saw hot Percy goad
His slow artillery up the Concord road,
A tale which grew in wonder year by year;
As every time he told it, Joe drew near
To the main fight, till faded and grown gray,
The original scene to bolder tints gave way;
Then Joe had heard the foe's scared double-quick
Beat on stove drum with one uncaptured stick,
And, ere death came the lengthening tale to lop,
Himself had fired, and seen a red-coat drop;
Had Joe lived long enough, that scrambling fight
Had squared more nearly to his sense of right,
And vanquished Perry, to complete the tale,
Had hammered stone for life in Concord jail.

EPIGRAMS OF HALPIN.

THE LAST RESORT.

A DRAMATIST declared he had got
So many people in his plot,
That what to do with half he had
Was like to drive him drama-mad!
'The hero and the heroine
Of course are married—very fine!
But with the others, what to do
Is more than I can tell—can you?"

His friend replied—"'Tis hard to say,
But yet I think there is a way.
The married couple, thank their stars,
And half the 'others' take the cars;
The other half you put on board
An Erie steamboat—take my word,
They 'll never trouble you again!"
The dramatist resumed his pen.

FEMININE ARITHMETIC.

LAURA.

On me he shall ne'er put a ring,
So, mamma, 'tis in vain to take trouble –
For I was but eighteen in spring,
While his age exactly is double.

MAMMA.

He 's but in his thirty-sixth year,
Tall, handsome, good-natured and witty,
And should you refuse him, my dear,
May you die an old maid without pity!

LAURA.

His figure, I grant you, will pass,
And at present he 's young enough plenty;
But when I am sixty, alas!
Will not he be a hundred and twenty?

THE MUSHROOM HUNT.

In early days, ere Common Sense
And Genius had in anger parted,
They made to friendship some pretense,
Though each, Heaven knows! diversely hearted.
To hunt for mushrooms once they went,
Through nibbled sheepwalks straying onward,
Sense with his dull eyes earthward bent,
While Genius shot his glances sunward!

Away they go! On roll the hours,
And toward the west the day-god edges;
See! Genius holds a wreath of flowers,
Fresh culled from all the neighboring hedges!
Alas! ere eve their bright hues flit,
While Common Sense (whom I so doat on!)
Thanked God "that he had little wit,"
And drank his ketchup with his mutton.

JUPITER AMANS.

DEDICATED TO VICTOR HUGO.

LONDON LEADER.

"Le Petit" call not him who by one act
Has turned old fable into modern fact.
Nap Louis courted Europe: Europe shied:
Th' imperial purple was too newly dyed.
"I'll have her though," thought he, "by rape or rapine;
Jove nods sometimes, but catch a Nap a napping!
And now I think of Jove, 't was Jove's own fix,
And so I'll borrow one of Jove's own tricks:
Old itching Palm I'll tickle with a joke,
And he shall lend me England's decent cloak."
'T was said and done, and his success was full;
He won Europa with the guise of Bull!

THE ORATOR'S EPITAPH.

LORD BROUGHAM.

"Here, reader, turn your weeping eyes,
My fate a useful moral teaches;
The hole in which my body lies
Would not contain one-half my speeches."

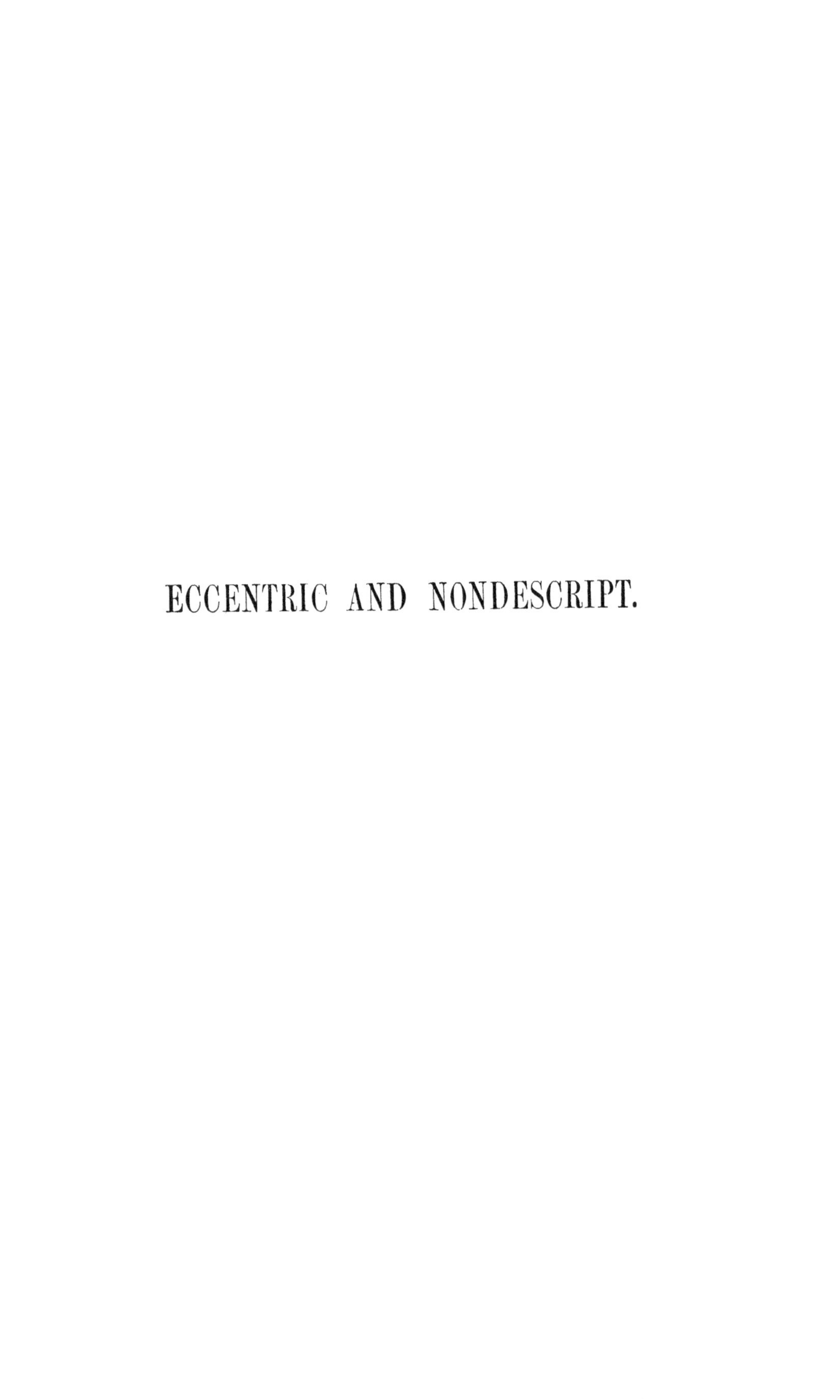

ECCENTRIC AND NONDESCRIPT.

ECCENTRIC AND NONDESCRIPT.

THE JOVIAL PRIEST'S CONFESSION.

TRANSLATED FROM THE LATIN OF WALTER DE MAPES,
TIME OF HENRY II.

LEIGH HUNT.

I DEVISE to end my days—in a tavern drinking,
May some Christian hold for me—the glass when I am shrinking,
That the cherubim may cry—when they see me sinking,
God be merciful to a soul—of this gentleman's way of thinking.

A glass of wine amazingly—enlighteneth one's intervals;
'Tis wings bedewed with nectar—that fly up to supernals;
Bottles cracked in taverns—have much the sweeter kernels,
Than the sups allowed to us—in the college journals.

Every one by nature hath—a mold which he was cast in;
I happen to be one of those—who never could write fasting;
By a single little boy—I should be surpass'd in
Writing so: I 'd just as lief—be buried; tomb'd and grass'd in.

Every one by nature hath—a gift too, a dotation:
I, when I make verses—do get the inspiration
Of the very best of wine—that comes into the nation:
It maketh sermons to astound—for edification.

Just as liquor floweth good—floweth forth my lay so;
But I must moreover eat—or I could not say so;
Naught it availeth inwardly—should I write all day so;
But with God's grace after meat—I beat Ovidius Naso.

Neither is there given to me—prophetic animation,
Unless when I have eat and drank—yea, ev'n to saturation;
Then in my upper story—hath Bacchus domination,
And Phœbus rushes into me, and beggareth all relation.

TONIS AD RESTO MARE.

ANONYMOUS.

AIR—"*Oh, Mary, heave a sigh for me.*"

O MARE æva si forme;
  Forme ure tonitru;
Iambicum as amandum,
  Olet Hymen promptu;
Mihi is vetas an ne se,
  As humano erebi;
Olet mecum marito te,
  Or *eta beta pi.*

Alas, plano more meretrix,
  Mi ardor vel uno;
Inferiam ure artis base,
  Tolerat me urebo.
Ah me ve ara silicet,
  Vi laudu vimin thus?
Hiatu as arandum sex—
  Illuc Ionicus.

Heu sed heu vix en imago,
  My missis mare sta;
O cantu redit in mihi
  Hibernas arida?
A veri vafer heri si,
  Mihi resolves indu:
Totius olet Hymen cum—
  Accepta tonitru.

DIC.

DEAN SWIFT.

DIC, heris agro at, an da quar to fine ale,
Fora ringat ure nos, an da stringat ure tale.*

* Dick, here is a groat, a quart o' fine ale,
For a ring at your nose, and a string at your tail.

MOLL.

DEAN SWIFT.

Mollis abuti,
Has an acuti,
No lasso finis,
Molli divinis.*

TO MY MISTRESS.

DEAN SWIFT.

O mi de armis tres,
Imi na dis tres.
Cantu disco ver
Meas alo ver?†

A LOVE SONG.

DEAN SWIFT.

Apud in is almi de si re,
Mimis tres I ne ver re qui re,
Alo veri findit a gestis,
His miseri ne ver at restis.‡

* Moll is a beauty,
Has an acute eye;
No lass so fine is,
Molly divine is.

† O my dear mistress
I am in a distress.
Can't you discover
Me as a lover?

‡ A pudding is all my desire,
My mistress I never require;
A lover I find it a jest is,
His misery never at rest is.

A GENTLE ECHO ON WOMAN.

IN THE DORIC MANNER.

DEAN SWIFT.

Shepherd. Echo, I ween, will in the woods reply,
And quaintly answer questions: shall I try?
Echo. Try.
Shepherd. What must we do our passion to express?
Echo. Press.
Shepherd. How shall I please her, who ne'er loved before?
Echo. Before.
Shepherd. What most moves women when we them address?
Echo. A dress.
Shepherd. Say, what can keep her chaste whom I adore?
Echo. A door.
Shepherd. If music softens rocks, love tunes my lyre.
Echo. Liar.
Shepherd. Then teach me, Echo, how shall I come by her?
Echo. Buy her.
Shepherd. When bought, no question I shall be her dear?
Echo. Her deer.
Shepherd. But deer have horns: how must I keep her under?
Echo. Keep her under.
Shepherd. But what can glad me when she's laid on bier?
Echo. Beer.
Shepherd. What must I do when women will be kind?
Echo. Be kind.
Shepherd. What must I do when women will be cross?
Echo. Be cross.
Shepherd. Lord, what is she that can so turn and wind?
Echo. Wind.
Shepherd. If she be wind, what stills her when she blows?
Echo. Blows.
Shepherd. But if she bang again, still should I bang her?
Echo. Bang her.
Shepherd. Is there no way to moderate her anger?
Echo. Hang her.
Shepherd. Thanks, gentle Echo! right thy answers tell
What woman is and how to guard her well.
Echo. Guard her well.

TO MY NOSE.

ANONYMOUS.

KNOWS he that never took a pinch,
Nosey! the pleasure thence which flows?
Knows he the titillating joy
Which my nose knows?

Oh, nose! I am as fond of thee
As any mountain of its snows!
I gaze on thee, and feel that pride
A Roman knows!

ROGER AND DOLLY.

BLACKWOOD.

YOUNG ROGER came tapping at Dolly's window—
Thumpaty, thumpaty, thump;
He begg'd for admittance—she answered him no—
Glumpaty, glumpaty, glump.
No, no, Roger, no—as you came you may go—
Stumpaty, stumpaty, stump.
O what is the reason, dear Dolly? he cried—
Humpaty, humpaty, hump—
That thus I'm cast off and unkindly denied?—
Trumpaty, trumpaty, trump—
Some rival more dear, I guess, has been here—
Crumpaty, crumpaty, crump—
Suppose there's been two, sir, pray what's that to you, sir?
Numpaty, numpaty, nump—
Wi' a disconsolate look his sad farewell he took—
Trumpaty, trumpaty, trump—
And all in despair jump'd into a brook—
Jumpaty, jumpaty, jump—
His courage did cool in a filthy green pool—
Slumpaty, slumpaty, slump—
So he swam to the shore, but saw Dolly no more—
Dumpaty, dumpaty, dump—

He did speedily find one more fat and more kind—
  Plumpaty, plumpaty, plump—
But poor Dolly 's afraid she must die an old maid—
  Mumpaty, mumpaty, mump.

THE IRISHMAN.

BLACKWOOD.

I.

There was a lady lived at Leith,
  A lady very stylish, man,
And yet, in spite of all her teeth,
  She fell in love with an Irishman,
    A nasty, ugly Irishman,
    A wild tremendous Irishman,
A tearing, swearing, thumping, bumping, ranting, roaring Irishman.

II.

His face was no ways beautiful,
  For with small-pox 't was scarred across:
And the shoulders of the ugly dog
  Were almost doubled a yard across.
    O the lump of an Irishman,
    The whiskey devouring Irishman—
The great he-rogue with his wonderful brogue, the fighting, rioting Irishman.

III.

One of his eyes was bottle green,
  And the other eye was out, my dear;
And the calves of his wicked-looking legs
  Were more than two feet about, my dear,
    O, the great big Irishman,
    The rattling, battling Irishman—
The stamping, ramping, swaggering, staggering, leathering swash of an Irishman.

IV.

He took so much of Lundy-foot,
  That he used to snort and snuffle—O,

And in shape and size the fellow's neck
  Was as bad as the neck of a buffalo.
      O, the horrible Irishman,
      The thundering, blundering Irishman—
The slashing, dashing, smashing, lashing, thrashing, hashing Irishman.

V.

His name was a terrible name, indeed,
  Being Timothy Thady Mulligan;
And whenever he emptied his tumbler of punch,
  He 'd not rest till he fill'd it full again,
      The boozing, bruising Irishman,
      The 'toxicated Irishman—
The whiskey, frisky, rummy, gummy, brandy, no dandy Irishman.

VI.

This was the lad the lady loved,
  Like all the girls of quality;
And he broke the skulls of the men of Leith,
  Just by the way of jollity,
      O, the leathering Irishman,
      The barbarous, savage Irishman—
The hearts of the maids and the gentlemen's heads were bothered
  I'm sure by this Irishman.

A *CAT*ALECTIC MONODY!

CRUIKSHANK'S OMNIBUS.

A *cat* I sing, of famous memory,
Though *cat*achrestical my song may be;
In a small garden *cat*acomb she lies,
And *cat*aclysms fill her comrades' eyes;
Borne on the air, the *cat*acoustic song
Swells with her virtues' *cat*alogue along;
No *cat*aplasm could lengthen out her years,
Though mourning friends shed *cat*aracts of tears.
Once loud and strong her *cat*echist-like voice
It dwindled to a *cat*call's squeaking noise;

Most *cat*egorical her virtues shone,
By *cat*enation join'd each one to one;—
But a vile *cat*chpoll dog, with cruel bite,
Like *cat*ling's cut, her strength disabled quite;
Her *cat*erwauling pierced the heavy air,
As *cat*aphracts their arms through legions bear;
'Tis vain! as *cat*erpillars drag away
Their lengths, like *cat*tle after busy day,
She ling'ring died, nor left in kit *kat* the
Embodyment of this *cat*astrophe.

A NEW SONG

OF NEW SIMILES.

JOHN GAY.

My passion is as mustard strong;
  I sit all sober sad;
Drunk as a piper all day long,
  Or like a March-hare mad.

Round as a hoop the bumpers flow;
  I drink, yet can't forget her;
For though as drunk as David's sow
  I love her still the better.

Pert as a pear-monger I 'd be,
  If Molly were but kind;
Cool as a cucumber could see
  The rest of womankind.

Like a stuck pig I gaping stare,
  And eye her o'er and o'er;
Lean as a rake, with sighs and care,
  Sleek as a mouse before.

Plump as a partridge was I known,
  And soft as silk my skin;
My cheeks as fat as butter grown,
  But as a goat now thin!

I melancholy as a cat,
  Am kept awake to weep;
But she, insensible of that,
  Sound as a top can sleep.

Hard is her heart as flint or stone,
  She laughs to see me pale;
And merry as a grig is grown,
  And brisk as bottled ale.

The god of Love at her approach
  Is busy as a bee;
Hearts sound as any bell or roach,
  Are smit and sigh like me.

Ah me! as thick as hops or hail
  The fine men crowd about her;
But soon as dead as a door-nail
  Shall I be, if without her.

Straight as my leg her shape appears,
  O were we join'd together!
My heart would be scot-free from cares,
  And lighter than a feather.

As fine as five-pence is her mien,
  No drum was ever tighter;
Her glance is as the razor keen,
  And not the sun is brighter.

As soft as pap her kisses are,
  Methinks I taste them yet;
Brown as a berry is her hair,
  Her eyes as black as jet.

As smooth as glass, as white as curds
  Her pretty hand invites;
Sharp as her needle are her words,
  Her wit like pepper bites.

Brisk as a body-louse she trips,
  Clean as a penny drest;
Sweet as a rose her breath and lips,
  Round as the globe her breast.

Full as an egg was I with glee,
  And happy as a king:
Good Lord! how all men envied me!
  She loved like any thing.

But false as hell, she, like the wind,
  Chang'd, as her sex must do;
Though seeming as the turtle kind,
  And like the gospel true.

If I and Molly could agree,
  Let who would take Peru!
Great as an Emperor should I be,
  And richer than a Jew.

Till you grow tender as a chick,
  I'm dull as any post;
Let us like burs together stick,
  And warm as any toast.

You'll know me truer than a die,
  And wish me better sped;
Flat as a flounder when I lie,
  And as a herring dead.

Sure as a gun she'll drop a tear
  And sigh, perhaps, and wish,
When I am rotten as a pear,
  And mute as any fish.

REMINISCENCES OF A SENTIMENTALIST.

THOMAS HOOD.

"My *Tables! Meat* it is, *I set it* down!"—HAMLET.

I THINK it was Spring—but not certain I am—
  When my passion began first to work;
But I know we were certainly looking for lamb,
  And the season was over for pork.

'T was at Christmas, I think, when I met with Miss Chase,
  Yes—for Morris had asked me to dine—
And I thought I had never beheld such a face,
  Or so noble a turkey and chine.

Placed close by her side, it made others quite wild
  With sheer envy, to witness my luck;
How she blushed as I gave her some turtle, and smiled
  As I afterward offered some duck.

I looked and I languished, alas! to my cost,
  Through three courses of dishes and meats;
Getting deeper in love—but my heart was quite lost
  When it came to the trifle and sweets.

With a rent-roll that told of my houses and land,
  To her parents I told my designs—
And then to herself I presented my hand,
  With a very fine pottle of pines!

I asked her to have me for weal or for woe,
  And she did not object in the least;—
I can't tell the date—but we married I know
  Just in time to have game at the feast.

We went to ———, it certainly was the sea-side;
  For the next, the most blessed of morns,
I remember how fondly I gazed at my bride,
  Sitting down to a plateful of prawns.

O, never may memory lose sight of that year,
  But still hallow the time as it ought!
That season the "grass" was remarkably dear,
  And the peas at a guinea a quart.

So happy, like hours, all our days seemed to haste,
  A fond pair, such as poets have drawn,
So united in heart—so congenial in taste—
  We were both of us partial to brawn!

A long life I looked for of bliss with my bride,
  But then Death—I ne'er dreamt about that!
O, there 's nothing is certain in life, as I cried
  When my turbot eloped with the cat!

My dearest took ill at the turn of the year,
  But the cause no physician could nab;
But something, it seemed like consumption, I fear—
  It was just after supping on crab.

In vain she was doctored, in vain she was dosed,
  Still her strength and her appetite pined;
She lost relish for what she had relished the most,
  Even salmon she deeply declined!

For months still I lingered in hope and in doubt,
  While her form it grew wasted and thin;
But the last dying spark of existence went out,
  As the oysters were just coming in!

She died, and she left me the saddest of men,
  To indulge in a widower's moan;
Oh! I felt all the power of solitude then,
  As I ate my first "natives" alone!

But when I beheld Virtue's friends in their cloaks,
  And with sorrowful crape on their hats,
O my grief poured a flood! and the out-of-door folks
  Were all crying—I think it was sprats!

FAITHLESS NELLY GRAY.

A PATHETIC BALLAD.

THOMAS HOOD.

Ben Battle was a soldier bold,
  And used to war's alarms;
But a cannon-ball took off his legs,
  So he laid down his arms!

Now, as they bore him off the field,
  Said he, "Let others shoot,
For here I leave my second leg,
  And the Forty-second Foot!"

The army-surgeons made him limbs:
  Said he, they 're only pegs:
But there 's as wooden members quite
  As represent my legs!"

Now, Ben he loved a pretty maid,
  Her name was Nelly Gray;
So he went up to pay his devours,
  When he devoured his pay!

But when he called on Nelly Gray,
  She made him quite a scoff;
And when she saw his wooden legs,
  Began to take them off!

"O, Nelly Gray! O, Nelly Gray
  Is this your love so warm?
The love that loves a scarlet coat
  Should be more uniform!"

Said she, "I loved a soldier once
  For he was blithe and brave;
But I will never have a man
  With both legs in the grave!

"Before you had those timber toes,
  Your love I did allow,
But then, you know, you stand upon
  Another footing now!"

"O, Nelly Gray! O, Nelly Gray!
  For all your jeering speeches,
At duty's call I left my legs,
  In Badajos's *breaches!*"

"Why then," said she, "you 've lost the feet
  Of legs in war's alarms,
And now you can not wear your shoes
  Upon your feats of arms!"

"O, false and fickle Nelly Gray!
  I know why you refuse:—
Though I 've no feet—some other man
  Is standing in my shoes!

"I wish I ne'er had seen your face;
  But now, a long farewell!
For you will be my death;—alas
  You will not be my *Nell!*"

Now, when he went from Nelly Gray,
  His heart so heavy got,
And life was such a burden grown,
  It made him take a knot!

So round his melancholy neck
  A rope he did entwine,
And, for his second time in life,
  Enlisted in the Line.

One end he tied around a beam,
  And then removed his pegs,
And, as his legs were off—of course,
  He soon was off his legs!

And there he hung, till he was dead
  As any nail in town—
For, though distress had cut him up,
  It could not cut him down!

A dozen men sat on his corpse,
  To find out why he died—
And they buried Ben in four cross-roads,
  With a *stake* in his inside!

NO!

THOMAS HOOD.

No sun—no moon!
No morn—no noon—
No dawn—no dusk—no proper time of day—
No sky—no earthly view—
No distance looking blue—
No road—no street—no "t' other side the way"—
No end to any Row—
No indications where the Crescents go—

No top to any steeple—
No recognitions of familiar people—
No courtesies for showing 'em—
No knowing 'em!
To traveling at all—no locomotion,
No inkling of the way—no notion—
"No go"—by land or ocean—
No mail—no post—
No news from any foreign coast—
No park—no ring—no afternoon gentility—
No company—no nobility—
No warmth, no cheerfulness, no healthful ease,
No comfortable feel in any member—
No shade, no shine, no butterflies, no bees.
No fruits, no flowers, no leaves, no birds,
November!

JACOB OMNIUM'S HOSS.

A NEW PALLICE COURT CHANT.

W. MAKEPEACE THACKERAY.

One sees in Viteall Yard,
Vere pleacemen do resort,
A wenerable hinstitute,
'Tis called the Pallis Court.
A gent as got his i on it,
I think will make some sport.

The natur of this Court
My hindignation riles:
A few fat legal spiders
Here set & spin their viles;
To rob the town theyr privlege is,
In a hayrea of twelve miles.

The Judge of this year Court
Is a mellitary beak,

He knows no more of Lor
  Than praps he does of Greek,
And prowides hisself a deputy
  Because he can not speak.

Four counsel in this Court—
  Misnamed of Justice—sits;
These lawyers owes their places to
  Their money, not their wits;
And there 's six attornies under them,
  As here their living gits.

These lawyers, six and four,
  Was a livin at their ease,
A sendin of their writs abowt,
  And droring in the fees,
When their erose a cirkimstance
  As is like to make a breeze.

It now is some monce since,
  A gent both good and trew
Possest a ansum oss vith vich
  He didn know what to do:
Peraps he did not like the oss,
  Perhaps he was a scru.

This gentleman his oss
  At Tattersall's did lodge;
There came a wulgar oss-dealer,
  This gentleman's name did fodge,
And took the oss from Tattersall's:
  Wasn that a artful dodge?

One day this gentleman's groom
  This willain did spy out,
A mounted on this oss,
  A ridin him about;
"Get out of that there oss, you rogue,"
  Speaks up the groom so stout.

The thief was cruel whex'd
  To find hisself so pinn'd;

The oss began to whinny,
  The honest groom he grinn'd;
And the raskle thief got off the oss
  And cut avay like vind.

And phansy with what joy
  The master did regard
His dearly bluvd lost oss again
  Trot in the stable yard!

Who was this master good
  Of whomb I makes these rhymes?
His name is Jacob Homnium, Exquire;
  And if *I*'d committed crimes,
Good Lord! I wouldn't ave that mann
  Attack me in the *Times!*

Now, shortly after the groomb
  His master's oss did take up,
There came a livery-man
  This gentleman to wake up;
And he handed in a little bill,
  Which hanger'd Mr. Jacob.

For two pound seventeen
  This livery-man eplied,
For the keep of Mr. Jacob's oss,
  Which the thief had took to ride.
"Do you see any think green in me?"
  Mr. Jacob Homnium cried.

"Because a raskle chews
  My oss away to robb,
And goes tick at your Mews
  For seven-and-fifty bobb,
Shall *I* be called to pay?—It is
  A iniquitious Jobb."

Thus Mr. Jacob cut
  The conwasation short;
The livery-man went ome,
  Detummingd to ave sport,
And summingsd Jacob Homnium, Exquire,
  Into the Pallis Court.

Pore Jacob went to Court,
  A Counsel for to fix,
And choose a barrister out of the four,
  An attorney of the six;
And there he sor these men of Lor,
  And watched 'em at their tricks.

The dreadful day of trile
  In the Pallis Court did come;
The lawyers said their say,
  The Judge looked wery glum,
And then the British Jury cast
  Pore Jacob Hom-ni-um.

O, a weary day was that
  For Jacob to go through;
The debt was two seventeen
  (Which he no mor owed than you),
And then there was the plaintives costs,
  Eleven pound six and two.

And then there was his own,
  Which the lawyers they did fix
At the wery moderit figgar
  Of ten pound one and six.
Now Evins bless the Pallis Court,
  And all its bold ver-dicks!

I can not settingly tell
  If Jacob swaw and cust,
At aving for to pay this sumb,
  But I should think he must,
And av drawn a cheque for £24 4*s.* 3*d.*
  With most igstreme disgust.

O Pallis Court, you move
  My pitty most profound.
A most emusing sport
  You thought it, I'll be bound,
To saddle hup a three-pound debt,
  With two-and-twenty pound.

Good sport it is to you,
  To grind the honest pore;
To pay their just or unjust debts
  With eight hundred per cent. for Lor;
Make haste and git your costes in,
  They will not last much mor!

Come down from that tribewn,
  Thou Shameless and Unjust;
Thou Swindle, picking pockets in
  The name of Truth, august;
Come down, thou hoary Blasphemy,
  For die thou shalt and must.

And go it, Jacob Homnium,
  And ply your iron pen,
And rise up Sir John Jervis,
  And shut me up that den;
That sty for fattening lawyers in,
  On the bones of honest men.

PLEACEMAN X.

THE WOFLE NEW BALLAD OF JANE RONEY AND MARY BROWN.

WILLIAM MAKEPEACE THACKERAY.

AN igstrawnary tail I vill tell you this veek—
I stood in the Court of A'Beckett the Beak,
Vere Mrs. Jane Roney, a vidow, I see,
Who charged Mary Brown with a robbin' of she.

This Mary was pore and in misery once,
And she came to Mrs. Roney it's more than twelve monce;
She adn't got no bed, nor no dinner, nor no tea,
And kind Mrs. Roney gave Mary all three.

Mrs. Roney kep Mary for ever so many veeks
(Her conduct disgusted the best of all Beax),
She kept her for nothink, as kind as could be,
Never thinking that this Mary was a traitor to she.

"Mrs. Roney, O Mrs. Roney, I feel very ill;
Will you jest step to the doctor's for to fetch me a pill?"
"That I will, my pore Mary," Mrs. Roney says she:
And she goes off to the doctor's as quickly as may be.

No sooner on this message Mrs. Roney was sped,
Than hup gits vicked Mary, and jumps out a bed;
She hopens all the trunks without never a key—
She bustes all the boxes, and vith them makes free.

Mrs. Roney's best linning gownds, petticoats, and close,
Her children's little coats and things, her boots and her hose,
She packed them, and she stole 'em, and avay vith them did flee.
Mrs. Roney's situation—you may think vat it vould be!

Of Mary, ungrateful, who had served her this vay,
Mrs. Roney heard nothink for a long year and a day,
Till last Thursday, in Lambeth, ven whom should she see?
But this Mary, as had acted so ungrateful to she.

She was leaning on the helbo of a worthy young man;
They were going to be married, and were walkin hand in hand;
And the church-bells was a ringing for Mary and he,
And the parson was ready, and a waitin' for his fee.

When up comes Mrs. Roney, and faces Mary Brown,
Who trembles, and castes her eyes upon the ground.
She calls a jolly pleaseman, it happens to be me;
I charge this young woman, Mr. Pleaseman, says she.

Mrs. Roney, o, Mrs. Roney, o, do let me go,
I acted most ungrateful I own, and I know,
But the marriage bell is a ringin, and the ring you may see,
And this young man is a waitin, says Mary, says she.

I don't care three fardens for the parson and clark,
And the bell may keep ringing from noon day to dark.
Mary Brown, Mary Brown, you must come along with me.
And I think this young man is lucky to be free.

So, in spite of the tears which bejewed Mary's cheek,
I took that young gurl to A'Beckett the Beak;
That exlent justice demanded her plea—
But never a sullable said Mary said she.

On account of her conduck so base and so vile,
That wicked young gurl is committed for trile,
And if she 's transpawted beyond the salt sea,
It 's a proper reward for such willians as she.

Now, you young gurls of Southwark for Mary who veep,
From pickin and stealin your ands you must keep,
Or it may be my dooty, as it was Thursday veek
To pull you all hup to A'Beckett the Beak.

PLEACEMAN X.

THE BALLAD OF ELIZA DAVIS.

W. MAKEPEACE THACKERAY.

GALLIANT gents and lovely ladies,
List a tail vich late befel,
Vich I heard it, bein on duty,
At the Pleace Hoffice, Clerkenwell.

Praps you know the Fondling Chapel,
Vere the little children sings:
(Lor! I likes to hear on Sundies
Them there pooty little things!)

In this street there lived a housemaid,
If you particklarly ask me where—
Vy, it was at four-and-tventy,
Guilford Street, by Brunsvick Square.

Vich her name was Eliza Davis,
And she went to fetch the beer:
In the street she met a party
As was quite surprized to see her.

Vich he vas a British Sailor,
For to judge him by his look:
Tarry jacket, canvas trowsies,
Ha-la Mr. T. P. Cooke.

Presently this Mann accostes
Of this hinnocent young gal—
Pray, saysee, Excuse my freedom,
You 're so like my Sister Sal!

You 're so like my Sister Sally,
  Both in valk and face and size;
Miss, that—dang my old lee scuppers,
  It brings tears into my hyes!

I 'm a mate on board a wessel,
  I 'm a sailor bold and true;
Shiver up my poor old timbers,
  Let me be a mate for you!

What 's your name, my beauty, tell me?
  And she faintly hansers, "Lore,
Sir, my name 's Eliza Davis,
  And I live at tventy-four."

Hofttimes came this British seaman,
  This deluded gal to meet:
And at tventy-four was welcome,
  Tventy-four in Guilford Street.

And Eliza told her Master
  (Kinder they than Missuses are),
How in marridge he had ast her,
  Like a galliant Brittish Tar.

And he brought his landlady vith him
  (Vich vas all his hartful plan),
And she told how Charley Thompson
  Reely was a good young man.

And how she herself had lived in
  Many years of union sweet,
Vith a gent she met promiskous,
  Valkin in the public street.

And Eliza listened to them,
  And she thought that soon their bands
Vould be published at the Fondlin,
  Hand the clergyman jine their ands.

And he ast about the lodgers
  (Vich her master let some rooms),
Likevise vere they kep their things, and
  Vere her master kep his spoons.

Hand this vicked Charley Thompson
  Came on Sundy veek to see her,
And he sent Eliza Davis
  Hout to vetch a pint of beer.

Hand while poor Eliza vent to
  Fetch the beer, dewoid of sin,
This etrocious Charley Thompson
  Let his wile accomplish hin.

To the lodgers, their apartments,
  This abandingd female goes,
Prigs their shirts and umberellas :
  Prigs their boots, and hats, and clothes.

Vile the scoundrle Charley Thompson,
  Lest his wictim should escape,
Hocust her vith rum and vater,
  Like a fiend in huming shape.

But a hi was fixt upon 'em
  Vich these raskles little sore;
Namely, Mr. Hide, the landlord
  Of the house at tventy-four.

He vas valkin in his garden,
  Just afore he vent to sup;
And on looking up he sor the
  Lodger's vinders lighted hup.

Hup the stairs the landlord tumbled;
  Something's going wrong, he said;
And he caught the vicked voman
  Underneath the lodger's bed.

And he called a brother Pleaseman,
  Vich vas passing on his beat,
Like a true and galliant feller,
  Hup and down in Guildford Street.

And that Pleaseman, able-bodied,
  Took this voman to the cell;
To the cell vere she was quodded,
  In the Close of Clerkenwell.

And though vicked Charley Thompson
  Boulted like a miscrant base,
Presently another Pleaseman
  Took him to the self-same place.

And this precious pair of raskles
  Tuesday last came up for doom;
By the beak they was committed,
  Vich his name was Mr. Combe.

Has for poor Eliza Davis,
  Simple gurl of tventy-four,
She, I ope, will never listen
  In the streets to sailors moar.

But if she must ave a sweet-art
  (Vich most evèry gurl expex),
Let her take a jolly Pleaseman,
  Vich is name peraps is—X.

LINES ON A LATE HOSPICIOUS EWENT.*

BY A GENTLEMAN OF THE FOOT-GUARDS (BLUE).

W. MAKEPEACE THACKERAY.

I PACED upon my beat
  With steady step and slow,
All huppandownd of Ranelagh-street;
  Ran'lagh, St. Pimlico.

While marching huppandownd
  Upon that fair May morn,
Beold the booming cannings sound,
  A royal child is born!

The Ministers of State
  Then presnly I sor,
They gallops to the Pallis gate,
  In carridges and for.

* The birth of Prince Arthur.

With anxious looks intent,
  Before the gate they stop,
There comes the good Lord President,
  And there the Archbishopp.

Lord John he next elights;
  And who comes here in haste?
'Tis the ero of one underd fights,
  The caudle for to taste.

Then Mrs. Lily, the nuss,
  Toward them steps with joy;
Says the brave old Duke, "Come tell to us,
  Is it a gal or a boy?"

Says Mrs. L. to the Duke,
  "Your Grace, it is *a Prince*."
And at that nuss's bold rebuke,
  He did both laugh and wince.

He vews with pleasant look
  This pooty flower of May,
Then says the wenerable Duke,
  "Egad, its my buthday."

By memory backards borne,
  Peraps his thoughts did stray
To that old place where he was born
  Upon the first of May.

Peraps he did recal
  The ancient towers of Trim;
And County Meath and Dangan Hall
  They did rewisit him.

I phansy of him so
  His good old thoughts employin;
Fourscore years and one ago
  Beside the flowin' Boyne.

His father praps he sees,
  Most musicle of Lords,
A playing maddrigles and glees
  Upon the Arpsicords.

Jest phansy this old Ero
  Upon his mother's knee!
Did ever lady in this land
  Ave greater sons than she?

And I shouldn be surprise
  While this was in his mind,
If a drop there twinkled in his eyes
  Of unfamiliar brind.

*   *   *   *

To Hapsly Ouse next day
  Drives up a Broosh and for,
A gracious prince sits in that Shay
  (I mention him with Hor!)

They ring upon the bell,
  The Porter shows his ed,
(He fought at Vaterloo as vell,
  And vears a veskit red.)

To see that carriage come
  The people round it press:
"And is the galliant Duke at ome?"
  "Your Royal Ighness, yes."

He stepps from out the Broosh
  And in the gate is gone,
And X, although the people push,
  Says wery kind "Move hon.

The Royal Prince unto
  The galliant Duke did say,
"Dear Duke, my little son and you
  Was born the self-same day.

"The lady of the land,
  My wife and Sovring dear,
It is by her horgust command
  I wait upon you here.

"That lady is as well
  As can expected be;

And to your Grace she bid me tell
 This gracious message free.

" That offspring of our race,
 Whom yesterday you see,
To show our honor for your Grace,
 Prince Arthur he shall be.

" That name it rhymes to fame;
 All Europe knows the sound:
And I could n't find a better name
 If you 'd give me twenty pound.

" King Arthur had his knights
 That girt his table round,
But you have won a hundred fights,
 Will match 'em, I 'll be bound.

" You fought with Bonypart,
 And likewise Tippoo Saib;
I name you then, with all my heart,
 The Godsire of this babe."

That Prince his leave was took,
 His hinterview was done.
So let us give the good old Duke
 Good luck of his god-son,

And wish him years of joy
 In this our time of Schism,
And hope he'll hear the royal boy
 His little catechism.

And my pooty little Prince
 That's come our arts to cheer,
Let me my loyal powers ewince
 A welcomin of you ere.

And the Poit-Laureat's crownd,
 I think, in some respex,
Egstremely shootable might be found
 For honest Pleaseman X.

THE LAMENTABLE BALLAD OF THE FOUNDLING OF SHOREDITCH.

W. MAKEPEACE THACKERAY.

COME, all ye Christian people, and listen to my tail,
It is all about a Doctor was traveling by the rail,
By the Heastern Counties Railway (vich the shares don't desire),
From Ixworth town in Suffolk, vich his name did not transpire.

A traveling from Bury this Doctor was employed
With a gentleman, a friend of his, vich his name was Captain
Loyd;
And on reaching Marks Tey Station, that is next beyond Colchest-
er, a lady entered into them most elegantly dressed.

She entered into the carriage all with a tottering step,
And a pooty little Bayby upon her bussum slep;
The gentlemen received her with kindness and siwillaty,
Pitying this lady for her illness and debillaty.

She had a fust-class ticket, this lovely lady said,
Because it was so lonesome she took a secknd instead.
Better to travel by secknd class than sit alone in the fust,
And the pooty little Baby upon her breast she nust.

A seein of her cryin, and shiverin and pail,
To her spoke this surging, the Ero of my tail;
Saysee you look unwell, ma'am, I'll elp you if I can,
And you may tell your case to me, for I 'm a meddicle man.

"Thank you, sir," the lady said, "I only look so pale,
Because I ain't accustom'd to traveling on the rale;
I shall be better presnly, when I 've ad some rest:"
And that pooty little Baby she squeeged it to her breast.

So in conwersation the journey they beguiled,
Capting Loyd and the medical man, and the lady and the child,
Till the warious stations along the line was passed,
For even the Heastern Counties' trains must come in at last.

When at Shoreditch tumminus at lenth stopped the train,
This kind meddicle gentleman proposed his aid again.

"Thank you, sir," the lady said, "for your kyindness dear;
My carridge and my osses is probbibly come here.

"Will you old this baby, please, vilst I step and see?"
The Doctor was a famly man: "That I will," says he.
Then the little child she kist, kist it very gently,
Vich was sucking his little fist, sleeping innocently.

With a sigh from her art, as though she would have bust it,
Then she gave the Doctor the child—wery kind he nust it;
Hup then the lady jumped hoff the bench she sat from,
Tumbled down the carridge steps and ran along the platform.

Vile hall the other passengers vent upon their vays,
The Capting and the Doctor sat there in a maze;
Some vent in a Homminibus, some vent in a Cabby,
The Capting and the Doctor vaited with the babby.

There they sat looking queer, for an hour or more,
But their feller passinger neather on 'em sore:
Never, never back again did that lady come
To that pooty sleeping Hinfant a suckin of his Thum!

What could this pore Doctor do, bein treated thus,
When the darling baby woke, cryin for its nuss?
Off he drove to a female friend, vich she was both kind and mild,
And igsplained to her the circumstance of this year little child.

That kind lady took the child instantly in her lap,
And made it very comforable by giving it some pap;
And when she took its close off, what d' you think she found?
A couple of ten pun notes sown up, in its little gownd!

Also, in its little close, was a note which did conwey,
That this little baby's parents lived in a handsome way:
And for its Headucation they reglary would pay,
And sirtingly like gentle-folks would claim the child one day,
If the Christian people who 'd charge of it would say,
Per adwertisement in the *Times*, where the baby lay.

Pity of this bayby many people took,
It had such pooty ways and such a pooty look;
And there came a lady forrard (I wish that I could see
Any kind lady as would do as much for me,

And I wish with all my art, some night in *my* night gownd,
I could find a note stitched for ten or twenty pound)—
There came a lady forrard, that most honorable did say,
She 'd adopt this little baby, which her parents cast away.

While the Doctor pondered on this hoffer fair,
Comes a letter from Devonshire, from a party there,
Hordering the Doctor, at its Mar's desire,
To send the little infant back to Devonshire.

Lost in apoplexity, this pore meddicle man,
Like a sensable gentleman, to the Justice ran;
Which his name was Mr. Hammill, a honorable beak,
That takes his seat in Worship-street four times a week.

"O Justice!" says the Doctor, "Instrugt me what to do,
I 've come up from the country, to throw myself on you;
My patients have no doctor to tend them in their ills,
(There they are in Suffolk without their draffts and pills!)

"I 've come up from the country, to know how I 'll dispose
Of this pore little baby, and the twenty-pun note, and the clothes,
And I want to go back to Suffolk, dear Justice, if you please,
And my patients wants their Doctor, and their Doctor wants his feez."

Up spoke Mr. Hammill, sittin at his desk,
"This year application does me much perplesk;
What I do adwise you, is to leave this babby
In the Parish where it was left, by its mother shabby."

The Doctor from his Worship sadly did depart—
He might have left the baby, but he had n't got the heart
To go for to leave that Hinnocent, has the laws allows,
To the tender mussies of the Union House.

Mother, who left this little one on a stranger's knee,
Think how cruel you have been, and how good was he!
Think, if you 've been guilty, innocent was she;
And do not take unkindly this little word of me:
Heaven be merciful to us all, sinners as we be!

PLEACEMAN X.

THE CRYSTAL PALACE.

W. MAKEPEACE THACKERAY.

With ganial foire
Thransfuse me loyre,
Ye sacred nymphths of Pindus,
The whoile I sing
That wondthrous thing
The Palace made o' windows!

Say, Paxton, truth,
Thou wondthrous youth,
What sthroke of art celistial
What power was lint
You to invint
This combineetion cristial.

O would before
That Thomas Moore
Likewoise the late Lord Boyron,
Thim aigles sthrong
Of Godlike song,
Cast oi on that cast oiron!

And saw thim walls,
And glittering halls,
Thim rising slendther columns,
Which I, poor pote,
Could not denote,
No, not in twinty vollums.

My Muse's words
Is like the birds
That roosts beneath the panes there;
Her wings she spoils
'Gainst them bright toiles,
And cracks her silly brains there.

This Palace tall,
This Cristial Hall,
Which imperors might covet,

Stands in Hide Park
Like Noah's Ark
A rainbow bint above it.

The towers and faynes,
In other scaynes,
The fame of this will undo,
Saint Paul's big doom,
St. Payther's Room,
And Dublin's proud Rotundo.

'Tis here that roams,
As well becomes
Her dignitee and stations,
Victoria great,
And houlds in state
The Congress of the Nations.

Her subjects pours
From distant shores,
Her Injians and Canajians;
And also we,
Her kingdoms three,
Attind with our allagiance.

Here comes likewise
Her bould allies,
Both Asian and Europian;
From East and West
They sent their best
To fill her Coornocopean.

I seen (thank Grace!)
This wondthrous place
(His Noble Honor Misteer
H. Cole it was
That gave the pass,
And let me see what is there.)

With conscious proide
I stud insoide
And look'd the World's Great Fair in,

Until me sight
Was dazzled quite,
And couldn't see for staring.

There 's holy saints
And window paints,
By Maydiayval Pugin;
Alhamborough Jones
Did paint the tones
Of yellow and gambouge in.

There 's fountains there
And crosses fair;
There 's water-gods with urrns;
There 's organs three,
To play, d' ye see,
"God save the Queen," by turns.

There 's statues bright
Of marble white,
Of silver and of copper,
And some in zink,
And some, I think,
That is n't over proper.

There 's staym Ingynes,
That stand in lines,
Enormous and amazing,
That squeal and snort,
Like whales in sport,
Or elephants a-grazing.

There 's carts and gigs,
And pins for pigs;
There 's dibblers and there 's harrows,
And plows like toys,
For little boys,
And illegant wheel-barrows.

For them genteels
Who ride on wheels,
There 's plenty to indulge 'em,

There 's Droskys snug
From Paytersbug
And vayhycles from Belgium.

There 's Cabs on Stands,
And Shandthry danns;
There 's wagons from New York here;
There 's Lapland Sleighs,
Have cross'd the seas,
And Jaunting Cars from Cork here.

Amazed I pass
From glass to glass,
Deloighted I survey 'em;
Fresh wondthers grows
Beneath me nose
In this sublime Musayum.

Look, here 's a fan
From far Japan,
A saber from Damasco;
There 's shawls ye get
From far Thibet,
And cotton prints from Glasgow.

There 's German flutes,
Marocky boots,
And Naples Macaronies;
Bohaymia
Has sent Bohay,
Polonia her polonies.

There 's granite flints
That 's quite imminse,
There 's sacks of coals and fuels,
There 's swords and guns,
And soap in tuns,
And Ginger-bread and Jewels.

There 's taypots there,
And cannons rare;
There 's coffins filled with roses:

There 's canvas tints,
Teeth instruments,
And shuits of clothes by MOSES.

There 's lashins more
Of things in store,
But thim I don't remimber;
Nor could disclose
Did I compose
From May time to Novimber.

Ah, JUDY thru!
With eyes so blue,
That you were here to view it!
And could I screw
But tu pound tu
'Tis I would thrait you to it.

So let us raise
Victoria's praise,
And Albert's proud condition,
That takes his ayse
As he surveys
This Crystal Exhibition.

THE SPECULATORS.

W. MAKEPEACE THACKERAY.

THE night was stormy and dark, The town was shut up in sleep: Only those were abroad who were out on a lark, Or those who 'd no beds to keep.

I pass'd through the lonely street, The wind did sing and blow; I could hear the policeman's feet Clapping to and fro.

There stood a potato-man In the midst of all the wet; He stood with his 'tato-can In the lonely Haymarket.

Two gents of dismal mien, And dark and greasy rags, Came out of a shop for gin. Swaggering over the flags:

Swaggering over the stones, These shabby bucks did walk; And I went and followed those seedy ones, And listened to their talk.

Was I sober or awake? Could I believe my ears? Those dismal beggars spake Of nothing but railroad shares.

I wondered more and more: Says one—"Good friend of mine, How many shares have you wrote for In the Diddlesex Junction line?"

"I wrote for twenty," says Jim, "But they wouldn't give me one;" His comrade straight rebuked him For the folly he had done:

"O Jim, you are unawares Of the ways of this bad town; *I* always write for five hundred shares, And *then* they put me down."

"And yet you got no shares," Says Jim, "for all your boast;" "I *would* have wrote," says Jack, "but where Was the penny to pay the post?"

"I lost, for I could n't pay That first instalment up; But here 's taters smoking hot—I say Let 's stop, my boy, and sup."

And at this simple feast The while they did regale, I drew each ragged capitalist Down on my left thumb-nail.

Their talk did me perplex, All night I tumbled and toss'd And thought of railroad specs, And how money was won and lost.

"Bless railroads everywhere," I said, "and the world's advance; Bless every railroad share In Italy, Ireland, France; For never a beggar need now despair, And every rogue has a chance."

LETTER

FROM MR. HOSEA BIGLOW TO THE HON. J. T. BUCKINGHAM, EDITOR OF THE BOSTON COURIER, COVERING A LETTER FROM MR. B. SAWIN, PRIVATE IN THE MASSACHUSETTS REGIMENT IN MEXICO.

JAMES RUSSELL LOWELL.

MISTER BUCKINUM, the follerin Billet was writ hum by a Yung feller of our town that wuz cussed fool enuff to goe atrottin inter Miss Chiff arter a Drum and fife. it ain't Nater for a feller to let on that he's sick o' any bizness that He went intu off his own free will and a Cord, but I rather cal'late he's middlin tired o' voluntearin By this Time. I bleeve u may put dependunts on his statemence. For I never heered nothin bad on him let Alone his havin what Parson Wilbur cals a *pongshong* for cocktales, and he ses it wuz a soshiashun of idees sot him agoin arter the Crootin Sargient cos he wore a cocktale onto his hat.

his Folks gin the letter to me and i shew it to parson Wilbur and he ses it oughter Bee printed. send It to mister Buckinum, ses he, i don't ollers agree with him, ses he, but by Time, says he, I *du* like a feller that ain't a Feared.

I have intusspussed a Few reflecckshuns hear and thair. We're kind o' prest with Hayin.

Ewers respecfly
HOSEA BIGLOW.

THIS kind o' sogerin' aint a mite like our October trainin',
A chap could clear right out from there ef 't only looked like rainin'.
An' th' Cunnles, tu, could kiver up their shappoes with bandanners,
An' send the insines skootin' to the bar-room with their banners,
(Fear o' gittin' on 'em spotted), an' a feller could cry quarter
Ef he fired away his ramrod arter tu much rum an' water.
Recollect wut fun we hed, you 'n I an' Ezry Hollis,
Up there to Waltham plain last fall, ahavin' the Cornwallis ?*
This sort o' thing aint *jest* like thet—I wish thet I wuz furder—†
Nimepunce a day fer killin' folks comes kind o' low fer murder
(Wy I've worked out to slarterin' some for Deacon Cephas Billins,
An' in the hardest times there wuz I ollers tetched ten shillins),
There 's sutthin' gits into my throat thet makes it hard to swaller,
It comes so nateral to think about a hempen collar;
It 's glory—but, in spite o' all my tryin to git callous,
I feel a kind o' in a cart, aridin' to the gallus.

* i hait the Site of a feller with a muskit as I du pizn But their *is* fun to a cornwallis I ain't agoin to deny it.—H. B.

† he means Not quite so fur i guess.—H. B.

But when it comes to *bein'* killed—I tell ye I felt streaked
The fust time ever I found out wy baggonets wuz peaked;
Here 's how it wuz: I started out to go to a fandango,
The sentinul he ups an' sez, "Thet 's furder 'an you can go."
"None o' your sarse," sez I; sez he, "Stan' back!" "Aint you a buster?"
Sez I, "I 'm up to all thet air, I guess I 've ben to muster;
I know wy sentinuls air sot; you aint agoin' to eat us;
Caleb haint no monopoly to court the seenoreetas;
My folks to hum air full ez good ez hisn be, by golly!"
An' so ez I wuz goin' by, not thinkin' wut would folly,
The everlastin' cus he stuck his one-pronged pitchfork in me
An' made a hole right thru my close ez ef I wuz an in'my.
Wal, it beats all how big I felt hoorawin' in ole Funnel
Wen Mister Bolles he gin the sword to our Leftenant Cunnle
(It 's Mister Secondary Bolles,* thet writ the prize peace essay;
Thet 's wy he did n't list himself along o' us, I dessay),
An' Rantoul, tu, talked pooty loud, but don't put *his* foot in it,
Coz human life 's so sacred thet he 's principled agin' it—
Though I myself can 't rightly see it 's any wus achokin' on 'em
Than puttin' bullets thru their lights, or with a bagnet pokin' on 'em;
How dreffle slick he reeled it off (like Blitz at our lyceum
Ahaulin' ribbins from his chops so quick you skeercely see 'em),
About the Anglo-Saxon race (an' saxons would be handy
To do the buryin' down here upon the Rio Grandy),
About our patriotic pas an' our star-spangled banner,
Our country's bird alookin' on an' singin' out hosanner,
An' how he (Mister B. himself) wuz happy fer Ameriky—
I felt, ez sister Patience sez, a leetle mite histericky.
I felt, I swon, ez though it wuz a dreffle kind o' privilege
Atrampin' round thru Boston streets among the gutter's drivelage;
I act'lly thought it wuz a treat to hear a little drummin',
An' it did bonyfidy seem millanyum wuz acomin'
Wen all on us got suits (darned like them wore in the state prison)
An' every feller felt ez though all Mexico wuz hisn.†

* the ignerant creeter means Sekketary; but he ollers stuck to his books like cobbler's wax to an ile-stone.—H. B.

† it must be aloud that thare's a streak o' nater in lovin' sho, but it sartinly is 1 of the curusest things in nater to see a rispecktable dri goods dealer (deekon

This 'ere 's about the meanest place a skunk could wal diskiver
(Saltillo 's Mexican, I b'lieve, fer wut we call Saltriver).
The sort o' trash a feller gits to eat doos beat all nater,
I 'd give a year's pay fer a smell o' one good bluenose tater;
The country here thet Mister Bolles declared to be so charmin'
Throughout is swarmin' with the most alarmin' kind o' varmin'.
He talked about delishis froots, but then it wuz a wopper all,
The holl on't 's mud an' prickly pears, with here an' there a chapparal;
You see a feller peekin' out, an', fust you know, a lariat
Is round your throat en' you a copse, 'fore you can say, "Wut air ye at?"*
You never see sech darned gret bugs (it may not be irrelevant
To say I 've seen a *scarabœus pilularius* † big ez a year old elephant),
The rigiment come up one day in time to stop a red bug
From runnin' off with Cunnle Wright—'t wuz jest a common *cimex lectularius.*
One night I started up on eend an' thought I wuz to hum agin,
I heern a horn, thinks I it 's Sol the fisherman hez come agin,
His bellowses is sound enough—ez I 'm a livin' creeter,
I felt a thing go thru my leg—'t wuz nothin' more 'n a skeeter!
Then there 's the yaller fever, tu, they call it here el vomito—
(Come, thet wun't du, you landcrab there, I tell ye to le' *go* my toe!
My gracious! it 's a scorpion thet 's took a shine to play with 't,
I dars n't skeer the tarnal thing fer fear he 'd run away with 't).
Afore I come away from hum I hed a strong persuasion
Thet Mexicans worn't human beans‡—an ourang outang nation,
A sort o' folks a chap could kill an' never dream on 't arter,
No more 'n a feller 'd dream o' pigs thet he hed hed to slarter;

off a chutch mayby) a riggin' himself out in the Weigh they du and struttin' round in the Reign aspilin' his trowsis and makin' wet goods of himself. E fany thin's foolisher and moor dicklus than militerry gloary it is milishy gloary.—H. B.

* these fellers are verry proppilly called Rank Heroes, and the more tha kill the ranker and more Herowick tha bekum.—H. B.

† it wuz "tumblebug" as he Writ it, but the parson put the Latten instid. i sed tother maid better meeter, but he said tha was eddykated peepl to Boston and tha would n't stan' it no how. idnow as tha *wood* and idnow *as* tha wood.—H. B.

‡ he means human beins, that's wut he means. i spose he kinder thought tha wuz human beans ware the Xisle Poles comes from.—H. B.

I 'd an idee thet they were built arter the darkie fashion all,
An' kickin'-colored folks about, you know, 's a kind o' national;
But when I jined I worn't so wise ez thet air queen o' Sheby,
Fer, come to look at 'em, they aint much diff'rent from wut we be,
An' here we air ascrougin' 'em out o' thir own dominions,
Ashelterin' 'em, ez Caleb sez, under our eagle's pinions,
Wich means to take a feller up jest by the slack o' 's trowsis
An' walk him Spanish clean right out o' all his homes an' houses;
Wal, it doos seem a curus way, but then hooraw fer Jackson!
It must be right, fer Caleb sez it 's reg'lar Anglo-saxon.
The Mex'cans don't fight fair, they say, they piz'n all the water,
An' du amazin' lots o' things thet is n't wut they ough' ter;
Bein' they haint no lead, they make their bullets out o' copper
An' shoot the darned things at us, tu, which Caleb sez aint proper;
He sez they 'd ough' to stan' right up an' let us pop 'em fairly
(Guess wen he ketches 'em at thet he 'll hev to git up airly),
Thet our nation 's bigger 'n theirn an' so its rights air bigger,
An' thet it 's all to make 'em free that we air pullin' trigger,
Thet Anglo Saxondom's idee 's abreakin' 'em to pieces,
An' thet idee 's thet every man doos jest wut he damn pleases;
Ef I don't make his meanin' clear, perhaps in some respex I can,
I know that "every man" don't mean a nigger or a Mexican;
An' there 's another thing I know, an' thet is, ef these creeturs,
Thet stick an Anglo-saxon mask onto State-prison feeturs,
Should come to Jaalam Center fer to argify an' spout on 't,
The gals 'ould count the silver spoons the minnit they cleared out on 't

This goin' ware glory waits ye haint one agreeable feetur,
An' ef it worn't fer wakin' snakes, I 'd home agin short meter;
O, would n't I be off, quick time, ef 't worn't thet I wuz sartin
They 'd let the daylight into me to pay me fer desartin!
I don't approve o' tellin' tales, but jest to you I may state
Our ossifers aint wut they wuz afore they left the Baystate ·
Then it wuz "Mister Sawin, sir, you 're middlin' well now, be ye?
Step up an' take a nipper, sir; I 'm dreffle glad to see ye;"
But now it' s "Ware 's my eppylet? here, Sawin, step an' fetch it!
An' mind your eye, be thund'rin' spry, or, damn ye, you shall ketch it!"
Wal, ez the Doctor sez, some pork will bile so, but by mighty,
Ef I hed some on 'em to hum, I 'd give 'em linkum vity,

I 'd play the rogue's march on their hides an' other music fol-
lerin'——
But I must close my letter here, for one on 'em 's a-hollerin',
These Anglosaxon ossifers—wal, taint no use ajawin',
I 'm safe enlisted fer the war,
Yourn,
BIRDOFREDOM SAWIN

A LETTER

FROM A CANDIDATE FOR THE PRESIDENCY IN ANSWER TO SUTTIN QUESTIONS PROPOSED BY MR. HOSEA BIGLOW, INCLOSED IN A NOTE FROM MR. BIGLOW TO S. H. GAY, ESQ., EDITOR OF THE NATIONAL ANTI-SLAVERY STANDARD.

JAMES RUSSELL LOWELL.

DEER SIR its gut to be the fashun now to rite letters to the candid 8s and i wus chose at a public Meetin in Jalaam to du wut wus nessary fur that town. i writ to 271 ginerals and gut ansers to 209. tha air called candid 8s but I don't see nothin candid about em. this here 1 which I send wus thought satty's factory. I dunno as it's ushle to print Poscrips, but as all the ansers I got hed the saim, I sposed it wus best. times has gretly changed. Formaly to knock a man into a cocked hat wus to use him up, but now it ony gives him a chance fur the cheef madgustracy.— H. B.

DEAR SIR—You wish to know my notions
On sartin pints thet rile the land;
There 's nothin' thet my natur so shuns
Ez bein' mum or underhand;
I 'm a straight-spoken kind o' creetur
Thet blurts right out wut 's in his head,
An' ef I 've one pecooler feetur,
It is a nose thet wunt be led.

So, to begin at the beginnin';
An' come directly to the pint,
I think the country's underpinnin'
Is some consid'ble out o' jint;
I aint agoin' to try your patience
By tellin' who done this or thet,
I don't make no insinooations,
I jest let on I smell a rat.

Thet is, I mean, it seems to me so,
  But, ef the public think I 'm wrong,
I wunt deny but wut I be so—
  An', fact, it don't smell very strong;
My mind 's tu fair to lose its balance
  An' say wich party hez most sense;
There may be folks o' greater talence
  Thet can't set stiddier on the fence.

I 'm an eclectic: ez to choosin'
  'Twixt this an' thet, I 'm plaguy lawth;
I leave a side thet looks like losin',
  But (wile there 's doubt) I stick to both;
I stan' upon the Constitution,
  Ez preudunt statesmun say, who 've planned
A way to git the most profusion
  O' chances ez to *ware* they 'll stand.

Ez fer the war, I go agin it—
  I mean to say I kind o' du—
Thet is, I mean thet, bein' in it,
  The best way wuz to fight it thru;
Not but wut abstract war is horrid,
  I sign to thet with all my heart—
But civlyzation *doos* git forrid
  Sometimes upon a powder-cart.

About thet darned Proviso matter
  I never hed a grain o' doubt,
Nor I aint one my sense to scatter
  So 's no one could n't pick it out;
My love fer North an' South is equil,
  So I 'll just answer plump an' frank,
No matter wut may be the sequil—
  Yes, sir, I *am* agin a Bank.

Ez to the answerin' o' questions,
  I 'am an off ox at bein' druv,
Though I aint one thet ary test shuns
  'll give our folks a helpin' shove;

Kind o' promiscoous I go it
  Fer the holl country, an' the ground
I take, ez nigh ez I can show it,
  Is pooty gen'ally all round.

I don't appruve o' givin' pledges;
  You 'd ough' to leave a feller free,
An' not go knockin' out the wedges
  To ketch his fingers in the tree;
Pledges air awfle breachy cattle
  Thet preudent farmers don't turn out—
Ez long 'z the people git their rattle,
  Wut is there fer 'm to grout about?

Ez to the slaves, there 's no confusion
  In *my* idees consarnin' them—
I think they air an Institution,
  A sort of—yes, jest so—ahem:
Do *I* own any? Of my merit
  On thet pint you yourself may jedge;
All is, I never drink no sperit,
  Nor I haint never signed no pledge.

Ez to my principles, I glory
  In hevin' nothin' o' the sort;
I aint a Wig, I aint a Tory,
  I 'm jest a candidate, in short;
Thet 's fair an' square an' parpendicler,
  But, ef the Public cares a fig
To hev me an' thin' in particler,
  Wy, I 'm a kind o' peri-wig.

P. S.

Ez we 're a sort o' privateerin',
  O' course, you know, it 's sheer an' sheer,
An' there is sutthin' wuth your hearin'
  I 'll mention in *your* privit ear;
Ef you git *me* inside the White House,
  Your head with ile I 'll kin' o' 'nint
By gittin' *you* inside the Light-house
  Down to the eend o' Jaalam Pint.

An' ez the North hez took to brustlin'
At bein' scrouged frum off the roost,
I 'll tell ye wut 'll save all tusslin'
An' give our side a harnsome boost—
Tell 'em thet on the Slavery question
I 'm RIGHT, although to speak I 'm lawth;
This gives you a safe pint to rest on,
An' leaves me frontin' South by North.

THE CANDIDATE'S CREED.

(BIGLOW PAPERS.)

JAMES RUSSELL LOWELL.

I DU believe in Freedom's cause,
Ez fur away ez Paris is;
I love to see her stick her claws
In them infarnal Pharisees;
It 's wal enough agin a king
To dror resolves and triggers,—
But libbaty 's a kind o' thing
Thet don't agree with niggers.

I du believe the people want
A tax on teas and coffees,
Thet nothin' aint extravygunt,—
Purvidin' I 'm in office;
For I hev loved my country sence
My eye-teeth filled their sockets,
An' Uncle Sam I reverence,
Partic'larly his pockets.

I du believe in *any* plan
O' levyin' the taxes,
Ez long ez, like a lumberman,
I git jest wut I axes:
I go free-trade thru thick an' thin,
Because it kind o' rouses
The folks to vote—and keep us in
Our quiet custom-houses.

I du believe it's wise an' good
  To sen' out furrin missions,
Thet is, on sartin understood
  An' orthydox conditions;—
I mean nine thousan' dolls. per ann.,
  Nine thousan' more fer outfit,
An' me to recommend a man
  The place 'ould jest about fit.

I du believe in special ways
  O' prayin' an' convartin';
The bread comes back in many days,
  An' buttered, tu, fer sartin;—
I mean in preyin' till one busts
  On wut the party chooses,
An' in convartin' public trusts
  To very privit uses.

I do believe hard coin the stuff
  Fer 'lectioneers to spout on;
The people 's ollers soft enough
  To make hard money out on;
Dear Uncle Sam pervides fer his,
  An' gives a good-sized junk to all—
I don't care *how* hard money is,
  Ez long ez mine 's paid punctooal.

I du believe with all my soul
  In the gret Press's freedom,
To pint the people to the goal
  An' in the traces lead 'em:
Palsied the arm thet forges yokes
  At my fat contracts squintin',
An' withered be the nose thet pokes
  Inter the gov'ment printin'!

I du believe thet I should give
  Wut 's his'n unto Cæsar,
Fer it 's by him I move an' live,
  From him my bread an' cheese air

I du believe thet all o' me
  Doth bear his souperscription,—
Will, conscience, honor, honesty,
  An' things o' thet description.

I du believe in prayer an' praise
  To him thet hez the grantin'
O' jobs—in every thin' thet pays,
  But most of all in CANTIN';
This doth my cup with marcies fill,
  This lays all thought o' sin to rest—
I *don't* believe in princerple,
  But, O, I *du* in interest.

I du believe in bein' this
  Or thet, ez it may happen
One way, or t' other hendiest is
  To ketch the people nappin';
It aint by princerples nor men
  My preudent course is steadied—
I scent wich pays the best, an' then
  Go into it baldheaded.

I du believe thet holdin' slaves
  Comes nat'ral tu a President,
Let 'lone the rowdedow it saves
  To have a wal-broke precedunt;
Fer any office, small or gret,
  I could 'nt ax with no face,
Without I 'd been, thru dry an' wet,
  The unrizziest kind o' doughface.

I du believe wutever trash
  'll keep the people in blindness,—
Thet we the Mexicans can thrash
  Right inter brotherly kindness—
Thet bombshells, grape, an' powder 'n' ball
  Air good-will's strongest magnets—
Thet peace, to make it stick at all,
  Must be druv in with bagnets.

In short, I firmly du believe
  In Humbug generally,
Fer it 's a thing thet I perceive
  To hev a solid vally;
This heth my faithful shepherd ben,
  In pasturs sweet heth led me,
An' this 'll keep the people green
  To feed ez they have fed me.

THE COURTIN'.

JAMES RUSSELL LOWELL.

ZEKLE crep' up, quite unbeknown,
  An' peeked in thru the winder,
An there sot Huldy all alone,
  'ith no one nigh to hender.

Agin' the chimbly crooknecks hung,
  An' in among 'em rusted
The ole queen's arm thet gran'ther Young
  Fetched back from Concord busted.

The wannut logs shot sparkles out
  Toward the pootiest, bless her!
An' leetle fires danced all about
  The chiny on the dresser.

The very room, coz she wuz in,
  Looked warm frum floor to ceilin'.
An' she looked full ez rosy agin
  Ez th' apple she wuz peelin'.

She heerd a foot an' knowd it, tu,
  Araspin' on the scraper—
All ways to once her feelins flew
  Like sparks in burnt-up paper.

He kin' o' l'itered on the mat,
  Some doubtfle of the seekle:
His heart kep' goin' pitypat,
  But hern went pity Zekle.

A SONG FOR A CATARRH.

PUNCH

By *B*ary A*ll*e is like the su*l*,
Whe*l* at the daw*l* it fli*l*gs
Its golde*l* s*b*iles of light upo*l*
Earth's gree*l* and lo*l*ely thi*l*gs.
I*l* vai*l* I sue, I o*l*ly wi*l*
Fro*b* her a scor*l*ful frow*l*,
But soo*l* as I *b*y prayers begi*l*,
She cries O *l*o! bego*l*e,
Yes! yes! the burthe*l* of her so*l*g
Is *l*o! *l*o! *l*o! bego*l*e!

By *B*ary A*ll*e is like the moo*l*,
Whe*l* first her silver shee*l*
Awakes the *l*ighti*l*gale's soft tu*l*e,
That else had sile*l*t bee*l*.
But *B*ary A*ll*e, like darkest *l*ight,
O*l* *b*e, alas! looks dow*l*;
Her s*b*iles o*l* others bea*b* their light,
Her frow*l*s are all *b*y ow*l*.
I've but o*l*e burthe*l* to *b*y so*l*g—
Her frow*l*s are all *b*y ow*l*.

EPITAPH ON A CANDLE.

PUNCH.

A *wicked* one lies buried here,
Who died in a *decline*;
He never rose in rank, I fear,
Though he was born to *shine*.

He once was *fat*, but now, indeed,
He's thin as any griever;
He died—the Doctors all agreed,
Of a most *burning* fever.

One thing of him is said with truth,
  With which I 'm much amused;
It is—that when he stood, forsooth,
  A *stick* he always used.

Now *winding-sheets* he sometimes made,
  But this was not enough,
For finding it a poorish trade,
  He also dealt in *snuff*.

If e'er you said " *Go out*, I pray,"
  He much ill nature show'd;
On such occasions he would say,
  " Vy, if I do, *I'm blow'd*."

In this his friends do all agree,
  Although you 'll think I 'm joking,
When *going out* 'tis said that he
  Was very fond of *smoking*.

Since all religion he despised,
  Let these few words suffice,
Before he ever was baptized
  They *dipp'd* him once or twice.

POETRY ON AN IMPROVED PRINCIPLE.

A RENCONTER WITH A TEA-TOTALLER.

PUNCH.

On going forth last night, a friend to see,
I met a man by trade a s-n-o-*b*;
Reeling along the path he held his way.
" Ho! ho!" quoth I, " he 's d-r-u-n-*k*."
Then thus to him—" Were it not better, far,
You were a little s-o-b-e-*r*?
'T were happier for your family, I guess,
Than playing of such rum r-i-g-*s*.
Besides, all drunkards, when policemen see 'em,
Are taken up at once by t-h-*e*-*m*."

"Me drunk!" the cobbler cried, "the devil trouble you!
You want to kick up a blest r-o-*w*.
Now, may I never wish to work for Hoby,
If drain I 've had!" (the lying s-n-*o-b!*)
I 've just return'd from a tee-total party,
Twelve on us jamm'd in a spring c-a-*r-t*.
The man as lectured, now, *was* drunk; why, bless ye,
He 's sent home in a c-h-a-i-*s-e*.
He 'd taken so much lush into his belly,
I 'm blest if he could t-o-dd-*l-e*.
A pair on 'em—hisself and his good lady;—
The gin had got into her h-e-*a-d*.
(My eye and Betty! what weak mortals *we* are;
They said they took but ginger b-e-*e-r!*)
But as for me, I 've stuck ('t was rather ropy)
All day to weak imperial p-*o-p*.
And now we 've had this little bit o' sparrin',
Just stand a q-u-a-r-t-e-*r-n!*"

ON A REJECTED NOSEGAY,

OFFERED BY THE AUTHOR TO A BEAUTIFUL YOUNG LADY, WHO RETURNED IT.

PUNCH.

WHAT! then you won't accept it, wont you? Oh!
No matter; pshaw! my heart is breaking, though.
My bouquet is rejected; let it be:
For what am I to you, or you to me?
'Tis true I once had hoped; but now, alas!
Well, well; 'tis over now, and let it pass.
I was a fool—perchance I am so still;
You won't accept it! Let me dream you will:
But that were idle. Shall we meet again?
Why should we? Water for my burning brain?
I could have loved thee—Could! I love thee yet
Can only Lethe teach me to forget?
Oblivion's balm, oh tell me where to find!
Is it a tenant of the anguish'd mind?
Or is it?—ha! at last I see it come;
Waiter! a bottle of your oldest rum.

A SERENADE.

PUNCH.

Smile, lady, smile! (*Bless me! what's that?*
Confound the cat!)—
Smile, lady, smile! One glance bestow
On him who sadly waits below,
To catch—(*A villain up above*
Has thrown some water on me, love!)
To catch one token—
(*Oh, Lord! my head is broken;*
The wretch who threw the water down,
Has dropped the jug upon my crown)—
To catch one token, which shall be
As dear as life itself to me.
List, lady, then; while on my lute
I breathe soft—(*No! I'll not be quiet;*
How dare you call my serenade a riot?
I do defy you)—while upon my lute
I breathe soft sighs—(*Yes, I dispute*
Your right to stop me—breathe soft sighs.
Grant but one look from those dear eyes—
(*There, take that stupid noddle in again;*
Call the police!—do! I'll prolong my strain),
We'll wander by the river's placid flow—
(*Unto the station-house!—No, sir, I won't go;*
Leave me alone!)—and talk of love's delight.
(*Oh, murder!—help! I'm locked up for the night!*)

RAILROAD NURSERY RHYME.

PUNCH.

Air—"*Ride a Cock Horse.*"

Fly by steam force the country across,
Faster than jockey outside a race-horse:
With time bills mismanaged, fast trains after slow,
You shall have danger wherever you go.

AN INVITATION TO THE ZOOLOGICAL GARDENS.

PUNCH.

I HAVE found out a gig-gig-gift for my fuf-fuf-fair,
I have found where the rattle-snakes bub-bub-breed;
Will you co-co-come, and I 'll show you the bub-bub-bear,
And the lions and tit-tit-tigers at fuf-fuf-feed.

I know where the co-co-cockatoo's song
Makes mum-mum-melody through the sweet vale;
Where the mum-monkeys gig-gig-grin all the day long
Or gracefully swing by the tit-tit-tit-tail.

You shall pip-pip-play, dear, some did-did-delicate joke
With the bub-bub-bear on the tit-tit-top of his pip-pip-pip-pole;
But observe, 'tis forbidden to pip-pip-poke
At the bub-bub-bear with your pip-pip-pink pip-pip-pip-pip-parasol!

You shall see the huge elephant pip-pip-play,
You shall gig-gig-gaze on the stit-stit-stately racoon;
And then did-did-dear, together we 'll stray
To the cage of the bub-bub-blue-faced bab-bab-boon.

You wished (I r-r-remember it well,
And I lul-lul-loved you the m-m-more for the wish)
To witness the bub-bub-beautiful pip-pip-pel-
ican swallow the l-l-ive little fuf-fuf-fish!

ΤΟ ΘΕ ΛΕΑΔΙΝΓ ΠΕΡΙΟΔΙΚΑΛ.*

PUNCH.

Θις κομπλιμεντ, γρεατ σιρ, ο τακε,
Υρε α βρικ ανδ νο μιστακε,
Ενεμι το καντ ανδ φυδγε.
Τιμε το θεε I νε'ερ βεγρυδγε,
Ανδ I ὠπε το σεε υρε ναμε
Φωρεμοστ ιν θε λιστς οφ Φαμε.

Τομ Σμιθ, Γρυβ στρεετ

* English words in Greek letters.

THE PEOPLE AND THEIR PALACE.

IMPROVISED BY A FINE GENTLEMAN.

PUNCH.

Oh dem that absawd Cwystal Palace! alas,
What a pity they took off the duty on glass!
It 's having been evaw ewected, in fact,
Was en-ti-a-ly owing to that foolish act.

Wha-evew they put it a cwowd it will dwaw,
And that is the weason I think it a baw;
I have no gweat dislike to the building, as sutch;
The People is what I object to sa mutch.

The People!—I weally am sick of the wawd:
The People is ugly, unpleasant, absawd;
Wha-evaw they go, it is always the case,
They are shaw to destroy all the chawm of the place.

Their voices are loud, and their laughter is hawse;
Their featyaws are fabsy, iwegulaw, cause;
How seldom it is that their faces disclose,
What one can call, pwopally speaking, a nose!

They have dull heavy looks, which appeaw to expwess
Disagweeable stwuggles with common distwess;
The People can't dwess, does n't know how to walk,
And would uttaly wuin a spot like the Pawk.

That I hate the People is maw than I 'll say;
I only would have them kept out of my way,
Let them stay at the pot-house, wejoice in the pipe,
And wegale upon beeaw, baked patatas, and twipe.

We must have the People—of that tha 's no doubt—
In shawt they could not be, pahaps, done without.
If 'twa not faw the People we could not have Boots.
Tha 's no doubt that they exawcise useful pasuits.

They are all vewy well in their own pwopa spheeaw,
A long distance off; but I don't like them neeaw;

The slams is the place faw a popula show;
Don't encouwage the people to spoil Wotten Wow.

It is odd that the DUKE OF AWGYLL could pasue,
So eccentwic a cawse, and LAD SHAFTESBUWY too,
As to twy and pwesawve the Glass House on its site,
Faw no weason on awth but the People's delight.

A "SWELL'S" HOMAGE TO MRS. STOWE

PUNCH.

A MUST wead *Uncle Tom*—a wawk
Which A 'm afwaid 's extwemely slow,
People one meets begin to talk
Of Mrs. HARWIETBEECHASTOWE.

'Tis not as if A saw ha name
To walls and windas still confined;
All that is meawly vulga fame:
A don't wespect the public mind.

But Staffa'd House has made haw quite
Anotha kind a pawson look,
A Countess would pasist, last night,
In asking me about haw book.

She wished to know if I admiawd
EVA, which quite confounded me;
And then haw Ladyship inqwaw'd
Whethaw A did 'nt hate LEGWEE?

Bai JOVE! A was completely flaw'd;
A wish'd myself, or haw, at Fwance;
And that 's the way a fella 's baw'd
By ev'wy gal he asks to dance.

A felt myself a gweat a fool
Than A had evaw felt befaw;
A 'll study at some Wagged School
The tale of that old Blackamaw!

THE EXCLUSIVE'S BROKEN IDOL.

PUNCH.

A don't object at all to War
  With a set a fellas like the Fwench,
But this dem wupcha with the Czar,
  It gives one's feeling quite a wench.

The man that peace in Yawwup kept
  Gives all his pwevious life the lie;
A fina fella neva stepped,
  Bai Jove, he 's maw than six feet high!

He cwushed those democwatic beasts;
  He 'd flog a Nun; maltweat a Jew,
Or pawsecute those Womish Pwiests,
  Most likely vewy pwoppa too.

To think that afta such a cawce,
  Which nobody could eva blame,
The Emp'wa should employ bwute fawce
  Against this countwy just the same!

We all consida'd him our fwiend,
  But in a most erwoneus light,
In shawt, it seems you can't depend
  On one who fancies might is wight.

His carwacta is coming out;
  His motives—which A neva saw—
Are now wevealed beyond a doubt,
  And we must fight—but what a baw!

THE LAST KICK OF FOP'S ALLEY.

PUNCH.

Air—"*Weber's Last Waltz.*"

My wawst feaws are wealized; the Op'wa is na maw,
And the wain of Donizetti and Tapischowe are aw!
No entapwising capitalist bidding faw the lot,
In detail at last the pwopaty is being sold by Scott.

Fahwell to *Anna Bolena;* to *Nauma*, oh, fahwell!
Adieu to *La Sonnambula!* the hamma wings haw knell;
I Puwitani, too, must cease a cwowded house to dwaw,
And they 've knocked down lovely *Lucia*, the *Bwide of Lammamaw.*

Fahwell the many twinkling steps; fahwell the gwaceful fawm
That bounded o'er the wose-beds, and that twipped amid the stawm;
Fahwell the gauze and muslin—doomed to load the Hebwew's bags;
Faw the *Times* assauts the wawdwobe went—just fancy—as old wags!

That ev'wy thing that's bwight must fade, we know is vewy twue,
And now we see what sublunawy glowwy must come to;
How twue was MAIDSTONE'S pwophecy; the Deluge we behold
Now that HAW MAJESTY'S Theataw is in cawse of being sold.

THE MAD CABMAN'S SONG OF SIXPENCE.*

PUNCH.

WOT 's this ?—wot hever is this 'ere ?
Eh ?—arf a suvrin !—feels like vun—
Boohoo! they won't let me have no beer!
Suppose I chucks it up into the sun !—
No—that ain't right—
The yaller 's turned wite!
Ha, ha, ho!—he 's sold and done—
Come, I say!—I won't stand that—
'Tis all my eye and BETTY MARTIN!
Over the left and all round my hat,
As the pewter pot said to the kevarten.

Who am I? HEMPRER of the FRENCH
LEWIS NAPOLEON BONYPART,
Old Spooney, to be sure—
Between you and me and the old blind oss
And the doctor says there ain't no cure.

* This inimitable burlesque was published soon after the cab fare had been reduced from eightpence to sixpence a mile.

D' ye think I care for the blessed Bench?—
From Temple Bar to Charing Cross?
Two mile and better—arf a crown—
Talk of screwing a feller down!
As for poor BILL, it's broke his art.
Cab to the Moon, sir? Here you are!—
That's—how much?—
A farthin' touch!
Now as we can't demand back fare.

But, guv'ner, wot can this 'ere be?—
The fare of a himperial carridge?
You don't mean all this 'ere for me!
In course you ain't heerd about my marridge—
I feels so precious keveer!
How was it I got that kick o' the 'ed?
I've ad a slight hindisposition
But a Beak ain't no Physician.
Wot's this 'ere, sir? wot's this 'ere?
You call yerself a gentleman? yer Snob!
He was n't bled:
And I was let in for forty bob,
Or a month, instead:
And I caught the lumbago in the brain—
I've been confined—
But never you mind—
Ho, ho, ho, ho, ho, ho! I ain't hinsane.

Vot his this 'ere? Can't no one tell?
It sets my ed a spinnin—
The QUEEN's eye winks—it ain't no sell—
The QUEEN's 'ed keeps a grinnin:
Ha, ha! 't was guv
By the cove I druv—
I vunders for wot e meant it!
For e sez to me,
E sez, sez e,
As I ort to be contented!
Wot did yer say, sir, wot did yer say?
My fare!—wot, that!
Yer knocks me flat.
Hit in the vind!—I'm chokin—give us air—
My fare? Ha, ha! My fare? Ho, ho! My fare?

Call that my fare for drivin yer a mile?
I ain't hinsane—not yet—not yet avile!
    Wot makes yer smile?
My blood is bilin' in a wiolent manner!
    Wot 's this I 've got?
    Show us a light—
    This 'ere is—wot?—
There 's sunthin the matter with my sight—
    It is—yes!—No!—
    'Tis, raly, though—
    Oh, blow! blow! blow!—
Ho, ho, ho, ho! it is, it is a Tanner!*

ALARMING PROSPECT

PUNCH.

To the Editor of "PUNCH."

SIR—You are aware, of course, that in the progress of a few centuries the language of a country undergoes a great alteration; that the Latin of the Augustan age was very different from that of the time of Tarquin; and no less so from that which prevailed at the fall of the Roman empire. Also, that the Queen's English is not precisely what it was in Elizabeth's days; to say nothing of its variation from what was its condition under the Plantagenets.

I observe, with regret, that our literature is becoming conversational, and our conversation corrupt. The use of cant phraseology is daily gaining ground among us, and this evil will speedily infect, if it has not already infected, the productions of our men of letters. I fear most for our poetry, because what is vulgarly termed *slang* is unfortunately very expressive, and therefore peculiarly adapted for the purposes of those whose aim it is to clothe "thoughts that breathe" in "words that burn;" and, besides, it is in many instances equivalent to terms and forms of speech which have long been recognized among poetical writers as a kind of current coin.

The peril which I anticipate I have endeavored to exemplify in the following

AFFECTING COPY OF VERSES (WITH NOTES).

GENTLY o'er the meadows prigging,[1]
  Joan and Colin took their way,
While each flower the dew was swigging,[2]
  In the jocund month of May.

Joan was beauty's plummiest[3] daughter;
  Colin youth's most nutty[4] son;
Many a nob[5] in vain had sought her—
  Him full many a spicy[6] one.

She her faithful bosom's jewel
  Did unto this young un'[7] plight;
But, alas! the gov'nor[8] cruel,
  Said as how he'd never fight.[9]

Soon as e'er the lark had risen,
  They had burst the bonds of snooze,[10]
And her daddle[11] link'd in his'n,[12]
  Gone to roam as lovers use.

In a crack[13] the youth and maiden
  To a flowery bank did come,
Whence the bees cut,[14] honey-laden,
  Not without melodious hum.

Down they squatted[15] them together,
  "Lovely Joan," said Colin bold,
"Tell me, on thy davy,[16] whether
  Thou dost dear thy Colin hold?"

"Don't I, just?"[17] with look ecstatic,
  Cried the young and ardent maid;
"Then let's bolt!"[18] in tone emphatic,
  Bumptuous[19] Colin quickly said.

"Bolt?" she falter'd, "from the gov'nor?
  Oh! my Colin, that won't pay;[20]
He will ne'er come down,[21] my love, nor
  Help us, if we run away."

"Shall we then be disunited?"
  Wildly shrieked the frantic cove;[22]
"Mull'd[23] our happiness! and blighted
  In the kinchin-bud[24] our love!

"No, my tulip![25] let us rather
  Hand in hand the bucket kick;[26]
Thus we'll chouse[27] your cruel father—
  Cutting from the world our stick!"[28]

Thus he spoke, and pull'd a knife out,
  Sharp of point, of edge full fine;
Pierc'd her heart, and let the life out—
  "Now," he cried, "here's into mine!"[29]

But a hand unseen behind him
  Did the fatal blow arrest.
Oh, my eye![30] they seize and bind him—
  Gentle Muse, conceal the rest!

In the precints of the prison,
  In his cold crib[31] Colin lies;
Mourn his fate all you who listen,
  Draw it mild, and mind your eyes![32]

1. "Prigging," stealing; as yet exclusively applied to petty larceny. "Stealing" is as well known to be a poetical term as it is to be an indictable offense: the Zephyr and the Vesper Hymn, *cum multis aliis*, are very prone to this practice.

2. "Swigging," drinking copiously—of malt liquor in particular. "Pearly drops of dew we drink."—OLD SONG.

3. "Plummiest," the superlative of "plummy," exquisitely delicious; an epithet commonly used by young gentlemen in speaking of a *bonne bouche* or "tit bit," as a mince pie, a preserved apricot, or an oyster patty. The transference of terms expressive of delightful and poignant savor to female beauty, is common with poets. "Death, that hath sucked the *honey of thy breath.*"—SHAKSPEARE. "Charley loves a pretty girl, *as sweet as sugar candy.*"—ANON.

4. "Nutty," proper—in the old English sense of "comely," "handsome." "Six *proper* youths, and tall."—OLD SONG.

5. "Nob," a person of consequence; a word very likely to be patronized, from its combined brevity and significancy.

6. "Spicy," very smart and pretty; it has the same recommendation, and will probably supplant the old favorite "bonny." "Busk ye, busk ye, my *bonny, bonny* bride."—HAMILTON.

7. "Young 'un," youth, young man. "A *youth* to fortune and to fame unknown."—GRAY.

8. "Gov'nor," or "guv'nor," a contraction of "governor," a father. It will, no doubt, soon supersede sire, which is at present the poetical equivalent for the name of the author of one's existence. See all the poets, *passim.*

9. "Said as how he'd never fight," the thing was out of the question; a metaphorical phrase, though certainly, at present, a vulgar one.

10. "Snooze," slumber personified, like "Morpheus," or "Somnus."

11. "Daddle."—Q. from δάκτυλος, a finger—*pars pro toto?*—Hand, the only synonym for it that we have, except "Paw," "Mawley," &c., which are decidedly *generis ejusdem.*

12. "His'n," his own; corresponding to the Latin *suus*, his own and nobody else's, so frequently met with in OVID and others.

13. "Crack," a twinkling, an extremely short interval of time, which was formerly expressed, in general, by a periphrasis; as, "Ere the leviathan can swim a league!"—SHAKSPEARE.

14. "Cut," sped. A synonym.

15. "Squatted," sat. Id.

16. "Davy," affidavit, solemn oath. Significant and euphonious, therefore alluring to the versifier.

17. "Don't I, just?" A question for a strong affirmation, as, "Oh, yes, indeed I do;" a piece of popular rhetoric, pithy and forcible and consequently almost sure to be adopted—especially by the pathetic writers.

18. "Bolt," run away. Syn.

19. "Bumptious," fearless, bold, and spirited; a very energetic expression; such as those rejoice in who would fair "*Denham's* strength with Waller's sweetness join."

20. "That won't pay," that plan will never answer. Metaph.

21. "Come down," disburse; also rendered in the vernacular by "fork out," etc. Id.

22. "Cove," swain. "Alexis shunn'd his fellow *swains*."—PRIOR. See also SHENSTONE *passim*.

23. "Mull'd," equivalent to "wreck'd," a term of pathos.

24. "Kinchin-bud," infant-bud. Metaph.; moreover, very tender, sweet, and touching, as regards the idea.

25. "My tulip," a term of endearment. "Fairest *flower*, all flowers excelling." *Ode to a Child:* COTTON.

26. "The bucket kick," pleonasm for die; as, "to breathe life's latest sigh."—"To yield the soul,"—"the breath,"—or, *ut apud antiq.* "Animam expirare," seu "efflare," etc.

27. "Chouse," cheat. Syn.

28. "Cutting . . . our stick." Pleon. ut supra.

29. "Here's unto mine!" A form of speech analogous to "Have at thee."—SHAKSPEARE, and the dramatists generally.

30. "Oh, my eye!" an interjectional phrase, tantamount to "Oh, heavens!" "Merciful powers!" etc.

31. "Cold crib," cold bed. "Go to thy cold bed and warm thee."—SHAK.

32. "Draw it mild," etc. Metaph. for "Rule your passions, and beware!"

I doubt not that it will be admitted by your judicious readers that I have substantiated my case. Our monarchical institutions may preserve our native tongue for a time, but if it does not become, at no very distant period, as strange a medley as that of the American is at present—to use the expressive but peculiar idiom of that people—"*it's a pity.*"

I am, sir, etc., P.

EPITAPH ON A LOCOMOTIVE.

BY THE SOLE SURVIVOR OF A DEPLORABLE ACCIDENT (NO BLAME TO BE ATTACHED TO ANY SERVANTS OF THE COMPANY).

PUNCH.

COLLISIONS four
Or five she bore,
The Signals wor in vain;
Grown old and rusted,
Her biler busted,
And smash'd the Excursion Train.

"HER END WAS PIECES."

THE TICKET OF LEAVE.

[AS SUNG BY THE HOLDER, AMID A CONVIVIAL CIRCLE IN THE SLUMS.]

PUNCH.

VEN a prig has come to grief,
He 's no call for desperation;
Though I 'm a conwicted thief,
Still I 've opes of liberation.
The Reverend Chapling to deceive
A certain dodge and safe resource is,
Whereby you gets a Ticket of Leave,
And then resumes your wicious courses.

(*Spoken.*) I vos lagged, my beloved pals, on a suspicion of burglary, 'ad up afore the Recorder, and got seven years' penal serwitude and 'ard labor. Hand preshus 'ard labor and 'ard lines I found it at first, mind you. Vell, I says to myself, blow me! I ain't a goin' to stand this 'ere, you know; but 'taint no use kickin' agin stone walls and iron spikes: wot I shall try and do is to gammon the parson.

"Ven a prig," etc.

Them parsons is so jolly green,
They 're sure to trust in your conwersion,
Which they, in course, believes 'as been
The consequence of their exertion.
You shakes your 'ead, turns up your eyes,
And they takes that to be repentance;
Wherein you moans, and groans, and sighs,
By reason only of your sentence.

(*Spoken.*) Wen in a state of wiolent prespiration smokin' 'ot from the crank, the Chapling comes into my cell, and he says, says he, "My man," he says, "how do you feel?" "'Appy, sir," says I, with a gentle sithe; "thank you, sir: quite 'appy." "But you seem distressed, my poor fellow," says he. "In body, sir," says I; "yes. But that makes me more 'appy. I'm glad to be distressed in body. It serves me right. But in mind I'm 'appy: leastways almost 'appy." "'Ave you hany wish to express," says he; "is there any request as you would like to make." "'AWKER'S *Hevening Potion*, sir," says I, "and the *Dairyman's Daughter:* if 'AWKER'S *Hevening Potion* was but mine—and the *Dairyman's Daughter*—I think, sir, I should be quite 'appy." "My friend," says the parson, "your desire shall be attended to," and hout he valked: me a takin' a sight at 'im be'ind 'is back; for as soon as I thought he wos out of 'earin', sings I to myself—

"Ven a prig," etc

In the chapel hof the Jug,
Then I did the meek and lowly,

Pullin' sitch a spoony mug
  That I looked unkimmon pure and 'oly.
As loud as ever I could shout,
  All the responses too I hutter'd,
Well knowing what I was about:
  So the reverend Gent I buttered.

(*Spoken.*) Won day he comes to me arter service, and axes me what I thought I could do for myself in the way of yarnin a honest liveliwood, if so be as I was to be allowed my liberty and to go back to the world. "Ah! sir," says I, "I don't think no longer about the world. 'Tis a world of sorrow and wanity. I havn't given a thought to what I should do in it." "Every one," says the Chapling "has his sphere of usefulness in society; can you think of no employment which you have the desire and ability to follow?" "Well, sir," says I "if there is a wocation which I should feel delight and pleasure in follerin' 'tis that of a Scripter Reader. But I ain't worthy to be a Scripter Reader. A coalporter of tracts and religious books, sir, I thinks that's what I should like to try and be, if the time of my just punishment was up. But there's near seven year, sir, to think about that—and p'raps 'tis better for me to be here." That's the way I used to soap the Chapling—Cos vy?

"Ven a prig," etc.

So he thought I kissed the rod,
  All the while my 'art was 'ardened;
And I 'adn't been very long in quod
  Afore he got me as good as pardoned;
And here am I with my Ticket of Leave,
  Obtained by shamming pious feeling,
Which lets me loose again to thieve,
  For I means to persewere in stealing.

(*Spoken.*) With which resolution, my beloved pals, if you please I'll couple the 'elth of the clergy; and may they hever continue to be sitch kind friends as they now shows theirselves to us when we gets into trouble. For,

"Ven a prig," etc.

A POLKA LYRIC.

BARCLAY PHILIPS.

Qui nunc dancere vult modo,
Wants to dance in the fashion, oh!
Discere debet—ought to know,
Kickere floor cum heel and toe,
    One, two, three,
    Hop with me,
Whirligig, twirligig, rapide.

Polkam jungere, Virgo, vis,
Will you join the polka, miss?
Liberius—most willingly,
Sic agimus—then let us try:
Nunc vide,
Skip with me,
Whirlabout, roundabout, celere.

Tum læva cito, tum dextra,
First to the left, and then t' other way;
Aspice retro in vultu,
You look at her, and she looks at you.
Das palmam
Change hands, ma'am;
Celere—run away, just in sham.

A SUNNIT TO THE BIG OX.

COMPOSED WHILE STANDING WITHIN 2 FEET OF HIM, AND A TUCHIN' OF HIM NOW AND THEN.

ANONYMOUS.

All hale! thou mighty annimil—all hale!
You are 4 thousand pounds, and am purty wel
Perporshund, thou tremenjos boveen nuggit!
I wonder how big you was wen you
Wos little, and if yure muther wud no you now
That you 've grone so long, and thick, and phat;
Or if yure father would rekognize his ofspring
And his kaff, thou elefanteen quodrupid!
I wonder if it hurts you mutch to be so big,
And if you grode it in a month or so.
I spose wen you wos young tha did n't gin
You skim milk but all the kreme you kud stuff
Into your little stummick, jest to see
How big yude gro; and afterward tha no doubt
Fed you on otes and ha and sich like,
With perhaps an occasional punkin or squosh!
In all probability yu don't no yure enny
Bigger than a small kaff; for if you did,

Yude brake down fences and switch your tail,
And rush around, and hook, and beller,
And run over fowkes, thou orful beast.
O, what a lot of mince pize yude maik,
And sassengers, and your tale,
Whitch kan't wa fur from phorty pounds,
Wud maik nigh unto a barrel of ox-tail soop,
And cudn't a heep of stakes be cut oph yu,
Whitch, with salt and pepper and termater
Ketchup, wouldn't be bad to taik.
Thou grate and glorious inseckt!
But I must klose, O most prodijus reptile!
And for mi admirashun of yu, when yu di,
I'le rite a node unto yore peddy and remanes,
Pernouncin' yu the largest of yure race;
And as I don't expect to have a half a dollar
Agin to spare for to pa to look at yu, and as
I ain't a ded head, I will sa, farewell.

ENIGMATIC.

ENIGMATIC.

RIDDLES BY MATTHEW PRIOR.

TWO RIDDLES.

Sphinx was a monster that would eat
Whatever stranger she could get;
Unless his ready wit disclos'd
The subtle riddle she propos'd.
Œdipus was resolv'd to go,
And try what strength of parts would do.
Says Sphinx, on this depends your fate;
Tell me what animal is that
Which has four feet at morning bright,
Has two at noon and three at night?
'Tis man, said he, who, weak by nature,
At first creeps, like his fellow creature,
Upon all-four; as years accrue,
With sturdy steps he walks on two;
In age, at length, grows weak and sick,
For his third leg adopts a stick.
Now, in your turn, 'tis just methinks,
You should resolve me, Madam Sphinx.
What greater stranger yet is he
Who has four legs, then two, then three;
Then loses one, then gets two more,
And runs away at last on four?

ENIGMA.

By birth I'm a slave, yet can give you a crown,
I dispose of all honors, myself having none:
I'm obliged by just maxims to govern my life,
Yet I hang my own master, and lie with his wife.

When men are a-gaming I cunningly sneak,
And their cudgels and shovels away from them take.
Fair maidens and ladies I by the hand get,
And pick off their diamonds, tho' ne'er so well set.
For when I have comrades we rob in whole bands,
Then presently take off your lands from your hands.
But, this fury once over, I 've such winning arts,
That you love me much more than you do your own hearts.

ANOTHER.

Form'd half beneath, and half above the earth,
We sisters owe to art our second birth:
The smith's and carpenter's adopted daughters,
Made on the land, to travel on the waters.
Swifter they move, as they are straiter bound,
Yet neither tread the air, or wave, or ground:
They serve the poor for use, the rich for whim,
Sink when it rains, and when it freezes swim.

RIDDLES BY DEAN SWIFT AND HIS FRIENDS.*

A MAYPOLE.

Deprived of root, and branch, and rind,
Yet flowers I bear of every kind:
And such is my prolific power,
They bloom in less than half an hour;
Yet standers-by may plainly see
They get no nourishment from me.

* The following notice is subjoined to some of those riddles, in the Dublin edition; "About nine or ten years ago (*i. e.* about 1724), some ingenious gentlemen, friends to the author, used to entertain themselves with writing riddles, and send them to him and their other acquaintance; copies of which ran about, and some of them were printed, both here and in England. The author, at his leisure hours, fell into the same amusement; although it be said that he thought them of no great merit, entertainment, or use. However, by the advice of some persons, for whom the author has a great esteem, and who were pleased to send us the copies, we have ventured to print the few following, as we have done two or three before, and which are allowed to be genuine; because we are informed that several good judges have a taste for such kind of compositions."

My head with giddiness goes round,
And yet I firmly stand my ground;
All over naked I am seen,
And painted like an Indian queen.
No couple-beggar in the land
E'er join'd such numbers hand in hand.
I join'd them fairly with a ring;
Nor can our parson blame the thing.
And though no marriage words are spoke,
They part not till the ring is broke:
Yet hypocrite fanatics cry,
I 'm but an idol raised on high;
And once a weaver in our town,
A damn'd Cromwellian, knock'd me down.
I lay a prisoner twenty years,
And then the jovial cavaliers
To their old post restored all three—
I mean the church, the king, and me.

ON THE MOON.

I with borrowed silver shine,
What you see is none of mine.
First I show you but a quarter,
Like the bow that guards the Tartar:
Then the half, and then the whole,
Ever dancing round the pole.

What will raise your admiration,
I am not one of God's creation,
But sprung (and I this truth maintain),
Like Pallas, from my father's brain.
And after all, I chiefly owe
My beauty to the shades below.
Most wondrous forms you see me wear,
A man, a woman, lion, bear,
A fish, a fowl, a cloud, a field,
All figures heaven or earth can yield;
Like Daphne sometimes in a tree;
Yet am not one of all you see.

ON INK.

I am jet black, as you may see,
The son of pitch and gloomy night;
Yet all that know me will agree,
I 'm dead except I live in light.

Sometimes in panegyric high,
Like lofty Pindar, I can soar,
And raise a virgin to the sky,
Or sink her to a filthy ——.

My blood this day is very sweet,
To-morrow of a bitter juice;
Like milk, 'tis cried about the street,
And so applied to different use.

Most wondrous is my magic power:
For with one color I can paint;
I'll make the devil a saint this hour,
Next make a devil of a saint.

Through distant regions I can fly,
Provide me but with paper wings;
And fairly show a reason why
There should be quarrels among kings;

And, after all, you 'll think it odd,
When learned doctors will dispute,
That I should point the word of God,
And show where they can best confute.

Let lawyers bawl and strain their throats
'Tis I that must the lands convey,
And strip their clients to their coats;
Nay, give their very souls away.

ON A CIRCLE.

I 'm up and down, and round about,
Yet all the world can't find me out;
Though hundreds have employ'd their leisure,
They never yet could find my measure.

I 'm found almost in every garden,
Nay, in the compass of a farthing.
There 's neither chariot, coach, nor mill,
Can move an inch except I will.

ON A PEN.

In youth exalted high in air,
Or bathing in the waters fair,
Nature to form me took delight,
And clad my body all in white.
My person tall, and slender waist,
On either side with fringes graced;
Till me that tyrant man espied,
And dragg'd me from my mother's side;
No wonder now I look so thin;
The tyrant stript me to the skin:
My skin he flay'd, my hair he cropt:
At head and foot my body lopt:
And then, with heart more hard than stone,
He pick'd my marrow from the bone.
To vex me more, he took a freak
To slit my tongue and make me speak:
But, that which wonderful appears,
I speak to eyes, and not to ears.
He oft employs me in disguise,
And makes me tell a thousand lies:
To me he chiefly gives in trust
To please his malice or his lust.
From me no secret he can hide:
I see his vanity and pride:
And my delight is to expose
His follies to his greatest foes.
All languages I can command,
Yet not a word I understand.
Without my aid, the best divine
In learning would not know a line:
The lawyer must forget his pleading;
The scholar could not show his reading.
Nay; man my master is my slave;
I give command to kill or save.

Can grant ten thousand pounds a-year,
And make a beggar's brat a peer.
But, while I thus my life relate,
I only hasten on my fate.
My tongue is black, my mouth is furr'd,
I hardly now can force a word.
I die unpitied and forgot,
And on some dunghill left to rot.

A FAN.

From India's burning clime I'm brought,
With cooling gales like zephyrs fraught.
Not Iris, when she paints the sky,
Can show more different hues than I:
Nor can she change her form so fast,
I'm now a sail, and now a mast.
I here am red, and there am green,
A beggar there, and here a queen.
I sometimes live in a house of hair,
And oft in hand of lady fair.
I please the young, I grace the old,
And am at once both hot and cold
Say what I am then, if you can,
And find the rhyme, and you're the man.

ON A CANNON.

Begotten, and born, and dying with noise,
The terror of women, and pleasure of boys,
Like the fiction of poets concerning the wind,
I'm chiefly unruly when strongest confined.
For silver and gold I don't trouble my head,
But all I delight in is pieces of lead;
Except when I trade with a ship or a town,
Why then I make pieces of iron go down.
One property more I would have you remark,
No lady was ever more fond of a spark;
The moment I get one my soul's all a-fire,
And I roar out my joy, and in transport expire.

ON THE FIVE SENSES.

All of us in one you 'll find,
Brethren of a wondrous kind;
Yet among us all no brother
Knows one title of the other;
We in frequent counsels are,
And our marks of things declare,
Where, to us unknown, a clerk
Sits, and takes them in the dark.
He 's the register of all
In our ken, both great and small;
By us forms his laws and rules,
He 's our master, we his tools;
Yet we can with greatest ease
Turn and wind him where you please.
One of us alone can sleep,
Yet no watch the rest will keep,
But the moment that he closes,
Every brother else reposes.
If wine's bought or victuals drest,
One enjoys them for the rest.
Pierce us all with wounding steel,
One for all of us will feel.
Though ten thousand cannons roar,
Add to them ten thousand more,
Yet but one of us is found
Who regards the dreadful sound.

ON SNOW.

From Heaven I fall, though from earth I begin.
No lady alive can show such a skin.
I 'm bright as an angel, and light as a feather,
But heavy and dark, when you squeeze me together.
Though candor and truth in my aspect I bear,
Yet many poor creatures I help to insnare.
Though so much of Heaven appears in my make,
The foulest impressions I easily take.
My parent and I produce one another,
The mother the daughter, the daughter the mother.

ON A CANDLE.

Of all inhabitants on earth,
To man alone I owe my birth,
And yet the cow, the sheep, the bee,
Are all my parents more than he:
I, a virtue, strange and rare,
Make the fairest look more fair;
And myself, which yet is rarer,
Growing old, grow still the fairer.
Like sots, alone I'm dull enough,
When dosed with smoke, and smear'd with snuff;
But, in the midst of mirth and wine,
I with double luster shine.
Emblem of the Fair am I,
Polish'd neck, and radiant eye;
In my eye my greatest grace,
Emblem of the Cyclops' race;
Metals I like them subdue,
Slave like them to Vulcan too;
Emblem of a monarch old,
Wise, and glorious to behold;
Wasted he appears, and pale,
Watching for the public weal:
Emblem of the bashful dame,
That in secret feeds her flame,
Often aiding to impart
All the secrets of her heart;
Various is my bulk and hue,
Big like Bess, and small like Sue:
Now brown and burnish'd like a nut,
At other times a very slut;
Often fair, and soft and tender,
Taper, tall, and smooth, and slender:
Like Flora, deck'd with various flowers,
Like Phœbus, guardian of the hours:
But whatever be my dress,
Greater be my size or less,
Swelling be my shape or small,
Like thyself I shine in all.
Clouded if my face is seen,
My complexion wan and green,

Languid like a love-sick maid,
Steel affords me present aid.
Soon or late, my date is done,
As my thread of life is spun;
Yet to cut the fatal thread
Oft revives my drooping head;
Yet I perish in my prime,
Seldom by the death of time;
Die like lovers as they gaze,
Die for those I live to please;
Pine unpitied to my urn,
Nor warm the fair for whom I burn;
Unpitied, unlamented too,
Die like all that look on you.

ON A CORKSCREW.

Though I, alas! a prisoner be,
My trade is prisoners to set free.
No slave his lord's commands obeys
With such insinuating ways.
My genius piercing, sharp, and bright,
Wherein the men of wit delight.
The clergy keep me for their ease,
And turn and wind me as they please.
A new and wondrous art I show
Of raising spirits from below;
In scarlet some, and some in white;
They rise, walk round, yet never fright.
In at each mouth the spirits pass,
Distinctly seen as through a glass.
O'er head and body make a rout,
And drive at last all secrets out;
And still, the more I show my art,
The more they open every heart.
  A greater chemist none than I
Who, from materials hard and dry,
Have taught men to extract with skill
More precious juice than from a still.
  Although I'm often out of case,
I'm not ashamed to show my face.

Though at the tables of the great
I near the sideboard take my seat;
Yet the plain 'squire, when dinner 's done,
Is never pleased till I make one;
He kindly bids me near him stand,
And often takes me by the hand.
 I twice a-day a-hunting go,
And never fail to seize my foe;
And when I have him by the poll,
I drag him upward from his hole;
Though some are of so stubborn kind,
I 'm forced to leave a limb behind.
 I hourly wait some fatal end;
For I can break, but scorn to bend.

AN ECHO.

Never sleeping, still awake,
Pleasing most when most I speak;
The delight of old and young,
Though I speak without a tongue.
Nought but one thing can confound me,
Many voices joining round me;
Then I fret, and rave, and gabble,
Like the laborers of Babel.
Now I am a dog, or cow,
I can bark, or I can low;
I can bleat, or I can sing,
Like the warblers of the spring.
Let the love-sick bard complain,
And I mourn the cruel pain;
Let the happy swain rejoice,
And I join my helping voice:
Both are welcome, grief or joy,
I with either sport and toy.
Though a lady, I am stout,
Drums and trumpets bring me out:
Then I clash, and roar, and rattle,
Join in all the din of battle.
Jove, with all his loudest thunder,
When I 'm vexed can't keep me under;

Yet so tender is my ear,
That the lowest voice I fear;
Much I dread the courtier's fate,
When his merit 's out of date,
For I hate a silent breath,
And a whisper is my death.

ON THE VOWELS.

We are little airy creatures,
All of different voice and features;
One of us in glass is set,
One of us you 'll find in jet.
T' other you may see in tin,
And the fourth a box within.
If the fifth you should pursue,
It can never fly from you.

ON A PAIR OF DICE.

We are little brethren twain,
Arbiters of loss and gain,
Many to our counters run,
Some are made, and some undone:
But men find it to their cost,
Few are made, but numbers lost.
Though we play them tricks forever,
Yet they always hope our favor.

ON A SHADOW IN A GLASS.

By something form'd, I nothing am,
Yet every thing that you can name;
In no place have I ever been,
Yet everywhere I may be seen;
In all things false, yet always true,
I 'm still the same—but ever new.
Lifeless, life's perfect form I wear,
Can show a nose, eye, tongue, or ear,
Yet neither smell, see, taste, nor hear.

All shapes and features I can boast,
No flesh, no bones, no blood—no ghost:
All colors, without paint, put on,
And change, like the chameleon.
Swiftly I come, and enter there,
Where not a chink lets in the air;
Like thought, I'm in a moment gone,
Nor can I ever be alone:
All things on earth I imitate
Faster than nature can create;
Sometimes imperial robes I wear,
Anon in beggar's rags appear;
A giant now, and straight an elf,
I'm every one, but ne'er myself;
Ne'er sad I mourn, ne'er glad rejoice,
I move my lips, but want a voice;
I ne'er was born, nor ne'er can die,
Then, pr'ythee, tell me what am I?

ON TIME.

Ever eating, ever cloying,
All-devouring, all-destroying
Never finding full repast,
Till I eat the world at last.

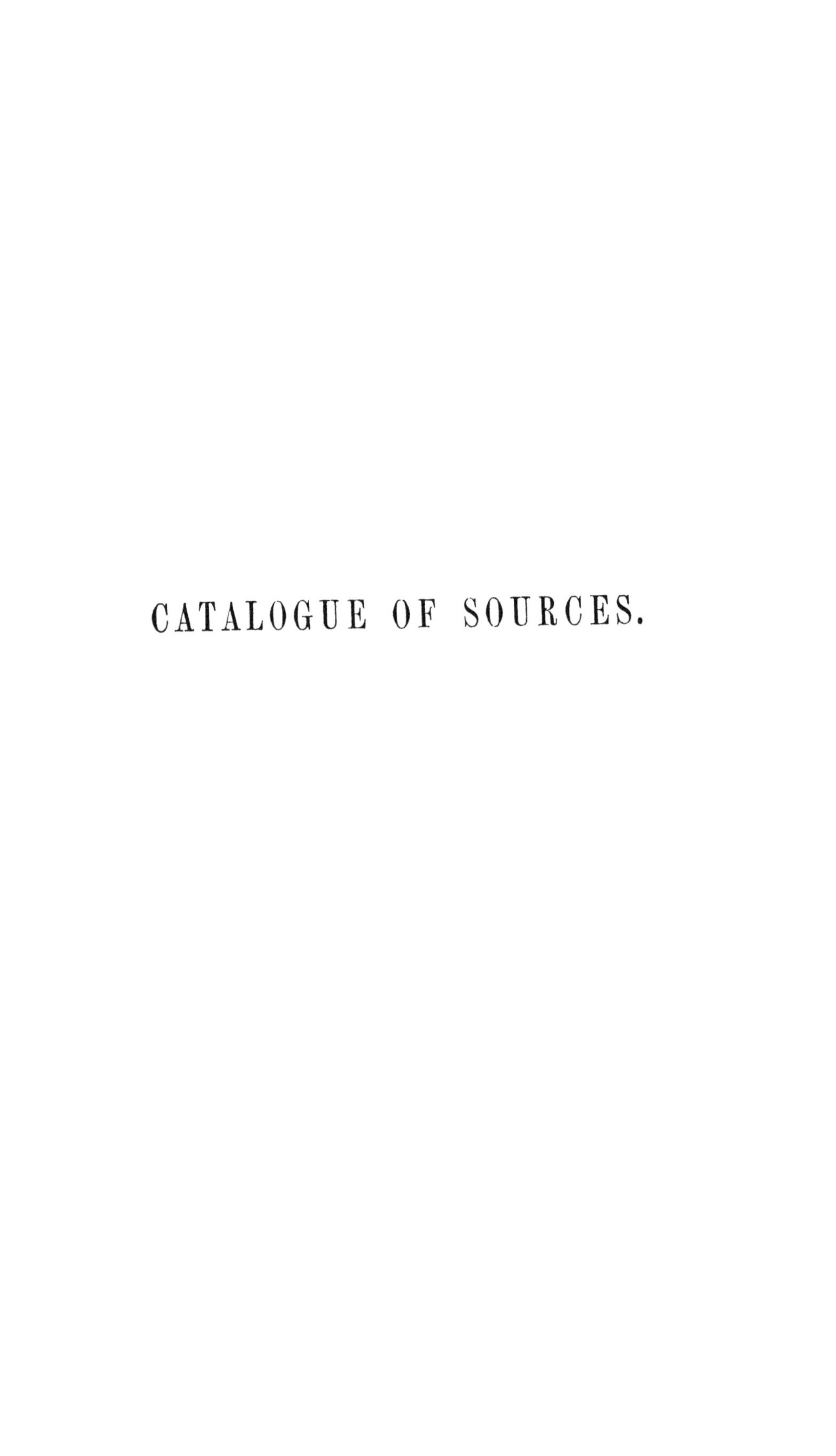

CATALOGUE OF SOURCES.

CATALOGUE OF SOURCES.

ADDISON, JOSEPH—The Essayist of the "Spectator;" born 1632; died 1708. Addison, though one of the most celebrated of English humorists, wrote scarcely a line of humorous verse. See p. 538.

ALLINGHAM, WILLIAM—An American writer; contributor to "Putnam's Magazine;" author of a volume of poems recently published in Hartford. See p. 70.

ANONYMOUS—To Punch's Almanac, for 1856, we are indebted for an account of this prolific writer:

Of ANON," says Punch, "but little is known, though his works are excessively numerous. He has dabbled in every thing. Prose and Poetry are alike familiar to his pen. One moment he will be up the highest flights of philosophy, and the next he will be down in some kitchen garden of literature, culling an Enormous Gooseberry, to present it to the columns of some provincial newspaper. His contributions are scattered wherever the English language is read. Open any volume of Miscellanies at any place you will, and you are sure to fall upon some choice little bit signed by 'Anon.' What a mind his must have been! It took in every thing like a pawnbroker's shop. Nothing was too trifling for its grasp. Now he was hanging on to the trunk of an elephant and explaining to you how it was more elastic than a pair of India-rubber braces; and next he would be constructing a suspension bridge with a series of monkey's tails, tying them together as they do pocket-handkerchiefs in the gallery of a theater when they want to fish up a bonnet that has fallen into the pit.

"Anon is one of our greatest authors. If all the things which are signed with Anon's name were collected on rows of shelves, he would require a British Museum all to himself. And yet of this great man so little is known that we are not even acquainted with his Christian name. There is no certificate of baptism, no moldy tombstone, no musty washing-bill in the world on which we can hook the smallest line of speculation whether it was John, or James, or Joshua, or Tom, or Dick, or Billy Anon. Shame that a man should write so much, and yet be known so little. Oblivion uses its snuffers, sometimes, very unjustly. On second thoughts, perhaps, it is as well that the works of Anon were not collected together. His reputation for consistency would not probably be increased by the collection. It would be found that frequently he had contradicted himself—that in many instances when he had been warmly upholding the Christian white of a question he had afterward turned round, and maintained with equal warmth the Pagan black of it. He might often be discovered on both sides of a truth, jumping boldly from the right side over to the wrong, and flinging big stones at any one who dared to assail him in either position. Such double-sidedness would not be pretty, and yet we should be lenient to such inconsistencies. With one who had written so many thousand volumes, who had twirled his thoughts as with a mop on every possible subject, how was it possible to expect any thing like consistency? How was it likely that he could recollect every little atom out of the innumerable atoms his pen had heaped up?

"Anon ought to have been rich, but he lived in an age when piracy was the fashion, and when booksellers walked about, as it were, like Indian chiefs, with the skulls of the authors they had slain, hung round their necks. No wonder, therefore, that we know nothing of the wealth of Anon. Doubtless he died in a garret, like many other kindred spirits, Death being the only score out of the many knocking at his door that he could pay. But to his immortal credit let it be said he has filled more libraries than the most generous patrons of literature. The volumes that formed the fuel of the barbarians' bonfire at Alexandria would be but a small book-stall by the side of the octavos, quartos, and duodecimos he has pyramidized on our book-shelves. Look through any catalogue you will, and you will find that a large proportion of the works in it have been contributed by Anon. The only author who can in the least compete with him in fecundity is Ibid." See pp. 569, 570, 571, 572, 584, 587, 646.

ANTI-JACOBIN, THE—Perhaps the most famous collection of Political Satires extant. Originated by Canning in 1797, it appeared in the form of a weekly newspaper, interspersed with poetry, the avowed object of which was to expose the vicious doctrines of the French Revolution, and to hold up to ridicule and contempt the advocates of that event, and the sticklers for peace and parliamentary reform. The editor was William Gifford, the vigorous and unscrupulous critic and poetaster the writers, Mr. John Hookham Frere, Mr. Jenkinson (afterward Earl of Liverpool); Mr. George

Ellis, Lord Clare, Lord Mornington (afterward Marquis Wellesley), Lord Morpeth (afterward Earl of Carlisle), Baron Macdonald, and others. These gentlemen spared no means, fair or foul, in their attempts to blacken their adversaries. Their most distinguished countrymen, if opposed to the Tory government of the time being, were treated with no more respect than foreign adversaries, and were held up to public execration as traitors, blasphemers, and debauchees. The period was one of great political excitement, a fierce war with republican France being in progress, the necessity for which divided the public into two great parties; national credit being affected, the Bank of England suspending cash payments, mutinies breaking out in the fleets at Spithead and the Nore, and Ireland at the verge of rebellion. Spain, also, had declared war against Britain, which was thus left to contend singly against the power of France. Party feeling running very high, the anti-Jacobins were by no means discriminating in their attacks, associating men together who really had nothing in common. Hence the reader is surprised to find Charles Lamb and other non-intruders into politics, figuring as congenial conspirators with Tom Paine. Fox, Sheridan, Erskine, and other eloquent liberals of the day, with Tierney, Horne Tooke, and Coleridge were at the same time writing and talking in the opposite extreme, and little quarter was given—certainly none on the part of the Tory wits. The poetry of the "Anti-Jacobin," however, was not exclusively political, comprising also parodies and burlesques on the current literature of the day, some being of the highest degree of merit, and distinguished by sharp wit and broad humor of the happiest kind. In these, Canning and his coadjutors did a real service to letters, and assisted in a purification which Gifford, by his demolition of the Della Cruscan school of poetry had so well begun. Perhaps no lines in the English language have been more effective or oftener quoted than Canning's "*Friend of Humanity and the Knife Grinder.*" Many of the celebrated caricatures of Gilray were originally designed to illustrate the Poetry of the Anti-Jacobin. It had, however, but a brief, though brilliant existence. Wilberforce and others of the more moderate supporters of the ministry became alarmed at the boldness of the language employed. Pitt (himself a contributor to the journal), was induced to interfere, and after a career of eight months, the "Anti-Jacobin" (in its original form), ceased to be. See pp. 384, 386, 387.

AYTOUN, WILLIAM—Professor of Polite Literature in the Edinburg University: editor of "Blackwood's Magazine:" son-in-law of the late Professor Wilson. Professor Aytoun was bred to the bar but, we believe, never came into practice. He is the author of several humorous pieces, and of many in which the intention to be humorous was not realized. He is what the English call a very *clever* man. Like many others who excel in ridicule and sarcasm, he is devoid of that kind of moral principle which makes a writer prefer the Just to the Dashing. Aytoun is a fierce Tory in politics—a snob on principle. The specimens of his humorous poetry contained in this collection were taken from the "Ballads of Bon Gaultier," and the "Idées Napoléoniennes," editions of both of which have been published in this country. See pp. 181, 345, 347, 503, 504, 506, 507, 510, 511, 512, 513, 514, 516, 576.

BARHAM, REV. RICHARD HARRIS—Author of the celebrated "Ingoldsby Legends," published originally in "Bentley's Miscellany," afterward collected and published in three volumes, with a memoir by a son of the author.

Mr. Barham was born at Canterbury, England, December 6th, 1788. His family is of great antiquity, having given its name to the well-known "Barham Downs," between Dover and Canterbury. He was educated at St. Paul's School in Canterbury, where he made the acquaintance of Richard Bentley, who afterward became his publisher. From this school, he went to Oxford, entering Brazennose College, as a gentleman commoner, where he met Theodore Hook, and formed a friendship with that prince of wits which terminated only with Hook's life. At the University, Barham led a wild, dissipated life—as the bad custom then was—and was noted as a wit and good fellow. Being called to account, on one occasion, by his tutor for his continued absence from morning prayer, Barham replied,

"The fact is, sir, you are too *late* for me."

"Too late?" exclaimed the astonished tutor.

"Yes, sir," rejoined the student, "I can not sit up till seven o'clock in the morning. I am a man of regular habits, and unless I get to bed by four or five, I am fit for nothing the next day."

The tutor took this jovial reply seriously, and Barham perceiving that he was really wounded, offered a sincere apology, and afterward attended prayers more regularly.

Entering the church, he devoted himself to his clerical duties with exemplary assiduity, and obtained valuable preferment, rising at length to be one of the Canons of St. Paul's Cathedral. This office brought him into relations with Sydney Smith, with whom, though Barham was a Tory, he had much convivial intercourse.

Very early in life Mr. Barham became an occasional contributor to Blackwood's Magazine, then in the prime of its vigorous youth. The series of contributions called "Family Poetry," which appear in the volumes for 1823, and subsequent years, were by him. Most of those humorous effusions have been transferred to this volume. In 1837 Mr. Bentley established his "Miscellany," and secured the services of his friend Barham, who, up to this time was unknown to the general public, though he had been for nearly twenty years a successful writer. The "Ingoldsby Legends" now appeared in rapid succession, and proved so popular that their author soon became one of the recognized wits of the day. A large number of these unique and excellent productions enrich the present collection. "As respects these poems," says Mr. Barham's biographer, "remarkable as they have been pronounced for the wit and humor which they display, their distinguishing attractions lies in the almost unparalleled flow and felicity of the versification. Popular phrases, sentences the most prosaic, even the cramped technicalities of legal diction, and snatches from well-nigh every language, are wrought in with an apparent absence of all art and effort that surprises, pleases, and convulses the reader at every turn. The author triumphs with a master hand over every variety of stanza, however complicated or exacting; not a word seems out of place, not an expression forced; syllables the most intractable, and the only partners fitted for them throughout the range of language are coupled together as naturally as those kindred spirits which poets tell us were created pairs, and dispersed in space to seek out their particular mates. A harmony pervades the whole, a perfect modulation of numbers, never, perhaps, surpassed, and rarely equaled in compositions of their class. This was the *forte* of Thomas Ingoldsby; a harsh line or untrue rhyme grated on his ear like the Shandean hinge." These observations are just. As a rhymer, Mr. Barham has but one equal in English literature—Byron.

Mr. Barham died at London on the 17th of June, 1845, in the fifty-seventh year of his age. He was an extremely amiable, benevolent character. It does not appear that his love of the humorous was ever allowed to interfere with the performance of his duties as a clergyman. Without being a great preacher, he was a faithful and kindly pastor, never so much in his element as when ministering to the distresses, or healing the differences of his parishioners. Unlike his friend, Sydney Smith, he was singularly fond of the drama, and for many years was a member of the Garrick Club. He was one of the few English writers of humorous verse, *all* of whose writings may be read aloud by a father to his family, and in whose wit there was no admixture of gall. See pp. 41, 44, 125, 129, 136, 146, 156, 164, 282, 287, 417, 418, 419, 568, 569.

"BENTLEY'S MISCELLANY"—A London Monthly Magazine, founded about twenty years ago by Mr. Bentley, the publisher. Charles

Dickens, and the author of the Ingoldsby Legends were among the first contributors. See p. 576.

BLACKWOOD'S MAGAZINE—First appeared in April, 1817. Founded by William Blackwood, a shrewd Edinburgh bookseller. Its literary ability and fierce political partisanship, soon placed it foremost in the ranks of Tory periodicals. Perhaps no magazine has ever achieved such celebrity, or numbered such a host of illustrious contributors. John Wilson, the world-famous "Christopher North," was the virtual, though not nominal editor, Blackwood himself retaining that title. It would be a long task to enumerate all, who, from the days of Sir Walter Scott and the Ettrick Shepherd, to those of Bulwer and Charles Mackay, have appeared in its columns. Maginn, Lockhart, Gillies, Moir, Landor, Wordsworth, Coleridge, Lamb, Bowles, Barry Cornwall, Gleig, Hamilton, Aird, Sym, De Quincey, Allan Cunningham, Mrs. Hemans, Jerrold, Croly, Warren, Ingoldsby (Barham), Elizabeth Barrett Browning, Milnes, and many others, of scarcely less note, found in Blackwood scope for their productions, whether of prose or verse. In its early days much of personality and sarcasm marked its pages, savage onslaughts on Leigh Hunt, and "the Cockney School of Literature," alternating with attacks on the Edinburgh Review, the Quarterly, and all Whigs and Whig productions whatever. The celebrated *Noctes Ambrosianæ*, a series of papers containing probably more learning, wit, eloquence, eccentricity, humor, and personality than have ever appeared elsewhere, formed part of the individuality of Blackwood. They were written by Wilson, Maginn, Lockhart, and Hogg, the two first named (and especially Wilson), having the pre-eminence. To the New York edition of this work, by Dr. Shelton Mackenzie (whose notes contain a perfect mine of information), we refer the reader for further particulars relative to Blackwood. See pp. 410, 412, 414, 587, 588.

BROUGHAM, LORD—The well-known member of the English House of Peers. It seems, from some jocularities attributed to his lordship, that he adds to his many other claims to distinction that of being a man of wit. See p. 580.

BRYANT, WILLIAM CULLEN—The most celebrated of American poets. Editor of the "New York Evening Post." Born 1794. See p. 58.

BURNS, ROBERT—Born 1750, died 1796. The best loved, most national, most independent, truest, and greatest of Scottish poets, of whom to say more here were an impertinence. See pp. 25, 243, 246, 247, 551, 552, 553.

BUTLER, SAMUEL—Born in 1612; the son of a substantial farmer in Worcestershire, England. Very little is known of the earlier portion of his life, as he had reached the age of fifty before he was so much as heard of by his cotemporaries. He appears to have received a good education at the cathedral school of his native county, and to have filled various situations, as clerk in the service of Thomas Jeffries of Earl's Croombe, secretary to the Countess of Kent, and general man of business to Sir Samuel Luke, of Cople Hoo, Bedfordshire, who, it is said, served as the model for his hero, Hudibras. The first part of this singular poem was published at the close of 1662, and met with extraordinary success. Its wit, its quaint sense and learning, its passages of sarcastic reflection on all manner of topics, and above all, its unsparing ridicule of men and things on the Puritan side, combined to render it a general favorite. The reception of Part II., which appeared a year subsequent, was equally flattering. Yet its author seems to have fallen into the greatest poverty and obscurity, from which he never was enabled to emerge. It appears to have been his strange fate to flash all at once into notoriety, which lasted precisely two years, to fill the court and town during that time with continuous laughter, intermingled with inquiries who and what he was, and then for seventeen long years to plod on unknown and unregarded, still hearing his *Hudibras* quoted, and still preparing more of it, or matter similar, with no result. He died, in almost absolute destitution, in 1680, and was buried at a friend's expense, in the church-yard of St. Paul's, Covent Garden. See pp. 199, 527, 528, 529, 530, 531, 532, 533.

BYROM—A noted English Jacobite. Born 1691. See p. 545.

BYRON, GEORGE GORDON NOEL—Born 1788, died in Greece, 1824. Respecting his celebrated Satire on the poet Rogers, which appears in this collection, we read the following in a London periodical:—"The satire on Rogers, by Lord Byron, is not surpassed for cool malignity, dexterous portraiture, and happy imagery, in the whole compass of the English language. It is said, and by those well informed, that Rogers used to bore Byron while in Italy, by his incessant minute dilettantism, and by visits at hours when Byron did not care to see him. One of many wild freaks to repel his unseasonable visits was to set his big dog at him. To a mind like Byron's, here was sufficient provocation for a satire. The subject, too, was irresistible. Other inducements were not wanting. No man indulged himself more in sarcastic remarks on his cotemporaries than Mr. Rogers. He indulged his wit at any sacrifice. He spared no one, and Byron, consequently did not escape. Sarcastic sayings travel on electric wings—and one of Rogers's personal and amusing allusions to Byron reached the ears of the poetic pilgrim at Ravenna. Few characters can bear the microscopic scrutiny of wit. Byron suffered. Fewer characters can bear its microscopic scrutiny when quickened by anger, and Rogers suffered still more severely.

"This, the greatest of modern satirical portraits in verse, was written before their final meeting at Bologna. Rogers was not aware that any saying of his had ever reached the ear of Byron, and Byron never published the verses on Rogers. They met like the handsome women described by Cibber, who, though they wished one another at the devil, are 'My dear,' and 'My dear,' whenever they meet. One doubtless considered his saying as something to be forgotten, and the other his verses as something not to be remembered. These verses are not included in Byron's works, and are very little known." See pp. 33, 34, 311, 567, 568.

CHAUCER lived in the thirteenth century, dying in 1400. He is designated the father of English poetry. The obsolete phraseology of his writings, though presenting a barrier to general appreciation and popularity, will never deter those who truly love the "dainties that are bred in a book" from holding him in affection and reverence. His chief work, the "Canterbury Pilgrimage," "well of English undefiled" as it is, was written in the decline of life, when its author had passed his sixtieth year. For catholicity of spirit, love of nature, purity of thought, pathos, humor, subtle and minute discrimination of character and power of expressing it, Chaucer has one superior—Shakspeare. See p. 21.

CHESTERFIELD, LORD—Born in 1794; died 1773. Courtier, statesman, and man of the world; famous for many things, but known to literature chiefly by his "Letters to his Son," which have formed three generations of "gentlemen," and still exert great influence. Chesterfield was a noted wit in his day, but most of his good things have been lost. See p. 546.

CLEVELAND, JOHN—A political writer of Charles the First's time; author of several satirical pieces, now known only to the curious. He died in 1659. See p. 546.

COLERIDGE, SAMUEL TAYLOR—Poet, plagiarist, and opium-eater. Born at Bristol, in 1770. Died near London in 1834. He was a weak man of genius, whose reputation, formerly immense, has declined since he has been better known. But "Christabel" and the "Ancient Mariner," will charm many generations of readers yet unborn. Most of the epigrams which appear in his works are *adapted* from Lessing. See pp. 104, 557, 558.

COWPER, WILLIAM—The gentle poet of religious England: born 1731; died 1800. Cowper was an elegant humorist, despite the gloominess of his religious belief. It is said, however, that his most comic effusions were written during periods of despondency. See pp. 99, 241, 242.

"CRUIKSHANK'S OMNIBUS"—A monthly Magazine, published at the period of the artist's greatest celebrity, principally as a vehicle for his pencil. Its editor was Laman Blanchard, a lively essayist, and amiable man, whom anticipations of pecuniary distress subsequently goaded to suicide. See pp. 431, 589.

DEVREAUX, S. H.—An American scholar. Translator of "Yriarte's Fables," recently published in Boston. See pp. 239, 241.

ERSKINE, THOMAS—One of the most eminent of English lawyers. Born 1750; died 1823. See p. 559.

FIELDING, HENRY—The great English Humorist; author of "Tom Jones;" born, 1707; died, 1754. See p. 382.

GAY, JOHN—A poet and satirist of the days of Queen Anne. Born 1688; died, 1732. His wit, gentleness, humor, and animal spirits appear to have rendered him a general favorite. In worldly matters he was not fortunate, losing £20,000 by the South Sea bubble; nor did his interest, which was by no means inconsiderable, succeed in procuring him a place at court. He wrote fables, pastorals, the burlesque poem of "Trivia," and plays, the most successful and celebrated of which is the "Beggar's Opera." Of this work there exists a sequel or second part, as full of wit and satire as the original, but much less known. Its performance was suppressed by Walpole, upon whom it was supposed tc reflect. See pp. 215, 350, 590.

GRAY, THOMAS—Author of the "Elegy written in a Country Church-yard;" Professor of Modern History in the University of Cambridge. Born in London, 1716; died, 1771. Gray was learned in History, Architecture, and Natural History. As a poet, he was remarkable for the labor bestowed on his poems, for his reluctance to publish, and for the small number of his compositions. Carlyle thinks he is the only English poet who wrote less than he ought. See p. 97.

HALPIN, ——— —A writer for the press, a resident of New York, author of "Lyrics by the Letter H," published a year or two since by Derby. See pp. 578, 579.

HOLMES, OLIVER WENDELL—A physician of Boston, Professor of Anatomy in Harvard University; born at Cambridge, Mass., in 1809. Dr. Holmes's humorous verses are too well known to require comment in this place. His burlesque, entitled "Evening, by a Tailor," is very excellent of its kind. See pp. 61, 340, 342, 517, 518.

HOOD, THOMAS—Author of the "Song of the Shirt," which Punch had the honor of first publishing. Born in 1798; died in 1845. Hood was the son of a London bookseller, and began life as a clerk. He became afterward an engraver, but was drawn gradually into the literary profession, which he exercised far more to the advantage of his readers than his own. His later years were saddened by ill-health and poverty. Some of his comic verses seem forced and contrived, as though done for needed wages. Hood was one of the literary men who should have made of literature a staff, not a crutch. It was in him to produce, like Lamb, a few very admirable things, the execution of which should have been the pleasant occupation of his leisure, not the toil by which he gained his bread. See pp. 45, 46, 289, 294, 307, 309, 422, 423, 425, 426, 592, 594, 596.

HUNT, JAMES HENRY LEIGH—English Journalist and Poet. Born in 1784. His father was a clergyman of the Established church, and a man of wit and feeling. See p. 583.

JOHNSON, DR. SAMUEL—Born 1709; died 1784. Critic, moralist, lexicographer, and, above all, the hero of Boswell's Life of Johnson. The ponderous philosopher did not disdain, occasionally, to give play to his elephantine wit. See p. 545.

JONSON, BEN—Born 1574; died 1637. Poet, play-wright, and friend of Shakspeare, in whose honor he has left a noble eulogium. A manly, sturdy, laborious, English genius, of whose dramatic productions, however, but one ("Every Man in his Humor") has retained possession of the stage. He is also the author of some exquisite lyrics. See pp. 525, 526.

LAMB, CHARLES—Born in London, 1775; died, 1832. As a humorous essayist, unrivaled and peculiar, he is known and loved by all who are likely to possess this volume. See pp. 29, 566.

LANDOR, WALTER SAVAGE—A living English writer of considerable celebrity, author of "Imaginary Conversations," contributor to several leading periodicals. Mr. Landor is now advanced in years. His humorous verses are few, and not of striking excellence See p. 572.

"LANTERN," THE—A comic weekly, in imitation of "Punch," published in this city a few years ago. The leading spirit of the "Lantern" was Mr. John Brougham, the well-known dramatist and actor. See p. 194.

"LEADER," THE—A London weekly newspaper, of liberal opinions; ably written and badly edited, and, therefore, of limited circulation. See p. 580.

LESSING, GOTTHOLD EPHRAIM—The well-known German author; born 1729; died 1781. The epigrams of Lessing have been so frequently stolen by English writers, that, perhaps, they may now be considered as belonging to English literature, and hence entitled to a place in this collection. At least we found the temptation to add them to our stock irresistible. See pp. 553, 554, 555, 556.

LINDSAY—A friend of Dean Swift. A polite and elegant scholar; an eminent pleader at the bar in Dublin, and afterward advanced to be one of the justices of the Common Pleas. See p. 544.

LOWELL, JAMES RUSSELL—The American Poet. Born at Boston, in the year 1819. To Mr. Lowell must be assigned a high, if not the highest place, among American writers of humorous poetry. The Biglow Papers, from which we have derived several excellent pieces for this volume, is one of the most ingenious and well-sustained *jeux d'esprit* in existence. See pp. 522, 578, 619, 623, 626, 629.

MAPES, WALTER DE—A noted clerical wit of Henry the Second's time. See p. 583.

MOORE, THOMAS—The Irish poet; born at Dublin in the year 1780. Moore has been styled the best writer of political squibs that ever lived. He was employed to write comic verses on passing events, by the conductors of the "London Times," in which journal many of his satirical poems appeared. The political effusions that gave so much delight thirty years ago are, however, scarcely intelligible to the present generation, or if intelligible, not interesting. But Moore wrote many a sprightly stanza, the humor of which does not depend for its effect upon local or cotemporary allusions. This collection contains most of them. See pp. 36, 37, 38, 39, 124, 259, 260, 261, 263, 266, 267, 269, 273, 276, 415, 560, 561, 562, 563, 564, 565.

MORRIS, GEORGE P—The father of polite journalism in this city, and the most celebrated of American Song-writers. Born in Pennsylvania about the beginning of the present century. See p. 196.

"PERCY RELIQUES"—A celebrated collection of ancient ballads, edited by Bishop Percy, a man of great antiquarian knowledge and poetic taste. The publication of the "Percy Reliques" in the last century, introduced the taste for the antique, which was gratified to the utmost by Sir Walter Scott, and which has scarcely yet ceased to rage in some quarters. See pp. 75, 77, 80.

PHILIPS, BARCLAY—A living English writer, of whom nothing is known in this country. See p. 645.

PINDAR, PETER—See Wolcott.

POPE, ALEXANDER—The poet of the time of Queen Anne; author of the "Dunciad," which has been styled the most perfect of satires. Born in London, 1688; died, 1744. See p. 539.

PRAED, WINTHROP MACKWORTH—An English poet, author of "Lillian," born in London about the year 1800. Little is known of Mr. Praed in this country, though it was here that his poems were first collected and published in a volume. His family is of the aristocracy of the city, where some of his surviving relations are still engaged in the business of banking. At Eton, Praed was highly distinguished for his literary talents. He was for some time the editor of "The Etonian," a piquant periodical published by the students. From Eton he went to Cambridge, where he won an unprecedented number of prizes for poems and epigrams in Greek, Latin, and English. On returning to London, he was associated with Thomas Babbington Macaulay in the editorship of "Knight's Quarterly Magazine," after the discontinuance of which he occasionally contributed to the "New Monthly." A few years before his death, Mr. Praed became a member of Parliament, but owing to his love of ease and society, obtained little distinction in that body.

Mr. N. P. Willis thus writes of the poet as he appeared in society: "We chance to have it in our power to say a word as to Mr. Praed's personal appearance, manners, etc. It was our good fortune when first in England (in 1834 or '35), to be a guest at the same hospitable country-house for several weeks. The party there assembled was somewhat a famous one—Miss Jane Porter, Miss Julia Pardoe, Krazinski (the Polish historian), Sir Gardiner Wilkinson (the Oriental traveler), venerable Lady Cork ('Lady Bellair' of D'Israeli's novel), and several persons more distinguished in society than in literature. Praed, we believe, had not been long married, but he was there with his wife. He was apparently about thirty-five, tall, and of dark complexion, with a studious bend in his shoulders, and of irregular features strongly impressed with melancholy.

His manners were particularly reserved, though as unassuming as they could well be. His exquisitely beautiful poem of 'Lillian' was among the pet treasures of the lady of the house, and we had all been indulged with a sight of it, in a choicely bound manuscript copy—but it was hard to make him confess to any literary habits or standing. As a gentleman of ample means and retired life, the kind of notice drawn upon him by the admiration of this poem, seemed distasteful. His habits were very secluded. We only saw him at table and in the evening; and, for the rest of the day, he was away in the remote walks and woods of the extensive park around the mansion, apparently more fond of solitude than of any thing else. Mr. Praed's mind was one of wonderful readiness—rhythm and rhyme coming to him with the flow of an improvisatore. The ladies of the party made the events of every day the subjects of charades, epigrams, sonnets, etc., with the design of suggesting inspiration to his ready pen; and he was most brilliantly complying, with treasures for each in her turn."

Mr. Praed died on the 15th of July, 1839, without having accomplished any thing worthy the promise of his earlier years—another instance of Life's reversing the judgment of College. As a writer of agreeable trifles for the amusement of the drawing-room, he has had few superiors, and it is said that a large number of his impromptu effusions are still in the possession of his friends unpublished. Two editions of his poems have appeared in New York, one by Langley in 1844, and another by Redfield, a few years later. See pp. 50, 52, 313, 316.

PRIOR, MATTHEW—Born 1664; died 1721. A wit and poet of no small genius and good nature—one of the minor celebrities of the days of Queen Anne. His "Town and Country Mouse," written in ridicule of Dryden's famous "Hind and Panther," procured him the appointment of Secretary of Embassy at the Hague, and he subsequently rose to be embassador at Paris. Suffering disgrace with his patrons he was afterward recalled, and received a pension from the University of Oxford, up to the time of his death. See pp. 85, 200, 201, 202, 534, 535, 536, 537, 651, 652.

"PUNCH"—Commenced in July, 1841, making its appearance just at the close of the Whig ministry, under Lord Melbourne, and the accession of the Tories, headed by Sir Robert Peel. Originated by a circle of wits and literary men who frequented the "Shakspeare's Head," a tavern in Wych-street, London. Mark Lemon, the landlord was, and still is, its editor. He is of Jewish descent, and had some reputation for ability with his pen, having been connected with other journals, and also written farces and dramatic pieces. Punch's earliest contributors were Douglas Jerrold, Albert Smith, Gilbert Abbot a'Beckett Hood and Maginn—Thackeray's *debût* occurring in the third volume. It is said that one evening each week was especially devoted to a festive meeting of these writers, where, Lemon presiding, they deliberated as to the conduct and course of the periodical. "Punch," however, was at first not successful, and indeed on the point of being abandoned as a bad speculation, when Messrs. Bradbury and Evans, two aspiring printers, now extensive publishers, purchased it at the very moderate price of one hundred pounds, since which time it has continued their property, and a valuable one. In those days it presented a somewhat different appearance from the present, being more closely printed, finer type used, and the illustrations (with the exception of small, black, *silhouette* cuts, after the style of those in similar French publications), were comparatively scanty. Soon, however, "Punch" throve apace, amply meriting its success. To Henning's drawings (mostly those of a political nature), were added those of Leech, Kenny Meadows, Phiz (H. K. Browne), Gilbert, Alfred Crowquill (Forrester), and others—Doyle's pencil not appearing till some years later. Chief of these gentlemen in possession of the peculiar artistic ability which has identified itself with "Punch" is unquestionably Mr. John Leech, of whom we shall subsequently speak, at greater length. He has remained constant to the journal from its first volume.

Jerrold's writings date from the commencement. Many essays and satiric sketches over fancy signatures, are from his pen. His later and longer productions, extending through many volumes, are "Punch's Letters to his Son," "Punch's Complete Letter Writer," "Twelve Labors of Hercules," "Autobiography of Tom Thumb," "Mrs. Caudle's Curtain Lectures," "Capsicum House for Young Ladies," "Our Little Bird," "Mrs. Benimble's Tea and Toast," "Miss Robinson Crusoe," and "Mrs. Bib's Baby," the last two of which were never completed. During the publication of the "Caudle Lectures," "Punch" reached the highest circulation it has attained. We have the authority of a personal friend of the author for the assertion that their heroine was no fictitious one. The lectures were immensely popular, Englishmen not being slow to recognize in Jerrold's caustic portraiture the features of a very formidable household reality. But with the ladies Mrs. Caudle proved no favorite, nor, in their judgment, did the "Breakfast-Table-Talk," of the Hen-pecked Husband (subsequently published in the Almanac of the current year), make amends for the writer's former productions.

Albert Smith's contributions to the pages of "Punch," were the "Physiologies of the London Medical Student," "London Idler," and "Evening Parties," with other miscellaneous matter. Much of the author's own personal experience is probably comprised in the former, and his fellow-students and intimates at Middlesex Hospital were at no loss to identify the majority of the characters introduced. Mr. Smith's connection with "Punch" was not of long continuance. A severe criticism appearing subsequently in its columns, on his novel of the "Marchioness of Brinvilliers" (published in "Bentley's Miscellany," of which journal he was then editor), he, in retaliation, made an onslaught on "Punch" in another story, the "Pottleton Legacy," where it figures under the title of the Cracker.

Mr. Gilbert a'Beckett, who had before been engaged in many unsuccessful periodicals, found in "Punch" ample scope for his wit and extraordinary faculty of punning. In "The Comic Blackstone," "Political Dictionary," "Punch's Noy's Maxims," and the "Autobiography, and other papers relating to Mr. Briefless," he put his legal knowledge to a comic use. Many fugitive minor pieces have also proceeded from his pen, and he has but few equals in that grotesque form of hybrid poetry known as Macaronic. He is now a London magistrate, and *par excellence*, the punster of "Punch."

The Greek versions of sundry popular ballads, such as "The King of the Cannibal Islands," were the work of Maginn. Hood's world-famous "Song of the Shirt," first appeared in "Punch's" pages.

Thackeray has also been an industrious contributor, Commencing with "Miss Tickletoby's Lectures" (an idea afterward carried out in a somewhat different fashion by a'Beckett in his "Comic History of England"), he, besides miscellaneous writings, produced the "Snob Papers," "Jeames's Diary," "Punch in the East," "Punch's Prose Novelists," "The Traveler in London," "Mr. Brown's Letters to a Young Man about Town," and "The Proser." Of the merits of these works it is unnecessary to speak. The "Book of Snobs" may rank with its author's most finished productions. "Jeames's Diary," suggested by the circumstance of a May-fair footman achieving sudden affluence by railroad speculations during the ruinously exciting period of 1846, may, however, be considered only a further carrying out of the original idea of "Charles Yellowplush." A ballad in it, "The Lines to my Sister's Portrait," is said, to use a vulgar, though expressive phrase, to have *shut up* Lord John Manners, who had achieved some small reputation as "one of the Young England poits." Thackeray parodied his style, and henceforth the voice of the minstrel was dumb in the land. Like Jerrold's "Caudle Lectures," of which many versions appeared at the London theaters, Jeames's adventures were dramatized. The "Prose Novelists" contain burlesque imitations of Bulwer, D'Israeli, Lever, James, Fennimore Cooper, and Mrs. Gore. The illustrations accompanying Thackeray's publications in "Punch," are by his own hand, as are also many other sketches scattered throughout the volumes. They may be generally distinguished by the insertion of a pair of spectacles in the corner. His articles, too, frequently bear the signature "SPEC." Not until the commencement of 1855 did Thackeray relinquish his connection with "Punch." An allusion to this, from his pen, contained in an essay on the genius of Leech, and published in the "Westminster Review," was commented upon very bitterly by Jerrold, in a notice of the article which appeared in "Lloyd's Weekly Newspaper," of which he is editor.

During the last five years, other writers, among which may be enumerated the Mayhew brothers, Mr. Tom Taylor, Angus Reach, and Shirley Brooks, have found a field for their talents in "Punch.' Only Jerrold, a'Beckett, and the editor, Mark Lemon, remain of the original contributors. Its course has been a varied, but perfectly independent one, generally, however, following the lead of the almighty "*Times*," that glory and shame of English journalism, on political questions. In earlier days it was every way more democratic, and the continuous ridicule both of pen and pencil directed against Prince Albert, was said to have provoked so much resentment on the part of the Queen, that she proposed interference to prevent the artist Doyle supplying two frescos to the pavilion at Buckingham Palace. "Punch's" impartiality has been shown by attacks on the extremes and absurdities of all parties, and there can be little question that it has had considerable influence in producing political reform, and a large and liberal advocacy of all popular questions. In behalf of that great change of national policy, the repeal of the Corn Laws, "Punch" fought most vigorously, not, however, forgetting to bestow a few raps of his *batôn* on the shoulders of the Premier whose wisdom or sense of expediency induced such sudden tergiversation as to bring it about. O'Connell's blatant and venal patriotism was held up to merited derision, which his less wary, but more honest followers in agitation, O'Brien, Meagher, and Mitchell, equally shared. Abolition (or at least modification) of the Game Laws, and of the penalty of death, found championship in "Punch," though the latter was summarily dropped upon a change in public opinion, perhaps mainly induced by one of Carlyle's "Latter Day" pamphlets. "Punch" has repeatedly experienced (and merited) the significant honor of being denied admission to the dominions of continental monarchs. Louis Philippe interdicted its presence in France, even (if we recollect aright) before the Spanish marriages had provoked its fiercest attacks—subsequently, however, withdrawing his royal *veto*. In Spain, Naples, the Papal Dominions, those of Austria, Russia, and Prussia, the hunch-backed jester has been often under ban as an unholy thing, or only tolerated in a mutilated form. Up to the commencement of the late war, strict measures of this kind were in operation upon the Russian frontier, but "Punch" now is freely accorded ingress in the Czar's dominions—

probably as a means of keeping up the feeling of antagonism toward England.

Its success has provoked innumerable rivals and imitators, from the days of "Judy," "Toby," "The Squib," "Joe Miller," "Great Gun," and "Puppet-Show," to those of "Diogenes" and "Falstaff." None have achieved permanent popularity, and future attempts would most likely be attended with similar failure, as "Punch" has a firm hold on the likings of the English people, and especially Londoners. It fairly amounts to one of their institutions. Like all journals of merit and independence, it has had its law troubles, more than one action for libel having been commenced against it. James Silk Buckingham, the traveler and author, took this course, in consequence of the publication of articles disparaging a club of his originating, known as the "British and Foreign Institute." A Jew clothes-man, named Hart, obtained a small sum as damages from "Punch." But Alfred Bunn, lessee of Drury Lane Theater, libretto-scribbler, and author of certain trashy theatrical books, though most vehemently "pitched into," resorted to other modes than legal redress. He produced a pamphlet of a shape and appearance closely resembling his tormentor, filled not only with quizzical, satirical, and rhyming articles directed against Lemon, a'Beckett, and Jerrold (characterizing them as Thick-head, Sleek-head, and Wrong-head), but with caricature cuts of each. Whether in direct consequence or not, it is certain that "the poet Bunn" was unmolested in future.

Our notice would scarcely be complete without a few lines devoted to the "Punch" artists, and more especially John Leech. Doyle (the son of H. B., the well-known political caricaturist), whose exquisite burlesque medieval drawings illustrative of the "Manners and Customs of ye Englishe," will be remembered by all familiar with "Punch's" pages, relinquished his connection with the journal and the yearly salary of eight hundred pounds, in consequence of the Anti-papal onslaughts which followed the nomination of Cardinal Wiseman to the (Catholic) Archbishop of Westminster. The artist held the older faith, and was also a personal friend of "His Eminence." His place was then filled by John Tenniel, a historical painter, who had supplied a cartoon to the Palace of Westminster, and is still employed on "Punch," he, in conjunction with John Leech, and an occasional outsider, furnishing the entire illustrations. John Leech, himself, to whom the periodical unquestionably owes half its success, has been constant to "Punch" from an early day. He has brought caricature into the region of the fine arts, and become the very Dickens of the pencil in his portrayal of the humorous side of life. Before his advent, comic drawing was confined to very limited topics, *outre* drawings and ugliness of features forming the fun—such as it was. Seymour's "Cockney Sportsmen," and Cruikshank's wider (yet not extensive) range of subjects, were then the best things extant. How stands the case now? Let "Punch's" twenty-nine volumes, with their ample store of pictorial mirth of Leech's creating, so kindly, so honest, so pleasant and graceful, answer. Contrast their blameless wit and humor with the *equivoque* and foul *double entendre* of French drawings, and think of the difference involuntarily suggested between the social atmospheres of Paris and London.

Leech is a good-looking fellow, approaching the age of forty, and not unlike one of his own handsome "swells" in personal appearance. The Royal Academy Exhibition of 1855 contained his portrait, painted by Millais, the chief of the pre-Raphaelite artists, who is said to be his friend. As may be gathered from his many sporting sketches, Leech is fond of horses, and piques himself on "knowing the points" of a good animal. (We may mention, by-the-by, that Mr. "Briggs" of equestrian celebrity had his original on the Stock Exchange.) He in summer travels considerably, forwarding his sketches to the "Punch" office, generally penciling the accompanying words on the wood-block. In one of the past volumes, dating some eight or ten years back, he has introduced himself in a cut designated "our artist during the hot weather," wherein he appears with his coat off, reclining upon a sofa, and informing a pretty servant-girl who enters the room, that "he is busy." Quizzical portraits of the writers of "Punch" have been introduced in its pages. In Jerrold's "Capsicum House" (vol. XII.), the author's portrait, burlesqued into the figure of "Punch," occurs more than once. And a double-page cut, entitled "Mr. Punch's Fancy Ball," in the early part of the same volume, comprises sketches of the then entire *corps* of contributors, artistic and literary. They are drawn as forming the orchestra, Lemon conducting, Jerrold belaboring a big drum, Thackeray playing on the flute, Leech the violin, and others extracting harmony from divers musical instruments. Again they appear at a later date, as a number of boys at play, in an illustration at the commencement of Vol. XXVII.

"Punch's" office is at 85 Fleet-street. The engraving, printing, and stereotyping is performed at Lombard-street, Whitefriars, where its proprietors have extensive premises. See pp. 56, 57, 321, 322, 324, 325, 327, 328, 330, 331, 333, 334, 336, 338, 339, 432, 433, 434, 435, 436, 437, 438, 439, 440, 441, 442, 443, 444, 445, 446, 447, 449, 450, 451, 453, 455, 456, 457, 458, 459, 460, 461, 462, 463, 464, 465, 466, 467, 468, 469, 470, 471, 472, 473, 474, 475, 478, 480, 485, 492, 496, 497, 498, 499, 572, 573, 574, 575, 576, 630, 631, 632, 633, 634, 635, 636, 637, 638, 640, 643, 644.

"REJECTED ADDRESSES," by James and Horace Smith, published in London, October, 1812. The most successful *jeu d' esprit* of modern times, having survived the occasion that suggested it for nearly half a century, and still being highly popular. It has run through twenty editions in England, and three in America. The opening of Drury-lane theater in 1802, after having been burned and rebuilt, and the offering of a prize of fifty pounds by the manager for the best opening address, were the circumstances which suggested the production of the "Rejected Addresses." The idea of the work was suddenly conceived, and it was executed in six weeks. In the preface to the eighteenth London edition the authors give an interesting statement of the difficulties they encountered in getting the volume published:

"Urged forward by our hurry, and trusting to chance, two very bad coadjutors in any enterprise, we at length congratulated ourselves on having completed our task in time to have it printed and published by the opening of the theater. But, alas! our difficulties, so far from being surmounted, seemed only to be beginning. Strangers to the arcana of the bookseller's trade, and unacquainted with their almost invincible objection to single volumes of low price, especially when tendered by writers who have acquired no previous name, we little anticipated that they would refuse to publish our 'Rejected Addresses,' even although we asked nothing for the copyright. Such, however, proved to be the case. Our manuscript was perused and returned to us by several of the most eminent publishers. Well do we remember betaking ourselves to one of the craft in Bond-street, whom we found in a back parlor, with his gouty leg propped upon a cushion, in spite of which warning he diluted his luncheon with frequent glasses of Madeira. 'What have you already written?' was his first question, and interrogatory to which we had been subjected in almost every instance. 'Nothing by which we can be known.' 'Then I am afraid to undertake the publication.' We presumed timidly to suggest that every writer must have a beginning, and that to refuse to publish for him until he had acquired a name, was to imitate the sapient mother who cautioned her son against going into the water until he could swim. 'An old joke—a regular Joe!' exclaimed our companion, tossing off another bumper. 'Still older than Joe Miller,' was our reply; 'for, if we mistake not, it is the very first anecdote in the facetiæ of Hierocles.' 'Ha, sirs!' resumed the bibliopolist, 'you are learned, are you? So, hoh!—Well, leave your manuscript with me; I will look it over to-night, and give you an answer to-morrow.' Punctual as the clock we presented ourselves at his door on the following morning, when our papers were returned to us with the observation—'These trifles are really not deficient in smartness; they are well, vastly well for beginners; but they will never do—never. They would not pay for advertising, and without it I should not sell fifty copies.'

"This was discouraging enough. If the most experienced publishers feared to be out of pocket by the work, it was manifest *à fortiori*, that its writers ran a risk of being still more heavy losers, should they undertake the publication on their own account. We had no objection to raise a laugh at the expense of others; but to do it at our own cost, uncertain as we were to what extent we might be involved, had never entered into our contemplation. In this dilemma, our 'Addresses,' now in every sense rejected, might probably have never seen the light, had not some good angel whispered us to betake ourselves to Mr. John Miller, a dramatic publisher, then residing in Bow-street, Covent Garden. No sooner had this gentleman looked over our manuscript, than he immediately offered to take upon himself all the risk of publication, and to give us half the profits, *should there be any;* a liberal proposition, with which we gladly closed. So rapid and decided was its success, at which none were more unfeignedly astonished than its authors, that Mr. Miller advised us to collect some 'Imitations of Horace,' which had appeared anonymously in the 'Monthly Mirror,' offering to publish them upon the same terms. We did so accordingly; and as new editions of the 'Rejected Addresses' were called for in quick succession, we were shortly enabled to sell our half copyright in the two works to Mr. Miller, for one thousand pounds! We have entered into this unimportant detail, not to gratify any vanity of our own, but to encourage such literary beginners as may be placed in similar circumstances; as well as to impress upon publishers the propriety of giving more consideration to the possible merit of the works submitted to them, than to the mere magic of a name."

The authors add, that not one of the poets whom they "audaciously burlesqued," took offense at the ludicrous imitation of their style. From "Sir Walter Scott," they observe, "we received favors and notice, both public and private, which it will be difficult to forget, because we had not the smallest claim upon his kindness. 'I certainly must have written this myself!' said that fine tempered man to one of the authors, pointing to the description of the Fire, 'although I forgot upon what occasion.' Lydia White, a literary lady, who was prone to feed the lions of the day, invited one of us to dinner; but, recollecting afterward that William Spencer formed one of the party, wrote to the latter to put him off; telling him that a man was to be at her table whom he 'would not like to meet.' 'Pray who is this whom I should not like to meet?' inquired the poet. 'O!' answered the lady, 'one of those men who have made that shameful attack upon you!' 'The very man upon earth I should like to know!' rejoined the lively and careless bard. The two individuals accordingly met, and have continued fast friends ever since. Lord Byron, too, wrote thus to Mr. Murray from Italy: 'Tell him we forgive him, were he twenty times our satirist.'

"It may not be amiss to notice, in this place, one criticism of a Leicester clergyman, which may be pronounced unique: 'I do not see why they should have been rejected,' observed the matter-of-fact annotator; 'I think some of them very good!' Upon the whole, few have been the instances, in the acrimonious history of literature, where a malicious pleasantry like the 'Rejected Addresses'—which the parties ridiculed might well consider more annoying than a direct satire—instead of being met by querulous bitterness or petulant retaliation, has procured for its authors the acquaintance, or conciliated the good-will, of those whom they had the most audaciously burlesqued."

James Smith died in London on the 29th of December, 1836, in the sixty-fourth year of his age. His brother survived him many years. Both were admired and ever-welcome members of the best society of London. See pp. 393, 396, 402, 408,

ROGERS, SAMUEL—The English poet and banker, recently deceased. Author of a "pretty poem," entitled, "The Pleasures of Memory." In his old age, he was noted for the bitter wit of his conversation. See p. 566.

SAXE, JOHN G—Editor of the "Burlington Gazette," and Wandering Minstrel. The witty poems of Mr. Saxe are somewhat in the manner of Hood. To be fully appreciated they must be heard, as they roll in sonorous volumes, from his own lips. His collected poems were published a few years ago by Ticknor & Fields, and have already reached a ninth edition. See pp. 68, 69, 343, 519, 577, 578.

SCOTT, SIR WALTER—Born 1771; died, 1832. Sir Walter Scott, though he excelled all his cotemporaries in the humorous delineation of character, wrote little humorous verse. The two pieces published in this volume are so excellent that one is surprised to find no more of the same description in his writings. See pp. 115, 559.

SHERIDAN, DR. THOMAS—Noted for being an intimate friend of Dean Swift, and the grandfather of Richard Brinsley Sheridan. Born in 1684; died in 1738. He was an eccentric, witty, somewhat learned, Dublin schoolmaster. He published some sermons and a translation of Persius; acquired great celebrity as a teacher; but through the imprudence that distinguished the family, closed his life in poverty. We may infer from the few specimens of his facetious writings that have been preserved that he was one of the wittiest of a nation of wits. One or two of his epigrams are exquisitely fine. See pp. 212, 545.

SHERIDAN, RICHARD BRINSLEY—Author of the "Rivals," and the "School for Scandal." Born at Dublin in 1751; died, 1816. Sheridan must have written more humorous poetry than we have been able to discover. It is probable that most of his epigrams and verified repartees have either not been preserved, or have escaped our search. Moore, in his "Life of Sheridan," gives specimens of his satirical verses, but only a few, and but one of striking excellence. See pp. 281, 559.

SMITH, HORACE—See "Rejected Addresses."

SMITH, JAMES—See "Rejected Addresses."

SMITH, REV. SYDNEY—The jovial prebendary of St. Paul's, the wittiest Englishman that ever lived; died in 1845. Except the "Recipe for Salad," and an epigram, we have found no comic verses by him. He "leaked another way." See pp. 40, 566.

SOUTHEY, ROBERT—The English poet and man of letters; born in 1774. Southey wrote a great deal of humorous verse, much of which is ingenious and fluent. He was amazingly dexterous in the use of words, and excelled all his cotemporaries, except Byron and Barham, in the art of rhyming. See pp. 26, 28, 105, 250, 388, 389, 390, 391, 392.

SWIFT, JONATHAN—Dean of St. Patrick's. Dublin. Born 1667; died, 1739. It were superfluous to speak of the career or abilities of this great but most unhappy man, who unquestionably ranks highest amid the brilliant names of that brilliant epoch. His works speak for him, and will to all time. Of his poetical writings it may be said that though only surpassed in wit and humor by his more universally known prose, they are infinitely *nastier* than any thing else in the English language. They have, however, the negative virtue of being nowise licentious or demoralizing—or at least no more so than is inseparable from the choice of obscene and repulsive subjects. Nearly all his unobjectionable comic verses may be found in this volume. See pp. 204, 205, 206, 358, 359, 360, 365, 539, 540, 541, 542, 543, 544, 585, 586, 652, 653, 654, 655, 656, 657, 658, 659, 660, 661, 662.

THACKERAY, WILLIAM MAKEPEACE—The greatest of living satirists. Born at Calcutta of English parents, in 1811. Most of Mr. Thackeray's comic verses appeared originally in "Punch." They have recently been collected and published in a volume with other and more serious pieces. This collection contains nothing more mirth-provoking than the "Ballads of Pleaceman X," by Mr. Thackeray. See pp. 54, 184, 191, 318, 319, 597, 601, 603, 606, 610, 613, 617.

WAKE, WILLIAM BASIL—An English writer, contributor to "Hone's Every Day Book." See p. 102.

WALLER, EDMUND—Born in Warwickshire, England, in 1608. Poet, man of fortune, member of the Long Parliament, and traitor to the People's Cause. He was fined ten thousand pounds and banished, but Cromwell permitted his return, and the poet rewarded his clemency by a panegyric. See pp. 533, 534

WESLEY, REV. SAMUEL—A clergyman of the Church of England; father of the celebrated John Wesley; author of a volume of poems, entitled "Maggots;" born in 1662; died in 1785. See p. 566.

WILLIAMS, SIR CHARLES HANBURY—A noted wit of George the Second's time; born in 1709; died, 1759. He was a friend of Walpole, sat in parliament for Monmouth, and rose to some distinction in the diplomatic service. An edition of his writings in three volumes was published in London in 1822. Time has robbed his satires of their point, by burying in oblivion the circumstances that gave rise to them. A single specimen of his writings is all that was deemed worthy of place in this volume. See p. 87.

WILLIS, N. P.—The well-known American poet and journalist. Mr. Willis has written many humorous poems, but only a few have escaped the usual fate of newspaper verses. Born at Portland, Maine, 1807. See pp. 60, 62, 63, 64, 65, 66.

WOLCOTT, JOHN (Peter Pindar), the most voluminous, and one of the best, of the humorous poets who have written in the English language. He was born in Devonshire, England, and flourished in the reign of George III., whose peculiarities it was his delight to ridicule. No king was ever so mercilessly and so successfully lampooned by a poet as George III. by Peter Pindar. Wolcott was by profession a Doctor of Medicine. In 1766, we find him accompanying his relative, Sir William Trelawney, to Jamaica, of which island Sir William had been appointed governor. While there, the rector of a valuable living died, and Dr. Wolcott conceived the idea of entering the church and applying for the vacant rectorship. To this end he began actually to perform the duties of the parish, reading prayers and preaching, and soon after returned to England to take orders, provideed with powerful recommendations. To his great disappointment, the Bishop of London refused him ordination, and the reader of Peter Pindar will not be at a loss to guess the reason of the refusal. Wolcott now established himself in Truro, and continued in the successful practice of medicine there for several years.

At Truro, he met the youthful Opie. "It is much to his honor," says one who wrote in Wolcott's own lifetime, "that during his residence in Cornwall, he discovered, and encouraged, the fine talents of the late Opie, the artist; a man of such modesty, simplicity of manners, and ignorance of the world, that it is probable his genius would have lain obscure and useless, had he not met, in Dr. Wolcott, with a judicious friend, who knew how to appreciate his worth, and to recommend it to the admiration of the world. The Doctor's taste in painting has already been noticed; and it may now be added, that perhaps few men have attained more correct notions on the subject, and the fluency with which he expatiates on the beauties or defects of the productions of the ancient or modern school, has been amply acknowledged by all who have shared in his company. The same taste appears to have directed him to some of the first subjects of his poetical satire, when he began to treat the public with the pieces which compose these volumes. The effect of these poems on the public mind will not be soon forgot. Here appeared a new poet, and a new critic, a man of unquestionable taste and luxuriant fancy, combined with such powers of satire, as became tremendously formidable to all who had the misfortune to fall under his displeasure. It was acknowledged at the same time, that amid some personal acrimony, and some affectionate preferences, not far removed, perhaps, from downright prejudice, he in general grounded his praise and censure upon solid principles, and carried the public mind along with him, although sometimes at the heavy expense of individuals."

Later in life Dr. Wolcott removed to London, where he died at an advanced age. His writings were, as may be supposed, eagerly read at the time of their publication, but since the poet's death, they have scarcely received the attention which their merits deserve. The present collection contains all of his best poems which are not of a character too local and cotemporary, or too coarse in expression, to be enjoyed by the modern reader. See pp. 21, 22, 24,

89, 90, 91, 93, 95, 216, 217, 218, 220, 222, 223, 226, 231, 233, 236, 238, 367, 546, 547, 548, 549, 550, 551.

YRIARTE, DON TOMAS DE—An eminent Spanish poet, born at Teneriffe about 1760. He is known to English readers chiefly through his "Literary Fables," of which, specimens, translated by Mr. Devereaux, are given in this volume. Yriarte also wrote comedies and essays. See pp. 239, 241.

www.ingramcontent.com/pod-product-compliance
Lightning Source LLC
LaVergne TN
LVHW021047110826
845150LV00001B/7